Mexican American LITERATURE

General Editor
Charles Tatum

HBJ Harcourt Brace Jovanovich, Publishers
Orlando   San Diego   Chicago   Dallas

Charles Tatum (Ph.D., University of New Mexico) is Head of the Department of Spanish and Portuguese at the University of Arizona. Born in El Paso, Texas, to a Mexican mother and an Anglo father, he spent his formative years in Mexico—firmly rooting him in the culture of his mother's people. His interest in Hispanic literature began when he was an undergraduate at the University of Notre Dame and led to a year of intensive study on a Fulbright Fellowship in Madrid, Spain. In 1980, he was awarded a National Endowment for the Humanities Fellowship that helped him to continue his studies. A scholar and teacher of Mexican American literature for over fifteen years, Tatum has written numerous articles and a book, *Chicano Literature*, tracing its history and trends.

Reviewers and Contributors

Juan Bruce-Novoa
University of California
Irvine, California

Michelle Giroux
Smoky Hill High School
Aurora, Colorado

Roseann Gonzalez
University of Arizona
Tucson, Arizona

Salvador Guereña
University of California
Santa Barbara, California

Rolando Hinojosa-Smith
University of Texas
Austin, Texas

Luis Leal
University of California
Santa Barbara, California

Francisco A. Lomeli,
University of California
Santa Barbara, California

Ann Moseley
East Texas State University
Commerce, Texas

Mary J. Nichols
Austin High School
Austin, Texas

Heida Serrano
Business and Management Center
Dallas, Texas

Gary Soto
University of California at Berkeley
Berkeley, California

Printed in the United States of America
ISBN 0-15-347499-8

Acknowledgments

For permission to reprint copyrighted material, grateful acknowledgment is made to the following sources:

Academy of American Franciscan History, Father James McManamon: From pp. 95–109 in *Writings of Junípero Serra*, Volume I, edited by Antonine Tibesar, O.F.M. Copyright 1955 by Academy of American Franciscan History.

Leonard Adame: "In December's Air" by Leonard Adame from *Speaking for Ourselves*, 2nd Edition. Published by Scott Foresman, 1971.

Professor Alurista: "mis ojos hinchados," "must be the season of the witch," and "when raza?" from *Floricanto en Aztlán* by Alurista. Copyright © 1971 by the Regents of the University of California.

The Americas Review: From "Ghosts and Voices: Writing from Obsession" by Sandra Cisneros in *The Americas Review*, Spring 1987. Copyright © 1987 by the Americas Review.

Rudolfo A. Anaya: "Salomon's Story" from *Tortuga* by Rudolfo A. Anaya. Published by The University of New Mexico Press, 1988.

Ronald Arias: "El Mago" by Ronald Arias from *El Grito: A Journal of Contemporary Mexican-American Thought*, Spring 1970.

Arte Público Press: "Refugee Ship" by Lorna Dee Cervantes from *Revista Chicano-Riqueña*, Spring 1975. Copyright © 1975 by Revista Chicano-Riqueña. Adapted from *The Flying Tortilla Man* by Denise Chávez. Copyright 1989 by Denise Chávez. "Boys and Girls," "The House on Mango Street," and "My Name" from *The House on Mango Street* by Sandra Cisneros. Copyright © 1986 by Sandra Cisneros. "Virginia Gill, Visual Artist Bakes a Cake for the Arts Committee Meeting" from *Woman, Woman* by Angela de Hoyos. Copyright © 1985 by Angela de Hoyos. "Bailando," "Graduation Morning," and "Mi Madre" from *Chants* by Pat Mora. Copyright © 1985 by Pat Mora. "Recuerdo: How I changed the war and won the game" by Mary Helen Ponce from *Woman of Her Word: Hispanic Women Write*, edited by Evangelina Vigil. Copyright © 1983 by *Revista Chicano-Riqueña*. "A Prayer" and "The Portrait" from *. . . y no se lo tragó la tierra (. . . and the earth did not devour him)* by Tomás Rivera, translated by Evangelina Vigil-Piñón. Copyright © 1987 by Consuelo Rivera; copyright © 1987 by Evangelina Vigil-Piñón. "Coming Back From It," "My Father Is a Simple Man," "Olivia," and "This Is What I Said" from *The Sadness of Days: Selected and New Poems* by Luis Omar Salinas. Copyright © 1987 by Luis Omar Salinas. "Old Man" and "Once" from *Selected Poems: Ricardo Sánchez* by Ricardo Sánchez. Copyright © 1985 by Ricardo Sánchez. "The Jacket" in *Small Faces* by Gary Soto. Copyright © 1986 by Gary Soto.

Susan Bergholz Literary Services: "Three Wise Guys: Un Cuento de Navidad / A Christmas Story" from *The Sky Has Little Eyes* by Sandra Cisneros.

Bilingual Review / Press: "Rafe Buenrostro Returns from Korea" from *Fair Gentlemen of Belken County* by Rolando Hinojosa, translated by Julia Cruz. © 1986 by Bilingual Press / Editorial Bilingüe. "Last Day in Viet Nam" by Leroy V. Quintana from *Five Poets of Aztlán*, edited by Santiago Daydí-Tolson. © 1985 by Bilingual Press / Editorial Bilingüe. Published by Bilingual Review / Press, Arizona State University, Tempe, AZ.

Contents

Contemporary Period *(1960–Present)* 285

Short Fiction 287

x

Drama 624

Guide to Spanish Pronunciation

If you have ever heard English spoken by a native of England or Australia, you likely noticed a striking difference between that person's pronunciation and your own. Like English, Spanish is pronounced differently depending on region. For example, the Spanish spoken in Mexico differs noticeably from the Spanish spoken in Spain. Pronunciation also varies regionally within Spain, Mexico, and other countries where Spanish is spoken—much as the Midwestern accent of a person from Chicago differs from the Southern accent of someone from Alabama.

The guidelines that begin below and continue on the following pages give the pronunciations most commonly used in Mexican Spanish. Because the sounds of one language cannot always identically reproduce those of another, guides such as this one are approximate. The phonetic respellings throughout the textbook give the nearest English equivalents of Spanish pronunciations.

In pronouncing Spanish words and names, it will be helpful to keep in mind that each vowel and diphthong (a vowel sound created when two or more vowels are glided together within a single syllable, as with *oy* in *boy*) will almost always retain the same sound quality regardless of where it appears within a word. For example, consider the English words *rat* and *rate*. If these were pronounced according to Spanish phonetics, the *a* in both words would have the same pronunciation, and the *e* in *rate*—silent in English—would be pronounced as well. With one exception (see the pronunciation given for the letter *u*), there are no silent vowels in Spanish.

The following explanations provide approximate equivalents in English for each letter and combination of letters used in Spanish.

a	Like **a** in **mama**: *mago, adobe.*
b	Like **b** in **bat**: *buena, Baca.*
c	Before **e** or **i**, like **s** in **sit**: *centavo, Cisneros;* before **a, o,** or **u,** like **c** in **cat**: *comadre, cuento.*
ch	Like **ch** in **child**: *chicharras, chanza.*
d	At the beginning of a word or after **n,** pronounced like **d** in **day**: *día, curandera;* in all other cases, like **th** in **than**: *nada, Adame.*
e	Like **e** in **yes**: *mecate, retablo.*

f	Like **f** in **fall**: *familia, Rodolfo*.
g	Before **a, o, u,** or a consonant, like **g** in **get**: *agua, mugres;* before **e** and **i**, like **h** in **help**: *geranio, magia*.
h	Silent except after **c** (see **ch**): *hombre, hoy*.
i	Like **ee** in **meet**: *mariachi, tilma*.
j	Like **h** in **help**: *bruja, Jiménez*.
k	Like **k** in **keep**; rarely appears in Spanish except in words taken from other languages.
l	Like **l** in **lift**: *español, Gonzales*.
ll	Like **y** in **yard**: *Llorona, manzanilla*.
m	Like **m** in **mat**: *mira, malecón*.
n	In most cases like **n** in **not**: *don, nieve;* in some cases before **c** and **g,** like **ng** in **singer**: *barranca, gringo*.
ñ	Like **ny** in **canyon**: *doña, piñon*.
o	Like **o** in **corn**: *choza, Soto*.
p	Like **p** in **part**: *palo, López*.
q	Like **k** in **keep**: *que, banquito* (always followed by **u,** which is silent, and **e** or **i**).
r	Like **rr** (see the next entry) when it appears at the beginning of a word or after **n, l,** or **s**: *ratón, Buenrostro;* in all other cases, like **rr** with a slight **d** sound at the end: *ahorita, Otero*.
rr	Strongly trilled, or vibrated, with a drawn-out **r** sound as in **hurry**: *carreta, urraca*.
s	Like **s** in **sit**: *hueso, masa*.
t	Like **t** in **tap**: *atole, tía*.
u	Like **oo** in **too**: *lucero, Ulica;* always silent when preceded by a **q**: *aquí, Quintana*.
v	Unless emphasis is desired at the beginning of a word (*¡viva!*), like **b** in **bat**: *verdad, Rivera*.
w	Rarely appears in Spanish except in words taken from other languages.
x	Usually like **x** in **ox**; sometimes like **h** in **help** as in the pronunciation of *México*.
y	Like **y** in **yard**: *yo, Anaya*.
z	Like **s** in **sit**: *raza, Zamora*.

Diphthongs

ai—ay	Like **i** in **I**, but drawn out slightly into the two sounds **ah** and **ee**: *paisanos, Fray.*
au	Like **ow** in **cow**: *Autoridades.*
ei—ey	Like **ay** in **say**: *rey.*
eu	Like **e** and **o** in **guess who**: *Eleuterio.*
ia—ya	Like **ya** in **yarn**: *acequia, Arias.*
ie—ye	Like **ye** in **yes**: *tierra, vieja.*
io—yo	Like **yo** in **yo-yo**: *barrio, arroyo.*
iu—yu	Like **yu** in **yule**: *cayuco.*
oa	Like **wa** in **want**: *Joaquín.*
oi—oy	Like **oi** in **oil**: *hoy, estoy.*
ua	Like **wa** in **wand**: *cahuama, Juan.*
ue	Like **we** in **went**: *Manuel, abuelito.*
ui—uy	Like **we** in **we**: *Luis, huiclamina.*

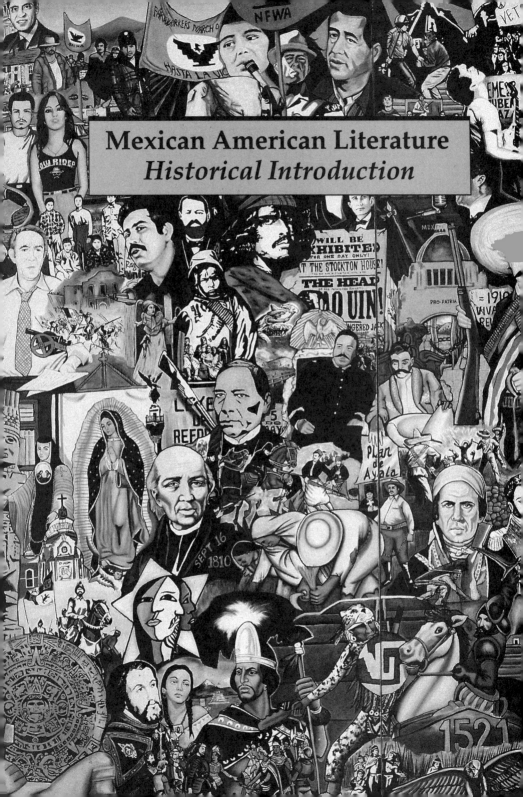

Mexican American Literature
Historical Introduction

The Spanish and Mexican Periods

Visions of Wealth

Christopher Columbus and his crew returned from their historic voyage to the New World eager to tell of exotic natives who lived surrounded by plants and animals unknown on the European continent. Columbus wrote in his journal of the myriad varieties of trees he had sighted, the wild and colorful parrots and other birds that sang enchanting songs in the lush greenery, and the brightly colored flowers whose scent filled the humid tropical air.

The Indians of the Caribbean islands on which Columbus and his men landed also enticed them with visions of great wealth, telling the Europeans what they wanted to hear—that gold, precious stones, and rich spices could be found in lands farther to the west. Perhaps the island natives told them this in order to get their unexpected and unwelcome visitors to leave them alone. We will never know, but what is important is that Columbus and his men returned to Spain determined to set forth on new voyages.

Columbus's official report to King Ferdinand and Queen Isabella of Spain paints an exciting tale of a journey to a land that Europeans could barely imagine at the time. He convinced Queen Isabella to finance another voyage in order to claim the wealthy lands west of the Caribbean islands as possessions of the Spanish Crown.

We know that Columbus made several voyages to the New World. Although he never discovered the riches he was seeking, he and other explorers who followed him created among their fellow Europeans an obsession to discover wealth in the New World. This dream launched dozens of expeditions, manned by thousands of sailors, soldiers, missionaries, and adventurers, throughout the sixteenth century. While many came to the New World for other reasons such as the desire to convert Indians to Christianity or to escape prosecution for their crimes, the majority were spurred on by visions of becoming wealthy and powerful.

The Conquest of Mexico

Under the leadership of Hernán Cortés, a small Spanish military expedition crossed over from the Caribbean islands to Mexico's Gulf coast, landing close to the present-day seaport of Veracruz in 1519. The coastal Indians that Cortés and his conquistadors encountered told them of the Aztecs, a fabulously prosperous people whose empire radiated out from its capital in Central Mexico for hundreds of miles in all directions. These reports fueled the Spaniards' dreams of discovering great deposits of mineral wealth that would bring glory to themselves and the Spanish Crown. As one conquistador declared, "We came here to serve God and the King, and also to get rich."

The Spaniards had brought with them horses as well as gunpowder, both of which were unknown in the New World prior to this time. Naturally, the Indians thought that these strange white men, mounted on unknown beasts and bearing weapons that flashed with fire and explosions, possessed some magical power. In addition, the Aztec religion had predicted that a bearded stranger would arrive in their land at about the same time that Cortés, who had an impressive full beard, appeared with his guns and horses.

The Aztec capital of Tenochtitlán was built upon a series of islands in the middle of a large lake and could be reached from the mainland by several causeways or bridges. Taking advantage of this position, the Aztecs had little difficulty defending themselves against hostile Indian tribes with whom they were constantly struggling. However, Cortés convinced the Aztec leader Moctezuma to allow him and his men to cross over into the city. Once there, they defeated the unsuspecting Aztec soldiers. By 1521, Cortés's small band of soldiers along with Indian enemies of the Aztecs had succeeded in totally defeating the mighty Aztec armies.

Spain Amasses Power in the New World

Cortés and his fellow Spaniards soon brought the Aztecs and other Mexican Indians under military control. To consolidate its territorial claims in the New World and to exert civilian rule over the conquered Indians, the Spanish Crown established a system of viceroyalties. These governing bodies were similar to the individual states in this country or the provinces that make up Canada today but were much larger. The ruling monarch in Spain appointed an official representative, or viceroy, to govern each of these territories. Much of present-day Mexico became the viceroyalty of New Spain, with its capital in what is now Mexico City and what had been, until 1521, the capital of the Aztec empire.

The Mexican Indians suffered greatly under Spanish rule. Within a hundred years of Cortés's arrival, several million had died from disease, exposure, and physical abuse in Spanish mines and on Spanish plantations. Yet, at the same time, the Spaniards mixed and intermarried with the native Indian population to form a new race of *mestizos*. Today's Mexicans and Mexican Americans trace their ancestry to this combination of races, languages, and cultures.

Cabeza de Vaca and the Spanish Presence in the Southwest

We can trace the Spanish presence in the southwestern United States to a military expedition led by Pánfilo de Narváez. He and approximately four hundred men set out in 1527 from Cuba to explore the southeast coast of the United States from Florida to the Rio Grande. Like many of the expeditions before them, they sought gold, silver, and precious stones to add to the Spanish Crown's increasing wealth plundered from the New World.

A violent storm shipwrecked the Narváez expedition off the coast of what is now Texas, where few survivors managed to struggle ashore. They proceeded to make rafts from the ship's wreckage and then set out again, probably in an attempt to make their way back to their home port. The rafts in turn were torn apart by the rough seas, and more men perished. The few left alive included a Spanish military official named Alvar Núñez Cabeza de Vaca.

During the next ten years, Cabeza de Vaca and the remaining members of the original Narváez expedition ventured overland through much of the lower southwestern United States. Cabeza de

Vaca left us a detailed account of their struggle to survive (see pages 79–94). He tells us of those who died from disease, injury, and exposure and of the handful who managed to persevere thanks to a combination of luck and common sense. They lived among both hostile and friendly Indian tribes before eventually reaching Mexico City, the seat of power in New Spain.

Like Christopher Columbus, Hernán Cortés, and many other Spaniards before him, Cabeza de Vaca marvelled at the wonders of the New World. He describes in rich detail extraordinary plant and animal life and varied Indian tribes, providing a treasury of reliable information for future explorers. He also tended to exaggerate the Indian accounts of gold and other mineral wealth, which always seemed to lie beyond the next mountain range.

Other Explorations of the Southwest and California

Although Cabeza de Vaca and his men had not actually seen any of the fabled wealth they had heard so much about, the tales they brought back to Mexico City fired the imaginations of other explorers. Pursuing these elusive riches and eager to extend its territories northward from the viceroyalty of New Spain, the Spanish Crown financed a stream of expeditions throughout the sixteenth, seventeenth, and eighteenth centuries.

Fray Marcos de Niza, Francisco de Coronado, Juan Rodríguez Cabrillo, Juan de Oñate, Diego de Vargas, Fray Eusebio Kino, and Juan de Anza are only a few of the Spaniards who played major roles in these expeditions. Throughout the Southwest and California today, hundreds of towns, forests, monuments, streets, and even shopping centers and hotels bear their names, providing a permanent record of their exploits.

By the end of the eighteenth century, Spanish ranchers and farmers had settled the coast of California from San Diego to San Francisco, along the Rio Grande in New Mexico, and throughout the territories that later became parts of Arizona and Texas. Many of the men on those expeditions continued mixing and intermarrying with the women of the less hostile Indian tribes, such as the

Pueblo Indians of New Mexico. This practice waned as Spanish women joined later expeditions bent on colonizing the new land. One of the most important contributions made by these early Spanish settlers was the establishment of the cattle industry, which continues to this day to play a key role in the economy of the western United States.

Mexico Declares Its Independence from Spain

Early in the nineteenth century, the *mestizo* population of New Spain as well as those who identified themselves as the sons and daughters of Spaniards—known as *criollos* [creoles]—began agitating for political change. The dramatic success of the French Revolution a few years earlier had launched a new wave of thought in Europe late in the eighteenth century, and the American Revolution had heralded the dawning of democracy in the emerging country of the United States just to the north of New Spain.

This explosion of struggles for independence, combined with political instability in Spain, emboldened leaders in all of Spain's viceroyalties to speak out against the Crown and to insist on a greater role in governing themselves. Increasing unrest and heated demands for change finally ignited revolutionary wars throughout Spain's New World territories. From the tip of South America to New Spain in the north, the flames of insurrection raged from about 1810 to the 1820s, searing the influence of the Spanish Crown from most of the New World forever and forging the independence of the new republics of Latin America.

After a bloody ten-year struggle, Mexico won its freedom in 1821—an event that is celebrated today by Mexicans and Mexican Americans alike. Unfortunately, independence did not bring peace. For the next thirty years the Spanish-speaking inhabitants of the northern territories continued fighting to gain greater autonomy—now from the central authorities of the new Republic, who fiercely resisted. The bitterness and division between Mexico City and its distant northern territories grew steadily as each region became increasingly convinced that the central government paid little heed to its particular circumstances and problems.

The Mexican American Period

American Expansionism and Mexico's Northern Territories

At the same time that hostilities were flaring between the northern territories and the central government of the Republic, Anglo-Americans began moving into areas of the Southwest and California. They came for many reasons—often, to search for gold and other riches and to settle on farms and ranches.

The Spanish-speaking population in each region of Mexico's northern territories responded differently to the new Anglo-American settlers. In Texas, for example, Stephen F. Austin and his followers were first welcomed and then later opposed when it became clear that they intended to try to establish an independent country. In New Mexico, the Mexican citizenry actively resisted the coming of the Anglo-Americans, while in California the Mexican population largely accepted them or at least did not offer resistance.

After the defeat of Mexican forces at the Battle of San Jacinto in 1836, the Republic of Texas declared its independence. That same year, Sam Houston was elected president of the Republic, which nine years later became the twenty-eighth state of the Union.

Anti-Mexican Feelings Peak and War Erupts

Encouraged by the aggressive expansionism of President James Polk and others, the American military and many Anglo-American citizens committed acts of violence and plunder against Mexican citizens in the Southwest. During the 1830s and 1840s, anti-Mexican feelings rose to a fever pitch in the United States. Many Anglo-Americans advocated the armed seizure of Mexican lands.

On the night of his inauguration, Polk told a close associate that it was his intention to bring California under the American flag during his term of office. He openly challenged and provoked the Mexican government by ordering General Taylor and his troops into Mexican territory in 1846. This action soon led to an incident that ignited the powder keg we know as the Texas-Mexican or Mexican-American War. Both American political parties, the Whigs and the Democrats, in the Senate and the House of Representatives overwhelmingly passed a war resolution.

Frederick Douglass, a former slave known for his passionate speaking and writing, denounced the war in his Rochester, New York, newspaper *North Star*, calling it "disgraceful, cruel, and iniquitous." Abraham Lincoln, then a recently elected Illinois congressman, openly challenged his President's motives.

Despite these and other protests against waging war with Mexico, American troops mobilized for battle. One large force landed at the Mexican east coast seaport of Veracruz after pounding it with naval artillery. Another force invaded New Mexico and then moved overland to California. A separate invasion was launched through Texas but was stalled after the Mexican Army fought it to a standstill in Monterrey. After catching the Mexican forces in a massive pincer action and on multiple fronts, the American army then marched on Mexico City. Faced with almost certain military defeat and plagued by its own internal divisions, the Mexican government soon surrendered.

The Treaty of Guadalupe Hidalgo of 1848

Mexico and the United States signed the Treaty of Guadalupe Hidalgo in 1848. Mexico was forced to accept the Rio Grande as the boundary between the two countries. In addition, it ceded to the United States in exchange for fifteen million dollars much of the present-day states of Arizona, California, Nevada, New Mexico, and Utah, as well as parts of Colorado. Four years later Mexico sold the remaining part of New Mexico and Arizona to the United States. By the middle of the nineteenth century, American expansionism had engulfed all of Mexico's northern territories.

The Aftermath
of the War

The Treaty of Guadalupe Hidalgo guaranteed the rights of a new group of citizens—Mexican Americans, those of Mexican descent in the Southwest who chose to become American citizens after 1848. Although these new citizens were allowed to freely practice their religion (in most cases, Roman Catholicism), American officials routinely violated many of their other constitutional rights, such as the free expression of their language and customs. Mexican Americans also suffered discrimination in education, employment, and housing.

The Spanish Crown had granted land to many families in the northern territories of New Spain before Mexico declared its independence from Spain in 1821. The Republic of Mexico had honored most of these claims. However, when the American government took control, officials conspired with bankers, investors and others to deprive Mexican American families of their rights to their land. Often, particularly in New Mexico, questionably legal means were employed to transfer title of these lands to Anglo-Americans.

Meanwhile, the Texas Rangers, a band of law officers formed originally to combat hostile Indians, enforced clearly illegal and repressive policies against the new Spanish-speaking citizens. To this day, many Mexican Americans in Texas harbor suspicion and resentment toward the Texas Rangers even though this law enforcement agency has made great strides toward changing its image.

Mexican American
Resistance

Throughout the period from about 1848 to the first quarter of this century, Mexican Americans resisted the violence, theft, and denial of their constitutional rights and guarantees. Across the Southwest and California, groups organized under such leaders as Juan N. Cortina, Gregorio Cortez, Elfego Baca, Tiburcio Vásquez, and Joaquín Murieta.

While Anglo-American historians and folklorists commonly have portrayed these men as bandits, the Spanish-speaking population has lionized them as symbols of resistance against domination by another culture. They play the same role among Mexican Americans in the Southwest that Robin Hood played in England centuries ago: foes and robbers of the rich, champions and benefactors of the defenseless poor. During their heyday, these leaders reigned as cultural heroes, much the same as rock stars or sports figures do today. Popular ballads, or *corridos*, about these heroes, which were composed over a hundred years ago, are still sung today on the radio, at festivals, and at social gatherings of Mexican Americans.

Resistance of the dominant Anglo culture sparked numerous incidents, such as the 1878 El Paso Salt War, seen by one Mexican American historian as a popular people's revolt against economic exploitation. In New Mexico, the paramilitary political organization known as *Las Gorras Blancas* [The White Hats] staged guerrilla raids against Anglo authorities they saw as unjust.

Work stoppages or strikes were another tactic used to protest the exploitation of Mexican and Mexican American labor in the factories and the fields. Prime examples include the berry strike of 1933 in El Monte, California, and the DiGiorgio strike at Arvin, California, in 1947. In both cases, workers rallied spontaneously to form effective labor associations that negotiated for better working conditions and higher pay.

Over one hundred Spanish-language newspapers sprung up in large towns and cities all over the Southwest and California and carried the banner for protest and resistance. In newspapers such as *La Regeneración* [Regeneration] and *El Clamor Público* [The Public Outcry], editors and popular community figures voiced their cultural pride, patriotism, anger, and passion for freedom. Between 1910 and 1920, the period of the Mexican Revolution, many Mexican intellectuals left their native country and found work writing and editing Spanish-language newspapers in the United States.

Special interest groups formed associations wherever Mexican Americans congregated. Known originally as *mutualistas*, they evolved into present-day organizations such as the League of United Latin American Citizens (LULAC) and the American GI Forum. Then, as now, these associations took public stands on educational, social, and political issues that affected Mexican Americans.

Change in the Mexican American Community After World War II

In general, the Mexican American population in the Southwest and California remained isolated in the midst of American society through the end of World War II. While some individuals and organizations continued to fight discrimination, they made few gains in truly integrating this ethnic and cultural minority into the United States mainstream.

After fighting their way across Europe and the Pacific between 1940 and 1945 and receiving numerous decorations for bravery, many thousands of Mexican American citizens returned home ready to participate fully in American society. They had spilled their blood on foreign ground in defense of their country's values and traditions, and now they demanded their rightful share of the American Dream—a considerably larger share than they had been dealt before the war. At the same time, the hundreds of thousands of Mexican Americans who had contributed to the war effort by laboring in factories, on farms, and throughout the economy had no intention of returning to their former secondary status.

A new awareness of their rights as citizens gripped Mexican Americans, who now resolved to become integrated into American society so that they could take advantage of all that life in the United States had to offer. Unfortunately, many Mexican Americans mistakenly thought that they had to surrender their language, traditions, and customs in the process of becoming acccul-turated in the post-war economy.

Many well-meaning parents wanted their children to forget their Spanish-Indian origin, insisting that they speak only English at home as well as in school. Consequently, many Mexican Americans of the "baby boom" generation born during the decade after World War II found themselves caught between their ethnic/cultural past and the demands of the present that they abandon this past. While their grandparents and many of their parents still spoke Spanish, they were taught that English, and English only, was the language of the American Dream.

The Contemporary Period

The 1960s Bring Important Changes

In the early 1960s, Mexican Americans began to reevaluate the attitudes and practices that had prevailed within their culture since about 1945. A new consciousness emerged, especially among younger Mexican Americans, who felt a resurgence of cultural pride. Questioning their parents' drive to try to become like the Anglos, this new generation placed value on speaking Spanish and studying the history of their people.

As a symbol of this new pride, they adopted the term "Chicano" instead of "Mexican American" or "Hispanic" to identify themselves. The choice of the word "Chicano" scandalized their parents and grandparents, who used it as a disparaging term for lower-class Mexicans who moved into rural areas of the United States after emigrating from Mexico. In terms of a comparison, "Chicano" had much the same connotation for older Mexican Americans that "white trash" had for urban Anglos. By identifying themselves as Chicanos, however, the members of the younger generation were acknowledging and, just as importantly, accepting with pride the Mexican Indian side of their heritage and not only the more socially acceptable Spanish/European part.

Political Militancy Comes of Age

The term "Chicano" came to be equated with political militancy in the urban barrios and on high-school and college campuses. Chicano political groups and student organizations sprang up all over the Southwest and California in the mid-1960s. Two prominent groups were the Mexican American Movement of Aztlán and the Chicano Student Movement of Aztlán. Students, teachers, and community leaders successfully petitioned for the creation of Chicano Studies programs that emphasized a non-Anglo version of Mexican and Mexican American history and culture.

Students and educators also supported rural and urban community leaders such as César Chávez, Rodolfo "Corky" Gonzales, Reies López Tijerina, and José Angel Gutiérrez who actively opposed economic exploitation and other forms of discrimination. In 1965, César Chávez organized the Mexican, Mexican American, and Filipino farm workers in California and led a successful national boycott of California-grown grapes. In 1967, the Brown Berets, a militant group of largely urban youth, began mobilizing in cities across California and the Southwest. Poet Rodolfo "Corky" Gonzales played a key role in rallying the Chicano community of Denver. (A portion of his best-known poem, *I Am Joaquín*, which is an epic tribute to his people, is included on pages 451–453.) In 1970, José Angel Gutiérrez and others founded La Raza Unida Party (The United Peoples Party) as a vehicle for self-determination independent of the Democrats and the Republicans. Within a few years, La Raza Unida succeeded in getting candidates elected to local and regional offices, especially in the state of Texas.

Mexican Americans
of Today

Americans of Mexican descent have made significant gains in this country during the past twenty years. While serious problems persist in education, employment, and housing, Mexican Americans as a group have gained much ground toward achieving equal status within American society. In addition, numerous individuals have achieved notable success, such as Mayor Henry Cisneros of San Antonio; Governors Jerry Apodaca and Tony Anaya of New Mexico; singer Linda Ronstadt; writer, movie producer, and director Luis Valdez; actors Edward James Olmos and Martin Sheen and his sons; the Olympic boxer Michael Carbajal; golfers Lee Trevino and Nancy López; and many, many others.

More important, Mexican Americans are entering colleges and universities in growing numbers to pursue professional careers as doctors, lawyers, engineers, architects, scientists, artists, and writers. Increasingly active in the political life of this country, Mexican Americans now constitute an influential voting block that can effectively promote their interests in both the Democratic and the Republican Parties.

No longer do Mexican Americans feel that they have to hide their cultural heritage or give up their language for fear of being rejected by the dominant culture. The image of the quiet, embarrassed man or woman who stands with head bowed is long past.

Overview of Mexican American Literature

The different periods of Mexican American literature primarily correspond to changes in the political order of the Southwest and California. The literature before 1821 (the date of Mexico's independence from Spain) is called "Spanish" because of its strong ties to Hispanic culture. The literature between 1821 and 1848 falls in the "Mexican Period" because during this time the northern territories were politically a part of Mexico. The Treaty of Guadalupe Hidalgo, signed in 1848, ceded much of northern Mexico to the United States, and the many Mexican citizens who lived in that region and who chose to remain there became American citizens. Therefore, the term "Mexican American" both accurately and appropriately identifies the literature dating from 1848 until the 1960s. The "Contemporary Period" begins in the 1960s and coincides not with a change in the national affiliation of the Southwest and California but with a rising tide of cultural and political consciousness expressed through acceptance of the word "Chicano."

The Oral Tradition

This anthology begins with the oral tradition because this genre belongs to no single period of Mexican American literature but rather has flourished in all periods, from the sixteenth century right up through the present.

Spanish explorers and settlers transplanted from the Iberian Peninsula a rich stock of oral literature that has remained vitally alive in the folk tales, poetry, and songs that have passed by word of mouth from generation to generation. Many of these oral works have been collected and transcribed. Some forms, like the very popular *corrido*, have evolved from earlier forms and reflect the strong presence of Hispanic culture in this country.

The Spanish and Mexican Periods

Hispanic literature took root in the Southwest with the arrival of the earliest Spanish explorers, missionaries, and soldiers. Alvar Núñez Cabeza de Vaca, an officer in the Spanish army, has left us a dramatic and moving record of his and his men's ten-year struggle to survive among the Indians of the Southwest. His *Adventures in the Unknown Interior of America* (1527–1537) provides not only a rich source of historical and geographical information but also imaginative descriptions of friendly and hostile Indian tribes as well as of the plant and animal life he and his men saw.

Gaspar Pérez de Villagrá's *Historia de la Nueva México* [The history of the New Mexico], published in Spain in 1610, is the first record of written poetry in the Southwest. The poet tells us in his long epic poem about the perilous journey undertaken by a Spanish military expedition overland from Mexico City through Mexico's central highlands to its northern territories. The poem also contains a short account of the performance of the first dramatic work written in the Southwest. A soldier named Capitain Farfán wrote a play, which his men performed on the banks of the Rio Grande not far from the present-day city of El Paso, Texas. In the play, they give thanks to God for protecting them on their trek.

From the 1600s until 1821, the Spaniards who explored and colonized the Southwest and California seemed eager to chronicle their adventures for future generations. They also shared their intimate thoughts and feelings in a wide variety of poetry.

The Mexican American Period

Much of the literature published during the earlier part of the Mexican American Period (from the mid-1850s to the 1930s) appeared in Spanish-language newspapers, which circulated in virtually every large town and city along the United States–Mexico border from Brownsville, Texas, to San Diego, California. Some lasted only a short time while others held on tenaciously for over twenty-five years.

Many of these newspapers regularly included splendid examples of short fiction, serialized novels, poetry, and even short plays by popular Hispanic writers. In addition, hundreds of works were contributed by anonymous and lesser-known local authors. While the quality of these works is uneven, they provide a rich tapestry of the values and concerns of the people who wrote them.

After the 1930s, Mexican American writers started producing more works in English, making them more accessible to a wider reading public. Some of these writers were published in popular magazines; others were associated with universities or professional associations which provided outlets for their literary talents.

Throughout the Mexican American Period, traveling theater companies, mainly from Mexico, toured the Southwest performing popular Spanish and Latin American works. Some of the larger cities eventually established modest resident theater companies that appealed to a Spanish-speaking audience. At the same time, local amateur groups continued to perform the traditional folk and religious plays that had their origins in the Spanish Period.

The Contemporary Period

In many ways, the poetry, novels, plays, short fiction, and other literary works written after 1965 represent a break with the works that preceded them. The chief source of this break lay in the Chicano movement's rejection of the efforts toward assimilation made by Mexican Americans after World War II through the early 1960s.

Writers in general began to commit themselves more earnestly to evaluating and portraying the socio-political circumstances in which they lived. They saw themselves playing a vital role in expanding their readers' political consciousness and overall awareness of the world around them.

In addition to publishing their work in the more-than-fifty Spanish-language newspapers that focused on social and political issues, writers joined together in informal associations and established journals and small publishing houses. For example, El Grupo Quinto Sol [The Fifth Sun Group] formed in Berkeley, California, in 1967 to define and promote new Chicano ideals. In the same year, writers and university professors launched *El Grito: A Journal of Contemporary Mexican-American Thought*, which published creative literature and important studies in the social sciences—all from a Chicano perspective.

In 1969, some of the same writers and intellectuals who had founded *El Grito* established Quinto Sol Publications, which published *El Espejo / The Mirror*, the first anthology of contemporary Chicano literature. Quinto Sol Publications quickly established an ambitious publishing program and a literary prize called the Premio Quinto Sol.

Writers and university professors soon launched other publishing ventures. *Revista Chicano-Riqueña* published its first issue in 1975. This journal, now renamed *The Americas Review*, still publishes some of the most interesting, innovative literature by Chicano and other Hispanic writers in the United States. *The Americas Review* is associated with Arte Público Press, which, along with Bilingual Press, publishes the bulk of Chicano literature today.

Contemporary Chicano literature has undergone significant changes during the last twenty years. More and more writers seem to be emphasizing formal literary aspects to a greater degree than before. Their works also tend to be more introspective than those published during the 1960s and the 1970s. While this dynamic literature constantly changes, Chicano writers remain deeply committed to their cultural heritage, and cultural pride and protest against discrimination continue to be common themes. Mexican American literature will undoubtedly continue to explore new dimensions of external and internal reality and in so doing will expand far beyond its regional confinement to the Southwest and California.

R:Tontonteanc.

P:Secondido.

P:Tabursa

Puertos

Ciuola.

S:Franc:

R:Albofeda

Bafos.

B:Canoas.

MAR
VERME
IO

B: de f: +

Ancoras.

B: de S:
Abad.

Vandras.

C +

Ciguata.

Balenas.

S:Tiago.

S:Tomas.

Aguataneo

Acapul

MAR DEL SVR.

NVEVA HISPANIA TABVLA NOVA

Portola-Serra, 1769-70   –––––––––

Marcos de Niza, 1539   ▬▬▬▬▬

The Oral Tradition

The Oral Tradition

Hispanic literature, like the literature of most cultures, was preceded by a rich oral tradition consisting of stories, poems, legends, and historical accounts that were passed along by word-of-mouth long before they were written down. Storytellers played a vital role in helping to preserve the folklore as well as the values, beliefs, and customs of rural communities. The earliest poets were not writers but performers who roamed the countryside and traveled from town to town, bringing news from other regions and entertaining their audiences with tales of heroic deeds, tragic loves, and great battles. Oral forms of literature were eventually recorded and became an integral part of written literature; however, in many cultures—Hispanic culture among them—the oral tradition has endured alongside the written tradition.

Many of the oral forms of literature that were prospering in Spain during the sixteenth and seventeenth centuries took root in New Spain and elsewhere in the New World. Brought to the New World by the first Spanish explorers and settlers, these forms evolved into a unique oral tradition that continues to thrive in Hispanic communities throughout the United States. Mexican American oral literature takes its distinctive regional flavor from the blending of Spanish and native Indian traditions as well as the contributions of individual communities and storytellers.

From the mountain villages of northern New Mexico and southern Colorado to the urban areas of Texas and California, the Mexican American oral tradition remains a vital presence, as seen in the arts of storytelling, poetry, and musical performance. Relatively isolated rural communities have preserved the authenticity of original Spanish customs, traditions, and language, while urban areas such as San Antonio and Los Angeles attract a steady flow of immigrants from Mexico and other Hispanic countries, keeping the language and culture of these cities in a constant state of change. As the Spanish language thrives, so does the oral tradition of Mexican American literature.

Folk Tales

Passed down from generation to generation, folk tales represent a vital part of the Mexican American oral tradition. Although such tales take a variety of different forms from region to region and from storyteller to storyteller, they often exhibit one or more of the following features.

- a hero or heroine who must answer a perplexing riddle to receive a reward such as marriage
- a humorous or satirical view of human weaknesses and follies
- animals that act and speak as people
- a lesson or a moral
- a fiendish villain who goes about playing cruel practical jokes
- magic and enchantment
- ghostly apparitions that frighten wayward people into mending their ways

The stories that appear on the following pages illustrate several of these traditional features. For example, one of the tales of the Weeping Woman relates two young men's eerie encounter with the legendary *La Llorona*—an apparition that indeed prompts them to reform their lives.

The Deer Thief

Have you ever had something stolen from you? If so, you probably felt shocked, angry, and—perhaps worst of all—helpless. In "The Deer Thief," a simple hunter is the victim of theft. However, as you shall see, he is far from helpless in bringing the thief to justice.

A hunter was out hunting one day and killed a deer. Since it was very late in the day, he couldn't take the deer home, so he skinned it and hung it as high as he could from the branch of a tall pine tree. The following day he returned for his deer, but the deer was gone. He searched the area for tracks. He inspected everything very carefully, and then he went to the Justice of the Peace to seek redress.

The Justice of the Peace asked him if he had any idea who stole the deer. The hunter replied that he had not seen the thief and he didn't know who it was, but he could give an accurate description of the man who stole the deer.

"If you know something, tell me what kind of man he is," the Justice of the Peace said.

"Well, he is shorter than I. He is older, and he had a yellow bulldog with him."

"But how do you know all that?"

"I know he is shorter than I because he had to put some logs beneath the tree to reach the deer," replied the hunter.

"And how do you know he is old?"

"Because he took short steps, like an old man."

"And how do you know he had a yellow dog?"

"I followed his tracks and I found yellow hair where the dog passed beneath low branches."

"But how do you know it was a bulldog?" the exasperated judge asked.

"Because when the old man was lowering the deer, the dog sat nearby and the way the stub of his tail dug into the ground told me it was a bulldog."

The judge was convinced and granted permission to look

for a man fitting that description. After searching for some time the hunter and the Justice of the Peace arrived at a house where they saw a yellow bulldog. They knocked on the door and a small, old man appeared. Then they searched his barn and found the stolen deer. So the hunter, by using his wits, had tracked down the thief who had stolen his deer.

retold by **Rudolfo A. Anaya**

For Study and Discussion

1. In this folk tale, a hunter becomes a detective who cleverly solves a crime by using close observation and logical deduction. **a.** In what ways are detectives like hunters? **b.** How does the hunter catch the deer thief?

2. The hunter's ability to identify specific details about the thief seems uncanny until the hunter explains how he has arrived at his conclusions. From the perspective of the storyteller, what is the purpose of initially withholding this information?

Literary Elements

The Folk Tale

A **folk tale** is an account, legend, or story of unknown authorship that is passed along orally from generation to generation. In communities where few if any people can read or write, folk tales and other folklore play an important role in preserving values, beliefs, historical knowledge, and other defining features of the group. As the culture changes and grows, so do its folk tales in the hands of creative storytellers: details are embellished or otherwise altered, and the stories emerge enriched with each retelling. What values, beliefs, and other cultural elements are evident in "The Deer Thief"?

Give some examples of traditional American folk tales. Who might some of these legendary folk heroes be in contemporary America? (For example, in modern times Johnny Appleseed might be an environmentalist who travels the country replanting forests destroyed by acid rain.) Choose one of these traditional tales and modernize it, keeping in mind that you are free to embellish it. After you have written an updated version of a folk tale, present it to the class, perhaps accompanied by visual props or sound effects (appropriate music, recordings of howling wind or ocean waves, maybe even sounds of city traffic).

Creative Writing

Writing a Detective Story

"The Deer Thief" is essentially a detective story. The hunter uncovers clues at the scene of the crime and then analyzes these clues to determine the thief's identity. His success, though surprising, is plausible because he has based his analysis on factual evidence and on logical methods of deduction. Write your own detective story, making sure to include the following basic elements of the form: a mystery (it need not be a crime), the collection of clues, and the analysis of those clues to arrive at a reasonable yet unexpected conclusion. Your "mystery" need not be a spectacular one; rather, you might want to write about the sort of mystery that people encounter in everyday life: a lost pet, a stolen bike, a missing cassette tape. Try to be inventive in constructing clues and in describing the progress of your detective's investigation.

Prewriting. As you think about possible plot lines for your story, write down ideas as they come to you. For example, if you have thought of a good ending for a story but have not worked out details of plot, character, and setting, you may want to write a version of this conclusion and then work backward to construct the beginning and middle. Or, you may want to compose a rough outline of the general plot of your story and a list of "clues" to your mystery before you decide on a conclusion.

Writing. Although your story will likely focus more on plot than on description, you will want to "flesh out" your narrative with details of setting and character to make it plausible and interesting to the reader. For example, if your story centered on a missing bicycle, you would want to describe the scene of the crime and the surrounding neighborhood as well as the "clues" (such as bicycle tracks leading to a nearby garage) that help your narrator to solve the mystery.

The Force of Luck

Which would you rather receive: two hundred dollars or "a worthless piece of lead"? Enlisted to settle an argument between two wealthy friends, a simple miller proves that apparent values can be deceptive. When you finish reading "The Force of Luck," see if you think that the argument between the two friends has been resolved.

Once two wealthy friends got into a heated argument. One said that it was money which made a man prosperous, and the other maintained that it wasn't money, but luck, which made the man. They argued for some time and finally decided that if only they could find an honorable man then perhaps they could prove their respective points of view.

One day while they were passing through a small village they came upon a miller who was grinding corn and wheat. They paused to ask the man how he ran his business. The miller replied that he worked for a master and that he earned only four bits a day, and with that he had to support a family of five.

The friends were surprised. "Do you mean to tell us you can maintain a family of five on only fifteen dollars a month?" one asked.

"I live modestly to make ends meet," the humble miller replied.

The two friends privately agreed that if they put this man to a test perhaps they could resolve their argument.

"I am going to make you an offer," one of them said to the miller. "I will give you two hundred dollars and you may do whatever you want with the money."

"But why would you give me this money when you've just met me?" the miller asked.

"Well, my good man, my friend and I have a long standing argument. He contends that it is luck which elevates a man to high position, and I say it is money. By giving you this money perhaps we can settle our argument. Here, take it, and do with it what you want!"

So the poor miller took the money and spent the rest of the day thinking about the strange meeting which had presented him with more money than he had ever seen. What could he possibly do with all this money? Be that as it may, he had the money in his pocket and he could do with it whatever he wanted.

When the day's work was done, the miller decided the first thing he would do would be to buy food for his family. He took out ten dollars and wrapped the rest of the money in a cloth and put the bundle in his bag. Then he went to the market and bought supplies and a good piece of meat to take home.

On the way home he was attacked by a hawk that had smelled the meat which the miller carried. The miller fought off the bird but in the struggle he lost the bundle of money. Before the miller knew what was happening the hawk grabbed the bag and flew away with it. When he realized what had happened he fell into deep thought.

"Ah," he moaned, "wouldn't it have been better to let that hungry bird have the meat! I could have bought a lot more meat with the money he took. Alas, now I'm in the same poverty as before! And worse, because now those two men will say I am a thief! I should have thought carefully and bought nothing. Yes, I should have gone straight home and this wouldn't have happened!"

So he gathered what was left of his provisions and continued home, and when he arrived he told his family the entire story.

When he was finished telling his story his wife said, "It has been our lot to be poor, but have faith in God and maybe someday our luck will change."

The next day the miller got up and went to work as usual. He wondered what the two men would say about his story. But since he had never been a man of money he soon forgot the entire matter.

Three months after he had lost the money to the hawk, it happened that the two wealthy men returned to the village. As soon as they saw the miller they approached him to ask if his luck had changed. When the miller saw them he felt ashamed and afraid that they would think that he had squandered the money on worthless things. But he decided to tell them the truth and as soon as they had greeted each other he told his story.

The men believed him. In fact, the one who insisted that it was money and not luck which made a man prosper took out another two hundred dollars and gave it to the miller.

"Let's try again," he said, "and let's see what happens this time."

The miller didn't know what to think. "Kind sir, maybe it would be better if you put this money in the hands of another man," he said.

"No," the man insisted, "I want to give it to you because you are an honest man, and if we are going to settle our argument you have to take the money!"

The miller thanked them and promised to do his best. Then as soon as the two men left he began to think what to do with the money so that it wouldn't disappear as it had the first time. The thing to do was to take the money straight home. He took out ten dollars, wrapped the rest in a cloth, and headed home.

When he arrived his wife wasn't at home. At first he didn't know what to do with the money. He went to the pantry where he had stored a large earthenware jar filled with bran. That was as safe a place as any to hide the money, he thought, so he emptied out the grain and put the bundle of money at the bottom of the jar, then covered it up with the grain. Satisfied that the money was safe he returned to work.

That afternoon when he arrived home from work he was greeted by his wife.

"Look, my husband, today I bought some good clay with which to whitewash the entire house."

"And how did you buy the clay if we don't have any money? he asked.

"Well, the man who was selling the clay was willing to trade for jewelry, money, or anything of value," she said. "The only thing we had of value was the jar full of bran, so I traded it for the clay. Isn't it wonderful, I think we have enough clay to whitewash these two rooms!"

The man groaned and pulled his hair.

"Oh, you crazy woman! What have you done? We're ruined again!"

"But why?" she asked, unable to understand his anguish.

"Today I met the same two friends who gave me the two hundred dollars three months ago," he explained. "And after I told them how I lost the money they gave me another two hundred. And I, to make sure the money was safe, came home and hid it inside the jar of bran—the same jar you have traded for dirt! Now we're as poor as we were before! And what am I going to tell the two men? They'll think I'm a liar and a thief for sure!"

"Let them think what they want," his wife said calmly. "We will only have in our lives what the good Lord wants us to have. It is our lot to be poor until God wills it otherwise."

So the miller was consoled and the next day he went to work as usual. Time came and went, and one day the two wealthy friends returned to ask the miller how he had done with the second two hundred dollars. When the poor miller saw them he was afraid they would accuse him of being a liar and a spendthrift. But he decided to be truthful and as soon as they had greeted each other he told them what had happened to the money.

"That is why poor men remain honest," the man who had given him the money said. "Because they don't have money they can't get into trouble. But I find your stories hard to believe. I think you gambled and lost the money. That's why you're telling us these wild stories."

"Either way," he continued, "I still believe that it is money and not luck which makes a man prosper."

"Well, you certainly didn't prove your point by giving the money to this poor miller," his friend reminded him. "Good evening, you luckless man," he said to the miller.

"Thank you, friends," the miller said.

"Oh, by the way, here is a worthless piece of lead I've been carrying around. Maybe you can use it for something," said the man who believed in luck. Then the two men left, still debating their points of view on life.

Since the lead was practically worthless, the miller thought nothing of it and put it in his jacket pocket. He forgot all about it until he arrived home. When he threw his jacket on a chair he heard a thump and he remembered the piece of lead. He took it out of the pocket and threw it under the table. Later that night after the family had eaten and gone to bed, they heard a knock at the door.

"Who is it? What do you want?" the miller asked.

"It's me, your neighbor," a voice answered. The miller recognized the fisherman's wife. "My husband sent me to ask you if you have any lead you can spare. He is going fishing tomorrow and he needs the lead to weight down the nets."

The miller remembered the lead he had thrown under the table. He got up, found it, and gave it to the woman.

"Thank you very much, neighbor," the woman said. "I promise you the first fish my husband catches will be yours."

"Think nothing of it," the miller said and returned to bed. The next day he got up and went to work without thinking any more of the incident. But in the afternoon when he returned home he found his wife cooking a big fish for dinner.

"Since when are we so well off we can afford fish for supper?" he asked his wife.

"Don't you remember that our neighbor promised us the first fish her husband caught?" his wife reminded him. "Well this was the fish he caught the first time he threw his net. So it's ours, and it's a beauty. But you should have been here when I gutted him! I found a large piece of glass in his stomach!"

"And what did you do with it?"

"Oh, I gave it to the children to play with," she shrugged.

When the miller saw the piece of glass he noticed it shone so brightly it appeared to illuminate the room, but because he knew nothing about jewels he didn't realize its value and left it to the children. But the bright glass was such a novelty that the children were soon fighting over it and raising a terrible fuss.

Now it so happened that the miller and his wife had other neighbors who were jewelers. The following morning when the miller had gone to work the jeweler's wife visited the miller's wife to complain about all the noise her children had made.

"We couldn't get any sleep last night," she moaned.

"I know, and I'm sorry, but you know how it is with a large family," the miller's wife explained. "Yesterday we found a beautiful piece of glass and I gave it to my youngest one to play with and when the others tried to take it from him he raised a storm."

The jeweler's wife took interest. "Won't you show me that piece of glass?" she asked.

"But of course. Here it is."

"Ah, yes, it's a pretty piece of glass. Where did you find it?"

"Our neighbor gave us a fish yesterday and when I was cleaning it I found the glass in its stomach."

"Why don't you let me take it home for just a moment? You see, I have one just like it and I want to compare them."

"Yes, why not? Take it," answered the miller's wife.

So the jeweler's wife ran off with the glass to show it to her husband. When the jeweler saw the glass he instantly knew it was one of the finest diamonds he had ever seen.

"It's a diamond!" he exclaimed.

"I thought so," his wife nodded eagerly. "What shall we do?"

"Go tell the neighbor we'll give her fifty dollars for it, but don't tell her it's a diamond!"

"No, no," his wife chuckled, "of course not." She ran to her neighbor's house. "Ah yes, we have one exactly like this," she told the miller's wife. "My husband is willing to buy it for fifty dollars—only so we can have a pair, you understand."

"I can't sell it," the miller's wife answered. "You will have to wait until my husband returns from work."

That evening when the miller came home from work his wife told him about the offer the jeweler had made for the piece of glass.

"But why would they offer fifty dollars for a worthless piece of glass?" the miller wondered aloud. Before his wife could answer they were interrupted by the jeweler's wife.

"What do you say, neighbor, will you take fifty dollars for the glass?" she asked.

"No, that's not enough," the miller said cautiously. "Offer more."

"I'll give you fifty thousand!" the jeweler's wife blurted out.

"A little bit more," the miller replied.

"Impossible!" the jeweler's wife cried, "I can't offer any more without consulting my husband." She ran off to tell her husband how the bartering was going, and he told her he was prepared to pay a hundred thousand dollars to acquire the diamond.

He handed her seventy-five thousand dollars and said, "Take this and tell him that tomorrow, as soon as I open my shop, he'll have the rest."

When the miller heard the offer and saw the money he

couldn't believe his eyes. He imagined the jeweler's wife was jesting with him, but it was a true offer and he received the hundred thousand dollars for the diamond. The miller had never seen so much money, but he still didn't quite trust the jeweler.

"I don't know about this money," he confided to his wife. "Maybe the jeweler plans to accuse us of robbing him and thus get it back."

"Oh, no," his wife assured him, "the money is ours. We sold the diamond fair and square—we didn't rob anyone."

"I think I'll still go to work tomorrow," the miller said. "Who knows, something might happen and the money will disappear, then we would be without money and work. Then how would we live?"

So he went to work the next day, and all day he thought about how he could use the money. When he returned home that afternoon his wife asked him what he had decided to do with their new fortune.

"I think I will start my own mill," he answered, "like the one I operate for my master. Once I set up my business we'll see how our luck changes."

The next day he set about buying everything he needed to establish his mill and to build a new home. Soon he had everything going.

Six months had passed, more or less, since he had seen the two men who had given him the four hundred dollars and the piece of lead. He was eager to see them again and to tell them how the piece of lead had changed his luck and made him wealthy.

Time passed and the miller prospered. His business grew and he even built a summer cottage where he could take his family on vacation. He had many employees who worked for him. One day while he was at his store he saw his two benefactors riding by. He rushed out into the street to greet them and ask them to come in. He was overjoyed to see them, and he was happy to see that they admired his store.

"Tell us the truth," the man who had given him the four hundred dollars said. "You used that money to set up this business."

The miller swore he hadn't, and he told them how he had given the piece of lead to his neighbor and how the fisherman had in return given him a fish with a very large diamond in its stomach. And he told them how he had sold the diamond.

"And that's how I acquired this business and many other things I want to show you," he said. "But it's time to eat. Let's eat first then I'll show you everything I have now."

The men agreed, but one of them still doubted the miller's story. So they ate and then the miller had three horses saddled and they rode out to see his summer home. The cabin was on the other side of the river where the mountains were cool and beautiful. When they arrived the men admired the place very much. It was such a peaceful place that they rode all afternoon through the forest. During their ride they came upon a tall pine tree.

"What is that on top of the tree?" one of them asked.

"That's the nest of a hawk," the miller replied.

"I have never seen one; I would like to take a closer look at it!"

"Of course," the miller said, and he ordered a servant to climb the tree and bring down the nest so his friend could see how it was built. When the hawk's nest was on the ground they examined it carefully. They noticed that there was a cloth bag at the bottom of the nest. When the miller saw the bag he immediately knew that it was the very same bag he had lost to the hawk which fought him for the piece of meat years ago.

"You won't believe me, friends, but this is the very same bag in which I put the first two hundred dollars you gave me," he told them.

"If it's the same bag," the man who had doubted him said, "then the money you said the hawk took should be there."

"No doubt about that," the miller said. "Let's see what we find."

The three of them examined the old, weatherbeaten bag. Although it was full of holes and crumbling, when they tore it apart they found the money intact. The two men remembered what the miller had told them and they agreed he was an honest and honorable man. Still, the man who had given him the money wasn't satisfied. He wondered what had really happened to the second two hundred he had given the miller.

They spent the rest of the day riding in the mountains and returned very late to the house.

As he unsaddled their horses, the servant in charge of

grooming and feeding the horses suddenly realized that he had no grain for them. He ran to the barn and checked, but there was no grain for the hungry horses. So he ran to the neighbor's granary and there he was able to buy a large clay jar of bran. He carried the jar home and emptied the bran into a bucket to wet it before he fed it to the horses. When he got to the bottom of the jar he noticed a large lump which turned out to be a rag covered package. He examined it and felt something inside. He immediately went to give it to his master who had been eating dinner.

"Master," he said, "look at this package which I found in an earthenware jar of grain which I just bought from our neighbor!"

The three men carefully unraveled the cloth and found the other one hundred and ninety dollars which the miller had told them he had lost. That is how the miller proved to his friends that he was truly an honest man.

And they had to decide for themselves whether it had been luck or money which had made the miller a wealthy man!

retold by **Rudolfo A. Anaya**

For Study and Discussion

1. At the end of the tale, the two friends must decide whether it is luck or money that has led to the miller's prosperity. **a.** What clue does the title provide as to which is responsible? **b.** Which do you think it is—luck or money?

2. In order to resolve their argument, the two wealthy men disrupt the life of a simple miller who, though poor, is content with his lot. Although he eventually prospers, the miller also experiences great distress as a result of this experiment. Do you think that the two men's manipulation of the miller is unjust? Refer to specific passages in the story to support your answer.

Writing About Literature

Analyzing Cause and Effect

The miller is eager to tell the two wealthy men "how the piece of lead had changed his luck and made him wealthy." Certainly, he is tremendously lucky to end up with a diamond in exchange for "a worthless piece of lead." Yet, the story provides ample evidence that the miller himself is largely responsible for his prosperity. Reread the story, noting the events that lead up to the miller's good fortune. To what extent does his "changed luck" trace to his own efforts and virtues? In an essay of two or three paragraphs, discuss and support your answer.

Prewriting. As you review the latter half of the story, ask yourself the following questions. At what point in the story does the miller's "luck" change? How is he responsible for his wife's receiving the fish? How does he bargain with the jeweler's wife? What does he do with the money once he receives it? Next, divide the things that happen to the miller into two categories: those events that are attributable to luck or chance and those that the miller himself brings about through prudence, ingenuity, and charity. Are there events whose causes are uncertain?

Writing. Word your thesis sentence carefully so that it clearly states the point that you intend to make in your essay. As you write, make sure that transitions between ideas are clear: use transitional expressions such as *however, likewise,* and *in addition* to link ideas and examples when appropriate.

Tales of *La Llorona*

Most cultures have legends of ghostly figures who inhabit the night. One such figure in Mexican American culture is *La Llorona* (lah yoh-roh'nah), the Weeping Woman. Many towns throughout Mexico as well as the Southwest and California have their own tales of this legendary figure. The most common version centers around an Indian woman who is betrayed by her deceitful husband. Insane with rage and anguish, she drowns their children and soon afterward dies in remorse. Her restless spirit takes human form and appears to unsuspecting people, usually around the lake or river where the drowning is supposed to have taken place. She is often dressed in a flowing white dress and is weeping or wailing, grieving the loss of her children.

La Llorona takes on different forms, which vary from locale to locale. For example, in Valencia County, New Mexico, she is supposed to have appeared as a beautiful woman to a man who happened to be looking out a window one warm summer evening. He hastened outside to search for her, but she had mysteriously disappeared and was nowhere to be found. Anglo and Mexican American cowboys in western New Mexico have described her as a very fetching horse-woman dressed in elegant riding clothes. The rural inhabitants of southern Colorado, on the other hand, have seen her as a weeping woman who would emerge from a big black rock at night. Enveloped in a white mist, she would grow taller and taller and then vanish.

In one form or another, *La Llorona* has haunted Mexico and the Southwest for a long time. While those who have investigated the legend disagree on its specific origin, they do agree that it seems to be a combination of European and Mexican Indian legends. Some trace *La Llorona* to the Greek Medea myth. Others claim that she resembles the legendary European "women in white" who are said to have disguised themselves in white to be able to move about freely at night when women were supposed to stay at home.

The two tales of *La Llorona* on the following pages come from the area around Austin, Texas, and present two of the themes commonly found in stories about the Weeping Woman throughout the Southwest.

The first opens with the underlying tragedy of *La Llorona,* the murder of her children. The remainder of the story tells of two young boys' frightening encounter with her. In the second story, the Weeping Woman again throws a scare into two friends, this time grown men; however, a somewhat understated vein of humor tempers the element of fright and leaves the reader with a smile at the close of the tale.

The Weeping Woman
(I)

Have you ever been on a camping trip and found yourself alarmed by strange noises in the night? If so, you can probably sympathize with the two boys in this tale. As you read, see if you think the boys let their imaginations run away with them . . . or if they really did have an encounter with La Llorona.

Do you know why La Llorona appears near the Colorado River?[1] Well, La Llorona was a woman who lived here in Austin. She had two children, but she didn't love them. One day she took them to the river and drowned them. She never repented, and that is why she appears there and cries for her children.

My son, Rodolfo, was ten or eleven years old when he and some other boys decided to spend the night out near the river. They went in a little cart and took some blankets.

At night they spread the blankets out on the ground and went to sleep. He says that after midnight all of them woke up at the same time and saw a shadow flit across them. Then they heard the piercing wail of La Llorona. They got up and came home immediately. My son was very frightened when he got home.

---

1. **Colorado River:** the small Colorado River in Texas; not the large Colorado River that flows from Colorado to California.

The Weeping Woman
(II)

As this tale illustrates, sometimes a brush with the ghostly Weeping Woman prompts people to mend their ways. The two men in this story get more than they bargained for when they decide to follow an "attractive woman" on their way into town. See if you can catch a note of humor in the startling outcome of their pursuit.

My brother had a very good friend who was a shoemaker. The two were heavy drinkers, and they liked to go out together to eat and drink.

Well, one night my brother went to see his friend about twelve-thirty and prevailed on him to go out to drink with him.

Shortly after the two had started out for their favorite saloon, they noticed that a very attractive woman was walking just ahead of them. They decided to follow her. The two followed for a long time, but they couldn't catch up with her. When it seemed that they were coming up even with the woman, she suddenly seemed to get about half a block ahead of them. Finally, my brother and his friend decided to turn back, but as a parting gesture they said, "Good-by, my dear!"

At the same time that the two said, "Good-by, my dear!" the attractive woman whom they had followed turned around. She had the face of a horse, her fingernails were shiny and tin-like, and she gave a long, piercing cry. It was La Llorona.

My brother would have run, but his friend had fainted, and he had to revive him. The two reformed after that encounter with La Llorona.

For Study and Discussion

The Weeping Woman (I)

1. This tale gives one version of *La Llorona*'s tragedy. Compare this version to the version discussed in the essay that begins on page 36. What elements are similar? What variations appear here?

2. According to this version, *La Llorona* drowned her children in the Colorado River. Why might she be likely to appear to two young boys near that river?

The Weeping Woman (II)

3a. The two men have no idea that the "attractive woman" they are following is *La Llorona*. What is the first clue in the tale that she is not an ordinary woman? **b.** Why do you think she allows them to follow her before she reveals her face?

4. Irony of situation involves a difference between the expected result of an action or situation and its actual result. How is this tale an example of irony of situation?

Creative Writing

Writing a Ghostly Tale

Like most tales of ghostly creatures, the legend of *La Llorona* has many variations, depending on the story's locale and the creative imagination of the storyteller. Write your own tale about *La Llorona* or about an eerie legend that is part of the folklore of your area.

Prewriting. Your tale might focus on the legendary history of a ghostly figure or on a specific encounter with the subject of the legend. Even if you are writing about a particular incident, you will want to give a brief description of the legend behind it. If you are writing about *La Llorona,* you can draw on the variations presented in this book to create your own version of the tale. If you choose to write about a legend that is set in your area, you may want to ask your parents, one of your teachers, or a local expert on folklore for additional information about the origins and variations of the legend. Remember that, as a storyteller, you are free to embellish or otherwise alter the tale to add interest to your story.

Writing and Revising. Choose your words carefully to create the desired atmosphere and effect. Try to avoid clichéd phrases such as "it was a dark and stormy night," focusing instead on specific details of setting and action to set the mood of your tale.

Folk Music and Poetry

Like folk tales, the music and poetry of the oral tradition continue to thrive wherever Spanish is spoken in the United States. Defined by a number of distinctive features, Mexican American folk songs and oral poetry fall into four categories: the *romance*, the *corrido*, the *décima*, and the *canción*.

The *romance* is a form of ballad that was originally sung by Spanish troubadours who traveled from region to region bringing news and relating stories. *Romances* sung today throughout California and the southwestern United States include children's nursery rhymes as well as ballads about religious miracles, tragic occurrences, and remarkable achievements.

The *corrido* is a popular musical form that has evolved from the *romance*. The traditional *corrido* is usually a fast-paced ballad that tells a story of tragedy, heroism, or adventure. "The Ballad of Gregorio Cortez" and "Ballad of the Death of Antonio Mestas," which appear on the following pages, are good examples of this kind of ballad. *Corridos* composed today deal with a variety of topics including legendary horse races, the travails of immigrants crossing the Mexican border into the United States, and the lives of popular figures such as the baseball player Fernando Valenzuela and President John F. Kennedy.

The *décima* and the *canción* are types of folk songs that, like the *romance*, originated in Spain. While the *décima* often employs a somewhat rigid metrical structure, the *canción* is more flexible and can take a variety of verse forms. Dealing predominantly with love and religious themes, these folk songs are heard mainly in New Mexico and southern Colorado.

El gato le dice al ratón / The Cat Says to the Mouse

Although this folk ballad takes the form of a simple rhyme, its last stanza reveals it to be a strong statement concerning political upheavals in nineteenth-century Mexico. Márquez, Mejía, and Miramón were conservative generals who supported Maximilian, an Austrian who was appointed emperor of Mexico in 1864. A majority of the Mexican people were opposed to Maximilian's reign and supported the reinstatement of Benito Juárez as their leader. Maximilian and his generals were eventually captured and shot by Juárez's soldiers in Querétaro, and Juárez—then a national hero—was reelected as president.

While ballads can be read as poems, they are usually set to music. The following musical notation gives the tune and lyrics for the first stanza of "El gato le dice al ratón."

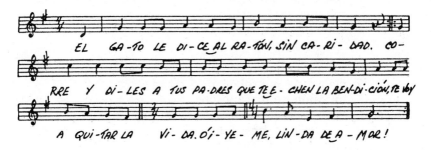

EL GA-TO LE DI-CE AL RA-TÓN, SIN CA-RI-DAD. CO-
RRE Y DI-LES A TUS PA-DRES QUE TE E-CHEN LA BEN-DI-CIÓN, TE VOY
A QUI-TAR LA VI-DA. ÓI-YE-ME, LIN-DA DE A-MOR!

El gato le dice
al ratón

1

El gato le dice al ratón, sin caridad.
El gato le dice al ratón, sin caridad.
Corre y díles a tus padres
que te echen la benedición,
te voy a quitar la vida.   5
¡Oyeme, linda de amor!

2

El ratón le dice al gato, sin caridad.
El ratón le dice al gato, sin caridad.
No me mates todavía,
déjame de hacer testamento   10
de toda mi lotería.
¡Oyeme, linda de amor!

3

El gato le dice al ratón, sin caridad.
El gato le dice al ratón, sin caridad.
Confiesa y dí tus pecados;   15
porque tienes que morir
en mis dientes apretados.
¡Oyeme, linda de amor!

4

Yo me acuso que robé, sin caridad.
Yo me acuso que robé, sin caridad.   20
De un cajón de marquesote
no esperando confesarme
con tan grande sacerdote.
¡Oyeme, linda de amor!

5

De esta sierra a la otra sierra, sin caridad.   25
De esta sierra a la otra sierra, sin caridad.

The Cat Says to the Mouse

1

The cat says to the mouse, without charity.
The cat says to the mouse, without charity.
Go and tell your parents
To give you their blessing;
I am going to take your life.   5
Hear me, my beautiful beloved!

2

The mouse says to the cat, without charity.
The mouse says to the cat, without charity.
Do not kill me yet,
Give me time to make my will   10
And bequeath all my belongings.
Hear me, my beautiful beloved!

3

The cat says to the mouse, without charity.
The cat says to the mouse, without charity.
Confess all of your sins;   15
For you're going to meet your death
In my clenched teeth.
Hear me, my beautiful beloved!

4

I accuse myself of theft, without charity.
I accuse myself of theft, without charity.   20
Of stealing a cake from a bin
Not expecting to confess
To such a great priest.
Hear me, my beautiful beloved!

5

From this mountain to the other, without charity.   25
From this mountain to the other, without charity.

¡Mueran Márquez y Mejía,
¡Mueran todos los queretanos,
Miramón y sus hermanos!
¡Oyeme, linda de amor!   30

Death to Márquez and Mejía,
Death to all the *Queretanos,*
Miramón and all his brothers![1]
Hear me, my beautiful beloved!   30

---

1. **Márquez, Mejía, Miramón** (mahr'kehs, meh-hee'ah, mee-rah-mohn'):
   These men were generals in the service of the conservatives supporting
   Maximilian against Juárez. The *Queretanos* were from Querétaro, where
   the generals and Maximilian were shot. (Rubén Cobos supplied these
   notes.)

For Study and Discussion

1. The refrain "Hear me, my beautiful beloved!" occurs at the end of each stanza. What is the effect of this refrain? How does it help to create the tone of the ballad and to unify its elements?

2. Although the last stanza may at first seem unrelated to the rest of the ballad, like the previous stanzas it contains a message of impending disaster. What parallel is drawn between the cat's prey and the individuals mentioned in the last stanza?

3. This ballad may remind you of nursery rhymes that you heard as a child. **a.** How is it like a nursery rhyme? **b.** What particular rhyme or rhymes does it remind you of, if any?

Literary Elements

Translation

Often, **connotations**—meanings and feelings that have become associated with words and phrases—are difficult to translate from one language into another. A **literal,** or word-for-word, translation accurately conveys the definition of a word or phrase but often does not capture its connotations. For this reason, translators often give a **figurative** interpretation—one that focuses on the intended meaning of a word or phrase rather than on its literal definition.

Translating a poetic work is particularly challenging because poets and songwriters often employ figures of speech and subtle ambiguities of meaning as well as complex sound patterns and stanza structures. In "The Cat Says to the Mouse," for example, the translator was not able to both preserve the ballad's original rhyme scheme and render the exact meanings of the lines. Look carefully at the ends of the lines in the Spanish version and the English translation. How does the rhyme scheme of the Spanish version compare to that of the translation?

El corrido de Gregorio Cortez / The Ballad of Gregorio Cortez

Like most ballads, "The Ballad of Gregorio Cortez" is based on recorded historical events. According to some, the "real" Gregorio Cortez was a peaceful, hard-working man who killed in self-defense and was unjustly pursued. According to others, he was a horse thief and a cold-blooded murderer. The true story probably lies somewhere in between these two versions. By all accounts, however, the fugitive Cortez was clever, courageous, and an exceedingly good shot. Although captured and tried for murder and horse theft, he eventually received a pardon. Shortly after his release, however, he died from undetermined causes— some people think he had a heart attack; others believe he was poisoned. As you read the ballad, notice how the composer's attitude toward Cortez influences his account. Does the composer portray Cortez in a sympathetic or an unsympathetic light?

While ballads can be read as poems, they are usually set to music. The following musical notation gives the tune and lyrics for the first stanza of "El corrido de Gregorio Cortez."

EN EL CON - DA - DO DEL CAR - MEN LA DES -

GRA - CIA HA SU CE - DI - DO MU - RIÓ EL CHE - RIFE

MA - YOR QUE - DAN - DO ROMÁN HERIDO

El corrido de Gregorio Cortez

1

En el condado del Carmen
la desgracia ha sucedido,
murió el Cherife Mayor
quedando Román herido.

2

En el condado del Carmen
la desgracia sucedió,
murió el Cherife Mayor,
no saben quién lo mató.

5

3

Salió con rumbo a Laredo
sin ninguna timidez:
—Síganme rinches cobardes,
yo soy Gregorio Cortez.

10

4

Decía Gregorio Cortez,
con su alma muy encendida:
—No siento haberlo matado,
la defensa es permitida.

15

5

Decía Gregorio Cortez,
con su pistola en la mano:
—No corran rinches cobardes
con un puro mexicano.

20

6

Como a las ocho serían,
como tres horas después,
supieron que el malhechor
era Gregorio Cortez.

The Ballad of Gregorio Cortez

1

In the county of El Carmen,
The misfortune has occurred;
The Major Sheriff died,
Leaving Román badly wounded.

2

In the county of El Carmen,
The misfortune occurred;
The Major Sheriff died;
It is not known who killed him.

3

He went out toward Laredo,[1]
Without showing any fear,
"Follow me, you cowardly rangers,
I am Gregorio Cortez."

4

Then said Gregorio Cortez,
And his soul was all aflame,
"I don't regret that I killed him;
A man must defend himself."

5

Then said Gregorio Cortez,
With his pistol in his hand,
"Don't run, you cowardly rangers,
From a real Mexican."

6

It must have been about eight o'clock,
About three hours afterward,
They found out that the wrongdoer
Had been Gregorio Cortez.

---

1. **Laredo** (lah-reh'doh): city and port of entry in South Texas.

7

Iban los americanos
por el viento que volaban
porque se iban a ganar
dos mil pesos que les daban.

8

Decían los americanos:
—Si lo hallamos ¿qué le haremos?
Si le entramos por derecho
Muy poquitos volveremos.

9

Iban los americanos
iban siguiendo la huella,
porque alcanzar a Cortez
era alcanzar a una estrella.

10

Decía Gregorio Cortez:
—¿Pa' qué se valen de planes?
No me pueden agarrar
ni con esos perros jaunes.

11

Gregorio le dice a Juan:
—Muy pronto lo vas a ver;
anda díles a los rinches
que me vengan a aprehender.

12

Allá por El Encinal
lo alcanzaron a rodear,
poquitos más de trescientos
y allí les brincó el corral.

13

Salió Gregorio Cortez,
salió con rumbo a Laredo,
no lo quisieron seguir
porque le tuvieron miedo.

7

The Americans were riding   25
Through the air as if they flew;
Because they wanted to get
Two thousand dollars they were offered.

8

Then the Americans said,
"If we find him, what shall we do?   30
If we fight him man to man
Very few of us will return."

9

The Americans were riding,
They were following the trail;
Because trying to overtake Cortez   35
Was like overtaking a star.

10

Then said Gregorio Cortez,
"What is the use of your scheming?
You cannot catch me,
Even with those bloodhounds."   40

11

Gregorio says to Juan,
"You will see it very soon;
Go tell the rangers
To come and arrest me."

12

Over by El Encinal[2]   45
They succeeded in surrounding him;
Quite a few more than three hundred,
But there he jumped their corral.

13

Gregorio Cortez went out,
He went out toward Laredo,   50
They decided not to follow
Because they were afraid of him.

---

2. **El Encinal** (ehl ehn-see-nahl'): literally "The Woods"; the name of a
village in South Texas.

14

Venían todos los rinches,
venían buscando a Cortez,
les preguntaban a muchos: 55
—¿Dónde está el Rancho El Ciprés?

15

Cuando llegaron los rinches
Gregorio se presentó:
—Por la buena sí me llevan,
porque de otro modo no.   60

16

Ya mataron a Cortez,
ya se acabó la cuestión,
la pobre de su familia,
lo lleva en el corazón.

17

Ya con ésta me despido   65
con las hojas del ciprés,
aquí termina el corrido
de don Gregorio Cortez.

_____

14

All the rangers were coming,
They were looking for Cortez;
They asked of many people,   55
"Where is the ranch of El Ciprés?"[3]

15

When the rangers arrived,
Gregorio gave himself up,
"You will take me if I'm willing,
But not any other way."   60

16

Now they have killed Cortez,
Now matters are at an end;
His poor family
Are suffering in their hearts.

17

Now with this I say farewell,   65
With the leaves of the cypress,
This is the end of the ballad
Of Don Gregorio Cortez.

---

3. El Ciprés (ehl see-prehs'): literally "The Cypress"; the name of a ranch
in South Texas.

For Study and Discussion

1. In oral as well as written literature, the words artists choose reflect their feelings about the events they describe. In the first stanza of this *corrido,* what sentiments does the composer express through the line, "The misfortune has occurred"?

2. Like many folk ballads, this *corrido* portrays its hero as a larger-than-life figure. What remarkable qualities does this ballad attribute to Gregorio Cortez? On the basis of this portrayal, what sort of person does Cortez seem to be? Refer to specific lines and stanzas of the poem to support your answer.

3. What sort of person do you think Gregorio Cortez actually was? How do you feel about the ballad's sympathetic representation of him?

Literary Elements

The Folk Ballad

Folk ballads are stories told in verse, usually meant to be sung. Their language is simple yet poetic, and their subject matter— which includes tales of tragic love, heroism, and adventure— springs from the lives and dreams of the common people. Like any oral literature, folk ballads are anonymous and are passed down from generation to generation, incorporating the creative additions and embellishments of successive tellers. Frequently, several versions of a single ballad will flourish in various locales. In what ways does this particular version of "El corrido de Gregorio Cortez" reflect the folk ballad form?

Research variations of "El corrido de Gregorio Cortez." (One source is Américo Paredes's *"With His Pistol in His Hand": A Border Ballad and Its Hero.*) How do these other versions differ from the one presented here? What elements do they share? What are some traditional American folk ballads? How do they compare in form and theme to "El corrido de Gregorio Cortez"?

Corrido de la muerte de Antonio Mestas / Ballad of the Death of Antonio Mestas

In contrast to "The Ballad of Gregorio Cortez," this ballad tells not of a legendary heroic figure but rather of a simple, good-natured young man whose death was mourned by all who knew him. As you read "Ballad of the Death of Antonio Mestas," notice the specific details that ground the ballad in historical fact. What do these details reveal about Antonio Mestas and the people in his community?

While ballads can be read as poems, they are usually set to music. The following musical notation gives the tune and lyrics for "Corrido de la muerte de Antonio Mestas."

Corrido de la muerte de Antonio Mestas

1

Año de mil ochocientos
ochenta y nueve pasó,
que el día cinco de julio,
mi Dios lo determinó,
que al finado Antonio Mestas   5
un caballo lo mató,
en el lugar de "El Mogote,"
ese lugar escogió.

2

Del "Rancho de los Ingleses"
salió el hombre bueno y sano   10
a dar rodeo a las reses
según la orden de su amo.
Joven, alegre y lozano,
fué resignado a su suerte;
salió a recibir la muerte   15
en el lomo de un caballo.

3

En su cama verdadera
se presentó en su agonía,
falto de su compañía,
no despertó al cocinero,   20
un amigo verdadero
qu'el en el fondo tenía;
se dijo que el mismo día
en visión vió al caballero.

Ballad of the Death of Antonio Mestas

1

In the year of eighteen hundred
And eighty-nine in July,
On the fifth day God determined
Antonio Mestas must die;
That he should be thrown from the saddle   5
And meet his death on the ground,
Near the ridge of El Mogote,[1]
And there his body was found.

2

From the ranch owned by the English
Antonio rode at dawn,   10
To round up a herd of cattle
Which from their range had gone.
Though young and handsome and happy,
Antonio to fate was resigned;
To die like a man and a cowboy   15
Was in Antonio's mind.

3

For as he slept in the bunkhouse
Antonio had a dream,
A dream of death in the mountains,
Beside a running stream.   20
The cook he did not waken,
Who was his bosom friend,
And who, they say, in a vision
Foresaw Antonio's end.

---

1. **El Mogote** (ehl moh-goh'teh): a mountain located in northern New
Mexico.

4

Otro día en la mañana   25
salen todos a buscarlo,
recorren montes y valles
y sótanos y cañadas;
por último, de las cansadas,
lo dejan para otro día.   30
Se ausentó la compañía,
y el muerto quedó tirado.

5

A "La Cebolla" volando
vino el despacho improviso,
dándole a la gente aviso   35
de lo que estaba pasando;
la gente salió llorando
de compasión alarmada
y toda muy empeñada
al muerto siguen buscando.   40

6

Mi Diós, que todo lo mira
y todo pone en acuerdo,
orillas de una colina
hizo que gorjeara un cuervo
diciendo:—Aquí está tu siervo   45
entre esos zacatonales,
hombres, sean *razonales*,
observen lo que yo observo.—

7

El día siete de julio
toda la gente lo halló   50
al finado Antonio Mestas,
un caballo lo mató.
La gente se estremeció
viendo con asombro el cuerpo
hinchado y desfigurado   55
y casi todo deshecho.

4

The next morn all went searching,   25
They searched the land in vain,
They searched the mountain forests,
They searched the sagebrush plain.
They searched from early morning
Until the darkness fell,   30
But finding nothing, departed
Although they had hunted well.

5

To La Cebolla[2] came flying
The unexpected word,
To give the people notice   35
Of what had just occurred.
The people came out crying
With pity and alarm,
And everyone was fearful
Antonio had suffered harm.   40

6

But God who watcheth and knoweth
The thing that the searchers seek,
Caused a crow who stood on the hilltop
These bitter words to speak:
"Below me lies your servant   45
Among the grasses tall;
Observe the thing that I see,
It's here your friend did fall."

7

July the seventh they found him,
And all with sorrow were filled,   50
As they viewed Antonio's body,
Who by a horse was killed.
They turned away in horror,
The blood within them froze,
For the body was swollen and rotting,   55
And torn by carrion crows.

---

2. **La Cebolla** (lah seh-boh'yah): a town located in northern New Mexico.

Ballad of the Death of Antonio Mestas 63

8

Llegó Bernabel Trujillo
y mirando tal espanto,
de ternura formó el llanto
diciéndole: —Hermano mío,   60
¿por qué te hallas tan *mustío*?
¿Qué es lo que yo estoy mirando,
un hermano de mi vida
en estos campos tirado?—

9

Ya salió Ambrosio Espinosa   65
que es un joven vigilante,
a darle a su gente parte
de muerte tan lastimosa,
y como ágil mariposa
voló en el viento veloz,   70
con la voluntad de Dios,
en noche tan tenebrosa,

10

Al llano llegó por fin,
donde su padre vivía,
y le dice: —Qué avería   75
le causé a don Agustín;
padrecito, usted por fin
se tomará este trabajo,
y váyase para abajo;
dé parte a don Agustín.—   80

11

Don Benito se salió
y para abajo se fué:
—Buenos días tenga usted,
¿cómo le va, amiguito?—
—Apéese, don Benito,—   85
le dice don Agustín,
aunque sin saber el fin
se enterneció ¡pobrecito!

8

Then came Bernabal Trujillo
And saw him where he lay;
In tenderness he lamented,
And crying out did say: 60
"My brother, what has befallen,
And what is this I see,
So dead and still in the meadow,
Can this thing really be?"

9

Ambrosio Espinosa,   65
A strong and vigilant youth,
Was sent to bear to the family
The stern and dreadful truth.
And like the agile butterfly,
He flew through the winds of the night,   70
And the will of God sustained him
With courage and with might.

10

At last he came to the valley
In which his father dwelt,
And thus he spoke of the matter,   75
And full of sadness he felt
"Please go, my *padrecito*,[3]
And tell Don[4] Agustín
His son lies dead in the mountains,
But gently please begin."   80

11

Don Benito did as requested,
To bear the news he went:
"Good day, little friend. How goes it?
With a message I am sent."
"Dismount, my friend Don Benito,"   85
Don Agustín calmly did speak;
But though, poor man, he knew nothing,
He suddenly felt weak.

---

3. *padrecito* (pah-threh-see'toh): dear father.
4. **Don** (dohn): a title of respect, formerly used for Spanish-speaking men
of high rank; now used as a title of courtesy.

12
—Dispense usted mi venida,
amigo, tan de mañana, 90
del hijo de sus entrañas
vengo a traerle una noticia.—
Y Mestas, muy asustado
le dice: —¿Que sucedió?—
Don Benito, recatado 95
de este modo respondió:

13
—Que al finado Antonio Mestas
un caballo lo mató
en el lugar de "El Mogote,"
ese lugar escogió.— 100

14
Mestas el llanto soltó,
desesperado lloró:
—Perdí todo mi caudal,
perdí todo mi tesoro,
y sólo a mi Dios imploro.— 105
Le dice a la Martinita
—Ya murió tu esposo, hijita,
ya se acabó tu decoro.—

15
La joven se desmayó
asustada y macilenta 110
de noticia tan violenta
que así a sus oídos llegó.
Su pecho en llanto rompió
y entre sollozos decía:
—¡Ay, esposo del alma mía, 115
qué es lo que te sucedió!

16
¡Ay, padrecito Atilano,
ay, padrecito Agustín,
ay, hermanos de mi vida,
amado Antonio, hasta el fin, 120
¿Qué más te podré decir,
esposo y fiel verdadero?

12

"Forgive me for coming so early,
I come to bring you word   90
Of your beloved Antonio,
Which I have just now heard."
And Mestas, greatly excited,
Explained, "What happened, I pray?"
And Don Benito responded   95
To Don Agustín this way:

13

"The late Antonio Mestas"—
Don Agustín's heart was chilled,
"On the mountain called 'El Mogote'
By a bronco has been killed."   100

14

Mestas cried out in anguish,
"I've lost my only joy;
I pray to God in my sorrow
That he may take my boy."
He went to tell Martinita   105
(She felt a sense of dread),
"Your happiness is finished,
Your husband dear is dead."

15

The poor young woman fainted
From shock, surprise, and fears,   110
At the violent news he related
Which thus had reached his ears.
And sighs and moanings of anguish
Came forth from this breast so true:
"Oh husband dear of my spirit,   115
What has become of you!

16

"My father Atilano,
And father Agustín,
Oh brothers of my childhood,
My grief is very keen.   120
Beloved husband Antonio,
My husband and faithful friend,

En Dios mi remedio espero,
¡ay, Antonito, hasta el fin!—

17

Sale don Agustín Mestas   125
pa' "La Cebolla" violento,
cubierto de sentimiento
para traer a su hijo al fin.

18

Salen don Agustín Mestas
y don Atilano Herrera   130
y repasando la Sierra,
pues ya no *vían* las cuestas;
ni cansancio pa' las bestias
este día no se sintió.
Al finado Antonio Mestas   135
un caballo lo mató.

19

Llegaron a "La Cebolla"
en donde hallaron el cuerpo,
Antonito preguntando
si lo sucedido es cierto;   140
más dormido que despierto
don Agustín le decía:
—¡Ay hijo del alma mía!
¿que de veras estás muerto?—

20

Agustín triste y confuso   145
a su hijo lo remiraba
y más ternezas le echaba
viendo su cuerpo difunto.
Y entre tanto, se dispuso
a ponerlo en el cajón   150
y traerlo sin dilación
sus páis como es el uso.

21

Mas mirando el cuerpo hinchado
indisponible al intento,
sufre nuevo sufrimiento   155
y lo deja sepultado,

In God is my only comfort,
Antonio, 'til the end."

17
Don Agustín saddled his pony,   125
Consumed with passionate grief,
To give his son the last honors
Would be his only relief.

18
Don Agustín rode northward
With Don Atilano his friend,   130
Went up to the town of Cebolla
Where the cowboy met his end.
And as they climbed the steep mountain,
The father lashed at his steed,
"Today I've no pity for the horses,   135
For a horse has done this deed."

19
They came at last to Cebolla
Where the cowboy had been brought,
And gazing down at his body,
The anguished father thought: 140
"Am I awake? Am I sleeping?
Is this a dream in my head?
An evil dream I am dreaming,
Or are you really dead?"

20
Don Agustín, sad and bewildered,   145
Looked down at the corpse of the lad,
And many a deep sigh escaped him,
And these are the thoughts that he had:
"I must take him home in a coffin,
I must take his body down,   150
And give him a Christian burial
In his own native town."

21
But seeing the swollen body,
Which would not go in a case,
He knew they must bury the body   155
At once in that very place.

Ballad of the Death of Antonio Mestas 69

deciéndole a su hijo amado
sus padres enternecidos:
—Adiós, hijito queridoa
que te nos has ausentado.— 160

22
Un grande acompañamiento
lo ha llevado al camposanto
y todos con tierno llanto
le dan sepultura al muerto.

23
Ahí fueron las ternuras 165
al golpe de las paladas
y atravesaban espadas
el pecho de esas criaturas;
despidiéndose muy puras
de este atinado arancel, 170
a quien un caballo cruel
condujo a la sepultura.

24
En fin, todo terminó
y hasta sus casas volvieron,
y todos se convinieron 175
que Antonio Mestas murió;
con más ternura lloró
doña Martinita Herrera
porque ni muerto siquiera
a verlo jamás volvió. 180

"Goodbye, beloved Antonio,
Good-bye, my dear little boy;
Alas, alas, you have left us
And taken all our joy."   160

22
In great and solemn procession,
The people from miles around
Accompanied him to the graveyard
And laid him there in the ground.

23
And then like swords of anguish,   165
The heavy spadefuls fell,
And shudders ran through the people
Who had known Antonio well.
They said farewell full of sorrow,
With pity they were filled,   170
At the memory of poor Antonio
Whom a wild horse had killed.

24
At last, when all had been finished
And they to their homes had returned,
And all of the young man's relations   175
His tragic fate had learned,
Antonio's wife Martinita
Raised up her voice in pain:
"I shall never see my dear husband
Returning home again."   180

For Study and Discussion

1. As this *corrido* illustrates, ballads need not focus on heroic deeds or extraordinary events. In your opinion, why did the death of Antonio Mestas, a "handsome and happy" yet ordinary young man, become the subject of a *corrido*?

2. Although this *corrido* concerns the events surrounding the death of Antonio Mestas, it also poignantly captures the grief of Antonio's friends and relatives. What does the *corrido* reveal about the sentiments, relationships, and customs of the people of the rural community in which Antonio lived? Give specific examples from the poem to support your answer.

3. According to the composer of the *corrido,* both Antonio and his close friend foresaw Antonio's death. **a.** What other supernatural event occurs in connection with his death? **b.** What effect do these unusual, mystical elements have on the narrative?

Creative Writing

Writing a Corrido

The subject of a *corrido,* or ballad, need not be a legendary figure or a famous historical event; in fact, many ballads deal with the lives of everyday people. Write a ballad of at least four stanzas that tells the story of an event in your life or the deeds (or misdeeds) of someone you know.

Prewriting. Your ballad may be tragic, exciting, or humorous, depending on the subject matter you choose. Draw on your own memories and experiences in choosing your theme. For example, do you have a relative who has become a family legend for his or her adventurous or daring deeds? Has there been a comical event in your life that you can recall as vividly as if it happened yesterday? Keep in mind that, like all composers of *corridos,* you are free to embellish the events of your story, even lending them mythic proportions. You may even want to try your hand at putting your *corrido* to music.

Writing. Because they are meant to be sung, *corridos* usually have a very pronounced rhythm and rhyme scheme. As you are writing your *corrido,* experiment with various rhyme patterns and refrains, choosing the form that you feel is best suited to your tale.

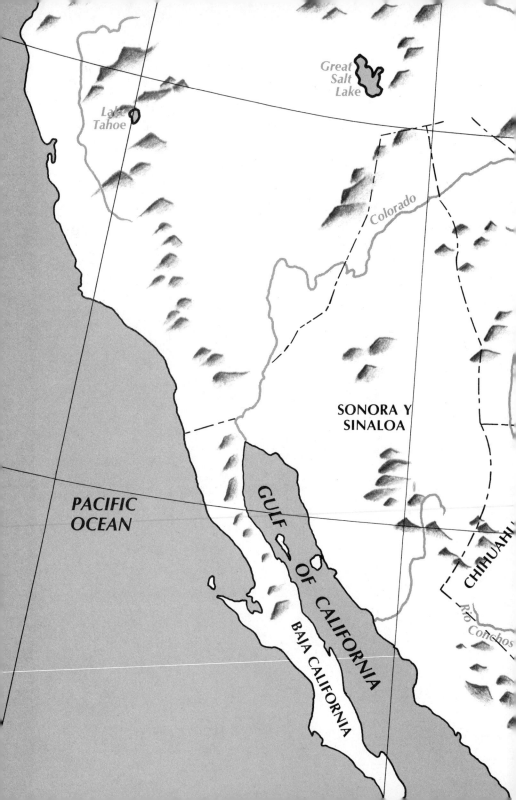

Great
Salt
Lake

Lake
Tahoe

Colorado

SONORA Y
SINALOA

PACIFIC
OCEAN

GULF OF CALIFORNIA

BAJA CALIFORNIA

CHIHUAHU

Río Conchos

Spanish and Mexican Periods
(1528-1848)

Missouri

Arkansas

Mississippi

NTA FE

Pecos

Red

Colorado

Brazos

TEJAS

Rio Grande

TAMAULIPAS

NUEVA
LEON

ZACATECAS

DURANGO

SAN

GULF
OF
MEXICO

Literature of the Spanish and Mexican Periods

Spanish poetry and drama in the Southwest and California trace back to 1598, when Juan de Oñate's expedition ventured into the northern territories of New Spain. The earliest written poem of this period, Gaspar Pérez de Villagrá's *Historia de la Nueva México*, records that the first Spanish drama in the New World was a simple play of religious thanksgiving performed by members of Oñate's expedition on the banks of the Rio Grande. Early dramas and poetry were primarily religious in nature, and in many cases dramatic performances played a strong role in the Spaniards' efforts to convert the native peoples to Christianity. Later secular, or nonreligious, plays and poems reflect changes in attitudes and allegiances in New Spain's northern territories, such as the Spanish population's growing resentment toward Texas Anglos in the 1840s.

Early prose works largely consist of the chronicles, reports, letters, logs, and diaries of Spanish adventurers who charted and settled the northern territories. Such discoverers as Alvar Núñez Cabeza de Vaca and Fray Junípero Serra chronicled their exploration of uncharted lands filled with rushing rivers, wide expanses of forest and desert, impassable mountain ranges, and splendorous sunrises and sunsets. They also described their struggles against hostile peoples who rose against the Spanish intruders. Explorers' exaggerated tales of vast riches captured the imagination of their countrymen and prompted centuries of further expeditions.

The three selections on the following pages illustrate the courageous, bold spirit that characterizes a whole age of Spanish exploration and colonization. Cabeza de Vaca's *Adventures in the Unknown Interior of America*, an account of his eight-year trek through the southeastern and southwestern United States, vividly describes both the harrowing and the rewarding adventures he and his men experienced on their journey. Fray Marcos de Niza's *The Story of the Discovery of the Seven Cities* recounts the author's failed quest for the fabled Seven Cities of Cíbola which, according to popular belief, contained untold wealth. Fray Junípero Serra's writings not only capture his fascination with the peoples, flora, and fauna he encountered but also drive home the bitter disappointments and boredom of relentless, hot marches over rough terrain.

Alvar Núñez Cabeza de Vaca
(1490–1557)

The call to high adventure quickened the pulse of many sixteenth-century Spaniards, Alvar Núñez Cabeza de Vaca (ahl'bahr noo'nyehs kah-beh'sah deh bah'kah) among them. His family had earned a name for itself in early Spanish history when one of Cabeza de Vaca's ancestors distinguished himself as a hero in the Battle of Navas de Tolosa, the famous and decisive battle in which the Spanish Christians defeated the Moors in 1212.

Born on Spain's southern coast in 1490, Cabeza de Vaca likely witnessed the sailing of the renowned explorer Ferdinand Magellan and others who embarked from Cádiz upon sea voyages that were to change the face of the world known to Europeans at that time. He joined the military as a teen-ager, saw action in several battles, and eventually gained the attention of his superior officers, which led to his receiving an important assignment to Spain's new territories overseas.

In 1527, Cabeza de Vaca sailed for the New World to join the Pánfilo de Narváez expedition on a quest to explore and claim for the Spanish Crown the area that is now Florida. Dazzled by the wealth that fellow Spaniards had begun amassing in Mexico, Narváez and his men set out for Florida the following year. Their dreams quickly vanished upon their arrival, however, when they met fierce opposition from hostile Indians. Narváez abandoned two hundred fifty of his men, one of whom was Cabeza de Vaca.

The marooned adventurers built rafts and slowly made their way around the Gulf Coast until a violent storm destroyed their makeshift vessels off the coast of Texas. Of the eighty remaining survivors, many fell victim to disease and to hostile Indians who forced Cabeza de Vaca and several other Spaniards into slavery.

Cabeza de Vaca recorded many of the adventures that he and his fellow Spaniards experienced among the various tribes of Indians they met during their westward journey. While historians disagree about their exact route, it is generally thought that they worked their way across Texas and southern New Mexico and Arizona to the Sonora River and then turned south. They were discovered by a party of Spanish slave hunters near the present-day Pacific coastal city of Culiacán in Mexico.

Cabeza de Vaca eagerly shared his adventures with all who were willing to listen, including the Spanish viceroy in Mexico City and, upon his return to Spain, powerful Spanish royalty. In 1540, he was named Governor of the Spanish territory in southern South America in recognition of his accomplishments in New Spain. After several years he was imprisoned for alleged misdeeds but was later pardoned. He died an honorable and honored man in 1557.

The selections on the following pages come from Cabeza de Vaca's exciting account *Adventures in the Unknown Interior of America*.

from **Adventures in the Unknown Interior of America**

According to Indian legend, somewhere in the northern territory (today the southwestern United States) stood seven cities rumored to have streets paved with gold and royal buildings filled with precious metals and jewels. Eager to bring glory and wealth to themselves and to the Throne, Spanish adventurers set out on land and sea, convinced that they would triumphantly return laden with untold treasures. Alvar Núñez Cabeza de Vaca was one of these men. However, his dreams—like those of many of his countrymen—never materialized. Instead, he spent eight long years fighting the elements, the terrain, hostile Indians, and all manner of adversity before reaching the haven of Mexico City. The following selections are taken from his account of his journey. The notes in brackets within the selections were provided by Cyclone Covey, the editor of Cabeza de Vaca's account, to clarify points in the narrative. In preparing these notes, Covey relied heavily on Cleve Hallenbeck's definitive research on Cabeza de Vaca, which was published in 1940.

How We Became Medicine-Men

The islanders wanted to make physicians of us without examination or a review of diplomas. Their method of cure is to blow on the sick, the breath and the laying-on of hands supposedly casting out the infirmity. They insisted we should do this too and be of some use to them. We scoffed at their cures and at the idea we knew how to heal. But they withheld food from us until we complied. An Indian told me I knew not whereof I spoke in saying their methods had no effect. Stones and other things growing about in the fields, he said, had a virtue whereby passing a pebble along the stomach could take away pain and heal; surely extraordinary men like us embodied such powers over nature. Hunger forced us to obey, but disclaiming any responsibility for our failure or success.

An Indian, falling sick, would send for a medicine-man, who would apply his cure. The patient would then give the medicine-man all he had and seek more from his relatives to give. The medicine-man makes incisions over the point of the pain, sucks the wound, and cauterizes it. This remedy enjoys high repute among the Indians. I have, as a matter of fact, tried it on myself with good results. The medicine-men blow on the spot they have treated, as a finishing touch, and the patient regards himself relieved.

Our method, however, was to bless the sick, breathe upon them, recite a *Pater noster*[1] and *Ave María*,[2] and pray earnestly to God our Lord for their recovery. When we concluded with the sign of the cross, he willed that our patients should directly spread the news that they had been restored to health.

In consequence, the Indians treated us kindly. They deprived themselves of food to give to us, and presented us skins and other tokens of gratitude.

My Years as a Wandering Merchant

After Dorantes and Castillo returned to the island [from the Han[3] oyster-eating season on the main], they rounded up all the surviving Christians, who were living somewhat separated from each other. They totaled fourteen. As I have said, I happened to be opposite on the main at that time participating in the Capoque blackberry-eating season. There I fell desperately ill. If anything before had given me hopes of life, this dashed them.

When the other Christians heard of my condition, they gave an Indian the wonderful robe of marten-skins we had taken from the *cacique*[4] [in that midnight brawl near Pensacola], to

---

1. *Pater noster* (pah'tehr nohs'tehr): prayer to God, beginning with "Our Father, who art in heaven. . . ."
2. *Ave María* (ah'beh mah-ree'ah): prayer to the Virgin Mary, beginning with "Hail Mary. . . . "
3. **Han:** a tribe of Indians that lived along the coast of Texas.
4. *cacique* (kah-see'keh): the equivalent of a prince or nobleman among the Indians.

bring them over to visit me. [The robe could have been, in reality, a bribe to make their getaway down the coast but, in any case, they would still need a guide to show them where the channel was shallow enough to wade, or a canoe if they were ferried.] Those who came were: Alonso del Castillo, Andrés Dorantes, [his cousin] Diego Dorantes, [Pedro de] Valdevieso [another cousin of Andrés], Estrada, Tostado, Chaves, Gutiérrez, Asturiano (a priest), Diego de Huelva, Estevánico the black [a Moor from the west coast of Morocco], and Benítez. When they reached the main, they found another of our company, Francisco de Leon [evidently a survivor of Cabeza de Vaca's barge, also kept by the Capoques].

The moment they had crossed, my Indians came to tell me and also brought word that Jerónimo de Alaniz [the notary] and Lope de Oviedo remained on the island. But sickness kept me from going [south] with my comrades; I did not even get to see them.

I had to stay with the Capoques more than a year. Because of the hard work they put me to, and their harsh treatment, I resolved to flee to the people of Charruco in the forests of the main. [Perhaps Cabeza de Vaca's illness bore on his change in status from a kindly treated medicine-man to a harshly treated slave; but he does not trace the transition for us. His comrades, living most of the time apart with the Han, apparently underwent the same drastic reduction in status.] My life had become unbearable. In addition to much other work, I had to grub roots in the water or from underground in the canebrakes. My fingers got so raw that if a straw touched them they would bleed. The broken canes often slashed my flesh; I had to work amidst them without benefit of clothes.

So I set to contriving how I might transfer to the forest-dwellers, who looked more propitious. My solution was to turn to trade.

[Escaping to Charruco about February 1530,] I did my best to devise ways of making my traffic profitable so I could get food and good treatment. The various Indians would beg me to go from one quarter to another for things they needed; their incessant hostilities made it impossible for them to travel cross-country or make many exchanges.

But as a neutral merchant I went into the interior as far as I pleased [the consensus is that he got as far as Oklahoma] and along the coast forty or fifty leagues [or at least, as Hallenbeck points out, between the impassable Sabine marshes to the north and perhaps not quite to Matagorda Bay to the south, where he would have learned far sooner than he did of three Spaniards who survived in that vicinity].

My principal wares were cones and other pieces of seasnail, conchs used for cutting, sea-beads, and a fruit like a bean [from mesquite trees] which the Indians value very highly, using it for a medicine and for a ritual beverage in their dances and festivities. This is the sort of thing I carried inland. By barter I got and brought back to the coast skins, red ochre which they rub on their faces, hard canes for arrows, flint for arrowheads, with sinews and cement to attach them, and tassels of deer hair which they dye red.

This occupation suited me; I could travel where I wished, was not obliged to work, and was not a slave. Wherever I went, the Indians treated me honorably and gave me food, because they liked my commodities. They were glad to see me when I came and delighted to be brought what they wanted. I became well known; those who did not know me personally knew me by reputation and sought my acquaintance. This served my main purpose, which all the while was to determine an eventual road out.

The hardships I endured in this journeying business were long to tell—peril and privation, storms and frost, which often overtook me alone in the wilderness. By the unfailing grace of God our Lord I came forth from them all. Because of them, however, I avoided the pursuit of my business in winter, a season when, anyway, the natives retire inside their huts in a kind of stupor, incapable of exertion. [Hallenbeck reasons that Cabeza de Vaca wintered on the Trinity River[5] or one of its western branches; the red ochre he acquired somewhere in that area is found in the woods around Nacogdoches.[6]]

I was in this [general coastal] region nearly six years [but in this particular vicinity from early winter 1528 to early winter 1532, a merchant for perhaps 22 months], alone among the Indians and naked like them. The reason I remained so long was my intention of taking the Christian, Lope de Oviedo, away

5. **Trinity River:** a river running through East Texas.
6. **Nacogdoches** (nah-kohg-doh'chehs): later settled as a small Spanish-Mexican colony in East Texas.

with me. His companion on the island Alaniz, whom Castillo, Dorantes, and the rest had left behind, died soon after their departure. To get Oviedo, the last survivor there, I passed over to the island every year and pleaded with him to come with me to attempt the best way we could contrive to find Christians. Each year he put me off, saying the next we would start.

The Journey to the Great Bay

At last, [on the fourth visit, in November 1532] I got him off, across the strait, and across four large streams on the coast [Bastrop Bayou, Brazos River, San Bernardo River, and Caney Creek]; which took some doing, because Oviedo could not swim.

So we worked along, with some Indians, until we came to a bay a league wide and uniformly deep. From its appearance we presumed it to be Espíritu Santo[7] [the name Pineda gave Matagorda Bay in 1519; Pineda's map, with which Cabeza de Vaca was familiar, mentions the conspicuous white sandhills beyond. They were guided not across the bay but across the Colorado River which flows into it.].

We met some Indians on the other side who were on their way to visit our late hosts. They told us that three men like us lived but a couple of days from here, and said their names. We asked about the others and were told that they were all dead. Most had died of cold and hunger. But our informants' own tribe had murdered Diego Dorantes, Valdevieso, and Diego de Huelva for sport because they left one house for another; and the neighboring tribe, where Captain Dorantes now resided, had, in obedience to a dream, murdered Esquivel [who had been in the Comptroller's barge] and Méndez [one of the four excellent swimmers who had set out, back in 1528, for Pánuco]. We asked how the living Christians fared. Badly, they replied; the boys and some of the Indian men enlivened their dreary idleness by constantly kicking, cuffing, and cudgeling the three slaves; such was the life they led.

We inquired of the region ahead and its subsistence. They said there was nothing to eat and that the few people [who evidently had not yet joined the nut-gathering exodus] were dying from the cold, having no skins or anything else to cover themselves with. They also told us that if we wished to see those

---

7. **Espíritu Santo** (ehs-pee'ree-too sahn'toh): Holy Spirit.

three Christians, the Indians who had them would be coming in about two days to eat nuts [pecans] on the river bank a league from here.

So we would know they had spoken the truth about the bad treatment of our fellows, they commenced slapping and batting Oviedo and did not spare me either. They would keep throwing clods at us, too, and each of the days we waited there they would stick their arrows to our hearts and say they had a mind to kill us the way they had finished our friends. My frightened companion Oviedo said he wanted to go back with the women who had just forded the bay with us (their men having stayed some distance behind). I argued my utmost against such a craven course, but in no way could keep him.

He went back, and I remained alone with those savages. They are called Quevenes and those with whom he returned, Deaguanes. [This is the last that was ever heard of the strongest man who had sailed in Cabeza de Vaca's barge.]

The Coming of the Indians with Dorantes, Castillo, and Estevánico

Two days after Lope de Oviedo departed, the Indians who had Alonso del Castillo and Andrés Dorantes reached the place we had been told of, to eat pecans. These are ground with a kind of small grain and furnish the sole subsistence of the people for two months of the year—and not every year, because the trees only bear every other year. The nut is the same size as that of Galicia; the trees are massive and numberless. [According to the *Joint Report,* these groves where the Indians began nutcracking were ten or twelve leagues above the Bay, i.e., on the lower Colorado, and tribes converged there from a distance of twenty and thirty leagues. In the course of the gathering season they worked a great distance up-river.]

An Indian [not one of those who had been manhandling Cabeza de Vaca but a recent arrival] told me secretly that the Christians had arrived at the appointed place and, if I wished to see them to steal away to a segment of the woods which he pointed out and that there he and his relatives would pick me up as they passed by. I decided to trust him, since he spoke a dialect distinct from the others. Next day, they found me hiding in the designated place and took me along.

As we approached their abode, Andrés Dorantes came out

to see who it could be; the Indians had told him a Christian was coming. When he saw me, he was terrified; for I had been considered long dead and the natives had confirmed my demise, he said [without mentioning that he was guilty of deserting a superior officer whom he had passed by without seeing in his presumed final illness]. But we gave many thanks to be alive together. This was a day of as great joy as we ever knew.

When we got to the place Castillo was, they asked me where I might be bound. To the land of Christians, I replied, and was seeking it right now. Andrés Dorantes said that he had long entreated Castillo and Estevánico to go forward, but that they overly dreaded the many bays and rivers they would have to cross, not knowing how to swim. Thus God our Lord had preserved me through all adversities, leading me in the end to the fellowship of those who had abandoned me, that I might lead them over the bays and rivers which obstructed our progress.

They warned me that if the Indians suspected my intention of going on they would murder me; to succeed, we would have to lie quiet until the end of six months, when these Indians would migrate to another part of the country for their season of picking prickly pears. People from parts farther on would be bringing bows to barter and, after making our escape, we could accompany them on their return. Consenting to this counsel, I stayed.

The prickly pear [or tuna, the fruit of the *Opuntia* cactus] is the size of a hen's egg, bright red and black in color, and good-tasting. The natives live solely on it three months of the year.

I was consigned as a slave to the Indian who had Dorantes. This Indian was squint-eyed; so were his wife and sons and another member of this household; so they were all, in a manner of speaking, semi-squinted. [The preceding sentence does not appear in the 1542 edition.] They were Mariames; the neighboring people who kept Castillo were Yguaces.

The Tribal Split and News of the Remaining Barge

When the six months I had been biding my time were up, the Indians proceeded to the prickly pears thirty leagues away [the vicinity of San Antonio], and the moment to execute our escape plan drew nigh. [This migration must have occurred in August 1533.] When we drew near the point of flight, our Indian masters quarreled over a woman. After a scuffle in which heads were bruised with fists and sticks, each took his lodge and went his own way. So we Christians found ourselves separated with no means of reuniting for another year.

During this year my lot was hard, as much from hunger as harsh treatment. Three times I had to run from my masters, who came after me with intent to kill; but each time, God our Lord preserved me. When the prickly pear season at last arrived again, we Christians came together with the aggregation of all the tribe in the cactus thickets.

We set a time for our escape, but that same day the Indians dispersed to different locales of the cactus country. I told my comrades I would wait for them at a certain spot among the prickly pear plants until the full moon. This day I was speaking to them was the new moon, September 1 [1534, in which year the new moon actually occurred on September 8]. I said that if they did not appear by the time the moon was full, I would go on alone. So we parted, each going with his Indian group.

On the thirteenth day of the moon, Andrés Dorantes came with Estevánico and told me they had left Castillo with other Indians nearby, called Anagados [Lanegados, 1555 edition]; that they had encountered great obstacles and got lost; that tomorrow the Mariames were going to move to the place where Castillo was and unite in friendship with this tribe which held him, having heretofore been at war with them. In this way we would recover Castillo.

The thirst we had all the while we ate the pears, we quenched with their juice. We caught it in a hole we hollowed out in the ground [surely in rock]. When the hole was full, we drank until slaked. The juice is sweet and must-colored. The Indians collect it like this for lack of vessels. There are many kinds of prickly pear, some very good; they all seemed so to me, hunger never leaving me the leisure to discriminate.

Aside from prickly pear juice, nearly all these people drink rain water, which lies about in puddles. There are rivers; but since the Indians know no fixed abode, they have no familiar places for getting water.

Over all the region we saw vast and beautiful plains that would make good pasture. I think the land would prove very productive if developed by civilized men. We saw no mountains.

When the tribes made their juncture next day, the [Anagado] Indians told us that another people, immediately ahead of us, called Camones, who came from close to the coast, had killed the men who landed in the barge of Peñalosa and Téllez. These men arrived so feeble that they could offer no resistance even while being slain, and the Camones slew them to a man. We were shown their clothes and arms and learned that the barge remained stranded where it landed. Now all five barges had been accounted for.

Our Escape

The second day after our juncture with the Anagados [i.e., on 22 September 1534], we commended ourselves to God our Lord and made our break. Although the season was late and the prickly pears nearly gone, we still hoped to travel a long distance on acorns which we might find in the woods.

Hurrying along that day in dread of being overtaken, we spied some smoke billows and headed in their direction. We reached them after vespers, to find one Indian. He fled when he saw us coming. We sent the Negro after him, and the Indian stopped when he saw only a lone pursuer. The Negro told him we were seeking the people who made those fires. He said their houses were nearby and he would guide us. We followed as he ran on to announce us.

We saw the houses at sunset. Two crossbow shots before reaching them, we found four Indians waiting to welcome us. We said in Mariame that we were looking for them. They appeared pleased with our presence and took us to their dwellings, where they lodged Dorantes and the Negro in the house of one medicine-man, and Castillo and me in that of another.

These people speak a different language and call themselves Avavares [also spelled Chavavares farther on]. They are the ones who carried bows to the Mariames and, although different in nation and tongue, understand Mariame. They had arrived that day, with their lodges, where we found them [on the upper Medina or Guadalupe River]. Right away they brought us a lot of prickly pears [prickly pears maturing progressively later westward], having heard of us and the wonders our Lord worked by us. If there had been nothing but these cures, they were enough to open ways for us through a poor region like this, find us guides for often uninhabited wastes, and lead us through immediate dangers, not letting us be killed, sustaining us through great want, and instilling in those nations the heart of kindness, as we shall see.

Our Success with Some of the Afflicted and My Narrow Escape

The very evening of our arrival, some Indians came to Castillo begging him to cure them of terrible headaches. When he had made the sign of the cross over them and commended them to God, they instantly said that all pain had vanished and went to their houses to get us prickly pears and chunks of venison, something we had tasted of precious little.

We returned many thanks to God, Whose compassion and gifts day by day increased. After the sick had been tended, the Indians danced and sang in festivity till sunrise. The celebration of our coming extended to three days.

When it ended, we inquired of the region farther on, of its people and subsistence. Prickly pears were plentiful throughout, they answered, but this season's had all been gathered by now and the tribes returned home. We would find the country very cold and skins scarce. Reflecting on this, and winter being already upon us, we concluded to stay with these Indians till spring.

Five days after our arrival, the tribe took us with them to gather more prickly pears, at a place where other peoples of different tongues converged. There being no fruit of any kind along the way, we walked five days in gnawing hunger, to a river [the Colorado], where we put up our houses and then went to look for the pods which grow on certain trees [mesquite].

The awkwardness of picking one's way in this vicinity of no paths slowed my own rounds and when, after dark, I went to join the others, who had returned to camp, I got lost. Thank God I found a burning tree, by the warmth of which I passed that cold night.

In the morning I loaded up with sticks and continued my search, carrying two burning brands. For five days I wandered in this way with my fire and my load; otherwise, had my wood failed me where none could be found, I would have lost my kindling fire by the time I located sticks elsewhere. This was all the protection I had against cold, as I wended my way naked as the day I was born.

I would go into the low woods by the river before sunset to prepare myself for the night. First I hollowed out a hole in the ground and threw in fuel, of which there was plenty from the fallen, dry trees in the woods. Then I built four fires around the hole in the form of a cross, and slept in this hole with my fuel supply, covering myself with bundles of the coarse grass which grows thick in those parts. Thus I managed shelter from the cold of night.

One night, the fire fell on the straw as I slept, and blazed so suddenly that it singed my hair in spite of my haste to get out. All this while, I tasted not a mouthful nor found anything to eat. My bare feet bled. By the mercy of God, the wind did not blow from the north in the whole time or I would have died.

At the end of the fifth day I reached the river bank where the Indians were then camped. The camp seems to have advanced daily. They and the Christians had given me up for dead, supposing I had been bitten by a snake. Everybody rejoiced to see me; my companions said it had been their great struggle with hunger that kept them from looking for me. All shared prickly pears with me that night, and the next morning we set out for a place where they still abounded. When we got there, we satisfied our great craving, and the Christians gave thanks to the Lord.

[Hallenbeck re-enacted Cabeza de Vaca's five-day adventure one October and reconstructs that he got lost on the Llano and made his bed on successive nights beside the Pedernales, tributaries of the Llano, the San Saba, the north fork of the San Saba, and tributaries of the last two.]

More Cures

A crowd of Indians came to Castillo next morning bringing five sick persons who had cramps. Each of the five offered his bow and arrows, and Castillo accepted them. At sunset [after all-day treatment, or postponing treatment to evening?] he blessed them and commended them to God our Lord. We all prayed the best we could for their health; we knew that only through Him would these people help us so we might emerge from this unhappy existence. And He bestowed health so bountifully that every patient got up the morning following as sound and strong as if he had never had an illness.

This caused great admiration and moved us to further gratitude to our Lord, Whose demonstrated mercy gave us a conviction that He would liberate us and bring us to a place where we might serve Him. I can say for myself that I had always trusted His providence and that He would lead me out of my captivity; I constantly expressed this to my companions.

The Indians having gone with their restored friends, we went over to some thickets where other tribesmen were eating prickly pears. These Indians were Cultalchulches and Malicones, who speak a different dialect. Adjoining them and opposite us were Coayos and Susolas and, on another side, Atayos, who were at war with the Susolas, daily exchanging arrow shots.

Since the Indians all through the region talked only of the wonders which God our Lord worked through us, individuals sought us from many parts in hopes of healing. The evening of the second day after our arrival at these thickets, some of the Susolas came to us and pressed Castillo to go treat their ailing kinsmen—one wounded, the others sick and, among them, a fellow very near his end. Castillo happened to be a timid practitioner—the more so, the more serious and dangerous the case—feeling that his sins would weigh and some day impede his performing cures. The Indians urged me to go heal them. They liked me, remembering I had ministered to them in the grove where they gave us nuts and skins when I first reunited with the Christians [meaning, apparently, on the Island of Doom].

So I had to go with them. Dorantes brought Estevánico and accompanied me. As we drew near the huts of the afflicted, I saw that the man we hoped to save was dead: many mourners were weeping around him, and his house was already down [to be burned with the deceased's possessions]—sure signs that the inhabitant was no more. I found his eyes rolled up, his pulse gone, and every appearance of death, as Dorantes agreed. Taking off the mat that covered him, I supplicated our Lord in his behalf and in behalf of the rest who ailed, as fervently as I could. After my blessing and breathing on him many times, they brought me his bow and a basket of pounded prickly pears.

The [local] natives then took me to treat many others, who

had fallen into a stupor, and gave me two more baskets of prickly pears. I, in turn, gave these to the [Susola] Indians who accompanied us. We returned to our lodgings, while the Indians whom we had given the fruit waited till evening to return.

When they got back that evening, they brought the tidings that the "dead" man I had treated had got up whole and walked; he had eaten and spoken with these Susolas, who further reported that all I had ministered to had recovered and were glad. Throughout the land the effect was a profound wonder and fear. People talked of nothing else, and wherever the fame of it reached, people set out to find us so we should cure them and bless their children.

When the Cultalchulches, who were in company with our [Avavare] Indians, were ready to return to their own heath, they left us all the prickly pears they had, without keeping one. They also gave us valuable cutting flints a palm and a half long, and begged us to remember them and pray to God that they might always be well. We promised. They departed the most contented beings in the world, having given us the best of all they had.

We lived with the Avavares eight months, reckoned by moons, during all which time people came seeking us from many parts and telling us we truly were children of the sun. Up to now, Dorantes and his Negro had not attempted to practice; but under the soliciting pressure of these pilgrims from diverse places, we all became physicians, of whom I was the boldest and most venturous in trying to cure anything. With no exceptions, every patient told us he had been made well. Confidence in our ministrations as infallible extended to a belief that none could die while we remained among them.

We told them we called this deity they spoke of, *Dios,*[8] and if they would call Him this and worship Him as we specified, it would go well with them. They replied they understood well and would do as we said. We ordered them to come down from the mountains fearlessly and peacefully, reinhabit the country and rebuild their houses and, among the latter, they should build one for God with a cross placed over the door like the one we had in the room and that, when Christians came among them, they should go to greet them with crosses in their hands instead of bows or other weapons, take them to their houses

---

8. *Dios* (dyohs): God, the Supreme Being.

and feed them, and the Christians would not harm them but be friends. The Indians told us they would comply.

The Captain [Díaz] concluded with a presentation of shawls and a repast, and they went back, taking the two captives who had served as emissaries. This parley took place before a notary in the presence of many witnesses.

The Great Transformation

As soon as these Indians got home, all the inhabitants of that province who were friendly to the Christians and had heard of us, came to visit, bearing beads and feathers. We commanded them to build churches with crosses; up to that time none had been erected. We also bade them bring their principal men to be baptized.

Then the Captain made a solemn covenant with God not to invade or consent to invasion, or enslave any of that region we had guaranteed safety; to enforce and defend this sacred contract until Your Majesty and Governor Nuño de Guzmán, or the Viceroy in your name, should direct further as to the service of God and Your Highness.

Indians came to us shortly with tidings that many people had descended from the mountains and were living again in the valleys; that they had erected churches with crosses, and were doing everything we required. Each day we heard further to the same effect.

Fifteen days after our taking up residence in this town, Alcaraz got back with his cohorts [possibly in response to peremptory orders sent out by Diaz]. They reported to the Captain the way the Indians had come down and repopulated the plain; how they would issue from their formerly deserted villages carrying crosses, take the visitors to their houses and give of what they had. The Christians even slept among these hosts overnight! They could not comprehend such a novelty. Since the natives said their safety had been officially assured, the Christians decided to depart quietly.

We are thankful to our merciful God that it should be in the days of Your Majesty's dominion that these nations might all come voluntarily to Him who created and redeemed us. We are convinced that Your Majesty is destined to do this much and that it is entirely within reason to accomplish. For in the 2,000 leagues we sojourned by land and sea, including ten months' ceaseless travel after escaping captivity, we found no sacrifices and no idolatry.

In that period, we crossed from sea to sea. The data we took great pains to collect indicate that the width of the continent, at its widest, may be 200 leagues [which would be an excellent estimate measuring at the latitude of Culiacán]; and that pearls and great riches are to be found on the coast of the South Sea, near which the best and most opulent of all nations flourishes.

Arrival in Mexico City

We stayed in San Miguel until May 15, the reason being that the devastated and enemy-ridden hundred leagues between there and Compostella, where Governor Nuño de Guzmán resided, required a convoy, which took time to arrange. Twenty mounted men escorted us forty leagues, and then six Christians, with five hundred slaves, escorted us the rest of the way. [A little over one hundred fifty miles on the road to Compostella, at the seaside town of Mazatlán, Cabeza de Vaca made his closest approach to the Pacific, which, however, could be sighted from the road sometime earlier.]

At Compostella the Governor received us graciously and outfitted us from his wardrobe. I could not stand to wear any clothes for some time, or to sleep anywhere but on the bare floor.

[Cabeza de Vaca does not mention quailing in the presence of five hundred Indian slaves the greater part of the trip from Culiacán, or that his gracious host was the prime mover of the slave raids in the Pima country. Guzmán was an extremely able man and, on occasion, charming, but also exceedingly cruel and predatory. Had the Narváez expeditionaries made it to Pánuco as they intended, they would have been received by Guzmán, who was then governor at that northernmost Spanish outpost. In the years Cabeza de Vaca ranged eastern Texas as a merchant, Guzmán founded Culiacán, the northernmost Spanish outpost in western Mexico (farther north than Pánuco). He also founded Compostella and Guadalajara, naming the latter after his own home town in Spain. He outraged the Spanish as well as the Indian population wherever he operated and had made mortal enemies of the other three most powerful men in New Spain: the Viceroy, Cortés, and the Archbishop. It was the licentiate

Diego Pérez de la Torre, however, who as special investigator was closing in on Guzmán at the time Cabeza de Vaca was his guest and who had the Governor in jail within eight months.]

After ten or twelve days, we left for Mexico City [now mounted, by Guzmán's generosity], and all the way enjoyed the hospitality of Christians, numbers of whom came out on the road to see us, giving thanks to God for preserving us through so many calamities. [Their route lay along the already-established highway, via Guadalajara—a total distance from Culiacán to Mexico City of slightly over 900 miles.]

We rode into Mexico City on Sunday [July 24], the day before the vespers of Santiago [Saint James] and were royally and joyously received by the Viceroy [the great first one, Antonio de Mendoza] and the Marqués del Valle [the great *conquistador*, Cortés], who gave us clothes and offered whatever else they had.

The day of Santiago was celebrated with a *fiesta*[9] and a bullfight.

---

9. *fiesta* (fyeh′stah): feast, entertainment.

For Study and Discussion

1. How would you describe Cabeza de Vaca's attitude toward the Indians he encountered during his wanderings?

2. Cabeza de Vaca's account of his trek, like the classic story of Robinson Crusoe's survival after being shipwrecked, is a stirring tale of adventure. What are some of the elements in Cabeza de Vaca's narrative that make it a good adventure story?

3. Throughout his account of his journey, Cabeza de Vaca tells of facing one ordeal after another—starvation, Indian attack, forced labor, severe weather, illness, and many, many others. A number of his trials were so severe that his endurance seems almost miraculous. In your opinion, what personal character traits and qualities enabled Cabeza de Vaca to survive? Give examples from the narrative to support your views.

4. Cabeza de Vaca relates several incidents in which he and his fellow adventurers appear to heal ailing Indians. **a.** According to his account, how do the Spaniards bring about these cures? **b.** What does the success of this type of treatment reveal about the Spaniards' and the Indians' respective beliefs about the cause and remedy of physical ailments?

Literary Elements

Forms of Discourse: Narration, Exposition, Description, Persuasion

Writing can be classified according to four types.

Narration presents a series of events. You can think of narration as storytelling.

Exposition provides information by explaining facts or ideas and showing their relationship to one another. How-to manuals and textbooks contain primarily exposition.

Description creates a clear impression of something, such as a person, setting, or object, by giving specific details that appeal to the five senses. For example, at the end of "The Coming of the Indians with Dorantes, Castillo, and Estevánico," Cabeza de Vaca describes the prickly pear.

Persuasion tries to convince an audience to act or think in a particular way. Examples of persuasion include advertisements and political speeches.

Writers rarely use only one form of discourse. Cabeza de Vaca combines exposition, narration, and description in recounting how he and the Indian medicine men treated the sick.

One way to understand the types of discourse is to think of them as different ways of talking about something, such as a tree.

Narration	"We planted that tree last spring."
Exposition	"That tree is a cedar."
Description	"Cedar trees have needlelike leaves and a distinct fragrance."

Alvar Núñez Cabeza de Vaca 95

Persuasion   "Cedar trees are so attractive that we should plant more of them."

Find a paragraph in "My Years as a Wandering Merchant" that contains at least two kinds of discourse. Identify the kinds of discourse, giving quotations to support your identification.

Writing About Literature

Analyzing a Writer's Purpose

In many cases, a simple factual account of an adventurer's exploits can grab and hold readers' attention. Nevertheless, explorers and others often embellish their tales to make them even more exciting and interesting to their audiences. To what extent does Cabeza de Vaca do this in *Adventures in the Unknown Interior of America?* Is his aim simply to inform his audience about what he has seen and experienced, or is he seeking to entertain his readers and appeal to their sense of adventure by choosing exciting details and relating them in a particularly dramatic fashion? Write a short essay three or four paragraphs long, giving your views on Cabeza de Vaca's purpose in writing his account. Be sure to provide specific evidence from the narrative to support your opinion.

Prewriting. To determine Cabeza de Vaca's purpose, you will need to analyze both the content (the details, examples, incidents, and other information he presents) and the form (the words, sentence structure, and other elements of writing) of his narrative. Does he seem to emphasize only the more thrilling aspects of his journey, or does he also cover a number of mundane, day-to-day details? Does he present his account in straightforward, objective wording, or does he use emotionally loaded words and phrases? Based on your analysis, draw a conclusion about Cabeza de Vaca's approach to his narrative, and state this conclusion clearly and concisely in a thesis sentence. Then organize specific details and quotations from the story under two to four categories that you can develop into paragraphs in your essay.

Writing and Revising. As you cite direct quotations from the narrative, make sure that you copy them accurately, including marks of punctuation, and that you always enclose them in quotation marks. Also take care to place the quotation marks properly in relation to other marks of punctuation—for example, commas and periods are always placed inside closing quotation marks.

Fray[1] Marcos de Niza

(1495–1558)

Little is known about the early life of
Fray Marcos de Niza (mahr'kohs deh
nee'sah) prior to when he set sail for the
territory of New Spain (present-day Mexico). Like many of his contemporaries, Fray Marcos, a native of Italy, came to the New World as part
of the Spanish missionary effort. Arriving in 1531, he mastered the
Spanish language and served in Peru and Guatemala before going on to
New Spain. He was already an elderly man in poor health when the
Bishop of New Spain asked him to take part in an expedition to the
northern frontier. Fray Marcos's skill as a cartographer (an expert with
maps and map making) and other special qualifications made him
uniquely suited for the expedition despite his physical frailty.

Fray Marcos selected Esteban (also known as Estevánico), the
Moorish slave who had accompanied Cabeza de Vaca, to be his guide.
They and the rest of the expeditionary force set out in 1538 to search
for the wealth that Cabeza de Vaca had reported several years before.
As the party entered what is today New Mexico, Esteban and a group of
Indians were sent ahead to report on possible dangers such as hostile
Indians. Upon nearing the site of the Zuni pueblo of Hawikuh (the
southwesternmost of the Zuni group of six villages), Esteban and his
patrol encountered the Zuni. Misjudging the Indians, Esteban antagonized them, and they attacked the patrol, killing most of the members.
When news of the incident reached Fray Marcos, he hastily returned to
Mexico City.

While it is clear that Esteban and his party had sighted the pueblo,

---

1. **Fray** (frai): Brother: a title given to a Spanish friar or monk.

historians hotly dispute whether Fray Marcos himself saw what he describes at the end of the following selection. His own contemporaries decided that he had not and gave him the unfortunate nickname of "The Lying Monk" because his description of a grand city bore little resemblance to what was nothing more than a pueblo of mud huts.

He reported that he had erected a cross on a hill not far from the "city," claiming it and all of the surrounding territory for Spain. Perhaps Fray Marcos had become a victim of the mania that had possessed so many other Europeans of his day: the obsession to gain fabulous riches and glory in the New World. Although the Spanish discovered much gold, silver, and other mineral wealth elsewhere in New Spain and in other viceroyalties in Central and South America, they mainly found only bitter frustration and a hostile environment in today's American Southwest.

from The Story of the Discovery of the Seven Cities

Cabeza de Vaca's account of his eight-year trek across what is now the American Southwest had helped to fuel rumors of vast wealth within the New World. Undaunted by reports of hostile Indians and barren wastelands to the North, a series of Spanish expeditions set out between 1538 and 1592 in search of the legendary Seven Cities of Cíbola,[1] which were thought to contain untold riches. One of the first of these expeditions was led by Fray Marcos de Niza, a Catholic friar appointed by the Governor of New Spain to put to rest the conflicting reports of wealth and desolation. The following selections are excerpts from Fray Marcos's account of his journey. As you read, notice how his use of eyewitness accounts adds to the appeal and the credibility of his narrative.

First News of Esteban's Disaster

Camp near Concho.
Tuesday, May 20

At this place there arrived an Indian, perspiring from head to foot, his face, his whole bearing a picture of darkest despair. We recognized him as the son of one of my headmen, who had left in the company of the Negro Esteban. This is what he told us:

---

1. **Cíbola** (see'boh-lah): tribal land of the Zuni Indians, which was rumored to contain seven cities of fabulous wealth.

Esteban at Cíbola, Monday, May 19

When Esteban was one day's journey out from Cíbola, he sent messengers ahead with his gourd. (This was his way of finding out what course of action to follow. This gourd of his had attached to it a red and a white feather and some strings with rattles.) Upon arriving at Cíbola, the messengers approached the representative of the Overlord and handed him the gourd. The ruler took it and began to examine the rattles. What he saw must have made him very angry. For he threw the gourd on the ground and told the messengers to leave without delay, and warn those people not to come into his city. If they did, he would kill them all. He knew the kind of men they were.

His Arrest

The messengers went back and told Esteban what had happened. But he said not to worry, for the ones who showed the greatest anger at first, invariably gave him the best reception.

So he persisted in going to the city. When he arrived there, he found a big crowd blocking his way, who took him and imprisoned him in a large house outside of the city, after depriving him of everything, his presents, his turquoises and whatever he had received from the Indians along the road.

There he had to remain all night, without a thing to eat or drink, either for himself or for those with him.

His End, May 20

When morning came along this Indian, feeling thirsty, left the house to get a drink in the river. After a while he chanced to look up and he saw Esteban running away, with the people from the city in pursuit and killing the Indians with him.

This Indian then went up the river and hid until he could sneak back on the road leading to the uninhabited region.

When the Indians heard this news, some began to raise a wailing. And as for me, the report of that disaster had me worried. Not that I feared the possible danger to my own life, but I did want to return and report about this great country, so that it could be made to obey God, and be added to our Holy Religion and to the realm of His Majesty. Therefore I did my best to quiet them, telling them not to believe everything the Indian said. But they sobbed that the Indian was telling nothing but what he had seen. I stepped aside to plead my cause with the Lord. I prayed for guidance and light, so that all would turn out for the best. Then I went back to the Indians and took the packs with the cloths and presents I had brought and with my knife cut the cords. (Till now I had not given away a thing.) I then gave a bit of everything to the headmen. I told them not to be afraid but to go on with me, which they finally agreed to do.

Second News of Esteban's Disaster

Camp near the Zuni River.[2]
Thursday, May 22

As we were traveling, with but one day's journey between us and Cíbola, two other Indians from Esteban's crowd met us. They were covered with blood and full of wounds. When they drew close, they raised such a pitiful and fearsome wail, which was answered by those with me, that I too could not hold back my tears. So many were crying that I could not ask about Esteban or about what had happened. I begged them to be quiet so that we could ascertain what had occurred. But they said how would it be possible to keep still, when they knew that their fathers, their sons, their brothers were dead, more than three hundred of those who had gone with Esteban. And now they would be able to go to Cíbola no longer. Nevertheless I tried my very best to quiet them and to take away their fear (although I must say, that I needed someone myself to take away my fear). I asked the wounded Indians about Esteban and about what had happened. They stood awhile without answering, continuing their wail with their countrymen. Finally they told me.

---

2. **Zuni River** (soo'nee): a river approximately ninety miles long that flows through New Mexico and Arizona.

Esteban at Zuni, May 19

When Esteban had come to within one day's journey of the city of Cíbola, he sent ahead his messengers to that town with the gourd to inform the Overlord of his arrival and of his intention to make a treaty with them and to cure their ailments. When they handed him the gourd, he noticed the rattles, and in great anger threw it to the ground. He said: "I understand these people, for these rattles are not of our kind. Tell them to go back immediately, otherwise not one man of them will survive." He was in a great rage.

The messengers returned sadly, and at first would tell Esteban nothing. But finally they did talk. He told them not to be afraid. He still intended to go there. Because, although they might talk mean, they would receive him well.

His Arrest

So he kept on and reached the city of Cíbola just before sunset. His crowd was with him, more than three hundred men and a good number of women. But they were not permitted to enter the city. Instead they were taken to a large house, a fair lodging place, outside the city. They immediately took away from Esteban all he had, saying that those were orders from the Overlord.

During that whole night, they gave us nothing to eat or drink.

His End, May 20

The following day, when the sun had risen to the height of a lance, Esteban, together with some of the headmen, left the house. Immediately a great crowd poured out of the city. At the sight of them he started to run. So did we. Those people then attacked us, wounding us with arrows and showering us with blows. We fell down and others fell on top of us, dead. We remained that way till dark, not daring to move. We could hear shouting and yelling in the city. We could also see many men and women on the flat roofs looking at us.

We saw nothing more of Esteban, but we believe that he and those with him were shot down by arrows.

We are the only ones to escape.

Fray Marcos de Niza 103

I realized what this all meant for my work, and how I could look for but little help to continue my journey. And how I did hate to give it up. God is my witness, how I longed for someone from whom I could ask advice. I confess I was at a loss.

I told them that Our Lord would punish Cíbola. And when the Emperor would find out what had happened, he would send many Christians against them. But they would not believe me. No one could crush the power of Cíbola. So they said. I just begged them to be consoled and to cease their wailings. I used up all my powers of oratory to reassure them. (To repeat what I said would be too tedious.)

Thereupon I left them and going away a stone's throw or two, recommended myself to God. I prayed an hour and a half. When I went back, I noticed one of the Indians who had come with me from Mexico, called Marcos, crying. He sobbed: "Padre,[3] they have decided to kill you, because it was on your account and on account of Esteban that so many of their relatives died. In fact not a man or a woman of the whole crowd survives."

I distributed the rest of my presents to regain their good will. Then I told them to remember that killing me would do me no harm, since dying as a Christian would lead me to Heaven. But my murderers would be made to pay the price, for Christians would come, looking for me, and, much as I would hate it, would kill them all. These and other arguments appeased them somewhat. All this while the wailing for the dead ones did not cease.

I asked for volunteers to continue the journey to Cíbola, to ascertain whether by chance any other Indians had escaped, and to find out what had happened to Esteban. But not a one offered to go.

Then I told them I just had to see the city of Cíbola. Their reply was that no one would go with me.

Finally my determined stand won the day, and two of the headmen did decide to accompany me.

---

3. **Padre** (pah'threh): Father; a Catholic priest.

Fray Marcos Views Cíbola
Friday, May 23

Accompanied by these and by my own Indians and interpreters, I completed the last lap of my journey, which brought me within sight of Cíbola.

This place is situated on the brow of a circular hill, arising out of a plain. It creates the impression of being a real city, the best, in fact, I have seen in these parts.

The houses are built exactly as the Indians had told me. They are built entirely of stone, in stories and with flat roofs. So it appeared to me when I looked at the city from a hill, which I had climbed.

The population is greater than that of Mexico City.

More than once was I tempted to go over to the city. I would have risked nothing more than my life, which I had already offered to my God, the very first day of my journey. But then if I should be killed, there would be available no information about this country, in my estimation, the greatest and best yet discovered.

When I told the headmen who had come with me how favorably I was impressed by Cíbola, they told me that it was but the smallest of the Seven Cities, and that Totonteac, with its countless buildings and inhabitants, was by far larger and better than all the seven combined.

While studying the city, the idea occurred to me to dedicate this country "The New Kingdom of St. Francis." With the help of the Indians I heaped up a great mound of stones, on top of which I placed a cross. It was rather small and scrimpy since I did not have the tools to make a better one. And I announced that I was erecting the cross and mound in the name of Don Antonio de Mendoza, Viceroy and Governor of New Spain, for the Emperor, for Our Lord, in token possession (as per instructions). I proclaimed that I was taking possession of all the Seven Cities, of the Kingdom of Totonteac, of Acus, and of Marata,[4] without visiting them, since I must return to give an account of my discoveries.

---

4. **Totonteac ... Acus ... Marata** (toh'tohn-tee'ahk ... ah'koos ... mah-rah'tah).

For Study and Discussion

1. In addition to relating his experiences, Fray Marcos de Niza also gives the first-person accounts of Indians who had been with Esteban's party. In what ways do these accounts make Fray Marcos's narrative more appealing and convincing to his readers?

2. Esteban holds an important place in American history because he is thought to be the first black person to set foot in the United States. Fray Marcos gives no actual description of Esteban in the three excerpts you have read, yet the Indians' eyewitness reports reveal details about his character and personality. What impression of Esteban do you get from the two accounts?

3. The Spaniards who conquered and colonized the New World gained much of the resolve and strength required for such an undertaking from their staunch belief that they were serving higher powers—the Christian church and the Spanish throne. Where in his narrative does Fray Marcos express this belief?

Writing About Literature

Analyzing the Personality of the Speaker in a Narrative

Fray Marcos de Niza gives very little specific information about himself; yet after having read a portion of his narrative, you probably have formed an opinion about his character and personality. How would you describe Fray Marcos? Was he a devout religious leader? a self-serving opportunist? an objective observer? Write a short description of Fray Marcos, using incidents and quotations from the narrative to support your view.

Prewriting. Brainstorm a list of words and phrases that you feel accurately describe Fray Marcos. Then, skim the narrative to find specific quotations and details that relate to these words and phrases. From your list, choose several descriptive terms that you feel best apply to Fray Marcos, and link these terms together in a single sentence. Use this sentence as your thesis statement, and organize your quotations and details in two or three groups that you can develop into paragraphs.

Writing and Revising. As you write and revise your description, avoid using the same word repeatedly. Consult a thesaurus and a dictionary to find synonymous words and phrases that will both add variety to your paper and bring your description into sharper focus. Before using a synonym that you find in a thesaurus, check its meaning in a dictionary to make sure that it has the precise denotation and connotation you wish to express.

Creative Writing

Writing a Journal Entry

Fray Marcos de Niza's narrative is written in the form of a daily journal. In the first two entries, Fray Marcos gives not only his own account of events but also those of Indians who had witnessed "Esteban's Disaster." Using these two entries as models, write a journal entry in which you give both your own commentary and someone else's first-person account of an actual event.

Prewriting. First, identify an actual event that you can comment on and that someone you know witnessed firsthand. Then, jot down notes for your introductory narrative in which you will identify the event, give your perspective on it, and lead into the first-person account. Next, ask an eyewitness to the event to tell you what he or she saw, felt, and thought about it. Take notes as you listen, recording as many of the witness's specific words and phrases as you can.

Writing. Assume that your reader knows nothing about the event. Make sure that you give a clear account that includes all the necessary facts, transitions between facts and descriptive details, and clear antecedents for all pronouns.

Fray[1] Junípero Serra

(1713–1784)

Following the expulsion of the Moors from the Iberian Peninsula (Spain and Portugal) in 1492, the religious zeal that had driven the Spanish Christians through long years of bitter conflict was rechanneled into converting the Indians in the New World. To carry out this aim, many Franciscan friars travelled to New Spain and the northern territories as missionaries. Like most of these friars, Fray Junípero Serra (hoo-nee'peh-roh sehr'rah) enthusiastically embraced this challenging task.

Born in 1713, Miguel Serra was frail and sickly as a child, leading him to devote most of his time to reading and contemplation. He soon discovered that he wished to devote his life to prayer and entered the Franciscan Order while in his teens. There he became convinced that he wanted to become a missionary and to die a martyr in the service of humanity and God. In 1731, he became a priest and assumed a new name, Junípero. After teaching philosophy and theology to his Franciscan brothers for several years, Fray Junípero finally received his assignment to the New World in 1749.

Apparently eager to begin a life of martyrdom, Fray Junípero made a pilgrimage on foot from the east coast of New Spain (present-day Mexico) to the capital at Mexico City, a distance of over three hundred miles. During this journey his leg became infected, resulting in an affliction that was to trouble him for the rest of his life.

He held a variety of assignments in and around Franciscan missions in New Spain until 1767, when he was appointed chief administrator

---

1. **Fray** (frai): Brother: a title given to a Spanish friar or monk.

for all missions in Baja California. Soon after that, he avidly accepted another more exciting assignment—an opportunity to accompany Gaspar de Portolá on his expedition to San Diego to establish more missions. Fray Junípero spent the rest of his life in the northern territory of Alta California, finally realizing his dream of becoming a missionary dedicated to serving God through endless toil and extreme physical hardship. He died peacefully in 1784, among the Indians along the coast of what is now southern California.

from Writings of Junípero Serra

The following selection gives several entries from the jour-
nal kept by Fray Junípero Serra as he accompanied an
expedition led by Gaspar de Portolá to San Diego in 1769.
As you read, notice the details that Fray Junípero deems
important enough to include in his narrative. You will
find that his concerns differ markedly from those of Cabeza
de Vaca and Fray Marcos de Niza.

[June] 12. We continued our journey; it was four hours of hard
going—nothing but ravines, steep climbing and sharp descents.
We saw no mescales[1] today, but quite a number of footprints
and gentile trails—showing there are many of them in this
region. Day by day this country seems to grow bigger and bigger
with great walls and fortress-like bastions rising up to defend
the west coast. They force us to make many detours thus more
than doubling the length of our march. For that reason today
we have travelled mostly toward the west, hoping to reach the
sea, but it continues to escape us. Midway in today's march we
passed a rivulet with green trees and very high alders, but
without water. And finally, from a summit we saw another
arroyo[2] even greener—the trees we took for cottonwoods—and
we felt sure of finding there some precious water. On arrival
we saw the trees were the same kind as we had seen before,
and that there was no water at all. It is late, and for the night
we are without water. Our halting place is on some rising land
near the river which we called San Nazario de los Alisos.[3]

    [June] 13. Feast of my beloved Saint Anthony of Padua.

---

1. **mescales** (mehs-kah'lehs): an Indian tribe.
2. **arroyo** (ahr-roh'yoh): small river or stream.
3. **San Nazario de los Alisos** (sahn nah-sah'ryoh deh lohs ah-lee'sohs):
   patron saint of Alisos; it was common for missionaries to name their
   mission cities after saints.

Yesterday men were sent on ahead to look for water with the tools necessary for digging water holes in case running water could not be found. We rose very early so that Mass was said before dawn, and before six o'clock in the morning our men and pack train had left the place. For about an hour we crossed gullies without number and medium-sized hills. We dropped down into a canyon, facing east most of the way. The march lasted a little more than two hours, and we found that our men sent ahead yesterday had dug a well, and seeing that its supply of water was insufficient they had opened another hole. We stopped there: eight animals satisfied their thirst at one well; a few more drank from the other. When we were all set to start again, we could not on account of an upset among the mule drivers. The cooking has been poorer than ordinarily on account of the lack of water for preparing meals; and in memory of these trials—or shall we call them blessings from heaven—we thought a suitable name for the place would be San Antonio de los Trabajos. Yet the great miracle worker among the saints thought well to temper our trials with heartening news from the men sent ahead; it came about three o'clock in the afternoon. They announced that two places with water were ready for the morrow—one at a distance of three leagues, and the second of five leagues. Both had running water in great abundance; there was also pasture for the animals. Blessed be God. The arroyo here is studded with very high and very leafy alders and affords good pasture. Likewise farther down it opens out into a broad plain, but lack of water makes it poor. Another Indian among those with the Captain of the expedition died here.

[June] 14. Being short of water we started very early again today. After a march of two hours we arrived at the first watering place. Here the animals satisfied to the full their consuming thirst. The road went through a succession of canyons and hills, all of pure soil as are all the mountains we saw today in all directions. Their number is beyond counting. Shortly before arriving at our stopping place one of our mule drivers discovered a silver mine which all declare to be very rich. May it bring them a fortune. This place has not only water but also plenty of fine pasture, and, dotted with shade trees, room for a good farm, to which we will give the name of San Basilio. The question arose of pushing on the same day to the next place, provided it was not too far away; but it was thought advisable to give the animals some easement and rest; and we stayed the whole day here. After midday, and after eating their dinner, at one fell swoop nine Indians who belonged to our company deserted: six of them from the San Borja Mission, and three others from Santa María de los Angeles Mission. About the middle of the afternoon their absence was noticed. We sent men to go after them, but not even tracks could be found. Questioning those who still remained as to the cause of so unexpected an event, seeing they were always given food and good treatment, and they had always given the impression of being well satisfied, the answer we got was this: that they did not know, but they rather suspected that, being near San Diego, they were afraid they would be forced to stay there without hope of returning to their own missions. May Our Lord God bless them for the services they have rendered us, and the way we will miss them in the future. At present there remain with us only five from Santa Gertrudis, three from San Borja, two from Santa María, and two boys who ride on their mules and act as scouts for the pack train. May God keep them with us, and protect them from all harm. Amen.

[June] 15. We set out at half past seven in the morning and after an hour's march arrived at the water hole we were aiming for—the one our men notified us of on Saint Anthony's Day. The road was like that of the day before. To get down to this place there is an immensely long grade; and, like so many others, in the rainy season it must be impassable. Even as it is the animals get stuck in the dust, and flounder around. So what must it be then?

This place is a valley whose length from north to south, if measured with a cord, would, in my judgment, be much more than two leagues; the width is in proportion, at least half a league. The soil is good throughout and fine for pasture. At the far north end, where I took a walk today, there are hundreds of cottonwoods and hundreds of live oaks, and of both kinds some of extraordinary size. All the hills around are green and covered with trees. There is an abundance of water. Not to mention what can be guessed at from the green hillsides around, I noticed today three springs which are very good. The first, where we are stopping, and about midway down the valley, is a spring from which the water rises with much force, and even now during the driest season of the year, it rises with considerable force in this manner. Without the construction of any dam or the expenditure of any labor it could be used for irrigation. The second is in about the same locality—perhaps a hundred yards farther on. Although it is fairly large, it has less water. The quality of the water in these two fountains is wonderful; it tastes good, fresh, delicious, surely the best we have tasted, as every one of us agrees. The third is likewise at the same northern end of the plain: it must be more than a mere spring of water, because, although I had no opportunity to make a close inspection of its origin while I was near it, as I will explain further on, from what can be clearly seen it irrigates more than a quarter of a league of reeds and sweet cypress which grow at the foot of the hill in the distance. There is quite a large brook full of water, overflowing all the time. This water by itself seems to be more than would supply our needs. In fine, this place seems to promise more for a mission than one could desire; and so would be a great credit to so grand a patron as Saint Anthony. That is the name we gave to it. If San Diego is close by, as we imagine, he will have in San Antonio a fine neighbor. For the farm, apart from what is in the vicinity of San Basilio, there is everything in abundance: thanks be to God. One thing only is lacking I find: there is no stone. Nor is there any in the neighboring mountains either. I do not know how they will manage for the buildings and corrals unless they make the corrals of wood— and there is plenty of it here—and the buildings of adobe.[4] Possibly after a careful search of the neighborhood, some hill might furnish the stone—a material quite plentiful in most parts of California.

While going to inspect the third source of water, we saw some gentile women. Keeping our eyes averted, we went straight ahead without speaking a word to them. But when we came to the end of the plain, from on top of the hill facing us, a number of Indians fully armed sprang up; and one of them began to shout unintelligible words with great violence. From his gestures we gathered that he wanted us to turn back. By signs and by shouting we tried to invite them to come down to us. It was all useless. If we had gone any farther forward, it would have brought us right to their feet. The Sergeant, my companion, buckled on his leather jacket, and was all set for a

4. **adobe** (ah-thoh'beh): mud brick that has been baked in the sun.

fight. He consulted me: should we go ahead or turn back? And I, realizing that this was no time for breaking with the poor Indians, nor was it a matter involving any disgrace, was all for letting them appear—regretfully however—to be victorious on the field of battle. And that is why we did not have a good look at the source of the water supply—the only thing we had in mind in coming there. The soldiers who went up there with their horses, and at the sight of which no gentile dared to remain in these hills to raise the war whoop, tell me that there is an abundance of Rose of Castile bushes, a bounteous supply of water and many natural attractions. Thanks be to God.

[June] 16. We remained here the better to get our animals into condition. Today at an early hour, the Sergeant, along with one soldier and a few Indians on foot, went ahead in quest of water holes for tomorrow and the days following. Six soldiers, who throughout the day were tending the animals as they fed, carefully inspected the said northern part of the district. They were at a loss for words properly to express the prospects for founding a mission, nay even a city of San Antonio de Padua. Furthermore they said that climbing a hill, near the bountiful river, and through an opening along its banks, they caught a glimpse of the ocean, and that, in their judgment, it must be a distance of four leagues away. They found little piles of sweet-tasting berries, which the Indians eat; they seemed very nice to me. They also found a large, flat bowl, with designs in the clay, wickerwork woven together firm and strong, and other pieces of pottery of fine, intricate workmanship, somewhat resembling the products of Guadalaxara.[5] However, no gentile was seen.

[June] 17. We went ahead, and, as we were leaving the plain, I noticed that one hillside had plenty of stone that will be of great help to the settlers of San Antonio. Farther on there was more. We travelled up and down in territory covered with live oak, hilly but not difficult. After an hour we discovered a valley more than a league in width, and in part so green that, if I did not know in what country I was, I would have taken it, without any hesitation, for land under cultivation. We dropped down to the valley, and we found in readiness a hut made of tree branches and the place prepared for a halt—all the handiwork of the Sergeant, who had also left a letter we found, giving

5. **Guadalaxara** (gwah-dah-lah-hah'rah): Guadalajara; city in west central Mexico.

a report of everything. At his request the place was named in honor of Saint Athenogenes, bishop and martyr, for whom he feels a special devotion. It was his Saint's feast day yesterday when he arrived here with his companions. At this place there is a spring of water that is always flowing. As it comes out, it is quite warm, but by the time it gets to the river below it is good drinking water for the animals; our men would drink it too, were it not that a little spring of fresh water is more convenient for them, flowing at the foot of a hill in the same valley. Moreover, we do not know how the countryside keeps so green, as we have not found any other water supply, no matter how hard we have looked. And in many spots the verdure seems to be permanent. In fine, I believe that if the places suitable for founding missions should be few, this place ought not be left out of the list; but seeing that San Antonio is so near, it might serve as a mission station, or as a second farming place, or in whatever way it may best please those who have the disposing of it. Or perhaps one day it might be a royal mining center—if these hills yield as they promise.

[June] 18. After taking our meal we started out. At the very time we were setting forth, the three Indians that remained with us from Mission San Borja—as I said on June 14—ran away. We had no notion why. And so, little by little, we find ourselves deprived of the services of these men, who are more useful than people realize, for only a person who is right on the spot can form a proper idea of how hard they have to work—on poor food and no salary. The march lasted three hours, entirely over hills. We have left many mountains behind us, but the west coast confronts us with many more that are still larger. Finally we halted on a hillside near a river bed covered with big live oaks. Yet we knew beforehand that tonight we would not have more water than what we carried in leather bottles from the previous stop. And that is why this morning, even after Mass we tarried there to give the animals a chance to have their fill of water. Anyway, after arriving, seeing that the river bed with the live oaks showed signs of some humidity, we took a chance and dug a well. Some water came out, but seeing it would be insufficient for the animals, we consoled ourselves by thinking it might serve for our men. On tasting it, it turned out to be brackish. So we finally left that improvement to the birds which flew there at once, and to any poor gentiles who might pass by before it was sucked up by sand and dryness. To this district which seems to afford some pasture at seasons when it is not so dry as now, we gave the name San Gervasio. These two last days we saw no gentiles, but many tracks of them.

[June] 19. We started very early. All the morning the way was up and down over mountains and down valleys, which has become a habit with us. After crossing the first ridge we ran into another arroyo full of live oaks, and some sycamores but short of water also, the general appearance being much the same as the spot where we slept last night. Passing there I gave it the name San Protasio, to keep company with his brother saint who was not far off. And so, seesawing between mountains and valleys, all dry, but dotted with trees, we traveled all the time today—a matter of a little more than three hours. During the last stretch we turned southward to get to the watering place that the Sergeant had found and sent us word about. His job is to go ahead and spot such places. But today he had more than he bargained for, as he had to sink a shaft and strengthen the walls so that we could lead down to it with security all the animals one by one. They all quenched their thirst to the full. At this place we found a note from the Sergeant saying that he had gone ahead three full days' march, and that he had got himself into some trouble with a band of armed gentiles, but that he had handled them diplomatically and succeeded in pacifying them. To this place—very much resembling our previous stop, with the exception that it has water—we have given the name of Santa Miguelina, or Michaelina. During today's march, one of the Governor's servants, born in Genoa and a cook by profession, proved the strength of his sword's steel by running it through the buttocks of a burro leaving it dead at his feet. It seems it got in his way, and brought his own animal to a standstill. Having taken the evidence of eyewitnesses, and the man pleading guilty of killing the animal, the Governor deprived him of his job, stripped him of his arms, and condemned him to follow the expedition on foot. Furthermore, he fined him four times the price of the animal—that is 40 pesos.[6] Here a pretty mare gave birth to a little mule; and seeing that the poor little animal could not possibly keep up with the other beasts, it was given to the Indians who immediately slaughtered

---

6. **pesos** (peh'sohs): monetary unit of some Latin American countries.

it. Cutting it up in pieces for a barbeque they made themselves a feast of its tender flesh. May it do them good.

[June] 20. We continued our journey which lasted five hours, crossing deep ravines, sometimes with the greatest difficulty, climbing up and down hills, without any intermission. After an hour, from a hilltop we saw the West Coast Sea that we had been so anxious to reach. And at the end of the day's march we camped upon the beach; although it was about a league from the water, I called it the beach, as it was all level ground up to the ocean. The place had pasture but no drinking water either for the men or the animals. We identified this place with what is called on the maps and sea charts: La Ensenada de Todos Los Santos.[7]

[June] 21. We pushed on following the direction of the shore from northeast to southwest. The road was all level, except for a deep ravine cutting right across our way, but it was not too bad. After two hours and a half of march, we arrived at the north horn of the said bay, and we pitched camp at a distance of a rifle-shot from the ocean. It is pleasant country, all good land, extending as far as the hills which are not very high. There are plenty of green trees along the river bank, which is dry at present; good and abundant water, sufficient for a town, but it is in large ponds at a level lower than the ground, but not much lower. Should a way be found for using this water for irrigation, or for impounding it at its source, great things could be accomplished with it. Even without it the countryside is covered with green grass and is able to retain considerable humidity, and it is a place where it rains. As a matter of fact this space is just waiting for a mission; what with the nearness to the ocean, its level stretch of beach and its fine bay, it would be situated wonderfully well to ship in and out produce and commodities of all kinds. For a long time, I have been anxious to dedicate a place to María Santísima, my Mother and Queen, and as we are now reminded of the commemoration of her Visitation or pilgrimage over the mountains of Judea, I gave it as my opinion that we should call this beautiful place La Visitación de María Santísima.[8]

---

7. **La Ensenada de Todos Los Santos** (lah ehn-seh-nah'thah deh toh'thohs lohs sahn'tohs): The Bay of All Saints.
8. **La Visitación de María Santísima** (lah bee-see-tah-syon' deh mah-ree'ah sahn-tee'see-mah): The Visitation of Mary the Most Holy.

Here we met the Sergeant, who, having gone ahead one more day's march, came back to make a report on the country, and to get provisions for pushing ahead.

[June] 22. We took the day off to rest the animals and give them their fill of food and drink. The rational beings also were looking forward to doing a little fishing and hunting for relaxation. But the fishermen did not hook a single fish, nor did the huntsmen—and rabbits and hares frisk playfully and plentifully around—hit a single mark. The Governor and I refreshed ourselves with *chía*[9] water, a present from the gentiles who had previously come to call on the Sergeant, and who now came to call on us, giving us much happiness and pleasure because of their cordiality, which till now they had never displayed.

[June] 23. We started from that place to re-enter the line of mountains encircling this end of the bay, and in less than an hour's marching, we found ourselves again on the seashore. We followed it the rest of the way—in all, three hours and a half—all good, level road on hard ground until it meets with a mountain which abuts against the ocean itself. At its foot, in a hollow, is a very green meadow with numerous pools of water, sweet and good. There we halted for the night. At this spot there is a large ranchería[10] of gentiles with whom we visited and were very much delighted: their fine stature, deportment, conversation and gaiety won the hearts of all of us. They loaded us down with fish and abalones;[11] they went out in their little canoes to fish especially for us; they put on their dances for our benefit and insisted we sleep there two nights. Anything we told them in Spanish they repeated to us very distinctly. In fact, all the gentiles have pleased me, but these in particular have won my heart. The mules alone excited their astonishment and a considerable amount of fear. While they were with us they were full of assurance, but if they saw any mules coming near they trembled all over. And having heard us call them by their name they would cry out: "Mule! mule!" and want to run off, till someone got up to chase them away. This place does not seem fit for any purpose other than what it now serves: a ranchería; and so we called it La Ranchería de San Juan. The women are

9. *chía* (chee'ah): a seed that, when put into water, tastes of sugar and lemon.
10. **ranchería** (rahn-cheh-ree'ah): a group of huts or cottages.
11. **abalones** (ah-bah-loh'nehs): large California mollusks.

very decently dressed, but the men are naked like the rest of them. They carry on their shoulders a quiver as you see in pictures. On their heads they wear a kind of circlet made of otter or other fine fur. Their hair is cut just like a wig and plastered with white clay, all done very neatly. May God make their souls attractive too! Amen.

[June] 24. Feast of the Holy Precursor, Saint John. After Mass there was an exchange of trinkets between the soldiers and gentiles, bartering pieces of white cloth—to which they are very partial—for basketfuls of fresh fish. In this they showed themselves to be real businessmen: if the piece of cloth was small, the amount of fish in exchange was less—with no arguing allowed. But when the piece was larger, they doubled the quantity of fish. We parted from our good hosts and started on our day's march—four hours and a half today—heading north, and turning our backs to the ocean as we set out. We marched first along a very rocky river bed for a time, then we soon climbed an exceedingly steep and rocky hill. After an hour's going we came in sight of the ocean again. It seemed near, but was at quite a distance should we have tried to get to it. We crossed a valley full of trees—alders and live oaks—but without water. Finally after crossing a number of ranges of hills, we arrived at an immense valley, with wonderful pasture, and at its extremities plenty of trees; there was a fair-sized river and lake of clear water. This place, it would appear, could support another good mission; we called it San Juan Bautista. We slept under the stout branches of a monster live oak; but here we did not enjoy the California privilege of being free from fleas, because we were covered with them and with ticks too. We met numbers of gentiles both along the road—on which we passed near a ranchería, and all came out to meet us without being invited—as well as after our arrival, for the gentiles from another place nearby also came. They all were just as friendly as those we had met before. Among other questions I asked them if they would like me to stay with them there. They answered they certainly would. I felt the greatest pity to see so many souls, so friendly as these gentiles were, and to have to leave them.

[June] 25. After Mass and other business that came up, we started out along a very hilly road, most of the time in sight of the ocean. The day's march lasted three hours and a half. We finally arrived at the valley, where we stopped. But to get down to it we had a long and steep road. We were skidding rather than walking, with the ground all around so insecure that it was nothing but dust in which the animals got stuck. At last we got out of it and we made our halting place in the lower part of a green and leafy plain which has the appearance of an already well-established mission, not only on account of the general aspect of the place but also on account of the numerous gentile huts scattered up and down. There are fine stretches of land, abundant feed, much water and trees everywhere, and from an enormous lake right in the middle a canal flows to the ocean. You can see the ocean through an opening between the hills in front; reckoning roughly the coast must be about two leagues away. A good deal of the ground is covered with rushes and tule reeds, and among the willows you see quantities of grapevines. On the north side is the beginning of a canyon which branches off according to the twists in the mountain range. It is choke-full of massive trees with enormous branches. We all agreed that it was a wonderful location for another mission. I called it San Juan de Capistrano.

For Study and Discussion

1. Throughout his account, Fray Junípero Serra gives detailed information about the terrain and other natural features of the country he was exploring. **a.** What does his choice of details reveal about the purpose of his expedition? **b.** How does the focus of Fray Junípero's account make his narrative different from those of Cabeza de Vaca and Fray Marcos de Niza?

2. Fray Junípero Serra was both a missionary and an explorer. His narrative contains numerous references to prayer, patron saints, and other aspects of religious worship as well as to natural features, pack animals, and other practical concerns regarding the expedition. In your opinion, was Fray Junípero primarily a spiritual man or a practical-minded one? Explain.

3. Nature plays a prominent role in both American and Latin American literature. Sometimes it is an inhospitable force against which characters must struggle to survive and prosper. At other times, nature provides a sanctuary, a refuge from the constraints of civilization. How does Fray Junípero Serra view nature, and what role does it play in his narrative?

Vocabulary

Finding Word Origins

Several of the words that Fray Junípero Serra uses to identify objects and natural features have their origins in Spanish and are now part of American English. For example, he refers to a *ranchería,* which in Spanish means "a collection of huts" and in American English has been shortened to *ranch*—a large farm with buildings, land, and facilities for raising livestock.

For each of the following words, use a dictionary to find the Spanish word from which it is derived along with its original meaning and its current meaning in American English.

canyon   burro   corral   barbecue

Find two other American English words that have their origins in Spanish, and give the same information about each of those two words.

Great
Salt
Lake

UTAH

Lake
Tahoe

Colorado

CALIFORNIA

NEW MEXICO

PACIFIC
OCEAN

GULF OF CALIFORNIA

Rio
Conchos

Mexican American Period (1848-1960)

KANSAS

Missouri

MISSOURI

Arkansas

ARKANSAS

Mississippi

Red

Pecos

Colorado

Brazos

TEXAS

LOUISIANA

Rio Grande

GULF
OF
MEXICO

Literature of the Mexican American Period

With the signing of the Treaty of Guadalupe Hidalgo in 1848, much of California and the Southwest became part of the United States. The Spanish-speaking inhabitants of the region suddenly and unexpectedly faced a decision that would deeply affect their lives: either to become U.S. citizens or to retain their Mexican citizenship and be forced to abandon their land and livelihood to move to Mexican territory. Most decided to stay.

Although the legal status of these new citizens of Mexican and Spanish descent changed overnight, they did not give up their language or their culture. They continued to speak Spanish and held tenaciously to their religion, values, and traditions, including their rich oral and literary tradition of folk music, poetry, and stories.

One measure of the strength and persistence of their culture was the appearance of Spanish-language newspapers throughout the Southwest and California. These publications afforded Mexican Americans a vital link to cultural, social, and political life across the border in Mexico and provided a vehicle for artistic and political expression. Some of these newspapers lasted for only a few years, while others spanned a large part of the Mexican American period from the mid-nineteenth to the mid-twentieth century.

Although Mexican Americans would later experience a brief but intense period of acculturation to mainstream Anglo society, most held to their culture and their language through the first part of the twentieth century. The literature of the Mexican American Period reflects this strong sense of cultural identity as well as a need to preserve and express a unique literary heritage.

Short Fiction of the
Mexican American Period

Fictional works written during the Mexican American Period reveal the struggles, dreams, and values of a people strongly rooted in their cultural past. Many of these works first appeared in Spanish-language newspapers throughout the southwestern United States and California—publications that offered Mexican Americans a forum for artistic expression as well as a glimpse of the wider Spanish-speaking world of letters. Although many Mexican American writers also began to publish in English, their works still reflected their Hispanic cultural traditions.

While some of these works, such as the comic sketches of Julio G. Arce (Jorge Ulica), contain sharp social and political commentary, most focus on more universal, time-honored subjects and themes such as love, family, and community, often expressing nostalgia for a simpler, idealized past. Nina Otero, for example, published short stories and narrative sketches that emphasized Hispanic customs and folklore. Later writers such as Juan Sedillo, Fray Angélico Chávez, and Sabine Ulibarrí also focused on Hispanic life, writing artful narratives that showed a new concern with literary craft.

During this period, several writers began to take a more introspective approach in their work, paying greater attention to character development and plot. Josephina Niggli, for example, displays deft familiarity with narrative techniques and with a wide variety of themes in both her fictional and her dramatic works.

Jorge Ulica
(1870–1926)

Unlike many writers of the Mexican American Period who assert their loyalty to their own people and culture, Jorge Ulica (hohr'heh oo-lee'kah) displays an ambivalent attitude that fluctuates between tolerance and criticism. Sometimes he defends fellow Mexican Americans against Anglo prejudice; at other times he chides them for what he sees as their lack of sophistication and their awkwardness in dealing with each other as well as with the Anglo culture.

Julio G. Arce, who wrote under the pen name Jorge Ulica, was born in Guadalajara, Mexico, into a family of distinguished physicians. While he followed in the family tradition by successfully completing a degree in pharmacy, he had already dedicated himself to his first love: the written word. When he was barely ten years old, he founded his first newspaper, a neighborhood gossip sheet. At fourteen, he launched his literary career in earnest as editor of an anti-government student newspaper called *El Hijo del Progreso* [The Son of Progress].

For the next thirty years, Ulica edited and published several newspapers in his native Guadalajara and elsewhere. His defiant stance toward government authorities kept him in hot water most of the time. After receiving a death threat in 1915, he left Mexico for Buenos Aires but ended up instead in San Francisco where he rapidly established himself as a journalist with a sharp tongue and a quick wit.

Until his death in 1926, he published a series of biting satirical sketches called *Crónicas diabólicas* [Diabolical chronicles]. Unfortunately, much of Ulica's irony and satiric humor in the original Spanish is based on plays on words and subtle linguistic nuances that are sometimes lost in English translations. Nevertheless, most readers find themselves often smiling and even laughing outright as they read translations such as the following two selections.

Touch-Down Extraordinario / An Extraordinary Touchdown

Comic writers such as Jorge Ulica often mix truth and exaggeration to point up the faults and failings of human nature. In his collection of short narratives titled Crónicas diabólicas *[Diabolical chronicles], Ulica pokes fun at some of the customs, institutions, and values of his adopted country. At the same time, his biting wit often targets what he views to be the innocence and gullibility of his fellow Mexican Americans as they adapt to life in an alien culture. As you read the following two selections from* Crónicas diabólicas, *consider whether Ulica's satires may apply to American society today. How many of Ulica's views do you find that you share?*

Touch-Down Extraordinario

Fue gran fortuna la mía la de encontrarme con un sujeto desconocido que, de primas a primera, me ofreció un boleto de entrada al famoso juego de foot-ball en que las dos grandes universidades californianas iban a disputarse el campeonato sublime de las patadotas. Por sólo un dólar puso en mis manos el ansiado—"ticket," cuando hubo desgraciados que tuvieron que pagar hasta veinticino por él. Hay días en que tiene uno el sol completamente de frente. ¡Ese era mi día frontisolar!

Poco antes de la hora de la lucha, tomé el ferryboat y me marché al lugar de los acontecimientos. Por un sin fin de puertas entraban al Stadium los curiosos y los aficionados, y quise colarme por la primera que hallé; pero alguien me preguntó por las letras cabalísticas de mi boleto. Lo vi y me encontré con que de cuanto signo contenía el diminuto billete, lo más aproximado al cabalismo era KLX.

Por la puerta K no me dejaron entrar.

No por la X.

Ni por la L.

Manifesté una cólera atroz y una desesperación intensísima, lo cual, notado por un gendarme, hizo que éste se pusiera al habla conmigo.

—¿Por qué está usted perturbando la paz?—me preguntó.

Le conté mis cuitas, y luego, mostrándole mi boleto le dije: ¿No es esto un boleto para presenciar el juego de foot-ball?

—Sí,—me contestó el dignísimo genízaro;—pero para "presenciarlo" por radio en la estación KLX.

Se me llenó la boca de letras representativas de la superira, principalmente de ches.

¡Seguía de cara al alma sol!

En este país se encuentra una con un filántropo en cada esquina. Unos edifican universidades, otros hospitales, otros bibliotecas y los más modestitos le regalan al menesteroso un par de calcetines sin mucho uso o le sueltan un nickel.

An Extraordinary Touchdown

It was my great fortune to run into a guy whom I didn't know, but who suddenly offered me a ticket to the famous football game in which the two great Californian universities were going to battle it out in the sublime championship of big kicks. He put the eagerly awaited ticket in my hand for just a dollar, when there were wretches who have had to pay up to twenty-five for it. There are days when the sun shines right above us. This was my sunny day!

Just before the fateful hour, I took the ferryboat, and I marched to the place where these mighty events would occur. There were fans and curious people entering the stadium through an infinity of doors. I tried to get in through the first one I came to, but someone asked me for the cabalistic letters on my ticket. I looked at it and found that, of all the signs on the little slip of paper, the closest thing to cabalism was "KLX."

They didn't let me in through gate K.

Nor through gate X.

Not even through L.

I was giving signs of an atrocious rage and a very intense desperation, when a policeman, who happened to notice me, paused to talk to me.

"Why are you disturbing the peace?" he asked me.

I told him my misfortunes and then, showing him my ticket, said, "Isn't this a ticket to watch the football game?"

"Yeah," answered the stately janizary, "but to watch' it by radio at station KLX."

My mouth filled with representative four-letter words.

But I wasn't about to give up my sunny day!

In this country one finds a philanthropist on every street corner. Some build universities; others, hospitals; and others, libraries; and the most modest ones hand out second-hand socks to the needy, or toss them a nickel.

Una dama filantrópica, alta, gruesa, gigantesca, se atravesó en mi camino, y viendo mi malestar, me llamó y me habló así . . .

—Supongo que usted desea entrar al Stadium y que no tiene boleto ni dinero . . .

—Tengo boleto, señora; pero de los de K.L.X., y con ésos no se entra. En cuanto a dinero, ha estado usted más acertada que la Pitonisa de Delfos.

—Pues venga usted conmigo. Tengo dos boletos de los mejores y veremos juntos el juego.

Entramos y tomamos asiento. Mientras principiaba el encuentro y las bandas soltaban torrentes de notas por las bocas de cornetones inmensos, conversamos la dama filantrópica y yo. Era viuda. Su marido había muerto de un golpe, a causa de un juego de foot-ball y la inconsolable esposa derramaba lágrimas a mares al recordarlo.

Sus penas la tornaron silenciosa. Despues de una larga pausa, en que sólo hubo sollozos, dejó oír de nuevo su voz.

—¿Usted sabe,—me interrogó,—dónde está situado el Sacro?

¡Sacro . . . ! Supongo que será abreviatura de Sacramento, la capital de California.

—No, hombre, no. ¡Sacro!

—No estoy muy fuerte en geografía.

—Hablo a usted del hueso, sacro . . . de un hueso nuestro.

—No sé por dónde anda . . .

—Pues bien, en el sacro recibió mi esposo la patada, el día de uno de estos juegos. El sacro viene a quedar donde estuviera la cola, si la tuviéramos los humanos.

—Muy mala parte, señora,—digo—para las patadas . . .

Pues allí recibió la patada míster Hilache, mi marido.

—Me sentí conmovido y estuve a punto de llorar con la viuda; pero el juego comenzaba en esos momentos.

Estaba yo por el team aureoazulado y cuando ganaban un punto los jugadores o ponían en derrota a los contrarios, daba tales voces y manifestaba tal entusiasmo que la viuda me llamaba al orden y aun me pellizacaba fuertemente las pantorrillas.

En uno de mis grandes entusiasmos, la dama se disgustó conmigo, me echó en cara mi inquietud y poco seso y acabó por decirme que ella estaba por los roji-blancos, que formaban el equipo contrario.

One such philanthropic lady—tall, stout, and gigantic—crossed my path and, seeing my poor condition, called out:

"I suppose that you want to enter the Stadium, but that you have neither the ticket nor the money . . ."

"I do have a ticket, ma'am, but it's a KLX ticket and they won't let me in with it. But you're more right about the money than the oracle at Delphi."

"Well then, come with me. I have two of the best tickets and we'll watch the game together."

We went in and sat down. While they were in pre-game preparation and the bands poured out streams of notes from the mouths of immense cornets, the philanthropical lady and I conversed. She was a widow. Her husband had died after receiving a blow—the result of a game of football—and the inconsolable wife still shed a sea of tears in his memory.

Her grief made her silent. After a long pause, broken only by sobs, she spoke up again.

"Do you know," she asked, "where the sacral is?"

"Sacral . . . ! I suppose that's short for Sacramento, the capital of California?"

"No, young man, no. *Sacral!*"

"I'm not very good at geography."

"I'm speaking to you about the *bone*, sacral—about a bone that we have."

"I don't know where it's located."

"Well anyway, it was in the sacral that my husband was kicked on the day of one of these games. The sacral is located where our tail would be, if we had one."

"That's a very bad place, ma'am—I mean, to be kicked . . ."

"Well that's where my husband, Mr. Hilache, was kicked."

I felt deeply moved and was on the verge of crying with the widow, but at that moment the game was just beginning.

I was for the blue-gold team, and whenever the players scored a point or otherwise turned back their adversaries I yelled so loud and showed so much enthusiasm that the widow chastened me and even pinched me hard in the calves.

In one of my biggest outbursts of enthusiasm, the lady became infuriated with me and reproached me for both my excitement and dull-wittedness, and finished by telling that she was for the opposing team, the ones in red and white.

Procuré contener mis manifestaciones; pero no lo logré del todo. Al terminar el encuentro, en que hubo empate, no dejé de saludar a los jugadores de mi oncena favorita, con aplausos y gritos de alegría.

Ya en esos momentos, la concurrencia empezaba a desalojar la gradería del Stadium. Tirios y troyanos se sentían satisfechos del resultado de la lucha, y las músicas, los gritos y las aclamaciones atronaban el espacio.

La viuda de Hilache aprovechó la desocupación de la grada que estaba arriba de la nuestra, subió a ella y me soltó el siguiente speech:

—Hace cinco años murió mi marido. El era partidario de los jugadores de "oro y azul" y yo de los "blanco y rojo." ¡Como usted,—gritós,—y como usted me lastimó el amor propio! Entonces yo, herida como estaba, le lancé la patada de la tarde, golpeándole el sacro. Horas después era cadáver . . .

Vi entonces que la dama tomaba vuelo con el pie y me apuntaba al sacro. Apenas pudo dar la patada en la nalga izquierda. ¡Tremenda patada! De darme en el sacro, estuviera haciendo compañia a míster Hilache.

He averiguado que esta señora filántropa va, año por año, al juego, llevando una víctima, a la que inevitablemente patea después del encuentro. ¡En memoria de su marido y como costumbre votiva! Unos pateados se ven malos y otros, como yo, sólo ligeramente contundidos. ¡Tenía al sol de frente!

Sin embargo, todavía no puedo sentarme a causa del magullamiento.

29 de noviembre, 1924

I tried to restrain my outbursts, but I wasn't completely successful. After the game—which ended in a tie—I couldn't stop cheering and applauding for my favorite team.

The crowd was already beginning to empty the stadium. Each opposing faction felt satisfied with the outcome of the match, and music, shouts, and acclamations thundered in the air.

Hilache's widow took advantage of the empty row above ours to climb up and address me from above:

"It was five years ago that my husband died. I was for the red and white team, and he was for the blue and gold. Just like you," she shouted, "and just like you he wounded my self-esteem! So, because I was so hurt, I gave him the biggest kick of the afternoon, and it hit him right in the sacral. A few hours later he was dead . . ."

I noticed that her foot had taken flight and was aimed right at my sacral. She was only able to hit my left cheek. What a kick! If it had landed on my sacral, I would have been at this moment accompanying Mr. Hilache.

I have since learned that this philanthropic lady takes a victim along every year to the game, whom she inevitably kicks after it's over. Some of the ones she kicks end up looking pretty bad, but others, like me, get off only lightly bruised. It was my sunny day, after all!

Nevertheless, I still can't sit because of the bruise.

November 29, 1924

---

translated by **Terry Martin**

I Didn't Cast My Vote, But I Sure Was Cast Out!

The elections have come and gone. Thank God. Now I can enjoy peace and quiet without hearing the doorbell ring every second and without having to respond to the calls of individuals and delegations soliciting votes.

Besides the election of 'high functionaries,' there were forty-three propositions put to vote in the last elections, in which, as it is easy to suppose, some people were pro and others were con. And the ones who were pro and the ones who were con went from house to house and place to place preaching in favor of their 'ideals.'

"Vote yes on Amendment X!"

"Don't vote against universal suffrage!"

"Support the municipal workers!"

"Vote yes!"

"Vote no!"

This was constantly repeated during the days before the election, and now that the thing is 'over,' as they say here, one can, frankly, breathe an atmosphere of undisturbed peace.

Of course I voted neither Yes nor No. I neither play, nor compose, the music of elections in this land.

* * *

The first to come to see me were the boxers. They talked to me about Dempsey and Willard, about Firpo and about Romero Rojas, about Gibbons and about Carpentier, and they made me cry when they referred to our compatriot Tony Fuentes. The final part of their speech was as follows:

"You know that the law only permits a maximum of four rounds of punches on the nose here. In four bouts you cannot always technically slap a guy until he is left 'snoring without ribs,' either with one jawbone less or his nostrils beaten to a pulp. So vote 'yes' on Amendment 7, which will allow twelve full rounds of pounding."

I was still crying when the delegation left, not because of the excitement that Tony's triumphs had caused, but because of the pats on the back that two or three of the boxers had given me when they thought they had obtained my vote. Each one of them had hit me as if he wanted to 'knock me out' with one stroke.

* * *

Then the firemen came. They demonstrated the necessity of voting for Amendment 40, the purpose of which was to raise their salaries, and promised me that if I voted "Yes," they would see that I was saved in the event of a fire at my home, with as little harm to me as possible.

They went up to my bedroom, looked out the windows, estimated my weight, and in order to show me their efficiency, threw me out the window onto a blanket that others were holding on the patio below. I was not hurt, except for a big bump on the back of my head.

The supporters of Amendment 43, who wanted to remove all the corpses from the old cemeteries in order to urbanize the sad places, also requested my vote, offering me in exchange a plot of land in any of the modern necropolises.

"Say 'Yes' to the rejection of the previous agreements!"

"But I have no intention of dying here," I declared to the generous donors.

"Why not? We will see that you give us the pleasure of always remaining among us," they replied sweetly. Then they added, "Otherwise, vote 'Yes' on Amendment 43."

Hours later, when the evening shadows appeared like mourning draperies on the horizon, another delegation arrived. It consisted of two gentlemen and a lady who were strangely dressed in black. The three were thin, pallid, and cadaverous, and their teeth chattered as though they were cold. In a hollow and cavernous voice, the woman declared, "Vote 'No' on Amendment 43."

"Vote 'No,' " repeated one of the two gentlemen.

"Vote 'No,' " resounded the echo from the lips of the third individual.

They immediately explained that it would be an atrocious offense to remove the dead from their holes and carry them off God knows where, thereby interrupting their sweet sleep of death. They spoke, gestured, and stared in such a way that they frightened me. I offered to vote for everything they wanted.

Jorge Ulica 135

They finally departed, leaving behind a card on the table, which read

CONFEDERATION OF CORPSES
THAT NEITHER WISH TO LEAVE,
NOR BE REMOVED.
Amendment 43
VOTE NO, NO, AND NO!

Since that day I have suffered from nightmares, and from midnight on I see gloomy phantoms . . . I hear mournful howls, too.

I am told that it is stray cats meowing, but who knows if it is not really the dead that wander around moaning. . . .

November 8, 1924

---

translated by **Terry Martin**

For Study and Discussion

An Extraordinary Touchdown

1. The speaker remarks that "in this country one finds a philanthropist on every street corner." **a.** What view does Ulica seem to take toward such people? **b.** How is it ironic that he refers to the widow as a "philanthropic lady"?

2. Writers often create comic effects through a play on words— that is, through the different ways that an ambiguous word or phrase can be interpreted. Although Ulica wrote "An Extraordinary Touchdown" in Spanish, the translator has rendered in English several plays on words that are important to the story. Identify at least two of these, and explain how they contribute to the humor of the story.

I Didn't Cast My Vote, But I Sure Was Cast Out!

3. The speaker states: "I neither play, nor compose, the music of elections in this land." In what way do the people soliciting votes play and compose "music" in their attempts to influence the speaker's vote? Why is their "music" so displeasing to the speaker?

4. Ulica uses a **simile**—a figure of speech that compares two basically unlike things—to foreshadow the arrival of the last "delegation." What is this simile, and how does it set the mood for the last few paragraphs of the story?

5. Based on his reactions to each group of solicitors, which group do you think the speaker is most impressed by? Does he seem to take any of them seriously, and if so, why?

Literary Elements

Satire

Satire is a kind of writing that holds up to ridicule the vices and follies of human beings. Ranging in tone from good-natured humor to bitter irony, satirical pieces can target individuals, groups, institutions, or humanity in general.

In the short pieces that make up his *Crónicas diabólicas*, Jorge Ulica satirizes what he sees as absurdities in American society and in general human behavior. For example, in "An Extraordinary Touchdown," he pokes fun at Americans' reverence for football through the character of the fanatical widow and also through the speaker himself. The "philanthropic lady" fatally kicked her husband for cheering the wrong team, and the speaker nearly suffers a similar fate as a result of his enthusiasm for the game. Ulica also satirizes human gullibility through his speaker, who twice allows himself to be duped for the sake of a football ticket.

What or whom does Ulica satirize in "I Didn't Cast My Vote, But I Sure Was Cast Out!"? What comic devices does he use to create this satirical effect?

Writing About Literature

Analyzing a Writer's Point of View

Although Ulica published his *Crónicas diabólicas* early in the twentieth century, you may find that some of his satirical observations about American society and humanity in general are still applicable today. In an essay of three or four paragraphs, discuss how the two selections you have read relate to your experiences of human nature and of modern American culture.

Prewriting. First, reread the stories and identify the people, institutions, and aspects of human behavior that Ulica satirizes. For example, what does he find ridiculous or objectionable about the exaggerated importance of football in American culture or about the American political process? What kinds of statements does he make about human nature? Next, consider your own feelings about Ulica's point of view. Are his observations accurate, or do they seem biased? If his views are exaggerated or otherwise distorted, do they nevertheless contain a note of truth? Do any of them reflect your own observations and experiences? If so, how do they apply?

Writing and Revising. As you write and revise your paper, concentrate on varying your diction. For example, rather than state repeatedly that the solicitors attempt to "get the speaker's vote," use alternative phrases such as "persuade the speaker to support their cause" or "harass the speaker into voting for their interests." Using specific rather than general terms can also help to add variety and clarity to your writing. For instance, if you are discussing "the election process," you can avoid using this phrase repeatedly by focusing on a particular aspect of the process. When discussing the people canvassing for votes, you could use the term *electioneering*. Similarly, you can refer to the speaker as an elector or as a member of the voting public.

Juan Sedillo
(1902–1982)

Some writers establish a name for themselves in the field of literature with a single work. Such is the case of Juan Sedillo (hwahn seh-thee'yoh) and his story "Gentleman of Río en Medio."

From the time of his birth in Socorro, New Mexico, until he became a member of the New Mexico state senate in 1932, little is known about Sedillo's life other than that he earned a law degree at Georgetown University. During the 1930s he served in the state senate for several years and practiced law in New Mexico. In the first half of the following decade, he fought in World War II as an officer in the United States Army, earning a Bronze Star Medal and five battle stars.

After the war, Sedillo acted as Chief of Legal Affairs in Germany from 1945–1948 and subsequently became a judge in the American zone in 1951. He also served in other posts in Europe over the next few years, including a position with the diplomatic corps in Morocco in 1957.

The appeal of service overseas finally waned in the late 1950s, and Sedillo returned to his native state of New Mexico to resume his law practice, which led to his again becoming a judge. From 1964 to 1968, he also wrote weekly articles about Mexico for New Mexico newspapers.

Creative pursuits—particularly writing and painting—played an important role in Sedillo's life. He kept his paintings private, never exhibiting them and sharing them only with his family. His writing, on the other hand, was quite public, consisting primarily of newspaper articles. The selection that begins on the following page, "Gentleman of Río en Medio," is believed to be his only piece of fiction and was inspired by a case that he handled as an attorney in Santa Fe, New Mexico.

Gentleman of Río en Medio[1]

Don Anselmo seems to have little sense for business when he insists on selling his land for half its worth. However, the American buyers soon discover that business is conducted quite differently in Río en Medio. As you read, you will find that they encounter a major problem when they take possession of the orchard. Consider what this problem and its solution reveal about the differences between Don Anselmo and the Americans.

It took months of negotiation to come to an understanding with the old man. He was in no hurry. What he had the most of was time. He lived up in Río en Medio, where his people had been for hundreds of years. He tilled the same land they had tilled. His house was small and wretched, but quaint. The little creek ran through his land. His orchard was gnarled and beautiful.

The day of the sale he came into the office. His coat was old, green and faded. I thought of Senator Catron,[2] who had been such a power with these people up there in the mountains. Perhaps it was one of his old Prince Alberts.[3] He also wore gloves. They were old and torn and his fingertips showed through them. He carried a cane, but it was only the skeleton of a worn-out umbrella. Behind him walked one of his innumerable kin—a dark young man with eyes like a gazelle.

The old man bowed to all of us in the room. Then he removed his hat and gloves, slowly and carefully. Chaplin[4] once

---

1. **Río en Medio** (ree'oh ehn meh'thyoh).
2. **Senator Catron:** Thomas Benton Catron, Senator from New Mexico (1912–1917).
3. **Prince Alberts:** long, double-breasted coats named after the English Prince Albert, who later became Edward VII.
4. **Chaplin:** Charlie Chaplin, renowned for his comic performances in silent movies.

did that in a picture, in a bank—he was the janitor. Then he handed his things to the boy, who stood obediently behind the old man's chair.

There was a great deal of conversation, about rain and about his family. He was very proud of his large family. Finally we got down to business. Yes, he would sell, as he had agreed, for twelve hundred dollars, in cash. We would buy, and the money was ready. "Don[5] Anselmo," I said to him in Spanish, "we have made a discovery. You remember that we sent that surveyor, that engineer, up there to survey your land so as to make the deed. Well, he finds that you own more than eight acres. He tells us that your land extends across the river and that you own almost twice as much as you thought." He didn't know that. "And now, Don Anselmo," I added, "these Americans are *buena gente*,[6] they are good people, and they are willing to pay you for the additional land as well, at the same rate per acre, so that instead of twelve hundred dollars you will get almost twice as much, and the money is here for you."

The old man hung his head for a moment in thought. Then he stood up and stared at me. "Friend," he said, "I do not like to have you speak to me in that manner." I kept still and let him have his say. "I know these Americans are good people, and that is why I have agreed to sell my house to them. But I do not care to be insulted. I have agreed to sell my house and land for twelve hundred dollars and that is the price."

I argued with him but it was useless. Finally he signed the deed and took the money but refused to take more than the amount agreed upon. Then he shook hands all around, put on his ragged gloves, took his stick and walked out with the boy behind him.

A month later my friends had moved into Río en Medio. They had replastered the old adobe[7] house, pruned the trees, patched the fence, and moved in for the summer. One day they came back to the office to complain. The children of the village were overrunning their property. They came every day and played under the trees, built little play fences around them, and

---

5. **Don** (dohn): a title of respect, formerly used for Spanish-speaking men of high rank; now used as a title of courtesy.
6. *buena gente* (bweh'nah hehn'teh).
7. **adobe** (ah-thoh'beh): mud brick that has been baked in the sun.

took blossoms. When they were spoken to they only laughed and talked back good-naturedly in Spanish.

I sent a messenger up to the mountains for Don Anselmo. I took a week to arrange another meeting. When he arrived he repeated his previous preliminary performance. He wore the same faded cutaway, carried the same stick and was accompanied by the boy again. He shook hands all around, sat down with the boy behind his chair, and talked about the weather. Finally I broached the subject. "Don Anselmo, about the ranch you sold to these people. They are good people and want to be your friends and neighbors always. When you sold to them you signed a document, a deed, and in that deed you agreed to several things. One thing was that they were to have the complete possession of the property. Now, Don Anselmo, it seems that every day the children of the village overrun the orchard and spend most of their time there. We would like to know if you, as the most respected man in the village, could not stop them from doing so in order that these people may enjoy their new home more in peace."

Don Anselmo stood up. "We have all learned to love these Americans," he said, "because they are good people and good neighbors. I sold them my property because I knew they were good people, but I did not sell them the trees in the orchard."

This was bad. "Don Anselmo," I pleaded, "when one signs a deed and sells real property one sells also everything that grows on the land, and those trees, every one of them, are on the land and inside the boundaries of what you sold."

"Yes, I admit that," he said. "You know," he added, "I am the oldest man in the village. Almost everyone there is my relative and all the children of Río en Medio are my *sobrinos* and *nietos*,[8] my descendants. Every time a child has been born in Río en Medio since I took possession of that house from my mother I have planted a tree for that child. The trees in the orchard are not mine, *Señor*,[9] they belong to the children of the village. Every person in Río en Medio born since the railroad came to Santa Fe owns a tree in that orchard. I did not sell the trees because I could not. They are not mine."

There was nothing we could do. Legally we owned the

---

8. *sobrinos . . . nietos* (soh-bree'nohs . . . nyeh'tohs): nephews . . . nieces; grandchildren.
9. *Señor* (seh-nyohr'): Sir, Mister.

trees but the old man had been so generous, refusing what amounted to a fortune for him. It took most of the following winter to buy the trees, individually, from the descendants of Don Anselmo in the valley of Río en Medio.

For Study and Discussion

1. The narrator is unable to convince Don Anselmo to take the additional money the Americans offer to pay him. Explain why Don Anselmo refuses to accept money that is rightfully his.

2. Throughout the story the narrator comments on Don Anselmo's appearance and behavior. Based on these comments, what does the narrator seem to think of Don Anselmo? Does he find the old man noble or ridiculous? How does he respond to Don Anselmo's manner of conducting business? Use specific examples from the story to support your answers.

3. By not informing the narrator that the trees on his land were not his to sell, Don Anselmo causes the Americans quite an inconvenience. Do you think Don Anselmo dealt honestly with the buyers of his property?

Writing About Literature

Analyzing Differences in Characters' Ethical Motivations

Don Anselmo's personal code of honor seems strange and impractical to the Americans who buy his property. Although Don Anselmo likes and respects his new neighbors, he refuses to compromise his convictions. In an essay two or three paragraphs long, discuss the differences between Don Anselmo's ethical code and that of the Americans.

Prewriting. Make a list of instances in the story in which Don Anselmo's convictions are at odds with those of the Americans. What underlying notions about money, property, and kinship cause these conflicts? Make sure that you can find specific examples in the story to illustrate your ideas.

Writing. As you analyze and contrast Don Anselmo's and the Americans' ethical codes, avoid statements of opinion such as the following: "Don Anselmo is foolish in stubbornly adhering to an antiquated gentlemanly code." Rather, focus on the perspectives and opinions of the characters themselves: "From the Americans' point of view, Don Anselmo's adherence to an antiquated code of honor may seem foolish and stubborn."

Nina Otero
(1882–1965)

One of the first Spanish-speaking
New Mexican women to hold prominent
public posts, Nina Otero (nee'nah
oh-teh'roh) distinguished herself as an
educator, suffragist, and writer during her long, productive life. She
played and active role in public affairs until her death, leaving an
indelible mark on the educational and political systems as well as the
literature of her time.

Otero was born in 1882 in Los Lunas, New Mexico—a town that
one of her ancestors founded. Descended from a long line of settlers
and political leaders, Otero was also a cousin of Governor Miguel Antonio Otero—another prolific writer of the Mexican American Period.
Like her famous cousin, Otero became involved in politics at an early
age. After graduating from Maryville College, a women's college in St.
Louis, Otero returned to New Mexico in 1917 to take a position as state
chair of a national suffragist organization.

Later that year, she became superintendent of schools in Santa Fe
County, a rather remarkable achievement for a woman of her time.
Otero went on to serve as an inspector with the Indian Service in the
Department of Interior and to supervise several adult education
programs. She held the position of education director of the Civilian
Conservation Corps and also of education director for the Works
Progress Administration in Puerto Rico. In 1938, Maryville College
recognized her contribution to Mexican American letters by awarding
her an honorary degree in literature.

"The Bells of Santa Cruz," which appears on the following pages, is
taken from *Old Spain in Our Southwest,* a collection of stories about
Otero's childhood in New Mexico. Interweaving romance and historical fact, this story retells a bittersweet legend that had been passed on

to Otero by her friend Doña Concepción. Although primarily a tale of tragic love, "The Bells of Santa Cruz" also offers a unique perspective from a Spanish point of view on an important facet of Mexican history: the Indians' violent revolt against Spanish domination in eighteenth-century New Mexico.

(For additional biographical information about Nina Otero, see page 237.)

The Bells of
Santa Cruz

*Set in eighteenth-century Spain and what is now New
Mexico, this story relates a legendary romantic tale concerning the history of the Santa Cruz church bells—bells
that are "rich not alone in metal, but in memories." As
you read, you may be reminded of other stories of tragic
love. Look for elements that make this tale a classic love
story. How does its historical backdrop lend it realism?*

In the ancient village of Santa Cruz there is an old saying—"The
toll of the bell is not for the dead, but to remind us that we,
too, may die tomorrow."

María Concepción told this story to me as we sat under
the roof of her *portal*[1] and watched the spring mist drift down
the *mesas.*[2]

Two hundred and thirty-nine years have passed since Don[3]
Diego de Vargas refounded this little village. It is recorded that
the church was built in 1733. But it was of the bells of this church
that María Concepción told—bells, rich not alone in metal, but
in memories, memories so old, so beautiful.

"That is the Angelus[4] ringing, Doña[5] Concepción."

"Ah, little one. Those bells tell of the loves of Castile and
of the sorrows that all great loves bring. I will tell you a story
that you may repeat it to your nieces and nephews, for perhaps
some day they will come here as you have come."

Drawing her shawl more tightly around her, she began:

"Many years ago, many more years than I can count,

---

1. *portal* (pohr-tahl'): porch.
2. *mesas* (meh'sahs): plateaus or flat surfaces on top of hills or mountains.
3. **Don** (dohn): a title of respect, formerly used for Spanish-speaking men
   of high rank; now used as a title of courtesy.
4. **Angelus** (ahn'heh-loos): a bell rung to call people to prayer.
5. **Doña** (doh'nyah): formal title of respect used before first names of
   women.

preparations were under way for the departure from Spain, from Castile, of three priests and a little band of soldiers. It must have been a wonderful sight, for it was a brave undertaking. Don Ángel, a young nobleman and a soldier, a nephew of Father Antonio Moreno who headed the missionary priests, was among those selected with other brave youths to undertake this perilous journey. Don Ángel wished to serve his God and his king! Short service he thought he would have, for, you know, youth feels it can conquer the world within a certain time.

"On his return, Don Ángel was to marry the beautiful noblewoman, Doña Teresa. Oh, they say that her beauty was the talk of the kingdom. She was like the flowers of Castile. Even heaven would rejoice in this union.

"The gayety of the farewell gathering, where gifts of gold and offerings of value were made to the members of the small band of loyal men, had but one sad note—the parting of the two lovers. Doña Teresa's laugh was her way of weeping to hide her sorrow. Don Ángel gave her a ring for her slender finger, and a chain and cross of gold. He kissed her hand. He waved a farewell to his friends and joined his companions.

"First they crossed the ocean. They tell me it was like flying in the blue sky. They crossed high mountains where unknown animals roamed and where unknown savages lived. Slowly and carefully this small band entered this country. At first the priests spoke to the Indians in symbols, and then instructed them and converted them to the Christian faith. In time Father Moreno started the building of a church. The church we now have is not the first one built, for that was destroyed when the Indians tired of the domination of the Spaniards, whose religion and form of government they did not understand. But this church was built by Father Moreno and his men in 1733 with the help of the converted Indians, and it is there in that tower that the bells hang which are so rich in memories. You know, Santa Cruz was the second big Catholic Mission built; the first was but a few miles north of here at San Juan of the Gentlemen.

"Time passed, and it was necessary for Father Moreno to return to old Spain, to report to his superiors the progress he had made in the establishment of churches, the number of converts to the Christian religion, and, important too, he must of necessity raise funds for further work in this New Spain, for the erection of churches to house his increasing flock. Don Ángel, having proved his ability as a soldier, his loyalty as a Spanish subject, was to accompany his uncle. Don Ángel, sleepless with anticipation and restless under delays, wrote Doña Teresa that he was returning to claim her love.

"But a few days before they were to start, the Indians made a surprise attack. At dawn, as the light made objects distinguishable, loud yells and shrill cries rent the air. The sound of war drums mingled with the war song of the Indian high priest. Arrows shot in every direction. Father Moreno entered the conflict, cross in hand. The young warriors of his band had a hand-to-hand encounter with the Indians whose yells grew louder and more fierce. The sound was as that of coyotes howling after a kill. A loyal Indian runner was sent to San Juan for reinforcements. Father Moreno was the target, and as young Don Ángel rushed to the aid of his uncle, an arrow whirled by the Padre and struck the young man. Don Ángel staggered forward and back and fell to the ground, the arrow deep in his side. Father Moreno ran and knelt to give absolution to the brave youth whose last words were: '*Tío*,[6] tell Teresa that my love was as great as my sacrifice!'

"Soldiers came from San Juan and they assisted in quieting the Indians. Since that time the Indians are our best neighbors. And why not? This ground was watered with the blood of martyrs and Indian braves and by tears of heaven which we call rain. This hallowed ground is also the resting place of the brave Castilian, Don Ángel.

"In Spain little was known of the struggle of this band of brave priests and soldiers. When the letters from her beloved stopped coming, Doña Teresa became anxious, but she kept her fear in her heart. If he was brave she, too, must show courage.

"Time passed; word came again from across the sea. A message for Doña Teresa from Padre Moreno:

" 'Gracious and courageous young lady:

" 'No words of grief and affection can express to you what my heart feels. As a brave and valiant soldier, Don Ángel has not to my knowledge been surpassed. God loved him even more than we, for He has called him to rest in the New World

---

6. *Tío* (tee'oh): Uncle.

in the shadow of the *Sangre de Cristo* Mountains[7] and the valley of the Holy Cross.' "

"Doña Teresa received the news in silence. For her no longer did snows have power to chill, nor the bright rays of the sun to warm. She walked alone in her garden crushing under foot the new sprouts in flower. There was a smell of earth, that earth which held her beloved gave forth of fragrance; it was the perfume of her heart in sorrow.

"For twelve years the Indians of the Río Grande del Norte had claimed the lovely valley of Santa Cruz. But after the conquest de Vargas sent new settlers and this soon became the largest community in this part of New Spain. Then Spanish people again knelt in peace before the altar of their holy religion.

"The beautiful church took years to build; thousands of *adobes*[8] are in those thick walls. The roof beams came from those *Sangre de Cristo* Mountains. It took several hundred men to put them in place. Oh, it was a labor of love, but when it was completed there were no bells to summon the people to Mass, no bells to announce the baptism of the Indians, or marriages according to the rites of our church. No bells to toll a benediction over their dead. So the priests sent to the Mother Country and there in Spain they held a celebration.

"People were invited to a great ceremony. Bells were to be molded to be sent to the New World. Friends and relatives of warriors and priests gathered in old Castile. A great fire was lighted, over which a huge caldron rested. A long pole was handled by one of the men in the crowd whose body became shiny from the sweat on his back, so hot was the fire that was to melt the metals.

"There was much merrymaking. It was the natural delight for a gift of such significance. And besides there was an opportunity for young people to meet and not be so closely guarded by their parents.

"Word reached Doña Teresa of the occasion for the celebration. Since the death of Don Ángel, she had never left her father's palace except to attend Holy Mass. She had been ill with a fever, a long illness which left her weak and frail, but she insisted on

---

7. *Sangre de Cristo* Mountains (sahn'greh deh krees'toh): high mountain range in northern New Mexico; southern extension of the Rocky Mountains.
8. *adobes* (ah-thoh'behs): mud bricks that have been baked in the sun.

taking part in this special celebration, much to the delight of her aged father.

"As young men linked their arms in those of young girls and danced around the caldron, the man stirred the molten metal, keeping time to the rhythm of the music. The fire was crackling. A lovely high coach driven by a team of sleek black horses drove up to the dancing group. It was like encountering the unknown dead when Doña Teresa, with the same charm but with the air of one tired and living in the past, stepped from the coach, accompanied by her father. A hush went over the crowd; a silence which not even the crackling of the burning wood seemed to shatter. Slowly they walked toward the great caldron. With a fixed melancholy expression Doña Teresa watched the seething mass. Ah, faces we see, hearts we do not know! Slowly she removed from her finger a gold ring, and over her head she slipped a gold chain on which hung a cross of gold. She pressed these, the parting gifts of Don Ángel, to her bosom for a minute and then threw them into the boiling metal, there to whisper a deeper note of melody and of love.

"A respect for those who mourn and a reverence for the dead you well know is the natural feeling of our old and of our young people. On seeing this act of courage and devotion, even the happy ones turned serious, and in a frenzy of awakened memories they all cast their jewels, silver and gold into the great caldron.

"What wonder that these bells have a different sound from all bells!

"A strange thing—those bells arrived here and were blessed on the day Doña Teresa died in Castile!

"When the Angelus rings, as we hear it now, and the streaks of rain sweep down from the *Sangre de Cristo* Mountains, there, in the mist, maybe the lovers meet—who knows?"

For Study and Discussion

1. Nina Otero describes the events surrounding the conquest and colonization of New Mexico from a Mexican point of view that draws on both Spanish and Indian perspectives. Does the point of view of her narrative seem to be closer to one of these perspectives than the other? How does she appear to view the Indians in their relationship to the Spaniards?

2. Otero idealizes Don Ángel, who represents what she believes to be the best traits of the Spanish character of the eighteenth century. How would you describe Don Ángel's character?

3. Although Doña Teresa exhibits great courage and restraint when faced with separation from her fiancé and his eventual death, she is deeply affected by her loss. How does the storyteller indicate Doña Teresa's true feelings?

Vocabulary

Understanding Connotations

In addition to their explicit meanings, or **denotations,** many words also have **connotations**—meanings and feelings that have come to be associated with a word over time.

In "The Bells of Santa Cruz," Doña Teresa receives a ring and a cross made of gold from her departing lover—gifts that she later throws into the molten metal that will be used to forge the Santa Cruz church bells. Although the explicit meaning of *gold* is "a yellow metallic element," the word *gold* also carries connotations of brilliance and purity, which enrich the meaning of the story. The gold metal of Doña Teresa's jewelry signifies the preciousness of her fiancé's memory and the depth and purity of her sacrifice when she relinquishes his parting gifts.

Each of the following words appears in the story. What connotations are connected to these words? What roles do these connotations play in the story?

bells   flock   mist   rain

Josephina Niggli

(1910–)

Dramatist, poet, and prose writer
Josephina Niggli (hoh-seh-fee'nah
neeg'glee) displayed a gift for writing at
an early age. Born near Hidalgo,
Mexico, where her father managed a
cement plant, Niggli came to the
United States with her parents during
the Mexican Revolution in 1913. Her mother, a concert violinist who
was originally from Virginia, taught her daughter at home until "Little
Niggli" (as she affectionately called Josephina) entered a Catholic high
school in San Antonio, Texas. Niggli's bicultural upbringing and uncon-
ventional education fostered in her a keen imagination and a deep understanding of Mexican American culture—two attributes that would
exert a powerful influence on her work as a writer.

Encouraged by her parents and by teachers, Niggli wrote prolifically
as a teen-ager, publishing short stories and poems in magazines such as
Ladies' Home Journal and *Mexican Life*. At eighteen, she published her
first poetry collection, *Mexican Silhouettes*.

When she entered the University of North Carolina to study play-
writing, her work as a dramatist began in earnest; many of the plays she
wrote during this time were produced. Her folk comedies and historical
plays reflect a detailed knowledge of Mexican traditions, history, and
lore as well as a keenly ironic insight into human failings.

In addition to being widely recognized as a playwright, Niggli has
received acclaim for her prose works. "The Quarry," which appears on
the following pages, is taken from *Mexican Village*—a highly successful
work that has been described both as a novel and as a collection of
short stories. The tales that make up *Mexican Village* are alternately
comic and tragic, ironic and compassionate in tone. Set in the Mexican

village of Hidalgo, these tales center on the character of Bob Webster, a half-Anglo, half-Mexican man who does not feel at home in either culture. When Webster takes the job of quarry master in Hidalgo, he gradually comes to embrace the villagers' way of life and to affirm his Mexican heritage.

The Quarry

When Bob Webster assumes the job of quarry master in Hidalgo the villagers recognize him as "a new type of jefe"[1]—one who understands his workers and treats them with respect. However, as the story progresses, it becomes clear that Webster has mixed feelings about being jefe. Notice the point at which the narrative shifts from the workers' point of view to Webster's. Based on Niggli's characterization of Webster, what kind of person do you think he is—that is, what are his true motivations and intentions?

By the end of the first work day, the men at the quarry discovered that they had a new type of *jefe*, a type they had never hitherto known. There had been many quarry masters in the ten years of the quarry's existence before 1913, when all work had ceased. There had been the martinet German, the casual Irishman, the homesick Englishman, the excitable Frenchman, and, of course, the drunken Italian.

With each new master came the changes. For two weeks the *jefe* would ride the mountain trails; he would set up what they called *La Sistema*,[2] the system. There would be much writing of papers and many speeches to the quarry men, especially on the subject of living in caves. But by the end of the two weeks the system would dissolve into the endless procession of slow days and nights. Speeches would be made to the women instead of the men; and bottles of golden cognac or colorless tequila[3] would take the place of the papers. And Don[4] Anselmo, the foreman, would see that the small red cars, fastened together by an endless chain, the rock-laden downward cars pulling up the empties, somehow reached the train tracks and that the rock was loaded on flatcars to be taken to the cement factory in Monterrey.

---

1. *jefe* (heh'feh): boss.
2. *La Sistema* (lah sees-teh'mah).
3. **tequila** (teh-kee'lah): a strong liquor distilled from the sap of the maguey plant.
4. **Don** (dohn): a title of respect, formerly used for Spanish-speaking men of high rank; now used as a title of courtesy.

Sometimes the *jefes* would remember to tell Don Anselmo that he was a good foreman, and would present him with a small bottle of liquor. The Italian had even looked with soft eyes on the ripening beauty of Candelaria. On that day Don Anselmo had fastened a block of wood to a tree and had shown the Italian some tricks of knife-throwing, and after that the Italian showed no further interest in Candelaria. That Anselmo, said the Inditos,[5] was a wise one. Candelaria was worth more than a casual sleeping on an office floor. A man from the village might not be such a rich one, but he would be Candelaria's husband long after a *jefe* had forgotten the color of Hidalgo's[6] mountains. And as for *La Sistema*, every master was entitled to his two weeks of amusement, but after that, well, the getting of stone from the quarry was a serious business and not to be entrusted to an outlander.

So the quarry men prepared themselves for the breaking in of the new *jefe*, who was, in himself, curious because he could speak Spanish, which no other quarry master had ever been able to do.

Their blank eyes hiding amusement, they watched Bob gallop up to the mesa[7] the second morning after his arrival. He called the foreman to him.

"Good morning, Don Anselmo."

A ripple of movement passed over the waiting crowd. What manner of *jefe* was this that he should call Anselmo Carvajal "Don"? The other *jefes* in their arrogance had never bothered to bestow a title of respect on the Inditos, even though old age demanded it of politeness. New interest came to the men, and they pressed closer as Bob said, "You doubtless have a method for taking the rock to the train?"

"That is so, *jefe*."

"It is a good method?"

"There have been no complaints from the cement factory in Monterrey, señor."

"Continue it, then, in the old manner. I will watch it, and if I am not pleased we can make changes later. But now I will need five men to help me here."

---

5. **Inditos** (een-dee'tohs): Indians; simple tribespeople like those working in the quarry.
6. **Hidalgo's** (ee-thahl'gohs).
7. **mesa** (meh'sah): a plateau or flat surface on top of a hill or mountain.

Don Anselmo, as curious as the rest, waved five men aside and took the others to the quarry; but during the day many, on one pretext or another, had to make little trips to the mesa, Don Anselmo with them, and what they saw amazed them. For the new *jefe* had ordered a fire, and the precious papers which had been so carefully guarded for seven years were tossed on the blazing wood.

The empty bottles were presented to the wide-eyed audience of children. And as for the women, well, that was the impossible thing. The new *jefe* gave them not so much as a passing glance as he went about his work. Nor did the audience seem to bother him. The other *jefes* had threatened all manner of punishment to keep children and old ones from the mesa—with the old ones they had been successful, never with the children. This new *jefe* accepted their attention without comment save to warn everyone to keep out of the working area. And once when a boy leaped forward with a shout to thrust his hand into the fire and show that even at nine years he was a man and not afraid of pain, the *jefe* had merely lifted him by the back of the neck and dropped him into the ditch that carried the irrigation water to Hidalgo. The child howled as the icy water flowed over him, and the *jefe* said mockingly, "You call yourself a man, and yet you scream at a drop of water."

All the old ones and the women laughed, and after that none of the children stepped across the line the *jefe* drew in the dirt.

When the sun was well overhead, the papers had been burned, the fire extinguished with water, and the furniture moved out of the shack. Then the *jefe* squatted on the ground like anyone else and drew from his pocket the package of food he had brought from the village.

For a long time the people rested in the shade of the mesquite trees, the men eating the food the women brought them, and the *jefe* listening quietly to the talk of the wise old ones, not once interrupting to show his superior wisdom, but listening with humility and silence as the young should listen to the old. There was talk of rain and crops, for the quarry people depended on the farms of Hidalgo for their food. And after a while there was talk of the Great Revolution[8] and what it would

---

8. **Great Revolution:** otherwise known as the Mexican Revolution of 1910, which created civil strife and suffering for over a decade.

mean to the Inditos, if it meant anything at all, which the old ones doubted; for, as the wisest said, through all the years there had been so many promises, and so many do-nothings. Now the Great Revolution was two years finished, and it, too, seemed to end in do-nothing.

Then at last the old ones were silent, and some of the younger men began to sing. At first the *jefe* listened to the songs, but when someone started the stirring song of Morelos[9] to which many soldiers had marched in the far-off days of 1812, the *jefe* surprised everyone by singing also, knowing both words and tune. His deep voice gave a bass to their light tenors, and he sang without effort as men sing who have known a song from childhood.

> *For a corporal I'd give twenty cents,*
> *For a sergeant I might give fifty.*
> *But for General Morelos*
> *I'd gladly give all my heart.*

At the finish he went without pause into the song of *The Flea*, the children adding their voices to the merriment:

> *With all the fleas I am most angry,*
> *They bite me when I am in bed.*
> *Ay! How they jump! Ay! How they leap!*
> *Ay! How they jump! Those wicked little fleas.*
>
> *All these fleas fill me with terror*
> *For the holes they bore into my skin.*
> *Ay! How they jump! Ay! How they leap!*
> *Ay! How they jump! Those wicked little fleas.*

Candelaria, watching him sing, pulled her shawl closer over her head. She had never seen eyes so somberly tragic in a man's face, and it seemed to her as though, during the music, some of the sadness left him; but it seemed also as though he went away from her into another world where she could not follow. And into her mind came the clear and bitter knowledge that all of her happiness rested in the cup of his hand, but that to him she would never be anything more than a cloud's shadow on the mountain slope.

---

9. **Morelos** (moh-reh'lohs): one of Mexico's national heroes. He led the struggle against Spain that resulted in Mexico's independence in 1821.

He rose, his arms lifted for a deep stretching of his body. "More work, friends. The hour of resting is over."

Earlier that morning the men had worked in silence, obedient to his orders, but curious. Now that he had sung with them they felt a greater ease. Secret laughter trembled among them, and words flowed from one to another. One man put the large desk chair on its side and showed how he could leap over it ten times without pause. Expressionless eyes swiveled to the *jefe's* face. Bob took a deep breath.

"After this, enough of games," he told them. Keeping his feet close together, he made twelve leaps back and forth across the chair, and there was no panting in his chest as he finished. The children mischievously sang the applause music,[10] and the women and the old ones obediently clapped.

Bob knew that the men were now ready to accept him on trial. He was their *jefe*. In all things he must be better than they were. This chair jumping was but the beginning of tests that would grow more difficult until they were satisfied that he was competent to lead them. His grandmother's wisdom flowed into his memory. *"And always the patrón,[11] the master, must ride with the least fear, throw the longest rope, climb the highest mountain. For is he not the patrón?"* Bob's mouth lifted in the slow sideways smile, and he waved his hand towards the shack. "Amuse yourself, my children. Storm this castle with fortitude. Make it as though it had never been. The glass from the window and the tin from the roof we will keep. But the boards can be broken up and put in the cooking fires."

The men looked at each other with little curious glances. The laughter passed out of them for the *jefe* had become a stranger again. To destroy this office was a terrible thing. Was it not the symbol of authority? Surely the mind of a *jefe* was a matter not understood by common Christians.

Bob felt the change in them. His fingers trembled with anger as he unfastened the door staples. Supposing they did want to keep the shack. He was the one who had to spend most of the day in it. What difference did it make what they did or

---

10. **applause music:** The last eight bars of the *Jarabe Tapatío*, known in the United States as the "Mexican Hat Dance." This music, called the "Diana," is always played in recognition of an outstanding feat, whether it be bull-fighting, a great speech, or anything else of value.
11. *patrón* (pah-trohn').

did not want? He was the *jefe,* he was the outlander, he was the stranger. For a year he would be a stranger, and then he would go away and forget them. Two hundred and fifty American dollars a month in salary. He could easily live on fifty. That left two hundred clear. Twelve times two hundred was twenty-four hundred. The letter from Tommy Eaton was very plain: "I tell you we could clean up in South America. With your Spanish and the way you understand these Latins it would be a cinch. And the whole world's going air-conscious. With me to fly the planes and you to manage the business on the ground, we'll be set. Of course we have to have capital to start with. But this flying circus I'm with now isn't bad. Besides what I can borrow, I should have about four thousand saved up by the end of the year if I can keep the wings sewn on my crate. Do you think you could swing at least two thousand by that time?"

Yes, the letter was plain, and Tommy Eaton would make a good partner. A little stupid, but the knowledge of airplanes was in his blood and his bones. And a year wasn't a long time to wait. Twelve months—three hundred and sixty-five days. Oh God, three hundred and sixty-five days of living in these mountains, of constantly proving that he was better than any quarry man, of seeing that endless cars of rocks were turned over to the care of the railroad. He'd be damned if he'd spend those days in a two-by-four shack that shut out the opalescent air and the blue arched sky. The door came loose from the jamb, and he let it fall to the ground. By evening the only reminder of the shack was a patch of hard-packed earth that marked the floor.

Don Anselmo, careful to make no reference to the desecration of the office, rode back to the village with him.

"It is in my mind," he told Bob, "that you would do well to purchase that horse. Don Fidencio, who keeps the blacksmith shop, has certain nags for hire, but they are of little value." He used the word *rocinante*[12] for nag, and Bob looked at him curiously.

"Is it possible that Don Quixote[13] has come to these mountains?" he asked.

"Don Quixote, señor? I do not know him. He is perhaps of Monterrey?"

---

12. *rocinante* (roh-see-nahn'teh).
13. **Don Quixote** (dohn kee-hoh'teh): the hero of a famous Spanish novel, who owned a horse named Rocinante.

"No matter. But Rocinante was the name of his horse."

"Indeed, señor. Now that is a strange thing. The horse of the young Castillo, Joaquín, you comprehend, not Alejandro, was also named Rocinante. Every day he rode it along the mountain trails. How he could ride, that one! And his horse was the finest of the Castillo blacks. He called it Rocinante for a little joke. And on Sunday mornings, for the sweetheart mass at twelve o'clock, he would ride that horse to the door and make it kneel in honor of the Blessed Virgin. Ay, he took much laughter with him when he left this valley."

"Where is he now?" Bob asked idly, not really curious.

"Dead, señor." The thin lips under the gray mustache closed tightly, as though afraid of giving away too much information. This, more than the words, attracted Bob's attention. What a strange place Hidalgo was, with its minor mysteries, and its feud with the neighboring valley. Well, it was no concern of Bob Webster's. But a horse was. He really needed a horse, and perhaps it would be better to buy one. The money problem was an item, but he could always sell it, and if he took good care of it, he might make a little profit. And besides, there should be some compensation for this twelve months' exile. He had always wanted to own a horse . . . ever since he had been old enough to comprehend what such an animal was. And his grandmother's voice came into him again: *"It was white, with tail and mane of cream. And when its hoofs struck the ground, sparks flew. I tell you such an animal has never been seen before or since."*

Bob said lightly, "As you say, this is a fine animal. But it is in my mind to buy a white horse."

"Ay, no, señor!" Don Anselmo hastily blessed himself. "To bring a white horse into these mountains is not wise. *El Caballo Blanco*[14] would not like it."

"*El Caballo Blanco* is dead. You yourself said this yesterday."

"Dead he may be in body, but the goatherds often see him on the trails in the moonlight, his hand on his gun, his hat on the back of his head, and his white horse between his knees."

"Have you ever seen him?"

---

14. *El Caballo Blanco* (ehl kah-bah'yoh blahn'koh): The White Horse. As revealed elsewhere in *Mexican Village*, this is a reference to Daniel Menendez, a bandit who rode a fine white horse that earned him the nickname *El Caballo Blanco* among the villagers.

"With my own eyes, no. But it would take a very brave soul to face his jealous anger. The men like you, señor. They think you will make a good *jefe*. They would not want to see you with your mind emptied of reason and foolish laughter on your mouth."

"A brave soul," Bob repeated thoughtfully. Perhaps a white horse would solve his difficulties with the men. If they saw him riding one without harm they would set no further tests for him, for they would know he was indeed the *jefe*, afraid not even of ghosts.

But his skeptical mind could not prevent the cold touch of fear within him that was a part of his heritage. "Eh, grandmother," he whispered, "shall I buy a white horse?" And the answer came out of his memory. *"When you are grown, young one, you, too, shall own a fine white horse, and the knowledge will console him[15] in purgatory."*

"Tomorrow I have business in Monterrey," Bob told the foreman. "See that the men do their work well, and clear me good blocks of stone for a new office. I will draw you a picture of what I have in mind."

---

15. *him:* a reference to Bob Webster's father, who is dead.

For Study and Discussion

1. Bob Webster is unlike any of the other *jefes* who have worked in the quarry. He wants to prove himself a good *patrón* (boss) by demonstrating his respect for the men, yet he knows that he must also establish his authority. **a.** How does Webster differ from the former *jefes*? **b.** What does he do to establish his authority over his workers? **c.** Do you think that his respectful treatment of the people at the quarry results from genuine concern for them or from more selfish motives? Explain.

2. As Webster tears down the shack, he reflects on his job as quarry master. **a.** Why did he take the job? **b.** How does he feel about being *jefe*? **c.** In light of his reasons for taking the job and his attitude toward being *jefe,* how would you characterize Bob Webster?

3. Webster decides to go to Monterrey on "business," presumably to buy a white horse despite Don Anselmo's warnings. **a.** What does Webster hope to accomplish by bringing a white horse into the Hidalgo Valley? **b.** Examining the thoughts that lead Webster to this decision, what can you determine about the way his mind works—about the factors he takes into consideration when making decisions?

Literary Elements

Anecdote

An **anecdote** is a very short story that is told to make a specific point. Within a larger work, an anecdote generally appears as a brief, self-contained tale that serves to illustrate some aspect of the narrative.

In "The Quarry," for example, the narrator relates an anecdote about Don Anselmo's response to one *jefe's* romantic interest in his daughter. According to this tale, Don Anselmo gave a demonstration of "tricks of knife-throwing" to intimidate the *jefe,* causing the man to show "no further interest" in the young Candelaria. An amusing tale in itself, this anecdote also sheds light on Don Anselmo's character. The reader learns from this anecdote that Don Anselmo is protective of his loved ones and yet is wise enough not to overtly challenge the quarry master's authority, using instead an indirect form of intimidation to put the *jefe* in his place.

Find another example of an anecdote in "The Quarry," and briefly explain its function in the story. What aspects of plot, character, or setting does it help to develop? Does it contribute to the theme, or meaning, of the story? Keep in mind that a tale must be able to stand on its own outside of its context in order to qualify as an anecdote.

Writing About Literature

Researching an Allusion

An **allusion** is a reference to a person, place, event, or literary work that a writer expects a reader to recognize. Allusions generally suggest a meaning rather than state it directly. They invite the reader to make connections and to draw comparisons that can lead to a fuller understanding of a work. Allusions to the Bible and to Greek and Roman deities are used throughout literature, as these are common frames of reference to many readers.

In "The Quarry," allusions are made to Don Quixote and his horse Rocinante. Write a short essay in which you discuss how these allusions provide insights into the theme, characters, plot, and other elements of the story.

Prewriting. Begin by locating information about Don Quixote and Rocinante. Since Cervantes's novel *Don Quixote* is too long to read in a short period of time, refer to an encyclopedia or a specialized reference book to obtain this information. Next, analyze Don Quixote and Rocinante. What special characteristics or features does each one possess? What type of man was Don Quixote? What were his ideals? What color was Rocinante? Was this horse a pure breed? Once you have become familiar with Don Quixote and Rocinante, you can then compare them to Bob Webster and the white horse he intends to buy. What insights into "The Quarry" do these comparisons provide?

Writing and Revising. Be careful to use clear pronoun references. When you use the word *he,* for example, clearly indicate to whom you are referring—Bob Webster or Don Quixote.

Sabine Ulibarrí
(1919–)

Sabine Ulibarrí (sah-bee'neh oo-lee-bahr-ree') has gained renown not only for his collections of short stories, but also for his poetry and essays. In all his work, he exhibits a strong allegiance to his Mexican American heritage. While Ulibarrí's stories and poetry express his longing for the Hispanic community of his youth, his essays establish him as a leading voice in contemporary Mexican American letters and culture. In the field of education, Ulibarrí took an early stand in support of bilingual education. He has long urged Mexican Americans not to abandon their native Spanish, because he is convinced that losing their language will surely alienate them from their heritage.

Born in 1919 in Santa Fe, New Mexico, Ulibarrí grew up in the northern New Mexican town of Tierra Amarilla. He taught for a time in this area and attended the University of New Mexico before joining the U.S. Air Force during the thick of World War II. He was awarded the Distinguished Flying Cross for his role as a gunner on thirty-five combat missions between 1942 and 1945. After the war, he returned to the University of New Mexico, where he earned his master's degree before going on to receive his doctorate in Spanish Literature in 1959 at UCLA. He has taught since then at the University of New Mexico, where he is now professor emeritus.

His many students over the years remember "Uli" as an affable and generous man whose oral recitations of Spanish poetry still echo through the halls of the buildings where he taught. He has written insightfully about literature and later in his career began devoting more of his time to writing both poetry and prose.

Ulibarrí published two books of poetry in 1966: *Al cielo se sube a pie* [You get to heaven on foot] and *Amor y Ecuador* [Love and

Ecuador]. Most of his poetry deals with solitude, uprootedness, the transitory nature of love, and the tragic consequences of progress. A strong nostalgic vein runs through his first and second collections of short stories: *Tierra Amarilla* (1964) and *Mi abuela fumaba puros* [My grandma smoked cigars] (1977). In both, he chronicles the traditional values, customs, and sentiments of the Spanish-speaking population of northern New Mexico where he was raised. He has commented that in his short stories he tries to reflect the Hispanic heritage that preceded by several centuries the arrival of the Anglos in the mid-1800s. Through his creative writing, he attempts to preserve this heritage in the face of a rapidly encroaching Anglo culture.

In many of his stories, Ulibarrí wistfully recounts incidents of his childhood in Tierra Amarilla with awe, humor, and excitement. The two selections on the following pages are strongly rooted in these rich childhood memories. In "My Wonder Horse," the author re-creates for us the legend of a fabulous white horse that roamed the countryside as a living symbol of beauty, strength, and freedom. "My Grandma Smoked Cigars" also focuses on a character forged from memory, another larger-than-life figure whom Ulibarrí recalls with a tone of admiration tinged with sadness. In both stories, the young narrator (undoubtedly representing Ulibarrí himself) gains key insights about himself and about life, insights that mark significant steps in his passage from youth to maturity.

My Wonder Horse

The transition from childhood to adulthood is often marked by "rites of passage"—challenging tests of skill, strength, and endurance. In "My Wonder Horse," the narrator tells a tale of how he met one such test and, in his victory and loss, triumphed. As you read "My Wonder Horse," notice how Ulibarrí uses vivid figures of speech to heighten the drama and the sense of rich personal experience in the story, which may, like much of his writing, reflect a boyhood memory of his own.

He was white. White as memories lost. He was free. Free as happiness is. He was fantasy, liberty, and excitement. He filled and dominated the mountain valleys and surrounding plains. He was a white horse that flooded my youth with dreams and poetry.

Around the campfires of the country and in the sunny patios of the town, the ranch hands talked about him with enthusiasm and admiration. But gradually their eyes would become hazy and blurred with dreaming. The lively talk would die down. All thoughts fixed on the vision evoked by the horse. Myth of the animal kingdom. Poem of the world of men.

White and mysterious, he paraded his harem through the summer forests with lordly rejoicing. Winter sent him to the plains and sheltered hillsides for the protection of his females. He spent the summer like an Oriental potentate in his woodland gardens. The winter he passed like an illustrious warrior celebrating a well-earned victory.

He was a legend. The stories told of the Wonder Horse were endless. Some true, others fabricated. So many traps, so many snares, so many searching parties, and all in vain. The horse always escaped, always mocked his pursuers, always rose above the control of man. Many a valiant cowboy swore to put his halter and his brand on the animal. But always he had to confess later that the mystic horse was more of a man than he.

I was fifteen years old. Although I had never seen the

Wonder Horse, he filled my imagination and fired my ambition. I used to listen open-mouthed as my father and the ranch hands talked about the phantom horse who turned into mist and air and nothingness when he was trapped. I joined in the universal obsession—like the hope of winning the lottery—of putting my lasso on him some day, of capturing him and showing him off on Sunday afternoons when the girls of the town strolled through the streets.

It was high summer. The forests were fresh, green, and gay. The cattle moved slowly, fat and sleek in the August sun and shadow. Listless and drowsy in the lethargy of late afternoon, I was dozing on my horse. It was time to round up the herd and go back to the good bread of the cowboy camp. Already my comrades would be sitting around the campfire, playing the guitar, telling stories of past or present, or surrendering to the languor of the late afternoon. The sun was setting behind me in a riot of streaks and colors. Deep, harmonious silence.

I sit drowsily still, forgetting the cattle in the glade. Suddenly the forest falls silent, a deafening quiet. The afternoon comes to a standstill. The breeze stops blowing, but it vibrates. The sun flares hotly. The planet, life, and time itself have stopped in an inexplicable way. For a moment, I don't understand what is happening.

Then my eyes focus. There he is! The Wonder Horse! At the end of the glade, on high ground surrounded by summer green. He is a statue. He is an engraving. Line and form and white stain on a green background. Pride, prestige, and art incarnate in animal flesh. A picture of burning beauty and virile freedom. An ideal, pure and invincible, rising from the eternal dreams of humanity. Even today my being thrills when I remember him.

A sharp neigh. A far-reaching challenge that soars on high, ripping the virginal fabric of the rosy clouds. Ears at the point. Eyes flashing. Tail waving active defiance. Hoofs glossy and destructive. Arrogant ruler of the countryside.

The moment is never ending, a momentary eternity. It no longer exists, but it will always live. . . . There must have been mares. I did not see them. The cattle went on their indifferent way. My horse followed them, and I came slowly back from the land of dreams to the world of toil. But life could no longer be what it was before.

That night under the stars I didn't sleep. I dreamed. How much I dreamed awake and how much I dreamed asleep, I do not know. I only know that a white horse occupied my dreams and filled them with vibrant sound, and light, and turmoil.

Summer passed and winter came. Green grass gave place to white snow. The herds descended from the mountains to the valleys and the hollows. And in the town they kept saying that the Wonder Horse was roaming through this or that secluded area. I inquired everywhere for his whereabouts. Every day he became for me more of an ideal, more of an idol, more of a mystery.

It was Sunday. The sun had barely risen above the snowy mountains. My breath was a white cloud. My horse was trembling with cold and fear like me. I left without going to mass. Without any breakfast. Without the usual bread and sardines in my saddle bags. I had slept badly, but had kept the vigil well. I was going in search of the white light that galloped through my dreams.

On leaving the town for the open country, the roads disappear. There are no tracks, human or animal. Only a silence, deep, white, and sparkling. My horse breaks trail with his chest and leaves an unending wake, an open rift, in the white sea. My trained, concentrated gaze covers the landscape from horizon to horizon, searching for the noble silhouette of the talismanic horse.

It must have been midday. I don't know. Time had lost its meaning. I found him! On a slope stained with sunlight. We saw one another at the same time. Together, we turned to stone. Motionless, absorbed, and panting, I gazed at his beauty, his pride, his nobility. As still as sculptured marble, he allowed himself to be admired.

A sudden, violent scream breaks the silence. A glove hurled into my face. A challenge and a mandate. Then something surprising happens. The horse that in summer takes his stand between any threat and his herd, swinging back and forth from left to right, now plunges into the snow. Stronger than they, he is breaking trail for his mares. They follow him. His flight is slow in order to conserve his strength.

I follow. Slowly. Quivering. Thinking about his intelligence. Admiring his courage. Understanding his courtesy. The afternoon advances. My horse is taking it easy.

Sabine Ulibarrí 169

One by one the mares become weary. One by one, they drop out of the trail. Alone! He and I. My inner ferment bubbles to my lips. I speak to him. He listens and is quiet.

He still opens the way, and I follow in the path he leaves me. Behind us a long, deep trench crosses the white plain. My horse, which has eaten grain and good hay, is still strong. Undernourished as the Wonder Horse is, his strength is waning. But he keeps on because that is the way he is. He does not know how to surrender.

I now see black stains over his body. Sweat and the wet snow have revealed the black skin beneath the white hair. Snorting breath, turned to steam, tears the air. White spume above white snow. Sweat, spume, and steam. Uneasiness.

I felt like an executioner. But there was no turning back. The distance between us was growing relentlessly shorter. God and Nature watched indifferently.

I feel sure of myself at last. I untie the rope. I open the lasso and pull the reins tight. Every nerve, every muscle is tense. My heart is in my mouth. Spurs pressed against trembling flanks. The horse leaps. I whirl the rope and throw the obedient lasso.

A frenzy of fury and rage. Whirlpools of light and fans of transparent snow. A rope that whistles and burns the saddle tree. Smoking, fighting gloves. Eyes burning in their sockets. Mouth parched. Fevered forehead. The whole earth shakes and shudders. The long, white trench ends in a wide, white pool.

Deep, gasping quiet. The Wonder Horse is mine! Both still trembling, we look at one another squarely for a long time. Intelligent and realistic, he stops struggling and even takes a hesitant step toward me. I speak to him. As I talk, I approach him. At first, he flinches and recoils. Then he waits for me. The two horses greet one another in their own way. Finally, I succeed in stroking his mane. I tell him many things, and he seems to understand.

Ahead of me, along the trail already made, I drove him toward the town. Triumphant. Exultant. Childish laughter gathered in my throat. With my newfound manliness, I controlled it. I wanted to sing, but I fought down the desire. I wanted to shout, but I kept quiet. It was the ultimate in happiness. It was the pride of the male adolescent. I felt myself a conqueror.

Occasionally the Wonder Horse made a try for his liberty,

snatching me abruptly from my thoughts. For a few moments, the struggle was renewed. Then we went on.

It was necessary to go through the town. There was no other way. The sun was setting. Icy streets and people on the porches. The Wonder Horse full of terror and panic for the first time. He ran and my well-shod horse stopped him. He slipped and fell on his side. I suffered for him. The indignity. The humiliation. Majesty degraded. I begged him not to struggle, to let himself be led. How it hurt me that other people should see him like that!

Finally we reached home.

"What shall I do with you, Mago?[1] If I put you into the stable or the corral, you are sure to hurt yourself. Besides, it would be an insult. You aren't a slave. You aren't a servant. You aren't even an animal."

I decided to turn him loose in the fenced pasture. There, little by little, Mago would become accustomed to my friendship and my company. No animal had ever escaped from that pasture.

My father saw me coming and waited for me without a word. A smile played over his face, and a spark danced in his eyes. He watched me take the rope from Mago, and the two of us thoughtfully observed him move away. My father clasped my hand a little more firmly than usual and said, "That was a man's job." That was all. Nothing more was needed. We understood one another very well. I was playing the role of a real man, but the childish laughter and shouting that bubbled up inside me almost destroyed the impression I wanted to create.

That night I slept little, and when I slept, I did not know that I was asleep. For dreaming is the same when one really dreams, asleep or awake. I was up at dawn. I had to go to see my Wonder Horse. As soon as it was light, I went out into the cold to look for him.

The pasture was large. It contained a grove of trees and a small gully. The Wonder Horse was not visible anywhere, but I was not worried. I walked slowly, my head full of the events of yesterday and my plans for the future. Suddenly I realized that I had walked a long way. I quicken my steps. I look ap-

---

1. **Mago** (mah'goh): Magician; one who possesses magical powers.

prehensively around me. I begin to be afraid. Without knowing it, I begin to run. Faster and faster.

He is not there. The Wonder Horse has escaped. I search every corner where he could be hidden. I follow his tracks. I see that during the night he walked incessantly, sniffing, searching for a way out. He did not find one. He made one for himself.

I followed the track that led straight to the fence. And I saw that the trail did not stop but continued on the other side. It was a barbed-wire fence. There was white hair on the wire. There was blood on the barbs. There were red stains on the snow and little drops in the hoofprints on the other side of the fence.

I stopped there. I did not go any further. The rays of the morning sun on my face. Eyes clouded and yet filled with light. Childish tears on the cheeks of a man. A cry stifled in my throat. Slow silent sobs.

Standing there, I forgot myself and the world and time. I cannot explain it, but my sorrow was mixed with pleasure. I was weeping with happiness. No matter how much it hurt me, I was rejoicing over the flight and the freedom of the Wonder Horse, the dimensions of his indomitable spirit. Now he would always be fantasy, freedom, and excitement. The Wonder Horse was transcendent. He had enriched my life forever.

My father found me there. He came close without a word and laid his arm across my shoulders. We stood looking at the white trench with its flecks of red that led into the rising sun.

For Study and Discussion

1a. What does the word "Wonder" in the title "The Wonder Horse" refer to? **b.** How does the sense of wonder associated with the horse influence the narrator of the story?

2. The capture of the Wonder Horse serves as a test, or "rite of passage," through which the young narrator seeks to prove his manhood. Ironically, it is the escape of the horse, rather than its capture, that indicates the narrator's growing maturity. What evidence can you find in the story that this is so?

3a. Following the narrator's rich descriptions and exalted dreams of the Wonder Horse, the horse's capture is unspectacular and somewhat of a letdown. Why does the author deliberately raise and then disappoint the reader's expectations? **b.** What key words and phrases does the author use to contrast the "legend" with the actual horse? Before answering this question, you may wish to make two lists of adjectives: those used by the author to describe the horse before its capture and those used to describe the horse during and after its capture.

Literary Elements

Figures of Speech: Similes and Metaphors

Writers often use figures of speech to express the symbolic significance of elements in a story. Two important figures of speech are similes and metaphors.

A **simile** uses words such as *like* or *as* to signal a comparison between things that are basically different but can be thought of as alike in some way. For example, in the simile "her heart fluttered like a hummingbird's wings," the girl's heart and the bird's wings are alike in that they both beat very rapidly.

In a **metaphor,** no signal word is used; instead, the comparison is stated directly. For example, in the metaphor "the tornado was a hungry giant, devouring everything in its path," the tornado is not compared to a hungry giant but is said to be a hungry giant. Similes and metaphors are two of the many creative tools that writers use to take advantage of both the literal meanings and the figurative connotations of words.

In "My Wonder Horse," Ulibarrí often describes the horse's physical appearance with similes and metaphors that reveal what the horse signifies for the young narrator. Identify three similes or metaphors that describe the Wonder Horse in the first three paragraphs of the story. When the narrator first sees the Wonder

Horse (page 168), what metaphors come to his mind? Explain how these similes and metaphors develop the idea that the horse is a "wonder."

Symbol

A **symbol** is a person, place, thing, or event that has a meaning in itself and that also stands for something larger than itself, such as an attitude, a belief, or a value. Writers often use a central symbol to develop or illustrate the major theme of a story. In "My Wonder Horse," a flesh-and-blood animal symbolizes important values, qualities, and ideals for the narrator. In the boy's eyes the horse is "fantasy, liberty, and excitement"; "pride, prestige, and art incarnate"; an "ideal . . . rising from the eternal dreams of humanity." These images of the horse rise from the narrator's own dreams of freedom, courage, and excitement. To capture the horse would mean, in a sense, gaining possession of the wonderful qualities the horse represents. What "clues" does the author give that the horse is a symbolic figure? Pay particular attention to the author's use of figurative language in describing the Wonder Horse as you formulate your answer.

My Grandma
Smoked Cigars

*Some people not only endure adversity but rise above it
to stand as models of strength and fortitude for those who
know them. The narrator's grandmother in this story is
one such person. Faced with tragic losses and "the winds
and storms of her full life," she steadfastly forges on,
mustering her strength through the eccentric, mystical
ritual that gives the story its title.*

The way I've heard it, my grandfather was quite a guy. There
are many stories about him. Some respectable, others not quite.
One of the latter goes as follows. That returning from Tierra
Amarilla to Las Nutrias,[1] after cups and cards, sometimes on
his buggy with its spirited trotters, sometimes on his *criollo*[2]
horse, he would take off his hat, hang it on a fence post, pull
out his six-gun and address himself to the stiff gentleman of
his own invention.

"Tell me, who is the richest man in all these parts?"

Silence.

"Well then, take this."

A shot. Splinters flew out of the post or a hole appeared
in the hat.

"Who's the toughest man around here?"

Silence.

"Well then, take this."

The same thing happened. He was a good shot. More questions of the same kind, punctuated with shots. When the sassy
post learned his lesson and gave my grandfather the answers
he wanted to hear, the ritual ended, and he went on his way,
singing or humming some sentimental song of the period. The

---

1. **Tierra Amarilla . . . Las Nutrias** (tyehr'rah ah-mah-ree'yah, lahs
   noo-tree-ahs'): towns in north central New Mexico.
2. *criollo* (kree-oh'yoh): domestic.

shooting was heard back in the town without it bothering anyone. Someone was sure to say with a smile, "There's don Prudencio doing his thing."

Of course my grandfather had other sides (the plural is intended) that are not relevant to this narrative. He was a civic, social and political figure and a family man twice over. What I want to do now is stress the fact that my relative was a real character: quarrelsome, daring and prankish.

He died in a mysterious way, or perhaps even shameful. I've never been able to find out exactly what streetcar my distinguished antecedent took to the other world. Maybe that wooden gentleman with his hat pulled over his eyes, the one who suffered the insults of the hidalgo[3] of Las Nutrias, gave him a woody and mortal whack. An hidalgo he was—and a father of more than four.

I never knew him. When I showed up in this world to present my Turriaga credentials, he had already turned his in. I imagine that wherever he is he's making violent and passionate love to the ladies who went to heaven—or hell, depending. . . . That is if my grandmother hasn't caught up with him in those worlds beyond the grave.

I don't think he and my grandmother had an idyllic marriage in the manner of sentimental novels where everything is sweetness, softness and tenderness. Those are luxuries, perhaps decadences, that didn't belong in that violent world, frequently hostile, of Río Arriba County[4] at the end of the past century. Furthermore, the strong personalities of both would have prevented it. I do believe they were very happy. Their love was a passion that didn't have time to become a habit or just friendship. They loved each other with mutual respect and fear, something between admiration and fury, something between tenderness and toughness. Both were children of their land and their times. There was so much to do. Carve a life from an unfriendly frontier. Raise their rebellious and ferocious cubs. Their life was an affectionate and passionate sentimental war.

I say all of this as a preamble in order to enter into my subject: my grandmother. I have so many and so gratifying

---

3. **hidalgo** (ee-thahl'goh): a Spanish nobleman of secondary rank.
4. **Río Arriba County** (ree'oh ahr-ree'bah): a county in northern New Mexico.

memories of her. But the first one of all is a portrait that hangs in a place of honor in the parlor of my memory.

She had her moments in which she caressed her solitude. She would go off by herself, and everyone knew it was best to leave her alone.

She always dressed in black. A blouse of lace and batiste up front. A skirt down to her ankles. All silk. A cotton apron. High shoes. Her hair parted in the middle and combed straight back, smooth and tight, with a round and hard bun in the back. I never saw her with her hair loose.

She was strong. As strong as only she could be. Through the years, in so many situations, small and big tragedies, accidents and problems, I never saw her bend or fold. Fundamentally, she was serious and formal. So a smile, a compliment or a caress from her were coins of gold that were appreciated and saved as souvenirs forever. Coins she never wasted.

The ranch was big business. The family was large and problematic. She ran her empire with a sure and firm hand. Never was there any doubt about where her affairs were going nor who held the reins.

That first memory: the portrait. I can see her at this moment as if she were before my eyes. A black silhouette on a blue background. Straight, tall and slender. The wind of the hill cleaving her clothes to her body up front, outlining her forms, one by one. Her skirt and her shawl flapping in the wind behind her. Her eyes fixed I don't know where. Her thoughts fixed on I don't know what. An animated statue. A petrified soul.

My grandfather smoked cigars. The cigar was the symbol and the badge of the feudal lord, the *patrón*.[5] When on occasion he would give a cigar to the foreman or to one of the hands on impulse or as a reward for a task well done, the transfiguration of those fellows was something to see. To suck on that tobacco was to drink from the fountains of power. The cigar gave you class.

They say that when my grandfather died my grandmother would light cigars and place them on ashtrays all over the house. The aroma of the tobacco filled the house. This gave the widow the illusion that her husband was still around. A sentimentalism and romanticism difficult to imagine before.

---

5. *patrón* (pah-trohn'): master.

As time went on, and after lighting many a cigar, a liking for the cigars seemed to sneak up on her. She began to smoke the cigars. At nightfall, every day, after dinner, when the tasks of the day were done, she would lock herself in her room, sit in her rocker and light her cigar.

She would spend a long time there. The rest of us remained in the living room playing the family role as if nothing were amiss. No one ever dared interrupt her arbitrary and sacred solitude. No one ever mentioned her unusual custom.

The cigar that had once been a symbol of authority had now become an instrument of love. I am convinced that in the solitude and in the silence, with the smell and the taste of the tobacco, there in the smoke, my grandmother established some kind of mystical communication with my grandfather. I think that there, all alone, that idyllic marriage, full of tenderness, softness and sweetness was attained, not possible while he lived. It was enough to see the soft and transfigured face of the grandmother when she returned to us from her strange communion, to see the affection and gentleness with which she treated us kids.

Right there, and in those conditions, the decisions were made, the positions were taken that ran the business, that directed the family. There in the light or in the shade of an old love, now an eternal love, the spiritual strength was forged that kept my grandmother straight, tall and slender, a throbbing woman of stone, facing the winds and storms of her full life.

When my parents married they built their home next to the old family house. I grew up on the windy hill in the center of the valley of Las Nutrias, with pine trees on all the horizons, with the stream full of beaver, trout and suckers, the sagebrush full of rabbits and coyotes, stock everywhere, squirrels and owls in the barns.

I grew up alongside my grandmother and far away from her, between tender love and reverent fear.

When I was eight years old, it was decided in the family that we should move to Tierra Amarilla so that my brothers and I could attend school. The furrows the tears left on my face still burn, and I still remember their salty taste the day we left my straight, tall and slender grandmother, waving her handkerchief, with the wind on her face on the hill in the center of the valley.

In Tierra Amarilla I was antisocial. Having grown up alone, I didn't know how to play with other children. I played with my dogs instead. In spite of this I did all right in school, and one day I was fifteen years old, more or less adapted to my circumstances.

One winter day we got ready to go to Las Nutrias. All with a great deal of anticipation. To visit my grandmother was always an event. The family would go with me in the car. My father with the sleigh and the hired hands. It was a matter of cutting fence posts.

We sang all the way. That is until we had to leave the highway. There was a lot of snow. The highway had been cleared, but the little road to Las Nutrias hadn't.

I put chains on the car, and we set out across the white sea. Now we were quiet and apprehensive. We soon got stuck. After a lot of shoveling and much pushing we continued, only to get stuck again farther on, again and again.

We were all exhausted and cold, and the day was drifting away. Finally we climbed the hill and came out of the pine grove from where we could see my grandmother's house. We got stuck again. This time there was no way of pulling the car out. My mother and the children continued on foot, opening their way through two and a half feet of soft snow. My brother Roberto pulled my sister Carmen on a small sled. It was getting dark. A trip of nine miles had taken us all day.

Juan Maes, the foreman quickly came with a team of horses and pulled me home.

I had barely come in and was warming up. My mother had brought me dry clothes, when we saw the lights of a car in the pine grove. We saw it approach slowly, hesitating from time to time. It was easier now; the road was now open.

It was my uncle Juan Antonio. The moment he came in we all knew he had bad news. There was a frightening silence. No one said a word. Everyone silent and stiff like wooden figures in a grotesque scene.

My mother broke the silence with a heart breaking "Alejandro!"

My uncle nodded.

"What happened?" It was my grandmother.

"Alejandro. An accident."

"What happened?"

"An accidental shot. He was cleaning a rifle. The gun went off."

"How is he?"

"Not good, but he'll pull through."

We all knew he was lying, that my father was dead. We could see it in his face. My mother was crying desperately, on the verge of becoming hysterical. We put our arms around her, crying. My uncle with his hat in his hands not knowing what to do. Another man had come with him. No one had noticed him.

That is when my grandmother went into action. Not a single tear. Her voice steady. Her eyes two flashing spears. She took complete control of the situation.

She went into a holy fury against my father. She called him ungrateful, shameless, unworthy. An inexhaustible torrent of insults. A royal rage. In the meantime she took my mother in her arms and rocked her and caressed her like a baby. My mother submitted and settled down slowly. We did too. My grandmother who always spoke so little did not stop talking that night.

I didn't understand then. I felt a violent resentment. I wanted to defend my father. I didn't because no one ever dared to talk back to my grandmother. Much less me. The truth is that she understood many things.

My mother was on the verge of madness. Something had to be done.

My grandmother created a situation, so violent and dramatic, that it forced us all, my mother especially, to fix our attention on her and shift it away from the other situation until we could get used to the tragedy little by little. She didn't stop talking in order not to allow a single aperture through which despair might slip in. Talking, talking, between abuse and lullaby, she managed that my mother, in her vulnerable state, fall asleep in the wee hours of the morning. As she had done so many times in the past, my grandmother had dominated the harsh reality in which she lived.

She understood something else. That my father didn't fire a rifle accidentally. The trouble we had to bury him on sacred ground confirmed the infallible instinct of the lady and mistress of Las Nutrias. Everything confirmed the talent and substance of the mother of the Turriaga clan.

The years went by. I was now a professor. One day we returned to visit the grandmother. We were very happy. I've said it before, visiting her was an event. Things had changed a great deal. With the death of my father, my grandmother got rid of all the stock. The ranch hands disappeared with the stock. Rubel and his family were the only ones who remained to look after her.

When we left the highway and took the little used and much abused road full of accustomed ruts, the old memories took possession of us. Suddenly we saw a column of black smoke rising beyond the hill. My sister shouted.

"Grandma's house!"

"Don't be silly. They must be burning weeds, or sage brush, or trash." I said this but apprehension gripped me. I stepped hard on the gas.

When we came out of the pine grove, we saw that only ruins remained of the house of the grandmother. I drove like a madman. We found her surrounded by the few things that were saved. Surrounded also by the neighbors of all the ranches in the region who rushed to help when they saw the smoke.

I don't know what I expected but it did not surprise me to find her directing all the activities, giving orders. No tears, no whimpers, no laments.

"God gives and God takes away, my son. Blessed be His Holy Name."

I did lament. The crystal chandeliers, wrecked. The magnificent sets of tables and washstands with marble tops. The big basins and water jars in every bedroom, destroyed. The furniture brought from Kansas, turned to ashes. The bedspreads of lace, crochet, embroidery. The portraits, the pictures, the memories of a family.

Irony of ironies. There was a jar of holy water on the window sill in the attic. The rays of the sun, shining through the water, converted into a magnifying glass. The heat and the fire concentrated on a single spot and set on fire some old papers there. And all of the saints, the relics, the shrines, the altar to the Santo Niño de Atocha, the palms of Palm Sunday, all burned up. All of the celestial security went up in smoke.

That night we gathered in what had been our old home. My grandmother seemed smaller to me, a little subdued, even a little docile: "Whatever you say, my son." This saddened me.

Sabine Ulibarrí 181

After supper my grandmother disappeared. I looked for her apprehensively. I found her where I could very well have suspected. At the top of the hill. Profiled by the moon. The wind in her face. Her skirt flapping in the wind. I saw her grow. And she was what she had always been: straight, tall and slender.

I saw the ash of her cigar light up. She was with my grandfather, the wicked one, the bold one, the quarrelsome one. Now the decisions would be made, the positions would be taken. She was regaining her spiritual strength. Tomorrow would be another day, but my grandmother would continue being the same one. And I was happy.

For Study and Discussion

1. "My Grandma Smoked Cigars" opens with a "preamble," or introduction, which focuses on the narrator's grandfather. The subject of the story, however, is the narrator's grandmother and her life. Why does the author begin with information about the grandfather rather than the grandmother?

2. News of her son's death triggers a startling and violent response in the narrator's grandmother. Why does the grandmother react in this way?

3. The title "My Grandma Smoked Cigars" is amusing and evokes images of an eccentric, perhaps even comical old woman. The woman the narrator describes, however, is quite different from this humorous figure suggested by the title. Discuss some of the grandmother's unique or surprising qualities. What makes her a memorable character and a figure who warrants respect?

4. The cigar is a powerful symbol in the story. Discuss what the cigar represents and how the grandmother's cigar-smoking relates to her inner strength.

Creative Writing

Writing from the First-person Point of View

In "My Grandma Smoked Cigars," the grandmother is a dominant figure who commands the respect of her family and all who knew her. Yet her inner life remains mysterious to the reader as well as to the narrator. Write about a significant incident in the story—such as the death of the grandmother's husband or son or the fire that destroys her home—from the grandmother's point of view. Writing in the first person, reveal her thoughts, emotions, and vulnerabilities. You might write your monologue in the form of a journal entry or a letter addressed to the grandmother's dead husband.

Prewriting. To help you gain a first-person perspective from the grandmother's point of view, you may wish to begin by writing a list of character traits that describe the grandmother, such as strong, brave, wise, persevering, caring. Next, identify the specific incident you will use from the story, and read the passages about that incident several times, looking for hints about the grandmother's reaction. Using your list of character traits, make notes on what a person who possesses those traits would think and feel about the incident. Finally, look for interrelationships among your notes and details from the story, and choose transitional words and phrases that state these relationships.

Writing and Revising. As you write and revise, keep in mind the grandmother's audience, or reader(s). Your choice of words, images, details, and even sentence structure will vary, depending on whether the grandmother is making a private journal entry or addressing another person. If she is writing to someone else, she would further adapt her language according to her relationship with that person, to the person's age, and to other characteristics of her reader(s).

Fray[1] Angélico Chávez

(1910–)

It was fitting that when Manuel E. Chávez joined the Franciscan Order, he took the name of Fray Angélico after the medieval Italian painter Fra Angélico da Fiesole, because like his namesake, Fray Angélico Chávez (ahn-heh'lee-koh chah'behs) has used his artistic talent to serve the Church. In addition to developing his skills as a painter of frescoes and murals, for more than half a century he has also lovingly and painstakingly penned literary portraits of his people.

Born in the isolated town of Wagon Mound in northern New Mexico, Chávez grew up in the midst of a Spanish community rich in traditions and fiercely protective of its heritage. While quite young, he discovered he had a religious calling, and at the age of fourteen, he left New Mexico for the St. Francis Seminary in Cincinnati, Ohio. His first assignment returned him to New Mexico, where he spent several years restoring the original Spanish religious art in rural village churches. He was ordained into the priesthood in 1937 and served for over three decades as a missionary in his native state and as a chaplain during World War II and the Korean War. Since his retirement from the priesthood, he has dedicated himself to his research and writing.

Until recently, many readers and critics have tended to dismiss Chávez's work as purely folkloric. Only now is he beginning to receive the recognition he deserves for the easy grace and engaging appeal of his poetry and stories. Fortunately, despite this previous lack of appreciation for his writing, he has made a large contribution to

---

1. **Fray** (frai): Brother: a title given to a Spanish friar or monk.

contemporary Mexican American literature, writing more than twenty books and numerous articles of fiction and nonfiction.

Like Sabine Ulibarrí, Chávez captures the unique texture of rural life in northern New Mexico, where the Spanish language, customs, and values of his ancestors have continued to thrive for five centuries. Chávez's tale "Hunchback Madonna," which begins on the following page, displays many of the finest features of his writing, giving this simple and sensitive story the timeless appeal of a popular legend.

Hunchback Madonna

According to the narrator, the appeal of the tiny, isolated village of El Tordo lies not in its quaint setting but in the village's most prized possession: a curiously "stoop-shouldered" image of the Madonna that hangs in the "old and crumbling" mission. The legend that lies behind this painting is the focus of Fray Angélico Chávez's tale. Like El Tordo's many pilgrims and sightseers, you too may be moved by the story of Mana Seda,[1] or "Sister Silk," the humble old woman who inspired the painting of the Madonna. As you read, consider how Mana Seda's life might stand as an inspiration to others.

Old and crumbling, the squat-built adobe[2] mission of El Tordo[3] sits in a hollow high up near the snow-capped Truchas.[4] A few clay houses huddle close to it like tawny chicks about a ruffled old hen. On one of the steep slopes, which has the peaks for a background, sleeps the ancient graveyard with all its inhabitants, or what little is left of them. The town itself is quite as lifeless during the winter months, when the few folks that live there move down to warmer levels by the Rio Grande; but when the snows have gone, except for the white crusts on the peaks, they return to herd their sheep and goats, and with them comes a stream of pious pilgrims and curious sightseers which lasts throughout the spring and summer weather.

They come to see and pray before the stoop-shouldered Virgin, people from as far south as Belén[5] who from some accident or some spinal or heart affliction are shoulder-bent and want to walk straight again. Others, whose faith is not so simple or who have no faith at all, have come from many parts of the

---

1. *Mana Seda* (mah-nah' seh'thah).
2. **adobe** (ah-thoh'beh): made of mud brick that has been baked in the sun.
3. **El Tordo** (ehl tohr'thoh).
4. **Truchas** (troo'chahs): mountains in New Mexico, northeast of Santa Fe.
5. **Belén** (beh-lehn'): a village in central New Mexico, on the Rio Grande.

country and asked the way to El Tordo, not only to see the curiously painted Madonna in which the natives put so much faith, but to visit a single grave in a corner of the *campo santo*[6] which, they have heard, is covered in spring with a profusion of wild flowers, whereas the other sunken ones are bare altogether, or at the most sprinkled only with sagebrush and tumbleweed. And, of course, they want to hear from the lips of some old inhabitant the history of the town and the church, the painting and the grave, and particularly of Mana Seda.

No one knows, or cares to know, when the village was born. It is more thrilling to say, with the natives, that the first settlers came up from the Santa Clara Valley long before the railroad came to New Mexico, when the Indians of Nambé and Taos still used bows and arrows and obsidian clubs; when it took a week to go to Santa Fe, which looked no different from the other northern towns at the time, only somewhat bigger. After the men had allotted the scant farming land among themselves, and each family raised its adobe hut of one or two rooms to begin with, they set to making adobes for a church that would shoulder above their homes as a guardian parent. On a high, untillable slope they marked out as their God's acre a plot which was to be surrounded by an adobe wall. It was not long before large pines from the forest nearby had been carved into beams and corbels and hoisted into their places on the thick walls. The women themselves mud-plastered the tall walls outside with their bare hands; within they made them a soft white with a lime mixture applied with the woolly side of sheepskins.

The padre, whose name the people do not remember, was so pleased with the building, and with the crudely wrought reredos behind the altar, that he promised to get at his own expense a large hand-painted *Nuestra Señora de Guadalupe*[7] to hang in the middle of the *retablo*.[8] But this had to wait until the next traders' ox-drawn caravan left Santa Fe for Chihuahua[9] in Old Mexico and came back again. It would take years, perhaps,

---

6. *campo santo* (kahm'poh sahn'toh): cemetery.
7. *Nuestra Señora de Guadalupe* (nwehs'trah seh-nyohr'ah deh gwah-thah-loo'peh): Our Lady of Guadalupe (the Virgin Mary), the patron saint of Mexico.
8. *retablo* (reh-tah'bloh): a shelf or ledge for holding altar ornaments.
9. **Chihuahua** (chee-wah'wah): a state in northern Mexico.

Fray Angélico Chávez 187

if there was no such painting ready and it must be made to order.

With these first settlers of El Tordo had come an old woman who had no relatives in the place they had left. For no apparent reason she had chosen to cast her lot with the emigrants, and they had willingly brought her along in one of their wooden-wheeled *carretas*,[10] had even built her a room in the protective shadow of the new church. For that had been her work before, sweeping the house of God, ringing the Angelus[11] morning, noon and night, adorning the altar with lace cloths and flowers, when there were flowers. She even persuaded the padre, when the first of May came around, to start an ancient custom prevalent in her place of origin: that of having little girls dressed as queens and their maids-in-waiting present bunches of flowers to the Virgin Mary every evening in May. She could not wait for the day when the Guadalupe picture would arrive.

They called her *Mana Seda*, "Sister Silk." Nobody knew why; they had known her by no other name. The women thought she had got it long ago for being always so neat, or maybe because she embroidered so many altar cloths. But the men said it was because she looked so much like a silk-spinning spider; for she was very much humpbacked—so bent forward that she could look up only sideways and with effort. She always wore black, a black shiny dress and black shawl with long leglike fringes and, despite her age and deformity, she walked about quite swiftly and noiselessly. "Yes," they said, "like the black widow spider."

Being the cause of the May devotions at El Tordo, she took it upon herself to provide the happy girls with flowers for the purpose. The geraniums which she grew in her window were used up the first day, as also those that other women had tended in their own homes. So she scoured the slopes around the village for wild daisies and Indian paint brush, usually returning in the late afternoon with a shawlful to spill at the eager children's feet. Toward the end of May she had to push deeper into the forest, whence she came back with her tireless, short-stepped spider-run, her arms and shawl laden with wild iris and cosmos, verbenas and mariposa lilies from the pine shadows.

This she did year after year, even after the little "queens"

---

10. *carretas* (kahr-reh′tahs): long, narrow carts.
11. **Angelus** (ahn′heh-loos): a bell rung to call people to prayer.

of former Mays got married and new tots grew up to wear their veils. Mana Seda's one regret was that the image of the Virgin of Guadalupe had not come, had been lost on the way when the Comanches or Apaches attacked and destroyed the Chihuahua–Santa Fe ox-train.

One year in May (it was two days before the close of the month), when the people were already whispering among themselves that Mana Seda was so old she must die soon, or else last forever, she was seen hurrying into the forest early in the morning, to avail herself of all the daylight possible, for she had to go far into the wooded canyons this time. At the closing services of May there was to be not one queen but a number of them with their attendants. Many more flowers were needed for this, and the year had been a bad one for flowers, since little snow had fallen the winter before.

Mana Seda found few blooms in her old haunts, here and there an aster with half of its petals missing or drought-toasted, or a faded columbine fast wilting in the cool but moistureless shade. But she must find enough flowers; otherwise the good heavenly Mother would have a sad and colorless farewell this May. On and on she shuttled in between the trunks of spruce and fir, which grew thicker and taller and closer-set as the canyon grew narrower. Farther up she heard the sound of trickling water; surely the purple iris and freckled lily flames would be rioting there, fresh and without number. She was not disappointed, and without pausing to recover her breath, began lustily to snap off the long, luscious stems and lay them on her shawl, spread out on the little meadow. Her haste was prompted by the darkness closing in through the evergreens, now turning blacker and blacker, not with approaching dusk, but with the smoky pall of thunderheads that had swallowed up the patches of blue among the tops of the forest giants.

Far away arose rumblings that grew swiftly louder and nearer. The great trees, which always whispered to her even on quiet, sunny days, began to hiss and whine angrily at the unseen wind that swayed them and swung their arms like maidens unwilling to be kissed or danced with. And then a deafening sound exploded nearby with a blinding bluish light. Others followed, now on the right or on the left, now before or behind, as Mana Seda, who had thrown her flower-weighted mantle on her arched back, started to run—in which direction she knew not, for the rain was slashing down in sheets that blurred the dark boles and boulders all around her.

At last she fell, whimpering prayers to the Holy Virgin with a water-filled mouth that choked her. Of a sudden, sunlight began to fall instead between the towering trees, now quiet and dripping with emeralds and sapphires. The storm had passed by, the way spring rains in the Truchas Mountains do, as suddenly as it had come. In a clearing not far ahead, Mana Seda saw a little adobe hut. On its one chimney stood a wisp of smoke, like a white feather. Still clutching her heavy, rain-soaked shawl, she ran to it and knocked at the door, which was opened by an astonished young man with a short, sharp knife in his hand.

"I thought the mountain's bowels where the springs come from had burst," she was telling the youth, who meanwhile stirred a pot of brown beans that hung with a pail of coffee over the flames in the corner fireplace. "But our most Holy Lady saved me when I prayed to her, *gracias a Dios*.[12] The lightning and the water stopped, and I saw her flying above me. She had a piece of sky for a veil, and her skirt was like the beautiful red roses at her feet. She showed me your house."

Her host tried to hide his amusement by taking up his work again, a head he had been carving on the end of a small log. She saw that he was no different from the grown boys of El Tordo, dark and somewhat lean-bodied in his plain homespun. All about, against the wall and in niches, could be seen several other images, wooden and gaily colored *bultos*,[13] and more *santos*[14] painted on pieces of wood or hide. Mana Seda guessed that this must be the young stranger's trade, and grew more confident because of it. As she spread out her shawl to dry before the open fire, her load of flowers rolled out soggily on the bare earth floor. Catching his questioning stare, she told him what they were for, and about the church and the people of El Tordo.

"But that makes me think of the apparition of Our Lady of Guadalupe," he said. "Remember how the Indian Juan Diego filled his blanket with roses, as Mary most holy told him to do? And how, when he let down his *tilma*[15] before the bishop, out

---

12. *gracias a Dios* (grah'syahs ah dyohs): thanks be to God.
13. *bultos* (bool'tohs): busts.
14. *santos* (sahn'tohs): images of saints.
15. *tilma* (teel'mah): a blanket used as a cloak.

fell the roses, and on it was the miraculous picture of the Mother of God?"

Yes, she knew the story well; and she told him about the painting of the Guadalupe which the priest of El Tordo had ordered brought from Mexico and which was lost on the way. Perhaps, if the padre knew of this young man's ability, he would pay him for making one. Did he ever do work for churches? And what was his name?

"My name is Esquipula," he replied. "Sí,[16] I have done work for the Church. I made the *retablo* of 'San Francisco' for his church in Ranchos de Taos, and also the 'Cristo' for Santa Cruz. The 'Guadalupe' at San Juan, I painted it. I will gladly paint another for your chapel." He stopped all of a sudden, shut his eyes tight, and then quickly leaned toward the bent old figure who was helping herself to some coffee. "Why do you not let me paint one right now—on your shawl!"

She could not answer at first. Such a thing was unheard of. Besides, she had no other *tápalo*[17] to wear. And what would the people back home say when she returned wearing the Virgin on her back? What would She say?

"You can wear the picture turned inside where nobody can see it. Look! You will always have Holy Mary with you, hovering over you, hugging your shoulders and your breast! Come," he continued, seeing her ready to yield, "it is too late for you to go back to El Tordo. I will paint it now, and tomorrow I and Mariquita will take you home."

"And who is Mariquita?" she wanted to know.

"Mariquita is my little donkey," was the reply.

Mana Seda's black shawl was duly hung and spread tight against a bare stretch of wall, and Esquipula lost no time in tracing with white chalk the outlines of the small wood-print which he held in his left hand as a model. The actual laying of the colors, however, went much slower because of the shawl's rough and unsized texture. Darkness came, and Esquipula lit an oil lamp, which he held in one hand as he applied the pigments with the other. He even declined joining his aged guest at her evening meal of beans and stale *tortillas*,[18] because he was not hungry, he explained, and the picture must be done.

---

16. *Sí* (see): yes.
17. *tápalo* (tah'pah-loh): a woman's shawl.
18. *tortillas* (tohr-tee'yahs): thin bread made of unleavened cornmeal.

Once in a while the painter would turn from his work to look at Mana Seda, who had become quite talkative, something the people back at El Tordo would have marveled at greatly. She was recounting experiences of her girlhood which, she explained, were more vivid than many things that had happened recently.

Only once did he interrupt her, and that without thinking first. He said, almost too bluntly: "How did you become hunchbacked?"

Mana Seda hesitated, but did not seem to take the question amiss. Patting her shoulder as far as she could reach to her bulging back, she answered, "The woman who was nursing me dropped me on the hard dirt floor when I was a baby, and I grew up like a ball. But I do not remember, of course. My being bent out of shape did not hurt me until the time when other little girls of my age were chosen to be flowermaids in May. When I was older, and other big girls rejoiced at being chosen May queens, I was filled with bitter envy. God forgive me, I even cursed. I at last made up my mind never to go to the May devotions, nor to mass either. In the place of my birth, the shores of the Rio Grande are made up of wet sand which sucks in every living creature that goes in; I would go there and return no more. But something inside told me the Lord would be most pleased if I helped the other lucky girls with their flowers. That would make me a flower-bearer every day. Esquipula, my son, I have been doing this for seventy-four Mays."

Mana Seda stopped and reflected in deep silence. The youth who had been painting absent-mindedly and looking at her, now noticed for the first time that he had made the Virgin's shoulders rather stooped, like Mana Seda's, though not quite so much. His first impulse was to run the yellow sun-rays into them and cover up the mistake, but for no reason he decided to let things stand as they were. By and by he put the last touches to his *oeuvre de caprice*,[19] offered the old lady his narrow cot in a corner, and went out to pass the night in Mariquita's humble shed.

The following morning saw a young man leading a gray burro through the forest, and on the patient animal's back swayed a round black shape, grasping her mantle with one hand

---

19. *oeuvre de caprice* (euh'vreh deh kah-prees'): French for "work of impulse."

while the other held tight to the small wooden saddle. Behind her, their bright heads bobbing from its wide mouth, rode a sack full of iris and tiger lilies from the meadow where the storm had caught Mana Seda the day before. Every once in a while, Esquipula had to stop the beast and go after some new flower which the rider had spied from her perch; sometimes she made him climb up a steep rock for a crannied blossom he would have passed unnoticed.

The sun was going down when they at last trudged into El Tordo and halted before the church, where the priest stood surrounded by a bevy of inquiring, disappointed girls. He rushed forth immediately to help Mana Seda off the donkey, while the children pounced upon the flowers with shouts of glee. Asking questions and not waiting for answers, he led the stranger and his still stranger charge into his house, meanwhile giving orders that the burro be taken to his barn and fed.

Mana Seda dared not sit with the padre at table and hied herself to the kitchen for her supper. Young Esquipula, however, felt very much at ease, answering all his host's questions intelligently, at which the pastor was agreeably surprised, but not quite so astonished as when he heard for the first time of Mana Seda's childhood disappointments.

"Young man," he said, hurriedly finishing his meal, "there is little time to lose. Tonight is closing of May—and it will be done, although we are unworthy." Dragging his chair closer to the youth, he plotted out his plan in excited whispers which fired Esquipula with an equal enthusiasm.

The last bell was calling the folk of El Tordo in the cool of the evening. Six queens with their many white-veiled maids stood in a nervous, noisy line at the church door, a garden of flowers in their arms. The priest and the stranger stood on guard facing them, begging them to be quiet, looking anxiously at the people who streamed past them into the edifice. Mana Seda finally appeared and tried to slide quietly by, but the padre barred her way and pressed a big basket filled with flowers and lighted candles into her brown, dry hands. At the same time Esquipula took off her black shawl and dropped over her gray head and hunched form a precious veil of Spanish lace.

In her amazement she could not protest, could not even move a step, until the padre urged her on, whispering into her ear that it was the Holy Virgin's express wish. And so Mana

Fray Angélico Chávez 193

Seda led all the queens that evening, slowly and smoothly, not like a black widow now, folks observed, but like one of those little white moths moving over alfalfa fields in the moonlight. It was the happiest moment of her long life. She felt that she must die from pure joy, and many others observing her thought so too.

She did not die then; for some years afterward, she wore the new black *tápalo* the padre gave her in exchange for the old one, which Esquipula installed in the *retablo* above the altar. But toward the last she could not gather any more flowers on the slopes, much less in the forest. They buried her in a corner of the *campo santo*, and the following May disks of daisies and bunches of verbenas came up on her grave. It is said they have been doing it ever since, for curious travelers to ask about, while pious pilgrims come to pray before the hunchback Madonna.

For Study and Discussion

1. Imagery consists of words or phrases that appeal to the reader's senses, thereby creating pictures, or images, in the reader's mind. In the first paragraph of this story, what images does Chávez use to describe the village of El Tordo? What impression of El Tordo do these images create?

2. The details associated with a particular setting—for instance, speech, dress, customs, and scenery—are known as **local color.** Give five examples of details that add local color to this story.

3. Although the story of Mana Seda is presented as a legend based on fact, it reads much like a **fable**—a tale told to present a moral or practical lesson. What moral lesson can be learned from Mana Seda's life? Try your hand at stating this moral in a single sentence, as morals are often stated at the end of fables.

4. Like many inspirational tales, this story concludes on a positive note. How do you feel about stories such as this one that have happy, uncomplicated endings?

Vocabulary

Using Hyphenation to Create Adjectives

When two or more words serve as a single adjective before a noun, they are often hyphenated. In "Hunchback Madonna," Fray Angélico Chávez uses such adjectives to create vivid descriptive phrases, for instance, "silk-spinning spider" and "flower-weighted mantle." **1.** Identify at least ten additional hyphenated adjectives used in the story, and write a short paragraph discussing how they contribute to the descriptive value of the narrative. **2.** Invent five of your own hyphenated adjectives, and use each in a sentence to describe a person, object, or scene.

Creative Writing

Writing a First-Person Narrative

Although "Hunchback Madonna" is told from a third-person point of view, the narrator offers glimpses of Mana Seda's thoughts and feelings. Write a narrative of two or three paragraphs from Mana Seda's point of view in which she reveals her inner reactions to events in the story.

Prewriting. Reread the story carefully, focusing on the descriptions that give a sense of Mana Seda's character. How does she feel about her life, her unfortunate deformity, her faith, and her service to others? What are her thoughts when Esquipula offers to paint a picture of the Madonna on her shawl? How does she feel as she leads the other May queens, and how does she feel afterward? Is she content to continue her accustomed way of life after "the happiest moment" is over?

Writing and Revising. Be sure to use language and diction that reflect Mana Seda's character and background. For example, you would not want to use slang or highly informal expressions that would be unfamiliar to her or unrepresentative of the rural community in which she lives.

Fray Angélico Chávez 195

Nonfiction of the
Mexican American Period

Whereas nonfiction works of the Spanish and Mexican Periods consist mainly of chronicles, logs, letters, and reports—writings that are informative rather than literary—essayists of the Mexican American Period began to write for a more general readership. Focusing on style as well as on content, these writers crafted descriptive, well-developed essays that give vivid accounts of Mexican American experience in the late nineteenth and early twentieth centuries.

These largely autobiographical works are often highly entertaining. For example, Miguel Antonio Otero's *My Life on the Frontier* and Andrew García's *Tough Trip Through Paradise* tell in lively, colorful prose of the authors' exploits in the wild, lawless West of the late 1800s. In narratives such as "Tucson, Arizona: El Hoyo," Mario Suárez gives a vivid sense of local color in his descriptions of Mexican American communities.

Several women writers stand out for their adept renderings of the folkloric aspects of life during the Mexican American Period. Concentrating on local and regional legends, customs, characters, and speech patterns, writers such as Nina Otero and Jovita González created skillful narratives that popularized for both Mexican American and Anglo readers a memorable if somewhat idealized view of Hispanic life.

Miguel Antonio Otero

(1859–1944)

Born in New Mexico into a politically
active and commercially successful family, Miguel Antonio Otero (mee-gwehl'
ahn-toh'nyoh oh-teh'roh) grew to become not only a respected
businessman and active politician but also one of the most prolific
Mexican American writers of the nineteenth and twentieth centuries.
Despite his parents' repeated attempts to give him a conventional formal education, Otero opted to learn about life through his experiences
in the streets of frontier towns throughout Kansas, Colorado, and New
Mexico. He gained practical business knowledge and skills by working
in the offices of one of his father's businesses, Otero, Stellar & Co.,
which he eventually took over following his father's death in 1880.

After several years of dabbling successfully in different commercial
ventures, Otero entered the world of politics at age twenty-four as an
elected clerk for the city of Las Vegas, New Mexico. He subsequently
held a series of political posts and in 1896, at the age of thirty-seven,
was appointed governor of the New Mexico Territory by President
William McKinley. Due partly to conflicting opinions between Otero
and President Theodore Roosevelt over the issue of statehood for New
Mexico and Arizona, Otero was not reappointed at the end of his
second term and stepped down from the governorship in January of
1907. Otero continued to be involved in politics, serving as an advisor
to many state and federal officials of both political parties.

In the 1920s, Otero began to write his memoirs, which were later
published as a two-volume work, *My Life on the Frontier.* In a lively
and energetic prose style, he recounts his experiences of growing up in
Kansas, Colorado, and New Mexico in the late nineteenth century.

He describes his years in boarding school; the coming of the great railroads; the many saloons, dance halls, and barbershops that lined the main streets of Western towns; and the legendary figures who set the boisterous, rough-and-tumble pace of life on the Western frontier. *My Life on the Frontier* received favorable reviews from magazines such as *Time* and *The New York Book Review.* Encouraged by these and other laudatory responses to his first work, Otero went on to publish *The Real Billy the Kid: With New Light on the Lincoln County War* in 1936 and, four years later, *My Nine Years as Governor of the Territory of New Mexico 1897–1906.*

In the following excerpt from *My Life on the Frontier,* Otero creates a colorful picture of life in Hays City, Kansas, during the late 1800s. He focuses on two well-known figures of the Wild West, Wild Bill Hickok and Calamity Jane, whom he places within the context of the lawlessness and "six-gun" justice that still prevailed during Otero's lifetime.

from My Life on the Frontier

A good friend of Wild Bill Hickok and an observant witness to the taming of the Wild West, Miguel Antonio Otero tells of life and death in the "wild and woolly" frontier town of Hays City, Kansas. The events and characters that Otero describes have held their legendary status from his day up to our own. Notice the specific details that the author gives to characterize the people, environment, and incidents in his narrative. See if you can think of any current notable people and events that could be characterized by these same descriptive details.

Hays City was, without doubt, a wild and woolly town from start to finish. Main Street was almost a solid row of saloons, dance halls, restaurants, barber shops and houses of prostitution kept by such notorious characters as "Calamity Jane," "Lousy Liz," "Stink-foot Mag," and "Steamboat."

Hundreds of freighting outfits had come to Hays City with the arrival of the railroad, and soon the surrounding country looked like a large tent city, except that covered wagons took the place of tents.

It was an impressive sight to see a thousand or more covered wagons camped around Hays City at the same time, all waiting to be loaded with freight for western Kansas, Colorado, New Mexico, Arizona and Mexico. At night the hundreds of blazing campfires made the scene look like a large illuminated city. Early in the evening, and frequently far into the night, we could hear the music of accordions, guitars, banjos and harmonicas, interspersed with songs—some sentimental, some boisterous.

On the whole, it was a collection of humanity seemingly happy, even in the face of danger. Money was plentiful; it came easy and went easy. The saloons, dance halls and gambling rooms all did a thriving business. They never closed. It was a

Miguel Antonio Otero 199

unique phase of life, this, of such terminal towns as Hays City, and its like will never be seen again.

During those busy days, firms doing business under the general designation of "Wholesale and Retail Grocers, Forwarding and Commission Merchants," remained open both day and night. This was necessary, since it usually took all day to load a large outfit, and after that there were many odds and ends that had to be attended to. The wagon-boss had to buy all his provisions for the trip, see that his wagons and animals were in good condition, sign the bills of lading for each wagon, obtain an advance of the money needed for incidental expenses on the trip, and give drafts on the merchants owning the goods. All this had to be done in time for the train of wagons to start at daybreak. To attend to these necessary details, the commission houses utilized two full sets of bookkeepers, salesmen, clerks and porters, one set working all day and the other all night.

Shortly after our arrival in Hays City, my father met his old New Mexico friend, Adolph Mennet, who was in company with two Frenchmen, John Lawrence ("French John") and John Villepigue. All three were living in a small log cabin a short distance from town and had a few milk cows. They were soldiers of fortune, having just escaped from Mexico, where they had been engaged in fighting under the banner of the Emperor Maximilian. My father hired all three of them, and they became employees of the commission house.

Buffalo hunters had not yet begun to make Hays City their rendezvous. Because of the Indians, that means of livelihood was much too dangerous to be comfortable. But a few hunters, more venturesome than the others, took the risk, since there was good money in hides. I have seen thousands of dead buffalo on the plains, killed solely for their hides, the carcasses left to rot or become food for the grey wolves, coyotes, badgers or ravens. The freighters were always well supplied with buffalo meat, and all the camps had much the appearance of a New England wash day with the fresh buffalo meat hanging on stretched ropes to dry so as to be available as jerked meat for the homeward journey.

Frequently, while living at Hays City, I saw large herds of buffalo come within a half-mile of the town. On such occasions every man owning a horse would ride out to kill some buffalo cows, yearlings or calves. This was called, in the argot of the time, a "run," which was certainly a descriptive expression, for it was a pell-mell dash of scores of men mounted on horses. When a hunter brought down a buffalo he did not stop to claim his animal but, dropping by its side his glove or his hat or some other article to attest his ownership, he rode on after others. Of course after such a hunt every home in town would be abundantly supplied with buffalo meat—saddles, quarters, whole calf, half a yearling, humps, tongues, to say nothing of hides to be tanned and made into overcoats or robes.

With such a conglomeration of humanity, it was no wonder that almost every morning there would be an announcement: "Another man for breakfast last night." It soon became necessary to act in the interest of law and order and to act vigorously. The best citizens of the town held a meeting in a store located at the eastern corner of Main Street. The summons that went out to the better class of citizens was mandatory and forcibly worded, the notice winding up with these three words: "No excuse taken."

When the meeting had been called to order, a leader was promptly chosen, and a binding oath administered to him by the oldest man in the room. The leader promptly took the chair and made a cool and emphatic statement of the necessity for immediate action. He then asked everyone present to stand up and raise his right hand. Then he administered to all the same oath he had taken. In this fashion the Vigilance Committee of Hays City was organized.

For a while the Vigilance Committee was very active in regulating the toughest characters the frontier ever saw together at one time, and did its work well. The first task undertaken by the committee was to serve notice on the undesirables then in town, giving them so many hours in which to leave. Anyone served who failed to comply was promptly hanged. It did not take the tough element long to realize that the Vigilance Committee of Hays City meant business, and after the first few lessons in law and order the number of hangings for the good of the community became greatly reduced. Nevertheless, it was not long before Hays City boasted a good-sized graveyard, not a single grave in which was occupied by anyone who had died a natural death.

The Vigilance Committee showed discretion and sound judgment in securing as town marshal the famous "Wild Bill"

Hickok. He had his hands full in keeping order in the ranks of that motley and unruly horde of humanity, but he was equal to the task and proved himself one of the most efficient peace officers the West has ever known.

It was in the year 1868 that I first met Wild Bill, and during my stay in Hays City I often came into contact with him. He dropped into the office of Otero & Sellar very frequently to talk to my father, who was a member of the Vigilance Committee. I took a great fancy to him and greatly enjoyed his company. At that time both my brother Page and myself had a stable with several fine saddle horses. No better horses could be found on the frontier, for they were trained buffalo hunters and seemed to enjoy the sport as much as the rider. You could fire off a gun between their ears without bothering them in the least. Wild Bill was very fond of good horses, and he was always welcome to any we had. Thus we became very good friends. He often took my brother and myself on buffalo hunts.

Wild Bill was one of the most perfect specimens of manhood I have ever seen. He was tall—about six feet two—and his bearing was always erect and confident, though in no wise haughty or severe. His features were regular, clean-cut and expressive. His voice was low, yet firm, and carried with it a suggestion of indomitable will power. He was strong, vigorous, agile; yet he was as gentle as a child except when in a fight, and even then he was calm and bold, without a sign of nervousness. He never became excited, always remaining as cool and deliberate as a judge passing sentence.

Beyond a shadow of doubt he was the most fearless, and perhaps the most dangerous, man in an encounter on the frontier, but never in any instance is it recorded that he started a quarrel. There was only one Wild Bill.

He was without a peer in the use of the rifle and the six-shooter. So quick was he on the draw and so perfect was his aim that almost every time he shot it meant death to his adversary.

Previous to my acquaintance with Wild Bill, he had engaged in two of his most famous fights—that with the McCandles crowd, in which he earned his nickname "Wild Bill," and that with the noted gunman, Dave Tutt, in which in fair fight Wild Bill killed his man at the first shot. He had also been one of Buffalo Bill's scouts in the campaign against Black Kettle, in which the latter was killed.

While I knew him in Hays City, he added to his record the killing of three men in single combat. The first was a man named Sam Strawhorn, a killer of note, who came to Hays City for the sole purpose of adding Wild Bill to his list of victims. He had but recently engaged in a fight with a peace officer at Ellsworth, Kans., and would have triumphed had it not been for Wild Bill, who assisted in subduing him. Wild Bill was playing cards in one of the saloons, having been appointed town marshal only a few days before. Strawhorn, having heard of the appointment and still smarting from what he termed interference on Wild Bill's part, was headed for revenge, determined to catch his intended victim off guard and kill him. Wild Bill had been notified about Strawhorn's numerous threats to shoot him on sight, and naturally was keeping a sharp look-out. On this particular occasion, Strawhorn entered the saloon and walked carelessly toward the bar. On getting within a few feet of Wild Bill he attempted to draw his gun, but Wild Bill was too quick for him and, before he could raise his gun, he dropped dead with a bullet through his brain. Strawhorn was notoriously bad and had already been marked by the Vigilance Committee. Wild Bill was complimented by all the best element in Hays City for getting rid of Strawhorn.

I was an eye-witness to Wild Bill's encounter with Bill Mulvey, and shall relate the details as they linger in my mind:

I was standing near Wild Bill on Main Street, when someone began "shooting up the town" at the eastern end of the street. It was Bill Mulvey, a notorious murderer from Missouri, known as a handy man with a gun. He had just enough red liquor in him to be mean and he seemed to derive great amusement from shooting holes into the mirrors, as well as the bottles of liquor behind the bars, of the saloons in that section of the street. As was usually the case with such fellows, he was looking for trouble, and when someone told him that Wild Bill was the town marshal and therefore it behooved him to behave himself, Mulvey swore that he would find Wild Bill and shoot him on sight. He further averred that the marshal was the very man he was looking for and that he had come to the "damn' town" for the express purpose of killing him.

The tenor of these remarks was somehow made known to

Wild Bill. But hardly had the news reached him than Mulvey appeared on the scene, tearing toward us on his iron-grey horse, rifle in hand, full cocked. When Wild Bill saw Mulvey he walked out to meet him, apparently waving his hand to some fellows behind Mulvey and calling to them: "Don't shoot him in the back; he is drunk."

Mulvey stopped his horse and, wheeling the animal about, drew a bead on his rifle in the direction of the imaginary man he thought Wild Bill was addressing. But before he realized the ruse that had been played upon him, Wild Bill had aimed his six-shooter and fired—just once. Mulvey dropped from his horse—dead, the bullet having penetrated his temple and then passed through his head.

During this episode I had been standing about twenty-five feet from Wild Bill. My joy in the outcome was boundless, for I had been afraid that Mulvey, with his rifle trained directly on Wild Bill, would pull the trigger.

The third killing was that of a man named Bill Thompson, with whom Wild Bill had had some difficulty of slight importance. Thompson was not a bad man or tough citizen. He was regarded as cowardly; consequently Wild Bill paid but slight heed to him. One day Wild Bill entered a restaurant and, while giving his order to the waiter, was surprised to see the waiter jump back. Hastily taking cognizance of the situation, he saw Thompson not more than five paces away with a pistol pointed at him. He quickly slipped from his chair to the floor, the bullet passing harmlessly through the space where his head had been a second before. Wild Bill had drawn his pistol as he slipped from the chair, and before Thompson could take a second shot Wild Bill's pistol rang out and Thompson dropped to the floor with a bullet through his brain.

My direct acquaintance with Wild Bill was not of long duration, for in 1870 he joined Buffalo Bill's Wild West Shows and left the country. He soon grew tired of the show life and went back to Abilene, Kans., becoming town marshal for another very lawless place. Finally he drifted north and spent the latter part of his life in Deadwood, So. Dak., where he later met his death at the hands of a cowardly assassin on August 2nd, 1876, at the comparatively early age of thirty-nine.

I have a friend living in Santa Fé, Frank M. Jones, who was at Deadwood when Wild Bill was murdered. From him I have gathered a first-hand account of that regrettable affair, which runs as follows:

"Wild Bill and myself were the very best of friends and frequently played cards together. Almost every night—frequently it was early morning—we would walk home together, since we roomed just across the street from each other.

"The night before the killing Wild Bill had been playing a game of casino with Jack McCall and had won all of McCall's money and gold dust, amounting to something less than two hundred dollars. In weighing the gold dust, it was found that McCall was short some eighteen dollars and Hickok asked him if that was all he had. McCall answered 'Yes,' and started for the front door of the saloon. Bill called him back and gave him some money, remarking in a joking manner:

" 'Jack, you may need some money to provide for your lodging and breakfast and I'll stake you.'

"McCall took the money, and they parted, apparently the best of friends.

"The following afternoon—I should say about two o'clock—Wild Bill and a few friends were playing poker. McCall entered the saloon. He was facing Bill, whom he greeted pleasantly as he passed. McCall made his way to the rear of the barroom. He at once turned and walked back toward the table where Bill was sitting. He came up directly behind Wild Bill's back while the latter was in the act of dealing the cards, quickly placed the muzzle of his pistol at the back of Bill's head—and fired, killing him instantly! At the same time he said:

" 'Damn you; take that.'

"The saloon in which this occurred belonged to Carl Mann, Jerry Lewis and Billy Nuttall, and was known as the 'No. 10 Saloon.'

"It was a well-known fact that Wild Bill had many enemies among the outlaws and bad men and was a marked man. They had even gone so far as to offer rewards for Bill's head, which would be paid to any man or group of men who would take the chance of catching Wild Bill off his guard. The probable explanation of McCall's cowardly act is that he was desirous of getting some of this money.

"He may have been specially instigated by some individual. Only a short time before, Wild Bill had incurred the enmity of a notorious gambler named Varnes. During a game of poker in which Bill, Varnes and Tim Healy participated, a dispute arose between Varnes and Healy. Varnes grabbed the pot, at the same time drawing his pistol, as Healy tried to interfere with him. Varnes had not counted on Wild Bill's interfering, since he knew that Healy and Bill were not on friendly terms.

"But he reckoned without his host, for Bill was always on the side of fair play and honest treatment, even in a game of cards. So his gun was out in a second, and, covering Varnes with it, he said:

" 'You can't get away with any such stuff in any game I'm playing in. Healy won that pot fairly, and I'll see he gets it.'

"Varnes sullenly put up his gun and Healy took the pot.

"This friendly act served to square all past differences between Bill and Healy; Varnes, however, became his mortal enemy. When McCall was tried and convicted, he admitted that Varnes had paid him a large sum of money for killing Wild Bill, and that the conspiracy between them had been arranged the very day of the killing. After this testimony had been given, Varnes left the country and was never heard of again.

"McCall, it is true, pled in his own defense at the Deadwood Miner's Court that acquitted him that Wild Bill had killed his brother near Fort Hays and that he had come to Deadwood for the sole purpose of revenge. He also claimed that he had been awaiting an opportunity and had finally killed him in the manner described, because he could not afford to take any chances with such a well-known man-killer as Wild Bill. It was discovered later that this was a fictitious story. Shortly after the trial, McCall was arrested on a warrant from the United States District Court and taken to Yankton, where he was tried before a jury, convicted of murder in the first degree, and hanged."

Mr. Jones describes Wild Bill as follows: "He was a handsome fellow, tall and well-built, about one hundred and eighty-five pounds in weight and about six feet tall, with wavy dark-brown hair and blue eyes. He was extremely quiet and seldom spoke of himself unless pressed by a friend to do so; he never cared to refer to his past life or to any of his many killings. Bill took an occasional drink, but he was not what you might call a drinking man, and I never saw him under the influence of liquor.

"Once in conversation about General George A. Custer he

told me of his taking up a piece of land which was open to settlement, just outside a United States Military Reservation and putting up a building for a saloon, where the soldiers might spend their money on pay-day. A few days after he had started his business he was ordered by the commanding officer to close up and move away, because it was claimed he was on Government land belonging to the Reservation. This Wild Bill denied, and consequently refused to obey the command, claiming that the land belonged to him. A small detachment of soldiers, led by Custer, who at the time was a line officer, appeared on the scene with orders to eject Wild Bill from the premises. In the fight that followed, three of the soldiers were killed.

"Wild Bill was arrested by the military authorities, tried for and convicted of murder, and ordered shot; but his case was taken to the civil court, where he was promptly acquitted, a survey having been made in which it was ascertained that the land was off the Reservation. Since the land belonged to him, the jury felt that he had a perfect right to defend his own property. In relating this incident, Wild Bill used to say that he might have killed Custer at the time, but he deliberately kept from firing at him because he liked him and regarded him as a fine soldier."

Hays City was not free from the threat of Indian attacks, although it does not seem to me that we lived in such constant dread as at Ellsworth, owing largely to the fact that Fort Hays was so near.

Between the town and Fort Hays ran a beautiful stream, known as Big Creek, which was not only a favorite place for swimming and bathing, but also a popular camping ground for the freighters. The large trees growing on both banks of Big Creek yielded a density of shade that reminded one of the tropics.

On one occasion a large horse-and-mule outfit arrived from New Mexico and established camp in the vicinity of the creek. The men had barely unharnessed the tired animals and started them down to the creek for water, when a band of wild Indians dashed out of the thicket and, in plain sight of the people of the town and the soldiers at the fort, shot and killed the herders. Then by shaking tin cans and dried buffalo-skin rattles, they caused a big stampede among the 800-odd frightened animals. The leader of the Indians caught the bell mare and rushed across the creek, the entire herd following while a group of Indians forced them from the rear. In a few minutes all that could be seen of the herd was a cloud of dust. Hundreds of citizens from the town, as well as a detachment of cavalry from the fort, went in pursuit, but they never recovered the animals. Otero & Sellar had to telegraph for several cars of Missouri mules to replace those the Indians had stolen.

No account of Hays City would be complete without some mention of "Calamity Jane," one of the frontier's most notorious characters. She dressed in a buckskin suit like a man, and was regarded by the community as a camp follower, since she preferred to ply her well-known profession among the soldiers rather than among the teamsters, freighters, herders, and the hunters. Calamity Jane's accomplishments as a "wild woman" were numerous: she could drink whiskey, smoke, chew tobacco, and swear better than the proverbial drunken sailor.

When I used to see her about Hays City in 1868, she was a comparatively young woman, perhaps twenty years of age or thereabouts, and still extremely good-looking. She was a fearless and excellent horsewoman, and a good shot with either rifle or pistol. Money seemed to mean little to her; she spent it recklessly in saloons or at the gambling table.

After a few years she left Hays City and moved from terminal town to terminal town along the advancing Kansas–Pacific Railroad, until she eventually reached Fort Carson. Then she drifted successively to Dodge City, Granada, and La Junta, towns along the Atchison, Topeka & Santa Fé Railroad. Early in 1876 she departed from La Junta for parts farther north. All the time she kept up her connection with the dance halls and continued in her old occupation. As she grew older, she developed into a rather bright woman.

There was one redeeming feature to those unfortunate women of the frontier: that was their charity. They were entirely unlike their male associates, the bad men of the frontier who were constantly wearing a chip on their shoulders and looking for a quarrel. These women in almost every instance took the part of the weak and would spend their last dollar to aid anyone in distress. Calamity Jane was no exception to the rule.

The class to which she belonged was numerous enough in the terminal towns. The majority of such women seemed to have had some sad experience back home, and this perhaps explains why they never used their family names. As a rule, they placed little value upon money and allowed their male companions to use all of their earnings in any way they pleased. When these courtesans grew old, or when their faces and bodies began to show the effects of a hard life of licentiousness and dissipation—many were old at thirty-five—they would be placed in the discard, with the immediate prospect of filling a drunkard's grave. Sometimes they chose to end it all without more ado by the morphine or strychnine route. In those days strychnine and other poisons were sold openly by the bottle and might be purchased in any store and by any person with the price, for they were largely used by hunters for killing grey wolves, coyotes, badgers, wildcats, skunks and other animals whose skins were in great demand.

So it was no common thing to hear of the death of some unfortunate woman, driven by force of circumstances into a life of degradation, ending her unhappy existence by first stupefying her mind with large quantities of poor whiskey, and then topping it off with a dose of poison sufficient to kill fifty grey wolves. In almost every instance these unfortunates would take the whole bottle of poison, their intention being to make the job certain.

This seems an appropriate point at which to give some account of that wholesale trafficking in female human flesh, which during those frontier days was more horrible than the atrocities committed by the wildest Indians. In order to keep the dance halls filled with girls, the owners would stake some woman to go back East and bring in a fresh lot of girls. They would be induced to come West under the pretext that they could obtain work in some hotel or private family at much better wages than they were receiving in their home towns. But when they reached their destination, they would find themselves forced to accept a life of debauchery, or be thrown into the street in a strange town, there to starve to death among the riff-raff.

It was no uncommon sight to see a group of gamblers, dance-hall owners, bad men and pimps gathered at the depot to meet the train on which their victims, a cargo of fresh young girls, were coming to their inevitable ruin. They gathered on such occasions chiefly for the purpose of being on the ground and seeing with their own eyes whether their orders had been properly filled. In order to expedite delivery, assignments were

Miguel Antonio Otero 209

generally made right on the depot platform by the smiling procuress who had conducted the party—much as a horseman would pick his horses or mules at a country fair. It was never long before the entire cargo had been initiated into the necessary accomplishments of the trade, drinking, smoking, snuff-dipping, as well as the art of roping in the improvident sucker.

For Study and Discussion

1. Miguel Otero paints a highly favorable, idealized portrait of Wild Bill Hickok. **a.** Judging by Otero's description, in what ways does Hickok qualify as a hero? **b.** What hints about Hickok's character and actions indicate that he was not as heroic as Otero portrays him? **c.** What kind of person do you think Hickok actually was?

2. As described by Otero, Hays City was indeed "a wild and woolly town" populated by many diverse and strong-willed people. **a.** What words and phrases would you use to characterize the inhabitants of Hays City? **b.** What differences do you see, if any, between the men as a group and the women? Refer to specific information in the narrative to support your view.

3. You have probably seen movies on television or in the theater about the Old West. How does Wild Bill Hickok as he is described in Otero's account compare to the heroes in the westerns you have seen?

Creative Writing

Writing a Memoir
In *My Life on the Frontier*, Miguel Otero relates incidents and details that he recollects from his years growing up in Hays City, Kansas. Such narratives which focus on personal accounts of

public events and important persons are called **memoirs**. A memoir differs from an **autobiography,** which primarily gives an account of the writer's own life. While a writer often includes firsthand observations and other personal information in a memoir, it is mainly concerned with matters that do not deal directly with the writer's personal life.

Write a descriptive account about a noteworthy event you have seen or a notable person who interests you. If you cannot think of a subject with which you have had firsthand experience, you may wish to base your memoir on something or someone you have seen on television or in a movie.

Prewriting. Begin by identifying the event or person you will write about. Be sure to choose a public event—perhaps an election, a major sports event, or a concert—or a newsworthy person. Brainstorm a list of details about the event or person. Arrange these details according to a specific relationship between them, such as time sequence, spatial relationship, or cause and effect. Before you start writing, skim Otero's narrative to get ideas about style, tone, diction, and content.

Writing. As you write, keep your focus on the event or person rather than on your reaction or relationship to your subject. In giving your account, you will likely make comments about your subject—in fact, such commentary is quite appropriate and can add appeal, as it does in Otero's account—however, do not let your commentary overshadow, outweigh, or otherwise dominate your subject.

Andrew García
(1853–1943)

Andrew García (gahr-see'ah) not only recorded the adventures and misadventures of outlaws and other colorful characters of the Old West, he *lived* such a life himself. Starting out as a *vaquero* [cowboy], he went on to become a fur trapper, a member of an outlaw band, a soldier in the frontier army, and finally a ranch owner.

Born close to the Texas–Mexico border, he left home as a boy to drive cattle north, and he never looked back. His autobiographical collection of stories, *Tough Trip Through Paradise,* tells of his rough-and-tumble exploits in the Wild West, or as he put it, "the melting pot of hell."

He spent more than ten years among the Nez Perce Indians in Montana, where he gained his nickname The Squaw Kid after marrying several Indian women during his stay with the tribe. García went on to ride with thieves, murderers, and assorted scoundrels yet preferred to be a witness to, rather than a participant in, their various illegal and underhanded activities.

Finally, in 1909 García decided to settle down. He bought a ranch, married a woman with four sons, and at the age of sixty began writing an account of his exciting life. Five years after his death, his manuscripts were discovered packed carefully in dynamite boxes. The loosely linked collection of stories was edited to become *Tough Trip Through Paradise,* which was published after his death. The selection on the following pages is the seventh chapter from García's book and gives his remembrance of one of the many times he found himself in mortal danger while riding with a gang of desperados.

Very Short on Law and Order

from **Tough Trip Through Paradise**

In story, song, and film, the outlaws of the Wild West have captured the imagination of Americans for generations. In this autobiographical account, the author tells of his adventures riding with desperados, such as the "notorious" Big Nose George, who had hearts "black as night" and "the stamp of evil . . . on their whiskered faces." Yet, the West did not long remain "very short on law and order," and nearly every one of these hard, treacherous men faced an early death, leaving only those who had known them—people like Andrew García—to tell the tale of their nefarious deeds and misdeeds.

So Red and I hit the trail. Again we had to put Beaver Tom in the pack string on his horse and drive him along that way. It was an awful sight to see this big husky man helpless. His love for whiskey had brought him lower down than a brute. He was now of no use, as he was as helpless and weak as a child and could hardly hold on to the saddle.

I bitterly thought, "What am I going to do if he dies? If this bunch will do as they say and let me leave them at the Musselshell, I will be alone with this pack string of stuff, and because I have *aparejos*,[1] I cannot put the packs on alone. Now I got sweet thoughts that La Brie is going to kill me anyway so why worry about the future, for I am as good as dead now."

In this happy frame of mind, we followed the trail which ran up Otter Creek for a while, then crossed another low divide and followed on down to the Sweet Grass. The way this trail kept winding and running into ups and downs made one think

---

1. *aparejos* (ah-pah-reh'hohs): harness, rigging.

that he who laid it out thought that time and steep climbing were no object. Upon coming to the Sweet Grass I thought they would expect to camp here, but they still kept on going, and when we came to the forks of the trail that went down the Sweet Grass, I could see that a large bunch of horses had gone down that trail, probably early that morning. It must have been the Crow war party; and so it was. In a little while we came to where they had camped last night. Now we were safe from them, and the trail to the Musselshell should have been clear, if a bunch of Piegans were not following them up for revenge.

It seemed that La Brie had wanted to take it out of us all that day. He kept on going till near sundown. We were a hungry and tired bunch as we sat around the fire eating fat venison, except Beaver Tom, who now seemed worse than this morning. The bunch said that he was going to get the shakes, and didn't seem any too glad for what was done, because now they had to feed Tom their valuable whiskey.

They had run the stolen horses up in the gulch past the camp where there was plenty of grass and they would not be bothered all night. Those horses were good and tired, besides sore-footed from this rough country. They did not feel like rambling off.

None of us had much to say. It was almost too quiet to feel good. La Brie rolled up in his blankets and had not spoken a word to anyone. Red and I had to go on guard together again, but before we left camp Reynolds came over to where I sat and told me to be careful and watch every move La Brie made. He was awful mad at me. There was no telling what that crazy half-breed might do. He was going to say some more to me but saw that La Brie, though rolled up in his blankets, was watching us with his beady eyes. Reynolds got up and left me. Now Red and I went on guard at the mouth of the canyon where the stolen horses were. Neither of us had much to say; he thought that Beaver Tom was going to croak, and that La Brie was a bad one. In this silent way we sat out our watch.

Reynolds and Shinnick came and relieved us. They cautioned me to watch out for La Brie in going into camp. But he was in his blankets when we got there and everything went all right. At daylight Brock Davis and La Brie woke the camp up and sent Red out to bring in the horses. This gave me a chance to cook breakfast and get some grub ready for the trail today.

Beaver Tom did not want to get up any more. They were giving him hot whiskey and soda as he was shaking like he had chills and could hardly keep the hot whiskey down. Red brought in the bunch and it was not long till we were saddled up. La Brie told Red to pack up and stay behind like we did yesterday, and to keep a sharp lookout behind. Brock Davis, Reynolds and Shinnick would round up the stolen bunch in the gulch and start out and La Brie would have to scout on ahead to see if everything was all right so we wouldn't run into any jackpots. Then the four of them rode out of camp.

It took Red and I some time to pack up. We were about ready to go, but Beaver Tom did not want to move or go as he was too sick. He did not get any sympathy from us. We pulled the blankets from him and put them in the packs and he soon changed his mind when we told him to climb on his horse or stay. He was so weak that it took both of us to get him into the saddle and to make sure that he would not fall off we lashed him tight and fast in the saddle. He bent over the saddle horn in a half-dead stupor.

I led off, driving some of the pack horses ahead of me and Red put Beaver Tom where he could watch him. When he came to the gulch where the stolen horses had fed all night I could see that they had got them and had taken the trail ahead with them. I kept on going. After traveling a mile or so, I was surprised when I caught up with Brock Davis, Reynolds and Shinnick, who were holding up the stolen bunch near the mouth of another gulch. When I stopped, they rode up to me and Brock Davis said to me, "We are sorry to do it, kid, but you have got to pull out from us here when you have the chance."

"You don't want to let the grass grow under your feet in doing it, for that Injun louse La Brie told George and Al yesterday that as soon as we get through this tough country, he is going to kill you and take your outfit. He wanted them to come in on the deal with him, and said it would be foolish for us to let you pull through with you knowing so much about us. When we came back, he said, we would have always to be on the lookout for you and he is not going to take any chances on you squealing. He says that he holds the edge on us: If we kill him for killing you, we can never make it alone through to the Northwest Territory without him to guide us. He said the Injuns would get us all, and even if we did make it through we could never sell those horses because we are strangers. George and Al strung him along and fooled him into thinking that they would do it with him to throw him off. We talked it over and it is as he says. He does hold the edge on us. It would not do you any good if we killed him after you are dead and though we are bad enough we don't stand for any murder or robbing a friend. La Brie is liable to come back if we don't move soon, and find us all here, and he will suspect that something is wrong.

"We will just have to plug La Brie," Brock Davis said, "but bad as he needs it, we don't want to do it if we can help it. Red will help you to start up this canyon; then we will drive the bunch over and cover up your trail. Go as far as you can; then camp and try to get Beaver Tom well again. Then you can both take the trail for the Musselshell. Here is a bottle of whiskey; give him as little as he will stand and try to get him eating again. We think he will pull through in a few days. We intend to take care of La Brie so that he don't come back tonight after he finds you gone. Still, don't be foolish enough to stick around your camp any more than you can help. Get away a distance and lay low. Keep a sharp lookout for two or three days. If he should try to sneak back, remember—kill him with the first shot, or it will be the last of you. Besides, should we meet any Indians, he is devil enough to send them after you to do you in. Keep your eyes open until you get out of here. Don't be mean enough to leave Beaver Tom and ride off. Stay with your outfit. We are going to tell La Brie that we started you back for the Yellowstone."

I shook hands with them all, and while they had done me dirt by roping me in with them at Bozeman, I still had to be thankful that they were not all like La Brie. I was sorry to leave them and had good cause to feel sorry for myself. They cut out their four pack horses and put them in the stolen bunch. That was the only way they could drive them along. I started my way up the canyon; they started the stolen horses and went on their way.

In the end their trail was to bring two of them, Reynolds and Henry Redman, or Red Murphy as he was called, under the hangman's tree. La Brie and Brock Davis shot it out when La Brie tried to doublecross the bunch out of its share of the plunder after they reached Canada. Brock Davis shot La Brie, but when he was on the ground dying, he still had enough of the devil left in him to shoot Brock Davis so that he died a day or two later. It all goes to show that the good old adage that crime does not pay still holds true. In the years to come, I was to hear more about some of them, when I was in the country where they had been. Except for Al Shinnick, from whom most of this information came, we were never to meet again.

Sitting here tonight, many years later, with more time than money, I think about those faces that pass before my eyes like it was yesterday. They remind me of the chances and temptations to become an outlaw. I sure came through a tough mill. I see those men as they stood in those old days of the Golden West—some of them in the springtime of their manhood, so beautiful and strong that it makes you wonder, because their hearts are as black as night, and they are cruel, treacherous and merciless as a man-eating tiger of the jungle. Others are ruffians, with the stamp of evil so plain on their whiskered faces that they make you shiver.

All of them died some kind of a violent death. It seems more real and horrid, because I knew them, and now stand like the sexton in the funeral train, for they have gone—all—all—all.

When I left Bozeman, how was I to know that the gent who called himself George Reynolds was one of the most notorious outlaws, and soon was to make history as Big Nose George in one of the most daring robberies in Montana?

The only thing that I picked up while I was with the bunch was that he had spent some of his younger life around St. Georges, Utah. Some writers have written about the career of Big Nose George and the Cohn Coulee robbery. They leave the reader in doubt. The story was told to me by one who said he was not in this hold-up, but everyone knew that he was.

Old Man Cohn ran the sutler's store in Old Fort Keough. He was not very well liked. It came to pass that he acquired many of the soldiers', and some of the none too honest civilians', hard-earned dollars. He had to buy more goods, but, unfortunately for him, the East where all the goods were wouldn't come to Old Man Cohn, so Cohn decided to go back East.

There was an army ambulance and some officers going through to Bismarck and they would travel with an escort of fifteen men, because the noble red man still had decided ideas of his own about his white brothers. Everything was lovely, safe and sure for Old Man Cohn, so he girded up his loins with all kinds of money. But in some way it soon came to be known to the shining lights in and around Old Miles and they communicated this valuable knowledge to the rest: that Cohn was going to take this trip, and take his money back to the predatory rich of the East. With righteous indignation they came to the conclusion that Old Man Cohn was not the proper person to take care of it. It would be a burning shame on this community of buffalo-hunting saints, for they could put all this money to better use in drinking red-eye rotgut and playing draw poker. They were all firm believers in patronizing home industry; this way, they would keep it in the family.

The hell of it was how to get it with fifteen cavalrymen guarding it; but a little thing like that did not bother those master minds. Undaunted, they called a council of war with Big Nose George in the chair, and vowed they would get that boodle even if they had to draft the only preacher in the town.

This bunch took no chances on the ambulance not stopping long enough in Miles. When with a flourish of trumpets the ambulance pulled out of Keough with a front and rear guard in regulation style, the Big Nose George missionaries had seen to it that every soldier in the guard was the proud possessor of a full quart bottle of Buffalo Hunter's Delight, which was also good for soldiers. The soldiers had been told to spare it not and, if the ambulance stopped long enough in Miles, their many friends would see that each soldier got another bottle of the Buffalo Hunter's Delight. It was not every day that the buffalo hunters got the chance to show how they appreciated the noble soldiers' friendship like they did that day.

The ambulance did stop, for whoever saw a trooper good and true that would refuse a shot of good old red-eye? What they put under their belts then and there, only themselves and the devil knew. Off started the ambulance on its long journey, and in it were the officers and Old Man Cohn, not forgetting the boodle. The guard was in the right position, just as a matter of form of course; for what danger could have come from the innocent buffalo hunters? This being an awfully dry country, the troopers, one by one, fell out of line and trailed along behind to sample the Buffalo Hunter's Delight.

It went this way until the ambulance came to a coulee, said to be located about eighteen miles from Miles. At this point the escort was scattered behind along the trail as drunk as lords.

Before the driver went down in the coulee, he thought that he saw a man's head on the opposite side of the coulee. He thought nothing of it until he drove to the bottom of the coulee, where he found out there was something in it, for now through the crisp Montana air came the words that all ambulance and stage drivers knew better be obeyed, "Hands up—light and hit the ground right side up." He pulled the four mules to their haunches. The head he thought he saw now turned out to be a determined road agent standing in the middle of the road with a cocked Winchester leveled at his manly bosom, and four more road agents, two on each side of the ambulance, with an awe-inspiring display of firearms in their hands. They told the occupants of the ambulance to come out the right side of the ambulance with hands up, and no monkey business about it either.

They promptly disarmed them and lined them up, but in no other way did they molest or do anything to the officers. They went after Cohn and were soon in possession of every dollar that he had with him. The amount he had with him was never rightly known to outsiders. Some writers say forty thousand dollars, others say more and some a little less, but the man who said that he was not there, but whom everyone knew was, said that they were all damn liars and were only talking through their hats, for he had heard that all the cash the cashier for the Big Nose George Company could make out of it was $16,218.75.

But the worst was still to come, and it showed that the cutthroats who did this robbery were well informed before of what Cohn intended to do. He had put in the ambulance a small keg of peach brandy for himself and the officers to drink on the trip. At the same time he put a small keg of whiskey in the boot of the ambulance for the soldiers to drink. Those hellions, after robbing the man of every cent, reached in the ambulance and brought out the keg of peach brandy. Cohn kicked on their taking that. He told them to take the keg in the boot, as it was the same kind of stuff. They promptly told him that he was a liar and that he could drink his own rotgut whiskey in the boot and see how he liked it, as they knew of the peach brandy for some time before this.

While the perpetrators of this crime were well known to most of the citizens of Miles City and the sheriff, nothing was

Andrew García 219

ever done to bring them to justice. Not because those good people wanted it so, but they were powerless in one way; the cutthroat friends of Big Nose George were too strong for them. They could not help knowing who those rascals were. All of this money was spent in Miles City with lavish generosity in gambling and drunken debauchery. It soon became a common joke. When you wanted to treat a friend, you said, "Come up, old boy, and have something on me, for I still have one of old Cohn's dollars left." Down the river from Miles City about eighteen miles there used to be a coulee, called Cohn's Coulee by the old-timers. Maybe it still goes by that name yet. If it is not, the good people of Miles City should put that name back on it. I know that it would please Old Man Cohn up in heaven. He sure to God paid enough for it.

After Big Nose George blowed in his share of the Cohn holdup he lit out with some of his own kind. He went back to his old trade of stealing horses. Down in Wyoming he rustled a bunch, but in doing so got into a fight and killed a deputy sheriff. He got away with the horses and made the drive through into Canada. Where he blowed in the money of this raid, no one knows.

Again he went to Wyoming where there was now a reward on his head, dead or alive. Although they were after him good and strong, it did not bother this knightly gentleman with a big nose, who rustled another bunch of horses. But his old-time luck went back on him. In some way the law got wise to George's aspirations, and the result was a fight in which one of his men got killed. In this fight Big Nose George and his youthful partner in crime managed to wound a deputy and kill another and get away with the bunch.

Now he found himself with just this young fellow who had no experience in whooping up a bunch of stolen horses, although he was pretty good at plugging deputy sheriffs. Big Nose found out that he had bit off more than he could chew. He dropped most of the horses with a squaw-man friend and started off with a small bunch that the two of them could handle. He headed for Miles City to rustle up another crew. There lived the genial Al Shinnick of whom I have already told you so much. While it did not bust up their friendship, Al had let a female come in between him and George. He was now the possessor of a highly cultured lady, even if she was somewhat careless and liberal with her virtue.

George showed up at Miles City on the quiet. He was not long in finding out that it was different robbing Old Man Cohn, who had real money to pass around, from bringing in a few stolen horses that were a drug on the market in Miles at the time. All friendship had ceased anyway as George's hide was now worth more to the uplifters of the law than his friendship. They were out to get him and earn the fat reward that was offered for him by the Territory of Wyoming. The honest and law-abiding people were getting stronger and putting it up to the upholders of the law that the time was coming when they would find out that they did not intend to stand for outlawry much longer. Big Nose George laid low at Al Shinnick's, but it was not long until it leaked out that Big Nose George was in and around Miles again. When the uplifters of the law found this out for sure, did they go and take this murderer and horse thief to his fate? They did nothing of the kind and for some days Big Nose George could have left and gone his way of crime and destruction and none would have stopped him.

Their scheme was to get a hooker, or harlot, of the town, to go and visit the Shinnick place and coax the young man who was with Big Nose George uptown with her. She did this for several days. Then the law got a man who had the guts to go and get the drop on Big Nose George, which he did as the two of them stood in the corral looking over the stolen horses. This man got a horse between him and Big Nose George, who had left his gun at the house, and told him to hold them up. Then the uplifters of the law, who were hiding in the brush nearby, bravely rushed over and captured Big Nose George, after this man had done the dangerous part. This was a brave act, for if Big Nose George had had his gun, the man never would have taken him alive, and probably would have lost his own life. It was an easy matter to capture Big Nose George's young partner uptown, and the law had both of them.

You may not understand that just because the good people called their town Miles City, it was not the beautiful city it is today. It was only a small town with a few houses and some shacks, for in those days anything was called a city and some of them had high-sounding names, like Ruby City which contained one magnificent lean-to-shack. At that time Miles City had only trappers, buffalo hunters and what was spent by the soldiers from Fort Keough to depend on. While there were some good, honest and God-fearing men and women there, the majority were the kind that the less said, the better. They were gamblers, tinhorns, and strong-arm men, with their prostitute partners who catered to the wants of the buffalo hunters and soldiers or anyone else, and what the gamblers did not get, those snuff-dipping vultures finished the job. In regard to the buffalo hunters and trappers, no one could tell who or what they had been. Some were good and a whole lot of them bad and as a rule stood in with the lower strata, as most of them were booze hounds who blowed in their money by gambling, and were very short on law and order. After the buffalo were all killed off, many of those gentry promptly took up horse stealing and cattle lifting as the next best job to buffalo hunting, and cost the stockman many a bloody battle and the loss of many thousands of dollars in stock before they got them hung upon trees, or run out of the country, and a few in the pen.

When the above kind of people are in the majority, they always see to it that their own kind of people are elected to enforce the law, and when they are not, they always seem to be able to elect them who will play on both sides of the fence. Where they had all the say in the election, you can imagine what chance for an honest deal the people got. It is no wonder that the justice you sometimes got was crooked and rotten as hell; and again those kind of people sure knew how to hold an election and get the full strength of them votes.

After letting every man and what few kids there were around vote two or three times, they now remembered that Phoebe's Baby Kid did not vote. . . . Two drunken brutes brought this little boy, maybe three or four years old for he still wore dresses, up to the window at the polls and made out a ticket for him to vote. To anyone but this drunken crowd of ruffians, it would have been a pitiful sight to see this little kid who had been raised in hell's cauldron, with a burly ruffian holding him by the hand.

The three judges were pretty full like the rest. The Republican judge now leered at them and said, "You Democrats have voted every man and boy two or three times in this burg today and I did not kick, but I'll be damned if I am going to see you vote Phoebe's Baby. I challenge this vote." Then two others amid the cheers of the crowd proved that the kid was twenty-one years old and of legal age, and voted him over the judge. And this goes to show that even Democracy can sometimes cover a multitude of sins.

After the Miles City capture of Big Nose George and his partner it was not long until officers from Wyoming came and took them to Rawlins to stand trial for their crimes.

The law was slow and Big Nose George got converted to religion to kill the time. So well did he play the hypocrite that he fooled the jailer and other officers. They did not take enough care in watching him. This desperate cutthroat took the steel shank from his boot and made a knife out of it. George watched like a cat for his chance which the careless deputy soon gave him. He repaid the man's kindness to him by springing on him and cutting him badly. He would have killed him only someone heard the racket in time to save his life. When the people of Rawlins heard this, they came that night and took Big Nose George out of the jail and hung him until he was dead. Big Nose George got what was coming to him.

It made me think what would have happened to me in the end if I had listened to him that night on the Big Timber, when he coaxed me to become a horse thief like himself.

For Study and Discussion

1. While the horse thieves in "Very Short on Law and Order" openly disobey many rules and proprieties of lawful society, they do adhere to their own code of honor. Give examples from the story that reveal this code and the outlaws' allegiance to it.

2. In remembering the group of men he once rode with, the narrator comments, "It all goes to show that the good old adage that crime does not pay still holds true." In what sense does crime "not pay" for these men?

3. The title of this selection, "Very Short on Law and Order," suggests that it will illustrate the lawlessness of the town that the

narrator describes. Give two examples from the narrative that indicate a lack of "law and order in Miles City." In what way do these incidents suggest the corruption and ineffectualness of the Miles City law enforcers?

Vocabulary

Recognizing Jargon

Jargon usually refers to the specialized vocabulary or idioms used by people in the same work, profession, or field of knowledge. "Very Short on Law and Order" contains several examples of cowboy jargon, such as *grub* (food) and *plug* (to shoot).

Locate and define seven other words or phrases from the story that are examples of cowboy jargon. Then choose three of these seven terms, and write an original sentence for each word or phrase.

Jovita González
(1899–1983)

In her writing, Jovita González (hoh-vee'tah gohn-sah'lehs) brings to life characters whose daily lives are woven from the same fabric as the many legends, folk tales, and songs that have been passed down through generations of her people.

Born in Roma, Texas, González is the descendant of original Spanish settlers in the American Southwest. Her great-great-grandfather, who lived to be 125 years old, received a large land grant from the Spanish king, placing her great-great-grandparents among the most prominent landholders along the Texas–Mexico border.

At a time when Mexican Americans had limited opportunities for an education, González obtained a teaching certificate. After teaching for some time at Saint Mary's Hall in San Antonio, she went on to earn a master's degree at the University of Texas at Austin. While attending the University in 1925, González became actively involved in the Texas Folklore Society where she met J. Frank Dobie, who encouraged her research into the Mexican folklore of Texas. In 1930, she became president of the Society, and her works were published regularly in the Society's publications and in the *Southwest Review*. Later, she received a grant from the Rockefeller Foundation to write a book about Mexican American life and lore along the Texas–Mexico border.

In addition to achieving recognition as a folklorist, González also made significant contributions to the field of education. She and her husband, Edmundo Mireles, developed the first Texas elementary school bilingual program. Her books *El Español Elemental* and the three-volume *Mi Libro Español* have been used to promote bilingual education throughout the southwestern United States.

From 1939 until her retirement in 1966, González taught Spanish and history at Ray High School in Corpus Christi, Texas. Today, her books and folklore are still being read and reprinted, and her ideas in education continue to guide the course of instructional programs.

Most of González's writings, including the selections from *Among My People* on the following pages, focus on the Spanish-speaking inhabitants of the Texas–Mexico border. In creating her memorable characters, González brought to life the individuals and scenes that formed an integral part of her growing-up years.

from **Among My People**

In her collection of tales titled Among My People, *Jovita González paints memorable scenes from her childhood among rural Hispanic folk along the Texas–Mexico border. Her tightknit community of characters inhabit the hot, sometimes inhospitable environment of the Rio Grande Valley, finding diversion in tall tales swapped beneath the moonlight and in the comical exploits of their neighbors. The stories on the following pages focus on several of these characters whose eccentricities have made them the stuff of local legends. As you read, notice the gentle, understated humor with which González portrays her characters. How does the author seem to feel about the people she describes? Why do you think she chose to write about these people in particular?*

Shelling Corn by Moonlight

In August, down towards the Rio Grande, the rays of the sun beat vertically upon the sandy stretches of land, from which all tender vegetation has been scorched, and the white, naked land glares back at the sun; the only palpitating things discoverable between the two poles of heat are heat devils. The rattlesnakes are as deeply holed up and as quiet as in midwinter. In the thickets of brush the roadrunners, rusty lizards, mockingbirds, and all other living things pant. Whirlwinds dance across the stretches of prairie interspersed between the thickets of thorn. At six o'clock it is hotter than at midday. Seven o'clock, and then the sun, a ball of orange-pink, descends below the horizon at one stride. The change is magical. A soft cooling breeze, the pulmotor of the Border lands, springs up from the south.

Down in the *cañada*,[1] which runs by the ranch, doves coo. Out beyond, cattle are grazing and calves are frisking. In the

---

1. *cañada* (kah-nyah'dah): a brook between mountains.

cottonwood tree growing beside the dirt "tank" near the ranch house the redbird sings. Children shout and play. From the corrals come the voices of vaqueros[2] singing and jesting. Blended with the bleatings of goats and sheep are the whistles and hisses of the *pastor* [3](shepherd). The locusts complete the chorus of evening noises. Darkness subdues them; then, as the moon rises, an uncounted mob of mongrel curs set up a howling and barking at it that coyotes out beyond mock.

It was on a night like this that the ranch folk gathered at the Big House to shell corn. All came: Tío[4] Julianito, the *pastor*, with his brood of sunburned half-starved children ever eager for food; Alejo the fiddler; Juanito the idiot, called the Innocent, because the Lord was keeping his mind in heaven; Pedro the hunter, who had seen the world and spoke English; the vaqueros; and, on rare occasions, Tío Esteban, the mail carrier. Even the women came, for on such occasions supper was served.

A big canvas was spread outside, in front of the kitchen. In the center of this canvas, ears of corn were piled in pyramids for the shellers, who sat about in a circle and with their bare hands shelled the grains off the cobs.

It was then, under the moonlit sky, that we heard stories of witches, buried treasures, and ghosts. I remember one in particular that sent chills up and down my spine.

"The night was dark, gloomy; the wind moaned over the treetops, and the coyotes howled all around. A knock was heard; the only occupant limped across the room and opened the door. A blast of cold wind put out the candle.

" 'Who is there?' he asked, looking out into a night as dark as the mouth of a wolf.

" 'Just a lost hermit,' answered a wailing voice. 'Will you give a stranger a lodging for the night?'

"A figure wrapped in a black cape entered, and as he entered, a tomblike darkness and coldness filled the room.

" 'Will you take off your hat and cape?' the host asked solicitously of his mysterious guest.

" 'No—but—I shall—take off my head.' And saying this,

---

2. **vaqueros** (bah-keh'rohs): cowboys.
3. *pastor* (pah-stohr').
4. **Tío** (tee'oh): Uncle.

the strange personage placed his head, a skull, upon the table nearby."

Then the *pastor* told of how he had seen spirits in the shape of balls of fire floating through the air. They were souls doing penance for their past sins. As a relief to our fright, Don[5] Francisco suggested that Tío Julianito do one of his original dances to the tune of Alejo's fiddle. A place was cleared on the canvas, and that started the evening's merriment.

Pedro the Hunter

Pedro was a wonderful person among all the people of the ranch. Besides being the most renowned hunter, he had seen the world, and conscious of his superiority, he strutted among the vaqueros and other ranch hands like an only rooster in a small barnyard. Besides, he spoke English, which he had learned on one of his trips up North. Yes, Pedro was a traveled man; he had been as far away as Sugar Land and had worked in the sugar-cane plantations. Many strange things he had seen in his travels. He had seen how the convicts were worked on the plantations and how they were whipped for the least offense. Yes, he, Pedro, had seen that with his own eyes.

He did not stay in the Sugar Land country long; the dampness was making him have chills. So he hired himself as a section hand. His auditors should have seen that big black monster, *el Tren Volador*.[6] It roared and whistled and belched fire and smoke as it flew over the land. He would have liked being a section hand on the railroads had it not been for the food—cornbread and salt pork.

He had been told that if he ate salt pork, he would soon learn to speak English. Bah! What a lie! He had eaten it three times a day and had only learned to say "yes." But being anxious to see a city, he came to Houston. As he walked through the downtown streets one Saturday evening, he saw some beautiful American ladies singing at a corner. What attracted his attention was that they played the guitar. And that made him homesick for the ranch. He stopped to listen, and the beautiful ladies talked to him and patted him on the back. They took him with them that night and let him sleep in a room above the garage.

---

5. **Don** (dohn): a title of respect, formerly used for Spanish-speaking men of high rank; now used as a title of courtesy.
6. *el Tren Volador* (ehl trehn boh-lah-dohr'): the Flying Train.

He could not understand them, but they were very kind and taught him to play the drum, and every evening the ladies, after putting on a funny hat, took the guitars and he the drum, and they went to town. They sang beautifully, and he beat the drum in a way that must have caused the envy of the passers-by, and when he passed a plate, many people put money in it. During the winter he learned English. But with the coming of spring he got homesick for the *mesquitales*,[7] the fragrant smell of the *huisache*,[8] the lowing of the cattle at sundown, and above all, for the mellow, rank smell of the corral. What would he not give for a good cup of black, strong ranch coffee, and a piece of jerky broiled over the fire! And so one night, with his belongings wrapped up in a blanket, he left south by west for the land of his youth. And here he was again, a man who had seen the world but who was happy to be at home.

The Mail Carrier

No people of the North feel cold more than do the Border people when the winter norther sweeps down. In the teeth of one of these northers we left Las Viboras ranch just before dawn, bound for the nearest railroad station, Hebbronville. The day proved to be as dreary as the dawn, and I amused myself counting the stiff jack rabbits that crossed our path. At a turn of the road the car almost collided with a forlorn-looking two-wheeled vehicle drawn by the sorriest-looking nag I had ever seen. On the high seat, perched like a bright-colored tropical bird, sat a figure wrapped up in a crazy quilt. On seeing us he stopped, motioned us to do the same, and in mumbled tones bade us good morning, asked where we were going, what might be the news at the ranches, and finally, were we all right. He seemed to ask these questions for the sake of asking, not waiting for a reply to any one of them. At last, having paused in his catechism long enough for some sort of reply to be given, he put out one of his hands gingerly from under his brilliant cape to wave us good-bye.

"That's Tío Esteban, the mail carrier," grandfather said. And that is how I met this employee of Uncle Sam. Six months later, suitcase and all, I rode with him twenty miles as a passenger, for the sum of two dollars and fifty cents. That summer

---

7. *mesquitales* (mehs-kee-tah'lehs): mesquite trees.
8. *huisache* (wee-sah'cheh): desert flowers.

we became intimate friends. He was the weather-beaten, brown-faced, black-eyed Cupid of the community. Often when some lovesick vaquero did not have a two-cent stamp to pay for the delivery of the love missive, he personally delivered the letter. Not only did he carry letters, but he served as secretary to those who could not write. He possessed a wonderful memory and could recite ballads and love poems by the hour. If the amorous outburst was in verse, his fee was double. He was a sly old fellow and knew all the love affairs of the community. I am not so sure of his honorableness as a mail carrier. I am afraid he sometimes opened the love missives. Once as he handed a love letter to Serafina, our cook, he said in a mellifluous voice, "My dear Serafina, as the poet says, we are like two cooing doves." Poor Serafina blushed even to the whites of her eyes. Later she showed me that very phrase in the letter.

Tío Esteban knew not only all the love affairs but also all the scandal of the two counties through which he passed. And because of that, he was the welcome guest of every ranch house. He made grandfather's house his headquarters and could always have a bed with the ranch hands. He needed little encouragement to begin talking. He usually sat on a low stool, cleared his throat, and went through all the other preliminaries of a long-winded speaker. Ah, how we enjoyed his news! What did he care for what the papers said? They told of wars in Europe, of thousands of boys killed in the trenches, of political changes, of the Kaiser's surrender.[9] But what was all this compared with what Tío Esteban had to tell us?

Did we know Chon had left his wife because she did not wash her face often enough? And about Felipe's hog eating all the soap his wife had made? Pablo's setting hen, which had all white Leghorn eggs, had hatched all black chickens. A strange event, but not so strange if you remembered that Pablo's sister-in-law had black chickens. And with such news he entertained us until the roosters began to crow.

Tío Pancho Malo

Tío Pancho Malo, they called him. After the fashion of these Mexican folk, the surname originated not from the fact that he was bad, but from the fact that he was different. No, he was

---

9. **Kaiser's surrender:** surrender of German armed forces at the end of World War I.

not bad. He merely had his own queer notions, his own ideas which he followed in his own peculiar way. And unconformity with the general tendencies and general customs is sufficient to make anyone an outlaw amid any group of folk.

Tío Pancho was a philosopher, and like all philosophers, he was at outs with the world and his fellowmen. I knew him as an old toothless, wizened creature, weak physically, but mentally sharp and alert. He spoke very little then. But as I went through the Border country, I would often hear, "as Tío Pancho Malo did," or "as Tío Pancho Malo said." If he himself was not willing to speak, those who knew him were only too glad to tell you, and always with a laugh, concerning the old man and his idiosyncrasies.

As a young married man he had lived near Mier, in Mexico, on his few ancestral acres of worthless alkaline land. "Bitter mesquites and poor folks' children are plentiful," is an old Border saying. And Tío Pancho's flock was more plentiful than the mesquite beans. His brood of boys were never bothered about keeping clean, for during the first two years of their life they were miniature Adams—except they wore no fig leaves—in a place far from being a Garden of Eden. When rebuked because of this indecency he permitted, he replied in a drawling voice, "Why should I interfere with the plans of my Creator? If he wanted children to wear clothes, he in his goodness would provide them."

When his wife died, she was buried without a coffin. "Who am I," he explained, "that I should prevent Nature from fulfilling her end? The sooner she mingles with Mother Earth, the sooner her destiny is fulfilled." After his wife's death he and his boys moved to Texas, where he became a *pastor* of goats. When the flock did not demand too much attention, he planted a few acres of land. One day, it is said, the ranch people were driven to hysterics by the appearance of his boys wearing gourds for hats.

"What is the object of a hat?" he asked. "Is it not protection from the elements? There in the shape of a gourd Nature has provided us with something that serves the same purpose and that does not cost anything."

He could neither read nor write; yet he composed poetry and expressed himself in a most flowery language. One day when he wanted an axe, he commanded one of his sons to bring him "that bright shiny object which man in his cruelty uses for the decapitation of defenseless trees."

When his boys grew up, his great exploit was the organization of a band. He did not know any music; neither did his sons. But what difference did that make? Their instruments were of the most rudimentary forms: reed flutes, handmade guitars, an old fife, a trombone, cymbals, and a drum. As director, Tío Pancho led this band from ranch to ranch, playing selections which they composed as the spirit moved them. Once they came to grandfather's ranch, and a more raggedy bunch I have never seen. They played a few selections, at the end of which grandfather asked them if they played by note.

"No," Tío Pancho Malo replied, "we play for chickens, beans, corn, or whatever the rancheros may have, but we never require a note."

He was very proud of his sons' accomplishments as musicians, and often paid them compliments but never in their presence.

"My Tirso," he said confidentially to grandfather, "plays the trombone with the strength of an ox."

Tío Pancho Malo went up and down the river playing his music and expounding his theories. As the years passed and the boys married off, the band disbanded and Tío Pancho was left alone. The last I heard of him he was at Alice, Texas, where he eked out a living as a water carrier. He was brought before the court by the society for the prevention of cruelty to animals, accused of having ill-treated his donkey.

"Your Honor," he told the judge, "these good ladies have accused me of cruelty towards my donkey, saying that I make the poor skinny creature work. But these ladies have not stopped to consider that I also am poor, skinny, and have to work. The donkey and I live for each other. Without me he would starve; without him I would die of hunger. We work together, and for each other. One of us is not any good without the other. If these ladies prevent his working, both of us will starve, and that in my mind would be not only cruelty to animals but cruelty to me."

The court could do nothing but let Tío Pancho Malo go his way.

Jovita González 233

For Study and Discussion

Shelling Corn by Moonlight

1. The author vividly captures the intense heat of the climate along the Rio Grande. **a.** What kinds of images does González use? **b.** What purpose do these descriptions serve in the tale?

2. In describing the corn-shelling, González also gives a picture of the rural community in which she lived. What do you learn about this community from the author's descriptions?

3. Tales of the supernatural are a vital part of the Mexican American oral tradition. Have you heard or read eerie tales that are similar to the one González relates?

Pedro the Hunter

4. Using an image that would be familiar to the rural people of her community, González describes Pedro as being "like an only rooster in a small barnyard." What does this comparison say about Pedro?

5. After seeing the "world," Pedro became "homesick" and returned to the ranch. What did he miss about the place where he grew up? Why did he finally decide to return home?

The Mail Carrier

6. As mail carrier, Tío Esteban forms a vital link between the rural community and the outside world. **a.** What other roles does he play within the community? **b.** Based on his actions, how would you characterize Tío Esteban?

7. Tío Esteban apparently cares little about "what the papers said" about "wars in Europe" and "political changes." **a.** What kind of news does Tío Esteban relay? **b.** Why do you think he deems this news more important than the news in the papers?

Tío Pancho Malo

8. The narrator says that Tío Pancho Malo "was a philosopher, and like all philosophers, he was at outs with the world and his fellowmen." **a.** Why is Tío Pancho Malo considered to be a philosopher? **b.** In what way is he "at outs with the world and his fellowmen"? Refer to specific passages in the story to support your answers.

9. Although Tío Pancho has "his own queer notions," he always gives seemingly reasonable arguments in defense of them. Based on hints in the story about other aspects of his character, do you think he really believes what he says? For example, do you think he really believes it is God's will that his children go without clothes?

Literary Elements

Irony

Verbal irony occurs when a writer or speaker says one thing and means something entirely different. González's descriptions of Pedro the hunter as "a traveled man" and as someone "who had seen the world" are examples of verbal irony. Clearly, Pedro has actually seen very little of the world; he has traveled only a short distance from his birthplace.

Dramatic irony is a different kind of irony in which the reader perceives something that a character in a story is not aware of. What is an example of dramatic irony in "Pedro the Hunter"? What is the basis for this irony?

Creative Writing

Writing a Description of Someone You Know

In *Among My People,* Jovita González describes several colorful figures from her childhood. González's descriptive language and understated humor capture the qualities that make these people memorable, captivating characters. Write your own short descriptive sketch focusing on an interesting person whom you know—

perhaps one who seems to aptly illustrate the notion that truth is stranger than fiction.

Prewriting. First, think of a person you would enjoy writing about. It may be a friend, a neighbor, a teacher, or perhaps someone in your family. Quite possibly, you will come up with several choices; choose the person about whom you could write the liveliest description. To safeguard the privacy of the person you are describing, you will want to avoid mentioning his or her name or to substitute a different name.

Brainstorm a list of the qualities, mannerisms, and behavior that characterize the person you have chosen. Then, decide upon the tone—humorous or serious—that your description will take. (You may want to adopt a mock-serious tone as González does, using verbal irony to express humor indirectly.) You can either give a general character sketch or describe a particular event that illustrates the person's striking qualities.

Writing and Revising. Always try to use adjectives, verbs, adverbs, and phrases that give a vivid picture of the person and that help to convey the tone of your description. Consider the following sentences:

a. My brother is tall.

b. My brother's towering height scarcely allows him to clear the doorways of our house.

a. Sarah knows a lot.

b. Sarah often seems like a walking encyclopedia, making her an unbeatable opponent in trivia games.

Nina Otero

(1882–1965)

Like many writers of the Mexican American Period, Nina Otero (nee'nah oh-teh'roh) often focused on the Hispanic folklore and traditions that formed an essential part of her heritage. Her stories incorporate both historical background and personal reminiscence to create memorable portraits of Mexican American life.

Otero's Spanish ancestors first settled in New Mexico during the seventeenth century. Drawing on knowledge of her own family history, she remarked that Hispanic people in Mexico and what is now the southwestern United States traditionally "lived close to the soil and to nature. They cherished the traditions that they had inherited from Spain and adapted to their new life." In an era when many Mexicans were becoming American citizens while at the same time struggling to retain their language and customs, Otero's dedication to the continuity of Hispanic culture helped keep the traditions of her people alive.

While some readers may feel that Otero's collection of stories *Old Spain in Our Southwest* paints a somewhat idealized picture of the Mexican American experience, her works nevertheless give insight into the powerful influence of Hispanic culture on Mexican American life and literature. "Asking for the Bride," which appears on the following pages, is taken from *Old Spain in Our Southwest* and traces the formal process that Hispanic couples traditionally went through to become engaged.

(For additional biographical information about Nina Otero, see page 145.)

Asking for the Bride

The Spanish marriage customs described in this account may seem strangely formal to you in light of modern-day American customs. Yet these customs and rituals served special purposes: "asking for the bride" in a formal manner was a family's way of showing that they endorsed their son's engagement. What are some modern American courtship rituals? How do they compare to those Nina Otero describes?

The Spaniard is dramatic in his love affairs. When a son of a *patrón* [1] wished to become engaged, his father and uncles made a visit to the father of the girl to ask for the parent's consent to an engagement, following the old custom as expressed in the Spanish law of 1766, that no young people could marry without the consent of their parents. This law was to prevent marriages between people of different social positions. It was the intention of Spain to perpetuate the ruling class in the New Possessions. The father and uncles on arriving at the home of the young girl were received most formally. This was an occasion when the formal reception room was made ready in advance, for a visit of this nature was never a surprise, although convention required that it seem so.

After an exchange of courtesies, the father of the would-be groom presented a letter which was received but not read. After a social visit, with wine and cookies served, the men departed, knowing only that a return visit would be made to deliver the answer before the month was over. The letter read:

"Most distinguished *Señor:* [2]
"Most esteemed *Doña:* [3]

"With our fitting regard and deserved affection, this

---

1. *patrón* (pah-trohn'): master, boss.
2. *Señor* (seh-nyohr'): Sir, Mister.
3. *Doña* (doh'nyah): formal title of respect used before first names of women.

238 Nina Otero

informal note comes with the sole object of making your illustrious selves aware that our son, Felipe, is favorably disposed to your pleasing young daughter, Consuelo. He wishes to place himself under your orders and to undergo the formality of the matrimonial ceremony in order better to serve you.

"We await, *señores*,[4] your answer in the hope that you will pledge to us the most precious jewel of your house. This is our prayer. We abide by your final decision when it is your pleasure to answer us.

"We are, with highest respects,
"At your orders,
"Yours with all courtesy,"

Time passed. The young girl asked for in marriage during this interval did not see the youth to whom she was to be pledged by her parents. Word was sent to the young man's father as to the date of the return visit, so that he should not be absent on such an important occasion. All the members of the household felt the dramatic effect, whether the answer were to be favorable or otherwise. There was a speculation in the house of Felipe, among the younger members of the family. Eduardo, the small brother, ran into the room of his aunt, a widow who lived with them—"*Tía*,"[5] the boy called, "today Felipe will know whether Consuelo will be his wife or not. You know, Felipe looked sad. I think he knows he will be given the *calabaza*[6]—the squash!"

"Do not be ridiculous," said his aunt. "Do you not know that the house of Aragón is the most distinguished in all this kingdom; that Felipe has cattle and sheep and horses and Indian slaves for his bride. No one could refuse such an offer!"

"But," continued Eduardo, "wouldn't it be funny for him to be given a squash? The yellow color would just suit Felipe and he is so jealous that he thinks if anyone visits in the hacienda of the Bacas he is in love with his *señorita*.[7] I want him to get

4. *señores* (seh-nyohr'ehs): sir and madam.
5. *Tía* (tee'ah): Aunt; older woman.
6. *calabaza* (kah-lah-bah'sah): a pumpkin, a squash; an ignorant person; **to be given the *calabaza*:** to be turned down as a suitor.
7. *señorita* (seh-nyohr-ee'tah): unmarried woman.

calabazas; he wouldn't be so everlastingly proud."

"His pride," said his aunt, "is of his family and his race."

"Look," said Eduardo, "here they come! See the big coach and oh! what lovely horses! I would rather have one of those horses than any girl."

The aunt had not heard this remark, as she was standing at a window looking at the guests.

The guests were received with great formality. Wine was served. No women ever took part in this special ceremony, though it was upon the mother's decision that the outcome depended. The visit was not a long one, for the answer, in the form of a beautifully written letter, was handed to Felipe's father.

After the guests had departed, the letter was eagerly read:

"Our Most Distinguished and
"Respected *Señor* and *Doña*:

"Greetings and happiness, and good returns in your business are our wishes.

"Most honored *Señor* and *Doña,* after greeting you we wish to notify you that we have made known to our young daughter, Consuelo, yours of date January 10, 1881, and have notified her that your son, Felipe, desires to be united with her by the bond of matrimony. She responded favorably to your request, and since we, because of the high respect in which we are pleased to hold you, have also agreed to your selection of our daughter, it is our duty as parents to make known to you our decision.

"Our doors will be open to you on the twenty-fifth of the present month at 2 o'clock in the afternoon, in order that you may be here to receive the pledge which you desire, and that you may arrange for the time when our children may pass on to be united by the means of the divine bond.

"With nothing more to say except to express the high respect in which we hold you,

"With sincerity, at your service,"

Preparations were immediately underway for the announcement of the engagement. This formal engagement is accompanied with as much ceremony frequently as the wedding itself.

The custom was for the groom-to-be to furnish the bride with a complete trousseau. Special marriage chests were carved and decorated. These were filled with fine linens, dainty underwear, house dresses, evening gowns, clothes for all occasions, of silks, satins, shoes of the latest pointed-toe styles. One chest contained the bridal outfit—a white satin gown trimmed with rose point-lace, a crown of wax orange blossoms to be placed over the sheer veil, white satin slippers, lace gloves. On top of the clothes were two velvet boxes, one containing a string of pearls for the bride and the other the wedding ring.

Servants were sent to the home of the bride-to-be with wagon loads of provisions to prepare for the wedding which took place shortly after the announcement of the engagement.

On the day set, there was great excitement everywhere. The trousseau was brought at that time, and often the girl was so young that her thoughts were entirely on her new clothes. The two mothers fitted the dresses on the girl at this time, left the many gifts to be admired and made final arrangements for the wedding feast. The wedding feast took place in the home of the bride, but the bridegroom's family was completely in charge, and furnished everything for the occasion.

At the announcement of the engagement, there was usually a dance given and at this time the bride might wear one of the dresses from her trousseau. A wedding feast was truly a gay time, for with the grandees the celebration would last a week or longer, even though the bridal couple might have left for their own hacienda.[8] The relatives particularly enjoyed it, for family relationships were cemented by the union.

---

8. **hacienda** (ah-syehn'dah): estate, large farm.

For Study and Discussion

1. Many marriage customs, such as that of "asking for the bride," were established for a particular reason. According to early Spanish law, what was the original purpose behind forbidding young people to marry without the consent of their parents?

2. As described by Otero, the custom of asking for the bride seems partriarchal, that is, male-dominated. Yet women, too, play an important role in this custom. In what ways do the women of the two families participate in the engagement between Felipe and Consuelo?

3. Filipe's aunt remarks that Consuelo's family would not refuse the marriage request because her nephew not only was from a distinguished family but also had "cattle and sheep and horses and Indian slaves." Why would these possessions be important to Consuelo's family?

Writing About Literature

Comparing Cultural Customs for Wedding Engagements

The strict formalities involved in arranging the engagement of two young people, as described in Nina Otero's "Asking for the Bride," may seem somewhat quaint and outdated to contemporary Americans. By the same token, the customary way in which modern American couples become engaged would likely seem quite strange and shockingly lax in the context of the culture Otero describes. In an essay of at least two paragraphs, compare the practices described in "Asking for the Bride" with the procedures and customs often followed today.

Prewriting. Reread the selection, looking for specific similarities and differences between the customs that are described and customs that are practiced today. Ask yourself questions such as, Is parental consent required or desired today? Is there any time today when the bride-to-be and her suitor are discouraged from seeing each other? Who covers the financial responsibilities of a wedding? What festivities today resemble the wedding feast? You might choose to devote one paragraph to similarities you find and another paragraph to differences. Or, you might elect to use one paragraph to discuss all similarities and differences and another paragraph to comment on your findings.

Writing. As you write, be sure to draw comparisons between specific types of customs and procedures. For example, if you give an example of a courtship ritual described in the selection, you will want to compare it to a modern-day custom that is similar in purpose.

Mario Suárez

(1925–)

The fiction and nonfiction of Mario Suárez (mah'ryoh swah'rehs) bridge the transition between the Mexican American Period and the Contemporary Period. His stories tend to concentrate on the local customs, colorful characters, and rich linguistic mixture of English and Spanish found in the barrio, while at the same time providing glimpses of a minority culture undergoing dramatic social change.

Suárez was born and raised in Tucson, Arizona, in a barrio still referred to today as *El Hoyo* [The Hole]. For Suárez, as for many Mexican American writers, the barrio represents a place of refuge and regeneration. Beneath its rough, shabby exterior, he finds the enduring soul of a people whose values and language have survived centuries of hardship, conflict, and social strife.

After graduating from high school, Suárez stayed in his hometown to attend the University of Arizona. He began to apply himself seriously to his writing during his undergraduate years, when he also devoted himself to the study of folklore. He continued to refine his writing skills after graduation, and in 1957 he received a John Jay Whitney Foundation Fellowship for creative writing. Currently, Suárez serves on the faculty of Chicano Studies at California Polytechnic College in Pomona, where he teaches English, history, and folklore.

Suárez's sketch *Tucson, Arizona: El Hoyo,* which begins on the following page, is judged by some readers to be his best work. In this insider's view of the barrio, Suárez skillfully captures the distinctive texture of sights, sounds, and smells he came to know so well during the many years he lived there.

Tucson, Arizona: El Hoyo[1]

A community is more than simply a collection of people who live in the same area. The bedrock of a community lies in the common bond that these people share. In this essay, Mario Suárez identifies such a bond as the "something more" at the heart of the barrio community of El Hoyo in Tucson, Arizona. As you read about El Hoyo, think about the community in which you live. How does the bond among the inhabitants of El Hoyo compare to the "something more" in your community?

From the center of downtown Tucson the ground slopes gently away to Main Street, drops a few feet, and then rolls to the banks of the Santa Cruz River. Here lies the section of the city known as El Hoyo. Why it is called El Hoyo is not very clear. In no sense is it a hole as its name would imply; it is simply the river's immediate valley. Its inhabitants are chicanos who raise hell on Saturday night and listen to Padre Estanislao on Sunday morning. While the term chicano is the short way of saying Mexicano, it is not restricted to the paisanos[2] who came from old Mexico with the territory or the last famine to work for the railroad, labor, sing, and go on relief. Chicano is the easy way of referring to everybody. Pablo Gutiérrez married the Chinese grocer's daughter and now runs a meat department; his sons are Chicanos. So are the sons of Killer Jones who threw a fight in Harlem and fled to El Hoyo to marry Cristina Méndez. And so are all of them. However, it is doubtful that all these spiritual sons of Mexico live in El Hoyo because of its scenic beauty—it is everything but beautiful. Its houses are simple affairs of unplastered adobe, wood, and abandoned car parts.

---

1. **El Hoyo** (ehl oh'yo): The Hole.
2. **paisanos** (pai-sah'nohs): countrymen, peasants.

Its narrow streets are mostly clearings which have, in time, acquired names. Except for some tall trees which nobody has ever cared to identify, nurse, or destroy, the main things known to grow in the general area are weeds, garbage piles, dark-eyed chavalos,[3] and dogs. And it is doubtful that the chicanos live in El Hoyo because it is safe—many times the Santa Cruz has risen and inundated the area.

In other respects living in El Hoyo has its advantages. If one is born with a weakness for acquiring bills, El Hoyo is where the collectors are less likely to find you. If one has acquired the habit of listening to Octavio Perea's Mexican Hour in the wee hours of the morning with the radio on at full blast, El Hoyo is where you are less likely to be reported to the authorities. Besides, Perea is very popular and sooner or later to everybody "Smoke In The Eyes" is dedicated between the pinto beans and white flour commercials. If one, for any reason whatever, comes on an extended period of hard times, where, if not in El Hoyo are the neighbors more willing to offer solace? When Teófila Malacara's house burned to the ground with all her belongings and two children, a benevolent gentleman carried through the gesture that made tolerable her burden. He made a list of five hundred names and solicited from each a dollar. At the end of a month he turned over to the tearful but grateful senora one hundred dollars in cold cash and then accompanied her on a short vacation. When the new manager of a local store decided that no more chicanas were to work behind the counters, it was the chicanos of El Hoyo who, on taking their individually small but collectively great buying power elsewhere, drove the manager out and the girls returned to their jobs. When the Mexican Army was enroute to Baja California and the chicanos found out that the enlisted men ate only at infrequent intervals, it was El Hoyo's chicanos who crusaded across town with pots of beans and trays of tortillas to meet the train. When someone gets married, celebrating is not restricted to the immediate friends of the couple. Everybody is invited. Anything calls for a celebration and a celebration calls for anything. On Armistice Day there are no less than half a dozen good fights at the Riverside Dance Hall. On Mexican Independence Day more than one flag is sworn allegiance to amid cheers for the queen.

---

3. **chavalos** (chah-bah'lohs): slang for "boys, youngsters, young men." (*Chavalas* is one feminine form.)

And El Hoyo is something more. It is this something more which brought Felipe Sánchez back from the wars after having killed a score of Germans with his body resembling a patchwork quilt to marry Julia Armijo. It brought Joe Zepeda, a gunner flying B-24's over Germany, back to compose boleros[4] He has a metal plate for a skull. Perhaps El Hoyo is proof that those people exist, and perhaps exist best, who have as yet failed to observe the more popular modes of human conduct. Perhaps the humble appearance of El Hoyo justifies the indifferent shrug of those made aware of its existence. Perhaps El Hoyo's simplicity motivates an occasional chicano to move away from its narrow streets, babbling comadres and shrieking children to deny the bloodwell from which he springs and to claim the blood of a conquistador while his hair is straight and his face beardless. Yet El Hoyo is not an outpost of a few families against the world. It fights for no causes except those which soothe its immediate angers. It laughs and cries with the same amount of passion in times of plenty and of want.

Perhaps El Hoyo, its inhabitants, and its essence can best be explained by telling a bit about a dish called capirotada.[5] Its origin is uncertain. But, according to the time and the circumstance, it is made of old, new or hard bread. It is softened with water and then cooked with peanuts, raisins, onions, cheese, and panocha.[6] It is fired with sherry wine. Then it is served hot, cold, or just "on the weather" as they say in El Hoyo. The Sermenos like it one way, the Garcias another, and the Ortegas still another. While it might differ greatly from one home to another, nevertheless it is still capirotada. And so it is with El Hoyo's chicanos. While being divided from within and from without, like the capirotada, they remain chicanos.

----

4. **boleros** (boh-leh'rohs): music for Mexican dances.
5. **capirotada** (kah-pee-roh-tah'thah).
6. **panocha** (pah-noh'chah): a coarse sugar made in Mexico.

For Study and Discussion

1. Although "divided from within and from without," the inhabitants of El Hoyo "remain chicanos" with strong community ties that regularly bring them together in celebration, in protest, or in some other group activity. Give several examples from the story that illustrate this community spirit.

2. Suárez does not paint an idealized or romanticized picture of El Hoyo. He points out that the residents do not live there "because it is safe" or "because of its scenic beauty." Yet Suárez also says that El Hoyo has "something more" that attracts people, keeps them there, and even draws them back after they have left. How would you describe this "something more"? Why would people choose to live in El Hoyo?

3. Suárez compares El Hoyo and its inhabitants to a particular dish whose ingredients vary "according to the time and the circumstance." What characteristics of this dish capture the essence of El Hoyo?

Writing About Literature

Using Sensory Details in a Description

In "Tucson, Arizona: El Hoyo," Mario Suárez describes the Mexican American neighborhood where he spent his childhood. He writes not simply from the perspective of an observer standing on a street corner taking in the sights, sounds, and smells of the barrio but from the heart of someone who has been a part of it. Using a rich blend of sensory details, he succeeds in conveying the shabbiness as well as the vitality of El Hoyo.

Write a short essay in which you use sensory details to describe your own hometown or a place you once visited and remember vividly.

Prewriting. Begin by recalling a place you once lived or visited that you feel strongly about. Thinking back to that location, jot down the first memories and associations that enter your mind. What details or incidents stand out in your memory? Pretend you are there again. What do you see? Whom, if anyone, do you see? Do you hear or smell anything? What is going on around you? How do you feel? Once you have a list of details, organize them by identifying relationships between them. Which details are most prominent? How are they related spatially? Are some details causes or effects of others? You might want to begin with a sentence such as the following: "It seems like just yesterday that I lived _____"; or "I can easily recall the day I visited _____ ." Or, you may even choose to build suspense by not fully revealing what or where your location is until the end of your essay.

Writing and Revising. As you write and revise your essay, pay special attention to your descriptive details. Rather than simply describing something as *colorful,* capture your reader's imagination with words like *dazzling, garish, exotic, gorgeous, lurid, gaudy,* or *iridescent.* Like all writers, you may have trouble thinking of such words. To help you do so, consult a thesaurus. But be careful; before you use a word, always check its definition in a dictionary to make sure it accurately expresses what you want to say.

Poetry of the Mexican American Period

Most of the poetry published during the Mexican American Period appeared in Spanish-language newspapers throughout the southwestern United States and California. Hundreds of poets—primarily males—published thousands of poems covering a wide variety of themes, such as love, religion, patriotism, death, family, cultural pride, and social protest. Most of these poets followed the traditional forms of the sonnet, quatrain, octave, and ten-line stanza.

Love poetry was the most popular. Virtually every newspaper that published any form of literature frequently carried selections in which the poet praised his beloved for her natural beauty and spiritual qualities. Another common theme focused on the poet's anguish when his sentiments were met with indifference by his beloved. This theme of unrequited love apparently held great appeal for readers at the time.

Melodrama and somewhat commonplace imagery dominated much of the love poetry. Many modern readers may find such imagery somewhat unoriginal, but it was quite popular a few decades ago. One poet's description of his true love's cherry-red lips and billowing hair or another's longing for his lady's seductive eyes and sweet smile appealed strongly to people whose own lives were dominated by the struggle to survive in an often-hostile environment. They reacted enthusiastically to exaggerated descriptions of the beloved and to highly sentimental expressions of love, not because they were uneducated or unsophisticated readers but rather because of the contrast that such poetry provided to their own lives as farmers, ranchers, and laborers.

The works on the following pages represent several features common to poetry of the Mexican American Period. For example, Manuel M. Salazar's "Canción," Jesús María H. Alarid's "Décima," and María Esperanza López de Padilla's "Separación" display the elevated language and imagery that characterizes love poetry of this period. Although most of the poetry published during this time was written by men, López de Padilla's poem illustrates that women writers also produced moving poetic works.

Whereas the speakers of "Separación" and "Canción" each voice their devotion to a beloved, the speaker of Jesús María H.

Alarid's "El idioma español" celebrates the beauty and dignity of the Spanish language. Alarid's poem embodies the sentiments of many Mexican Americans who, while pledging their loyalty to the United States, also declared their allegiance to their cultural traditions and native language. Eleuterio Baca's "America"—which, like many poems of this period, was written in Spanish—also reflects this dual loyalty, expressing a deep love of America from a distinctively Mexican American perspective.

Jesús María H. Alarid

(1842–?)

Not only in the arts but also in politics, law, and education, Jesús María H. Alarid (heh-soo's mah-ree'ah ah-lah'reed) helped to shape the history of his native New Mexico. He had an ideal opportunity to do this because his long life spanned all three of New Mexico's major modern historical periods: as a northern extension of the Mexican Republic, as a territory of the United States, and as the forty-seventh state of the Union.

Born in Santa Fe, Alarid began practicing law there at a young age. During the American Civil War, he served as an officer in the Union Army; then in 1863, he returned to New Mexico to become the official recorder for the House of Representatives in the territorial legislature and, a year later, the official librarian of the territory.

In addition to following in the footsteps of his father, who had held a high office in the Mexican government, Alarid played an active role in political causes. One prime example was his involvement in *El Movimiento del Pueblo* [The People's Movement], a loosely organized association of Spanish-speaking New Mexicans who struggled to secure their land titles and civil rights.

Outside of his political activities, Alarid taught in public and private schools for many years. He also contributed to the cultural scene in New Mexico as a director of a string orchestra and as a published poet.

In "El idioma español," which begins on page 254, Alarid passionately defends Mexican Americans' right to speak their native language. "Décima," which follows "El idioma español," focuses on a more personal theme: the tragic death of Alarid's wife shortly after their wedding. Together these two poems illustrate the many sides of a poet whose emotions and beliefs were inseparable from his art.

El idioma español[1] /
The Spanish Language

Alarid's eloquent defense of his native tongue is itself a testimony to the "grace" of the Spanish language. Although some of the beauty of the original poem is inevitably lost in translation, the English version nevertheless manages to capture the passionate tone of the writer's appeal. As you read, consider the speaker's arguments for the preservation of Spanish. What compromises does the speaker propose in order to establish "equality" for Spanish-speaking Americans?

---

1. **El idioma español** (ehl ee-thyoh'mah ehs-pah-nyohl').

El idioma español

Hermoso idioma español
¿Qué te quieren proscribir?
Yo creo que no hay razón
Que tú dejes de existir.

El idioma castellano   5
Fue originado en Castilla
Creencia que da al mejicano
Su gramática hoy en día
Pero quieren a porfía
Que quede un idioma muerto   10
No se declaran de cierto
Pero lo quieren quitar
Siendo un idioma tan lento
Y tan dulce para hablar.

Afirmo yo que el inglés   15
Como idioma nacional
No es de sumo interés
Que lo aprendamos hablar
Pues se debe de enseñar
Como patriotas amantes   20
Y no quedar ignorantes
Mas, no por eso dejar
Que el idioma de Cervantes
Se deje de practicar.

¿Cómo es posible señores   25
Que un nativo mejicano
Aprenda un idioma estraño?
En las escuelas mayores
Dicen, "Vendrán profesores
Para enseñar el inglés   30
El alemán y el francés
Y toditas las idiomas
Se me hace como maromas
Que voltean al revés.

The Spanish Language

Why would they do away with you
Oh lovely Spanish language?
I believe there is no reason
That you should simply vanish.

The language called Castilian   5
Had its origins in Castile
The Mexican his grammar
These roots provide him still
But there are those that in their prejudice
A dead language they'd see it become   10
They won't honestly declare this
But away with it they'd be done
Away with its slow and measured pace
Away with its sweetly spoken grace.

I declare that English   15
As language of this nation
Though we learn to speak it
Will not elevate our station
Of course we ought to teach it
As any loving patriot would agree   20
And not remain in ignorance
But this does not mean that we
Should refrain to practice
The language of Cervantes.

Sirs, how is it possible   25
That in the upper schools
A Mexican born and bred
Can learn another language's rules?
"Professors will come to teach you
German, French and English"   30
They say this, and for me all these tongues
Like a spinning dancer's dervish
Inside my head they jump and twist
And leave me in a whirling mist.

Jesús María H. Alarid 255

¿Cómo podrá el corazón   35
Sentir otro idioma vivo?
Un lenguaje sensitivo,
Es muy fácil de entender
Para poder comprender
Lo que se estudia y se aprende   40
Pero si uno no lo entiende
Lo aprende nomás a leer.

Todavía en la ocasión
Existe una mayoría
Que habla el idioma español   45
Y sostiene su hidalguía
Hablaremos á porfía
Nuestro idioma primitivo
Que siempre, siempre, esté vivo
Y exista en el corazón   50
Repito, que no hay razón
El dejar que quede aislado
¡Brille en la constitución
Del Estado Separado!

Cuando el mejicano entiende   55
Bien el idioma materno
Muy fácil será que aprenda
El idioma del gobierno
Rogaremos al eterno
Que nos dé sabiduría   60
Y que se nos llegue el día
De poder hablar inglés
Pues señores justo es
Que lo aprendamos hablar
Y siempre darle lugar   65
Al idioma nacional
Es justo y es racional
Pero les hago un recuerdo
Para a San Pablo adorar
No desadoren a San Pedro.   70

Hoy los maestros mejicanos
Estamos muy atrasados
Pocos de nuestros paisanos
Obtienen certificados
Pues hemos sido educados   75

256 *Jesús María H. Alarid*

How will the heart be able   35
To feel another tongue alive?
In a language that is sensitive
Understanding is not denied
And can be used to comprehend
What one studies and one learns   40
But without this understanding
One learns to read but can't read to learn.

A majority who speak Spanish
There still exists today
They preserve their noble convictions   45
Through stubborn ways, we could say
Our dear mother tongue
May it always, always live
And in our hearts exist
I repeat, there is no reason I can give   50
That it should remain isolate
May it shine on in the constitution
Of the Separated State!

When the Mexican is able
His maternal language to discern   55
The language of the government
Will be easy for him to learn
We pray to the Almighty Father
For it is his wisdom that we seek
That the day will come to us   60
When English we will speak
For certainly it is just
That we learn to speak it
And always give rightful place
To the language of the nation   65
It is just and it is rational
But I would also remind
That one must not rob Peter
Simply to pay Paul's fine.

Nowadays, as Mexican teachers   70
We find ourselves lagging behind
Few of our fellows have obtained
Official certificates signed
This is certainly due to our own education

Jesús María H. Alarid   257

En el idioma español
Yo creo fuera mejor
Si se trata de igualdad
Que el tiempo de examinar
Fuera en español e inglés
Pues es de grande interés
Que el inglés y el castellano
Ambos reinen a la vez
En el suelo americano.

1889

Which was given to us in Spanish   75
I think that it would be a better situation
If equality is to be established
That when it comes time for examination
It be given in English and in Spanish
For certainly it is a great gain   80
That both English and Castilian
On American soil jointly reign.

1889

Décima[1] / Décima

Following the loss of his wife after "one brief month" of marriage, the speaker in this poem struggles with the pain and "bitter disillusion" brought on by her death. A mournful tribute, this poem expresses the intense grief and sense of shock felt by any person who has lost a loved one.

---

1. **Décima** (deh'see-mah): a traditional Spanish verse form with a set metrical structure.

Décima

Yo no creo que estás muerta
Creo . . . Sí . . . que estás dormida
Dulce amor mía ¡Dispierta!
Carolina de mi vida,
Granito de oro esculpido   5
En mi amante corazón
Tengo sobrada razón
De dicirte "esposa fina"
Aquí está mi eterno amor
¡Resucita . . . Carolina   10
Ni el silencio de la tumba
Me podrá á mí convencer,
Que se ha muerto mi mujer
Pues vive en mi corazón!
¡Dios mío! os pido perdón.   15

Sabiendo Tú que yo la amo,
Por eso yo la reclamo
Pero Tú oh Dios no quisiste,
Entonces . . . Por qué me diste
Tan amargo desengaño . . .   20
28 días no más
Permitiste que estuviera,
A mi lado . . . eso si es cierto
Mas yo quisiera haber muerto
Pues vivir en este mundo   25
Es vivir en decierto
Sumergido en caos profundo.

Resucita Carolina
O también moriré
Aquí en el mundo estaré   30
Sin consuelo . . . noche y día
Sóla la Virgen María
Será mi único consuelo
Pues ya tu alma está en el Cielo
Y allá rogarás por mí   35
Siendo tú mi único anhelo
No podré vivir sin ti.

Décima

I don't believe that you are dead
But only sleeping; oh, my wife,
Sweet love of mine, awake!
Precious Caroline of my life,
Little grain of sculptured gold,   5
My loving heart with tenderness
Has every reason to profess
That you in truth were very fine.
Here lies my eternal love.
Come back to life, my Caroline   10
Even the silence of the tomb
Is unable to convince me
That my fair one's passed away,
For she still lives in my heart today.
Gracious God, please forgive me.   15

You, who know how well I love her
And the need I still have of her,
Did not allow her to remain;
Why did You give me so much pain
And such bitter disillusion?   20
Only one brief month you granted—
Twenty eight days you let her pass
Together happily at my side—
Now I wish instead that I had died,
For this world is but a desert mound,   25
And I a victim trapped inside
A chaos barren and profound.

Come back to life, sweet Caroline
Or I know that I will also die
Alone and comfortless by and by,   30
Insensible to sympathy,
Only the blessed Virgin Mary
Will be my constant consolation
While with earnest supplication
Your soul in heaven entreats for mine   35
Since you're my only aspiration
I'll die without you, Caroline.

Jesús María H. Alarid 261

For Study and Discussion

El idioma español / The Spanish Language

1. The speaker staunchly defends the Spanish language against those who would "do away" with it. **a.** Why does he feel that Mexican Americans should speak their native tongue? **b.** What is his attitude toward the English language?

2. In lines 52–53, the speaker refers to a provision in the New Mexico constitution making Spanish the official state language. In light of this provision, why might he refer to New Mexico as the "Separated State"?

3. The speaker feels that he and other Mexican teachers are at a disadvantage in the United States. **a.** How does he propose to establish "equality"? **b.** Why does he feel that equal opportunity for Mexican teachers would be a "great gain" for America?

Décima / Décima

4. In the first stanza, the speaker expresses disbelief that his wife has died. Why does he have difficulty accepting her death?

5. The speaker says that his wife's death has transformed the world into "a desert mound." Why is the image particularly appropriate in describing the speaker's feelings?

6. The speaker consoles himself with the hope that he will soon join his wife. How will this come about?

Literary Elements

Elegy

An **elegy** is a poem of mourning, usually over the death of an individual. Often, as in "Décima," the speaker in the poem expresses extreme sorrow at the loss of a loved one and has difficulty accepting that he or she is gone forever. What words and phrases does the speaker in "Décima" use to express his grief? In addition to the first three lines, where else in the poem does he reveal his inability to accept her death? Why does he find his wife's death particularly hard to bear?

Writing About Literature

Writing a Persuasive Essay on the Value of Mastering Two Languages

In "El idioma español," Alarid gives several reasons why Mexican Americans should speak and learn Spanish while also mastering the language of their adopted country. In a short persuasive essay, comment on Alarid's argument in favor of bilingual education for Hispanic Americans, and give your own viewpoint on the subject.

Prewriting. As you consider Alarid's argument, you may want to refer to the **For Study and Discussion** questions that focus on "El idioma español." In what situations does Alarid feel that Mexican Americans should continue to use Spanish? In what contexts does he agree that English is more appropriate?

Did you or a friend or relative grow up speaking two languages? Based on your experiences or on those of someone you know, what are the pros and cons of speaking and studying another language? Do you think bilingual children should continue to study both languages? Why or why not? You may discover that you have mixed feelings on the subject; if so, address these feelings in your essay.

You can organize your essay in one of two ways: devote one paragraph to Alarid's viewpoint and one to your own, or use examples from Alarid's poem throughout a general discussion to reinforce or add to your own argument.

Writing and Revising. As you write and revise your paper, feel free to add new ideas or additional examples as you think of them. Before making additions, review what you have already written so that you can determine where they will best fit.

Manuel M. Salazar

(1854–1911)

Like a number of other Mexican American writers whose works have survived over the past hundred years, Manuel M. Salazar (mah-nwehl′ sah-lah-sahr′) wrote prose and poetry not as a profession but more as a hobby or avocation.

Born in the northern New Mexico town of Puertecito, Salazar was a descendant of one of the region's oldest Hispanic families. Receiving his education prior to the advent of public schooling in the territory, he attended a parochial school in Santa Fe—St. Michael's, which still exists today.

Upon earning his high-school diploma, Salazar went into business for a short time before becoming a teacher in 1874. Four years later, he moved to Cimarron, New Mexico, where he continued teaching and also served as county recorder. His marriage in 1881 accompanied yet another move within his native state. Salazar again obtained a teaching position and also held a post as county recorder as well as a post in municipal government. From 1884 until 1895, he served five consecutive terms as recorder for Colfax County, New Mexico, and occupied several positions in local municipal and county governments. In 1895, he opened a general store, which he operated until his death in 1911.

In addition to poetry, Salazar also wrote but never published *Aurora y Gervacio, o sea la historia de un caminante* [Aurora and Gervacio, or the story of a wanderer], which is probably the first and perhaps the only novel by a native Hispanic New Mexican prior to the twentieth century.

Following the custom of his day, Salazar published his work in Spanish. His poem "Canción" [Song] appears on the following pages in both its original Spanish and an English translation.

Canción[1] / Song

At one time or another, for a variety of reasons, lovers often must part. Throughout the ages, poets have tried to capture the emotional intensity of such partings in verse and frequently in song, as Manuel Salazar does in this selection. How closely do the sentiments in Salazar's "Canción" [Song] match the sentiments expressed in songs that you listen to? Is Salazar's expression of these sentiments similar to or different from the way that they are expressed in the songs you enjoy?

---

1. **Canción** (kahn-syohn′).

Canción

Me voy mas no te olvido
Sí, siento mi partida
Al ver que entristecida
Te tienes que quedar.

Adiós celeste aurora   5
Febo lucido adiós
Adiós encantadora
Querida mía adiós.

Saldré triste y quejoso
De tu mansión querida,   10
Al ver que enternecida
Te tengo que dejar.

Si en mi retiro muero
No olvides a quien te ama
Pues él llora y exclama   15
Que te ama y te ha de amar.

En fin celeste aurora
De mi pecho delicia,
Escucha y ven propicia
Mis penas á calmar.   20

Song

It sorrows me, my love,
That shortly I must leave you;
I would not thus bereave you,
But you'll be on my mind.

Goodbye, my pale blue dawn   5
My bright Phoebus,[1] goodbye
Goodbye my charming one
My dearest love, goodbye

I'll leave our cherished dwelling
Dejected and complaining   10
To see my love remaining
Pathetically behind.

If far away I perish,
Do not forget the one who
Cries and says he loves you   15
And will love you throughout time.

So please, my pale blue dawn,
My heart's delight, come quickly
And tell me that you'll miss me
And make me feel fine.   20

---

1. **Phoebus** (fee'bus): personification of the sun; refers specifically to
   Apollo in his role as Greek god of the sun.

For Study and Discussion

1. The title of this poem is "Canción," which translates into English as "Song." In what ways is this poem like a song?

2. As a literary form, the *canción*, or song, often deals with a subjective state—that is, personal feelings or thoughts. What subjective state does the poet focus on in this poem?

3. You have probably heard popular songs that express the same theme found in this poem—the sorrow felt by lovers when they are about to be separated. How do the sentiments expressed in the poem compare to those in the songs you have heard? What is your reaction to such poems and songs? Do you find them trite and rather overly sentimental, or do you sympathize with the emotions they express?

Creative Writing

Writing a Short Story Based on a Poem

In "Song," the speaker and his beloved find themselves in circumstances that will cause their separation. Though the situation is not described, some hints about it are given. Embellish these hints to create a short story one or two pages long, revealing why the speaker must leave and perhaps guessing the fate of the two lovers after their separation.

Prewriting. Begin by identifying the hints that are given about the circumstances surrounding the lovers' separation. Make sure that you take into account the emotional responses of the speaker and his beloved. Next, you may wish to choose the time frame in which the story takes place—perhaps in the present, during World War II, in the Middle Ages, during the Spanish conquest of Mexico, or even in the near or distant future. Then imagine the lovers in an appropriate setting and situation for that time. Whether you make your story realistic or fanciful, be sure to clearly show how the events in your story lead into and follow from one another.

Writing and Revising. As you write and revise your story, additional details may occur to you. Feel free to insert this new information, but be careful to fit it smoothly into your story line, making sure that it does not conflict or seem out of place with other elements in your story.

Eleuterio Baca

(1853–?)

Although poet and translator Eleuterio Baca (eh-lehoo-teh'ryoh bah'kah) was rather well-known in his day, little information can be found concerning his life. He was a descendant of a long-established New Mexico family that had founded the town of Las Vegas, New Mexico. In 1867, Baca entered St. Louis University in Missouri and graduated from there five years later with the highest honors in his class. From the 1890s to the early 1920s, he lived in the northeastern part of New Mexico, close to his hometown of Las Vegas, and taught in the public schools in San Miguel County. For a short time he left his native state to teach in public schools in West Texas and then later returned to New Mexico.

Baca dedicated himself to his poetry and published his work for many years in several Spanish-language newspapers in New Mexico. His facility with language—both Spanish and English—served him well as a translator, too. In addition to translating songs and other musical compositions, he also translated nonfiction works, such as *Historia illustrada de Nuevo México* [The illustrated history of New Mexico] by the noted New Mexican historian Benjamin Read.

Like many other Mexican American writers of his era, Baca strongly expressed his patriotism for the United States. His patriotic allegiance is evidenced in the selection on the following pages, "America," which in large part mirrors the well-known American song of the same name. However, as you will notice, Baca has applied the creative bent that underlies his poetry to make his "America" speak for the special circumstances and experiences of Mexican American citizens of the United States.

America[1] / America

Like Samuel Francis Smith's popular song "America," this poem expresses the writer's sentiments toward his "beloved country." As you read the poem, consider how Baca's imagery reflects his unique perspective toward the landscape and spirit of his country. In Baca's eyes, what qualities make America a "blessed" country for him as it was for his forefathers?

---

1. **America** (ah-meh′ree-kah).

America

Tuyo, oh! mi patria amada,
De libertad morada,
  Es mi cantar;
Tierra de mis abuelos.
Su orgullo, sus anhelos,   5
Tiene el eco en tus cielos
  De libertad.

Tu nombre es, patria mía
Dulce amor alegría
  Del libre rogar;   10
Tus peñas, tus praderas,
Tus bosques, tus laderas,
Mi corazón de veras
  Rapto ha de amar!

Hínchese el leve viento   15
Al musical acento
  De tu canción;
Todo mortal despierte
Al eco vivo, fuerte,
Y hasta la piedra inerte,   20
  Prolongue el son.

A ti, Eterna, Deidad,
Autor de Libertad,
  Canta mi voz;
Sobre nos derramad   25
La sacra claridad
De recia libertad,
  Gran Rey, Gran Dios!

23 de diciembre, 1910

America

Oh! my beloved country,
Sweet abode of liberty,
  To you I sing;
My forefathers' land,
With pride and yearning manned,   5
In your skies echoes grand
  Freedom's ring.

Your name, oh country blessed!
Is sweet love and happiness
  For those who seek thereof;   10
To see your forested hills,
Your meadows and your rills,
My heart truly fills
  With raptest love.

Let the light breeze augment   15
The musical accent
  Of your dearest song;
Awaken, listen, everyone,
To the strongly echoed tone;
Let even the silent stone   20
  Prolong the sound.

To Thee, Eternal Deity
Author of our liberty
  My voice does sing;
Confer on those who worship Thee   25
The sacred clarity
Of incomparable liberty,
  Great God, Great King!

December 23, 1910

For Study and Discussion

1. You are probably familiar with at least the first verse and the refrain of the popular patriotic song "America" by Samuel Francis Smith. Compare the first verse in his song with the first verse of Baca's "America."

> *My country, 'tis of thee,*
> *Sweet land of liberty,*
> *Of thee I sing.*
> *Land where my fathers died,*
> *Land of the pilgrims' pride,*
> *From every mountainside*
> *Let freedom ring.*

a. How are the song and the poem alike? How are they different? **b.** What do these similarities and differences reveal about Baca's perspective as a Mexican American as compared with the sentiments expressed in Smith's "America"?

2. In the third stanza, Baca refers to the "dearest song" of America. **a.** What is this "song"? **b.** How does the natural imagery in the poem reflect the spirit of this "song"?

Literary Elements

Rhyme

Poets often create a musical quality in their work through the use of **rhyme**—the repetition of sounds in two or more words or phrases that appear near each other. Rhyme that occurs at the ends of lines is called **end rhyme,** as in the first two lines in Baca's "America":

> *Tuyo, oh! mi patria amada,*   *Oh! my beloved country,*
> *De libertad morada,*   *Sweet abode of liberty,*

The rhyme in these lines is called **perfect,** or **exact, rhyme** because the words *amada / morada* and *country / liberty* end in the same vowel sounds.

The end rhyme in the first two lines of the second stanza of the translated version of Baca's poem "America" is called **approximate rhyme** (also **slant rhyme** or **off rhyme**) because the final sounds are similar but not identical—*blessed* (pronounced *blest*) and *happiness.*

The pattern of end rhymes in a poem is called **rhyme scheme**. To identify the rhyme scheme of a poem, the letter *a* is assigned to the first rhyme, the letter *b* to the second rhyme, and so on.

a   *Oh! My beloved country,*
a   *Sweet abode of liberty,*
b   *To you I sing;*
c   *My forefathers' land,*
c   *With pride and yearning manned,*
c   *In your skies echoes grand*
b   *Freedom's ring.*

How does the rhyme scheme in the English translation of Baca's "America" compare with the rhyme scheme in the original Spanish? How does the rhyme scheme in Baca's poem compare with the rhyme scheme in Samuel Francis Smith's "America"?

Identify five examples of perfect rhyme and one example of approximate rhyme in the English version of Baca's "America."

María Esperanza López de Padilla

(1918–)

Like fellow poet Manuel Salazar, María Esperanza López de Padilla (mah-ree'ah ehs-peh-rahn'sah loh'pehs deh pah-thee'yah) can trace her family's roots to the original Hispanic settlers of New Mexico. She grew up in the county of Río Arriba where Spanish still prevails to this day as the spoken language in the relatively isolated mountain villages of the northwestern part of the state. Deeply devoted to her Hispanic heritage, she has spoken out against the threat that she believes the dominant Anglo culture presents to the traditions, language, and customs of her people.

As a child, María Esperanza worked alongside her father in the fields of southern Colorado and northern New Mexico. In the little free time they had, her mother taught her to read and write both Spanish and English. An eager student, she sharpened her skills by reading the Spanish-language newspaper *Nuevo Mexicano* [New Mexican] and listening to her father and his friends improvise and recite poetry. Despite the constant disruption and rather unorthodox nature of her early education, she managed to graduate from high school.

María Esperanza has continued to keep busy throughout her life. She wrote most of her poetry during the 1940s and has raised a family of five children. Pursuing her lifelong thirst for education, she eventually attended the University of New Mexico, graduating in 1974.

As a woman writing at the end of the Mexican American Period, María Esperanza brings a unique view to the poetry of that era, which was primarily written by males. Over the years many readers have been touched by the devotion expressed in her poem "Separación," which appears in both Spanish and English on the following pages.

Separación[1] / Separation

Like life itself, the fragile "flame" of love is all too easily extinguished. Faced with separation from her lover, the speaker in this poem seeks to guard this "precious flame" from doubts and "silly demands" that threaten it. As you read, notice the images she uses to describe how she will bear her lover's absence.

---

1. **Separación** (seh-pah-rah-syohn').

María Esperanza López de Padilla 277

Separación

Tan corta es la vida
Tan lijero su brillante vuelo
Que no hay suficiente tiempo
Para acariciarte y amarte
Tan aprisa se va la noche   5
Que debo jurar nunca dudarte.

Abrázame cerca, muy cerca
A tu pecho para que se imprente
Nuestro amor en mi corazón
Y me sostenga contra el tiempo   10
Que vendrá cuando tendrás
Que ausentarte muy lejos de aquí.

No hay tiempo para dudas
Cada hora debe de ternura rebozar
Más no vaya la preciosa llama   15
Del amor apagarse por necias demandas
Debo ser fuerte y mandarle a mi ser
Que se envuelva con manto de esperanza y fe
Hasta el día que regreses al nuestro hogar.

Separation

Life is so brief
Its brilliant flight so light
That there is not enough time
To caress and to love you
The night passes so quickly   5
That I should swear never to doubt you.

Hold me close, very close
To your chest so as to print
Our love deeply onto my heart
And so as to sustain me against the time   10
That will come when you will have
To go very far away.

There is no time for doubts
Every hour should be wrapped in tenderness
Let the precious flame of love   15
Not be extinguished by silly demands
I must be strong and command myself
To be covered in a mantle of hope and faith
Until the day that you return home.

María Esperanza López de Padilla 279

For Study and Discussion

1. The speaker takes an urgent tone in expressing her anguish about the anticipated separation from her lover. How does the poet create this sense of urgency? Give specific examples.

2. The poet uses the image of the "precious flame of love" in the last stanza. Why are the words "precious flame" particularly appropriate for describing love in this poem?

3. Anticipating the pain she will feel upon the separation from her lover, the speaker encourages and even commands herself "To be covered in a mantle of hope and faith." How will this "mantle" help her bear their separation?

Writing About Literature

Comparing the Treatment of the Same Theme in Two Poems

As discussed in the essay on page 250, most poems published during this era were written by men. "Separación," however, brings a female perspective to a theme highly popular among readers of the time: the pain of separation from a loved one. In a short essay, compare the treatment of this theme in López de Padilla's "Separation" and Manuel Salazar's "Song" (page 267).

Prewriting. What attitude does each poet take toward his or her subject? In what way do these attitudes reflect the gender and the circumstances of each speaker? Make a list of points of comparison between the two poems, and then develop this list into a paragraph or two of discussion.

Writing. Keep in mind the difference between a quotation and a paraphrase. Any word or phrase that you have altered from the poem—for example, by changing the tense of a verb—should not be enclosed in quotation marks.

The Voice of
the Hispano

*Have you ever been unjustly accused of something, such
as disloyalty to a friend or an ideal? If so, you probably
felt compelled to defend yourself—to make your own
"voice" be heard. As you read this poem, consider the
speaker's response to the "opinions / Against the Hispanic
people." What examples does the speaker give of the loyalty,
patriotism, and bravery exhibited by Mexican Americans?*

Many are the opinions
Against the Hispanic people
And they accuse them of betraying
The American government.

Making an experiment,   5
They will be disillusioned,
Our brave native men
Do not refuse to be soldiers.

It matters not what is said
Or how our fame is insulted,   10
As they will fight with pleasure
For the American eagle.

They accuse our native people
Of being rabble,
But they have not proven to be so   15
On the battlefield.

Like good countrymen
And faithful Americans,
We will free from that yoke
The humble Cubans.   20

For Study and Discussion

1. During the late nineteenth and early twentieth centuries, Hispanic Americans reacted strongly to accusations that they were not "faithful Americans." **a.** How is this poem a reaction to "opinions / Against the Hispanic people"? **b.** How does the speaker appear to feel about America?

2. During the Spanish-American War, many Mexican Americans fought on the side of the United States to secure Cuban independence from Spain. **a.** Where does the speaker allude to this conflict? **b.** What is significant about his declaration of loyalty to the United States in the war against Spain?

Writing About Literature

Writing a Personal Response to an Issue Addressed in a Poem

Although "The Voice of the Hispano" was written in the late nineteenth century, the poem also reflects the experiences and sentiments of many modern-day Hispanic Americans. For example, numerous Mexican Americans who felt that they were treated as second-class citizens in the United States nevertheless fought bravely for their country in Korea and Vietnam, where they continued to encounter prejudice. Write an essay discussing why, in your opinion, Mexican Americans such as those in "The Voice of the Hispano" would "fight with pleasure" for their country even though they feel it has treated them unfairly.

Prewriting. To gain a broader perspective on this issue, you may want to look ahead to two poems by contemporary Mexican American writers: Luis Omar Salinas's "Death in Viet Nam" on page 467 and Rolando Hinojosa-Smith's "The Eighth Army at the Chongchon" on page 605. If you choose to bring one or both of these poems into your discussion, you will want to consider how the sentiments expressed in them compare to those expressed in "The Voice of the Hispano." How does each writer seem to feel about his country's treatment of Mexican Americans during wartime? What distinctions, if any, does each make between the ideals of America and the reality of their experiences as Mexican Americans?

As you consider your own perspective, imagine yourself in the place of one of these writers or of someone you know who has been in a similar situation. What positive aspects of American society would you wish to "fight" for? How would your patriotism be affected by your experiences of prejudice or discrimination?

Revising. As you revise each draft of your essay, keep in mind the basic revising techniques: adding, deleting, or replacing words, sentences, or ideas; and rearranging words, sentences, or paragraphs.

NEBRASKA

IOWA

★ Cheyenne

Contemporary Period (1960-Present)

Denver

Kansas City •

Missouri

Colorado Springs

KANSAS

LORADO

MISSOURI

eblo

•Wichita

Tulsa •

OKLAHOMA

Arkansas

★
Oklahoma City

ARKANSAS

•Lubbock

Dallas
•

•Texarkana
•Shreveport

Mississippi

TEXAS

Colorado

Brazos

Red

Pecos

Austin ★

LOUISIANA

Rio Grande

Houston •
San Antonio

New Orleans

•Laredo Corpus Christi

EXICO

•Brownsville

Monterrey

**GULF
OF
MEXICO**

Saltillo •

Literature of the Contemporary Period

In the early 1960s, a new age dawned for Mexican American literature. During this time, the word *Chicano* came to represent for many Mexican Americans the most positive aspects of their newly rediscovered cultural past. The social and political activities of the Chicano movement sparked in Mexican American writers and artists a heightened awareness of their Hispanic and Indian heritage, generating an intense and exciting renaissance of Mexican American literature and art. Far from abating, this creative surge continues to grow stronger and more cohesive as increasing numbers of Mexican Americans seize the opportunities created for them during the 1960s. Today, Chicano literature is widely recognized as a distinctive and significant segment of contemporary American literature.

Within the past five years, contemporary Mexican American novelists, poets, and dramatists have enjoyed much-deserved renown, many of them receiving appointments to university posts and winning prestigious literary fellowships and awards. Rolando Hinojosa-Smith, for example, currently directs a new creative writing program at the University of Texas at Austin, and Alberto Ríos recently received a Guggenheim Fellowship, a much-coveted award given to only a few writers annually. Other Chicano writers such as Sandra Cisneros, Lucha Corpi, Gary Soto, Denise Chávez, and Pat Mora have also received national recognition both by public agencies and by private foundations such as the National Endowment for the Arts and the Kellogg Foundation.

Major publishing houses across the country are taking an increasing interest in Mexican American writers, recognizing both their talent and their contribution to American letters. Teachers and critics also have begun to discover not only the works of these contemporary writers but also the wealth of Mexican American literature that has existed in its many forms, tracing back several centuries. Like the culture itself, Mexican American literature commands an increasingly vital role in American history and experience.

Short Fiction of the Contemporary Period

Unlike the nostalgic, folkloric stories of the preceding period, contemporary Mexican American short fiction often focuses on the more painful aspects of Mexican American experience, including the harsh realities of poverty and prejudice. At the same time, many writers interweave this stark realism with satire, allegory, fantasy, and myth, creating multifaceted and highly imaginative works.

Many contemporary short stories focus on the everyday lives and struggles of ordinary people, often with a strong undercurrent of social commentary. The works of Daniel Garza and Francisco Jiménez, for example, illustrate the plight of thousands of migrant farmworkers in the southwestern United States and California. While some of these stories describe the upheaval, uncertainty, and thwarted dreams that haunt the lives of migrant workers, others deal with the prejudice and indifference encountered by Mexican Americans in Anglo communities.

Writers such as Sandra Cisneros, Mary Helen Ponce, Alberto Ríos, and Denise Chávez often write stories based on their own memories and experiences. Many of Cisneros's works recall her girlhood in a Chicago barrio—a life filled with constant instability, loneliness, and the limitations of poverty, yet also with humor and hope. Like Cisneros, Ponce and Ríos write from a childhood point of view, creating clever, imaginative characters. Chávez, who is represented in the contemporary drama section of this anthology, relates in her short stories bittersweet recollections of growing up in New Mexico.

Ron Arias's stories illustrate the merging of fantasy and realism that marks much contemporary Hispanic fiction. Drawing on his experience as a journalist and script writer, Arias displays a medley of different tones, moods, and perspectives in his short stories.

Like contemporary American fiction as a whole, Mexican American fiction is an exciting genre in rapid transition. Without abandoning their cultural identity or the social message of the Chicano movement, many Mexican American writers are experimenting with new forms and themes, producing works that are at the same time complex and accessible, imaginative and realistic.

Daniel Garza

(1938–)

Daniel Garza (dah-nyehl' gahr'sah)
has published little in comparison with
most of the other authors in this anthology, yet he has succeeded in capturing
in his writings the tension that exists
between Mexican Americans and Anglos in the many agricultural
communities of the southwestern United States.

Garza was born and raised in one of these communities close to
Hillsboro, Texas. His family had emigrated from Mexico to settle in
Texas in the early 1900s. He attended public school before leaving for
a few years to study at Texas Christian University in Ft. Worth and,
later, to serve as an officer in the U.S. Army.

Garza was recognized for his writings on Mexican Americans in
1962 when he received the *Harper's Magazine* Southwest Literature
Award for his article on seasonal cotton pickers, "Saturday Belongs to
the *Palomia.*" This article as well as several of his other works of nonfiction and fiction (including "Everybody Knows Tobie," which begins on
the following page) have been anthologized numerous times during the
past twenty years.

Everybody
Knows Tobie

As you read "Everybody Knows Tobie," you may be surprised to discover that this story focuses not on Tobie but on the experiences of his younger brother Joey, from whose point of view the story is told. Consider what the title suggests about the role Tobie plays in his younger brother's life.

When I was thirteen years old my older brother, Tobie, had the town newspaper route. Everyone in the town knew him well because he had been delivering their papers for a year and a half. Tobie used to tell me that he had the best route of all because his customers would pay promptly each month, and sometimes, he used to brag that the nice people of the town would tip him a quarter or maybe fifty cents at the end of the month because he would trudge up many stairs to deliver the paper personally.

The other newspaper boys were not as lucky as Tobie because sometimes their customers would not be at home when they went by to collect payment for that month's newspapers, or maybe at the end of the month the customers would just try to avoid the paper boys to keep from paying.

Yes, Tobie had it good. The biggest advantage, I thought, that Tobie had over all the newspaper boys was that he knew the Gringos[1] of the town so well that he could go into a Gringo barbershop and get a haircut without having the barber tell him to go to the Mexican barber in our town or maybe just embarrassing him in front of all the Gringo customers in the shop as

---

1. **Gringos** (green'gohs): foreigners who speak English, especially persons from the United States. It is sometimes used as a strongly negative term but not always; in this story it could be interchanged with the word *Anglo*.

they often did when Chicano[2] cotton pickers came into their places during the fall months.

The Gringo barbers of my town were careful whom they allowed in their shops during the cotton harvest season in the fall. September and October and cotton brought Chicanos from the south to the north of Texas where I lived, and where the cotton was sometimes plentiful and sometimes scarce. Chicanos is what we say in our language, and it is slang among our people. It means the Mexicans of Texas. These Chicano cotton pickers came from the Rio Grande Valley in South Texas, and sometimes, even people from Mexico made the trip to the north of Texas. All these Chicanos came to my little town in which many Gringos lived, and a few of us who spoke both English and Spanish.

When the Chicanos came to my town on Saturdays after working frightfully in the cotton fields all week, they would go to the town market for food, and the fathers would buy candy and ice cream for their flocks of little black-headed ones. The younger ones, the *jóvenes,*[3] would go to the local movie house. And then maybe those who had never been to the north of Texas before would go to the Gringos' barbershops for haircuts, not knowing that they would be refused. The Gringo barbers would be very careful not to let them come too close to their shops because the regular Gringo customers would get mad, and sometimes they would curse the Chicanos.

"Hell, it's them damn pepper bellies again. Can't seem to get rid of 'em in the fall," the prejudiced Gringos of my town would say. Some of the nicer people would only become uneasy at seeing so many Chicanos with long, black, greasy hair wanting haircuts.

The barbers of the town liked Tobie, and they invited him to their shops for haircuts. Tobie said that the barbers told him that they would cut his hair because he did not belong to that group of people who came from the south of Texas. Tobie understood. And he did not argue with the barbers because he knew how Chicanos from South Texas were, and how maybe Gringo scissors would get all greasy from cutting their hair.

During that fall Tobie encouraged me to go to the Gringo's

---

2. **Chicano** (chee-kah'noh): Mexican American.
3. *jóvenes* (hoh'beh-nehs).

place for a haircut. "Joey, when are you going to get rid of that mop of hair?" he asked.

"I guess I'll get rid of it when Mr. López learns how to cut flat-tops."

"Golly, Joey, Mr. López is a good ole guy and all that, but if he doesn't know how to give flat-tops then you should go to some other barber for flat-tops. Really, kid-brother, that hair looks awful."

"Yeah, but I'm afraid."

"Afraid of what?" Tobie asked.

"I'm afraid the barber will mistake me for one of those guys from South Texas and run me out of his shop."

"Oh, piddle," Tobie said. "Mr. Brewer . . . you know, the barber who cuts my hair . . . is a nice man, and he'll cut your hair. Just tell him you're my kid-brother."

I thought about this new adventure for several days, and then on a Saturday, when there was no school, I decided on the haircut at Mr. Brewer's. I hurriedly rode my bike to town and parked it in the alley close to the barbershop. As I walked into the shop, I noticed that all of a sudden the Gringos inside stopped their conversation and looked at me. The shop was silent for a moment. I thought then that maybe this was not too good and that I should leave. I remembered what Tobie had told me about being his brother, and about Mr. Brewer being a nice man. I was convinced that I belonged in the Gringo barbershop.

I found an empty chair and sat down to wait my turn for a haircut. One Gringo customer sitting next to me rose and explained to the barber that he had to go to the courthouse for something. Another customer left without saying anything. And then one, who was dressed in dirty coveralls and a faded khaki shirt, got up from Mr. Brewer's chair and said to him, "Say, Tom, looks like you got yourself a little tamale to clip."

Mr. Brewer smiled only.

My turn was next, and I was afraid. But I remembered again that this was all right because I was Tobie's brother, and everybody liked Tobie. I went to Mr. Brewer's chair. As I started to sit down, he looked at me and smiled a nice smile.

He said, "I'm sorry, sonny, but I can't cut your hair. You go to Mr. López's. He'll cut your hair."

Mr. Brewer took me to the door and pointed the way to

López's barbershop. He pointed with his finger and said, "See, over there behind that service station. That's his place. You go there. He'll clip your hair."

Tears were welling in my eyes. I felt a lump in my throat. I was too choked up to tell him I was Tobie's brother, and that it was all right to cut my hair. I only looked at him as he finished giving directions. He smiled again and patted me on the back. As I left, Mr. Brewer said, "Say hello to Mr. López for me, will you, sonny?"

I did not turn back to look at Mr. Brewer. I kept my head bowed as I walked to Mr. López's because tears filled my eyes, and these tears were tears of hurt to the pride and confidence which I had slowly gained in my Gringo town.

I thought of many things as I walked slowly. Maybe this was a foolish thing which I had done. There were too many Gringos in the town, and too few of us who lived there all the year long. This was a bad thing because the Gringos had the right to say yes or no, and we could only follow what they said. It was useless to go against them. It was foolish. But I was different from the Chicanos who came from the south, not much different. I did live in the town the ten months of the year when the other Chicanos were in the south or in Mexico. Then I remembered what the barber had told my brother about the South Texas people, and why the Gringo customers had left while I was in Mr. Brewer's shop. I began to understand. But it was very hard for me to realize that even though I had lived among Gringos all of my life I still had to go to my own people for such things as haircuts. Why wouldn't Gringos cut my hair? I was clean. My hair was not long and greasy.

I walked into Mr. López's shop. There were many Chicanos sitting in the chairs and even on the floor waiting their turn for a haircut. Mr. López paused from his work as he saw me enter and said, "Sorry, Joey, full up. Come back in a couple of hours."

I shrugged my shoulders and said O.K. As I started to leave I remembered what Mr. Brewer had told me to say to Mr. López. "Mr. López," I said, and all the Chicanos, the ones who were waiting, turned and looked at me with curious eyes. "Mr. Brewer told me to tell you hello."

Mr. López shook his head approvingly, not digesting the content of my statement. The Chicanos looked at me again and began to whisper among themselves. I did not hear, but I understood.

I told Mr. López that I would return later in the day, but I did not because there would be other Chicanos wanting haircuts on Saturday. I could come during the week when he had more time, and when all the Chicanos would be in the fields working.

I went away feeling rejected both by the Gringos and even my people, the entire world I knew.

Back in the alley where my bike was parked I sat on the curb for a long while thinking how maybe I did not fit into this town. Maybe my place was in the south of Texas where there were many of my kind of people, and where there were more Chicano barbershops and less Gringo barbers. Yes, I thought, I needed a land where I could belong to one race. I was so concerned with myself that I did not notice a Chicano, a middle-aged man dressed in a new chambray shirt and faded denim pants, studying me.

He asked, "*Qué pasó, Chamaco?*"[4]

"*Nada,*"[5] I answered.

"Maybe the cotton has not been good for you this year."

"No, *señor*.[6] I live here in the town."

And then the Chicano said, "Chico, I mistook you for one of us."

Suddenly the Chicano became less interested in me and walked away unconcerned.

I could not have told him that I had tried for a haircut at the Gringo's because he would have laughed at me, and called me a *pocho*,[7] a Chicano who prefers Gringo ways. These experienced Chicanos knew the ways of the Gringos in the north of Texas.

After the Chicano had left me, I thought that maybe these things which were happening to me in the town would all pass in a short time. The entire cotton crop would soon be harvested, and the farmers around my town would have it baled and sold.

---

4. *Qué pasó, Chamaco?* (keh pah-soh', chah-mah'koh?): What happened, boy?
5. *Nada* (nah'thah): nothing.
6. *señor* (seh-nyohr'): sir, mister.
7. *pocho* (poh'choh).

Then the Chicanos would leave the north of Texas and journey back to their homes in the valley in the south and to Mexico.

My town would be left alone for ten more months of the year, and in this time everything and everybody would be all right again. The Gringo barbers would maybe think twice before sending me to Mr. López's.

Early in November the last of the cotton around my town had been harvested. The people of South Texas climbed aboard their big trucks with tall sideboards and canvas on the top to shield the sun, and they began their long journey to their homes in the border country.

The streets of the little town were now empty on Saturday. A few farmers came to town on Saturday and brought their families to do their shopping; still the streets were quiet and empty.

In my home there was new excitement for me. Tobie considered leaving his newspaper route for another job, one that would pay more money. And I thought that maybe he would let me take over his route. This was something very good. By taking his route I would know all the Gringos of the town, and maybe . . . maybe then the barbers would invite me to their shops as they had invited Tobie.

At supper that night I asked Tobie if he would take me on his delivery for a few days, and then let me deliver the newspaper on my own.

Tobie said, "No, Joey. You're too young to handle money. Besides, the newspaper bag would be too heavy for you to carry on your shoulder all over town. No, I think I'll turn the route over to Red."

My father was quiet during this time, but soon he spoke, "Tobie, you give the route to Joey. He knows about money. And he needs to put a little muscle on his shoulders."

The issue was settled.

The next day Tobie took me to the newspaper office. Tobie's boss, a nice elderly man wearing glasses, studied me carefully, scratched his white head, and then asked Tobie, "Well, what do you think?"

"Oh," Tobie said, "I told him he was too young to handle this job, but he says he can do it."

"Yes, sir," I butted in enthusiastically.

Tobie's boss looked at me and chuckled, "Well, he's got enough spunk."

He thought some more.

Tobie spoke, "I think he'll make you a good delivery boy, sir."

A short silence followed while Tobie's boss put his thoughts down on a scratch pad on his desk.

Finally, the boss said, "We'll give him a try, Tobie." He looked at me. "But, young 'un, you'd better be careful with that money. It's your responsibility."

"Yes, sir," I gulped.

"O.K., that's settled," the boss said.

Tobie smiled and said, "Sir, I'm taking him on my delivery for a few days so he can get the hang of it, and then I'll let him take it over."

The boss agreed. I took his hand and shook it and promised him that I would do my extra best. Then Tobie left, and I followed behind.

In a few days I was delivering the *Daily News* to all the Gringos of the town, and also to Mr. Brewer.

Each afternoon, during my delivery, I was careful not to go into Mr. Brewer's with the newspaper. I would carefully open the door and drop the paper in. I did this because I thought that maybe Mr. Brewer would remember me, and this might cause an embarrassing incident. But I did this a very few times because one afternoon Mr. Brewer was standing at the door. He saw me. I opened the door and quickly handed him the newspaper, but before I could shut the door he said, "Say, sonny, aren't you the one I sent to Mr. López's a while back?"

"Yes, sir," I said.

"Why'd you stay around here? Didn't your people go back home last week? You do belong to 'em, don't you?"

"No, sir," I said. "I live here in the town."

"You mean to say you're not one of those . . .?"

"No, sir."

"Well, I'll be durned." He paused and thought. "You know, sonny, I have a young Meskin boy who lives here in town come to this here shop for haircuts every other Saturday. His name is . . . durn, can't think of his name to save my soul . . ."

"Tobie?"

"Yeah, yeah, that's his name. Fine boy. You know him?"

Daniel Garza 295

"Yes, sir. He's my older brother."

Then Mr. Brewer's eyes got bigger in astonishment, "Well, I'll be doubly durned." He paused and shook his head unbelievingly. "And I told you to go to Mr. López's. Why didn't you speak up and tell me you was Tobie's brother? I woulda put you in that there chair and clipped you a pretty head of hair."

"Oh, I guess I forgot to tell you," I said.

"Well, from now on, sonny, you come to this here shop, and I'll cut your hair."

"But what about your customers? Won't they get mad?"

"Naw. I'll tell 'em you're Tobie's brother, and everything will be all right. Everybody in town knows Tobie, and everybody likes him."

Then a customer walked into the barbershop. He looked at Mr. Brewer, and then at me, and then at my newspaper bag. And then the Gringo customer smiled a nice smile at me.

"Well, excuse me, sonny, got a customer waitin'. Remember now, come Saturday, and I'll clip your hair."

"O.K., Mr. Brewer. Bye."

Mr. Brewer turned and said good-bye.

As I continued my delivery I began to chuckle small bits of contentment to myself because Mr. Brewer had invited me to his shop for haircuts, and because the Gringo customer had smiled at me, and because now all the Gringos of the town would know me and maybe accept me.

Those incidents which had happened to me during the cotton harvest in my town: Mr. Brewer sending me to Mr. López's for the haircut, and the Chicano cotton picker avoiding me after discovering that I was not one of his people, and the Gringo customers leaving Mr. Brewer's barbershop because of me; all seemed so insignificant. And now I felt that delivering the *Daily News* to the businessmen had given me a place among them, and all because of the fact that everybody in my town knew Tobie.

For Study and Discussion

1. Because he is familiar to them, the "Gringos" of the town like and accept Tobie. **a.** In your experience, is it common for people who are prejudiced against another group of people to make exceptions for individuals of that group? **b.** If so, in what circumstances or situations does this happen?

2. In the story, Joey is subjected to the prejudice of the Anglo townspeople as well as that of a Chicano migrant worker. **a.** In what way is Joey "different from the Chicanos" but "not much different"? **b.** How does being excluded from both groups affect his feelings about himself and about his sense of his place in the world?

3. As Joey is delivering papers shortly after taking over Tobie's old route, he begins to "chuckle small bits of contentment to himself." Mr. Brewer's acceptance of him makes the earlier slights from the "Gringos" and the Chicano worker seem "insignificant." By the end of the story, has Joey resolved his conflicts regarding his identity as a Mexican American?

Literary Elements

First-person Point of View

In literature, **point of view** refers to the vantage point from which a story is told. In the **first-person point of view,** the story is told from the perspective of one of the characters in his or her own words. In "Everybody Knows Tobie," the reader views events from the perspective of its narrator and protagonist, Joey. As in this story, the first-person point of view creates a sense of immediacy; the reader is allowed inside the thoughts of the main character. How does this point of view limit the scope of the story? How would the story be different if it were told by an **omniscient,** or all-knowing, third-person narrator? How do you

Daniel Garza 297

think an older, wiser Joey would interpret the events of his life that are described in "Everybody Knows Tobie"?

Creative Writing

Writing from the First-person Point of View

Pretend that you are Tobie, Joey's older brother. Write a brief account of how you managed to become so well-liked by the Anglo community and of your ambitions for the future. Also discuss your predictions for your brother Joey's future.

Prewriting. Reread the story carefully, focusing on descriptions, dialogue, and events that help to characterize Tobie. You may want to brainstorm a list of Tobie's important characteristics before you begin writing. What sort of person does Tobie seem to be? How does he feel about himself, his brother Joey, and the community in which they live? What might his hopes be for Joey's future and for his own?

Writing and Revising. As you write and revise your narrative, be sure to use language and diction that reflect Tobie's character, background, and age. For example, you would not want to use slang words or regional dialect that would be unfamiliar to Tobie or unrepresentative of the area in which he lives.

Francisco Jiménez
(1943–)

Failing first grade and being mistakenly labeled by school officials as mentally retarded because he did not know English were only two of the setbacks that Francisco Jiménez (frahn-sees'koh hee-meh'nehs), now a distinguished educator, administrator, and writer, had to face in his youth.

Jiménez was born in San Pedro Tlaquepaque, Jalisco, Mexico, but moved with his family when he was four to California where jobs were available for migrant workers. The family called Santa Maria, California, home but moved frequently from one migrant camp to another, often having to sleep in garages, tents, or other makeshift shelters as they followed the crops each season. When Jiménez was six, he, too, began laboring from sunup to sundown with the rest of his family in the California fields. He could enroll in school for only a few months out of each year when the harvest season ended.

Since visas cost more money than his family could afford, only Jiménez's father had one during their first years in the United States. As illegal aliens, Jiménez and his mother, brothers, and sisters faced the constant threat of deportation. Their fears came true one day in 1958— a day that remains etched in Jiménez's memory. Immigration authorities took him from his eighth-grade classroom to deliver him to his family who were told they had only one week in which to leave the country. The family left for Mexico but were able to return legally to Santa Maria several months later with permanent resident visas.

While attending Santa Maria High School, Jiménez did exceedingly well in his studies and worked as a janitor to help support his family. He graduated from high school in 1962 with three college scholarships and then continued his education at Santa Clara University (SCU) in

California, graduating with honors in 1966. On a Woodrow Wilson fellowship grant, he pursued graduate studies at Columbia University in New York, where he eventually earned his Ph.D. Jiménez returned to SCU in 1973 to join the faculty of the Modern Language Department, where he serves as director of the Division of Arts and Humanities.

Jiménez has been honored many times since his entrance into the field of education. In 1976, he was selected by Governor Jerry Brown to become a member of the California Commission on Teacher Credentialing, on which he served as vice chairman and twice as chairman. Two years later, Jiménez received the President's Special Recognition Award at SCU and in 1985 was awarded an SCU Presidential Research Grant.

The next year, the California legislature honored him for his ten years of leadership on the credentialing commission, and SCU awarded him the prestigious Sanfilippo Chair.

In addition to being a devoted educator and administrator, Jiménez is also an acclaimed writer of literary criticism and short stories. He has published four books and numerous articles of literary criticism; his short stories have appeared in several anthologies.

Jiménez currently lives in Santa Clara with his wife and three sons. He is still a professor at SCU and also serves as an editorial advisor to the *Bilingual Press* and as the West Coast editor of the *Bilingual Review,* which he helped to found.

The Circuit

The migrant workers of this story follow the circuit of crop harvests from region to region, seeking jobs as pickers. As you read the story, consider how the title "The Circuit" applies to the narrator and his family in a deeper sense as well. In what way is the narrator's life a "circuit"—a journey that circles back to its starting point?

It was that time of year again. Ito, the strawberry sharecropper, did not smile. It was natural. The peak of the strawberry season was over and the last few days the workers, most of them braceros,[1] were not picking as many boxes as they had during the months of June and July.

As the last days of August disappeared, so did the number of braceros. Sunday, only one—the best picker—came to work. I liked him. Sometimes we talked during our half-hour lunch break. That is how I found out he was from Jalisco,[2] the same state in Mexico my family was from. That Sunday was the last time I saw him.

When the sun had tired and sunk behind the mountains, Ito signaled us that it was time to go home. "Ya esora,"[3] he yelled in his broken Spanish. Those were the words I waited for twelve hours a day, every day, seven days a week, week after week. And the thought of not hearing them again saddened me.

As we drove home Papá did not say a word. With both hands on the wheel, he stared at the dirt road. My older brother, Roberto, was also silent. He leaned his head back and closed his eyes. Once in a while he cleared from his throat the dust that blew in from outside.

Yes, it was that time of year. When I opened the front door to the shack, I stopped. Everything we owned was neatly packed in cardboard boxes. Suddenly I felt even more the weight of

---

1. **braceros** (brah-seh′rohs): contract farm laborers.
2. **Jalisco** (hah-lees′koh): a state in west central Mexico.
3. **Ya esora** (yah ehs-oh′rah): *Ya es hora* [It's time].

Francisco Jiménez 301

hours, days, weeks, and months of work. I sat down on a box. The thought of having to move to Fresno and knowing what was in store for me there brought tears to my eyes.

That night I could not sleep. I lay in bed thinking about how much I hated this move.

A little before five o'clock in the morning, Papá woke everyone up. A few minutes later, the yelling and screaming of my little brothers and sisters, for whom the move was a great adventure, broke the silence of dawn. Shortly, the barking of the dogs accompanied them.

While we packed the breakfast dishes, Papá went outside to start the "Carcanchita."[4] That was the name Papá gave his old '38 black Plymouth. He bought it in a used-car lot in Santa Rosa in the winter of 1949. Papá was very proud of his little jalopy. He had a right to be proud of it. He spent a lot of time looking at other cars before buying this one. When he finally chose the "Carcanchita," he checked it thoroughly before driving it out of the car lot. He examined every inch of the car. He listened to the motor, tilting his head from side to side like a parrot, trying to detect any noises that spelled car trouble. After being satisfied with the looks and sounds of the car, Papá then insisted on knowing who the original owner was. He never did find out from the car salesman, but he bought the car anyway. Papá figured the original owner must have been an important man because behind the rear seat of the car he found a blue necktie.

Papá parked the car out in front and left the motor running. "Listo,"[5] he yelled. Without saying a word, Roberto and I began to carry the boxes out to the car. Roberto carried the two big boxes and I carried the two smaller ones. Papá then threw the mattress on top of the car roof and tied it with ropes to the front and rear bumpers.

Everything was packed except Mamá's pot. It was an old large galvanized pot she had picked up at an army surplus store in Santa María the year I was born. The pot had many dents and nicks, and the more dents and nicks it acquired the more Mamá liked it. "Mi olla,"[6] she used to say proudly.

I held the front door open as Mamá carefully carried out

---

4. **Carcanchita** (kahr-kahn-chee'tah).
5. **Listo** (lees'toh): Ready; all set.
6. **Mi olla** (mee oh'yah): My pot.

her pot by both handles, making sure not to spill the cooked beans. When she got to the car, Papá reached out to help her with it. Roberto opened the rear car door and Papá gently placed it on the floor behind the front seat. All of us then climbed in. Papá sighed, wiped the sweat off his forehead with his sleeve, and said wearily: "Es todo."[7]

As we drove away, I felt a lump in my throat. I turned around and looked at our little shack for the last time.

At sunset we drove into a labor camp near Fresno. Since Papá did not speak English, Mamá asked the camp foreman if he needed any more workers. "We don't need no more," said the foreman, scratching his head. "Check with Sullivan down the road. Can't miss him. He lives in a big white house with a fence around it."

When we got there, Mamá walked up to the house. She went through a white gate, past a row of rose bushes, up the stairs to the front door. She rang the doorbell. The porch light went on and a tall husky man came out. They exchanged a few words. After the man went in, Mamá clasped her hands and hurried back to the car. "We have work! Mr. Sullivan said we can stay there the whole season," she said, gasping and pointing to an old garage near the stables.

The garage was worn out by the years. It had no windows. The walls, eaten by termites, strained to support the roof full of holes. The dirt floor, populated by earthworms, looked like a gray road map.

That night, by the light of a kerosene lamp, we unpacked and cleaned our new home. Roberto swept away the loose dirt, leaving the hard ground. Papá plugged the holes in the walls with old newspapers and tin can tops. Mamá fed my little brothers and sisters. Papá and Roberto then brought in the mattress and placed it on the far corner of the garage. "Mamá, you and the little ones sleep on the mattress. Roberto, Panchito, and I will sleep outside under the trees," Papá said.

Early next morning Mr. Sullivan showed us where his crop was, and after breakfast, Papá, Roberto, and I headed for the vineyard to pick.

Around nine o'clock the temperature had risen to almost one hundred degrees. I was completely soaked in sweat and my

---

7. **Es todo** (ehs toh'thoh): That's all.

mouth felt as if I had been chewing on a handkerchief. I walked over to the end of the row, picked up the jug of water we had brought, and began drinking. "Don't drink too much; you'll get sick," Roberto shouted. No sooner had he said that than I felt sick to my stomach. I dropped to my knees and let the jug roll off my hands. I remained motionless with my eyes glued on the hot sandy ground. All I could hear was the drone of insects. Slowly I began to recover. I poured water over my face and neck and watched the dirty water run down my arms to the ground.

I still felt a little dizzy when we took a break to eat lunch. It was past two o'clock and we sat underneath a large walnut tree that was on the side of the road. While we ate, Papá jotted down the number of boxes we had picked. Roberto drew designs on the ground with a stick. Suddenly I noticed Papá's face turn pale as he looked down the road. "Here comes the school bus," he whispered loudly in alarm. Instinctively, Roberto and I ran and hid in the vineyards. We did not want to get in trouble for not going to school. The neatly dressed boys about my age got off. They carried books under their arms. After they crossed the street, the bus drove away. Roberto and I came out from hiding and joined Papá. "Tienen que tener cuidado,"[8] he warned us.

After lunch we went back to work. The sun kept beating down. The buzzing insects, the wet sweat, and the hot dry dust made the afternoon seem to last forever. Finally the mountains around the valley reached out and swallowed the sun. Within an hour it was too dark to continue picking. The vines blanketed the grapes, making it difficult to see the bunches. "Vámonos,"[9] said Papá, signaling to us that it was time to quit work. Papá then took out a pencil and began to figure out how much we had earned our first day. He wrote down numbers, crossed some out, wrote down some more. "Quince,"[10] he murmured.

When we arrived home, we took a cold shower underneath a waterhose. We then sat down to eat dinner around some wooden crates that served as a table. Mamá had cooked a special

---

8. **Tienen que tener cuidado** (tyehn'ehn keh teh-nehr' kwee-thah'thoh): You have to be careful.
9. **Vámonos** (bah'moh-nohs): Let's go.
10. **Quince** (keen'seh): fifteen.

meal for us. We had rice and tortillas with "carne con chile,"[11] my favorite dish.

The next morning I could hardly move. My body ached all over. I felt little control over my arms and legs. This feeling went on every morning for days until my muscles finally got used to the work.

It was Monday, the first week of November. The grape season was over and I could now go to school. I woke up early that morning and lay in bed, looking at the stars and savoring the thought of not going to work and of starting sixth grade for the first time that year. Since I could not sleep, I decided to get up and join Papá and Roberto for breakfast. I sat at the table across from Roberto, but I kept my head down. I did not want to look up and face him. I knew he was sad. He was not going to school today. He was not going tomorrow, or next week, or next month. He would not go until the cotton season was over, and that was sometime in February. I rubbed my hands together and watched the dry, acid stained skin fall to the floor in little rolls.

When Papá and Roberto left for work, I felt relief. I walked to the top of a small grade next to the shack and watched the "Carcanchita" disappear in the distance in a cloud of dust.

Two hours later, around eight o'clock, I stood by the side of the road waiting for school bus number twenty. When it arrived I climbed in. Everyone was busy either talking or yelling. I sat in an empty seat in the back.

When the bus stopped in front of the school, I felt very nervous. I looked out the bus window and saw boys and girls carrying books under their arms. I put my hands in my pant pockets and walked to the principal's office. When I entered I heard a woman's voice say: "May I help you?" I was startled. I had not heard English for months. For a few seconds I remained speechless. I looked at the lady who waited for an answer. My first instinct was to answer her in Spanish, but I held back. Finally, after struggling for English words, I managed to tell her that I wanted to enroll in the sixth grade. After answering many questions, I was led to the classroom.

Mr. Lema, the sixth-grade teacher, greeted me and assigned me a desk. He then introduced me to the class. I was so nervous

---

11. **carne con chile** (kahr'neh kohn chee'leh): a dish made of meat, beans, and red peppers.

and scared at that moment when everyone's eyes were on me that I wished I were with Papá and Roberto picking cotton. After taking roll, Mr. Lema gave the class the assignment for the first hour. "The first thing we have to do this morning is finish reading the story we began yesterday," he said enthusiastically. He walked up to me, handed me an English book, and asked me to read. "We are on page 125," he said politely. When I heard this, I felt my blood pressure rush to my head; I felt dizzy. "Would you like to read?" he asked hesitantly. I opened the book to page 125. My mouth was dry. My eyes began to water. I could not begin. "You can read later," Mr. Lema said understandingly.

For the rest of the reading period I kept getting angrier and angrier with myself. I should have read, I thought to myself.

During recess I went into the restroom and opened my English book to page 125. I began to read in a low voice, pretending I was in class. There were many words I did not know. I closed the book and headed back to the classroom.

Mr. Lema was sitting at his desk correcting papers. When I entered he looked up at me and smiled. I felt better. I walked up to him and asked if he could help me with the new words. "Gladly," he said.

The rest of the month I spent my lunch hours working on English with Mr. Lema, my best friend at school.

One Friday during lunch hour Mr. Lema asked me to take a walk with him to the music room. "Do you like music?" he asked me as we entered the building.

"Yes, I like corridos,"[12] I answered. He then picked up a trumpet, blew on it and handed it to me. The sound gave me goose bumps. I knew that sound. I had heard it in many corridos. "How would you like to learn how to play it?" he asked. He must have read my face because before I could answer, he added: "I'll teach you how to play it during our lunch hours."

That day I could hardly wait to get home to tell Papá and Mamá the great news. As I got off the bus, my little brothers and sisters ran up to meet me. They were yelling and screaming. I thought they were happy to see me, but when I opened the door to our shack, I saw that everything we owned was neatly packed in cardboard boxes.

---

12. **corridos** (kohr-ree'thohs): ballads

For Study and Discussion

1. The narrator's comments about the family car—a "little jalopy" named "Carcanchita"—reveal that the father has great pride in his one valuable possession. **a.** What other details in the story help to characterize the narrator's parents? **b.** Based on these details, what kind of people do you think the parents are?

2. At the beginning of the story, the narrator makes friends with one of the braceros but must leave just as he is getting to know him. How does this **foreshadow,** or hint at, the story's ending?

3. Although the narrator works hard at his studies, his attempts to gain an education are thwarted by his family's constant moving. **a.** Based on the events of the story, what do you think will become of the narrator? **b.** Can you suggest ways in which he might break out of the "circuit," or fixed, circular path, of his life as a migrant worker?

4. Not only migrant workers but people from many walks of life—such as engineers, military personnel, entertainers, and oil-field workers—have occupations that require them to move frequently. Does anyone in your family or does anyone you know have such an occupation? If so, what are the positive and negative features of having to move? If you have never had such an experience yourself, you may want to speculate on the good points and bad points of leaving a familiar place for a new life.

Creative Writing

Writing a Different Ending to a Story

At the end of "The Circuit," the narrator comes home to find everything "neatly packed in cardboard boxes." Write a short narrative describing what you think would have happened to the narrator if his family had stayed in the same place for another six months.

Prewriting. Consider the narrator's circumstances toward the end of the story and the turns his life might take if he were able to stay in school. If his family remained in Fresno, would he continue his lessons with Mr. Lema? Would another six months be enough time for the narrator to find a way out of the "circuit" of his life, or would he, at the end of that time, find himself again moving on to the next harvest? In your narrative, you may want to adopt the organizational structure and tone used in "The Circuit," relating the events of your story in chronological order from the protagonist's point of view.

Writing and Revising. Be sure to pay close attention to pronoun references as you write and revise. If you have chosen to write your story from the first-person point of view, consistently use the pronouns *I* and *me* to identify the main character as the narrator of the story. If you are writing from the third-person point of view, use *he* and *him* only when the context clearly indicates which character you are referring to. For example, if you are describing an exchange between the protagonist and Mr. Lema, make sure that *he* definitely refers to either the protagonist or Mr. Lema.

Ron Arias

(1941–)

Born in 1941 in Los Angeles, California, Ronald Francis Arias (ah'ryahs)
spent much of his childhood living in El
Paso with his grandmother. During these
early years Arias whiled away countless
hours soaking up the exciting family stories she told him, sparking his
life-long interest in writing.

His stepfather's career as an Army officer, however, kept the family
moving. Arias attended high school in several states and graduated from
Stuttgart American High School in Germany in 1959. Over the years,
Arias acquired a taste for the adventure of frequent moves and eagerly
looked forward to traveling on his own. Upon graduating from high
school, he set out to tour Spain and while there met Ernest Hemingway
in Pamplona.

In 1962, Arias moved to Buenos Aires, Argentina, after being
awarded an Inter-American Press Association Scholarship. He wrote for
the English-language *Buenos Aires Herald* as well as for several
American newspapers, including the *New York Times,* until later that
year when he joined the Peace Corps and moved to a small village near
Cuzco in Peru. During his years in Peru, Arias traveled extensively
throughout the country, writing for various national and international
wire services and for the Copley newspapers. His ability to master different tones, moods, and techniques helped him greatly in writing many
human-interest features, business profiles, travelogues, and interviews.

In 1967, Arias received a B.A. in Spanish from the University of
California at Los Angeles and then earned his M.A. in journalism from
the same school the following year. In 1969, Arias's desire to travel
once again overwhelmed him. He moved to Caracas, Venezuela,
where he wrote for the *Caracas Daily Journal* for almost a year before

moving on to Washington, D.C., to become an editor for the Inter-American Development Bank. In 1971, he returned to California and began teaching writing and literature at San Bernardino Valley College and later at Crafton Hills College in Yucaipa.

Not until Arias was in his early thirties did he seriously start writing fiction. He has published many of his stories as well as his first novel, *The Road to Tumazunchale,* which was nominated for the prestigious National Book Award. Arias has also tried his hand at scriptwriting, preparing two full-length scripts and three television texts for shows such as "Quincy" and "Hill Street Blues." Today, Arias lives in Connecticut with his wife and son and works as a senior editor for *People* magazine. He recently completed his second novel, *Five Against the Sea,* which is based on the true story of five men who survived several months adrift on the open sea.

The following selection is one of Arias's first short stories. This work features a character—the *mago,* or magician—who particularly intrigues Arias. In "El Mago," Arias expertly blurs the borders between illusion and reality by describing the relationship that develops when two young girls meet with a mysterious but gentle old man.

El Mago[1]

*A number of contemporary Hispanic writers have earned
a name for themselves in the new genre of* magic realism—
*fiction in which elements of magic or the fantastic are
blended so smoothly with realistic details that the line
between reality and fantasy becomes undistinguishable.
"El Mago" falls within this exciting new genre. As you
read, pay close attention to Don Noriega and the other
characters' reactions to him, particularly at the end of the
story. Is he a magician, a charlatan, a true healer—is he
even real when Luisa returns to visit him?*

Luisa's father called him el curandero.[2] Sally's mother called
him an unfortunate. The girls simply called him El Mago.

There was no odor of age about him, though he was older
than the girls could imagine, only the smell of papered hairless
skin, it seemed. He was squat, fat and had nicotine stains on
one hand. Luisa remembered he had a harsh brittle cough; years
later she thought his chest was like an empty milk carton filled
with tiny bone particles.

This Sunday, like many Sundays before, the two girls sat
fidgeting in their blue corduroy jumpers and plain white
blouses, just behind the nuns, listening to words about Christ
and God and the Virgin and so many saints they would never
keep count, sat watching a fly rub together what looked like its
hands, watching the sleepy altar boy with his shoelaces untied,
sat playing silent games with their fingers and feet, folding and
unfolding catechism pamphlets, waiting, finally tiring, and
waiting some more. They had gone to Mass by themselves. Their
parents, who were at home asleep or making perfunctory love,
would attend later in the day.

Luisa and Sally had been best friends since third grade,
and often told strangers they were twins, even though Luisa
was darker and smaller, Sally being rounder and the "guera."[3]

---

1. **El Mago** (ehl mah'goh): the magician.
2. **el curandero** (ehl koo-rahn-deh'roh): a folk healer; someone who
   practices the art of medicine without a medical license.
3. **guera** (gweh'rah): a person with light-colored hair and skin.

The first thing El Mago told them was that they weren't twins. He said it in a friendly way, not trying to hurt, and told them it was good to play sisters.

El Mago, whose clients called him Don Noriega, lived alone in a shabby-looking wooden house halfway up a steep hill overlooking the old streetcar line to Glendale. The community knew him since two generations back when he arrived from an obscure town in northern Durango.[4] A hypnotist, a soothsayer and doctor of sorts, he rarely left his house, receiving payment usually in the form of food or small gifts. Around the sides of his house and in back he grew all the herbs, spices and exotic plants he needed for his cures. His living—or reception—room was lavishly decorated with thick Moroccan rugs, plaster sphinxes, pictures and figurines from pre-Colombian cultures, soft plushy chairs and odd-shaped lamps. On one side was a water-filled glass tank with tiny, slender fish from the Amazon. On the other side were two cages of birds from New Guinea and the rainforests of Panama. An adjoining room was lined, and divided, with filled bookcases.

Luisa and Sally met him the time they accompanied Sally's grandmother on a visit about her migraines and pains in her vesiculas. Don[5] Noriega, instead of immediately attending to business, devoted a few minutes to the girls. He overcame their shyness by giving them each a piece of biznaga candy, and then in a raspy voice told them not to worry about breaking things in the house. He insisted they explore whatever attracted their curiosity. When Luisa, the more awkward of the two girls, tipped over a metal stand with zodiac charts on it, Don Noriega helped her replace the stand. Gently and with a wink, he said all things can be repaired. It's the damage here, and he pointed over his heart, that cannot be fixed. Then he sat down to chat with the old woman, and the girls were left to their own.

After standing fascinated before the tank of colored fish, the girls moved on to another room which was dimly lighted, cluttered with boxes and books, and saturated with a strange incense. Sally's grandmother could be heard laughing in the other room. The girls began poking around, running their fingers across dusty surfaces, looking into corners. With an

---

4. **Durango** (doo-rahn'goh): a northern Mexican state.
5. **Don** (dohn): a title of respect, formerly used for Spanish-speaking men of high rank, now used as a title of courtesy.

innocent curiosity they held the tiny statues of half-men and animals which they had taken timidly from the shelves.

It wasn't long before Sally shrieked and came running out with a terrified look on her face.

"Mamá! Un hombre muerto, muerto de a tiro!"[6] she screamed.

Puzzled, the old woman looked to Don Noriega for an explanation. He sat back in his deep chair, and after an unhurried draw on his cigarette, told Sally and her grandmother that it was a fake mummy of a boy, not even a man. He gingerly explained what a mummy was and why people long ago used to preserve bodies. It was as a reminder, he said, for the dead must leave something behind to remind the living of those once known and loved.

But the old woman, with Sally still trembling in her arms, was set on leaving. Don Noriega went into the other room to tell Luisa she would have to go too, and that they were waiting for her. He found her standing beside a desk tinkering with the beads on the taut wires of a small box-like instrument. In a corner, on the other side of the room, was the opened mummy case propped up against the wall. Don Noriega told Luisa she would have to go, but that she could come another day. He promised to play music for her on the little instrument.

She raised her eyes. "Why do you have so many funny-looking things?" she asked.

Don Noriega looked down at her wonder-filled face. Luisa could see the thin lines deepen at the corners of his mouth, his eyes become friendlier. "If you like these things," he said, "why do you ask?"

At the door the old woman was still comforting Sally, who now eyed Don Noriega the way she might watch some unpredictable ogre. Luisa, biting her lips in thought, waved goodbye to him from the sidewalk.

When the story of the mummy was told, the girls' parents forbid them ever to visit Don Noriega again.

For months afterward Luisa was torn between wanting to see him and not wanting to disobey her parents. The girls had to pass by Don Noriega's street every Sunday after Mass, but

---

6. **Mamá! Un hombre muerto, muerto de a tiro!** (mah-mah'! oon ohm'breh mwehr'toh, mwehr'toh deh ah tee'roh!): Mom! A dead man, a really dead man!

Luisa never told Sally about her private wish. Walking along the weeded-over streetcar tracks, Sally would invariably poke fun at "that crazy old mago who slept with mummies and who was seen at night flying around with one of his birds." Luisa always kept silent, not knowing what to say about such things.

* * *

As usual, this Sunday the girls left the church eager for daylight and make-believe games along the pass through the hills on the way home. But more than that, today Luisa had firmly made up her mind. She would visit Don Noriega. When they approached the street on which he lived she would simply say goodbye to Sally and leave. Unconsciously she somehow felt that seeing him was worth the risk of a strapping from her father's belt.

"Luisa! You'll get in trouble," Sally warned. "What d'you want to see that old guy for?"

"Nothing will happen if you don't tell," Luisa replied calmly.

"Aren't you scared?"

Luisa looked down at the gravel between the track ties, her mind pulsing with excitement. "No," she said, trying to sound casual. "He even asked me to come back."

"Oh, Luisa, I wouldn't do that," Sally said, clutching her hands together.

"Go ahead and tell," Luisa challenged. "I won't get mad." She started up the hill. "Go on, Sally. Don't wait for me."

Sally stood watching her friend climb the long sidewalk and turn at Don Noriega's house.

The place was cluttered with scattered and charred boards, cans, pieces of cloth, blackened books, metal, chairs and sofas exuding tufts of wool, bottles and jars with dried dead plants. The front door was boarded closed, as were the broken windows to each side. Luisa looked like a waif standing in front of a ruined dream. She felt limp and bewildered, not yet sensing the numbness of death within the paint-peeled walls.

She stepped around a marble lamp base and picked her way along the side of the house to the rear. There was no back door, only a blackened doorway. She knocked softly, almost unheard, on the frame. Into the quiet she called hello. The darkness in there was still. After a moment, a wheezing brittle voice, filled with entreaty, came from within. Luisa hesitated, then stepped in. She was careful not to trip, though she bumped into strange objects at every turn, going from room to room, cautiously looking into every corner and closet. A painting fell down, a plaster statue tipped over. She fought to control her fear. In the front room, behind the door to the street, she saw the waterfilled fish tank. The little creatures were still there, floating on the surface. Luisa pursed her lips. With her forefinger she pushed one of the slivers and it slipped past the others, bumping into the side of the tank.

In the silence she heard a cough. The floorboards creaked as she stepped through the room where the mummy was, now resting on the floor. She went into the hallway, which was pierced with soft light through holes between the skeletal roof timbers. There, in the first room to the left, sat Don Noriega. He was on the edge of a metal cot which had no mattress. Luisa stood in the doorway, unable to speak but trying to smile.

"Siéntate, niña,"[7] he said and patted the space next to him on the cot. He had been waiting for her, Luisa thought, and would play that strange instrument. Afterward she would kiss him just above his whiskery eyebrows, saying, or not saying, thank you. He would ask her how things had been with her, and she would say fine. She would be as friendly and bright as possible. Maybe she could cheer him and make him forget about the house.

Now she moved toward the cot and sat down. A quiet music came from the delicate box beside her on the cot. The sunlight filtered in, and the notes from the strings seemed to dance and slip and twine themselves around the pale white rays in short bursts of joy, in what Don Noriega, she thought, might have felt had he played. She sat for a long while listening to the music.

But there was another voice, a human one, calling her faintly. I have to go now, she whispered, sitting straight all of a sudden, her small amber eyes losing that vision of awe. For a moment she could not move. Something held her back, something weighed in her chest and throat, and Luisa began to cry. The blurred image before her placed the small box lightly in her open hands.

In the hallway Luisa groped toward the back porch. The

---

7. **Siéntate, niña** (syehn'tah-teh, nee'nyah): Sit down, girl.

smell of incense and spices was strong. The hot autumn wind blew through the house like a warm voice wiping dry her moist skin.

Sally was out front, hands on hips, calling Luisa. Luisa came from around back, stepping over the mess on the ground and holding a black piece of wood in her hands, two metal strings dangling.

"What's that?" Sally demanded impatiently.

Luisa seemed surprised. "What's what?"

"That thing, what you got in your hand."

"Oh this . . ." and she held it up for Sally to inspect. "A present."

"A what?"

"A present I picked up."

"Oh." Sally moved her eyes to the house. "Looks like his place burned down. What d'you find inside?"

"Just this," Luisa said, gazing blankly at the house.

"What d'you want that for?"

Luisa pulled a wire loose and after a pause seemed to speak to herself. "Nothing, I guess. It's no good anymore," and knelt down to place it on the ground, remembering that after all it was not her heart she was laying down, as Don Noriega might say. It was only a thing, a piece of charred wood.

"Come on!" Sally whined. "Place gives me the creeps."

For Study and Discussion

1. The two girls in the story, Luisa and Sally, often claim to be twins; yet, as Don Noriega is quick to point out, they are not. **a.** In what ways do the two girls differ? **b.** In your opinion, why does Luisa react differently to Don Noriega than Sally does?

2. As Luisa is leaving Don Noriega's home at the end of the story, she loses her "vision of awe," and Don Noriega becomes a "blurred image" when he hands her the music box she had been listening to. In light of the fact that the box turns out to be "a

piece of charred wood," do you think that Don Noriega was really there, or was he a phantom? Explain.

3. Luisa and Sally respond in markedly different ways to Don Noriega and his house. How do you think you would react in their place? Have you ever met a mysterious person like Don Noriega who was reputed to have magical powers, or have you ever been to a place like Don Noriega's house? If so, how did you feel at the time? Did your feelings change as time passed? How do you feel about the experience now?

Vocabulary

Analyzing Words in the Context of a Story

To fully understand a story and interpret it accurately, you need to know exactly how the author uses particular words and phrases in context. Consult a dictionary and the Glossary at the back of this book to help you answer the following questions about words that appear in "El Mago."

1. Don Noriega is said to have come from "an obscure town in northern Durango." **a.** What does *obscure* mean in this context? **b.** How does the word *obscure* help to reinforce the characterization of Don Noriega?

2. When the girls ask about the mummy they find, Don Noriega "gingerly" explains what a mummy is. **a.** What does *gingerly* mean in this context? **b.** Why does Don Noriega feel that he must explain "gingerly"?

3. When walking near Don Noriega's house, Sally "would invariably poke fun at 'that crazy old mago.' " **a.** What is the definition of *invariably*? **b.** What does the word *invariably* indicate about Sally's attitude toward Don Noriega?

4. Luisa is likened to a "waif standing in front of a ruined dream" as she prepares to enter Don Noriega's house toward the end of the story. **a.** What is a waif? **b.** What does the word *waif* suggest about how Luisa looked and felt as she viewed Don Noriega's destroyed house?

5. Don Noriega's voice is described as "filled with entreaty" when he calls to Luisa from inside the ruined house. **a.** What is an "entreaty"? **b.** How would Don Noriega's voice sound if it were "filled with entreaty"? **c.** Why would Don Noriega have a note of entreaty in his voice?

Sandra Cisneros

(1954–)

Sandra Cisneros (sahn'drah sees-neh'rohs) believes that writing has, in a sense, chosen her. As far back as her early childhood, she began to mentally chronicle and embellish the everyday events of her life and, in the process, began to create her unique narrative voice. A gifted poet, prose writer, and teacher, Cisneros impresses students and readers alike with the vitality, directness, and humor she brings to her work.

Born in Chicago to a Mexican father and Mexican American mother, Cisneros was the only girl among six brothers. As she discusses in her essay "Ghosts and Voices" (see page 356), her loneliness and her family's economic hardships led her to escape into the world of books— a world that seemed far more interesting to her than her own "dull" life. Drawing on the plots of children's stories, she wove an elaborate fantasy world in which she saw herself and her family as "the fairy-tale victims of an evil curse." She believed that someday the spell would "wear off," enabling them to live like the happy, well-off families she saw on television.

Ironically, Cisneros now writes powerful poems and stories about the circumstances that seemed so intolerable to her as a child. As a young writer, she discovered that her true "voice" emerged when she wrote about the subjects she knew best—her own colorful experiences growing up in the rougher sections of Chicago. She began to rebel against formal literary language and traditional themes, choosing, instead, to write about "third-floor flats, and fear of rats, and drunk husbands sending rocks through windows, anything as far from the poetic as possible." She also began to draw consciously on the rich possibilities of her bilingual upbringing, incorporating into her work elements of Spanish syntax and diction.

The encouragement of her family greatly influenced Cisneros's decision to pursue a writing career. After graduating from Loyola University with a degree in English, she attended the University of Iowa's Writers Workshop—a program that has graduated many well-known contemporary writers. While there, she completed the manuscript for *My Wicked Wicked Ways,* which was published in 1987.

Cisneros has taught both high school and college; for a time she directed the Latino Alternative High School of Chicago, a program for dropouts returning to school to finish their education. In addition, she taught students in grades two through twelve for the Arts-in-the-School Program sponsored by the Illinois Arts Council. She has lectured and given readings from her work at colleges and universities in the United States and Mexico and has won numerous fellowships, grants, and awards for her writing. Her publications include two books of poems and a book of short stories; she is currently working on two new books of fiction.

The first three selections on the following pages are taken from *The House on Mango Street,* a collection of stories published in 1983, and the fourth selection, "The Three Wise Guys: Un Cuento de Navidad / A Christmas Story," comes from an untitled collection of stories forthcoming from Random House Press.

(For additional biographical information about Sandra Cisneros, see pages 355 and 545.)

The House on Mango Street

from The House on Mango Street

Writers often develop stories through the use of description—writing that provides a sensory impression about the appearance of a person, an object, or a place. In this story, Sandra Cisneros describes several places from her childhood. Much of her descriptive imagery in the story provides visual impressions. What other senses—hearing, smell, taste, touch—do the images appeal to?

We didn't always live on Mango Street. Before that we lived on Loomis on the third floor, and before that we lived on Keeler. Before Keeler it was Paulina, and before that I can't remember. But what I remember most is moving a lot. Each time it seemed there'd be one more of us. By the time we got to Mango Street we were six—Mama, Papa, Carlos, Kiki, my sister Nenny and me.

The house on Mango Street is ours and we don't have to pay rent to anybody or share the yard with the people downstairs or be careful not to make too much noise and there isn't a landlord banging on the ceiling with a broom. But even so, it's not the house we'd thought we'd get.

We had to leave the flat on Loomis quick. The water pipes broke and the landlord wouldn't fix them because the house was too old. We had to leave fast. We were using the washroom next door and carrying water over in empty milk gallons. That's why Mama and Papa looked for a house, and that's why we moved into the house on Mango Street, far away, on the other side of town.

They always told us that one day we would move into a house, a real house that would be ours for always so we wouldn't have to move each year. And our house would have running water and pipes that worked. And inside it would have real stairs, not hallway stairs, but stairs inside like the houses on T.V. And we'd have a basement and at least three washrooms so when we took a bath we didn't have to tell everybody. Our house would be white with trees around it, a great big yard and grass growing without a fence. This was the house Papa talked about when he held a lottery ticket and this was the house Mama dreamed up in the stories she told us before we went to bed.

But the house on Mango Street is not the way they told it at all. It's small and red with tight little steps in front and windows so small you'd think they were holding their breath. Bricks are crumbling in places, and the front door is so swollen you have to push hard to get in. There is no front yard, only four little elms the city planted by the curb. Out back is a small garage for the car we don't own yet and a small yard that looks smaller between the two buildings on either side. There are stairs in our house, but they're ordinary hallway stairs, and the house has only one washroom, very small. Everybody has to share a bedroom—Mama and Papa, Carlos and Kiki, me and Nenny.

Once when we were living in Loomis, a nun from my school passed by and saw me playing out front. The laundromat downstairs had been boarded up because it had been robbed two days before and the owner had painted on the wood YES WE'RE OPEN so as not to lose business.

Where do you live? she asked.

There, I said pointing up to the third floor.

You live *there?*

There. I had to look to where she pointed—the third floor, the paint peeling, wooden bars Papa had nailed on the windows so we wouldn't fall out. You live *there?* The way she said it made me feel like nothing. *There.* I lived *there.* I nodded.

I knew then I had to have a house. A real house. One I could point to. But this isn't it. The house on Mango Street isn't it. For the time being, Mama said. Temporary, said Papa. But I know how those things go.

For Study and Discussion

1. The narrator describes an incident that took place on Loomis Street in which a nun from her school asked where she lived. How did the narrator react to the nun's surprise and implied disapproval of the narrator's home?

2. Repetition is one method writers use to emphasize key points in a story. In recounting the incident with the nun, the narrator repeats the word *there* several times. **a.** In what other way is *there* emphasized? **b.** What is the purpose of this emphasis?

3. As it is commonly used, the word *real* means "actual or existing in fact." **a.** In what sense does the narrator use the word *real*? **b.** Which house is more "real" to the narrator—the house she hopes to have or the house in which she lives?

Literary Elements

Description

Writers often use the description of physical objects to reveal a character's thoughts and feelings and to develop the theme of a story. To be successful, such descriptions must contain specific details that appeal to the reader's senses. In "The House on Mango Street," Sandra Cisneros gives descriptions that create clear pictures of two houses: the house the narrator's family dreams of and the house that they actually get. List the specific details the author uses to describe each house. How do these details reveal the differences between the "dream house" and the actual house? How do they indicate the narrator's reaction to these differences?

Creative Writing

Writing Description

Using the descriptive passages in "The House on Mango Street" as a model, write a description of the house you would like to live in. Although the details that you furnish will likely be quite different from those used by the narrator in the story, be sure to make them specific in order to paint a clear, vivid picture of your dream house.

Prewriting. To help in identifying and organizing your details, you may wish to pretend you are walking through your dream house. For example, imagine that you are standing at the front door. What does the outside of the house look like? Is the house made of wood, brick, or some other material? How big is the yard? What kind of windows does the house have? Now, open the front door and step inside. Are you in a hallway, a foyer, the living room? How big is the space or room? How high are the ceilings? Is the floor carpeted, tiled, or wooden?

Proceed through your dream house, asking yourself similar questions as you enter each room. You may also wish to give details about furniture, wall hangings, light fixtures, appliances, and anything else you would want in a house.

Writing and Revising. As you write and revise your description, be as specific as possible. Instead of saying "wood paneling," for example, give the particular kind of wood—such as pine, birch, or mahogany. Specifying the features of your dream house in this way will help your reader to visualize it more clearly and will make your description more interesting.

My Name

from The House on Mango Street

Your name is one of your most personal possessions. Yet, you probably had no say in choosing it. If you could choose, would you stick with the name you have, or would you, like the narrator in this story, pick a new one?

In English my name means hope. In Spanish it means too many letters. It means sadness, it means waiting. It is like the number nine. A muddy color. It is the Mexican records my father plays on Sunday mornings when he is shaving, songs like sobbing.

It was my great-grandmother's name and now it is mine. She was a horse woman too, born like me in the Chinese year of the horse—which is supposed to be bad luck if you're born female—but I think this is a Chinese lie because the Chinese, like the Mexicans, don't like their women strong.

My great-grandmother. I would've liked to have known her, a wild horse of a woman, so wild she wouldn't marry until my great-grandfather threw a sack over her head and carried her off. Just like that, as if she were a fancy chandelier. That's the way he did it.

And the story goes she never forgave him. She looked out the window all her life, the way so many women sit their sadness on an elbow. I wonder if she made the best with what she got or was she sorry because she couldn't be all the things she wanted to be. Esperanza. I have inherited her name, but I don't want to inherit her place by the window.

At school they say my name funny as if the syllables were made out of tin and hurt the roof of your mouth. But in Spanish my name is made out of a softer something like silver, not quite as thick as my sister's name Magdalena which is uglier than mine. Magdalena who at least can come home and become Nenny. But I am always Esperanza.

I would like to baptize myself under a new name, a name more like the real me, the one nobody sees. Esperanza as Lisandra or Maritza or Zeze the X. Yes. Something like Zeze the X will do.

Sandra Cisneros 325

For Study and Discussion

1. The name *Esperanza* means "hope" in English; however, it has many negative associations for the young girl in this story. What are some of these associations?

2. Although the narrator is dissatisfied with her name, she nevertheless takes a certain pride in it. **a.** What is the source of this pride? **b.** What aspects of her name and its origins might she wish to preserve?

3. The young narrator selects a new name, "Zeze the X," to replace "Esperanza." What does the new name represent to her?

4. The narrator's use of imagery expresses some of her feelings about being Hispanic and female. In this light, discuss the meaning of the following images in "My Name": "the way so many women sit their sadness on an elbow" and "as if the syllables were made out of tin and hurt the roof of your mouth."

Creative Writing

Writing an Essay About Your Name

Write an essay about your name. Like the narrator in the story, were you named after a relative? What does your name mean? Trace the linguistic origins, or roots, of your name. Would you choose a new name for yourself if you could? If so, what name would you choose, and why?

Prewriting. Before you begin writing, jot down your initial responses to the questions above. Most likely you will have to go to the library to consult books that list names and their meanings, such as *The Name Dictionary* and *The Dictionary of Given Names,* to find information about the origin of your name. Once you have located your information and have answered all the questions, you can then organize your outline. The length of your essay will depend upon the amount of information you gather, but you should have at least two paragraphs, one tracing the origin of your name and another discussing whether or not you would change your name.

Writing and Revising. Be sure that you connect your sentences and paragraphs with transitions that clearly state the relationships between your ideas and information. For example, if your feelings about your name are based on information about its origin, indicate this relationship with a connecting sentence or clause such as *"Because my name means 'joy,'* I have good feelings about it and would like to keep it."

Boys and Girls

from The House on Mango Street

Do you think it is possible for people to grow up in the same house and yet "live in separate worlds"? In this story the narrator focuses on the "separate worlds" in which she, her brothers, and her sister live. As you read "Boys and Girls," identify the differences that cause this separation. What things could the narrator share with a "best friend" that she cannot share with her brothers or sister?

The boys and the girls live in separate worlds. The boys in their universe and we in ours. My brothers, for example. They've got plenty to say to me and Nenny inside the house. But outside they can't be seen talking to girls. Carlos and Kiki are each other's best friend . . . not ours.

Nenny is too young to be my friend. She's just my sister and that was not my fault. You don't pick your sisters, you just get them and sometimes they come like Nenny.

She can't play with those Vargas kids or she'll turn out just like them. And since she comes right after me, she is my responsibility.

Some day I will have a best friend all my own. One I can tell my secrets to. One who will understand my jokes without my having to explain them. Until then I am a red balloon, a balloon tied to an anchor.

For Study and Discussion

1. Referring to her younger brothers, the narrator says that boys live "in their universe and we in ours." **a.** In what way do boys and girls "live in separate worlds"? **b.** Does this separation change with age?

2. The narrator says that Nenny is "too young to be my friend. She's just my sister" and therefore "my responsibility." **a.** How does the narrator's metaphor of "a red balloon tied to an anchor" express her feelings about this responsibility? **b.** Younger brothers and sisters obviously can learn much from older siblings. What can an older brother or sister learn from one who is younger? Discuss the pros and cons of having a younger brother or sister. What are the advantages and disadvantages?

Writing About Literature

Analyzing Autobiographical Detail in a Story

Sandra Cisneros has commented that she writes "about those ghosts inside that haunt" her. Her "ghosts" include the insistent memories of the often troubling and disappointing experiences of her childhood. Several of these "ghosts" appear in "The House on Mango Street," "My Name," and "Boys and Girls." Discuss in two or three paragraphs the reasons the narrator in these stories gives for her dissatisfaction with her childhood and the remedies she imagines will dispel her feelings of discontent. Be sure to use specific examples from the stories to support your answers.

Prewriting. As you reread the selections, ask yourself, What exactly makes the narrator feel dissatisfied? What does she propose to do to remedy her dissatisfaction? Devoting one sheet of paper to each selection, write answers to these questions, including specific quotations from the story. You can then pull information from each sheet to create your outline. You can group your ideas in one of several ways. For example, if you choose to organize your information in two paragraphs, you can devote the first paragraph to the reasons for the narrator's dissatisfaction and the second paragraph to her remedies for her discontent. Or, you may wish to organize your paper in three paragraphs, analyzing one story per paragraph.

Writing and Revising. When using specific quotations, be sure to identify the story from which you take each one. Also, check to ensure that each quotation is given verbatim as it appears in the story and is enclosed in quotation marks.

Three Wise Guys: Un Cuento de Navidad[1] / A Christmas Story

When a large, mysterious Christmas box arrives at the home of the González family, each family member daydreams about what it might contain. You may be as surprised as the González family is to discover what the gift turns out to be. See if you think that the gift givers were "wise" in their choice.

The big box came marked DO NOT OPEN TILL XMAS, but the mama said not until the Day of the Three Kings. Not until El Día de los Reyes,[2] the 6th of January, do you hear? That is what the mama said exactly, only she said it all in Spanish. Because in Mexico where she was raised it is the custom for boys and girls to receive their presents on January 6th, and not Christmas, even though they were living on the Texas side of the river now. Not until the 6th of January.

Yesterday the mama had risen in the dark same as always to reheat the coffee in a tin saucepan and warm the breakfast tortillas. The papa had gotten up coughing and spitting up the night, complaining how the evening before the buzzing of the *chicharras*[3] had kept him from sleeping. By the time the mama had the house smelling of oatmeal and cinnamon the papa would be gone to the fields, the sun already tangled in the trees and the *urracas*[4] screeching their rubber-screech cry. The boy Rubén and the girl Rosalinda would have to be shaken awake for school. The mama would give the baby Gilberto his bottle and then she would go back to sleep before getting up again to

---

1. **Un Cuento de Navidad** (oon kwehn'toh deh nah-bee-thath').
2. **El Día de los Reyes** (ehl dee'ah deh lohs reh'ehs).
3. *chicharras* (chee'chahr-rahs): cicadas, which are cricket-like insects.
4. *urracas* (oor-rah'kahs): magpies; birds having long, graduated tails and black-and-white plumage.

Sandra Cisneros 331

the chores that were always waiting. That is how the world had been.

But today the big box had arrived. When the boy Rubén and the girl Rosalinda came home from school, it was already sitting in the living room in front of the television set that no longer worked. Who had put it there? Where had it come from? A box covered with red paper with green Christmas trees and a card on top that said: *Merry Christmas to the González Family. Frank, Earl, and Dwight Travis. P.S. DO NOT OPEN TILL XMAS.* That's all.

Two times the mama was made to come into the living room, first to explain to the children and later to their father how the brothers Travis had arrived in the blue pickup and how it had taken all three of those big men to lift the box off the back of the truck and bring it inside and how she had had to nod and say thank-you thank-you thank-you over and over because those were the only words she knew in English. Then the brothers Travis had nodded as well the way they always did when they came and brought the boxes of clothes or the turkey each November or the canned ham on Easter ever since the children had begun to earn high grades at the school where Dwight Travis was the principal.

But this year the Christmas box was bigger than usual. What could be in a box so big? The boy Rubén and the girl Rosalinda begged all afternoon to be allowed to open it, and that is when the mama had said the sixth of January, the Day of the Three Kings. Not a day sooner.

It seemed the weeks stretched themselves wider and wider since the arrival of the big box. The mama got used to sweeping around it because it was too heavy for her to push in a corner, but since the television no longer worked ever since the afternoon the children had poured iced tea through the little grates in the back, it really didn't matter if it obstructed the view. Visitors that came inside the house were told and told again the story of how the box had arrived, and then each was made to guess what was inside.

It was the *comadre*[5] Elodia who suggested over coffee one afternoon that the big box held a portable washing machine that could be rolled away when not in use, the kind she had seen in

---

5. *comadre* (koh-mah'threh): woman friend; also refers to a child's godmother.

her Sears Roebuck catalogue. The mama said she hoped so because the wringer washer she had used for the last ten years had finally gotten tired and quit. These past few weeks she had had to boil all the clothes in the big pot she used for cooking the Christmas tamales. Yes. She hoped the big box was a portable washing machine. A washing machine, even a portable one, would be good.

But the neighborman Cayetano said, What foolishness, *comadre*. Can't you see the box is too small to hold a washing machine, even a portable one. Most likely God has heard your prayers and sent a new color t.v. With a good antenna you could catch all the Mexican soap operas, the neighborman said. You could distract yourself with the complicated troubles of the rich and then give thanks to God for the blessed simplicity of your poverty. A new t.v. would surely be the end to all your miseries.

Each night when the papa came home from the fields he would spread newspapers on the cot in the living room where the boy Rubén and the girl Rosalinda slept, and sit facing the big box in the center of the room. Each night he imagined the box held something different. The day before yesterday he guessed a new record player. Yesterday an ice chest filled with beer. Today the papa sat with his bottle of beer, fanning himself with a magazine and said in a voice as much a plea as a prophecy: air conditioner.

But the boy Rubén and the girl Rosalinda were sure the big box was filled with toys. They had even punctured a hole in one corner with a pencil when their mother was busy cooking, although they could see nothing inside but blackness.

Only the baby Gilberto remained uninterested in the contents of the big box and seemed each day more fascinated with the exterior of the box rather than the interior. One afternoon he tore off a fistful of paper which he was chewing when his mother swooped him up with one arm, rushed him to the kitchen sink, and forced him to swallow handfuls of lukewarm water in case the red dye of the wrapping paper might be poisonous.

When Christmas Eve finally came, the family González put on their good clothes and went to midnight mass. They came home to a house that smelled of tamales and atole,[6] and

---

6. **atole** (ah-toh'leh): hot corn cereal.

everyone was allowed to open one present before going to sleep, but the big box was to remain untouched until the 6th of January.

On New Year's Eve the little house was filled with people, some related, some not, coming in and out. The friends of the papa came with bottles, and the mama set out a bowl of grapes to count off the New Year. That night the children did not sleep in the living room cot as they usually did because the living room was crowded with big-fannied ladies and fat-stomached men sashaying to the accordion music of the Midget Twins from McAllen. Instead the children fell asleep on a lump of handbags and crumpled suit jackets on top of the mama and the papa's bed, dreaming of the contents of the big box.

Finally the 5th of January. And the boy Rubén and the girl Rosalinda could hardly sleep. All night they whispered last minute wishes. The boy thought perhaps if the big box held a bicycle, he would be the first to ride it since he was the oldest. This made his sister cry until the mama had to yell from her bedroom on the other side of the plastic curtains, Be quiet or I'm going to give you each the stick, which sounds worse in Spanish than it does in English. Then no one said anything. After a very long time, long after they heard the mama's wheezed breathing and their papa's piped snoring, the children closed their eyes and remembered nothing.

The papa was already in the bathroom coughing up the night before from his throat when the *urracas* began their clownish chirping. The boy Rubén awoke and shook his sister. The mama frying the potatoes and beans for breakfast nodded permission for the box to be opened.

With a kitchen knife the boy Rubén cut a careful edge along the top. The girl Rosalinda tore the Christmas wrapping with her fingernails. The papa and the mama lifted the cardboard flaps and everyone peered inside to see what it was the brothers Travis had brought them on the Day of the Three Kings.

There were layers of balled newspaper packed on top. When these had been cleared away the boy Rubén looked inside. The girl Rosalinda looked inside. The papa and the mama looked.

This is what they saw: the complete *Encyclopaedia Britannica Junior*, twenty-four volumes in red imitation leather with gold-embossed letters beginning with volume 1, Aar-Bel, and ending with volume 24, Yel-Zyn. The girl Rosalinda let out a sad cry as if her hair was going to be cut again. The boy Rubén pulled out volume 4, Ded-Fem. There were many pictures and many words, but there were more words than pictures. The papa flipped through volume 22, but because he could not read English words, simply put the book back and grunted, What can we do with this? No one said anything and shortly after, the screen door slammed.

Only the mama knew what to do with the contents of the big box. She withdrew volumes 6, 7, and 8, marched off to the dinette set in the kitchen, placed two on Rosalinda's chair so she could better reach the table, and put one underneath the plant stand that danced.

When the boy and the girl returned from school that day they found the books stacked into squat pillars against one living room wall and a board placed on top. On this were arranged several plastic doilies and framed family photographs. The rest of the volumes the baby Gilberto was playing with, and he was already rubbing his sore gums along the corners of volume 14.

The girl Rosalinda also grew interested in the books. She took out her colored pencils and painted blue on the lids of all the illustrations of women and with a red pencil dipped in spit she painted their lips and fingernails red-red. After a couple of days when all the pictures of women had been colored in this manner, she began to cut out some of the prettier pictures and paste them on looseleaf paper.

One volume suffered from being exposed to the rain when the papa improvised a hat during a sudden shower. He forgot it on the hood of the car when he drove off. When the children came home from school they set it on the porch to dry. But the pages puffed up and became so fat, the book was impossible to close.

Only the boy Rubén refused to touch the books. For several days he avoided the principal because he didn't know what to say in case Mr. Travis were to ask how they were enjoying the Christmas present.

On the Saturday after New Year's the mama and the papa went into town for groceries and left the boy in charge of watching his sister and baby brother. The girl Rosalinda was stacking books into spiral staircases and making her paper dolls descend them in a fancy manner.

Perhaps the boy Rubén would not have bothered to open the volume left on the kitchen table if he had not seen his mother wedge her name-day[7] corsage in its pages. On the page where the mama's carnation lay pressed between two pieces of kleenex was a picture of a dog in a space ship. FIRST DOG IN SPACE the caption said. The boy turned to another page and read where cashews came from. And then about the man who invented the guillotine. And then about Bengal tigers. And about clouds. All afternoon the boy read, even after the mama and the papa came home. Even after the sun set until the mama said time to sleep and put the light out.

In their bed on the other side of the plastic curtain the mama and the papa slept. Across from them in the crib slept the baby Gilberto. The girl Rosalinda slept on her end of the cot. But the boy Rubén watched the night sky turn from violet. To blue. To grey. And then from grey. To blue. To violet once again.

---

7. **name-day:** the church feast day of the saint after whom one is named.

For Study and Discussion

1. Many cultures have unique customs and traditions surrounding the celebration of Christmas. What forms of celebration described in the story reflect the family's cultural background?

2. Each family member has different hopes about what the mysterious box contains—hopes that reflect their particular needs and wants. Accordingly, each person puts the actual contents of the box to a different use. How do these varied uses reflect the personality and interests of each family member?

3. In contrast to the family's true needs and wants, the Travis brothers' choice of a gift seems sadly inappropriate. In light of the story's ending, do you think their choice was a "wise" one after all? Discuss.

4a. What imagery does the author use in the last paragraph of the story to suggest that Rubén is deeply affected, even changed, by what he has read in the books? Discuss. **b.** What do you think Rubén is thinking and feeling as he lies awake?

Writing About Literature

Analyzing Ambiguous Statements

A statement is considered *ambiguous* if it can readily be interpreted in more than one way. For example, if a friend enthusiastically asks for your opinion about a new shirt that you find rather unattractive, you may truthfully remark, "I've never seen anything like it." This comment is ambiguous: you express your true opinion, yet your friend can interpret your response as a compliment. Writers often employ deliberate ambiguity in their works to leave the meaning open to several different interpretations. The title "Three Wise Guys," for example, has several possible meanings. In a short essay, discuss possible interpretations of this title.

Prewriting. First, determine the different meanings the title suggests, based on the context of the story. How do the "three wise guys" of the title relate to the three wise men in the Biblical story? to the three Travis brothers? How does the informal expression "wise guys" contribute to the ambiguity of the title and of the story itself?

Writing. Be careful not to create unintentional ambiguities in your own writing: choose your words carefully to make sure that your meaning is clear.

Alberto Ríos

(1952–)

*The more I wrote, the more I realized
I had been writing almost all my life—I
simply had had no name for it.*

Alberto Ríos (ahl-behr'toh ree'ohs)
made this comment about his first
writing courses in college—classes he
had chosen simply because they seemed to be the "easiest" in the
catalog. Having grown up in a town where "people who wrote were
called names," Ríos had never considered himself a writer, least of all a
poet. He little suspected that those first poetry and fiction classes not
only would challenge and inspire him but also would uncover talents
he had possessed all along.

Nogales, Arizona, the town where Ríos grew up, sits directly on the
Mexican border: he could put "one foot in Mexico and one foot in the
United States, at the same time." Born to a Mexican father and an
English mother, Ríos stood between cultures in a larger sense as well—
a dimension of his experience that has deeply influenced his writing.

In addition to his short story collection, *The Iguana Killer,* Ríos has
published three books of poems. He has won several awards for both
his poetry and his fiction and recently has received a Guggenheim
Fellowship that will allow him to take time from his teaching career to
concentrate more fully on writing.

The story "The Iguana Killer," which appears on the following pages,
draws on his father's reminiscences about growing up in a small village
in Mexico—stories that Ríos had heard many times as a child but that
acquired new meaning for him when he began to view them through a
writer's eyes.

(For additional biographical information about Alberto Ríos, see
page 563.)

The Iguana Killer

In this story, a young boy, Sapito, uses his keen imagination to devise a practical use for a puzzling Christmas gift. With his new "iguana-killer," Sapito not only helps to feed his family but also impresses his friends and earns extra money. As you read the story, watch for other examples of Sapito's inventiveness in dealing with unfamiliar objects and novel situations.

Sapito had turned eight two weeks before and was, at this time, living in Villahermosa,[1] the capital city of Tabasco.[2] He had earned his nickname because his eyes bulged to make him look like a frog, and besides, he was the best fly-catcher in all Villahermosa. This was when he was five. Now he was eight, but his eyes still bulged and no one called him anything but "Sapito."

Among their many duties, all the boys had to go down to the Río Grijalva[3] every day and try to sell or trade off whatever homemade things were available and could be carried on these small men's backs. It was also the job of these boys to fish, capture snails, trick tortoises, and kill the iguanas.

Christmas had just passed, and it had been celebrated as usual, very religious with lots of candle smoke and very solemn church masses. There had been no festivities yet, no laughing, but today would be different. Today was the fifth of January, the day the children of Villahermosa wait for all year. Tomorrow would be the *Día de los Reyes Magos,*[4] the Day of the Wise Kings, when presents of all sorts were brought by the Kings and given to friends. Sapito's grandmother, who lived in Nogales[5] in the United States, had sent him two packages. He had seen them, wrapped in blue paper with bearded red clown faces. Sapito's grandmother always sent presents to his family, and she always

---

1. **Villahermosa** (bee-yah-ehr-moh'sah).
2. **Tabasco** (tah-bahs'koh): state of southeastern Mexico.
3. **Río Grijalva** (ree'oh gree-hahl'bah).
4. ***Día de los Reyes Magos*** (dee'ah deh lohs ray'ehs mah'gohs).
5. **Nogales** (noh-gahl'ehs): city in southern Arizona.

seemed to know just what Sapito would want, even though they had never met.

That night, Sapito's mother put the packages under the bed where he slept. It was not a cushioned bed, but rather, a hammock, made with soft rattan leaves. Huts in Villahermosa were not rented to visitors by the number of rooms, but, instead, by the number of hooks in each place. On these hooks were hung the hammocks of a family. People in this town were born and nursed, then slept and died in these hanging beds. Sapito could remember his grandfather, and how they found him one afternoon after lunch. They had eaten mangoes together. Sapito dreamed about him now, about how his face would turn colors when he told his stories, always too loud.

When Sapito woke up, he found the packages. He played up to his mother, the way she wanted, claiming that the *Reyes* had brought him all these gifts. *Look and look, and look here!* he shouted, but this was probably the last time he would do this, for Sapito was eight now, and he knew better, but did not tell. He opened the two packages from Nogales, finding a baseball and a baseball bat. Sapito held both gifts and smiled, though he wasn't clearly sure what the things were. Sapito had not been born in nor ever visited the United States, and he had no idea what baseball was. He was sure he recognized and admired the ball and knew what it was for. He could certainly use that. But he looked at the baseball bat and was puzzled for some seconds.

It was an iguana-killer. *"¡Mira, mamá! un palo para matar iguanas!"*[6] It was beautiful, a dream. It was perfect. His grandmother always knew what he would like.

In Villahermosa, the jungle was not far from where Sapito lived. It started, in fact, at the end of his backyard. It was not dense there, but one could not walk far before a machete became a third hand, sharper, harder, more valuable than the other two in this other world that sometimes kept people.

This strong jungle life was great fun for a boy like Sapito, who especially enjoyed bringing coconuts out of the tangled vines for his mother. He would look for monkeys in the fat palm trees and throw rocks at them, one after the other. To get back,

---

6. *¡Mira, mamá! un palo para matar iguanas!* (¡mee'rah, mah-mah'! oon pah'loh pah'rah mah-tahr' ee-gwah'nahs!): Look, mama! a stick to kill iguanas!

the monkeys would throw coconuts back at him, yelling terrible monkey-words. This was life before the iguana-killer.

Every day for a week after he had gotten the presents, Sapito would walk about half a mile east along the Río Grijalva with Chachi, his best friend. Then they would cut straight south into the hair of the jungle.

There is a correct way to hunt iguanas, and Sapito had been well-skilled even before the bat came. He and Chachi would look at all the trees until the tell-tale movement of an iguana was spotted. When one was found, Sapito would sit at the base of the tree, being as quiet as possible, with baseball bat held high and muscles stiff.

The female iguana would come out first. She moved her head around very quickly, almost jerking, in every direction. Sapito knew that she was not the one to kill. She kept the little iguanas in supply—his father had told him. After a few seconds, making sure everything was safe, she would return to the tree and send her husband out, telling him there was nothing to worry about.

The male iguana is always slower. He comes out and moves his head to one side and just stares, motionless, for several minutes. Now Sapito knew that he must take advantage, but very carefully. Iguanas can see in almost all directions at once. Unlike human eyes, both iguana eyes do not have to center in on the same thing. One eye can look forward, and one backward, like a clown, so that they can detect almost any movement. Sapito knew this and was always careful to check both eyes before striking. Squinting his own eyes which always puffed out even more when he was excited, he would not draw back his club. That would waste time. It was already kept high in the air all these minutes. When he was ready, he would send the bat straight down as hard and as fast as he could. Just like that. And if he had done all these things right, he would take his prize home by the tail to skin him for eating that night.

Iguanas were prepared like any other meat, fried, roasted, or boiled, and they tasted like tough chicken no matter which way they were done. In Tabasco, and especially in Villahermosa, iguanas were eaten by everybody all the time, even tourists, so hunting them was very popular. Iguana was an everyday supper, eaten without frowning at such a thing, eating lizard. It was not different from the other things eaten here, the turtle

Alberto Ríos 341

eggs, *cahuamas*,[7] crocodile meat, river snails. And when iguanas were killed, nobody was supposed to feel sad. Everybody's father said so. Sapito did, though, sometimes. Iguanas had puffed eyes like his.

But, if Sapito failed to kill one of these iguanas, he would run away as fast as he could—being sad was the last thing he would think of. Iguanas look mean, they have bloodshot eyes, and people say that they spit blood. Sapito and his friends thought that, since no one they knew had ever been hurt by these monsters, they must not be so bad. This was what the boys thought in town, talking on a summer afternoon, drinking coconuts. But when he missed, Sapito figured that the real reason no one had ever been hurt was that no one ever hung around afterward to find out what happens. Whether iguanas were really dangerous or not, nobody could say for certain. Nobody's parents had ever heard of an iguana hurting anyone, either. The boys went home one day and asked. So, no one worried, sort of, and iguanas were even tamed and kept as pets by the old sailors in Villahermosa, along with the snakes. But only by the sailors.

The thought of missing a hit no longer bothered Sapito, who now began carrying his baseball bat everywhere. His friends were impressed more by this than by anything else, even candy in tin boxes, especially when he began killing four and five iguanas a day. No one could be that good. Soon, not only Chachi, but the rest of the boys began following Sapito around constantly just to watch the scourge of the iguanas in action.

By now, the bat was proven. Sapito was the champion iguana-provider, always holding his now-famous killer-bat. All his friends would come to copy it. They would come every day asking for measurements and questioning him as to its design. Chachi and the rest would then go into the jungle and gather fat, straight roots. With borrowed knives and machetes, they tried to whittle out their own iguana-killers, but failed. Sapito's was machine made, and perfect.

This went on for about a week, when Sapito had an idea that was to serve him well for a long time. He began renting out the killer-bat for a *centavo*[8] a day. The boys said yes yes right away, and would go out and hunt at least two or three

---

7. *cahuamas* (kah-wah'mahs): giant sea turtles.
8. *centavo* (sehn-tah'boh): a cent.

iguanas to make it worth the price, but really, too, so that they could use the bat as much as possible.

For the next few months, the grown-ups of Villahermosa hated Sapito and his bat because all they ate was iguana. But Sapito was proud. No one would make fun of his bulging eyes now.

Sapito was in Nogales in the United States visiting his grandmother for the first time, before going back to Tabasco, and Villahermosa. His family had come from Chiapas on the other side of the republic on a relative-visiting vacation. It was still winter, but no one in Sapito's family had expected it to be cold. They knew about rain, and winter days, but it was always warm in the jungle, even for these things.

Sapito was sitting in front of the house on Sonoita Avenue, on the sidewalk. He was very impressed by many things in this town, especially the streetlights. Imagine lighting up the inside *and* the outside. It would be easy to catch animals at night here. But most of all, he was impressed by his rather large grandmother, whom he already loved very much. He had remembered to thank her for the iguana-killer and the ball. She had laughed and said, *"Por nada, hijo."*[9] As he sat and thought about this, he wrapped the two blankets he had brought outside with him tighter around his small body. Sapito could not understand or explain to himself that the weather was cold and that he had to feel it, everyone did, even him. This was almost an unknown experience to him since he had never been out of the tropics before. The sensation, the feeling of cold, then, was very strange, especially since he wasn't even wet. It was actually hurting him. His muscles felt as if he had held his bat up in the air for an hour waiting for an iguana. Of course, Sapito could have gone inside to get warm near the wood-burning stove, but he didn't like the smoke or the smell of the north. It was a different smell, not the jungle.

So Sapito sat there. Cold had never been important in his life before, and he wasn't going to let it start now. With blankets he could cover himself up and it would surely pass. Covered up for escape, he waited for warmness, pulling the blankets over his head. Sometimes he would put out his foot to see if it was okay yet, the way the lady iguana would come out first.

---

9. *Por nada, hijo* (pohr nah'thah, ee'hoh): You're welcome, son.

Then, right then in one fast second, Sapito seemed to feel, with his foot on the outside, a very quiet and strange moment, as if everything had slowed. He felt his eyes bulge when he scrunched up his face to hear better. Something scary caught hold of him, and he began to shiver harder. It was different from just being cold, which was scary enough. His heartbeat was pounding so much that he could feel it in his eyes.

He carefully moved one of the blankets from his face. Sapito saw the sky falling, just like the story his grandmother had told him the first day they had been there. He thought she was joking, or that she didn't realize he was already eight, and didn't believe in such things anymore.

Faster than hitting an iguana Sapito threw his blankets off, crying as he had not cried since he was five and they had nicknamed him and teased him. He ran to the kitchen and grabbed his mother's leg. Crying and shivering, he begged, "*¡Mamá, por favor, perdóneme!*"[10] He kept speaking fast, asking for forgiveness and promising never to do anything wrong in his life ever again. The sky was falling, but he had always prayed, really he had.

His mother looked at him and at first could not laugh. Quietly, she explained that it was *nieve,*[11] snow, that was falling, not the sky. She told him not to be afraid, and that he could go out and play in it, touch it, yes.

Sapito still didn't know exactly what this *nieve* was, but now his mother was laughing and didn't seem worried. In Villahermosa, *nieve* was a good word, it meant ice cream. There was a *nieve* man. Certainly the outside wasn't ice cream, but the white didn't really look bad, he thought, not really. It seemed, in fact, to have great possibilities. Sapito went back outside, sitting again with his blankets, trying to understand. He touched it, and breathed even faster. Then, closing his eyes, which was not easy, he put a little in his mouth.

Sapito's family had been back in Villahermosa for a week now. Today was Sunday. It was the custom here that every Sunday afternoon, since there were no other amusements, the

---

10. *¡Mamá, por favor, perdóneme!* (¡mah-mah', pohr fah-bohr', pehr-thohn'eh-meh!): Mama, please forgive me!
11. *nieve* (nyeh'beh).

band would play on the *malecón*,[12] an area something like a park by the river, where the boats were all loaded.

Each Sunday it was reserved for this band—that is, the group of citizens that joined together and called themselves a band. It was a favorite time for everyone, as the paddle boat lay resting on the river while its owner played the trumpet and sang loud songs. The instruments were all brass, except for the marimba, which was the only sad sounding instrument. Though it was hit with padded drumsticks, its song was quiet, hidden, always reserved for dusk. Sapito had thought about the marimba as his mother explained about snow. Her voice had its sound for the few minutes she spoke, and held him. Before the marimba, before dusk, however, the brass had full control.

As dusk came, it was time for the *verbenas*,[13] when the girls, young and old, would come in and walk around the park in one direction and the boys would walk the opposite way, all as the marimba played its songs easily, almost by itself. On these Sundays no one was a man or a woman. They were all boys and girls, even the women who always wore black. This was when all the flirting and the smiling of smiles bigger than people's faces took place. Sapito and Chachi and the rest of the smaller boys never paid attention to any of this, except sometimes to make fun of someone's older sister.

An old man, Don[14] Tomasito, the baker, played the tuba. When he blew into the huge mouthpiece, his face would turn purple and his thousand wrinkles would disappear as his skin filled out. Sapito and his friends would choose by throwing fingers, and whoever had the odd number thrown out, matching no one else, was chosen to do the best job of the day. This had become a custom all their own. The chosen one would walk around in front of Don Tomasito as he played, and cut a lemon. Then slowly, very slowly, squeeze it, letting the juice fall to the ground. Don Tomasito's lips would follow.

On this first Sunday afternoon after he had returned, Sapito, after being chased by Señor[15] Saturnino Cantón, who was normally the barber but on Sunday was the policeman,

---

12. *malecón* (mah-leh-kohn').
13. *verbenas* (ber-beh'nahs): festivals or carnivals.
14. **Don** (dohn): a title of respect, formerly used for Spanish-speaking men of high rank, now used as a title of courtesy.
15. **Señor** (seh-nyohr'): Mr.

pulled out his prize. Sapito had been preparing his friends all day, and now they were yelling to see this new surprise. This was no iguana-killer, but Sapito hoped it would have the same effect.

Some of the people in Villahermosa used to have photographs of various things. One picture Sapito had particularly remembered. Some ladies of the town, who always made their own clothes, once had a picture taken together. They were a group of maybe ten ladies, in very big dresses and hats, some sitting and some standing. What Sapito recalled now was that they were all barefoot. They were all very serious and probably didn't think of it, but now, Sapito, after traveling to the north and seeing many pictures at his grandmother's house, thought their bare feet were very funny, even if shoes were hard to get and couldn't be made like dresses could. Sapito knew about such things now. He remembered that people in Nogales laughed at him when he was barefoot in the snow.

But now, Sapito had a photograph, too. This was his surprise. Well, what it was, really, was a Christmas card picturing a house with lots of snow around. He had gotten the picture from his grandmother and had taken great care in bringing it back home. He kept the surprise under his shirt wrapped in blue paper against his stomach, so it would stay flat. Here was a picture of the *nieve*, just like he had seen for himself, except there was a lot more of it in the picture. An awful lot more.

At the end of this Sunday, making a big deal with his small hands, he showed this prize to his friends, and told them that *nieve*, which means both snow and ice cream in the Spanish of those who have experienced the two, would fall from the sky in Nogales. Any time at all. His bulging eyes widened to emphasize what he was saying, and he held his bat to be even more convincing.

No one believed him.

"Pues, miren, ¡aquí está!"[16] He showed them the picture, and added now that it was a picture of his grandmother's house where he had just visited.

When Chachi asked, as Sapito had hoped, if it came down

---

16. *Pues, miren, ¡aquí está!* (pwehs, meer'ehn, ¡ah-kee' ehs-tah'!): Well, look for yourselves, here it is!

in flavors, he decided that he had gone this far, so why not. *"Vainilla,"*[17] he stated.

As the months went by, so did new stories, and strawberry and pistachio, and he was pretty sure that they believed him. After all, none of them had ever been up north. They didn't know the things Sapito knew. And besides, he still owned the iguana-killer.

Three months after the snow-picture stories had worn off, Señora[18] Casimira, with the help of the town midwife, had a baby girl. The custom here was that mother and baby didn't have to do any work for forty days. No one ever complained. Mostly the little girls would help in the house, doing the errands that were not big enough to bother the boys or the big girls with. They'd throw water out front to quiet the dust. Neighbors would wash the clothes.

For the boys, usually because they could yell louder and didn't want to work with the girls, their job was to go and bring charcoal from the river, to bring bananas and coconuts, and whatever other food was needed. Every morning Sapito and his friends would stand outside the door of Señora Casimira's house, with luck before the girls came, and call in to her, asking if she needed anything. She would tell them yes or no, explaining what to bring if something was necessary.

Spring was here now, and today was Saturday. Sapito thought about this, being wise in the way of seasons now, as he looked down on the Casimira *choza,*[19] the palm-thatched hut in which they lived. Señora Casimira was sure to be there today, he figured. There was no need to hang around, probably. Sapito had saved a little money from renting the killer-bat, and he suggested to his friends that they all go to Puerto Alvarado[20] on the paddle boat. They were hitting him on the back and laughing yes! even before he had finished.

The Río Grijalva comes down from the Sierra Madre mountains, down through the state of Tabasco, through Villahermosa, emptying through Puerto Alvarado several miles north into the Gulf of Mexico. The boys looked over at the Casimira *choza,* then backward at this great river, where the paddle boat was getting

---

17. *Vainilla* (bai-nee'yah): vanilla.
18. **Señora** (seh-nyoh'rah): Mrs.
19. *choza* (choh'sah).
20. **Puerto Alvarado** (pwehr'toh ahl-bah-rah'thoh).

ready to make its first trip of the day to Puerto Alvarado. They ran after it, fast enough to leave behind their shadows.

Sapito and his friends had been in Alvarado for about an hour when they learned that a *cahuama*, a giant sea turtle, was near by. They were on the rough beach, walking toward the north where the rocks become huge. Some palm trees nodded just behind the beach, followed by the jungle, as always. Sometimes Sapito thought it followed him, always moving closer.

Climbing the mossy rocks, Chachi was the one who spotted the *cahuama*. This was strange because the turtles rarely came so close to shore. In Villahermosa, and Puerto Alvarado, the money situation was such that anything the boys saw, like iguanas or the *cahuama*, they tried to capture. They always tried hard to get something for nothing, and here was their chance— not to mention the adventure involved. They all ran together with the understood intention of dividing up the catch.

They borrowed a rope from the men who were working farther up the shore near the palm trees. "*¡Buena suerte!*"[21] one of the men called, and laughed. Sapito and Chachi jumped in a *cayuco,*[22] a kayak built more like a canoe, which one of the fishermen had left near shore. They paddled out to the floating turtle, jumped out, and managed to get a rope tied around its neck right off. Usually, then, a person had to hop onto the back of the *cahuama* and let it take him down into the water for a little while. Its burst of strength usually went away before the rider drowned or let go. This was the best fun for the boys, and a fairly rare chance, so Sapito, who was closest, jumped on to ride this one. He put up one arm like a tough cowboy. This *cahuama* went nowhere.

The two boys climbed back into the *cayuco* and tried to pull the turtle, but it still wouldn't budge. It had saved its strength, and its strong flippers were more than a match for the two boys now. Everyone on shore swam over to help them after realizing that yells of how to do it better were doing no good. They all grabbed a part of the rope. With pure strength against strength, the six boys sweated, but finally outpulled the stubborn *cahuama*, dragging it onto the shore. It began flopping around on the sand until they managed to tip it onto its back. The turtle seemed to realize that struggling was a waste of its last fat-man

---

21. *¡Buena suerte!* (¡bweh'nah swehr'teh!): good luck!
22. *cayuco* (kah-yoo'koh).

energy, and started moving like a slow motion robot, fighting as before but, now, on its back, the flippers and head moved like a movie going too slow.

The *cahuama* had seemed huge as the boys were pulling it, fighting so strong in the water, but it was only about three feet long when they finally took a breath and looked. Yet, they all agreed, this *cahuama* was very fat. It must have been a grandfather.

Chachi went to call one of the grown-ups to help. Each of the boys was sure that he could kill a *cahuama* and prepare it, but this was everybody's, and they wanted it cut right. The men were impressed as the boys explained. The boys were all nervous. Maybe not nervous—not really, just sometimes they were sad when they caught *cahuamas* because they had seen what happens. Like fish, or iguanas, but bigger, and bigger animals are different. Sad, but they couldn't tell anyone, especially not the other boys, or the men. Sapito looked at their catch.

These sailors, or men who used to be sailors, all carried short, heavy machetes, specially made for things taken from the sea. Chachi came back with a man who already had his in hand. The blade was straight because there was no way to shape metal, no anvil in Alvarado. The man looked at Sapito. "*Préstame tu palo,*"[23] he said, looking at Sapito's iguana-killer. Sapito picked it up from where he had left it and handed it to the man, carefully. The fisherman beat the turtle on the head three times fast until it was either dead or unconscious. Then he handed the bat back to Sapito, who was sort of proud, and sort of not.

The man cut the *cahuama's* head off. Some people eat the head and its juice, but Sapito and his friends had been taught not to. No one said anything and it was tossed to the ground. The flippers continued their robot motion.

He cut the side of the turtle, where the underside skin meets the shell. He then pulled a knife out of his pocket, and continued where the machete had first cut, separating the body of the turtle from the shell. As he was cutting he told the boys about the freshwater sac that *cahuamas* have, and how, if they were ever stranded at sea, they could drink it. They had heard the story a hundred times, but nobody knew anybody who really did it. The boys were impatient. Then he separated the

---

23. *Préstame tu palo* (prehs'tah-meh too pah'loh): Hand me your club.

underpart from the inside meat, the prize. It looked a little redder than beef. The fins were then cut off—someone would use their leather sometime later.

The man cut the meat into small pieces. The boys took these pieces and washed them in salt water to make the meat last longer. Before cooking them, they would have to be washed again, this time in fresh water to get all the salt off. In the meantime, the saltwater would keep the meat from spoiling. One time Sapito forgot, or really he was in too much of a hurry, and he took some *cahuama* home but forgot to tell his mother. It changed colors, and Sapito had to go get some more food, with everybody mad at him. The boys knew that each part of the *cahuama* was valuable, but all they were interested in now was what they could carry. This, of course, was the meat.

The man gave each of the boys some large pieces, and then kept most of it for himself. The boys were young, and could not argue with a grownup. They were used to this. The fisherman began to throw the shell away.

"No, por favor, dámelo,"[24] Sapito called to him. The man laughed and handed the shell to Sapito, who put his pieces of meat inside it and, with the rest of the boys, wandered back to the river to wait for the paddle boat. The shell was almost too big for him. The boys were all laughing and joking, proud of their accomplishment. They asked Sapito what he was going to do with the shell, but he said that he wasn't sure yet. This wasn't true. Of course, he was already making big, very big, plans for it.

They got back early in the afternoon, and everyone went home exhausted. Sapito, before going home, went into the jungle and gathered some green branches. He was not very tired yet—he had a new idea, so Sapito spent the rest of the afternoon polishing the shell with sand and the hairy part of some coconuts, which worked just like sandpaper.

When it was polished, he got four of the best branches and whittled them to perfection with his father's knife. Sapito tied these into a rectangle using some *mecate*,[25] something in between rope and string, which his mother had given him. The shell fit halfway down into the opening of the rectangle. It was

---

24. *No, por favor, dámelo* (noh, pohr fah-bohr', dah'meh-loh): No, please, give it to me.
25. *mecate* (meh-kah'teh).

perfect. Then, onto this frame, he tied two flat, curved branches across the bottom at opposite ends. It moved back and forth like a drunk man. He had made a good, strong crib. It worked, just right for a new-born baby girl.

Sapito had worked hard and fast with the strength of a guilty conscience. Señora Casimira just might have needed something, after all. It was certainly possible that her husband might have had to work today. All the boys had known these facts before they had left, but had looked only at the paddle boat—and it had waved back at them.

Sapito took the crib, hurrying to beat the jungle dusk. Dusk, at an exact moment, even on Sundays, owned the sky and the air in its own strange way. Just after sunset, for about half an hour, the sky blackened more than would be normal for the darkness of early night, and mosquitoes, like pieces of sand, would come up out of the thickest part of the jungle like tornadoes, coming down on the town to take what they could. People always spent this half hour indoors, Sundays, too, even with all the laughing, which stopped then. This was the signal for the marimba's music to take over.

Sapito reached the *choza* as the first buzzings were starting. He listened at the Casimira's door, hearing the baby cry like all babies. The cradle would help. He put it down in front of the wooden door without making any noise, and knocked. Then, as fast as he could, faster than that even, he ran back over the hill, out of sight. He did not turn around. Señora Casimira would find out who had made it. And he would be famous again, thought Sapito, famous like the other times. He felt for the iguana-killer that had been dragging behind him, tied to his belt, and put it over his right shoulder. His face was not strong enough to keep away the smile that pulled his mouth, his fat eyes all the while puffing out.

For Study and Discussion

1. Sapito and his friends have assigned "duties" that they perform to help their families, such as hunting, fishing, and selling or trading homemade goods. Young people in many cultures are expected to take on responsibilities for looking after younger siblings, doing chores around the house, and a wide variety of other tasks. How do Sapito's duties compare to those for which you and your friends are responsible? Explain.

2. Although he has never heard of baseball and is quite puzzled by his grandmother's gift, Sapito succeeds in putting his new bat to good use. **a.** What does this inventiveness indicate about Sapito? **b.** How is his life changed by the "iguana-killer"?

3. At several points in the story, Sapito identifies with the iguanas. Citing specific examples, discuss the empathy Sapito feels toward the iguanas: why does he identify himself with them, and what does this identification suggest about Sapito as a character?

4. Sapito is careful not to harm the female iguanas. What does this indicate about his relationship to his environment?

Literary Elements

Characterization

Writers often use action to develop **characterization**—that is, to reveal the personality of a character. In "The Iguana Killer," Alberto Ríos characterizes Sapito partly through description of his actions. For example, Sapito's reactions to the cold and snow when he visits his grandmother indicate that he is cautious yet resourceful when faced with the unknown. "Covered up for escape" from the strange sensation of cold, he hesitantly tests the air with one foot. Although panic-stricken at the sight of "the sky falling," he conquers his fear and later uses tales of his experience to impress his friends. This ability to deal with unfamiliar objects and experiences and to put them to practical use is an important element of Sapito's character.

In a short essay, compare Sapito's iguana killing with his role in the killing of the *cahuama*. What aspects of Sapito's character do these actions illustrate? How does Sapito's experience in killing the turtle reveal a development of his personality?

Writing About Literature

Analyzing a Symbol

A **symbol** is a person, thing, or event that has a literal meaning and also stands for something larger than itself. In "The Iguana Killer," Sapito's bat plays an important role both as an object and as a symbolic means for characterizing Sapito. Sapito's bat not only brings him much prestige but also represents the self-confidence he gains from his "champion iguana-provider" status. The bat lends Sapito a sense of identity and an air of authority that extend beyond the realm of iguana killing. His friends believe his tales of "ice cream" falling out of the sky up north because they have never seen snow, "and besides, he still owned the iguana-killer." The bat also represents Sapito's imagination and ingenuity: although "puzzled for some seconds" as to its purpose, he quickly invents a practical use for it that is more appropriate to his life in the jungle than its intended use would be.

Choose another symbol from "The Iguana Killer," and discuss its meaning in a short essay. Possible choices include: the iguanas themselves; Sapito's Christmas card; the giant sea turtle; the crib that Sapito makes from the turtle's shell.

Prewriting. After you choose a symbol, make sure that you understand the literal meaning of the object, person, or event. What is its literal significance in the story? Next, consider its symbolic meaning. What larger concept or theme might the symbol represent in the story? Have you encountered a similar symbol in other works or in your life experience? How does an analysis of this symbol increase your understanding of the story?

Writing. Your interpretation of a symbol will depend largely on your experience and on other reading you have done. Indicate that your interpretation of the symbol you have chosen is partly a subjective, or personal, reading of that symbol by using phrases such as *seems to, might represent, I think that,* and *in my opinion.*

Nonfiction of the
Contemporary Period

Like other literature of this period, contemporary Mexican American nonfiction reflects the artistic growth and heightened social awareness generated by the Chicano movement. Whereas the autobiographies and descriptive essays of the preceding period focused on surface features of Mexican American culture, many nonfiction works by contemporary writers delve deeper into social, artistic, and philosophical issues.

Through autobiographies, critical essays, and interviews, contemporary writers explore a broad range of themes such as personal identity, activism and social change, and creative voice. Sandra Cisneros, for example, writes about her experiences of growing up Mexican American as well as her adult perspectives on Mexican American culture and art. The richly detailed autobiographical works of Ernesto Galarza and Gary Soto also re-create childhood perceptions and events. Unlike the nostalgic narratives that marked the Mexican American Period, these works realistically portray the more painful aspects of the authors' early years, such as poverty, loneliness, and alienation.

Many of the nonfiction works of the Contemporary Period provide a meaningful context for understanding and interpreting Mexican American literature as a whole. As writers reflect on their experiences and on their own and others' works, they often shed light on the cultural and personal forces that shape Mexican Americans' lives and art.

Sandra Cisneros

(1954–)

Sandra Cisneros (sahn'drah sees-neh'rohs) says that while growing up, she had little opportunity to read or hear about people who, like herself, came from a working-class Mexican American background. As she comments in the essay on the following pages, she often wondered why her family was not like those she saw on television, whose homes were "all green lawns and white wood" and whose lives differed so greatly from hers.

As a Chicana writer concerned with women's issues, Cisneros has come to embrace her cultural background and to be particularly empathetic toward minority women whose experience mirrors her own. Like poet Gary Soto, she tries to speak both to and for the many working-class Mexican Americans whose lives would otherwise remain unknown to mainstream society. In presenting accurate, realistic images of Mexican American culture, she hopes to dispel limiting stereotypes and lend support and encouragement to her people.

Cisneros says that she particularly enjoys reading the works of minority and women writers. She finds that these writers not only address powerful, relevant themes but also speak directly to her personal experience.

Although mainly a poet and short story writer, Cisneros has also published a number of nonfiction pieces, including articles, interviews, and book reviews. In the following selection, "Ghosts and Voices," she discusses how her personal background has influenced her writing.

(For additional biographical information about Sandra Cisneros, see pages 319 and 545.)

Ghosts and Voices: Writing from Obsession

Writers draw inspiration from many different sources. The "ghosts" and "voices" of this essay's title refer to the often painful childhood experiences that "haunt" the author's memory. As you read, consider how the author's "obsession" with her past figures into her writing. How have these experiences helped to form her creative voice?

I like to think one of the circumstances that led me to my writing is the fact I was born an only daughter in a family of six sons—two older, four younger. There was a sister, born next in sequence after me, but she died when she and I were both so young I hardly remember her, except as an image in a few blurred photographs.

The six brothers soon paired themselves off. The oldest with the second-oldest, the brother beneath me with the one beneath him and the youngest two were twins, genetically as well as socially bound. These three sets of men had their own conspiracies and allegiances, leaving me odd-woman-out forever.

My parents would be hard-pressed to recall my childhood as lonely, crowded as the nine of us were in cramped apartments where there were children sleeping on the living room couch and fold-out Lazy Boy, and on beds set up in the middle room, where the only place with any privacy was the bathroom. A second or third-floor flat, but invariably the top floor because "noise travelled down," or so we naively believed, convinced us it was wiser to be the producer of noise rather than its victim.

To make matters worse, we were constantly moving back and forth between Chicago and Mexico City due to my father's compulsive "home-sickness." Every couple of years we would have to pack all our things, store the furniture I don't know where, pile into the station wagon, and head south to Mexico. It was usually a stay of a few months, always at the

356 *Sandra Cisneros*

grandparents' house on La Fortuna, número 12. That famous house, the only constant in the series of traumatic upheavals we experienced as children, and, no doubt for a stubborn period of time, my father's only legitimate "home" as well.

In retrospect, my solitary childhood proved important. Had my sister lived or had we stayed in one neighborhood long enough for a friendship to be established, I might not have needed to bury myself in books the way I did. I remember, I especially liked reading about "the olden times" because the past seemed more interesting than my dull present.

But in school we were also required to take books out of our class library. Since our school was poor, so were the choices. As a result I read a lot of books I might not have read otherwise; the lives of saints, or very stodgy editions of children's stories published in the 1890s—usually didactic, Horatio Alger-type tales which I enjoyed all the same because of the curious English.

About this time I began hearing a voice in my head, a narrator—just like the ones in the books,—chronicling the ordinary events that made up my life: "I want you to go to the store and get me a loaf of bread and a gallon of milk. Bring back all the change and don't let them gyp you like they did last time." In my head my narrator would add: . . . *she said in a voice that was neither reproachful nor tender. Thus clutching the coins in her pocket, our hero was off under a sky so blue and a wind so sweet she wondered it didn't make her dizzy.* This is how I glamorized my days living in the third-floor flats and shabby neighborhoods where the best friend I was always waiting for never materialized.

One of the most important books in my childhood (and still a favorite now) was Virginia Lee Burton's *The Little House,* a picture book that tells the story of a house on a country hill whose owner promises never to sell her "for gold or silver" and predicts his great, great grandchildren will live in her.

Stable and secure in the country, the little house is happy witnessing the changes of seasons and generations, although curious about the distant lights of the big city. The sun and changing moons across the top of the page as well as the alterations in the landscape and dress fashion, make us aware time is passing. Finally, the city that has been growing ever larger, catches up with the little house, until she finds she is no longer in the country but eventually surrounded by tall buildings and

Sandra Cisneros 357

noisy traffic. The inhabitants move away, and the little house, no longer able to see the stars at night, grows sad; her roof sags and the doorstep droops; the windows that serve as eyes, one on either side of the door, are broken. Fortunately, the great-granddaughter of the man who built the house rescues her in one of the best moments in the book. Traffic is halted on the busy boulevard for the little house to be wheeled away to the country and settled on a hill just like the one it originally sat on, happy and once again loved.

Wasn't *The Little House,* the house I dreamed of, a house where one family lived and grew old and didn't move away? One house, one spot. I read and reread that book, sometimes taking the book out of the library seven times in a row. Once my brother and I even schemed to keep it. If we lied and told the librarian we'd lost it, we would simply be fined the price of the book, and then it would be ours forever without the anxiety of the rubber-stamped due date. That was the plan, a good one, but never executed—good, guilty Catholics that we were. (I didn't know books could be legitimately purchased somewhere until years later. For a long time I believed they were so valuable as to only be dispensed to institutions and libraries, the only place I'd seen them.)

The Little House was my own dream. And I was to dream myself over again in several books, to re-invent my world according to my own vision. I dreamed our family as the fairy-tale victims of an evil curse, the cause of our temporary hard times. "Just for a spell," we were told, and in my head my narrator interpreted, "Just a spell."

"Don't play with those kids," my mama and papa warned. "Don't hang around with that kind. We didn't raise you to talk like that. That's how *gente baja*[1] behave. Low class." As if it didn't have anything to do with us.

I dreamed myself the sister in the "Six Swans" fairy tale. She too was an only daughter in a family of six sons. The brothers had been changed into swans by an evil spell only the sister could break. Was it no coincidence my family name translated "keeper of swans?" I dreamed myself Andersen's "Ugly Duckling." Ridiculous, ugly, perenially the new kids. But one

---

1. *gente baja* (hen'teh bah'hah): low-class people.

day the spell would wear off. I kept telling myself. "Temporary."

There were other books that spoke to me. Hugh Lofting's *Doctor Doolittle* series. Imagine being able to talk to animals. Didn't it seem as if they were the only ones who understood you anyway. And *The Island of the Blue Dolphins*, the survival story of a lonely girl who inhabits a one-citizen island. *Hittie: Her First 100 Years*, a century account of a wooden doll who is whisked through different homes and owners but perseveres. And *Alice and Wonderland & Through the Looking Glass* for the wonderful way of transforming the everyday into the fantastic.

As a young writer in college I was aware I had to find my voice, but how was I to know it would be the voice I used at home, the one I acquired as a result of one English-speaking mother and one Spanish-speaking father. My mother's English was learned in the Mexican/Italian neighborhood she grew up in on Chicago's near south side, an English learned from playmates and school, since her own parents spoke Spanish exclusively. My father, on the other hand, spoke to us in a Spanish of grandmothers and children, a language embroidered with the diminutive. To give you an example:

> *My mother:* "Good lucky I raised you kids right so you wouldn't hang around with the punks and floozies on the corner and wind up no good to nobody."

> *My father:* (translated more or less from the Spanish): "Eat a little bit more, my heaven, before leaving the table and fill your tum-tum up good."

These two voices at odds with each other—my mother's punch-you-in-the-nose English and my father's powdered-sugar Spanish—curiously are the voices that surface in my writing. What I'm specially aware of lately is how the Spanish syntax and word choice occurs in my work even though I write in English.

It's ironic I had to leave home to discover the voice I had all along, but isn't that how it always goes. As a poor person growing up in a society where the class norm was superimposed on a t.v. screen, I couldn't understand why our home wasn't all green lawn and white wood like the ones in "Leave It To Beaver" or "Father Knows Best." Poverty then became the ghost and in an attempt to escape the ghost, I rejected what was at hand and

Sandra Cisneros 359

emulated the voices of the poets I admired in books: big, male voices like James Wright and Richard Hugo and Theodore Roethke, all wrong for me.

It wasn't until Iowa and the Writers Workshop that I began writing in the voice I now write in, and, perhaps if it hadn't been for Iowa I wouldn't have made the conscious decision to write this way. It seems crazy, but until Iowa I had never felt my home, family, and neighborhood unique or worthy of writing about. I took for granted the homes around me, the women sitting at their windows, the strange speech of my neighbors, the extraordinary lives of my family and relatives which was nothing like the family in "Father Knows Best." I only knew that for the first time in my life I felt "other." What could I write about that my classmates, cultivated in the finest schools in the country like hot house orchids, could not? My second-rate imitations of mainstream voices wouldn't do. And imitating my classmates wouldn't work either. That was their voice, not mine. What could I write about that they couldn't? What did I know that they didn't?

During a seminar titled "On Memory and the Imagination" when the class was heatedly discussing Gustav Bachelard's *Poetics of Space* and the metaphor of a house—*a house, a house,* it hit me. What did I know except third-floor flats. Surely my classmates knew nothing about that. That's precisely what I chose to write: about third-floor flats, and fear of rats and drunk husbands sending rocks through windows, anything as far from the poetic as possible. And this is when I discovered the voice I'd been suppressing all along without realizing it.

Recently, talking with fellow writer and friend Norma Alarcón, we agreed there's no luxury or leisure in our lives for us to write of landscapes and sunsets and tulips in a vase. Instead of writing by inspiration, it seems we write by obsession, of that which is most violently tugging at our psyche.

If I were asked what it is I write about, I would have to say I write about those ghosts inside that haunt me, that will not let me sleep, of that which even memory does not like to mention. Sometimes it seems I am writing the same story, the same poem, over and over. I found it curious that Cherríe Moraga's new book is titled *Giving up the Ghost.* Aren't we constantly attempting to give up the ghost, to put it to sleep once and for all each time we pick up the pen.

Perhaps later there will be time to write by inspiration. In the meantime, in my writing as well as in that of other Chicanas and other women, there is the necessary phase of dealing with those ghosts and voices most urgently haunting us, day by day.

Lecture, Indiana University—11/11/86

For Study and Discussion

1. In "Ghosts and Voices," Cisneros uses the metaphor of "ghosts" in several different contexts. Referring to specific passages in the essay, discuss the ways in which her family's poverty and her difficult childhood have become "ghosts" to her, as well as the author's suggestion that we are all, to some extent, "haunted" by our pasts.

2. The author says that she initially turned to literature as an escape from her "solitary childhood." **a.** In what way did she begin to incorporate the "ghosts" of her childhood experiences into her own writing? **b.** How have the author's unique personal experiences and her Mexican American heritage influenced the development of her "voice" as a writer?

3. Sandra Cisneros claims that she writes not so much by "inspiration" as by "obsession." **a.** What does she mean by this, and how does this sense of being "driven" toward certain subjects relate to the "ghosts and voices" of her past? **b.** Although the word usually has negative connotations, the author uses "obsession" in a mostly positive sense. Have you ever felt compelled to write down your feelings about a significant experience you have had? How did you feel when you were writing, and how did you feel afterward?

Creative Writing

Experimenting with Voice

The **voice** in a work of literature is the language style adopted by the author to create the effect of a particular speaker. Although a writer's voice is often shaped by his or her subject matter, it is also—as Sandra Cisneros indicates in "Ghosts and Voices"—a unique aspect of the writer's personal style.

Write a poem or a short piece of fiction that reflects either your personal writing voice or the voice of a writer you admire.

Prewriting. If you are unsure of your personal voice, use the following suggestions to discover the writing voice you find most comfortable. First, think about the language and syntax of your everyday speech. Do you change your voice to suit different situations? If you keep a journal, what kind of voice do you use when you write in it? Choosing a subject with which you are comfortable may also help you to find your voice as a writer.

If you are imitating a specific writer's voice, examine several works by that author and make a list of any striking characteristics you discover. For example, a list of the elements that make up Cisneros's writing voice would likely include:

1. informal diction;
2. imaginative imagery drawn from her personal experience;
3. hypenated compound adjectives, many she coins herself.

Writing and Revising. Your **diction,** or choice of words, should reflect the voice you intend to adopt. For example, formal, elevated diction would probably be inappropriate for a description of your first fishing trip. If you have chosen a writing voice and a subject that are familiar to you, your diction will probably naturally adapt to your topic. If you are imitating the voice of another writer, you many need to refer frequently to your list of characteristics to determine the appropriate word choices.

Ernesto Galarza
(1905–1984)

In his varied roles as a labor leader, educator, community activist, and writer, Ernesto Galarza (ehr-nehs'toh gah-lahr'sah) devoted most of his life to helping working people, especially those of Hispanic background. He was born in Mexico and at the age of six immigrated with his family to the United States. Finding that Mexican workers were a source of inexpensive labor, the railroad and farming industries eagerly welcomed newly arriving immigrants. This raised false hopes for families like Galarza's who fled revolution-torn Mexico in search of a more peaceful and prosperous life.

The Galarza family settled on the edge of a barrio in Sacramento, California, where young Ernesto quickly adapted to American culture. He learned English, attended local schools, and often acted as an interpreter for local Spanish-speaking Mexicans. When Galarza's mother and uncle died of influenza, he worked in migrant camps and at other sundry jobs to support himself. His memories of the harsh and dehumanizing conditions in labor camps remained with him for the rest of his life.

Despite having to work hard to support his family, Galarza finished high school and received a scholarship to Occidental College in Los Angeles. While studying Latin American history there, he published his first scholarly work at the age of twenty-three. Galarza went on to earn a graduate degree from Stanford University and then enrolled at Columbia University, where he received a Ph.D.

After completing his doctoral degree, Galarza worked in the fields of education, labor, and Latin American studies before moving to Washington, D.C., to join the Pan American Union (PAU) in 1936. He worked with the PAU for eleven years and then moved to San Jose,

California, to take a position with the newly founded National Farm Labor Union (NFLU). Serving as research director and, later, as secretary-treasurer and vice president, Galarza remained with the NFLU for the next twelve years.

During his years of union work, Galarza engrossed himself in the problems of the agricultural worker. He wrote numerous reports documenting the unjust treatment of farm workers, held many leadership positions in unions, led several strikes, and campaigned against government officials who sought to pass discriminatory right-to-work laws. When, after many years of intense effort, Galarza succeeded in helping to end a program that condoned the industry-wide abuse of farm laborers, he withdrew from the NFLU to devote more time to reading and writing.

Galarza wrote steadily throughout the 1960s and 1970s, publishing several books based on his extensive research into the struggles of the farm worker. He also played an active role in the development of Spanish-language teaching materials and bilingual education programs. In addition to his scholarly publications, Galarza wrote a collection of children's stories and his autobiographical work *Barrio Boy*. The following selection is an excerpt from *Barrio Boy* in which Galarza recalls his and his family's struggles to survive in the working-class environment of the barrio.

On the Edge
of the Barrio[1]

from Barrio Boy

*Life can be hard "on the edge of the barrio," as Ernesto
Galarza reveals in this autobiographical narrative of his
youth. Yet, despite the tragedy and hardships that beset
him, he kept alive his hopes and dreams for a better life
and later made them come true. As you read, consider the
events the author describes. How do you think you would
react in such circumstances?*

To make room for a growing family it was decided that we
should move, and a house was found in Oak Park, on the far
side of town where the open country began. The men raised
the first installment for the bungalow on Seventh Avenue even
after Mrs. Dodson explained that if we did not keep up the
monthly payments we would lose the deposit as well as the
house.

The real estate broker brought the sale contract to the
apartment one evening. Myself included, we sat around the
table in the living room, the gringo[2] explaining at great length
the small print of the document in a torrent of words none of
us could make out. Now and then he would pause and throw
in the only word he knew in Spanish: "Sabee?"[3] The men
nodded slightly as if they had understood. Doña[4] Henriqueta

---

1. **Barrio** (bahr'ryoh): one of the districts into which a large town or city is divided.
2. **gringo** (green'goh): a foreigner who speaks English, especially a person from the United States.
3. **Sabee?** (sah'bee?): You know?
4. **Doña** (doh'nyah): formal title of respect used before first names of women.

was holding firmly to the purse which contained the down payment, watching the broker's face, not listening to his words. She had only one question. Turning to me she said: "Ask him how long it will take to pay all of it." I translated, shocked by the answer: "Twenty years." There was a long pause around the table, broken by my stepfather: "What do you say?" Around the table the heads nodded agreement. The broker passed his fountain pen to him. He signed the contract and after him Gustavo and José. Doña Henriqueta opened the purse and counted out the greenbacks. The broker pocketed the money, gave us a copy of the document, and left.

The last thing I did when we moved out of 418 L was to dig a hole in the corner of the backyard for a tall carton of Quaker Oats cereal, full to the brim with the marbles I had won playing for keeps around the *barrio*. I tamped the earth over my buried treasure and laid a curse on whoever removed it without my permission.

Our new bungalow had five rooms, and porches front and back. In the way of furniture, what friends did not lend or Mrs. Dodson gave us we bought in the secondhand shops. The only new item was an elegant gas range, with a high oven and long, slender legs finished in enamel. Like the house, we would be paying for it in installments.

It was a sunny, airy spot, with a family orchard to one side and a vacant lot on the other. Back of us there was a pasture. With chicken wire we fenced the back yard, turned over the soil, and planted our first vegetable garden and fruit trees. José and I built a palatial rabbit hutch of laths and two-by-fours he gathered day by day on the waterfront. A single row of geraniums and carnations separated the vegetable garden from the house. From the vacant lots and pastures around us my mother gathered herbs and weeds which she dried and boiled the way she had in the pueblo.[5] A thick green fluid she distilled from the mallow that grew wild around us was bottled and used as a hair lotion. On every side our windows looked out on family orchards, platinum stretches of wild oats and quiet lanes, shady and unpaved.

We could not have moved to a neighborhood less like the *barrio*. All the families around us were Americans. The grumpy

5. **pueblo** (pweh'bloh): town, village.

retired farmer next door viewed us with alarm and never gave us the time of day, but the Harrisons across the street were cordial. Mr. Harrison loaned us his tools, and Roy, just my age but twice my weight, teamed up with me at once for an exchange of visits to his mother's kitchen and ours. I astounded him with my Mexican rice, and Mrs. Harrison baked my first waffle. Roy and I also found a common bond in the matter of sisters. He had an older one and by now I had two younger ones. It was a question between us whether they were worse as little nuisances or as big bosses. The answer didn't make much difference but it was a relief to have another man to talk with.

Some Sundays we walked to Joyland, an amusement park where my mother sat on a bench to watch the children play on the lawn and I begged as many rides as I could on the roller coaster, which we called in elegant Spanish "the Russian Mountain." José liked best the free vaudeville because of the chorus girls who danced out from the stage on a platform and kicked their heels over his head.

Since Roy had a bicycle and could get away from his sister by pedaling off on long journeys I persuaded my family to match my savings for a used one. Together we pushed beyond the boundaries of Oak Park miles out, nearly to Perkins and the Slough House. It was open country, where we could lean our wheels against a fence post and walk endlessly through carpets of golden poppies and blue lupin. With a bike I was able to sign on as a carrier of the *Sacramento Bee,* learning in due course the art of slapping folded newspapers against people's porches instead of into the bushes or on their roofs. Roy and I also became assistants to a neighbor who operated a bakery in his basement, taking our pay partly in dimes and partly in broken cookies for our families.

For the three men of the household as well as for me the bicycle became the most important means for earning a living. Oak Park was miles away from the usual places where they worked and they pedaled off, in good weather and bad, in the early morning. It was a case of saving carfare.

I transferred to the Bret Harte School, a gingerbread two-story building in which there was a notable absence of Japanese, Filipinos, Koreans, Italians, and the other nationalities of the Lincoln School. It was at Bret Harte that I learned how an English sentence could be cut up on the blackboard and the pieces placed on different lines connected by what the teacher called a diagram. The idea of operating on a sentence and re-arranging its members as a skeleton of verbs, modifiers, subject, and prepositions set me off diagraming whatever I read, in Spanish and English. Spiderwebs, my mother called them, when I tried to teach her the art.

My bilingual library had grown with some copies of old magazines from Mexico, a used speller Gustavo had bought for me in Stockton, and the novels my mother discarded when she had read them. Blackstone was still the anchor of my collection and I now had a paperback dictionary called *El Inglés sin Maestro*.[6] By this time there was no problem of translating or interpreting for the family I could not tackle with confidence.

It was Gustavo, in fact, who began to give my books a vague significance. He pointed out to me that with diagrams and dictionaries I could have a choice of becoming a lawyer or a doctor or an engineer or a professor. These, he said, were far better careers than growing up to be a *camello*,[7] as he and José always would be. *Camellos*, I knew well enough, was what the *chicanos*[8] called themselves as the worker on every job who did the dirtiest work. And to give our home the professional touch he felt I should be acquiring, he had a telephone installed.

It came to the rest of us as a surprise. The company man arrived one day with our name and address on a card, a metal tool box and a stand-up telephone wound with a cord. It was connected and set on the counter between the dining room and the parlor. There the black marvel sat until we were gathered for dinner that evening. It was clearly explained by Gustavo that the instrument was to provide me with a quick means of reaching the important people I knew at the Y.M.C.A., the boy's band, or the various public offices where I interpreted for *chicanos* in distress. Sooner or later some of our friends in the *barrio* would also have telephones and we could talk with them.

"Call somebody," my mother urged me.

With the whole family watching I tried to think of some

---

6. *El Inglés sin Maestro* (ehl een-glehs' seen mah-ehs'troh): *English Without a Teacher.*
7. *camello* (kah-meh'yoh): camel.
8. *chicanos* (chee-kah'nohs): Mexican Americans.

important person I could ring for a professional conversation. A name wouldn't come. I felt miserable and hardly like a budding engineer or lawyer or doctor or professor.

Gustavo understood my predicament and let me stew in it a moment. Then he said: "Mrs. Dodson." My pride saved by this ingenious suggestion, I thumbed through the directory, lifted the earpiece from the hook, and calmly asked central for the number. My sisters, one sitting on the floor and the other in my mother's arms, never looked less significant; but they, too, had their turn saying hello to the patient Señora[9] Dodson on the other end of the line.

Every member of the family, in his own way, missed the *barrio*. José and Gustavo could no longer join the talk of the poolrooms and the street corners by walking two blocks down the street. The sign language and simple words my mother had devised to communicate with the Americans at 418 L didn't work with the housewives on 7th Avenue. The families we had known were now too far away to exchange visits. We knew no one in Oak Park who spoke Spanish. Our street was always quiet and often lonely with little to watch from our front porch other than boys riding bicycles or Mrs. Harrison hanging out her wash. Pork Chops and the Salvation Army never played there.

I, too, knew that things were different. There was no corner where I could sell the *Union* and my income from running errands and doing chores around the rooming house stopped. There were no alleys I could comb for beer bottles or docks where I could gather saleable or edible things. The closest to Big Singh I could find was a runty soothsayer in Joyland who sat on a rug with a feather in his turban and told your fortune.

We now had an infant boy in the family who with my two sisters made four of us. The baby was himself no inconvenience to me, but it meant that I had to mind the girls more, mostly chasing them home from the neighbors. If I had been the eldest girl in the family I would have stepped into my mother's place and taken over the management of all but the youngest. But being a boy, the female chores seemed outrageous and un-Mexican. Doña Henriqueta tried telling me that I was now the *jefe de familia*[10] of all the juniors. But she was a gentle mother

---

9. Señora (seh-nyoh'rah): Mrs.
10. *jefe de familia* (heh'feh deh fah-mee'lyah): head of the family.

and the freedom of the house, the yard, and my personal property that she gave the two girls did nothing to make them understand that I was their *jefe*. When Nora, the oldest of the two,
demolished my concertina with a hammer (no doubt to see
where the notes came from) I asked for permission to strangle
her. Permission was denied.

During the first year we lived at Oak Park we began to
floor and partition the basement. Some day, we knew, the
López's would come through and we would have a temporary
home ready for them. With three-and-a-half men in the house
earning wages, if work was steady, we were keeping up with
the installments and saving for the reunion.

An epidemic erased the quiet life on 7th Avenue and the
hopes we had brought with us.

I had been reading to the family stories in the *Bee* of the
Spanish influenza. At first it was far off, like the war, in places
such as New York and Texas. Then the stories told of people
dying in California towns we knew, and finally the *Bee* began
reporting the spread of the "flu" in our city.

One Sunday morning we saw Gustavo coming down the
street with a suitcase in his hand, walking slowly. I ran out to
meet him. By the front gate, he dropped the suitcase, leaned on
the fence, and fainted. He had been working as a sandhog on
the American River, and had come home weak from fever.

Gustavo was put to bed in one of the front rooms. José set
out to look for a doctor, who came the next day, weary and
nearly sick himself. He ordered Gustavo to the hospital. Three
days later I answered the telephone call from the hospital telling
us he was dead. Only José went to Gustavo's funeral. The rest
of us, except my stepfather, were sick in bed with the fever.

In the dining room, near the windows where the sunlight
would warm her, my mother lay on a cot, a kerosene stove at
her feet. The day Gustavo died she was delirious. José bicycled
all over the city, looking for oranges, which the doctor said were
the best medicine we could give her. I sweated out the fever,
nursed by José, who brought me glasses of steaming lemonade
and told me my mother was getting better. The children were
quarantined in another room, lightly touched by the fever, more
restless than sick.

Late one afternoon José came into my room, wrapped me
in blankets, pulled a cap over my ears, and carried me to my

mother's bedside. My stepfather was holding a hand mirror to her lips. It didn't fog. She had stopped breathing. In the next room my sister was singing to the other children, "A birdie with a yellow bill/hopped upon my windowsill/cocked a shiny eye and said/Shame on you you sleepy head."

The day we buried Doña Henriqueta, Mrs. Dodson took the oldest sister home with her. The younger children were sent to a neighbor. That night José went to the *barrio*, got drunk, borrowed a pistol, and was arrested for shooting up Second Street.

We did not find out what had happened until I bicycled the next morning to Mrs. Dodson to report that José had not come home. By this time our friends in the *barrio* knew of José's arrest and a telephone call to a bartender who knew us supplied the details. Nothing serious, Mrs. Dodson repeated to me. Nobody had been hurt. She left me in charge of my sister and went to bail out my uncle.

They returned together. Gently, Mrs. Dodson scolded José, who sat dejectedly, his eyes closed so he would not have to look her in the eye, cracking the joint of his fingers, chewing on his tight lips, a young man compressing years of hard times and the grief of the past days in a show of manhood.

When the lecture was nearly over, Mrs. Dodson was not talking of drunkenness and gunplay, but of the future, mostly of mine, and of José's responsibility for it. She walked with us down the front stairway. Pushing my bicycle I followed him on foot the miles back to Oak Park, keeping my distance, for I knew he did not want me to see his face. As he had often told me, "Men never cry, no matter what."

A month later I made a bundle of the family keepsakes my stepfather allowed me to have, including the butterfly sarape, my books, and some family pictures. With the bundle tied to the bars of my bicycle, I pedaled to the basement room José had rented for the two of us on O Street near the corner of Fifth, on the edge of the *barrio*.

José was now working the riverboats and, in the slack season, following the round of odd jobs about the city. In our basement room, with a kitchen closet, bathroom, and laundry tub on the back porch and a woodshed for storage, I kept house. We bought two cots, one for me and the other for José when he was home.

Ernesto Galarza 371

Our landlords lived upstairs, a middle-aged brother and sister who worked and rented rooms. As part payment on our rent I kept the yard trim. They were friends of Doña Tránsito, the grandmother of a Mexican family that lived in a weather-beaten cottage on the corner. Doña Tránsito was in her sixties, round as a barrel, and she wore her gray hair in braids and smoked hand-rolled cigarettes on her rickety front porch. To her tiny parlor *chicanos* in trouble came for advice, and the firm old lady with the rasping voice and commanding ways often asked me to interpret or translate for them in their encounters with the *Autoridades*.[11] Since her services were free, so were mine. I soon became a regular visitor and made friends with her son, Kid Felix, a prizefighter who gave free boxing lessons to the boys in the neighborhood.

Living only three houses from Doña Tránsito, saying my *saludos*[12] to her every time I passed the corner, noticing how even the Kid was afraid to break her personal code of *barrio* manners, I lived inside a circle of security when José was away. On her front porch, summer evenings, the old Mexican dame talked about people such as I had known in the pueblo and asked how I was doing in school and where I was working.

It was Doña Tránsito who called in the *curandera*[13] once when the child of a neighbor was dying. I had brought a doctor to the house and was in the sick room when he told the family there was nothing more he could do. Doña Tránsito ordered me at once to fetch the old crone who lived on the other side of the railroad tracks towards the river and who practiced as a healer.

With Doña Tránsito I watched the ritual from a corner of the sick room. The healer laid on a side table an assortment of bundled weeds, small glass jars, candles, and paper bags tied with strings. On the floor next to her she placed a canvas satchel. A bowl and some cups were brought to her from the kitchen. She crumpled stems of herbs into one of the cups and mixed them with oil from one of her jars. She hooked her finger into another jar and pulled out a dab of lard which she worked into a powder in another cup to make a dark paste. Two candles were lighted and placed at the head of the bed. The electric light

---

11. *Autoridades* (ow-toh-ree-thah'thehs): authorities; public officials.
12. *saludos* (sah-loo'thohs): salutations, greetings.
13. *curandera* (koo-rahn-deh'rah): someone who practices the art of medicine without a medical license.

was turned off. She opened the satchel and took out a framed picture of the Virgin of Guadalupe, which was hung on the wall over the sick child's head. The window blind pulled down.

The little girl was uncovered. She lay naked, pale and thin on the sheet, her arms straight down her sides. Around her the healer arranged a border of cactus leaves, which she took out of her satchel one by one, cutting them open around the edge. She warmed the cup with the powdered herbs and rubbed the concoction on the soles of the child's bare feet. With the paste, which she also warmed over the candle, the healer made a cross on the forehead of the patient and another on her chest. A blanket was then laid over her, leaving only the head uncovered.

The healer knelt before the picture of the Virgin and began to pray. The parents of the child, some relatives who were there, Doña Tránsito and I formed a circle around the room, on our knees.

We had been praying a long while when the healer arose and bent over the bed, looking intently at the wasted face. To nobody in particular she said the child was not sweating. She wrapped her black shawl around her head and shoulders, left the room, and closed the street door quietly behind her. In the morning the child died.

Through Doña Tránsito I met other characters of the *barrio*. One of them was Don[14] Crescencio, stooped and bony, who often stopped to chat with my neighbor. He told us stories of how he had found buried treasure with two twigs cut from a weeping willow, and how he could locate an underground spring in the same way, holding the twigs just so, feeling his way on bare feet over the ground, watching until the twigs, by themselves, crossed and dipped. There were the Ortegas, who raised vegetables on a sandlot they had bought by the levee, and explained to Doña Tránsito, who knew a great deal about such matters herself, what vegetables did better when planted according to different shapes of the moon. The Kid gave us lectures and exhibitions explaining jabs and left hooks and how he planned to become the world's Mexican champion. In our basement José gathered his friends to listen to songs of love, revenge, and valor, warmed with beer and tequila.

When troubles made it necessary for the *barrio* people to

---

14. **Don** (dohn): a title of respect, formerly used for Spanish-speaking men of high rank, now used as a title of courtesy.

deal with the Americans uptown, the *Autoridades,* I went with them to the police court, the industrial accident office, the county hospital, the draft board, the county clerk. We got lost together in the rigamarole of functionaries who sat, like *patrones,*[15] behind desks and who demanded licenses, certificates, documents, affidavits, signatures, and witnesses. And we celebrated our successes, as when the worker for whom I interpreted in interviews that lasted many months, was awarded a thousand dollars for a disabled arm. Don Crescencio congratulated me, saying that in Mexico for a thousand American dollars you could buy the lives of many peons.

José had chosen our new home in the basement on O Street because it was close to the Hearkness Junior High School, to which I transferred from Bret Harte. As the *jefe de familia* he explained that I could help earn our living but that I was to study for a high school diploma. That being settled, my routine was clearly divided into schooltime and worktime, the second depending on when I was free from the first.

Few Mexicans of my age from the *barrio* were enrolled at the junior high school when I went there. At least, there were no other Mexican boys or girls in Mr. Everett's class in civics, or Miss Crowley's English composition, or Mrs. Stevenson's course. Mrs. Stevenson assigned me to read to the class and to recite poems by Amado Nervo, because the poet was from Tepic and I was, too. Miss Crowley accepted my compositions about Jalcocotán and the buried treasure of Acaponeta while the others in the class were writing about Sir Patrick Spence and the Beautiful Lady without Mercy, whom they had never met. For Mr. Everett's class, the last of the day, I clipped pieces from the *Sacramento Bee* about important events in Sacramento. From him I learned to use the ring binder in which I kept clippings to prepare oral reports. Occasionally he kept me after school to talk. He sat on his desk, one leg dangling over a corner, behind him the frame of a large window and the arching elms of the school yard, telling me he thought I could easily make the debating team at the high school next year, that Stanford University might be the place to go after graduation, and making other by-the-way comments that began to shape themselves into my future.

---

15. *patrones* (pah-troh'nehs): masters or bosses.

Afternoons, Saturdays, and summers allowed me many hours of worktime I did not need for study. José explained how things now stood. There were two funerals to pay for. More urgently than ever, Doña Esther and her family must be brought to live with us. He would pay the rent and buy the food. My clothes, books and school expenses would be up to me.

On my vacations, and when he was not on the riverboats, he found me a job as water boy on a track gang. We chopped wood together near Woodland and stacked empty lug boxes in a cannery yard. Cleaning vacant houses and chopping weeds were jobs we could do as a team when better ones were not to be had. As the apprentice, I learned from him how to brace myself for a heavy lift, to lock my knee under a loaded hand-truck, to dance rather than lift a ladder and to find the weakest grain in a log. Like him I spit into my palms to get the feel of the axe handle and grunted as the blade bit into the wood. Imitating him I circled a tree several times, sizing it up, *tante-ando*,[16] as he said, before pruning or felling it.

Part of one summer my uncle worked on the river while I hired out a farmhand on a small ranch south of Sacramento. My senior on the place was Roy, a husky Oklahoman who was part-time taxi driver and full-time drinker of hard whiskey. He was heavy-chested, heavy-lipped and jowly, a grumbler rather than a talker and a man of great ingenuity with tools and automobile engines. Under him I learned to drive the Fordson tractor on the place, man the gasoline pump, feed the calves, check an irrigation ditch, make lug boxes for grapes and many other tasks on a small farm. Roy used Bull Durham tobacco which he rolled into the same droopy cigarettes that Doña Eduvijes smoked in Jalco and Doña Tránsito on her front porch.

Roy and I sat under the willow tree in front of the ranch house after work, I on the grass, he on a creaky wicker chair, a hulking, sour man glad for the company of a boy. He counseled me on how to avoid the indulgences he was so fond of, beginning his sentences with a phrase he repeated over and over, "as the feller says." "Don't aim to tell you your business," he explained, "but, as the feller says, get yourself a good woman, don't be no farmhand for a livin', be a lawyer or a doctor, and don't get to drinkin' nohow. And there's another thing, Ernie.

---

16. *tanteando* (tahn-teh-ahn'doh): examining with care.

If nobody won't listen to you, go on and talk to yourself and hear what a smart man has to say."

And Roy knew how to handle boys, which he showed in an episode that could have cost me my life or my self-confidence. He had taught me to drive the tractor, walking along side during the lessons as I maneuvered it, shifting gears, stopping and starting, turning and backing, raising a cloud of dust wherever we went. Between drives Roy told me about the different working parts of the machine, giving me instructions on oiling and greasing and filling the radiator. "She needs to be took care of, Ernie," he admonished me, "like a horse. And another thing, she's like to buck. She can turn clear over on you if you let 'er. If she starts to lift from the front even a mite, you turn her off. You hear?"

"Yes, sir," I said, meaning to keep his confidence in me as a good tractor man.

It was a few days after my first solo drive that it happened. I was rounding a telephone pole on the slightly sloping bank of the irrigation ditch. I swung around too fast for one of the rear tracks to keep its footing. It spun and the front began to lift. Forgetting Roy's emphatic instructions I gunned the engine, trying to right us to the level ground above the ditch. The tractor's nose kept climbing in front of me. We slipped against the pole, the tractor, bucking, as Roy said it would.

Roy's warning broke through to me in my panic, and I reached up to turn off the ignition. My bronco's engine sputtered out and it settled on the ground with a thump.

I sat for a moment in my sweat. Roy was coming down the ditch in a hurry. He walked up to me and with a quick look saw that neither I nor the tractor was damaged.

"Git off" he said.

I did, feeling that I was about to be demoted, stripped of my rank, bawled out, and fired.

Roy mounted the machine, started it, and worked it off the slope to flat ground. Leaving the engine running, he said: "Git on."

I did.

"Now finish the discing," he said. Above the clatter of the machine, he said: "Like I said, she can buck. If she does, cut 'er. You hear?" And he waved me off to my work.

Except for food and a place to live, with which José

provided me, I was on my own. Between farm jobs I worked in town, adding to my experience as well as to my income. As a clerk in a drug store on Second and J, in the heart of the lower part of town, I waited on *chicanos* who spoke no English and who came in search of remedies with no prescription other than a recital of their pains. I dispensed capsules, pills, liniments, and emulsions as instructed by the pharmacist, who glanced at our customers from the back of the shop and diagnosed their ills as I translated them. When I went on my shift, I placed a card in the window that said "Se habla Español."[17] So far as my *chicano* patients were concerned it might as well have said "Dr. Ernesto Galarza."

From drugs I moved to office supplies and stationery sundries, working as delivery boy for Wahl's, several blocks uptown from skid row. Between deliveries I had no time to idle. I helped the stock clerk, took inventory, polished desks, and hopped when a clerk bawled an order down the basement steps. Mr. Wahl, our boss, a stocky man with a slight paunch, strutted a little as he constantly checked on the smallest details of his establishment, including myself. He was always pleasant and courteous, a man in whose footsteps I might possibly walk into the business world of Sacramento.

But like my uncles, I was looking for a better *chanza*,[18] which I thought I found with Western Union, as a messenger, where I could earn tips as well as wages. Since I knew the lower part of town thoroughly, whenever the telegrams were addressed to that quarter the dispatcher gave them to me. Deliveries to the suites on the second floor of saloons paid especially well, with tips of a quarter from the ladies who worked there. My most generous customer was tall and beautiful Miss Irene, who always asked how I was doing in school. It was she who gave me an English dictionary, the first I ever possessed, a black bound volume with remarkable little scallops on the pages that made it easy to find words. Half smiling, half commanding, Miss Irene said to me more than once: "Don't you stop school without letting me know." I meant to take her advice as earnestly as I took her twenty-five cent tip.

It was in the lower town also that I nearly became a performing artist. My instructor on the violin had stopped giving

---

17. **Se habla Español** (seh ah-blah ehs-pah-nyohl'): Spanish is spoken here.
18. *chanza* (chahn'sah): chance.

me lessons after we moved to Oak Park. When we were back on O Street he sent word through José that I could work as second fiddler on Saturday nights in the dancehall where he played with a mariachi.[19] Besides, I could resume my lessons with him. A dollar a night for two hours as a substitute was the best wages I had ever made. Coached by my teacher, I second-fiddled for sporting *chicanos* who swung their ladies on the dance floor and sang to our music. Unfortunately I mentioned my new calling to Miss Crowley when I proposed it to her as a subject for a composition. She kept me after school and per-suaded me to give it up, on the ground that I could earn more decorating Christmas cards during the vacation than at the dancehall. She gave me the first order for fifty cards and got subscriptions for me from the other teachers. I spent my Christmas vacation as an illustrator, with enough money saved to quit playing in the saloon.

It was during the summer vacation that school did not interfere with making a living, the time of the year when I went with other *barrio* people to the ranches to look for work. Still too young to shape up with the day-haul gangs, I loitered on skid row, picking up conversation and reading the chalk signs about work that was being offered. For a few days of picking fruit or pulling hops I bicycled to Folsom, Lodi, Woodland, Freeport, Walnut Grove, Marysville, Slough House, Florin, and places that had no name. Looking for work, I pedaled through a countryside blocked off, mile after mile, into orchards, vineyards, and vegetable farms. Along the ditchbanks, where the grass, the morning glory, and the wild oats made a soft mattress I unrolled my bundle and slept.

In the labor camps I shared the summertime of the lives of the *barrio* people. They gathered from barrios of far-away places like Imperial Valley, Los Angeles, Phoenix, and San Antonio. Each family traveling on its own, they came in trucks piled with household goods or packed in their secondhand *fotingos* and *chevees*.[20] The trucks and cars were ancient models, fresh out of a used-car lot, with license tags of many states. It was into these jalopies that much of the care and a good part of the family's earnings went. In camp they were constantly being fixed, so

---

19. **mariachi** (mah-ryah'chee): Mexican street band.
20. *fotingos* . . . *chevees* (foh-teen'gohs . . . cheh'vees): Fords . . . Chevies.

378 *Ernesto Galarza*

close to scrap that when we needed a part for repairs, we first went to the nearest junkyard.

It was a world different in so many ways from the lower part of Sacramento and the residences surrounded by trim lawns and cool canopies of elms to which I had delivered packages for Wahl's. Our main street was usually an irrigation ditch, the water supply for cooking, drinking, laundering, and bathing. In the better camps there was a faucet or a hydrant, from which water was carried in buckets, pails and washtubs. If the camp belonged to a contractor, and it was used from year to year, there were permanent buildings—a shack for his office, the privies, weatherworn and sagging, and a few cabins made of secondhand lumber, patched and unpainted.

If the farmer provided housing himself, it was in tents pitched on the bare baked earth or on the rough ground of newly plowed land on the edge of a field. Those who arrived late for the work season camped under trees or raised lean-to's along a creek, roofing their trucks with canvas to make bedrooms. Such camps were always well away from the house of the ranchero,[21] screened from the main road by an orchard or a grove of eucalyptus. I helped to pitch and take down such camps, on some spot that seemed lonely when we arrived, desolate when we left.

If they could help it, the workers with families avoided the more permanent camps, where the seasonal hired hands from skid row were more likely to be found. I lived a few days in such a camp and found out why families avoided them. On Saturday nights when the crews had a week's wages in their pockets, strangers appeared, men and women, carrying suitcases with liquor and other contraband. The police were called by the contractor only when the carousing threatened to break into fighting. Otherwise, the weekly bouts were a part of the regular business of the camp.

Like all the others, I often went to work without knowing how much I was going to be paid. I was never hired by a rancher, but by a contractor or a straw boss who picked up crews in town and handled the payroll. The important questions that were in my mind—the wages per hour or per lug box, whether the beds would have mattresses and blankets, the price of meals,

---

21. **ranchero** (rahn-cheh'roh): landowner.

how often we would be paid—were never discussed, much less answered, beforehand. Once we were in camp, owing the employer for the ride to the job, having no means to get back to town except by walking and no money for the next meal, arguments over working conditions were settled in favor of the boss. I learned firsthand the chiseling techniques of the contractors and their pushers—how they knocked off two or three lugs of grapes from the daily record for each member of the crew, or the way they had of turning the face of the scales away from you when you weighed your work in.

There was never any doubt about the contractor and his power over us. He could fire a man and his family on the spot and make them wait days for their wages. A man could be forced to quit by assigning him regularly to the thinnest pickings in the field. The worst thing one could do was to ask for fresh water on the job, regardless of the heat of the day; instead of iced water, given freely, the crews were expected to buy sodas at twice the price in town, sold by the contractor himself. He usually had a pistol—to protect the payroll, so it was said. Through the ranchers for whom he worked, we were certain that he had connections with the *Autoridades*, for they never showed up in camp to settle wage disputes or listen to our complaints or to go for a doctor when one was needed. Lord of a rag-tag labor camp of Mexicans, the contractor, a Mexican himself, knew that few men would let their anger blow, even when he stung them with curses.

As a single worker, I usually ate with some household, paying for my board. I did more work than a child but less than a man, neither the head nor the tail of a family. Unless the camp was a large one I became acquainted with most of the families. Those who could not write asked me to chalk their payroll numbers on the boxes they picked. I counted matches for a man who transferred them from the right pocket of his pants to the left as he tallied the lugs he filled throughout the day. It was his only check on the record the contractor kept of his work. As we worked the rows or the tree blocks during the day, or talked in the evenings where the men gathered in small groups to smoke and rest, I heard about *barrios* I had never seen but that must have been much like ours in Sacramento.

The only way to complain or protest was to leave, but now and then a camp would stand instead of run, and for a few hours or a few days work would slow down or stop. I saw it happen in a pear orchard in Yolo when pay rates were cut without notice to the crew. The contractor said the market for pears had dropped and the rancher could not afford to pay more. The fruit stayed on the trees, while we, a committee drafted by the camp, argued with the contractor first and then with the rancher. The talks gave them time to round up other pickers. A carload of police in plain clothes drove into the camp. We were lined up for our pay, taking whatever the contractor said was on his books. That afternoon we were ordered off the ranch.

In a camp near Folsom, during hop picking, it was not wages but death that pulled the people together. Several children in the camp were sick with diarrhea; one had been taken to the hospital in town and the word came back that he had died. It was the women who guessed that the cause of the epidemic was the water. For cooking and drinking and washing it came from a ditch that went by the ranch stables upstream.

I was appointed by a camp committee to go to Sacramento to find some *Autoridad* who would send an inspector. Pedaling my bicycle, mulling over where to go and what to say, I remembered some clippings from the *Sacramento Bee* that Mr. Everett had discussed in class, and I decided the man to look for was Mr. Simon Lubin, who was in some way a state *Autoridad*.

He received me in his office at Weinstock and Lubin's. He sat, square-shouldered and natty, behind a desk with a glass top. He was half-bald, with a strong nose and a dimple in the center of his chin. To his right was a box with small levers into which Mr. Lubin talked and out of which came voices.

He heard me out, asked me questions and made notes on a pad. He promised that an inspector would come to the camp. I thanked him and thought the business of my visit was over; but Mr. Lubin did not break the handshake until he had said to tell the people in the camp to organize. Only by organizing, he told me, will they ever have decent places to live.

I reported the interview with Mr. Lubin to the camp. The part about the inspector they understood and it was voted not to go back to work until he came. The part about organizing was received in silence and I knew they understood it as little as I did. Remembering Durán in that camp meeting, I made my first organizing speech.

The inspector came and a water tank pulled by mules was parked by the irrigation ditch. At the same time the contractor began to fire some of the pickers. I was one of them. I finished that summer nailing boxes on a grape ranch near Florin.

When my job ended I pedaled back to Sacramento, detouring over country lanes I knew well. Here and there I walked the bicycle over dirt roads rutted by wagons. The pastures were sunburned and the grain fields had been cut to stubble. Riding by a thicket of reeds where an irrigation ditch swamped I stopped and looked at the red-winged blackbirds riding gracefully on the tips of the canes. Now and then they streaked out of the green clump, spraying the pale sky with crimson dots in all directions.

Crossing the Y Street levee by Southside Park I rode through the *barrio* to Doña Tránsito's, leaving my bike hooked on the picket fence by the handle bar.

I knocked on the screen door that always hung tired, like the sagging porch coming unnailed. No one was at home.

It was two hours before time to cook supper. From the stoop I looked up and down the cross streets. The *barrio* seemed empty.

I unhooked the bicycle, mounted it, and headed for the main high school, twenty blocks away where I would be going in a week. Pumping slowly, I wondered about the debating team and the other things Mr. Everett had mentioned.

For Study and Discussion

1. Throughout the trials and tragedies that his family faced, Galarza played an important role in several respects. **a.** In what ways did he help his family during times of crisis? **b.** In light of Galarza's later achievements as described in the biographical sketch about him on page 363, what do you think he gained from these experiences?

2. Even when relating what must have been some of the most sorrowful and momentous events in his life, such as the death of his mother, Galarza maintains an objective tone throughout his narrative. What does the author's tone suggest about his perspective on life?

3. While Galarza gives detailed descriptions of life "on the edge of the barrio," he does not make many evaluative statements about it. What words and phrases would you use to characterize the circumstances and environment of Galarza's life after he and José moved to O Street?

4. You have probably heard or read stories like Galarza's in which the main character and his or her family were beset with troubles and yet endured. What is your reaction to such stories? Do they seem idealized and unrealistic? Do you find them inspirational and true to life?

Writing About Literature

Analyzing Theme in a Narrative

Often, the main aim of a nonfiction narrative is simply to present an interesting, accurate account of a specific course of events. However, many narratives also have a **theme**—a general idea or insight that the author wishes to express. Frequently, as in Galarza's autobiographical narrative, this main idea is not stated directly and must be inferred from the work. Write a short essay three or four paragraphs long explaining what you think is the theme underlying "On the Edge of the Barrio."

Prewriting. Skim through "On the Edge of the Barrio" two, three, or more times to get an overall impression of Galarza's purpose in writing his narrative. What underlying idea ties together or runs through the events and details he presents? What specific information in Galarza's account leads you to recognize this central, unifying idea? State your interpretation of the theme in a single sentence. Then find quotations and specific information in the narrative to support your interpretation, and organize these

Ernesto Galarza 383

references in a logical order to create an outline that you can follow in writing your paper.

Writing and Revising. Make sure that you clearly indicate to your reader how the supporting information you give is logically related to your ideas. To get some distance from your paper so that you can see it as much as possible from a reader's perspective, set it aside for a day or two before going back over it and making your final revisions.

Mary Helen Ponce

(1938–)

Mary Helen Ponce (pohn'seh) says that
as a child she was "always writing,
either on paper or in the dirt." She
learned to write not from teachers or
textbooks but from constant reading.
The more she read, the more she came to realize that everyday events
were worth writing about—that the stories that made up her own life
were, in their own way, "history." To this day, Ponce feels that books
are her "best friends" because they allow her to explore new places and
ideas and inspire her to express her own creative talents.

Born in Pacoima, California, into a large Mexican American family,
Ponce has described her childhood as "terribly happy." Her experiences while growing up in a small barrio have led her to empathize
with other ethnic Americans whose families have had to adjust to the
language and customs of a new country. Her autobiographical writings
reflect this experience of acculturation as well as Ponce's strong ties to
her Hispanic heritage.

While raising her family of four children, Ponce continued to read
avidly—up to ten books per week—and to write her own short stories.
In 1974, she decided to start college. She says that this decision owes
partly to the encouragement of her children (her oldest son was already
in college) and partly to the inspiration she drew from the Chicano
movement. Ponce received undergraduate and graduate degrees in
Mexican American Studies from California State University at
Northridge. In addition to acquiring a strong interest in Latin American
literature, she also began to concentrate on women's issues, particularly
the concerns of minority women. Her intensive studies soon led to a
teaching career at the same university, where she offered classes in

writing and Chicana literature from 1983 to 1987. Ponce now lives in New Mexico and continues to write.

Arte Público Press published Ponce's first book of fiction in 1987. "Recuerdo," the story that begins on the following page, will appear in a forthcoming book of autobiographical stories. Like many of Ponce's stories, "Recuerdo" vividly captures the flavor of life in a barrio from a young girl's point of view.

Recuerdo: How I changed the war and won the game.

When the demands of the adult world interfere with "an important ball game," the narrator of this story arrives at an inventive compromise. As you read, consider how you would respond to the narrator's bit of creative translation if you were one of the elderly women in the story.

During World War II, I used to translate the English newspaper's war news for our adopted grandmother Doña[1] Luisa and her friends. All of them were *señoras de edad,*[2] elderly ladies who could not read English, only their native Spanish.

Every afternoon they would gather on Doña Luisa's front porch to await Doña Trinidad's son who delivered the paper to her promptly at 5 P.M. There, among the *geranios*[3] and pots of *yerba buena*[4] I would bring them the news of the war.

At first I enjoyed doing this, for the *señoras* would welcome me as a grown-up. They would push their chairs around in a semicircle, the better to hear me. I would sit in the middle, on a *banquito*[5] that was a milk crate. I don't remember how I began to be their translator but because I was an obedient child and at eight a good reader, I was somehow coerced or selected.

I would sit down, adjust my dress, then slowly unwrap the paper, reading the headlines to myself in English, trying to decide which news items were the most important, which to tell first. Once I had decided, I would translate them into my best Spanish for Doña Luisa and her friends.

---

1. **Doña** (doh'nyah): formal title of respect used before first names of women.
2. *señoras de edad* (seh-nyoh'rahs deh eh-thahth').
3. *geranios* (heh-rah'nyohs): geraniums.
4. *yerba buena* (yehr'bah bweh'nah): mint; peppermint.
5. *banquito* (bahn-kee'toh): a stool.

The news of a battle would bring sighs of *Jesús, María y José, Ay Dios Mío,*[6] from the ladies. They would roll their eyes toward heaven, imploring our Lord to protect their loved ones from danger. In return they vowed to light candles or to make a *manda,*[7] a pilgrimage to *la Virgen de San Juan*[8] in the nearby town of Sunland. Once I had read them the highlights of the war I was allowed to play ball with my friends.

One day we had an important ball game going, our team was losing, and it was my turn at bat. Just then Doña Luisa called me. It was time for *las noticias.*[9] Furious at this interruption yet not daring to disobey, I dropped the bat, ran to the porch, ripped open the paper, pointed to the headlines and in a loud voice proclaimed: "Ya están los japoneses en San Francisco . . . los esperan en Los Angeles muy pronto,"[10] or "The Japanese have landed in San Francisco; they should be in Los Angeles soon."

"Jesús, María y José, Sangre de Cristo, Ave María, Purísima"[11] chanted las señoras as I dashed off to resume my game. *"Dios mío ya vámonos, ya vámonos"*[12] they said as chairs were pushed aside, *"vamos a la Iglesia . . . a rezarle al Señor."*[13]

After that I was able to translate according to whim—and depending on whether or not I was up to bat when the paper arrived.

---

6. *Jesús, María y José, Ay Dios Mío* (heh-soos', mah-ree'ah ee hoh-seh', ai dyohs mee'oh): Jesus, Mary and Joseph, oh dear God.

7. *manda* (mahn'dah): a petition.

8. *la Virgen de San Juan* (lah beer'hehn deh sahn hwahn): the Virgin of San Juan.

9. las noticias (lahs noh-tee'syahs): the information; news.

10. Ya están los japoneses en San Francisco . . . los esperan en Los Angeles muy pronto (yah ehs-tahn' lohs hah-poh-neh'sehs ehn sahn frahn-sees'koh . . . lohs ehs-peh'rahn ehn lohs ahn'heh-lehs mwee prohn'toh).

11. . . . *Sangre de Cristo, Ave María, Purísima* (sahn'greh deh krees'toh, ah'beh mah-ree'ah, poo-ree'see-mah): These are exclamations similar to "oh my God" and "goodness gracious."

12. *Dios mío ya vámonos, ya vámonos* (dyohs mee'oh yah bah'moh-nohs, yah bah'moh-nohs): My God let's go, let's go.

13. *vamos a la Iglesia . . . a rezarle al Señor* (bah'mohs ah lah ee-gleh'syah . . . ah reh-sahr'leh ahl seh-nyohr'): we're going to the church . . . to pray to the Lord.

For Study and Discussion

1. This story is told from the point of view of an eight-year-old girl, reflecting her perspective and concerns. **a.** How does the narrator's view of the reading sessions and of the war headlines contrast with that of the "señoras de edad" whose loved ones are involved in the war? **b.** Seen from the women's point of view, is the narrator's invented translation of the headlines amusing?

2. In some respects the narrator is quite precocious—that is, unusually mature for her age. In several instances, though, she thinks and reacts as any eight-year-old child might. **a.** Give three examples from the story of the narrator's intelligence and maturity. **b.** Cite several instances in which she thinks and behaves like a typical eight-year-old child.

3. *Recuerdo* means "remembrance." Although the writer narrates the story from the perspective of her eight-year-old self, the story is nevertheless recalled through a distance of many years. Can you recall times in your life when your perspective was very different from your current way of looking at things—instances in which you placed great importance on things that now seem silly or insignificant to you?

Creative Writing

Writing a Reminiscence

In describing events from an eight-year-old's point of view, Mary Helen Ponce is able to capture both the perspective she had as a child and the humor that these memories take on from a distance. Referring to **For Study and Discussion** question 3, write a first-person account of an amusing incident that you remember from your childhood.

Prewriting. In thinking back, try to remember exactly how you felt and what you thought about the events that come to your mind. Can you recall an incident that now seems funny to you but at the time seemed quite serious and important? To help you recapture the way that you felt at that time in your life, brainstorm a list of details about the incident, including the response(s) you had to them. Then compose your narrative from this childhood point of view as if it had happened only a few days ago. You may also wish to include a final paragraph commenting on the events in your narrative and telling why the memory of them seems amusing to you now.

Writing. As you write your story, refer to "Recuerdo" to see what stylistic devices Ponce uses to capture an eight-year-old's perspective. For example, consider the simple diction and straightforward manner of her narrative, as in the sentence: "One day we had an important ball game going, our team was losing, and it was my turn at bat." The phrase "important ball game" conveys that this was a crucial moment for Ponce at the time.

Gary Soto

(1952–)

I write because those I live and work among can't write. I only have to think of the . . . factory worker I worked with in L.A. or the toothless farm laborer I hoed beside in the fields outside Fresno . . . they're everything.

As this quotation from Gary Soto (soh'toh) suggests, his writing draws on his rich, often painful personal history and yet also addresses the lives of many, particularly those of Mexican American migrant workers. Born in Fresno, California, Soto has experienced firsthand the grim realities of mind-deadening factory work and farm labor—experiences he vividly describes in his first book of poems, *The Elements of San Joaquin*. Using precise language and skillfully crafted imagery, his poetry explores a variety of themes—from observations of the natural world to expressions of the inner landscape of his childhood memories and dreams.

Graduating with honors from California State University in 1974, Soto went on to study creative writing at the University of California, Irvine, and began to publish his poems in magazines across the country. Upon graduating from the University of California, he became a college lecturer. He has won numerous awards for his poetry.

Soto's autobiographical story "The Jacket," which begins on the following page, describes a painful time in his early life when he felt that he was a social outcast. While the narrative focuses mainly on his unhappiness, it also contains a note of humor that is characteristic of Soto's nonfiction.

(For additional biographical information about Gary Soto, see page 524.)

The Jacket

*The growing-up years Gary Soto describes in this story
were "a sad time for the heart"—a time marked by loneliness and dejection. Humiliated by his "ugly" jacket, Soto
felt himself to be a ridiculous figure, mocked and rejected
by teachers as well as peers. Although some of this ridicule
may have been imagined, the depth of his unhappiness was
quite real. He did, however, survive this painful time and,
as an adult, even manages to introduce a note of wry
humor into some of his descriptions. See if you can detect
this comic element in the figurative language he uses to
describe the jacket.*

My clothes have failed me. I remember the green coat that I
wore in fifth and sixth grades when you either danced like a
champ or pressed yourself against a greasy wall, bitter as a
penny toward the happy couples.

When I needed a new jacket and my mother asked what
kind I wanted, I described something like bikers wear: black
leather and silver studs with enough belts to hold down a small
town. We were in the kitchen, steam on the windows from her
cooking. She listened so long while stirring dinner that I thought
she understood for sure the kind I wanted. The next day when
I got home from school, I discovered draped on my bedpost a
jacket the color of day-old guacamole.[1] I threw my books on the
bed and approached the jacket slowly, as if it were a stranger
whose hand I had to shake. I touched the vinyl sleeve, the collar,
and peeked at the mustard-colored lining.

From the kitchen mother yelled that my jacket was in the
closet. I closed the door to her voice and pulled at the rack of
clothes in the closet, hoping the jacket on the bedpost wasn't
for me but my mean brother. No luck. I gave up. From my bed,
I stared at the jacket. I wanted to cry because it was so ugly and

---

1. **guacamole** (gwah-kah-moh'leh): a thick, yellowish-green paste made of
   mashed avocados.

so big that I knew I'd have to wear it a long time. I was a small kid, thin as a young tree, and it would be years before I'd have a new one. I stared at the jacket, like an enemy, thinking bad things before I took off my old jacket whose sleeves climbed halfway to my elbow.

I put the big jacket on. I zipped it up and down several times, and rolled the cuffs up so they didn't cover my hands. I put my hands in the pockets and flapped the jacket like a bird's wings. I stood in front of the mirror, full face, then profile, and then looked over my shoulder as if someone had called me. I sat on the bed, stood against the bed, and combed my hair to see what I would look like doing something natural. I looked ugly. I threw it on my brother's bed and looked at it for a long time before I slipped it on and went out to the backyard, smiling a "thank you" to my mom as I passed her in the kitchen. With my hands in my pockets I kicked a ball against the fence, and then climbed it to sit looking into the alley. I hurled orange peels at the mouth of an open garbage can and when the peels were gone I watched the white puffs of my breath thin to nothing.

I jumped down, hands in my pockets, and in the backyard on my knees I teased my dog, Brownie, by swooping my arms while making bird calls. He jumped at me and missed. He jumped again and again, until a tooth sunk deep, ripping an L-shaped tear on my left sleeve. I pushed Brownie away to study the tear as I would a cut on my arm. There was no blood, only a few loose pieces of fuzz. Damn dog, I thought, and pushed him away hard when he tried to bite again. I got up from my knees and went to my bedroom to sit with my jacket on my lap, with the lights out.

That was the first afternoon with my new jacket. The next day I wore it to sixth grade and got a D on a math quiz. During the morning recess Frankie T., the playground terrorist, pushed me to the ground and told me to stay there until recess was over. My best friend, Steve Negrete, ate an apple while looking at me, and the girls turned away to whisper on the monkey bars. The teachers were no help: they looked my way and talked about how foolish I looked in my new jacket. I saw their heads bob with laughter, their hands half-covering their mouths.

Even though it was cold, I took off the jacket during lunch and played kickball in a thin shirt, my arms feeling like braille

Gary Soto 393

from goose bumps. But when I returned to class I slipped the jacket on and shivered until I was warm. I sat on my hands, heating them up, while my teeth chattered like a cup of crooked dice. Finally warm, I slid out of the jacket but a few minutes later put it back on when the fire bell rang. We paraded out into the yard where we, the sixth graders, walked past all the other grades to stand against the back fence. Everybody saw me. Although they didn't say out loud, "Man, that's ugly," I heard the buzz-buzz of gossip and even laughter that I knew was meant for me.

And so I went, in my guacamole jacket. So embarrassed, so hurt, I couldn't even do my homework. I received Cs on quizzes, and forgot the state capitols and the rivers of South America, our friendly neighbor. Even the girls who had been friendly blew away like loose flowers to follow the boys in neat jackets.

I wore that thing for three years until the sleeves grew short and my forearms stuck out like the necks of turtles. All during that time no love came to me—no little dark girl in a Sunday dress she wore on Monday. At lunchtime I stayed with the ugly boys who leaned against the chainlink fence and looked around with propellers of grass spinning in our mouths. We saw girls walk by alone, saw couples, hand in hand, their heads like bookends pressing air together. We saw them and spun our propellers so fast our faces were blurs.

I blame that jacket for those bad years. I blame my mother for her bad taste and her cheap ways. It was a sad time for the heart. With a friend I spent my sixth-grade year in a tree in the alley waiting for something good to happen to me in that jacket, which had become the ugly brother who tagged along wherever I went. And it was about that time that I began to grow. My chest puffed up with muscle and, strangely, a few more ribs. Even my hands, those fleshy hammers, showed bravely through the cuffs, the fingers already hardening for the coming fights. But that L-shaped rip on the left sleeve got bigger; bits of stuffing coughed out from its wound after a hard day of play. I finally scotch-taped it closed, but in rain or cold weather the tape peeled off like a scab and more stuffing fell out until that sleeve shriveled into a palsied arm. That winter the elbows began to crack and whole chunks of green began to fall off. I showed the cracks to my mother, who always seemed to be at the stove with steamed-up glasses, and she said that there were children in Mexico who would love that jacket. I told her that this was America and yelled that Debbie, my sister, didn't have a jacket like mine. I ran outside, ready to cry, and climbed the tree by the alley to think bad thoughts and watch my breath puff white and disappear.

But whole pieces still casually flew off my jacket when I played hard, read quietly, or took vicious spelling tests at school. When it became so spotted that my brother began to call me "camouflage," I flung it over the fence into the alley. Later, however, I swiped the jacket off the ground and went inside to drape it across my lap and mope.

I was called to dinner: steam silvered my mother's glasses as she said grace; my brother and sister with their heads bowed made ugly faces at their glasses of powdered milk. I gagged too, but eagerly ate big rips of buttered tortilla that held scooped up beans. Finished, I went outside with my jacket across my arm. It was a cold sky. The faces of clouds were piled up, hurting. I climbed the fence, jumping down with a grunt. I started up the alley and soon slipped into my jacket, that green ugly brother who breathed over my shoulder that day and ever since.

For Study and Discussion

1. The narrator of "The Jacket" blames his "guacamole"-colored jacket for all of the painful experiences he has while he wears it. **a.** What are some of these experiences? **b.** In what way is the jacket indirectly responsible for the speaker's difficulties? **c.** To what extent do you think he exaggerates the role the jacket plays in his unhappy adolescence? Explain.

2. Toward the end of the story, the narrator says, "I blame that jacket for those bad years. I blame my mother for her bad taste and her cheap ways." What do you think are some of the mother's possible reasons for purchasing this particular jacket for her son?

In your opinion, is the narrator fair in blaming his mother for his "bad years"? Discuss the events in the story from her point of view.

Literary Elements

Narrative Writing

Narrative writing relates a series of events—that is, it tells a story. Narration is usually associated with fiction; however, plays, poetry, and nonfiction can also use a narrative form. Gary Soto's "The Jacket" is an autobiographical story that relates a series of events from the author's childhood—a string of disappointments and humiliations that result from his having to wear an unattractive, ill-fitting jacket that his mother had bought for him.

Like most narratives, this one follows a chronological order, tracing the days and years through which the narrator suffers wearing "that green ugly brother." Note the words and phrases in the story that help you to follow the order of events: "The first afternoon," "That winter," and so forth.

What words and phrases introduce passages that give an overview of the events and time frame of the story? How does the author combine narrative writing with descriptive details to make the story come alive for the reader? Cite specific examples from the story to support your answers.

Juan Bruce-Novoa

(1944–)

As a Mexican American deeply affected by the Chicano movement, Juan Bruce-Novoa (hwahn broos-noh-boh'ah) brings a unique "critical edge" to his perspective on American history and literature. His minority background has led him to realize that written history does not always reflect the realities of American society—that the experiences of minority cultures constitute an "unspoken history" of the United States. In his critical studies, he is committed to representing the communal interests of Chicano culture. Although his concerns as a writer and critic are primarily artistic or literary, he believes that "art is always political" in that it reflects the culture that produces it and often opposes the prevailing view of mainstream society.

Bruce-Novoa's family background has exerted a powerful influence on his life and work. He grew up in Denver, Colorado, in a family of artists—painters, writers, and musicians—whose constant lively discussions helped to kindle in him a passionate concern with the arts. These interests revealed themselves early on when he wrote his first short stories in elementary school. As a young adult, he also explored his musical talents, working as a rock-and-blues musician until he graduated from college in 1966.

After receiving his undergraduate degree in history from Regis College, Bruce-Novoa began graduate studies in Contemporary Mexican Literature at the University of Colorado. He received his Ph.D. in 1974 and went on to pursue a teaching career as a professor of Chicano and Mexican Literature at Yale University. Currently, he is teaching at Trinity University in San Antonio, Texas. He has published numerous short stories, poems, reviews, and critical studies, which have brought him wide acclaim as both an insightful writer of and a perceptive commentator on Mexican American literature.

The following selection is taken from Bruce-Novoa's *Chicano Authors,* an informative, compelling collection of interviews in which well-known Mexican American writers—such as poet and novelist Rolando Hinojosa-Smith—reflect candidly on their lives, their culture, and their art.

An Interview with Rolando Hinojosa-Smith

What is Mexican American literature? How does it differ from other American literature and particularly the literature of other minorities? What distinctive perspective on life does Mexican American literature offer? What are the strengths and weaknesses of Mexican American literature? In the following interview, Rolando Hinojosa-Smith answers these and other vital questions concerning the literature of his people. As you read Hinojosa-Smith's comments, think back on selections you have read in this anthology. To what extent do they reflect his ideas? Do you think that he has overlooked any significant features of Mexican American literature?

In addition to being a critic, Hinojosa-Smith is also a writer. Look at the short story and the poems by him included in this book on pages 414 and 605. How would you evaluate his work, especially in light of the standards he sets forth in this interview?

Q *How do you perceive your role as a writer vis-à-vis: (a) the Chicano[1] community or movement; (b) U.S. society; (c) literature itself?*

A My role as a writer . . . I've not given much thought to this one so I'll probably ramble. My role—if that is what it is—is to write. There are some eternal verities and anyone who writes wants to state them for himself and for his time. In my home state there is something called the Texas Academy of Arts and Letters—I may not have the title right, but it's that type of thing,

---

1. **Chicano** (chee-kah'noh): Mexican American.

and some of the people in it are Larry King, Larry McMurtry, Bill Moyers, and so on. Now, I don't believe that they as Texans have read Chicano literature, and so their view of Texas is lacking in one big respect. That aside, they, as Texans, are writing about other verities in Texas and they certainly know what they are writing about. I write about Belken County [a fictional county in South Texas] and its people . . . who knows them as well as I do? No one; my role is to write and then to try to get the stuff published; in the meantime, I keep writing. I'm not setting myself as an example; I see myself as a writer, and, as I have just said, I try to get published.

Q *What is the place of Chicano literature within U.S. literature?*

A I don't know what the place is—or that there's *one* place. Some universities use my *Estampas* (the English version by Gustavo Valadez) in English departments; others in the Department of Spanish and Portuguese or Modern Languages or Ethnic Studies. Some use the writing as just an extension of Spanish American literature. This is what's happening to Chicano literature; it's being read in the universities for the most part. It is read outside, of course, but at this stage, Chicano literature is being discussed in universities through symposia, colloquia, seminars, etc. This, I suspect, is due to the dual language aspect. Maybe the succeeding Chicano generation of writers will write in English and thus take a place in U.S. literature, if that's what the author wants. It could probably stand alone, again because of the language.

Q *What is the relationship of Chicano literature to Mexican literature?*

A Chicano literature's relationship to Mexican literature would have to depend on the Chicano author. The first consideration is the language, but Chicano literature does not restrict itself to Spanish, as you know, so it depends on the author and his roots. These may be superficial in some cases and deep in others, but the Chicano author will usually write about the Chicano's life in his native land, the United States. Mexico would probably never be the main locale of a novel—

unless a Chicano sets it there and writes about a Chicano's life in Mexico—the point is that Chicano literature is not Mexican literature . . . Mexican literature may serve as an educational background, but not, necessarily, as the base. It is merely one of the many elements of the present Chicano writers.

Q *Do you perceive yourself and your work as political?*

A Some of my work may be perceived as political; I perceive it as my work and let others perceive it as they wish. Some say it isn't political—maybe they mean not political enough . . . who knows? I can't stop to worry over this aspect of my work. I do know one thing—it isn't didactic; my experience in reading political literature is that it tends to be didactic and, hence, intramural. The last thing that literature should find itself is between walls—no matter who builds them.

Q *Does the Chicano author have anything in common with the majority group writers? Differences?*

A I guess that by majority group writers you mean non-Chicanos . . . I can't say Anglo because where does that put Roth or Bellow, who write in most instances of the Jewish experience in the United States? Or where does this put Salinger or Heller, whose characters may or may not be Jewish? So I say non-Chicano because I certainly couldn't include Richard Wright or Hughes or Baldwin as Anglos . . . Is the last one a majority writer? And let's see . . . there's Robert Penn Warren, John Hersey, certainly; Capote . . . Katherine Ann Porter . . . now they are Anglo, but I don't see them as Anglos or as anything else . . . they're writers. It would be ridiculous for me to write as if I were an American Jew . . . or as if I were a Kentuckian or a Tennessean . . . I could write about sports, I guess, since that has little to do with the reality of daily living . . . But to write of Mississippi? The Philadelphia Main Line? I wouldn't know where to begin. That's better left to people who know what they are writing about. You seldom see a serious writer writing out of his element; that's for television and for popular magazines. Do I sound snobbish? Petulant? I'm neither . . . it is a matter of established fact that a writer had damn well better know what he's writing about or it won't be good writing. The writer should know or sense or suspect when he's fooling around or when he's on shaky ground. It may be that someone may think this is medieval in that it begs for the shoemaker to stick to his last . . . well, how many novels did O'Neill write? How many plays did Faulkner produce? I guess that Cervantes has got to be the best example of a writer who tried drama and poetry for years before he found himself in his novel. Don't forget the Byzantine type he came up with in the *Persiles* was written by the same right hand that wrote both parts of the *Quijote.*

Now . . . the Chicano writer who decries his lack of popularity or of recognition had better decide to do something else with his life. This is not a Spanish-speaking country for the most part; if he wants recognition then he better sell his wares to Mexico, Central and South America, and Spain. If he does and if he does it well, good for him, but will he still be a Chicano? Perhaps . . . who's to know?

Q *Does Chicano literature share common ground with Black literature? Differences?*

A Black writers, majority group writers? I think I've said it all or as much as I could. I think I understand and appreciate their writing, but then I also think I understand and appreciate *Dead Souls* by Gogol and *Vidas secas* by Graciliano Ramos, the Northeast Brazilian. Writers are writers. Look, I've never been to Germany and yet when Böll speaks of "the Beast" in *Billiards at Half Past Nine,* I understand . . . I'll say I do . . . It's loud and clear as a bell. When a Black says he suffers, I see and understand. When a Black critic tells me I don't *feel* then I must tell that critic, Black or not, that if I don't *feel,* then *that* is the writer's fault. Pure and simple.

Q *Is there any relationship with the literature of other Spanish-speaking groups?*

A I don't mean to be either picky or cute here, but do you mean an affinity for and with other Spanish-speaking groups? In the U.S.? I'm very interested in the Chicano urban experience in Los Angeles and elsewhere . . . the urban Chicano . . . When the Chicanos from Chicago, Gary, Hammond, Detroit, or the

75,000 in Iowa, or the Chicanos in El Paso, Phoenix, Denver, Kansas City, Wichita, come out with their work then I'll begin to see what Chicano literature is like there—in those places. The Puerto Ricans? Those who have never been to the Island? That's a coming thing. And how about the young Cubans who came here with their parents in 1959 and after? It will be interesting to see what acculturation or assimilation takes place . . . At present there is a Chicano–Boricua[2] publication—the *Revista Chicano-Riqueña*—out of Indiana University put out by Luis Davila, a Chicano, and Nicolás Kanellos, a Boricua. The relationships are new, and, once again, on an individual basis. I'm in touch with Manuel Ramos Otero, a Boricua who lives and works in New York, and he in turn will put me in contact with others and I will let them know of others and so on.

I have read of the Brazilian interest in Chicano literature. I've seen some general critical reviews of Chicano literature in Mexico . . . not much. The relationships are just beginning, that is, the formal relationships. The blood has been there for years.

Q *Does Chicano literature have a distinctive perspective on life? What effect does it have on the literature?*

A I would say that Chicano literature has its own perspectives on life, but then so does any other literature. The uninformed say that the themes and perspectives of Chicano literature are restricted to agricultural settings. Well now, that type of assertion is naïve, self-revealing, and parochial . . . Chicano literature is like varietal wine . . . The effect of variety is that it tends to present many shades and hues of the central theme: our life here, in our native land.

Q *Does Chicano literature improve communication between Chicanos and Anglo Americans?*

A It may, but I've seen little evidence of literature teaching anybody anything other than the way people live. I don't believe that one should write with the idea of communicating . . . It probably boils down to this: communication is a personal thing . . . it is based on personal relationships not on government

2. **Boricua** (boh-ree'kwah): a general term for Puerto Ricans, derived from Borinquen, the Taíno name for the island.

edict. I was in my teens when World War II was grinding down and I still recall reading about Eisenhower's non-fraternization rule . . . he was a cynical old man . . . through his knowledge of history he knew full well that it was unenforceable and yet he made a big show of it to the so-called "folks back home." The first GI, and who knows what color he was, and his fraulein were already communicating before Ike's prattle . . . I don't know if literature improves communication and as for teaching . . . well, it doesn't appear as if we have learned to employ all that we know.

Q *Does Chicano literature reevaluate, attack, or subvert the value system of the majority society? Is it a revolutionary literature? Thematically? Technically?*

A All serious literature—and some funny literature is serious stuff, right?—and anyway, all serious literature usually assesses our present life. The author tells his tale, but there is an assessment, an evaluation, yes, perhaps a reevaluation of society. It may also attack or subvert certain elements of that society or bring them to light, and this depends on style and manner—satire, wit, sarcasm—or the chosen genre—prose, poetry, the essay, and so on. Revolutionary? Yes and even totalitarian as is some criticism by Chicano critics. However, when someone offers a writer a chance to publish and stipulates that the writing must be socially and politically relevant, then the writer isn't given much of a chance to be creative, is he? But let me switch here . . . I think that Chicano literature is as technically revolutionary as the Chicano writer is able—or dares—or cares—or knows . . . In *Estampas*, I wrote a novel—in four parts . . . each part has a different title and three of the parts are different in structure from each other. Are you familiar with it? *Estampas* is different from *Cosas* and both are different from *Rafa*. *Vidas* resembles *Estampas*, but that's all, a resemblance. I still hold to the word *novel* in the original intent of *novella, algo nuevo*[3] [something new], something dynamic, ever changing . . . And yet I hear *Estampas* referred to as *cuentos*[4] or *vignettes* or short pieces or as a *new* genre, for crying out loud. Oh, it's true all right . . . some teachers debated about it in a conference in New Orleans

---

3. *algo nuevo* (ahl'goh nweh'boh).
4. *cuentos* (kwehn'tohs): stories or tales.

. . . what a waste of time. *Estampas* is a novel and that's it. There's a bit of fooling around with time and space, but the plots are there—there's no novelistic statute that says I have to end a novel in one tome or two . . . I have just finished another novel—you have the manuscript [*Klail City y sus alrededores*]— and I'm starting another one—I use epistles, dialogues, monologues, a prologue here and there at the beginning of each division and anything that can help me to tell my story—and that is it—anything that can help you to tell your story is one of the keys to writing. If my multiple use of forms helps other writers, fine, but they had better come up with a plot for the characters or it won't go anywhere . . . It comes to that, as always; one must have something to say irrespective of the form.

Q *Are Chicanos at a disadvantage in trying to practice the art of writing?*

A Only if they have nothing to say. A writer—even when he's not writing it down—is thinking and that's working at writing. It isn't writing, but it's working at it. If one's eight-to-five job is so demanding that one can't even think about writing, that's a tragedy, not a disadvantage. The main disadvantage certainly is finding no Chicano publishing outlets . . . but if by disadvantage you mean economic disadvantage then the answer is yes . . . Es una desgracia.[5] [It's a disgrace.]

Q *What are the most outstanding qualities of Chicano literature? Weaknesses?*

A The weaknesses of Chicano literature must always lie with the authors. If the author is not able to appreciate or to be aware of the universality of the Chicano's life, then what can one expect? Pearl Buck's *Good Earth* was set in China, certainly, but it went beyond the Great Wall . . . Chicano literature should be treated by Chicano writers in that light . . . beyond our own walls, whatever they may be. Some well-meaning people fret that Anglos may not receive a good impression of us—their own words—in some of the episodes of *Estampas*. They do not

---

5. **Es una desgracia** (ehs oo'nah dehs-grah'syah).

recognize that their reservations are weaknesses. That's taking your hat off and going to see the boss to say, "See what I have here? I'm being a good boy." If the Chicano writer tries to please that part of the Chicano public, he's in trouble. He's also in trouble if he tries to please any one special sector of the Chicano population. The writer should write the best he can; if he has weaknesses in his writing they'll show up soon enough. Chicano literature in all its phases and through all its genres may be a reflection of the Chicano and his life; however, what weaknesses there are must be leveled toward the authors who couldn't—or wouldn't—present the verities (as they honestly saw them) of all Chicanos: rural, urban, young, old, good, bad, sick, well, at home, at work, in love . . .

Outstanding qualities? The presence of the Chicano and his endurance—write about that and, at the risk of being intramural, you will have captured, through literature, the most outstanding qualities of the Chicano's life. In passing, one of the weaknesses is the lack of a truly first-rate work of Chicano literary critique by Chicanos.

For Study and Discussion

1. Hinojosa-Smith points out that writers should base their work on settings, topics, and experiences drawn from their own lives and should stick to the form—novel, drama, poetry, or whatever—that suits the individual writer. Do you agree or disagree with Hinojosa-Smith? Be prepared to explain your answer, using examples of specific works and writers.

2. One criticism commonly leveled at Mexican American literature is that it takes a primarily agricultural perspective on life. Hinojosa-Smith disagrees and claims instead that Mexican American literature presents "many shades and hues" of Mexican American life. Based on selections you have read, identify other perspectives encountered in Mexican American literature and give specific examples of where and how they are expressed.

3. Hinojosa-Smith believes that all serious literature "assesses our present life." In what ways does literature provide evaluations or assessments of life? Consider the themes, characters, plots, and other features of Mexican American works that you have read. How are these literary elements used in the works to evaluate the customs, values, and beliefs of American society, and particularly of Mexican American culture?

Vocabulary

Identifying Words in Context

Each of the words in the following list appears in Juan Bruce-Novoa's interview with Rolando Hinojosa-Smith. Look up the meaning of each word in a dictionary. Then choose the word that best fits in the blank for each of the sentences given after the list.

verities	parochial	symposia
varietal	superficial	subvert
didactic	stipulates	decries
statute	irrespective	acculturation

   1. The contract _____ that the work must be completed before June.

   2. The separate provinces will never reach an agreement among themselves if they insist on asserting their _____ interests.

   3. Although the report was quite lengthy, it provided only a _____ treatment of the subject.

   4. The radicals sought to _____ the duly elected government.

   5. In drafting the Constitution, the Founding Fathers asserted what they felt were the fundamental _____ of a free society.

   6. Aesop's fables are obviously _____ ; in fact, each one has its moral clearly stated at the end.

7. Learning how to speak English usually speeds up the process of _____ for most people who immigrate to the United States.

8. Anna insisted on following her original plan, _____ of the consequences.

9. The legislature enacted a comprehensive _____ concerning the disposal of toxic waste.

10. Although that candidate _____ the exploitation of immigrant workers, he doesn't seem to have any plan for improving the situation.

Creative Writing

Conducting an Interview

Using Juan Bruce-Novoa's interview with Hinojosa-Smith as a model, conduct an interview of your own, choosing someone who is accomplished in a field that interests you. Then transcribe your interview, following the format used by Bruce-Novoa.

Prewriting. Do not assume that the person will be available and willing to be interviewed. Always call or write to the person, and request to set up a time when you may either visit or telephone him or her.

Once you have arranged a time with the interviewee, write ten or twelve questions that you would like to ask. Avoid asking questions that can be answered with a simple *yes* or *no*. Instead, devise open-ended questions that call for the interviewee to provide detailed information.

Make sure that you arrive or call on time and are prepared. If you would like to tape-record the interview, you must first receive permission from the interviewee to do so. When taking notes, either during the interview or later from a recording, make sure that you quote the interviewee verbatim so that you do not misrepresent what he or she tells you. If you are unsure about an answer, ask the interviewee to repeat that portion of what he or she said. When you complete the interview, ask if the interviewee would like to add anything.

Writing and Revising. When writing your account, you may wish to omit unnecessary information. In such cases, use ellipses (. . .) to indicate the omission, and be sure to get the interviewee's approval of your deletions. Whether you wish to delete information or not, it is good practice to send the interviewee a copy of the account before submitting it in class. To differentiate between the questions and the answers, put the letter Q before each question and the letter A before each answer.

After you get the interviewee's approval, recopy or type the interview, making any changes requested by the interviewee. Pay particularly close attention to accuracy so that you do not create errors in your final version.

The Novel of the Contemporary Period

Like other genres of this period, the contemporary novel reflects the powerful influence of the Chicano movement. The reawakening of their cultural pride prompted the first novelists to concentrate more on social and cultural issues than on literary craft—an understandable emphasis considering the turbulent period during which these initial works were written. Gradually, however, novelists began to explore additional themes and to concentrate more on the formal and creative aspects of their writing. Social backdrops and one-dimensional characters gave way to well-developed settings and characters of greater substance and credibility.

Nevertheless, just as the poets of the Contemporary Period remained committed to social change, the novelists did not turn their backs on the injustice and socioeconomic problems faced by their people. As contemporary novelists have taken a more literary approach to writing, their works have become increasingly compelling and realistic, enabling them to convey social messages even more powerfully.

Two significant writers of the early part of the Chicano Period are José Antonio Villarreal and Oscar Zeta Acosta. Villarreal's first novel, *Pocho* [an Americanized person of Mexican descent], traces the experiences of a Mexican family that flees Mexico during the 1910 Revolution to settle in the United States. The members of this family, particularly the young male protagonist, find themselves torn between their deeply imbedded native culture and the culture of their adopted country. Acosta was a lawyer and Chicano activist in California during the late 1960s, a time of social upheaval. After abandoning his law career to write, he published two highly autobiographical novels, *The Autobiography of a Brown Buffalo* and *The Revolt of the Cockroach People*.

The early 1970s saw the publication of three novels that heartened and inspired many young Chicano writers. Tomás Rivera's *. . . y no se lo tragó la tierra* [. . . and the earth did not devour him], Rudolfo Anaya's *Bless Me, Ultima*, and Rolando Hinojosa-Smith's *Estampas del valle y otras obras* [Sketches of the valley and other works] all received the prestigious Quinto Sol Literary Prize. The twelve thematically unified sections of Rivera's work present a collective voice that shouts out in protest against the exploitation of migrant farm workers. Anaya's narrative focuses on a Mexican American boy's painful journey into manhood and his abandonment of his family's values. Set in a fictional county in Texas, Hinojosa-Smith's novel describes a difficult but generally cheerful way of life that closely parallels the author's own experiences of growing up in the southwestern United States.

Miguel Méndez and Ron Arias are two other novelists who deserve special mention. Méndez's novels *Peregrinos de Aztlán* [Pilgrims from Aztlán] and *Santa María de las Piedras* [Saint Mary of the Rocks] draw on aspects of life in both Mexico and the United States. Arias's only novel, *The Road to Tamazunchale*, immerses the reader in the dreams and surreal fantasies of its fatally ill protagonist. Like Arias's short fiction, this novel reflects important experimental currents not only in Mexican American writing but also in contemporary Hispanic literature as a whole.

Rolando Hinojosa-Smith

(1929–)

Rolando Hinojosa-Smith's (roh-
lahn'doh ee-noh-hoh'sah) Spanish
ancestors first settled in the Rio Grande
Valley—then the northern territories of New Spain—in 1749. To this
day, many of his relatives still live in the Valley on both sides of the
Texas–Mexico border. His fictional works reflect these deep roots in
Hispanic culture and tradition as well as his personal experiences of
growing up in the Rio Grande Valley. In his novels, he has skillfully
created a fictional place—Belken County, Texas—whose inhabitants go
about their daily lives dealing as best they can with the conflicts that
arise from racial strife and cultural misunderstanding.

Born in Mercedes, Texas, to a Mexican American father and an
Anglo mother, Hinojosa-Smith began his education in a private
Mexican school run by Mexican exiles—an experience that strongly
reinforced his ties to Mexican culture. Often sick as a child, he spent
many school days at home where he read constantly. His first attempts
at writing began at the local public high school; these early writings are
still available in the school's library. After graduating from high school
in 1946, he moved away from the Rio Grande Valley, but he did not
leave it. He has made return pilgrimages to his birthplace many times
during the past forty years. Like a sacred shrine, the Rio Grande Valley
is part of Hinojosa-Smith's psyche and has formed the backdrop for the
intricate narrative tapestries he weaves in his novels.

After serving two years in the Army during the 1940s, Hinojosa-
Smith attended the University of Texas for a short time before he was
recalled to military service in 1950. He saw combat in the Korean War
and after his release from the service returned to the University of Texas

to work toward his degree. Later, he attended New Mexico Highlands University and earned a Ph.D. in Spanish from the University of Illinois in 1969. Rising rapidly in the academic ranks, Hinojosa-Smith became Vice President for Academic Affairs at Texas A & I University in Kingsville, Texas. He currently directs the creative writing program at the University of Texas at Austin.

In addition to achieving recognition as a teacher and administrator, Hinojosa-Smith has received international acclaim as a writer of both poetry and prose. His first novel, *Estampas del valle y otras obras* [Sketches of the valley and other works], won the 1973 Quinto Sol Prize—one of the most prestigious awards given in contemporary Chicano letters. His second novel, *Klail City y sus alrededores* [Klail City and its surroundings], earned him the international Casa de las Americas award in 1976.

The following selection is an excerpt from *Claros varones de Belken* [Fair gentlemen of Belken County], which was published in 1986 as the fourth part of a series of interrelated works that Hinojosa-Smith calls his "Klail City Death Trip." The novel is a collection of dialogues and monologues that focus on four characters' memories of their pasts and reflections on their present lives. In this excerpt, the main character, Rafe Buenrostro, reveals his thoughts as he eases back into life in the Lower Rio Grande Valley after a harrowing tour of duty in Korea.

(For additional biographical information about Rolando Hinojosa-Smith, see page 604.)

Rafe Buenrostro[1]
Returns from Korea

from Fair Gentlemen of Belken County

After serving for three years as a soldier in Korea, Rafe Buenrostro at last returns home to his family and friends. However, war has left its indelible mark on Rafe in the form of painful memories and personal losses that continue to haunt him. As you read, consider how Rafe's close ties to family and community help him to bear these losses and resume his life in the valley.

Rafe Buenrostro I

Israel and Susana came for me up at the Missouri-Pacific station; fifteen years later, there'd be no more passenger service, but for now, one couldn't even imagine such a thing. If one comes to the Valley[2] by train, from Monterrey to Barrones, Tamaulipas, (mostly desert) south to north, or up from William Barrett, north to south (again, mostly desert), the Valley looks like an oasis. It's near the Gulf and with the Río Grande gently flowing, and surrounded by a semi-desert what one sees seems out of place: palm trees, citrus groves, Valley bananas, cotton, if it's summer, and all kinds of vegetables, all year round. The mesquite trees and wisterias grow like weeds there; from time to time the scraggly retamas and white goose-foot shrubs and the strong, firm scrub oaks surround some of the pasture land. And there's willows, chinaberry, and ebony. The fertility is also due to underground water. There are sugar cane and sorghum crops towards Edgerton where cantaloupes and watermelons are also a steady crop. Relámpago usually brings the first bale of cotton;

---

1. **Rafe Buenrostro** (rah'feh bwehn-rohs'troh).
2. **the Valley:** the Rio Grande Valley.

in Ruffing, it's onions and strawberries. Each Valley town has some distinction in this regard and Klail City has the sweetest navel oranges and best cabbage anywhere.

I was home after three years and more; discharge papers in the barrack's bag somewhere. The plan was to stay with Israel and Aaron at El Carmen for a year. After that, no telling.

That, anyway, was what I had told myself while in Korea and at Tokyo General. As I stepped down off the platform, I vaguely remembered my last two weeks in Japan: saying good-bye to friends, tending to some personal business and whatnot; a sort of pilgrimage, somehow. But that had been another life, and now I was home, I was in the Valley.

At the station, *abrazos*[3] and taps on the back; this had happened before, when I returned from my first army discharge soon to marry Conce Guerrero.

Israel picked up my barrack's bag, and I told him I'd sent some other things from Fort Lewis; he said they were home already, two boxes and a duffel bag.

Susana laughed and said: "Here, take *this* bundle." *Their* Rafe.

Israel laughed: "Your namesake. The first time you got wounded, remember? We gave him your name."

"Just in case?"

"Just in case . . . we didn't tell anyone you were wounded, by the way."

Susana: "He'll be three in September. Looks like you've got your health back, Rafe. Hungry?"

"No. How about Israel here? Behaving himself, is he?"

"Ha! He's a load and a half, your brother is. You and Aaron should pay me a salary. Right, Milo?"

Israel laughed again. "And I'm the best one of the lot. I'll tell you who's going to be a handful—and you're carrying him right there. He's asleep and he looks like an angel, but he's going to be something, he is."

The usual talk: you'd think I'd never been away. That, now that I think back on it, hadn't changed then and hasn't changed now.

The next day I told Israel I planned to stay put, at home, on the ranch. The university plans were to be postponed for a

---

3. *abrazos* (ah-brah'sohs): hugs, embraces.

year; two maybe, but no more than three. I went on: that I'd go to Klail once in a while; that I'd call on some people; but that I'd be staying at the ranch as much as possible.

"I think that's the best thing, Rafe. I like the idea of your staying here. We've always been a close family, you know that. I don't think any of us know each other very well; maybe it isn't even important, necessary. It's love, Rafe; and, we're family. I'm, what? thirteen years older than you? That was quite a difference when I was twenty-three and you were ten, but not now. You're around twenty-one or so, and now we're closer in age, right?"

"Ah-hah. The other Buenrostros . . ."

"Not that many, Rafe. Uncle Julian had Melchor and I buried both of them . . . Dad had *us;* you, me, and Aaron. And that's it. As for the other Buenrostros, we're not even first cousins to any of them. They're family, sure, and we get along, but we're the ones . . ."

"From El Carmen . . ."

"Right; from El Carmen. It's just the three of us, and Aaron is five years younger than you are."

Susana stepped out into the porch to tell us that Jehú had just called from William Barrett; that he'd be in Klail in a couple of days and that he wanted to eat *buñuelos* . . .[4]

"*Buñuelos?* What's the occasion?"

"Because when we were in Japan and Korea, homecooking was what we all talked about. It's as simple as that. Jehú's going through the same thing, that's all. Did he say he was going to William Barrett?"

"No. He called from there. He's been there a week already. He was discharged at Fort Ben."

So Jehú would be here in two-three days; it'd been a long time, thirty months and more: another uniformed man getting off the train . . . Man? Yeah; we were men already. We'd come to that.

Rafe Buenrostro II

With don[5] Celso, Charlie Villalón's father.

I called on him a week after I came home; we spoke for a

---

4. *buñuelos* (boo-nyweh'lohs): fritters made of flour and eggs.
5. **don** (dohn): a title of respect, formerly used for Spanish-speaking men of high rank; now used as a title of courtesy.

long time before and after supper. Around nine or so, the three girls came out to the porch.

What were those places like, Rafe?

Charlie, in a postcard, said that it got really cold over there.

You two had Japanese girlfriends, right? And one of them had a younger brother who was blind, right?

In one of the snapshots, Pepe Vielma had a mustache; we hardly recognized him.

Sonny Ruiz, in a letter a long time ago, sent us some Japanese paper money.

Don Celso blew his nose a couple of times and chuckled now and then at the things Charlie used to do; we then reminisced about the time a calf threw me into the cactus patch; he, don Celso, had pulled me out and there I was, all covered with thorns. We turned in around ten; one of the girls said my room was ready; it was Charlie's old room.

The next day, around seven, I was already on the porch when I spotted don Celso coming in from the goat pens. He waved with his hat and said: "What? Have you had breakfast already? Good. Let's have an extra cup of coffee."

When he saw my suitcase, he asked if I were planning to leave so soon; I said I wasn't, the presents were inside the suitcase.

"Let's see; what've you got there?"

The first thing was a snapshot of the four of us, dressed in civilian clothes. We were standing in front of a park in Nagoya, two months before the war.

"What are Sonny and Pepito Vielma laughing about?"

"No idea, don Celso . . . maybe only mainly on account of because, as we used to say."

"Ah . . . Charlie came out really well in this one, didn't he? (handkerchief again).

"What else have you got, son?"

"This is a personal gift, don Celso."

"How does it work?"

"Look here, you point it this way and push this little button over here."

"Is it German?"

"No, no. It's Japanese."

"And what about these other doo-dads?"

"Those, you turn with the left hand . . . see? When what

you're pointing at is in focus, it'll figure out the distance auto-matically and there, it's ready to take a picture. It aims for you."

"Like for a deer?"

"Something like that . . ."

"But it must be more complicated than that."

"Well, somewhat; yes. But it's for a lifetime."

"That's true, too; so, the camera is Japanese, huh? Who'd think those shorties could come up with something like that, right?"

"These three jackets are for the girls; they're somewhat loud but that's how they make them over there."

"Else! Ana! Girls! Come here . . . look at what Rafe brought."

"This lighter is for you, too, don Celso. And this . . ."

"But it's Charlie, Rafe. Exactly. How did they make it? Is it made of stone?"

"I don't know how they make it . . . We took that picture in color, and the Japanese have developed a process which makes pictures come out in relief and then they cover them like this, in clear glass."

"Those Japanese are really something. I appreciate it, Rafe. I really do."

He had his handkerchief out by the time the girls came out; they loved the jackets but Charlie's picture stole the show.

"Look at Charlie! He . . . he's real."

"You're pure gold, Rafe . . . Pure gold."

"You're your father's son."

Else said: "It's close to eight, Dad. You haven't had a thing to eat yet. I'll bring out some *empanadas*,[6] right away. Anita, Lema, come on. And thanks again, Rafe."

Don Celso: "I'd like to talk to you about Charlie. I mean, I wish you'd tell me about it. Not right now, no; next week. Are you free?"

"Absolutely. You can count on it."

"I couldn't talk about him now, son. Ah, here come the girls again. And thank you, Rafe. Again."

---

6. *empanadas* (ehm-pah-nah'thahs): pies filled with meat and/or vegetables.

Rafe Buenrostro III

Susana had another son and no complications, so she was home three days later. They named him Juan after an old Peralta, and Luciano after a Buenrostro who had been one of the godfathers at my father's confirmation at the Salineño de los Conde Mission in Dellis County.

My sister-in-law was Señor[7] and Señora[8] de Andrea's only child; her mother, doña[9] Barbarita was a Farías from the Edgerton Farias' and had come to stay at El Carmen with us to help out. Her husband, don Odón de Andrea, was one of the 1927 Mexican exiles who'd made a living operating a rather small print shop and by teaching at a neighborhood Mexican school in Klail City.

Doña Barbarita had known my father; she was a few years younger than he: "Yes, I knew him well. I used to see him at family affairs, as you can imagine. The Campoys and we always got along well. More so in the case of the Vilches, I grew up on the Vilches ranch, and that's why I know all of this land like the back of my hand. Do you remember the salt water well, Rafe?"

"The one close to the monument, you mean?"

"No, not that one; the closer one. Did you know the Bohigas family? The ones with the bulging eyes?"

"I know who they are but I don't know them well. They lost that land near Bascom to the Leguizamóns, right?"

"Child! How do you know about those things? Anyway, from those lands you go along the river, going east, but before you get to the sand dunes, there, by the bridge. Do you know what I'm talking about?"

"Yes."

"Well, that's the salt water well I'm talking about. There, your father when he was a boy—younger than you—saved my father's life. I was just a toddler then. My father's horse had shied or something and knocked my father off. When he came to, his head was bandaged and he saw 'Quieto' holding a rattlesnake. Your father had whipped it to death. What happened

---

7. Señor (seh-nyohr'): Mr.
8. Señora (seh-nyoh'rah): Mrs.
9. doña (doh'nyah): formal title of respect used before first names of women.

was that when your father saw the frightened horse, he followed and lassoed it; calming it down, he released it and followed it again; they got to the shortcut, followed the tracks, and found my dad there.

That horse was called "Little Drum." My father gave it to Quieto as a present. As a matter of fact, the bloodline of many of the horses in your Uncle Julian's herd come down from it. Did you know that?"

"No. Did you know my great-grandfather on my father's side of the family?"

"The first Rafael? Oh, no, child. He died about five years before I was born. But I knew doña Benita, your great-grandmother Campoy because she was younger, just like your great-grandfather on your mother's side, don José; I knew him, too."

"Did you also know Luciano Buenrostro?"

"Of course, and his twin, Justo, too. They both lived to be no less than eighty years old. Luciano, when he was a youngster, confirmed your dad, as was the custom, at the salt lake at the Conde's Mission. That's the monument you mentioned.

"Now then, those old Buenrostros, and all of you Buenrostros are all related; they held that property near El Ebano."

"Yes, I know where it is. I used to work there in the summers; I'd stay with doña Virginia . . ."

"Justo's second wife who happens to be my mother's sister."

"Is that how we are related?"

"In part, that's how we're related on that side. Your mother-in-law, Modesta, may she rest in peace, was a first cousin of mine. And you know your Conce—may she rest in peace—was a Guerrero on her father's side, the coastal Mexican, but your Conce was also a Vidaurri on the side of doña Enriqueta, the one who just died."

At that moment, Israel came out and told me he had to go to Klail. "No, it has nothing to do with Susana; I'm going to Ralston Feed. You want to go or stay?"

Doña Barbarita's string of names ended up with Conce and her family. While in Japan and Korea, I thought little about her; here it was another matter. Ten months of marriage is nothing but her memory of her drowning and her parents' drowning in the river was brought back alive . . .

We got married soon after my first discharge. The plans were for me to go to college in Jonesville. The following year, Easter Sunday, the families had gathered near the river. The day began like any other in March in the Valley: Cool, somewhat sunny inland but with dark clouds over the Gulf. The families gathered near the Vilches' river bend ranch in Toluca; I'd gone with Israel to Río Rico to get who knows what for that afternoon, when a rain and hail storm caught up with us on the way back. It took over an hour and a half to make the usual twenty to thirty minute trip.

When we did get back, Israel and I were laughing, soaked clear through and covered with mud. When we got back to the picnic ground we knew something was up, something serious. Deadly.

Aaron, who must have been close to fourteen at the time, came running to us unable to talk. Israel got down immediately and ran to the river bank. I stayed behind with Aaron trying to find out what had happened. He kept repeating don Gervasio's and doña Modesta's names but said nothing about Conce. I remember this clearly.

I left him there and, before I got to where the families were, Israel, head down, came walking towards me.

Rafe Buenrostro IV

When the reserve called us up, (months before the war) that was the last time the Vielma family saw their son Pepe. We'd left Klail in civilian clothes; when we got to William Barrett, they took us straight to Fort Ben and back in uniform; two months later, Pier 92 in Seattle and bound for Japan.

When I got back from Korea, the first family I called was the Vielmas, but they weren't home; Israel thought they might be up in Austin on a visit. He knew, he said, that they planned to go to William Barrett before returning to Klail.

I asked Israel how the Vielmas had taken Pepe's death. They took it well enough, he said; they'd never get over it, but at least they were resigned to it. What else *could* they do?

"Did you hear Ventura got married? You didn't? To a Mexican girl from Jonesville; he met her up in Austin. They live there; she works for the state."

"Did he get his degree in architecture?"

"I think he's got a year to go; Ventura's got himself a part-time job in Austin working for a Mexican architect from San

Antonio. I haven't seen him for a couple of years. You'll see him when you go up to Austin."

"And Ángela?"

"About the same. The last I heard, she was in an accident but nothing serious. She hasn't married yet, and it looks like she's taken after that aunt a' hers on her mother's side; the one who owns that export-import business at the Jonesville port."

"Águeda."

"That's the one . . . But the Vielmas are doing all right."

I asked him if he remembered the time when the twins wanted to quit school. I knew Israel was going to laugh and it was good seeing him like that. Suddenly, he turned and said:

"You must've been about seven years old about the time Aaron fell down the stairs . . . Well, around that time, Dad said that don Prudencio was 'a good person.' Yeah, you must've been seven when you started to eat over there on Tuesday evenings. I remember Dad saying 'It's O.K. for him to eat over there; it's just like home.' Dad then called out to Aunt Matilda: 'It'd be a good idea to have the twins over for dinner, too, at least José Augusto. He and Rafe get along well. You pick the day, Mattie, and talk to Beba.' "

I'd forgotten about that; it could also be I never knew about it. The years we ate dinner together belonged to a life long gone. I couldn't even remember the first time Pepe and I started the Tuesday evening meals. It had gone on until we joined the army.

Pepe Vielma. It's hard to name him, to remember him. The army was another life, though. And there, Pepe Vielma was Joey Vielma; the Joey Vee who knew parts of Kobe and Nagoya better than anyone; he, who had read just about everything. Joey Vee: "That two gun's firing short; bring it up two clicks." And the time we got drunk with the chaplain, that, too, was Joey Vee. Not the dead man, however; the dead man was Pepe Vielma.

Israel's low voice, almost a whisper: "Hey . . . where were you?"

I told him about the wake at the military cemetery, and then I asked him for the keys: "I'm going to see Esteban."

"You brought Echevarría a present?"

"Yep; a bottle of Japanese wine and a lighter."

"He'll like that. Say 'hi!' for me; I've got to go, Rafe. I'll see you tonight, tomorrow morning."

Israel headed toward the river to see how the new irrigation pumps were working out.

I then went upstairs to pick up the presents and my eyes went straight to my Aunt Matilda Buenrostro's photograph. I barely knew my own mother, and so, I called my aunt "mother." As my father's sister, she ran the house. Ours was somewhat like the Vielma's in cleanliness and order and also in a certain ambience. While we didn't have the Vielma's strictness, we did have the same peace and quiet. At our house, problems were thought out; no yelling of any kind, not even when Uncle Julian brought my father (dead, atop the horse) just prior to my eighth birthday.

From what I do remember, my father was capable of spending hours in the company of friends, saying scarcely a word when they came to see him or when he himself paid them a call; something he did often.

Suddenly, the door was pushed open: My namesake, young Rafe, stared at me and then ran over for a hug. "Let's go look for your mother; I've got to go to Klail. Is she in the back yard, the patio?"

"Yes."

"You've got a gravelly voice, young Rafe."

"Yes."

"Yes."

Rafe Buenrostro V

I'd brought several snaps of Pepe as well as a book on primitive Japanese art to the Vielmas; don Prudencio said he knew the name of the publisher. Of the photos, they already had a copy of one of them where Pepe and I were sitting at a sidewalk restaurant. Doña Genoveva said that they'd send that one to Buenaventura.

The Vielma's house, a lot smaller than I remembered it, was as neat as usual with everything in place. The door to the twins' bedroom, immediately to the right, was closed.

Don Prudencio took me to a small living room; he looked older somehow; Doña Genoveva, on the other hand, looked unchanged. At the time of my visit, she must have been fifty-eight or so, and don Prudencio some five years older. As we entered the living room, Ángela came out of the kitchen; a smile and a hug. Doña Genoveva joined us then.

The four of us hardly spoke; it seemed as if we were all waiting for someone else to come in. After a while, don Prudencio rose and this was the sign for us to go to the dining room. Without a word, he and I set about opening the windows that faced the east and the west while the table was being laid out.

After dinner, he and I went to the porch. The visit wasn't turning out the way I had imagined it. Little or nothing was said about Pepe—José Augusto—and I felt as no other time in that family, where frankness was a code and a tradition, that the silence was oppressive. Years later, after the university, I learned that the silence was not due to Ángela's way of life. Not at all. It was Pepe's death in Korea. Everything functioned as before: amenities, grace and courtesy; but the silence was deadly.

When I said goodnight on the porch, don Prudencio alone, walked me to Israel's car: "You look well, Rafe. Do you *feel* well?"

I said I did, and I promised I'd see him again. To this, don Prudencio said:

"This is your house as it's always been, and in the same way that yours was . . . Pepe's."

Hearing him not say "José Augusto" surprised me, and, even more than his use of "Pepe," the timber of his voice. The conversation held no plan, no direction; it was depressing. Don Prudencio must've noticed it. He took my hand; this was followed by a silent hug. This, so natural in most people, was completely out of character; out of character for the don Prudencio I knew or thought I knew.

"I don't need to go to Jonesville tomorrow; they no longer need me at my age; the younger men do it all."

I didn't know what to say. The truth is that I, too, had nothing to say. At last I said: "Don Prudencio, *you're* the Herald. It needs *you*, not the other way round."

I was going to say more when he interrupted me: "What are you saying, boy? No, no. That's not true."

But it was true, and if he no longer exercised the power, the neatness, the accuracy of the Spanish section was there and it was due to him.

"I won't keep you any longer, Rafe. But do tell me this: Were you there? When José Augusto died, were you there?"

"Yes . . ."

"Was he the only one?"

"No, don Prudencio. There were others; a sergeant and a corporal died, too. And, there were several wounded."

"And you were one of these, right? Little Aaron told me. Yes. By the way, did you know Galindo wrote some verses in Spanish?"

"No."

"I'll give you a copy; maybe you can render them in English, Rafe."

"Me?"

"Yes, you. Look, tomorrow, since I'm not going to Jonesville, and if it's not too much trouble . . ."

"Whatever you say, don Prudencio."

"As I said, if it isn't too much trouble, come by, say around nine tomorrow morning?"

"Whenever you say."

"You know the gifts are appreciated, and most of all, the company."

It seemed he'd acquired something of a military bearing; he remained erect and when I shook his hand, I thought he was going to salute.

Standing by the car door, don Prudencio spoke again: "It's a consolation, knowing he didn't suffer; and, too, knowing you were there, Rafe. Look, Rafe, Genoveva and I want to see you again. It's a lot to ask, I know. You're young and you've got your own life, of course; but this is your home. Whenever you have time or whenever you think about it, come by."

I said I would and I did; I did so until I left for Austin, for the university, years later.

For Study and Discussion

1. Hinojosa-Smith's narrative technique can be likened to the weaving of a tapestry: within the framework of his story, he integrates many small yet telling threads of detail that together create a larger picture of Rafe Buenrostro's life and family. Give specific examples of this technique found in the section "Rafe Buenrostro III."

2. The family is of central importance in Mexican American culture. What role does the family unit play in Rafe Buenrostro's life? Give specific details to support your answer.

3. Although many of the characters in this novel are outwardly reserved, seeming at times emotionless, this apparent lack of emotion is deceiving. What details does the author use to indirectly reveal the depth of their feelings?

Writing About Literature

Analyzing Theme in Fiction

The soldier's return from war is a theme that traces back to the beginnings of written literature and quite likely long before. Tales that focus on this theme often describe the difficulties the soldier faces upon returning to family and society after a long absence and after experiencing the harrowing realities of war. In an essay of three or four paragraphs, discuss how this theme is developed in "Rafe Buenrostro Returns from Korea."

Prewriting. You will want to focus on the events and emotions that surround Rafe's homecoming as well as on the contrast between Rafe's war experiences and the life he returns to in the Valley. What ordeals did Rafe undergo while he was in Korea? What did he miss about the Valley? How does he feel about returning to a familiar, nonthreatening environment? What painful memories of the war and of events before the war continue to haunt him? What or who helps him to settle back into life in the Valley? How does Rafe feel toward his family and friends when he returns? How do these feelings differ from those he felt toward his famly and friends before he left for Korea?

Writing and Revising. When using quotations from the work, quote only as much of a passage as is necessary to support your statement. Use ellipsis points (. . .) to indicate omitted words or phrases in a sentence or passage, placing a period before the ellipsis points if they occur at the end of a sentence. Also use a period before the ellipsis points if they mark the omission of at least one sentence or more within the quotation.

Rudolfo A. Anaya

(1937–)

Myth, magic, and landscape flow together in the fiction of Rudolfo Anaya (roo-dohl'foh ah-nah'yah) to create a powerful current of mystery that is distinctively Hispanic and yet at the same time universal.

Born in northeastern New Mexico, Anaya has lived his entire life in his home state, where he currently teaches at the University of New Mexico. He has given readings from his works throughout the Southwest and, in 1980, at the White House. His own state recognized his contribution to the arts that same year by bestowing upon him the Governor's Award for Achievement in Literature.

His award-winning novel *Bless Me, Ultima* (1972) has brought him wide acclaim both for its literary merit and for its perceptive insights into Hispanic culture. After *Bless Me, Ultima,* Anaya published two more novels, *Heart of Aztlán* (1976) and *Tortuga* (1979). In addition, he has published a collection of short stories, *The Silence of the Llano* (1983), and has had two plays produced in New Mexico. Currently, he is working on his fourth novel.

The selection on the following pages, "Salomon's Story," is taken from *Tortuga* and exhibits Anaya's characteristic use of setting to develop a mythic story line. The common diction and simple syntax in the story give it an almost primitive style that is well suited to the brutal world of Salomon and his tribe of native hunters. Primarily, however, "Salomon's Story" illustrates Anaya's dedication to the process and art of storytelling itself.

Salomon's Story

from Tortuga

"Salomon's Story" is an excerpt from Anaya's novel Tor-
tuga, the story of a boy's recovery from a serious accident
that serves as his rite of passage into adulthood. Tortuga
meets Salomon in a hospital for crippled children, where
Salomon tells his story. Like Tortuga, Salomon undergoes
a painful experience that leads to a spiritual awakening.

Before I came here I was a hunter, but that was long ago. Still,
it was in the pursuit of the hunt that I came face to face with
my destiny. This is my story.

We called ourselves a tribe and we spent our time hunting
and fishing along the river. For young boys that was a great
adventure. Each morning I stole away from my father's home
to meet my fellow hunters by the river. My father was a farmer
who planted corn on the hills bordering the river. He was a
good man. He kept the ritual of the seasons, marked the path
of the sun and the moon across the sky, and he prayed each day
that the order of things not be disturbed.

He did his duty and tried to teach me about the rhythm in
the weather and the seasons, but a wild urge in my blood drove
me from him. I went willingly to join the tribe along the river.
The call of the hunt was exciting, and daily the slaughter of the
animals with the smell of blood drove us deeper and deeper
into the dark river. I became a member of the tribe, and I forgot
the fields of my father. We hunted birds with our crude weapons
and battered to death stray raccoons and rabbits. Then we
skinned the animals and filled the air with the smoke of roasting
meat. The tribe was pleased with me and welcomed me as a
hunter. They prepared for my initiation.

I, Salomon, tell you this so that you may know the meaning
of life and death. How well I know it now, how clear are the
events of the day I killed the giant river turtle. Since that day I
have been a storyteller, forced by the order of my destiny to

reveal my story. I speak to tell you how the killing became a horror.

The silence of the river was heavier than usual that day. The heat stuck to our sweating skin like a sticky syrup and the insects sucked our blood. Our half-naked bodies moved like shadows in the brush. Those ahead and behind me whispered from time to time, complaining that we were lost and suggesting that we turn back. I said nothing, it was the day of my initiation, I could not speak. There had been a fight at camp the night before and the bad feelings still lingered. But we hunted anyway, there was nothing else to do. We were compelled to hunt in the dark shadows of the river. Some days the spirit for the hunt was not good, fellow hunters quarreled over small things, and still we had to start early at daybreak to begin the long day's journey which would not bring us out until sunset.

In the branches above us the bird cries were sharp and frightful. More than once the leader lifted his arm and the line froze, ready for action. The humid air was tense. Somewhere to my left I heard the river murmur as it swept south, and for the first time the dissatisfaction which had been building within me surfaced. I cursed the oppressive darkness and wished I was free of it. I thought of my father walking in the sunlight of his green fields, and I wished I was with him. But it was not so; I owed the tribe my allegiance. Today I would become a full member. I would kill the first animal we encountered.

We moved farther than usual into unknown territory, hacking away at the thick underbrush; behind me I heard murmurs of dissension. Some wanted to turn back, others wanted to rest on the warm sandbars of the river, still others wanted to finish the argument which had started the night before. My father had given me an amulet to wear and he had instructed me on the hunt, and this made the leader jealous. Some argued that I could wear the amulet, while others said no. In the end the jealous leader tore it from my neck and said that I would have to face my initiation alone.

I was thinking about how poorly prepared I was and how my father had tried to help, when the leader raised his arm and sounded the alarm. A friend behind me whispered that if we were in luck there would be a deer drinking at the river. No one had ever killed a deer in the memory of our tribe. We held our breath and waited, then the leader motioned and I moved forward to see. There in the middle of the narrow path lay the biggest tortoise any of us had ever seen. It was a huge monster which had crawled out of the dark river to lay its eggs in the warm sand. I felt a shiver, and when I breathed the taste of copper drained my mouth and settled in my queasy stomach.

The giant turtle lifted its huge head and looked at us with dull, glintless eyes. The tribe drew back. Only I remained facing the monster from the water. Its slimy head dripped with bright green algae. It hissed a warning. It had come out of the water to lay its eggs, now it had to return to the river. Wet, leathery eggs fresh from the laying clung to its webbed feet, and as it moved forward it crushed them into the sand. Its gray shell was dry, dulled by the sun, encrusted with dead parasites and green growth; it needed the water.

"Kill it!" the leader cried, and at the same time the hunting horn sounded its too-rou which echoed down the valley. Ah, its call was so sad and mournful I can hear it today as I tell my story. . . . Listen, Tortuga, it is now I know that at that time I could have forsaken my initiation and denounced the darkness and insanity that urged us to the never-ending hunt. I had not listened to my father's words. The time was not right.

"The knife," the leader called, and the knife of the tribe was passed forward, then slipped into my hand. The huge turtle lumbered forward. I could not speak. In fear I raised the knife and brought it down with all my might. Oh, I prayed to no gods, but since then how often I have wished that I could undo what I did. One blow severed the giant turtle's head. One clean blow and the head rolled in the sand as the reptilian body reared back, gushing green slime. The tribe cheered and pressed forward. They were as surprised as I was that the kill had been so swift and clean. We had hunted smaller tortoises before and we knew that once they retreated into their shells it took hours to kill them. Then knives and spears had to be poked into the holes and the turtle had to be turned on its back so the tedious task of cutting the softer underside could begin. But now I had beheaded the giant turtle with one blow.

"There will be enough meat for the entire tribe," one of the boys cried. He speared the head and held it aloft for everyone to see. I could only look at the dead turtle that lay quivering on the sand, its death urine green blood staining the damp earth.

"He has passed his test," the leader shouted, "he did not

need the amulet of his father. We will clean the shell and it will be his shield! And he shall now be called the man who slew the turtle!"

The tribe cheered, and for a moment I bathed in my glory. The fear left me, and so did the desire to be with my father on the harsh hills where he cultivated his fields of corn. He had been wrong; I could trust the tribe and its magic. Then someone shouted and we turned to see the turtle struggling toward us. It reared up, exposing the gaping hole where the head had been, then it charged, surprisingly swift for its size. Even without its head it crawled toward the river. The tribe fell back in panic.

"Kill it!" the leader shouted, "Kill it before it reaches the water! If it escapes into the water it will grow two heads and return to haunt us!"

I understood what he meant. If the creature reached the safety of the water it would live again, and it would become one more of the ghosts that lurked along our never-ending path. Now there was nothing I could do but stand my ground and finish the killing. I struck at it until the knife broke on its hard shell, and still the turtle rumbled toward the water, pushing me back. Terror and fear made me fall on the sand and grab it with my bare hands. Grunting and gasping for breath I dug my bare feet into the sand. I slipped one hand into the dark, bleeding hole where the head had been and with the other I grabbed its huge feet. I struggled to turn it on its back and rob it of its strength, but I couldn't. Its dark instinct for the water and the pull of death were stronger than my fear and desperation. I grunted and cursed as its claws cut into my arms and legs. The brush shook with our violent thrashing as we rolled down the bank towards the river. Even mortally wounded it was too strong for me. At the edge of the river, it broke free from me and plunged into the water, trailing frothy blood and bile as it disappeared into the gurgling waters.

Covered with turtle's blood, I stood numb and trembling. As I watched it disappear into the dark waters of the river, I knew I had done a wrong. Instead of conquering my fear, I had created another shadow which would return to haunt us. I turned and looked at my companions; they trembled with fright.

"You have failed us," the leader whispered. "You have angered the river gods." He raised his talisman, a stick on which hung chicken feathers, dried juniper berries and the rattler of a snake we had killed in the spring, and he waved it in front of me to ward off the curse. Then they withdrew in silence and vanished into the dark brush, leaving me alone on that stygian bank.

Oh, I wish I could tell you how lonely I felt. I cried for the turtle to return so I could finish the kill, or return its life, but the force of my destiny was already set and that was not to be. I understand that now. That is why I tell you my story. I left the river, free of the tribe, but unclean and smelling of death.

That night the bad dreams came, and then the paralysis. . . .

For Study and Discussion

1. The giant turtle symbolizes a powerful force in "Salomon's Story." **a.** What is this force? **b.** How does Salomon deal with this force, and what is the result of his actions?

2. This story illustrates a basic contrast between two ways of life. **a.** What are these two ways of life? **b.** What two characters best represent them? **c.** Using specific examples from the story, discuss the values and rewards of each way of life.

3. Both Salomon and the young narrator in "My Wonder Horse" (page 167) undergo tests that serve as initiations, or "rites of passage," into manhood. However, the tests themselves, as well as their results for the two boys, differ greatly. **a.** In what way are the tests alike? **b.** In what way do they differ? **c.** To what extent do the two boys succeed or fail?

Writing About Literature

Identifying the Tone in a Short Story

Tone refers to the attitude a writer takes toward his or her subject, characters, or readers. The tone in the short biographies of the authors in this anthology, for example, is objective. Other examples of tone that writers may use in a story, poem, or play, include ironic, humorous, bitter, compassionate, detached, grim, and smug. A writer's choice of descriptive detail, point of view, diction, and setting all contribute to establishing tone.

In "Salomon's Story," the narrator's purpose for telling his tale sets the tone, which is then reinforced by other elements of the story. In a short essay, identify the tone in "Salomon's Story," and discuss how at least three literary elements help to establish that tone.

Prewriting. Begin by determining the narrator's purpose for telling his story. Is he trying to entertain, to amuse, to persuade, to inform, or does he have some other purpose? Next, ask yourself, "What is the narrator's attitude toward his subject?" He certainly does not take a lighthearted or amused view. Use two or three adjectives to identify his attitude, or in other words, his tone. Now, look at other elements in the story, such as the setting, other characters, symbolism, description, and diction. How do they help convey the narrator's tone? Once you have answered these questions, choose the three literary elements that most strongly express the narrator's tone and find specific examples of where they do so in the story. Finally, organize your ideas and details in an outline.

Writing and Revising. In addition to varying your diction, or choice of words, vary your sentence structure as well. For example, a series of short, choppy sentences can be combined into longer, more concise statements through the use of subordination:

> **Choppy:** The narrator in this story does not take a lighthearted view. His tone is not satirical either. He takes his subject quite seriously.

> **Better:** Far from adopting a lighthearted or satirical tone, the narrator in this story takes his subject quite seriously. (first two sentences combined in a subordinate phrase)

Tomás Rivera
(1935–1984)

Tomás Rivera (toh-mahs′ ree-beh′rah) has exerted a powerful influence on Chicano literature, not only through his writing but also in the model he himself provided for aspiring young Mexican American writers whose backgrounds were similar to his own.

Born in Crystal City, Texas, to migrant worker parents, Rivera often labored in the fields, attending school when he could. Beginning in his early childhood, he read whatever he could find—sports and adventure stories, discarded books that he fished out of trash dumps, old magazines that his father collected from neighbors. In high school, he developed a keen interest in American writers such as Ernest Hemingway, John Steinbeck, and the nineteenth-century poet Walt Whitman. Rivera wrote his first story when he was about twelve years old—a story that he later pronounced "crummy" but that sparked what would become a lifelong love of writing.

Although Rivera entered college with the intention of becoming an art teacher, he later changed his major to English, earning his undergraduate degree in 1958. Not until his graduate studies did he begin to focus on the works of Hispanic writers. He eventually received a Ph.D. in Romance languages and literature with an emphasis on Spanish studies. In 1979, he was appointed chancellor of the University of California at Riverside and served in that capacity until his death.

During his career as a writer and educator, Rivera published many stories, poems, and essays, as well as one novel. In his fiction, Rivera tried to capture "the suffering and the strength and the beauty" of the people he grew up among—migrant workers who, like his own family, endured poverty, mistreatment, and constant uprooting as they traveled across the United States in search of work. His award-winning novel

. . . y no se lo tragó la tierra [. . . and the earth did not devour him] uses simple yet evocative language to explore the struggles and hardships of working-class Mexican Americans. On the following pages are two excerpts—"A Prayer" and "The Portrait"—from this realistic and compelling work.

A Prayer

from . . . and the earth did not devour him

Although deeply personal, prayers often express universal human experiences and emotions. The entreaties of the speaker in this prayer echo the anguish of many people throughout history whose loved ones have gone to war.

Dear God, Jesus Christ, keeper of my soul. This is the third Sunday that I come to implore you, beg you, to give me word of my son. I have not heard from him. Protect him, my God, that no bullet may pierce his heart like it happened to Doña[1] Virginia's son, may he rest in God's peace. Take care of him for me, Dear Jesus, save him from the gunfire, have pity on him who is so good. Since he was a baby, when I would nurse him to sleep, he was so gentle, very grateful, never biting me. He's very innocent, protect him, he does not wish to harm anyone, he is very noble, he is very kind, may no bullet pierce his heart.

Please, Virgin Mary, you, too, shelter him. Shield his body, cover his head, cover the eyes of the Communists and the Koreans and the Chinese so that they cannot see him, so they won't kill him. I still keep his toys from when he was a child, his little cars, little trucks, even a kite that I found the other day in the closet. Also his cards and the funnies that he has learned to read. I have put everything away until his return.

Protect him, Jesus, that they may not kill him. I have made a promise to the Virgen de San Juan to pay her homage at her shrine and to the Virgen de Guadalupe,[2] too. He also wears a

---

1. **Doña** (doh'nyah): formal title of respect used before first names of women.
2. **Virgen de Guadalupe** (beer'hehn deh gwah-thah-loo'peh): The references in this paragraph to several Virgins reflect the belief that the Virgin Mother has appeared to the faithful many times in different places, where she has answered their prayers. The Virgen de Guadalupe is the most popular of these reported visions among Mexican and Mexican American Roman Catholics.

Tomás Rivera 437

little medallion of the Virgen de San Juan del Valle and he, too, has made a promise to her; he wants to live. Take care of him, cover his heart with your hand, that no bullet may enter it. He's very noble. He was very afraid to go, he told me so. The day they took him, when he said his farewell he embraced me and he cried for a while. I could feel his heart beating and I remembered when he was little and I would nurse him and the happiness that I felt and he felt.

Take care of him for me, please, I beseech you. I promise you my life for his. Bring him back from Korea safe and sound. Cover his heart with your hands. Jesus Christ, Holy God, Virgen de Guadalupe, bring him back alive, bring me back his heart. Why have they taken him? He has done no harm. He knows nothing. He is very humble. He doesn't want to take away anybody's life. Bring him back alive, I don't want him to die.

Here is my heart for his. Here is my heart. Here, in my chest, palpitating. Tear it out if blood is what you want, but tear it out of *me*. I sacrifice my heart for his. Here it is. Here is my heart! Through it runs his very own blood . . .

Bring him back alive and I will give you my very own heart.

The Portrait

from . . . and the earth did not devour him

Unscrupulous salespeople often operate under the principle that "a fool and his money are soon parted." In this story, a portrait salesman learns that applying this principle is not always as easy as it might seem: cornered by his irate victim, Don[1] Mateo, he must "produce the goods." When you finish the story, see if you think Don Mateo has, after all, gotten the "portrait" he paid for.

As soon as the people returned from up north the portrait salesmen began arriving from San Antonio. They would come to rake in. They knew that the workers had money and that was why, as Dad used to say, they would flock in. They carried suitcases packed with samples and always wore white shirts and ties; that way they looked more important and the people believed everything they would tell them and invite them into their homes without giving it much thought. I think that down deep they even longed for their children to one day be like them. In any event, they would arrive and make their way down the dusty streets, going house to house carrying suitcases full of samples.

I remember once I was at the house of one of my father's friends when one of these salesmen arrived. I also remember that that particular one seemed a little frightened and timid. Don Mateo asked him to come in because he wanted to do business.

"Good afternoon, traveler. I would like to tell you about something new that we're offering this year."

"Well, let's see, let's see . . ."

---

1. **Don** (dohn): title of respect, formerly used for Spanish-speaking men of high rank, now used as a title of courtesy.

"Well, sir, see, you give us a picture, any picture you may have, and we will not only enlarge it for you but we'll also set it in a wooden frame like this one and we'll shape the image a little, like this—three dimensional, as they say."

"And what for?"

"So that it will look real. That way . . . look, let me show you . . . see? Doesn't he look real, like he's alive?"

"Man, he sure does. Look, vieja.[2] This looks great. Well, you know, we wanted to send some pictures to be enlarged . . . but now, this must cost a lot, right?"

"No, I'll tell you, it costs about the same. Of course, it takes more time."

"Well, tell me, how much?"

"For as little as thirty dollars we'll deliver it to you done with inlays just like this, one this size."

"Boy, that's expensive! Didn't you say it didn't cost a lot more? Do you take installments?"

"Well, I'll tell you, we have a new manager and he wants everything in cash. It's very fine work. We'll make it look like real. Shaped like that, with inlays . . . take a look. What do you think? Some fine work, wouldn't you say? We can have it all finished for you in a month. You just tell us what color you want the clothes to be and we'll come by with it all finished one day when you least expect, framed and all. Yes, sir, a month at the longest. But like I say, this man, who's the new manager, he wants the full payment in cash. He's very demanding, even with us."

"Yes, but it's much too expensive."

"Well, yes. But the thing is, this is very fine work. You can't say you've ever seen portraits done like this, with wood inlays."

"No, well, that's true. What do you think, vieja?"

"Well, I like it a lot. Why don't we order one? And if it turns out good . . . my Chuy . . . may he rest in peace. It's the only picture we have of him. We took it right before he left for Korea. Poor m'ijo,[3] we never saw him again. See . . . this is his picture. Do you think you can make it like that, make it look like he's alive?"

---

2. **vieja** (byeh'hah): old lady; in this context, an affectionate term for "wife."
3. **m'ijo** (mee'hoh): a contraction of *mi hijo* [my son].

"Sure, we can. You know, we've done a lot of them in soldier's uniforms and shaped it, like you see in this sample, with inlays. Why, it's more than just a portrait. Sure. You just tell me what size you want and whether you want a round or square frame. What do you say? How should I write it down?"

"What do you say, vieja, should we have it done like this one?"

"Well, I've already told you what I think. I would like to have m'ijo's picture fixed up like that and in color."

"All right, go ahead and write it down. But you take good care of that picture for us because it's the only one we have of our son grown up. He was going to send us one all dressed up in uniform with the American and Mexican flags crossed over his head, but he no sooner got there when a letter arrived telling us that he was lost in action. So you take good care of it."

"Don't you worry. We're responsible people. And we understand the sacrifices that you people make. Don't worry. And you just wait and see, when we bring it, you'll see how pretty it's gonna look. What do you say, should we make the uniform navy blue?"

"But he's not wearing a uniform in that picture."

"No, but that's just a matter of fixing it up with some wood fiber overlays. Look at these. This one, he didn't have a uniform on but we put one on him. So what do you say? Should we make it navy blue?"

"All right."

"Don't you worry about the picture."

And that was how they spent the entire day, going house to house, street by street, their suitcases stuffed with pictures. As it turned out, a whole lot of people had ordered enlargements of that kind.

"They should be delivering those portraits soon, don't you think?"

"I think so, it's delicate work and takes more time. That's some fine work those people do. Did you see how real those pictures looked?"

"Yeah, sure. They do some fine work. You can't deny that. But it's already been over a month since they passed by here."

"Yes, but from here they went on through all the towns picking up pictures . . . all the way to San Antonio for sure. So it'll probably take a little longer."

"That's true, that's true."

And two more weeks had passed by the time they made the discovery. Some very heavy rains had come and some children, who were playing in one of the tunnels leading to the dump, found a sack full of pictures, all worm-eaten and soaking wet. The only reason that they could tell that these were pictures was because there were a lot of them and most of them the same size and with faces that could just barely be made out. Everybody caught on right away. Don Mateo was so angry that he took off to San Antonio to find the so and so who had swindled them.

"Well, you know, I stayed at Esteban's house. And every day I went with him to the market to sell produce. I helped him with everything. I had faith that I would run into that son of a gun some day soon. Then, after I'd been there for a few days, I started going out to the different barrios[4] and I found out a lot that way. It wasn't so much the money that upset me. It was my poor vieja, crying and all because we'd lost the only picture we had of Chuy. We found it in the sack with all the other pictures but it was already ruined, you know."

"I see, but tell me, how did you find him?"

"Well, you see, to make a long story short, he came by the stand at the market one day. He stood right in front of us and bought some vegetables. It was like he was trying to remember who I was. Of course, I recognized him right off. Because when you're angry enough, you don't forget a face. I just grabbed him right then and there. Poor guy couldn't even talk. He was all scared. And I told him that I wanted that portrait of my son and that I wanted it three dimensional and that he'd best get it for me or I'd let him have it. And I went with him to where he lived. And I put him to work right then and there. The poor guy didn't know where to begin. He had to do it all from memory."

"And how did he do it?"

---

4. **barrios** (bahr'ryohs): districts into which large towns or cities are divided.

"I don't know. I suppose if you're scared enough, you're capable of doing anything. Three days later he brought me the portrait all finished, just like you see it there on that table by the Virgin. Now tell me, how do you like the way my boy looks?"

"Well, to be honest, I don't remember too well how Chuy looked. But he was beginning to look more and more like you, isn't that so?"

"Yes, I would say so. That's what everybody tells me now. That Chuy's a chip off the old block and that he was already looking like me. There's the portrait. Like they say, one and the same."

For Study and Discussion

1. Throughout "A Prayer," the mother describes her son as a nonviolent, sensitive young man who is hardly the kind of person suited to become a soldier. **a.** Give several examples that illustrate this characterization of the son. **b.** If the son's character is as the mother describes, he probably would not fare well in combat. Is any evidence given in the story as to his fate?

2. In "The Portrait," what evidence can you find to show that the portrait salesman is a smooth talker who cheats gullible people by telling them what they want to hear and by appealing to their emotions?

3. Although somewhat gullible, Don Mateo in "The Portrait" proves himself to be a determined man who does not give up easily. **a.** Cite an incident in the story that shows that he is gullible. **b.** What incidents in the story reveal his determination? **c.** Give three adjectives, other than *gullible* and *determined,* that you think describe Don Mateo. Be prepared to give specific examples from the story to support your choices.

4. Some readers think that "The Portrait" ends with a touch of humor. What development or detail in the story can be seen as humorous?

Literary Elements

Point of View

Point of view is the vantage point from which a story is told. In the **first-person point of view,** one of the characters tells the story in his or her own words, which gives the work a sense of immediacy and intimacy. Since the story is presented from this one character's perspective, the reader can learn from the narrative only what this character knows and perceives. In the **third-person point of view,** the story is narrated by someone who stands outside of the action of the story. Sometimes the third-person narrator tells the story from a **limited point of view,** focusing on the thoughts and actions of a single character. In other cases, the narrator takes an **omniscient,** or all-knowing, perspective and describes what *all* of the characters think and do.

Writers always choose point of view carefully in order to give their stories a particular effect. Tomás Rivera, for example, uses different points of view in "A Prayer" and "The Portrait" to help create the particular effect he wanted in each story. What points of view does he use in these two stories? Why is his choice of point of view appropriate for each selection?

Writing About Literature

Analyzing Character

A prayer is a very personal form of expression which often reveals much about the person who is saying it. In Tomás Rivera's "A Prayer," we are given several insights into the mother's character which enable us to recognize qualities that she possesses. For example, when we read that she keeps her son's "toys from when he was a child" and has "put everything away until his return," we can gather that she is sentimental. Using specific clues from the story, write a two- or three-paragraph essay discussing two qualities you find in the mother.

Prewriting. Before you begin writing, reread the story several times, looking for evidence about the mother's character. As you read, make a list of quotations that indicate specific character traits. Next, group these quotations under particular traits. You can then use these groupings as a rough outline for two paragraphs. You may want to add a concluding paragraph to sum up the main points of your character analysis.

Writing and Revising. When you give specific quotations, be sure that you use the exact words and punctuation that appear in the story.

Poetry of the Contemporary Period

Many poets at the beginning of the Contemporary Period championed the Chicano movement of the late 1960s and early 1970s. These socially committed poets wrote to affirm their culture and to defend its traditions and values. Their poetry is often defiantly combative, exalting Mexican Americans' Indian heritage and challenging Anglo society to accept them as *mestizos* (the descendants of New World Indians and European Spaniards).

During the Mexican American Period, Spanish-language newspapers assumed an important role in openly voicing the social unrest that spread throughout the Mexican American community. The Chicano movement brought renewed interest to this print medium, as both professional and amateur writers sought an outlet for artistic and political expression. *Corridos, décimas,* and other traditional and contemporary poetry appeared in the pages of newspapers such as *El Malcriado* [The Brat], the official publication of the farm workers union led by César Chávez.

Several themes dominate in the poetry published during the height of the Chicano movement:

- the identification of Mexican Americans with both contemporary Mexico and its indigenous Aztec and Mayan cultures;
- the struggles and deprivation suffered by Mexican Americans in the barrios;
- the family as a source of comfort, strength, and traditional values and customs;
- *carnalismo* [brotherhood, camaraderie, solidarity] among Mexican Americans;
- unity achieved through political action aimed to preserve the values and traditions of Mexican Americans.

Poetic expression during the early part of the Contemporary Period is simple and direct, devoid of florid and affected language. Poets frequently used *code-switching* (a linguistic pattern of alternating rapidly between English and Spanish) to emphasize the uniqueness of Mexican American Spanish. By speaking in the traditional language of their culture in their art, Mexican American poets asserted the inherent value and dignity of this culture. They also affirmed the many and varied experiences of Mexican Americans by using the particular idioms that reflect these experiences, such as *caló*, or barrio slang. The use of *caló* lent authenticity to the poets' accounts of barrio life, which dealt with the daily experience of the thousands of unemployed and undereducated Mexican American youth.

Well-known, socially committed poets of the late 1960s and early 1970s include Rodolfo "Corky" Gonzales, Alurista, Ricardo Sánchez, and Tino Villanueva. Gonzales, organizer of the Denver-based militant organization Crusade for Justice, brings together many of the themes and motifs of the early Contemporary Period in his epic poem *Yo soy Joaquín* [I am Joaquín]. Alurista, a key figure in early Chicano poetry, experiments boldly with a creative mixture of English, Spanish, barrio slang, and Nahuatl (the language of the Aztecs and their contemporary Mexican descendants), producing surprising imagery and unique verbal effects. Sánchez's poetry urges Chicanos to unite in the spirit of *carnalismo* to resist oppression. His language is often like the blast of a loud horn: it jars and jolts the reader, commanding attention. Much of Villanueva's early poetry focuses on Mexican American urban and rural poverty. He sees the *pachuco*—a barrio Chicano characterized by flamboyant dress, distinctive slang, and a defiant stance—as a prime symbol of resistance to assimilation.

Beginning in the mid-1970s, poets began to focus less on specific societal ills and more on a broader spectrum of themes. They were no less politically committed than the poets of a few years before, but their works began to reflect a greater concern with their role as artists and with the formal elements of their craft such as poetic language and imagery. This trend has become even more pronounced in the 1980s as a greater number of poets begin to experiment with the technical aspects of writing.

In general, the poets of the later phase of the Contemporary Period tend to explore themes from a more personal point of view. The works of Luis Omar Salinas, for example, investigate the plight of the individual in the face of death, loneliness, and despair. Villanueva's later poetry is highly philosophical in its probing of topics such as death, love, time, and beauty. Drawing upon their experiences in Korea and Vietnam, respectively, poets Rolando Hinojosa-Smith and Leroy Quintana reflect on the human costs and the bitter ironies of war. The richly symbolic works of Alberto Ríos and Ray González challenge the reader to uncover deeper levels of meaning in seemingly simple images. Gary Soto's poems often emphasize poetic images that stem from his personal memories and the connections he perceives between his outer environment and his inner self. Like Soto, poet Leonard Adame often describes his boyhood in California, using finely crafted language that lends both beauty and precision to his works. Many of Jimmy Santiago Baca's poems are "meditations" on the continuity and wholeness of Hispanic life on the fringes of a New Mexico city.

Poetry by Mexican American women has grown into a strong and distinctive voice during the past decade. Writing from both a social and an individual perspective, many women poets have come to identify themselves as *chicanas*—a term that expresses both their pride in their heritage and their unique concerns as women in Mexican American culture. Angela de Hoyos and Bernice Zamora, for example, often focus on the role of women in modern society as well as on a variety of personal and philosophical themes. Poets Lorna Dee Cervantes, Sandra Cisneros, Pat Mora, and Rosemary Catacalos reflect on experiences they had while growing up in Mexican American urban communities, drawing upon images ingrained in memory to create works that take a highly personal approach to universal themes. Lucha Corpi represents a more introspective current in Chicano poetry, using precise language and imagery to explore her inner life and perceptions. Like other poets of the Contemporary Period, many Mexican American women poets not only address specific social and cultural issues but also offer insights into the whole of human experience.

Rodolfo "Corky" Gonzales

(1928–)

I Am Joaquín became a historical essay, a social statement . . . It is a mirror of our greatness and our weakness, a call to action as a total people, emerging from a glorious history, traveling through social pain and conflicts, confessing our weaknesses while we shout about our strength. . . .

This statement from Rodolfo "Corky" Gonzales's (roh-dohl'foh gohn-sah'lehs) introduction to his well-known poem expresses the depth of his commitment to his people. A poet, political activist, and ex-prizefighter, Gonzales brought the same aggressive drive to his civil rights work in the 1960s and 1970s that he had brought to his boxing career, setting him at the forefront of the Chicano movement.

Born in Denver, Colorado, to migrant worker parents, Gonzales took up boxing at age fifteen as a way of escaping the dead-end poverty of life in the barrio. He started boxing competitively after World War II, winning sixty-five of his seventy-five fights before his retirement from the sport in 1953. Following a brief comeback in 1957, he launched into his political career.

Gonzales held numerous important political positions throughout the early 1960s and was the first Mexican American district captain of the Denver Democratic Party. However, his fight for minority rights soon led him to adopt a more radical stance, often involving the organization of protests against discrimination. In 1966, he founded the Crusade for Justice, a service-oriented cultural center that soon evolved into a powerful and far-reaching voice for Mexican Americans. The Crusade for Justice sponsored the First Annual Chicano Youth Conference in 1969—a historical event that was attended by approximately fifteen hundred people.

In his civil rights work, Gonzales has focused on immediate social problems such as poverty, discrimination, and police brutality against Chicano youths, as well as on related issues of ethnic identity and cultural pride. Through social programs and active protest, he has urged Mexican Americans to both embrace their Mexican heritage and fight for their rights as American citizens.

Gonzales's writing is inseparable from his activism. With a single book-length poem, *I Am Joaquín,* he has greatly influenced the development of Chicano literature and has spoken to the hearts of countless Mexican Americans. As Gonzales himself states, *I Am Joaquín* is as much a social and historical document of Chicano culture as it is a literary work.

Gonzales currently lives in Denver, Colorado, where he is working on his autobiography and a collection of poems.

from I Am Joaquín[1]

Reflecting the powerful cultural reawakening of the Chicano movement, I Am Joaquín expresses the speaker's deeply rooted pride in his Mexican American heritage. As you read this excerpt, consider the many diverse elements that make up Joaquín's cultural identity. What aspects of his culture does he embrace? How does he preserve his sense of identity within the "whirl" of modern society?

I am Joaquín,
lost in a world of confusion,
caught up in the whirl of a
              gringo[2] society,
confused by the rules,   5
scorned by attitudes,
suppressed by manipulation,
and destroyed by modern society.
My fathers
    have lost the economic battle   10
and won
    the struggle of cultural survival.
And now!
    I must choose
              between   15
    the paradox of
victory of the spirit,
despite physical hunger,
              or
    to exist in the grasp   20
of American social neurosis,
sterilization of the soul
    and a full stomach.
Yes,
I have come a long way to nowhere,   25

---

1. Joaquín (hwah-keen').
2. gringo (green'goh): a foreigner who speaks English, especially a person from the United States.

unwillingly dragged by that
monstrous, technical,
industrial giant called
        Progress
and Anglo[3] success. . . .   30
I look at myself.
I watch my brothers.
I shed tears of sorrow.
I sow seeds of hate.
I withdraw to the safety within the   35
circle of life—
        MY OWN PEOPLE.
I am Cuauhtémoc,[4]
proud and noble,
        leader of men,   40
king of an empire
civilized beyond the dreams
    of the gachupín[5] Cortés,[6]
who also is the blood,
    the image of myself.   45
I am the Maya[7] prince.
I am Nezahualcóyotl,[8]
great leader of the Chichimecas.[9]
I am the sword and flame of Cortés
            the despot.   50
            And
I am the eagle and serpent of
        the Aztec civilization.
I owned the land as far as the eye
could see under the crown of Spain,   55
and I toiled on my earth

---

3. **Anglo:** an inhabitant of the United States whose native language is English and whose culture is of English origin.
4. **Cuauhtémoc** (kwow-tehm'ohk): last of the Aztec emperors.
5. **gachupín** (gah-choo-peen'): a native of Spain (Mexican slang).
6. **Cortés** (kohr-tehs'): Spanish conqueror of Mexico.
7. **Maya** (mah'yah): name of the native language and ancient civilization of the Yucatan.
8. **Nezahualcóyotl** (neh-sah-wahl-koh'yohtl): refined "poet king" of the Mexican city of Texcoco who ruled from 1418–1472.
9. **Chichimecas** (chee-chee-meh'kahs): barbaric nomads who acquired more civilized ways under the reign of Nezahualcóyotl.

and gave my Indian sweat and blood
  for the Spanish master
who ruled with tyranny over man and
beast and all that he could trample.   60
          But . . .
   THE GROUND WAS MINE.
I was both tyrant and slave.

For Study and Discussion

1. Joaquín feels that he speaks both for himself and for an entire culture. With what aspects of Mexican American history and experience does the speaker identify himself?

2. Joaquín embraces several seemingly contradictory aspects of his heritage. For example, he identifies with both the Spanish conqueror Cortés and the Indian peoples conquered by the Spaniards. What are some other conflicting elements of his heritage, and how does Joaquín reconcile them within himself?

3. The presence of conflict is a central element in *I Am Joaquín*. **a.** With what is the speaker in conflict and why? **b.** Where does he find refuge from strife?

Literary Elements

Parallelism

Parallelism is a kind of repetition in which a writer uses phrases and clauses that are similar in structure or meaning. For example, in the first stanza of *I Am Joaquín*, the poet uses a series of structurally similar phrases that begin with the participles *lost, caught, confused, scorned, suppressed,* and *destroyed.* This parallelism helps to create rhythm, emphasis, and unity in the stanza.

    Where else in the poem does Gonzales use parallelism? In each case, what is the effect of the parallel structure? What elements of the poem does it emphasize or unify?

Rodolfo "Corky" Gonzales 453

Alurista

(1947–)

One of the most prolific contemporary Mexican American poets, Alurista (ah-loo-rees'tah) has had more than ten books of his poetry published. Throughout these works he conducts linguistic experiments mixing English, Spanish, and barrio slang to create a rich variety of poetic voices. In fact, he even conducted one of these experiments on his given name, Alberto Urista, which he combined to form his pen name.

Like a number of other Mexican American writers, he was born in Mexico and began his schooling there. During his adolescent years, he moved with his family to San Diego, California. Alurista remained in the San Diego area through his college years and received an undergraduate degree in psychology, after which he went on to earn a doctorate in Spanish Literature.

In his early books of poetry such as *Floricanto en Aztlán* [Flowersong in Aztlán] and *Nationchild Plumaroja* [Nationchild redplumage], Alurista explores the meaning of his indigenous Indian roots, skillfully manipulating Indian motifs to symbolically merge the ancient and modern worlds. His exploration of his roots coincided with his active involvement in the Chicano movement, one of whose main precepts is the acceptance and glorification of the Mexican American's Indian heritage. Deeply dedicated to the Chicano movement, Alurista embraces the concept of "the great refusal," which entails the rejection of the dominant American culture in favor of traditional Mexican American customs and ideals. Much of his later poetry is less confrontational in its assertion of Chicano principles, yet it continues to exhibit wonderfully creative metaphorical and linguistic experimentation.

In addition to being a poet, dramatist, author of children's books, and community activist, Alurista has taught at several colleges and universities. He currently lives in California where he continues to teach, do research on Mexican American and Latin American literature, and write poetry.

The three selections by Alurista on the following pages, all from his earlier poetry, burst with surprising imagery and provocative uses of language. They convey the collective sadness and impatience of a people who have a proud ancestry yet suffer the humiliation of second-class status in the United States.

when raza?[1]

The speaker of this poem poses an urgent question: "when" will his race—the Mexican American people—gain their freedom? In answer, the speaker insists that his people must act "now," not "mañana" [tomorrow] —that Mexican Americans must "define" their future today.

when raza?
when . . .
     yesterday's gone
and
     mañana[2]   5
mañana doesn't come
     for he who waits
no morrow
     only for he who is now
to whom when equals now   10
he will see a morrow
mañana La Raza
     la gente que espera[3]
no verá mañana[4]
our tomorrow es hoy[5]   15
     ahorita[6]
que VIVA LA RAZA[7]
     mi gente[8]
our people to freedom
     when?   20
now, ahorita define tu mañana hoy[9]

---

1. **raza** (rah'sah): race.
2. **mañana** (mah-nyah'nah): tomorrow.
3. **la gente que espera** (lah hen'teh keh ehs-peh'rah): the people who wait.
4. **no verá mañana** (noh beh-rah' mah-nyah'nah): will not see tomorrow.
5. **es hoy** (ehs oy): is today.
6. **ahorita** (ah-ohr-ee'tah): this very moment.
7. **que VIVA LA RAZA** (keh vee'bah lah rah'sah): long live the race.
8. **mi gente** (mee hen'teh): my people.
9. **tu mañana hoy** (too mah-nyah'nah oy): your tomorrow today.

456 *Alurista*

must be the season of the witch

Drawing on a powerful image from Mexican American folklore, Alurista identifies the "witch" of this poem as La Llorona [The Weeping Woman]. According to legend, La Llorona drowned her children and now haunts the place where they were killed, weeping in grief over their loss. (For more information about this legend, see page 36.) As you read, consider what "the witch" represents. Why "must" the current age "be the season of the witch"?

---

must be the season of the witch
    la bruja[1]
    la llorona[2]
she lost her children
    and she cries   5
en las barrancas[3] of industry
    her children
devoured by computers
and the gears
must be the season of the witch   10
    i hear huesos[4] crack
in pain
    y lloros[5]
la bruja pangs
    sus hijos han olvidado[6]   15
la magia de durango[7]

---

1. **la bruja** (lah broo'hah): the witch.
2. **la llorona** (lah yoh-roh'nah): the weeping woman.
3. **en las barrancas** (ehn lahs bahr-rahn'kahs): in the ravines.
4. **huesos** (weh'sohs): bones.
5. **y lloros** (ee yoh'rohs): and weeping.
6. **sus hijos han olvidado** (soos ee'hohs ahn ohl-bee-thah'thoh): her children have forgotten.
7. **la magia de durango** (lah mah'hyah deh doo-rahn'goh): the magic of Durango.

Alurista 457

y la de moctezuma[8]
—el huiclamina[9]
must be the season of the witch
la bruja llora[10]   20
sus hijos sufren; sin ella[11]

---

8. y la de moctezuma (ee lah deh mohk-teh-soo'mah): and that of
Moctezuma (Montezuma, emperor of Mexico).
9. el huiclamina (ehl wee-klah-mee'nah): the second name of Montezuma I.
10. la bruja llora (lah broo'hah yoh'rah): the witch cries.
11. sus hijos sufren; sin ella (soos ee'hohs soo'frehn; seen eh'yah): her
children suffer; without her.

mis ojos hinchados[1]

*In this poem, the speaker feels a painful conflict between
his sense of personal freedom and his realization that, as
long as his race bears the "scars" of oppression, he cannot
truly be free. Have you ever felt a similar kind of conflict—a sense that, although you are personally free, you
are limited by your circumstances—perhaps by your age
or environment? How does Alurista's poetic imagery help
to express the speaker's conflict?*

Mis ojos hinchados
   flooded with lágrimas[2]
de bronce[3]
melting on the cheek bones
of my concern   5
   razgos indígenas[4]

---

1. mis ojos hinchados (mees oh'hohs een-chah'thohs): my swollen eyes.
2. lágrimas (lah'gree-mahs): tears.
3. de bronce (deh brohn'seh): of bronze.
4. razgos indígenas (rahs'gohs een-dee'heh-nahs): Indian features.

458 *Alurista*

the scars of history on my face
and the veins of my body
that ache
        vomito sangre[5]   10
y lloro libertad[6]
I do not ask for freedom
I *am* freedom
        no one
not even Yahweh[7]   15
and his thunder
can pronounce
        and on a stone
la ley del hombre esculpir
        no puede   20
mi libertad[8]
and the round tables
        of ice cream
                hot dog
        meat ball lovers meet   25
to rap
        and rap
and I hunger
        y mi boca está seca[9]
el agua cristalina[10]   30
        y la verdad[11]
transparent
in a cup
        is never poured
dust gathers on the shoulders   35
        of dignitaries
y de dignidad[12]

---

5. **vomito sangre** (boh'mee-toh sahn'greh): I vomit blood.
6. **y lloro libertad** (ee yoh'roh lee-behr-tahth'): and cry liberty.
7. **Yahweh** (yah'weh *or* way): Jehovah; sacred Hebrew name for God.
8. **la ley del hombre esculpir / no puede / mi libertad** (lah leh dehl ohm'breh ehs-kool-peer' / noh pweh'theh / mee lee-behr-tahth'): the law of man / cannot carve / my freedom.
9. **y mi boca está seca** (ee mee boh'kah ehs-tah' seh'kah): and my mouth is dry.
10. **el agua cristalina** (ehl ah'gwah krees-tah-lee'nah): the crystal water.
11. **y la verdad** (ee lah behr-thahth'): and the truth.
12. **y de dignidad** (ee deh deeg-nee-thahth'): and of dignity.

no saben nada[13]
muertos en el polvo[14]
they bite the earth   40
and return
to dust

---

13. **no saben nada** (noh sah'behn nah'thahth): they don't know anything.
14. **muertos en el polvo** (mwehr'tohs ehn ehl pohl'boh): dead in the dust.

For Study and Discussion

when raza?

1. The word *mañana* [tomorrow] has a special meaning in this poem. **a.** What does *mañana* represent for the speaker and for "La Raza"? **b.** According to the speaker, what must his "gente" [people] do to bring about "tomorrow"?

2. The speaker urges his people to recognize that "when equals now." **a.** What does he mean by this? **b.** How does the last line of the poem sum up his message?

3. At some time in your life, you have probably felt compelled to bring about a change in your personal life or your environment. What did you do to realize your goal? Did you find it difficult to take action?

must be the season of the witch

4. Through the image of *La Llorona* (see explanation in headnote) Alurista makes a strong statement about modern society. **a.** What or whom does *La Llorona* represent in the poem? **b.** Who are her "children"?

5. In this poem, *La Llorona*, or "la bruja" [the witch], has "lost her children." **a.** In what way(s) have her children been lost? **b.** What way of life have her children "olvidado" [forgotten]?

460 Alurista

mis ojos hinchados

6. The speaker says he bears "the scars of history" on his face. In light of his Mexican American heritage, what aspects of personal and racial history might these "scars" represent?

7. Although described in physical terms, the speaker's suffering is emotional or spiritual in nature. What seems to be the cause of his "lágrimas" [tears]?

8. The image of "dust" gathering "on the shoulders / of dignitaries" contrasts with "el agua cristalina" [the crystal water] that the speaker thirsts for. **a.** What do dust and water traditionally symbolize? **b.** What do these images represent in "mis ojos hinchados"?

Literary Elements

Code-Switching

The interplay between Spanish and English is common in the everyday speech of many Hispanic Americans, particularly those who live along the Mexico–United States border. As a natural extension of these speech patterns, many Mexican American authors alternate between Spanish and English in their writing. When this alternation occurs within a single poem or work of prose, it is called **code-switching.**

At the onset of the Chicano movement, writers such as Alurista consciously began to employ code-switching as a strong social statement—as a means of affirming their culture through their works. For example, in "when raza?" Alurista alternates between Spanish and English within the title and throughout the poem to express his commitment to "La Raza" [The Race]. His use of code-switching creates a poetic voice that speaks directly to Mexican Americans, urging them to fight for their rights as a culture within Anglo society.

Alurista 461

Find three examples of code-switching within individual lines in Alurista's "must be the season of the witch." How does the use of code-switching in these three lines relate to the theme of the poem?

Writing About Literature

Writing a Paraphrase of a Poem

In analyzing a poem, it is sometimes helpful to write a paraphrase—that is, to restate the poem in your own words. Although a paraphrase often cannot capture the stylistic effects and subtle ambiguities of meaning found in poetry, stating a poem's message in simpler language can help provide a better understanding of the poem as a whole. With this added understanding, you can return to the poem and view it in a new light. For example, the following is one possible paraphrase of lines 22–34 of Alurista's "mis ojos hinchados":

> While others gather around tables to talk about trivialities over empty foods, the speaker hungers and thirsts for the truth, which is like pure, clear water. Physical hunger is easy to satisfy, but longing for truth is not so readily quenched—particularly when the truth is unjustly withheld from those who seek it.

Write a paraphrase of Alurista's "when raza?"

Prewriting. As you reread the poem, pay particular attention to figurative language and to meanings that the poet suggests but does not actually state. For example, in lines 22–34 of "mis ojos hinchados," Alurista does not directly draw a contrast between the ice cream and hot dogs eaten by others and the "transparent" water of the truth; yet the juxtaposition of these images within the poem suggests such a contrast.

Writing and Revising. After you write a first draft of your paraphrase, reread the poem carefully to be sure that you have not misread or misrepresented the poet's words. For example, a misreading of line 28 of "mis ojos hinchados" might lead to a paraphrased statement that the speaker hungers for hot dogs and ice cream, whereas the object of the verb "hunger" is "la verdad" [the truth], which appears later, in line 31. Also, if you use any Spanish words from the poem in your paraphrase, be sure to insert the proper *diacritical marks*—marks such as ñ or á used in Spanish, usually to indicate pronunciation.

Creative Writing

Writing a Poem About a Symbolic Cultural Figure

In "must be the season of the witch," Alurista uses the powerful image of *La Llorona* as a symbol for the age in which he lives. As discussed in the introductory note for the poem, *La Llorona*—the "witch" of the title—forms the basis for countless legends in Mexican American folklore. In labeling his time "the season of the witch," Alurista emphasizes the importance of traditional aspects of his culture that he feels have been abandoned by members of the younger generation of Mexican Americans.

What figure from American culture do you think best represents modern American society? For example, is this "the season of" the astronaut, the entrepreneur, the environmentalist, the feminist? Write a poem approximately twenty lines long, revealing how the particular figure you choose represents your time.

Prewriting. Think about the events and trends that characterize the current age. What political and social currents, scientific advances, and prevailing attitudes seem most typical of contemporary society? Make a list of figures—either individual people or types of people—that you feel represent important aspects of American culture. Which of these figures do you feel most clearly represents our current age? Why exactly does this figure symbolize the present time?

Alurista 463

Luis Omar Salinas

(1937–)

Luis Omar Salinas (lwees oh'mahr sah-lee'nahs) drew great inspiration from the many books he read during his youth. By the age of fourteen, he had read the complete works of Jack London and was well on his way toward fulfilling his dream of becoming an accomplished writer.

Salinas was born in Robstown, Texas, and four years later moved with his family to Mexico. After the death of his mother the following year, Salinas was adopted by an aunt and uncle who returned with him to the United States to live in California. In the mid 1950s, Salinas graduated from Bakersfield High School and went to work at various odd jobs to support himself while he took classes at several California colleges. While at Fresno State University, he worked for a year as the editor of *Backwash,* one of the University's literary magazines, and became part of the Chicano literary and social movements that were active on the campus. Salinas also enrolled in creative writing courses and began to write many of the poems that later appeared in the first collection of his work, *Crazy Gypsy,* which was published in 1971.

The 1970s were prolific years for Salinas. In addition to coediting the Chicano anthology *From the Barrio,* he published several of his poems in a collection titled *Entrance: 4 Chicano Poets.* His poems have also appeared in numerous anthologies, journals, and newspapers. In much of his poetry, Salinas dwells on the feelings of alienation, exploitation, and loss of identity that many Mexicans have experienced after immigrating to the United States.

Perhaps the most distinguishing feature of his work is his abstract, metaphysical style. The influence of surrealist poets such as Pablo Neruda, César Vallejo, and Miguel Hernández is apparent in many of

Salinas's works. He uses striking and unsettling metaphors, often formed from the unexpected juxtaposition of images, to startle his readers from the comfort of their customary perceptions of life. Deftly contrasting and entwining the real and the unreal, Salinas casts his readers into a dreamlike atmosphere, leaving their familiar world far behind them. He feels that only through such a powerful change of perspective can readers be free from their fixed views of social order and see the injustices taking place around them.

In the 1980s Salinas began to create works with more conventional content and structure, using metaphors and images that were less shocking than those found in his earlier poems. Today, Salinas lives in Sanger, California, where he works part-time as a freelance Spanish translator and continues to write poetry.

Death in Viet Nam

A large number of young Mexican Americans fought and
died in the Vietnam War. While the sacrifice of soldiers
in battle is always a grievous loss, the sacrifice made by
these young men often seemed particularly bitter in light
of the exploitation and poverty suffered by many of them
and their families in the United States.

the ears of strangers
            listen
fighting men tarnish the ground
    death has whispered
                 tales to the young   5
and now choir boys are ringing
              bells
    another sacrifice for America
    a Mexican
    comes home   10
his beloved country
    gives homage
and mothers sleep
         in cardboard houses

    let all anguish be futile   15
tomorrow it will rain
and the hills of Viet Nam
resume
    the sacrifice is not over

Olivia

*In this touching poem on the death of his mother, the poet
reveals the memories of his childhood that he associates
with her and the deep sense of emptiness that he still feels
at her loss. As you read "Olivia," notice how the poet
weaves together specific details and abstract images to express the confusion he felt as a child and the grief he
continues to feel.*

I walk on the edge
of my mother's grave
sadly touching her rain
as if it were her dress
disguised as silk, I   5
wander on, a shadow
speaks as softly
as my hands
and we must leave off
where it began   10
the coughing
and my four year old
arms ready to please
mother you have
made the cold into fire   15
and your beauty the talk
of the town
I know death like I know
you mother
leavened bread in the oven   20
a dog,
my sister Irma,
and the neighbors
wailing like our kitchen
I didn't come to this world   25
to be frightened
yet your death sticks

468 *Luis Omar Salinas*

in my stomach
and I must clean the kitchen
with my hands   30
and I must wander on
into the night of leavened bread
and pursue truth
like a tube needing air.

My Father Is
a Simple Man

*Now and as you grow older, you will undoubtedly en-
counter times when reality is for you—as it is for the
speaker in this poem—"bitter-hard" and perhaps even
"punishing." At such times, do you think that you, like
the speaker, will find comfort in talking to one of your
parents or to some other adult who has a firm grasp on
"the simple facts" of life?*

I walk to town with my father
to buy a newspaper. He walks slower
than I do so I must slow up.
The street is filled with children.
We argue about the price   5
of pomegranates, I convince
him it is the fruit of scholars.
He has taken me on this journey
and it's been lifelong.
He's sure I'll be healthy   10
so long as I eat more oranges,
and tells me the orange
has seeds and so is perpetual;

Luis Omar Salinas 469

and we too will come back
like the orange trees.   15
I ask him what he thinks
about death and he says
he will gladly face it when
it comes but won't jump
out in front of a car.   20
I'd gladly give my life
for this man with a sixth
grade education, whose kindness
and patience are true . . .
The truth of it is, he's the scholar,   25
and when the bitter-hard reality
comes at me like a punishing
evil stranger, I can always
remember that here was a man
who was a worker and provider,   30
who learned the simple facts
in life and lived by them,
who held no pretense.
And when he leaves without
benefit of fanfare or applause   35
I shall have learned what little
there is about greatness.

_____

This Is What I Said

The speaker in this poem says that he has "difficult thoughts" that sometimes cause him to doubt whether he will ever be able to figure them out. He also has powerful memories he finds difficult to "translate." Do you ever have such thoughts and feelings "deep inside" you? How successful are you at gaining an understanding of them?

"I'm a very metaphysical cat,
someday I'll be slicing apples
in heaven," I tell my companion
the Estonian. The night
is just right for this, and   5
he laughs, and we both laugh.
Deep inside me, I think
difficult thoughts and wonder
whether my intellect is sharp
enough for this, or if I can   10
translate the feeling that
overcame me when my grandfather died,
or the time I had a high fever
and saw ghosts in the garden
and my mother consoled me.   15
There was a time when I chased
butterflies in Mexico, and the
mad nearby grinned with huge
faces which seemed to be made
of my mother's apron.   20
I realize I'm nothing;
yet if something kind were
to come from nowhere,
I'd start believing all over
again, and smile at a girl's   25
fancifulness, gather myself,
and make a life.

Luis Omar Salinas 471

Coming Back from It

While walking outdoors, thinking private thoughts, you may have sensed strong yet elusive connections between the natural world around you and the inner world of your ideas and feelings. As you read this poem, look for such connections between the speaker's inner and outer worlds. How does the natural world reflect or influence the speaker's thoughts?

I've been thinking about falling
in love, but the weather has been harsh,
a hair shirt of sorts, some ashes,
and I've noticed
a blind leaf fall on my black boots.   5
I catch my breath, lift
my white handkerchief up to my face
and look at my palm, where ambition crosses
and recrosses like the traffic at 5:00.

The cat from up the street   10
breaks toward a bird
and the sunlight catches
at my pulse
like a leaf puzzled in the air.

For Study and Discussion

Death in Viet Nam

1. The poem opens with the image of "the ears of strangers" listening. Who are these "strangers"?

2. Many young Mexican Americans were killed in action serving their country in the Vietnam War. What makes their sacrifice a bitterly ironic loss?

Olivia

3. The speaker says in lines 18 and 19, "I know death like I know / you mother." How do lines 20–24 relate to this statement?

4. The death of a parent often has a deep and lasting effect on a young child. In what ways did the death of the mother in "Olivia" affect the speaker?

5. "Death in Viet Nam" and "Olivia" both consist of a combination of concrete and abstract images. These images are often connected loosely or abruptly to convey not only meaning but also tone and feeling in the two poems. Do you prefer poems that have this kind of structure or ones that have regular sentence structure like that found in prose?

My Father Is a Simple Man

6. The speaker in the poem relates that his father has "a sixth / grade education" yet "The truth of it is, he's the scholar." Obviously, the father is not highly educated. In what way, then, is he a scholar?

7. The speaker's father draws an analogy between the "perpetual" orange and human life. Explain this analogy. How does it apply specifically to the speaker and his father?

8. Characterize the speaker in the poem. What is suggested about him in lines 2 and 3 when he says that he "must slow up" because his father walks more slowly?

This Is What I Said

9. In the first line of the poem, the speaker identifies himself as a "metaphysical cat." **a.** What does he mean by this? **b.** What specific details does he give that support this assertion?

10. The speaker says that "if something kind were / to come from nowhere" he would "start believing all over / again." What do you think he would "start believing"?

Luis Omar Salinas 473

Coming Back from It

11. In line 3, the speaker describes the weather as "a hair shirt of sorts." **a.** What is a hair shirt? **b.** In using this image, what effect is the speaker saying the weather has on him?

12. The first stanza of the poem seems quite different from the second stanza not only in length but also in its point of view and theme. How do the two stanzas combine to express a unified message, or theme, in the poem?

Literary Elements

Free Verse

In his poetry, Salinas attempts to capture the free association of perceptions, thoughts, and feelings that constantly takes place in most people's minds. To express this free interaction, he writes in **free verse,** which is unrhymed verse that has no metrical pattern or has an irregular pattern. The loose, anything-goes structure of free verse allows Salinas to put special emphasis on particular words or phrases by isolating them on their own lines or by placing them in pivotal positions to create striking images that can yield a variety of interpretations. For example, line 6 in "Olivia" ends with "a shadow," which can refer to "I" in line 5 or can be the subject of the verb *speaks* in line 7, thereby emphasizing the word *shadow* by placing it in a pivotal position between the lines that precede and follow it.

The many short lines in "Death in Viet Nam" not only emphasize the words in those lines but also create a choppy, abrupt rhythm in the poem. How does this rhythm contribute to the statement that Salinas is making about death in Vietnam?

Find another example of how Salinas uses the loose structure of free verse to place special emphasis on a word or phrase in "My Father Is a Simple Man," "This Is What I Said," or "Coming Back from It," and explain how this emphasis contributes to the **theme,** or overall message of the poem.

Vocabulary

Analyzing Words in the Context of a Poem

In "Death in Viet Nam," the poet's use of complex language places special importance on understanding the particular words that he chooses. Consult a dictionary to answer the following questions about specific words in "Death in Viet Nam."

1. In line 3, the poet says that "fighting men tarnish the ground." **a.** What does the word *tarnish* mean? **b.** In what way or ways can combat soldiers "tarnish the ground"?

2. In line 12, the country is said to give "homage" to the Mexican American soldiers killed in battle. **a.** What does the word *homage* mean? **b.** How do the origins of this word add meaning to Salinas's use of it in this poem?

3. The second stanza opens with the statement "let all anguish be futile." **a.** What do the two words *anguish* and *futile* mean? **b.** Who has anguish? **c.** Why is anguish futile in the context of the poem? Do you agree or disagree with the poet's statement in this line?

4. The next-to-last line in the poem consists of only one word— "resume." **a.** The subject of this verb is "hills"; does *resume* have an object? **b.** How can "the hills of Viet Nam / resume," or what do they resume?

Writing About Literature

Comparing the Development of the Same Theme in Two Poems

In both "My Father Is a Simple Man" and "This Is What I Said," Salinas comes to a similar conclusion regarding the value of the intellect compared with the ability to grasp the everyday realities of life. Write a short essay on the conclusion he reaches, using specific quotations from the two poems to support your views.

Prewriting. Begin by identifying Salinas's view on education and the intellect. Of what value is scholarship and intellect in gaining an understanding and appreciation of life? What faith does he place in his own intellectual abilities? Based on specific quotations from the poems, write one or two sentences stating what you think is Salinas's view. Next, look in the poems for examples of an alternative way of approaching life. Again, compose one or two sentences stating this alternative approach. Finally, determine which approach—the intellectual or the alternative— Salinas thinks is the better, and state Salinas's views in one or two sentences. You can now organize your paper in three paragraphs, using the sentences you have written for each idea to state the topic for each paragraph. The body of each paragraph can be developed with specific citations from the two poems to support the topics you have stated.

Writing and Revising. As you write and revise your paper, make sure that you clearly indicate to your reader exactly how the supporting quotations and examples in each paragraph relate to your discussion of them. For instance, introducing an explanation with the words "this shows" often does not clearly indicate what exactly "this" refers back to. To make such a statement clear, add a word or phrase that specifies "this"—such as, "this statement of the speaker's doubt . . ." or "the doubt expressed by the speaker in this line. . . ."

Creative Writing

Writing a Poem About a Person Who Has Been a Guiding Influence

Poets and other writers often create works that express their feelings toward their parents and others who have had a significant influence on them. In "Olivia," the speaker reveals the deep sense of loss he continues to feel many years after the death of his mother. In "My Father Is a Simple Man," he pays loving tribute to his father. Write a poem (it need not be as long as "Olivia" or "My Father Is a Simple Man") that expresses your feelings or thoughts about one of your parents or a person who has guided you in growing up.

Prewriting. First, sit back and think a moment about the lasting influence that your parents and other important people in your life have had on you. You might recall fond memories of a teacher, a grandparent, a coach, or a scout leader. Quickly jot down a number of specific details, images, and traits that you associate with one particular person. Choose several key items from your list that play a significant role in your memories, thoughts, or feelings about that person. Then bring your imagination into play to find links between the items you have chosen from your list.

Writing and Revising. Writing poetry differs markedly from writing prose. Prose is generally created from a well-organized plan or outline. Poetry, on the other hand, often flows from the free expression of imagination and then is molded into shape by both the imagination and the objective intellect. Consequently, you will likely wish to write your first draft (and maybe a second, third, or even more) rather quickly and then go back over it numerous times—adjusting, adding, deleting, and doing other fine tuning in revisions.

Writing About Thoughts Related to Environment

In "Coming Back from It," Salinas weaves together his thoughts with images of his surroundings, showing how elements of the environment reflect and perhaps even help to determine his state of mind. You have undoubtedly had an experience similar to Salinas's in which the world around you seemed to express or influence your mood or ideas. Write a short poem ten to fifteen lines long or a short narrative not more than a page long focusing on a thought or thoughts you have had that related directly to your surroundings.

Luis Omar Salinas 477

Prewriting. Think back on times when you were in an environment that had a particularly strong effect on you. Then recall specific details about that environment—specific sights, sounds, and smells or perhaps lack of them; the weather or decor; people or animals; the time of day or year; features in the sky. Concentrate on these details and try to bring to mind ideas that you associate with them. Analyze these associations. How or why did some element of the environment trigger a particular idea? Although you may wish simply to suggest rather than to specify links between your surroundings and your ideas, be sure that you have given these associations some thought so that you can focus on details that will clearly show how your ideas stem from your environment.

Writing and Revising. Draw upon the clear picture in your mind of the environment to choose words that make it come alive for your reader. Rather than simply saying that something is red, describe it as crimson or rust-colored or fire-engine red.

Angela de Hoyos

(1945–   )

Like many contemporary Mexican American poets, Angela de Hoyos (ahn' heh-lah deh oh'yohs) became involved in the cultural revolution of the 1960s, speaking out publicly against racism and social oppression. Her poems reflect her deep commitment to her cultural roots and her firm belief that Mexican Americans must preserve their heritage and language lest they lose their personal identity.

Born in Mexico, de Hoyos moved with her family to San Antonio, Texas, after World War II. While she was growing up, de Hoyos was greatly influenced by the poetry her mother read to her. Eventually de Hoyos began to write poems and short stories of her own, several of which she published in her high school's newspaper. Her reputation as a gifted poet soon spread beyond her local audience as she began to publish in magazines and give readings of her works.

De Hoyos's first two books, *Arise, Chicano! And Other Poems* and *Chicano Poems: For the Barrio,* were both published in 1975. Written in a mixture of Spanish and English, many of these poems depict the painful realities of Chicano experience and the tragic loss of identity that often results from Mexican Americans' assimilation into mainstream Anglo society. In these poems as in her later works, de Hoyos often uses satire and ironic humor to explore both serious and light themes. Her third collection, *Selected Poems / Selecciones,* takes a more introspective turn, frequently addressing life and death as personified, none-too-friendly forces that attempt to foil the speaker's happiness. In his introduction to her latest work, *Woman, Woman,* Rolando Hinojosa-Smith remarks that her poems are both "understated" and "very, very personal." He affirms that with Angela de Hoyos "we're in the hands of a poet, and one we can trust to startle and surprise us."

After her first three books were published, de Hoyos was invited to read her works throughout the southwestern United States and California as well as in Mexico and Europe. She has won a number of awards for her poetry, which has been translated into several languages and has received considerable critical study. De Hoyos continues to devote her time to writing as well as to painting and part-time work as a graphic artist in San Antonio. She is also general editor of a small publishing house, MandA Publications, and is active in promoting cultural activities within the community.

The poem on the following pages is taken from *Woman, Woman,* which was published in 1985.

Virginia Gill, Visual Artist Bakes a Cake for the Arts Committee Meeting

Virginia Gill's desserts tempt the speaker with their visual as well as their culinary appeal. Notice that de Hoyos also shapes her poem to make it visually appealing. How does the shape of the poem imitate the things it describes?

---

dark chocolate
ribbons
swirling
      around fingerlicking
      y y y u m m m m y y y   5
      white meringue
can melt away
the strongest case
of human resistance

Virginia bakes   10
and bakes
in frank disguise:
      Banana Nut Bread
      German Coffee Cake
      Creme de Menthe Pie   15
      Pane Italiano

    Ageless delights, these!
    All made from scratch

. . . and how logical
      the switch   20

Angela de Hoyos 481

:to exchange
ceramic kiln
for kitchen oven.
                    To produce
edible works of art   25
love-crafted
that rival
the clay sculpture
            in lak ech[1]
masterpieces of joy   30
that grace
the gallery
of her garden . . .

        Mangiamo![2] Virginia
            . . . truth is, you are out   35
            to sabotage my diet
            but my taste buds drool
            in shame:
                        May I have a
                        second helping?   40

_____

1. **in lak ech:** Mayan for "you are my other self."
2. **Mangiamo!** (mahn-gyah′moh!): Italian for "Let's eat!"

For Study and Discussion

1. An **analogy** is a comparison between two things that are in some way similar. **a.** What analogy does Angela de Hoyos draw in her poem? **b.** How are the two things she compares alike? How are they different? Refer to specific details in the poem in giving your answer.

2. The speaker says that Virginia Gill "bakes / in frank disguise." In what sense is she in "disguise"? How is her disguise a "frank" one—that is, not really a disguise at all?

3. As revealed in line 29, Angela de Hoyos feels a strong identification with fellow artist Virginia Gill. Have you ever felt that a poet's or visual artist's work spoke to you directly—as if that person were, in some sense, your "other self"?

Literary Elements

Poetic Use of Punctuation: Ellipsis Points

Ellipsis points are three successive periods (. . .) that serve several purposes in writing. Most commonly, they are used to indicate that words or phrases have been omitted from quoted material or that a quoted passage has been excerpted from a longer work. In works that contain dialogue, ellipsis points can indicate a pause or interruption in speech or a trailed-off remark. A third, more poetic usage of ellipsis points, as seen in Angela de Hoyos's poem, suggests a pause in thought or a transition between related ideas.

Examine each use of ellipsis points in de Hoyos's poem, and determine whether it indicates a pause, a transition, or both. What different ideas or continuations of thought do the ellipsis points link?

Ricardo Sánchez

(1941–)

Poet Ricardo Sánchez (ree-kahr'thoh
sahn'chehs) is an outspoken and
controversial figure in contemporary
Mexican American literature. Deeply
involved in the Chicano movement, he
views his writing as both a means of self-expression and a vehicle for
social protest. His poems are alternately lyrical and strident, nostalgic
and defiant; like his turbulent life, they are never dull.

Born in El Paso, Texas, Sánchez made yearly visits to his parents'
native New Mexico. He recalls feeling the stark contrast between the
beauty of the New Mexican landscape and the poverty, violence, and
racism he encountered in urban barrios. As a teen-ager, he rebelled
against the dominant Anglo culture that seemed to consign Mexican
Americans to a limited and degrading role in society. Although his love
of reading and writing began at an early age, his defiance in high
school prompted his teachers to label him as a troublemaker. He
received no support or encouragement for his creative efforts and grew
bitterly disillusioned, finally dropping out of school altogether.

After a brief stint in the Army and the devastating experience of
several deaths in his family, Sánchez ran afoul of the law and served
time in prison. Nevertheless, he continued to write and to fight for
social change, much to the displeasure of the legal authorities. The
birth of his first son shortly after Sánchez was sentenced to prison
strengthened his resolve to escape from the trap of menial labor yet at
the same time increased the urgency of his finding a way to support his
family.

In the years following his release from prison, Sánchez received fellowships that enabled him to both provide for his family and pursue his
writing career. Though he possessed only a high-school equivalency

diploma, he managed to earn a Ph.D. in little over a year of intensive study and has become widely recognized as a poet and lecturer. He published his first book of poetry, *Obras* [Works], in 1971; several other volumes followed, including a collection released by a Chicano publishing house that Sánchez helped to found.

Now acclaimed as a talented and prolific poet, Sánchez continues to speak out against social injustice. He has drawn analogies in his works between the poverty and oppression endured by many Mexican Americans living in barrios and the stifling despair he suffered during his years in prison. Sánchez is living proof, however, that Mexican Americans and other minorities can emerge triumphant from adversity with their humanity intact.

Sánchez currently lives in El Paso, Texas, where he writes a column for the *El Paso Herald-Post* and is completing a semi-autobiographical prose work. The two poems on the following pages, "Old Man" and "Once," are taken from Sánchez's *Selected Poems*, which was published in 1985.

Old Man

In a sense, each of us is a product of all our forebears, extending back through the long history of our family. The speaker in this poem pays tribute to his grandfather, who was his personal link to his ancestors. Perhaps you, too, are fortunate enough to have an older relative or friend of the family who has helped you forge such bonds with your "roots."

remembrance (smiles/hurts sweetly)
October 8, 1972

old man
with brown skin
talking of past
    when being shepherd
    in utah, nevada, colorado and new mexico   5
was life lived freely;

old man,
  grandfather,
wise with time
running rivulets on face,   10
deep, rich furrows,
  each one a legacy,
deep, rich memories
of life . . .
        "you are indio,[1]   15
            among other things,"
      he would tell me
          during nights spent
    so long ago
          amidst familial gatherings   20
    in albuquerque . . .

---

1. **indio** (een'dyoh): Indian.

486   Ricardo Sánchez

old man, loved and respected,
he would speak sometimes
of pueblos,[2]
  san juan, santa clara,   25
  and even santo domingo,
and his family, he would say,
came from there:
  some of our blood was here,
  he would say,   30
  before the coming of coronado,[3]
other of our blood
  came with los españoles,[4]
and the mixture
was rich,   35
  though often painful . . .

old man,
who knew earth
 by its awesome aromas
and who felt   40
the heated sweetness
 of chile verde[5]
by his supple touch,
gone into dust is your body
 with its stoic look and resolution,   45
but your reality, old man, lives on
in a mindsoul touched by you . . .

Old Man . . .

---

2. **pueblos** (pweh'blohs): towns, villages; also people, races, nations. The reference here is to Indian pueblos in central and northern New Mexico.
3. **coronado** (koh-roh-nah'thoh): Francisco de Coronado, sixteenth-century Spanish explorer who led an expedition into what is now the American Southwest.
4. **los españoles** (lohs ehs-pah-nyohl'ehs): the Spaniards.
5. **chile verde** (chee'leh behr'deh): green pepper.

Once

The speaker in this poem remembers and celebrates the imaginative inner world of his childhood. He also compares his childhood imaginings to the concerns of his "funny adult brain." What kinds of things did you think about and dream of as a small child? Would the thoughts and dreams you now have seem "funny" to your childhood self?

SLC, Utah, rumblings
25 de noviembre de 1980

once
long ago,
then
when my face
was fresh, un-bearded,   5
i used to make up words
for the worlds
i would dream,
    life in my barrio[1]
    was a joyful thing sometimes,   10
    and words
    would come and go,
        and i would sing
        nonsensical things
of when the world   15
was dinosaurs
and flying chickens

and all the people
were neither tiny, big nor medium size,
they were just people   20

---

1. **barrio** (bahr'ryoh): one of the districts into which a large town or city is divided.

who loved to dance, sing,
and oftentimes
ride
upon the backs
of monkey-like horses,   25
it was easy then
to sing
for i was young and full of life,
not that the youthful energy i had
has gone, mind you,   30
no, no, it hasn't,
it's just
that my songs now
fly
into soup, watermelon syrup,   35
and other funny things,
so i try to keep things simple,
if you please,
and in so doing find
that i need   40
once more
to return
to long ago
childhood dreams
in order to be free, alive   45
and able to sing
those dreams
which hide
within my funny adult brain. . . .

For Study and Discussion

Old Man

1. Ricardo Sánchez has said that Chicanos should present a "strong and real imagery" of themselves, using language "creatively, movingly, and truthfully." What images does the poet use to convey a sense of the old man's dignity and rich store of experience, as well as his strong roots in Mexican American culture?

2. In one sense, "Old Man" is an **elegy**—a poem of mourning over the death of a loved one. It is also, however, a poem of celebration and affirmation. What language and imagery does the speaker use to affirm that the grandfather's "reality"—his words and experiences, as well as the heritage he represents—has not died with his body?

3. The relationship between the speaker and his grandfather is central to the poem. In addressing his grandfather, the speaker refers to himself as "a mindsoul touched by you." What does he mean by a "mindsoul," and in what ways has he been "touched" by the presence and memory of his grandfather?

Once

4. The speaker in "Once" contrasts the "nonsensical things" of his childhood with the things that now concern him as an adult. However, his wish "to keep things simple" leads him to return—at least in spirit—to the simple, unstructured world of his "childhood dreams." **a.** How does the speaker's point of view express his desire "to keep things simple"? **b.** What sort of language, punctuation, and syntax does the poet use to evoke the fanciful, unstructured world of his childhood?

5. Line breaks help to guide the reading of a poem by regulating rhythm, creating emphasis, and highlighting ambiguities of meaning. In the third stanza of "Once," for example, the poet isolates the active verbs "ride," "to sing," and "fly," emphasizing the liveliness of the speaker's imagination and creating a rhythmic pattern in the poem. Reread the poems "Once" and "Old Man," paying careful attention to line breaks. Referring to specific lines in the poems, discuss the poet's use of line breaks to create desired effects.

Writing About Literature

Analyzing Tone

The **tone** of a work is the attitude the writer takes toward his or her subject, characters, and readers. The author's tone greatly affects our reading of a work because it encourages us to view the author's subject in a certain way. In poetry, tone is often expressed through syntax, rhythm, word choice, and imagery instead of through character and plot. In a short essay of two or three paragraphs, compare the tone of "Old Man" with that of "Once."

Prewriting. As you read through the poems, ask yourself the following questions. What attitude does the poet take toward his subject? How is this attitude evidenced by the poet's use of the language? For each poem, make a list of the words, images, rhythms, and kinds of syntax that help to create the tone of the poem.

It may be helpful to organize your essay into the following sections.

1. An introductory sentence that states the comparison you intend to draw.
2. Two paragraphs devoted to the analysis of specific elements of tone in each poem.
3. A concluding paragraph discussing the similarities and differences in tone between the two poems.

Writing and Revising. When you write about a poem, be sure to distinguish between the poet and the speaker. Elements of form and language should be attributed to the poet, while ideas, impressions, and attitudes that are expressed in the poem should be attributed to the speaker.

Creative Writing

Writing a Poem About an Everyday Object or Event

In "Once," Ricardo Sánchez suggests that everyday things such as "soup" and "watermelon syrup" are worthy of poetry. Many poets—particularly Imagist poets such as Ezra Pound, H.D. (Hilda Doolittle), and William Carlos Williams—have devoted their poetry to the rediscovery and celebration of the ordinary. Write a poem about a small, everyday object or event, such as a piece of ripe fruit you've just tasted, an old shoe on the roadside, or a rivulet of water running down a windowpane.

Prewriting. Before you begin writing, spend a minute or two examining your subject closely. Gather impressions with as many senses as possible—touch, smell, hearing, taste, sight—and allow your mind to associate freely. What does the object or event remind you of? For example, the taste of a certain kind of apple may evoke memories of fall, or of some unusual event during which you were eating just such an apple. After you have "meditated" on your subject for a few moments, sit down and begin to write, allowing yourself to jot down whatever associations come into your head, no matter how unlikely or "silly" they may seem. After composing this list of impressions, examine the list with a more critical eye and decide which of these images you would like to incorporate into your poem.

Writing. Try to focus on precise sensory images in your descriptions as well as on stanza and line breaks. Keep in mind that even "free verse" poetry often uses internal patterns of sound and rhythm.

Tino Villanueva
(1941–)

A gifted artist, critic, and poet, Tino
Villanueva (tee'noh bee-yah-nweh'bah)
has steadily gained recognition since the
publication of his first book of poems,
Hay Otra Voz Poems [There is another
voice poems], in 1972. Using carefully crafted imagery, he explores in
his poetry the unique perspective and heritage of Mexican Americans
as well as the common humanity of all people. He feels that Mexican
American literature, like all literature, should not just address the
experiences of a particular group but should overcome cultural barriers,
thereby opening lines of communication between people of diverse
backgrounds and experiences.

Villanueva was born in San Marcos, Texas. While he was still quite
young, his parents adopted the exhausting, nomadic life of migrant farm
workers. Often laboring in the fields himself, he attended school
irregularly and gained little from his academic courses. He did, however, excel at sports in high school and longed to follow in the footsteps
of his baseball heroes. He says that this dream "was an ardent fantasy to
overcome . . . immediate economic misery."

After high school, Villanueva struggled on his own to further his
education despite the demands of a full-time job. Drafted into the Army
in 1964, he spent two years in the Panama Canal Zone, where he took
extension courses from Florida State University. Upon his return to the
United States, he enrolled at Southwest Texas State University to complete his B.A. degree. It was here, he says, that he first began to write
poetry. He wryly describes his first poems as "exaggerated rhymes,
dripping with feigned sentimentalism and a self-evoked nostalgia."

Reading the work of other writers, particularly that of the lyrical poet
Dylan Thomas, helped him to mature as a poet and to develop his own

distinctive voice. Throughout college, he read widely, particularly the work of modern poets, and developed a lasting enthusiasm for "the delights of literature." Pursuit of these "delights" led to his earning a doctoral degree in Spanish and eventually to his becoming a college professor.

As a writer, he draws on his rich cultural heritage as well as his literary studies, remaining true to the language and experiences of Mexican Americans while at the same time addressing universal human themes. Reflecting this inclusive focus, his poetry covers a variety of topics from the plight of the migrant worker ("Day-Long Day") to the certainty of human mortality ("My Certain Burn Toward Pale Ashes"). Villanueva addresses these topics in a voice that is both lyrical and plain-spoken, complex and precise.

Day-Long Day

Stooping over the "Summer-long rows" of cotton, the migrant pickers described in this poem face mind-numbing toil day after day. By using repetitive imagery and sound patterns, the poet seeks to instill in the reader a sense of the laborers' unrelenting suffering. After you read this poem, close your eyes and try to see, feel, and hear the poet's descriptions.

> *"Again the drag of pisca.[1] pisca . . pisca*
> *. . . Daydreams border on sunfed halluci-*
> *nations, eyes and hands automatically*
> *discriminate whiteness of cotton from*
> *field of vision. Pisca, pisca."*
>
> *"Un hijo del sol",[2] Genaro Gonzales.*

Third generation timetable.
Sweat day-long dripping into open space;
sun blocks out the sky, suffocates the only breeze.
From *el amo desgraciado,*[3] a sentence:

«I wanna bale a day, and the boy here   5
don't haf'ta go to school.»

           * * *

In time binding motion—
a family of sinews and backs,
row-trapped,
zig-zagging through Summer-long rows   10
of cotton: Lubbock by way of Wharton.
«*Está como si escupieran fuego*»,[4] a mother moans
in sweat-patched jeans,

---

1. **pisca** (pees'kah): a term for "picking cotton."
2. *Un hijo del sol* (oon ee'hoh dehl sohl): a son of the sun.
3. *el amo desgraciado* (ehl ah'moh dehs-grah-syah'thoh): the wretched master.
4. *Está como si escupieran fuego* (ehs-tah' koh'moh see ehs-koo-pyeh'rahn fweh'goh): It is as though it were spitting fire.

stooping
with unbending dreams.   15
«Estudia para que no seas burro como nosotros»,[5]
our elders warn, their gloves and cuffs
leaf-stained by seasons.

* * *

Bronzed and blurry-eyed by
the blast of degrees,   20
we blend into earth's rotation.
And sweltering toward saturday, the
day-long day is sunstruck by 6:00 P.M.
One last chug-a-lug from a water jug
old as grandad.   25
Day-long sweat dripping into open space:
Wharton by way of Lubbock.

----

5. *Estudia para que no seas burro como nosotros* (ehs-too'thyah pah'rah
   keh noh seh'ahs boor'roh koh'moh noh-soh'trohs): Study so you won't be
   a beast of burden like us.

Pachuco Remembered

During the 1940s and 1950s, groups of young Mexican Americans asserted their identity by embracing the flamboyant, rebellious life style of the pachuco gang. Even today, the mystique of the pachucos continues to stir the imagination of many. Their distinctive "pachuquismo" slang and "fierce stance" of defiance mark them as forerunners of Chicano social protest.

¡Ese![1]
Within your will-to-be culture,
incisive,
aguzado,[2]
clutching the accurate click &   5
fist-warm slash of your filero[3]
(hardened equalizer gave you life,
opened up countercultures U.S.A.).

Precursor.

Vato loco alivianado[4]—a legend in your   10
own time flaunting early mod, sleazy,
but rigid,
with a message,
in a movement of your own,
in your gait sauntering,   15
          swaying,
          leaning the wrong way
          in assertion.

Baroque carriage between
waving-to-the-wind ducktails &   20

---

1. **¡Ese!** (¡eh'seh!): Hey, man! (pachuco slang).
2. **aguzado** (ah-goo-sah'thoh): shrewd, cunning (pachuco slang).
3. **filero** (fee-leh'roh): knife—specifically, a switchblade (pachuco slang).
4. **Vato loco alivianado** (bah'toh loh'koh ah-lee-byah-nah'thoh): crazy, hip dude (pachuco slang).

double-sole calcos[5]
buttressing street corners as any would-be
pillar of society.
Aesthetics existential:
    la lisa[6] unbuttoned,   25
    zoot suit with pegged tramos,[7]
    a thin belt holding up the
    scars of your age—
a moving target for la jura[8] brutality;
brown anathema of high-school principals.   30
Your fierce stance
            vs.
                starched voices:

    "Take those taps off!"
    "Speak English damn it!"   35
    "Button up your shirt!"
    "When did you last cut your hair?"
    "Coach, give this punk 25 licks!"

Emotion surging silent on your stoic tongue;
machismo-ego punished, feeling your fearful   40
eyes turn blue in their distant stare.

Day to day into the night, back to back grief,
& the railroad tracks a /Meskin/Dixon line/
hyphenating
the skin of your accent.   45
Sirol,[9] you heard the train on time
                tearing
through every map of hope SW U.S.A.,
but your poised blood, aware, in a
bitter coming-of-age: a juvenile La Causa   50
in your wicked
            stride . . .

---

5. **calcos** (kahl'kohs): shoes (pachuco slang).
6. **la lisa** (lah lee'sah): the shirt (pachuco slang).
7. **tramos** (trah'mohs): trousers (pachuco slang).
8. **la jura** (lah hoo'rah): the police (pachuco slang).
9. **Sirol** (see'rohl): yes (pachuco slang).

My Certain Burn Toward Pale Ashes

The poet's "certain burn" toward death—his, and all creatures', inescapable mortality—seems to negate the value of life: he is "drawn destoyed" from the mouth of creation. As you read, consider how the poet's speech—the poem itself—is both a defiance of death and an affirmation of life.

My certain burn
  toward pale ashes, is told by the
  hand that whirls the sun; each
  driving breath beats with the quick
  pulsing face.   5

My falling stride
  like sand toward decision,
  drains heavy with fixed age; each
  ghostly grain a step in time that
  measures tongues.   10

My ruddy sea
  that streams to dryness, bares
  bewildered its clay bone; each
  vessel's roar at God's speed drowns
  by force.   15

My waking light
  began when the fertile lips spun
  my pulse; and I, with muted tongue,
  was drawn destroyed from the making-
  mouth into this mass.   20

And held below
  by nature, the sweeping hand now
  turns my dust-bound youth; tell the
  world that I was struck by the
  sun's grave plot.   25

For Study and Discussion

Day-Long Day

1. The poet describes the field workers as "a family of sinews and backs." **a.** List additional phrases and images that the poet uses to characterize the workers. **b.** How does the characterization of the workers and their work relate to the tone of the poem?

2. Sunlight, normally a positive image, is an oppressive presence in this poem. What patterns of imagery does the poet use to describe the heat of the "day-long day"?

Pachuco Remembered

3. The poet honors the pachuco culture as a "precursor" of the Chicano movement. In what way can the pachuco counterculture, like the Chicano movement, be viewed as a form of social protest? Refer to specific images in the poem to support your answer.

4. Throughout the poem, Villanueva alternates use of pachuco slang with use of more formal English. In the first stanza, for example, he follows the word "incisive," which means "sharp or keen," with "aguzado"—pachuquismo slang for "shrewd or cunning." Reread the poem and note transitions the poet makes between the colorful slang of the pachucos and the more detached language of his commentary. What is the effect of this interplay of language? In your opinion, does it add to or detract from the effectiveness of the poem?

My Certain Burn Toward Pale Ashes

5. In this poem, the poet uses vivid, elemental imagery to explore the relationship between life and death. He argues that each moment of life is a "falling" toward old age and a "certain burn" toward death. **a.** What images in the poem convey a sense of time's passage? **b.** What images suggest a struggle between the forces of life and the forces of time?

6. Although this poem focuses on the inevitability of death, it also contains strong images of creation. For example, in the fourth stanza, the phrase "fertile lips spun / my pulse" evokes the image of a creator whose very act of speaking creates life. **a.** In what way is the poet also a creator? What does he create? **b.** How is his creativity a defiance of death? Refer to specific words and images in the poem to support your answers.

Vocabulary

Finding Synonyms for Slang Words

In "Pachuco Remembered," Villanueva's use of pachuco slang, or "pachuquismo," both characterizes and affirms the pachuco culture. **Slang** is informal, often colorful language that is not part of standard usage. As with the pachucos, slang is often used by members of particular groups to establish their identity and set them apart from others. Discuss the slang that you and your peers have created or inherited from older siblings or from television, movies, books, or other sources. Give synonyms in your own slang—the slang you and your peers commonly use—for the pachuco slang in Villanueva's poem.

Writing About Literature

Analyzing the Relationship Between Character and Environment

People have different ways of reacting to real or perceived oppression: they may yield to their circumstances, ignore them as much as possible, rebel against them, or affirm them. Situations or conditions that seem intolerably unjust to one person may seem perfectly reasonable or unremarkable to someone else. The circumstances in the Colonies that led to the American Revolution, for example, did not seem overly oppressive to Tories who considered themselves British citizens and preferred to remain under British rule. To those who fought for independence, however, British rule was intolerable. Colonists who went about their business with little concern about the issue of independence illustrate yet another way of reacting to one's circumstances.

Each of the three poems by Villanueva portrays people who are subject to forces larger than themselves. In an essay of three or four paragraphs, identify these forces and discuss how the characters in each poem react to their circumstances.

Prewriting. As you reread each poem, look for language that suggests a conflict between the characters and some aspect of their environment or condition of their existence. What verbs does the poet use? What tone does he create in the poem through the use of alliteration and other devices? For example, the lines "Bronzed and blurry-eyed by / the blast of degrees" in "Day-Long Day" establish the workers as passive victims of the sun's heat. Alliteration and passive verb forms in these lines emphasize the oppressiveness of the heat and, more important, indicate that the working conditions inflicted upon the laborers are dehumanizing. List the specific images and literary devices that have led to your interpretations of the poems. Although there is no single correct interpretation of each poem, an analysis of the forces at work in the poems must be based on close readings and careful analysis of details.

Writing. Because you will be dealing with several different poems, be sure to give clear title references when you refer to a particular poem. You can either incorporate the poem's title into an introductory statement or give the title directly after a quotation from the work. Also be sure to cite the correct line number(s) for each quotation that you use.

Jimmy Santiago Baca

(1952–)

Jimmy Santiago Baca (sahn-tyah'goh bah'kah) burst onto the scene in mainstream American poetry in 1986 with the publication of *Martín and Meditations on the South Valley,* for which he received the Vogelstein Literature Award and an American Book Award. Since the publication of this book of his poetry he has been much in demand on the lecture tour circuit, giving readings of his work throughout North America from Anchorage, Alaska, to Chihuahua City, Mexico.

Abandoned as a child by his parents, Baca was forced to live for short periods of time with his grandparents and with other relatives in different places throughout New Mexico. When he was barely ten, he ran away, spending the next few years living by his wits as he wandered from state to state. Baca was in and out of detention facilities several times and seemed destined for a life on the edge of society. Fortunately, however, he discovered and began to nurture his imaginative and creative talent. At the age of eighteen, he started to take an interest in writing poetry and received vital encouragement from mentors who recognized his great potential.

Baca eventually returned to Albuquerque, New Mexico, where he now lives. While pursuing his writing, he completed an undergraduate degree in English literature at the University of New Mexico. Soon after marrying, he passionately devoted himself to building a house in the city's South Valley, vowing to create the kind of secure homestead for himself and his family that he had lacked as a child.

After writing every day from daybreak to midday, Baca devotes much of his remaining time to his family and to helping his fellow

Mexican Americans and Chicanos. He strongly believes that his success has given him the obligation to contribute to his community. In addition to rebuilding houses and finding jobs for the poor, Baca has set up a scholarship fund for young writers.

Baca's reputation as a poet does not rest solely on his success with *Martín and Meditations on the South Valley*. He has also had several other collections of his poetry published—notably *Immigrants in Our Own Land*, in which he reflects on the troubled times he spent as a young outcast from society. Recently, he has finished another collection of poetry—*Black Mesa Poems*—and is hard at work on a trilogy of novels. In addition, he is working on a play for the Los Angeles Theater Center.

The selection that begins on the following page comes from Baca's highly autobiographical *Martín and Meditations on the South Valley* and traces the alternating moments of despair and hope he has experienced in his fight to overcome the self-destructiveness of his youth.

from Martín[1] and Meditations on the South Valley

Martín IV

The speaker in this poem tells of his troubled boyhood as an orphan. Shuttling back and forth between relatives, he felt "caught in the middle" between two very different worlds. Finding no home anywhere, he finally struck out on his own. As you read this poem, notice the speaker's use of imagery. Judging by the images he draws, where is his heart, his spirit, at home?

Grandma Lucero at the table
smokes Prince Albert cigarette
rolled from a can,
sips black coffee from metal cup,
and absorbs hours of silence   5
like prairie sky absorbs campfire smoke.
Death hangs over her shoulders
a black cow's hide
slung over the fence to dry.
She had once been a brimming acequia[2]   10
her four sons drank from
like bighorn sheep.

Conversations in her kitchen
about my mother I overheard as a boy,
made me sniff around the screen door to hear more,   15
like a coyote smells a cave he had been born in once.
My animal eyes and skin

---

1. **Martín** (mahr-teen′).
2. **acequia** (ah-seh′kyah): irrigation canal or ditch.

twitched with fear. I created myself in a field,
beside the house, where lizard and rabbit
breathed in my ear   20
stories of eagles and arrowheads. My heart
became an arroyo,[3] and my tears cut deep cracks
in my face of sand, when tía[4] Jenny came to take me away
from grandma. With rocks in my pockets
earth had bit off for me like soft bread   25
for the long journey,
I left Estancia for the orphanage.

                    As we drove through Tijeras[5] Mountains,
I looked back,
distant fields grooved with hoofpaths   30
of grazing cattle and sheep.
Grandma's knee-length gray hair,
she brushed and brushed every morning,
braided, bunned, and wrapped
with a black tápalo.[6]   35
Long gray rain clouds hung over
the crumbling train-track town—
then lightning crackled
like the slap of new lumber stacks,
and rain darkened   40
the plaster cracks of grandma's adobe[7] house.

I had an image of mother in the morning
dancing in front of the mirror
in pink panties,
masking her face with mascara,   45
squeezing into tight jeans.
Her laughter rough as brocaded cloth
and her teeth brilliant as church tiles.

On visiting days with aunts and uncles,
I was shuttled back and forth—   50
between Chavez bourgeois in the city

---

3. **arroyo** (ahr-roh'yoh): small river or stream.
4. **tía** (tee'ah): aunt, older woman.
5. **Tijeras** (tee-heh'rahs).
6. **tápalo** (tah'pah-loh): shawl.
7. **adobe** (ah-thoh'beh): made of mud brick that has been baked in the sun.

and rural Lucero sheepherders,
new cars and gleaming furniture
and leather saddles and burlap sacks,
noon football games and six packs of cokes   55
and hoes, welfare cards and bottles of goat milk.

I was caught in the middle—
between white skinned, English speaking altar boy
at the communion railing,
and brown skinned, Spanish speaking plains nomadic child   60
with buffalo heart groaning underworld earth powers,
between Sunday brunch at a restaurant
and burritos eaten in a tin-roofed barn,
between John Wayne on the afternoon movie
rifle butting young Braves,   65
and the Apache whose red dripping arrow
was the altar candle in praise of the buck
just killed.

Caught between Indio–Mejicano[8] rural uncles
who stacked hundred pound sacks of pinto beans   70
on boxcars all day, and worked the railroad tracks
behind the Sturgis sheds, who sang Apache songs
with accordions, and Chavez uncles and aunts
who vacationed and followed the Hollywood model
of My Three Sons for their own families,   75
sweeping the kitchen before anyone came to visit,
looking at photo albums in the parlor.

When I stayed with the Chavez'
I snuck out of the house, wandered at will,
heading south to the ditches of the South Valley,   80
and when they caught up with me days later,
I smelled of piñon[9] bark
from wood piles I had played on,
and the red brown clay stuck to my shoes
from corrals I had entered to pet a horse,   85
smeared over the new interior car carpet.
They stopped inviting me out.

---

8. **Indio–Mejicano** (een'dyoh–meh-hee-kah'noh): Mexican Indian.
9. **piñón** (pee-nyohn'): pine nut.

On my cot one night at the orphanage,
I dreamed my spirit was straw and mud,
a pit dug down below my flesh   90
to pray in,
and I prayed on beads of blue corn kernels,
slipped from thumb to earth,
while deerskinned drumhead of my heart
gently pounded and I sang   95
                    all earth is holy,
                    all earth is holy,
                    all earth is holy,
                    all earth is holy,
until a nun shook me awake.   100

Next day I ran away,
and drifted barrios[10] of Burque,[11]
stealing food from grocery stores,
sleeping in churches, and every dark dawn,
walking and walking and walking,   105
my eyes shaded with fear and my life
dimmed to a small shadow—
an old coal mine shaft
that kept falling in on me,
burying me in black sands of a murky past.   110

---

10. **barrios** (bahr'ryohs): districts into which a large town or city is divided.
11. **Burque** (boor'keh): short for Albuquerque, a city in central New Mexico.

For Study and Discussion

1. Throughout the poem, the speaker uses images drawn from nature to describe his boyhood experiences. What does the choice of these images suggest about the speaker?

2. The speaker says that he "was shuttled back and forth" between the Lucero side of his family and the Chavez side. **a.** What two, virtually opposite ways of life do these two sides of the speaker's family represent? **b.** Which does the speaker prefer? Why, in your opinion, does he have this preference?

3. In the final stanza, the speaker says that his life had "dimmed to a small shadow—/ an old coal mine shaft / that kept falling in." **a.** How does this image relate to the image he used to describe his spirit in the previous stanza? **b.** What does this image express about his reaction to the events he describes in the poem?

Literary Elements

Figurative Language

In "Martín IV," Baca creates several images using **figurative language,** or words and phrases that are not intended to be interpreted in a literal sense. For example, when the speaker says that his grandmother had been "a brimming acequia," he does not mean, of course, that she had in fact been a full waterway. Instead, he is creating a **metaphor,** which is a figure of speech that makes a comparison between two things that are basically dissimilar.

Another form of figurative language is the **simile,** which is a comparison of essentially unlike things through the use of a specific word of comparison, such as *like, as, than,* or *resembles*—for example, "lightning crackled / like the slap of new lumber stacks."

Writers use figurative language to give readers imaginative insights into the meaning or significance of something. In this poem the speaker's close ties to nature and his personal feelings or impressions are revealed through Baca's choice of figurative language.

Lines 13–27 contain several examples of figurative language that relates the speaker's boyhood self to nature. Identify one simile and one metaphor in these lines. What do the images in the second stanza suggest about the boy's attitude toward himself, nature, and his place in the world?

Lucha Corpi

(1945–)

In her poetry, Lucha Corpi (loo'chah kohr'pee) often expresses her personal struggles as a woman caught between two cultures. Born and raised in Mexico, Corpi immigrated to the United States with her husband when she was nineteen years old. Like many Mexican Americans, she was torn between two conflicting sets of values: those of her native Mexican culture and those of modern American society. She found it particularly difficult to reconcile her deeply ingrained traditional values with the relative freedom and equality experienced by women in the United States. Her painful divorce from her husband in 1970 intensified these conflicts, leading her to deeply question her role as a woman—specifically her identity as a Mexican woman in her adopted American culture.

Corpi's first attempts at writing coincided closely with her increasing involvement in the Chicano movement at the University of California at Berkeley and in the Mexican American community in Oakland, California. As she has come to identify herself as a Chicana, she has to some extent been able to merge the two halves of her cultural experience. She wrote her first short story in 1970 and has since published stories and poems in numerous magazines and journals. Her award-winning poetry has appeared in several anthologies of Chicano and women's literature, and a collection of her poems was published in *Fireflight: Three Latin American Poets* in 1976. Her book *Palabras de Mediodia / Noon Words* was published in 1980. Written in Spanish and translated into English, these critically acclaimed poems are lyrical and highly expressive with striking and original imagery. Recently, she published her first novel, *Delia's Song.*

Corpi earned a degree in literature from the University of California at Berkeley as well as a graduate degree in World and Comparative Literature from San Francisco State University. She currently lives in Oakland, California, where she teaches English as a Second Language in the public schools and continues to write and to give readings of her works.

The two poems by Corpi on the following pages are given in both Spanish and English, as they appeared originally in her collection *Palabras de Mediodia / Noon Words.*

Del Ajedrez[1] / Chess

Have you ever played or watched the game of chess? If so, you will probably particularly enjoy this poem. As you read, notice how the poet relates the strategies of the "ambitious king" and "persevering knights" to the world of human beings. Consider what the "armies" of pawns and the spider that weaves its web over the board might represent in human terms.

---

1. **Del Ajedrez** (dehl ah-heh-threhs').

Del Ajedrez

A Arturo Carrillo

En esta tibia obscuridad
nada se agranda
nada se altera
Cada pieza reclama su lugar
en el tablero silencioso.   5

La reina duerme
su sueño de madera
ante el ojo pretencioso
de obispos alcahuetes
y tenaces caballeros.   10

El despiesado consorte
con los ojos en blanco
trata de seducir
a la araña para que
con sus hilos infinitos   15
le conceda la virtud
de Mercurio.

Los soldados en fila india
se cuentan pequeñas tragedias
y grandes hazañas   20
de cuando heroicamente
aniquilaron a algún señor
obteniendo así el laurel
y el galardón del vencido.

Ahí los dos bandos   25
blanco y negro
en espera del reto
que desencadene la lucha
para cobrar con sangre
siglos de inhumanidad.   30

Chess

To Arturo Carrillo

In this intimate shadow
nothing grows
nothing changes.
Each piece claims its place
on the silent board.   5

The queen sleeps
her wooden sleep
under the pretentious eyes
of pandering bishops
and persevering knights   10

Her hobbled consort
with his sightless eyes
tries to cajole
the spider
into granting him   15
with its infinite threads
the wings of Mercury.

The pawns in Indian file
recount small tragedies
and great deeds done when they   20
were heroes in the conquest
of some great lord,
capturing the laurels
and plundering the prize
of the defeated.   25

There they are, two armies
black and white
drawn up and waiting
for the call to battle
hoping to collect in blood   30
payment for centries of inhumanity.

Curioso es que en esta
semiobscuridad
la araña que ajena
a los deseos
del rey ambicioso
los ve a todos igual
sigue bordando
su tela de seda fina
hacia la inmensidad.

35

Strangely enough,
the spider
untouched by the wheedling
of the ambitious king   35
sees both as equal
in the semidarkness
and goes on stretching
her silken fabric
toward infinity.   40

Emily Dickinson /
Emily Dickinson

*You have likely read at least one poem by the nineteenth-
century writer Emily Dickinson. A shy, solitary person,
Dickinson created powerful works that reveal an intense
inner life. Her poems often draw connections between small
events in the everyday world and the timeless spiritual
truths she saw reflected in them. As you read Corpi's poem,
consider why she might feel that she is "like" Dickinson.
What do the two poets have in common?*

Emily Dickinson

Como tú, soy de ayer,
de las bahías en donde
se ancla el día a
esperar su propia hora.

Como yo, eres de hoy,   5
del andar de esa hora
en la que apenas palpita
lo que aún no ha nacido.

Somos cultivadoras de
indecibles, tejedoras   10
de singulares, campesinas
migratorias en busca de
chinampas aún sin
siembra y sin cosecha.

Emily Dickinson

Like, you, I belong to yesterday,
to the bays where
day is anchored to
wait for its hour.

Like me, you belong to today,   5
the progression of that hour
when what is unborn
begins to throb.

We are cultivators of
the unsayable, weavers   10
of singulars, migrant
workers in search of
floating gardens as yet
unsown, as yet unharvested.

For Study and Discussion

Del Ajedrez / Chess

1. Corpi personifies the pieces on the chess board—that is, she gives them human qualities. **a.** How does she characterize the "two armies"? **b.** What facets of human nature might these armies represent?

2. The "two armies" of chess pieces wait to be called into battle. **a.** What "payment" do they hope to collect for "centuries of inhumanity?" **b.** What is ironic about their means of avenging the inhumanity of others?

3. "Untouched" by the armies' ambitions, the spider weaves her web over the miniature world of the chessboard. What might the spider represent in the poem?

Emily Dickinson / Emily Dickinson

4. Emily Dickinson's poems often describe abstract concepts, such as death, eternity, and forces of nature, in terms of everyday objects and events. In light of this aspect of Dickinson's work, what do you think Corpi means when she refers to Dickinson and herself as "cultivators of / the unsayable" and "weavers / of singulars"?

5. Corpi feels a kinship with Emily Dickinson, whose poems seem to mirror Corpi's own inner thoughts and emotions that "wait" for their hour to be born in a poem. Do you feel drawn to a particular poet whose works you have read in this book or elsewhere? If so, what do you feel you have in common with that poet? What facets of the poet's work reflect your own thoughts, feelings, or experiences?

Vocabulary

Explaining Words in Context

Poets choose their words carefully in order to create precise images that are rich in meaning. For example, in "Chess," Corpi refers to the "intimate shadow" that engulfs the chessboard. *Intimate* means "familiar or highly private and personal." "Intimate shadow," then, suggests a dim, isolated corner in which the chess pieces play out their own game of ambition and intrigue unnoticed by the rest of the world.

Corpi says that "the queen sleeps / . . . / under the pretentious eyes" of her bishops and knights. What does *pretentious* mean? In what way might these chess pieces be considered "pretentious?"

The queen's "hobbled consort / . . . / tries to cajole the spider" into freeing him. Define *hobbled, consort,* and *cajole.* Who is the queen's "consort," and why is he "hobbled"? In your opinion, why did Corpi use *hobbled* instead of a different word that has a similar meaning? How does the word *cajole* help to characterize the consort?

The pawns tell tales of "capturing the laurels / and plundering the prize / of the defeated." What do laurels traditionally represent, and how did they acquire this meaning? What does *plundering* mean? Why are these two words appropriate for describing the pawns' conquests?

The spider pays no attention to the "wheedling / of the ambitious king." What does *wheedling* mean, and how does it relate to *cajole* in line 13?

Writing About Literature

Using Personal Knowledge and Experience to Interpret a Poem

Each reader brings a unique perspective to a work of literature, depending on his or her own experience, thoughts, and emotions. Consequently, a certain phrase or image will call forth different feelings and associations in different people, leading them to interpret its meaning in different ways. For example, a person who enjoys playing chess will likely visualize and interpret Corpi's descriptions in light of the function of each chess piece and the rules and strategies of the game. Others who are less familiar with chess may enjoy different aspects of the poem, focusing more on Corpi's use of language and her insightful comments about human nature.

In "Emily Dickinson," Corpi concludes the poem with a **metaphor,** or figurative comparison, that identifies her and Emily Dickinson as

> . . . migrant
> workers in search of
> floating gardens as yet
> unsown, as yet unharvested.

In an essay of two or three paragraphs, discuss the meaning of these lines. What effect does your knowledge or experience of migrant workers' lives have on your interpretation? How might Corpi's own background have helped to determine her choice of metaphors?

Prewriting. Although your essay will focus largely on your personal response to the lines in the poem, you will first want to be sure that you grasp what they mean in themselves and in the context of the poem. For instance, you would have to know what a migrant worker is and who is being identified as a migrant worker within the poem before you could begin to interpret Corpi's metaphor.

Brainstorm a list of the things you know about migrant workers. For example, who are migrant workers? What kind of lives do they live, and what hardships do they suffer? Next, consider how your knowledge affects your reading of the lines. Why would migrant workers be searching for "floating gardens as yet / unsown, as yet unharvested"? How does the image of "floating gardens" contrast with the reality of field labor? In what way does Corpi's Mexican American heritage lend special significance to this metaphor?

Writing and Revising. Rather than assume that the reader will follow your train of thought, clearly state the links between your own experience and your reading of Corpi's lines. For example, if you are drawing on your knowledge of the constant uprooting that migrant workers experience, use a phrase such as "the fact that migrant workers must move from harvest to harvest suggests to me that . . ." or "in light of the frequent upheaval that migrant workers experience. . . ." Introducing your interpretation of the poem in this manner will ensure that the reader understands why and how you have reached a particular conclusion.

Gary Soto

(1952–)

I don't separate the craft of writing from subject matter. They must go hand in hand . . . . By craft I don't necessarily mean rhyme and meter, but just exactness of language.

In this comment about Chicano poetry, poet Gary Soto (soh'toh) reveals an important feature of his own work. Always aiming for "exactness of language" in his writing, Soto creates clear, powerful images that imprint themselves on the reader's mind. His lyrical yet terse style is well suited to his subject matter, which often deals with the harsher realities of Mexican American life in both urban and rural settings.

Soto was not always the careful, skilled poet he is today—in fact, he describes his first poems as "awkward" and "ungrammatical" with "inflated language and ideas." Determined to improve, he devoted years of study and hard work to perfecting his craft. Throughout college he read constantly and learned from the work of other writers, particularly other Hispanic poets such as Federico García Lorca and Pablo Neruda.

The selections on the following pages, with the exception of "Black Hair" and "Oranges," are taken from *The Elements of San Joaquin,* a book-length poem that won the United States Award of the International Poetry Forum in 1976. "Oranges" and "Black Hair" are taken from *Black Hair,* a collection of poems that was published in 1985.

(For additional biographical information about Gary Soto, see page 391.)

from **The Elements of San Joaquin**[1]

As parts of a single long work, the following selections from The Elements of San Joaquin *share in common a number of literary features and themes. Their setting is California's San Joaquin Valley, where poet Gary Soto has lived and worked for much of his life. Based on Soto's own experiences and perceptions, these poems explore a single speaker's experiences, memories, and observations of the world around him. "History" and "Braly Street," for example, both focus on "elements" of the speaker's personal history—from memories of his hard-working, stoical grandmother to reflections on the time-altered landscape of his childhood street. In "Sun," "Stars," and "Wind," the speaker meditates on elements of the natural world— sometimes as a detached observer, sometimes as an integral part of the environment he describes. "Field" and "Field Poem" express a less harmonious relationship with the environment: the speaker in these poems feels defeated by his back-breaking, dehumanizing labor as a migrant worker in the fields of San Joaquin.*

As you read these poems, notice the motifs—*recurring images—that bind them together.*

Field

The wind sprays pale dirt into my mouth
The small, almost invisible scars
On my hands.
The pores in my throat and elbows
Have taken in a seed of dirt of their own.   5

---

1. **San Joaquin** (sahn hwah-keen'): a fertile valley in central California where many Mexican Americans work as migrant field hands.

After a day in the grape fields near Rolinda[1]
A fine silt, washed by sweat,
Has settled into the lines
On my wrists and palms.

Already I am becoming the valley,   10
A soil that sprouts nothing
For any of us.

---

1. **Rolinda:** a small agricultural community outside of Fresno, California.

Wind

A dry wind over the valley
Peeled mountains, grain by grain,
To small slopes, loose dirt
Where red ants tunnel.

The wind strokes   5
The skulls and spines of cattle
To white dust, to nothing,

Covers the spiked tracks of beetles,
Of tumbleweed, of sparrows
That pecked the ground for insects.   10

Evenings, when I am in the yard weeding,
The wind picks up the breath of my armpits
Like dust, swirls it
Miles away

And drops it   15
On the ear of a rabid dog,
And I take on another life.

Wind

When you got up this morning the sun
Blazed an hour in the sky,

A lizard hid
Under the curled leaves of manzanita
And winked its dark lids.

Later, the sky grayed,
And the cold wind you breathed
Was moving under your skin and already far
From the small hives of your lungs.

Stars

At dusk the first stars appear.
Not one eager finger points toward them.
A little later the stars spread with the night
And an orange moon rises
To lead them, like a shepherd, toward dawn.

Sun

In June the sun is a bonnet of light
Coming up,
Little by little,
From behind a skyline of pine.

The pastures sway with fiddle-neck   5
Tassels of foxtail.

At Piedra[1]
A couple fish on the river's edge,
Their shadows deep against the water.
Above, in the stubbled slopes,   10

---

1. **Piedra** (pyeh'thrah): a park area outside of Fresno, California.

Cows climb down
As the heat rises
In a mist of blond locusts,
Returning to the valley.

Field Poem

When the foreman whistled
My brother and I
Shouldered our hoes,
Leaving the field.
We returned to the bus   5
Speaking
In broken English, in broken Spanish
The restaurant food,
The tickets to a dance
We wouldn't buy with our pay.   10

From the smashed bus window,
I saw the leaves of cotton plants
Like small hands
Waving good-bye.

History

Grandma lit the stove.
Morning sunlight
Lengthened in spears
Across the linoleum floor.
Wrapped in a shawl,   5
Her eyes small
With sleep,

She sliced papas,[1]
Pounded chiles[2]
With a stone   10
Brought from Guadalajara.[3]
            After
Grandpa left for work,
She hosed down
The walk her sons paved   15
And in the shade
Of a chinaberry,
Unearthed her
Secret cigar box
Of bright coins   20
And bills, counted them
In English,
Then in Spanish,
And buried them elsewhere.
Later, back   25
From the market,
Where no one saw her,
She pulled out
Pepper and beet, spines
Of asparagus   30
From her blouse,
Tiny chocolates
From under a paisley bandana,
And smiled.

That was the '50s,   35
And Grandma in her '50s,
A face streaked
From cutting grapes
And boxing plums.
I remember her insides   40
Were washed of tapeworm,
Her arms swelled into knobs
Of small growths—

---

1. **papas** (pah'pahs): potatoes.
2. **chiles** (chee'lehs): red peppers.
3. **Guadalajara** (gwah-thah-lah-hah'rah): capital of the state of Jalisco in west central Mexico.

Her second son
Dropped from a ladder   45
And was dust.
And yet I do not know
The sorrows
That sent her praying
In the dark of a closet,   50
The tear that fell
At night
When she touched
Loose skin
Of belly and breasts.   55
I do not know why
Her face shines
Or what goes beyond this shine,
Only the stories
That pulled her   60
From Taxco to San Joaquin,
Delano to Westside,[4]
The places
In which we all begin.

---

4. **Taxco . . . Westside** (tahs'koh): migrant workers come from towns such
as Taxco in Mexico to work in the fields around San Joaquin, Delano,
Westside, and other locations in the United States.

Braly Street

Every summer
The asphalt softens
Giving under the edge
Of boot heels and the trucks
That caught radiators   5
Of butterflies.
Bottle caps and glass
Of the '40s and '50s
Hold their breath
Under the black earth   10
Of asphalt and are silent
Like the dead whose mouths
Have eaten dirt and bermuda.

Every summer I come
To this street   15
Where I discovered ants bit,
Matches flare,
And pinto beans unraveled
Into plants; discovered
Aspirin will not cure a dog   20
Whose fur twitches.

It's 16 years
Since our house
Was bulldozed and my father
Stunned into a coma . . .   25
Where it was,
An oasis of chickweed
And foxtails.
Where the almond tree stood
There are wine bottles   30
Whose history
Is a liver. The long caravan
Of my uncle's footprints
Has been paved
With dirt. Where my father   35
Cemented a pond
There is a cavern of red ants
Living on the seeds
The wind brings
And cats that come here   40
To die among
The browning sage.

It's 16 years
Since bottle collectors
Shoveled around   45
The foundation
And the almond tree
Opened its last fruit
To the summer.
The houses are gone,   50
The Molinas, Morenos,
The Japanese families
Are gone, the Okies gone

Who moved out at night
Under a canopy of   55
Moving stars.

In '57 I sat
On the porch, salting
Slugs that came out
After the rain,   60
While inside my uncle
Weakened with cancer
And the blurred vision
Of his hands
Darkening to earth.   65
In '58 I knelt
Before my father
Whose spine was pulled loose.
Before his face still
Growing a chin of hair,   70
Before the procession
Of stitches behind
His neck, I knelt
And did not understand.

Braly Street is now   75
Tin ventilators
On the warehouses, turning
Our sweat
Towards the yellowing sky;
Acetylene welders   80
Beading manifolds,
Stinging the half-globes
Of retinas. When I come
To where our house was,
I come to weeds   85
And a sewer line tied off
Like an umbilical cord;
To the chinaberry
Not pulled down
And to its rings   90
My father and uncle
Would equal, if alive.

For Study and Discussion

Field

1. The speaker says that his pores "Have taken in a seed of dirt of their own," describing himself as if he were a field that is planted with earth. **a.** What other words and phrases in the selection echo this imagery? **b.** How does the speaker's inability to grow or create relate to his laboring in the grape fields? What is ironic about this relationship?

Wind / Wind

2. In the first selection titled "Wind," the "dry wind" erodes mountains, scatters animal bones, and covers the tracks of tumbleweed, sparrows, and insects. How does the wind act on the speaker of the poem? In what way does the speaker "take on another life"?

3. In the second "Wind" selection, the transformation of the sky is a gradual, somewhat ominous darkening. **a.** What images does the poet use to describe this transformation? **b.** What does the poem's final image suggest about the effect of the change of weather on the speaker?

4. The two selections titled "Wind" are meditations on different facets of a single element. Giving examples from the two selections, discuss the imagery the poet uses to create the tone of each meditation.

Stars

5. In "Stars," the nightly movement of the stars is presented as a kind of life cycle. What are the three stages of this "life cycle"?

6. The poet likens the moon to a shepherd who leads the stars "toward dawn." **a.** What does this simile suggest about the eventual fate of the stars? **b.** How does the meaning of dawn in the poem contrast with the meaning usually associated with dawn?

Gary Soto 533

Sun

7. The visual images of "a bonnet of light," swaying "Tassels of foxtail," and a couple whose shadows are "deep against the water" all create a sense of serenity. Discuss how the final image of the poem—"a mist of blond locusts"—relates to these earlier images. How does this image affect the tranquil mood of the poem?

Field Poem

8. The brothers speak to each other "In broken English, in broken Spanish." **a.** What does the imagery of "broken" speech suggest about their emotional and physical states as they leave the field? **b.** What phrase in the last stanza echoes this imagery?

9. Through the bus window, the speaker watches the cotton plants that are "Like small hands / Waving good-bye." What tone does this final image create?

10. The selections "Field" and "Field Poem" use different patterns of imagery to explore similar subjects. Citing specific images from both selections, compare the imagery and the thematic messages of the two poems.

History

11. As the title of the poem suggests, the speaker's memories of his grandmother are a significant part of his personal "history." What do the poem's last two lines suggest about the connection between the speaker's grandmother and his heritage as a Mexican American? To whom does the "we" refer in the last line?

12. Unearthing her "Secret cigar box," the grandmother counts her money "In English, / Then in Spanish" before reburying the box in a different spot. What does this description suggest about the grandmother and about the economic conditions under which she has lived?

13. The accidental death of the grandmother's second son is clearly one source of her grief. **a.** What images in the poem

534 *Gary Soto*

suggest that she has many private "sorrows" that cause her to grieve in secret? **b.** What does this privateness indicate about the grandmother?

Braly Street

14. The repetition of "Every summer" in the first stanza emphasizes the passing of time, which is marked by the speaker's periodic returns to Braly Street. **a.** What other repetitive images and phrases in the poem reinforce the sense that much time has passed since the speaker lived on Braly Street? **b.** What is the effect of this repetition?

15. Growing up on Braly Street was a process of discovery for the speaker: it was where he learned that "ants bit" and that "Aspirin will not cure a dog / Whose fur twitches," as well as larger and more painful truths about the nature of life and death. **a.** What has the speaker "discovered" during his visits to Braly Street as an adult? **b.** In your opinion, why does he return "Every summer"?

Literary Elements

Point of View

The **point of view** in a work of literature is the vantage point from which the work is told. In the **first-person point of view,** a character speaks in his or her own words, using pronouns such as *I* and *me.* In a work told from the **third-person point of view,** the narrator is not a character in the work and uses pronouns such as *he, she,* and *it.*

First-person and third-person points of view are the most common; however, writers sometimes choose the **second-person point of view,** which directly links the reader to the experiences of the speaker, as in the second of Gary Soto's "Wind" poems. His use of the pronoun *you* serves to generalize the experiences of the speaker. Although it is not literally the reader who "got up this morning," and breathed in "the cold wind," the poem's second-person point of view helps the reader to identify and empathize with the speaker. What other purposes might the use of *you* serve in this poem? How would the poem be different if it were written in the first or third person?

Choose another poem from *The Elements of San Joaquin,* and discuss its point of view. What is the relationship between the speaker and the content of the poem? Why do you think the poet chose that particular point of view? How would the tone and thematic content of the poem be altered by use of a different point of view?

Writing About Literature

Analyzing Motif

A **motif** is a recurring feature—such as an image, a phrase, or an idea—that appears in a literary work or group of works. A motif often helps to develop and emphasize a larger theme. Several of Gary Soto's poems, for example, contain recurring images of burial—of people and things that are literally and figuratively being covered over by soil, plant growth, and asphalt.

In "Field," the speaker has been toiling in grape fields, and the dirt settles on his skin like "A fine silt," filling the lines of his palms. He concludes, "Already I am becoming the valley, / A soil that sprouts nothing / For any of us." The speaker's potential for growth cannot surface when his identity is buried beneath the weight of mindless toil. The "seed of dirt" that the earth plants in him "sprouts nothing," just as his mind and spirit cannot grow because they are improperly nourished.

"History" contains images of burial as well: the grandmother has "Unearthed" her cigar box full of money, only to bury it again in a different place. Her second son "Dropped from a ladder / And was dust"—thereby himself becoming earth, just as the speaker of "Field" is becoming part of the very soil that he farms.

In "Braly Street," the street on which the speaker grew up holds many memories for him, but many once-familiar places are being buried "Under the black earth / Of asphalt" or are becoming overgrown with weeds. His uncle's footprints have been "paved / With dirt," and his uncle and father, now dead, are buried beneath the earth. He describes his dying uncle's hands as "Darkening to earth." As in "History," evidence of the speaker's origins now exist largely in memory; signs of his past, and of the people and things he loved, are "gone" from sight.

In a short essay, examine and discuss a motif other than the burial imagery that occurs in one or several of Gary Soto's poems.

Prewriting. As you read the poems, consider the following questions. What specific image, idea, phrase, or even point of view recurs in the poem or poems? What is the significance of this element in relation to the poem as a whole and—if you are examining several poems—in relation to the other poems? What general theme does this motif help to develop?

Writing and Revising. Be sure to attribute quotations to their proper sources. If you are analyzing a group of poems, take special care to specify the particular poem from which you have taken a passage. Also, if you are quoting a word, phrase, or line within a sentence of your essay, check to see that the quotation fits smoothly into your own sentence and that the verb tenses inside and outside of the quotation match.

Creative Writing

Writing a Poem About a Place

As Gary Soto's poems illustrate, a sense of place—of the elements of one's environment—can deeply influence one's personal experiences and memories. In "Braly Street," for example, changes in the landscape of the speaker's old neighborhood awaken memories of his childhood and of the people and experiences that helped to shape him. The landscape of Braly Street corresponds to his own emotional landscape: like Braly Street, he has been changed by time, his memories covered over with layers of experience just as his dead uncle's footprints have been "paved / With dirt." He returns to Braly Street "Every summer" not only to witness its changes but also to uncover his own memories of the past.

Write a short poem (ten to sixteen lines long) that focuses on a particular place that influenced you when you were younger and that you have not seen for at least a year. In your poem, explore your relationship to that place and the ways in which it had an influence on you.

Prewriting. You may want to focus on a particular street, a house, or a whole town. As you think about the place you have chosen, consider the following questions. What emotions do you associate with this place? What significant things happened to you while you were there? How did the landscape and people affect your thoughts and feelings? Would you like to return there? What do you think you would find if you did return? With these questions in mind, brainstorm a list of details that describe the place and your experience(s) there. Keep in mind that good poetry uses specific details and images to create a vivid description of its subject.

Writing. Carefully choose the adjectives and verbs that you use in your descriptions, considering the connotative meanings of words and the moods, or feelings, that they create. The verb tense you choose—past, present, or future—will help to determine the focus of your poem.

Black Hair

"The triple and hard slide, / The gloves eating balls into double plays"—these and other images describe the fast-paced action of a game that was "more than baseball" to the speaker of this poem. Watching from the bleachers, he worshipped the strength and skill of the players—represented by a fictional Mexican player, Hector Moreno—and vicariously shared in his heroes' triumphs. As you read "Black Hair," notice how the poet uses many active verbs to capture the enthusiasm and excitement he feels for the game.

At eight I was brilliant with my body.
In July, that ring of heat
We all jumped through, I sat in the bleachers
Of Romain Playground, in the lengthening
Shade that rose from our dirty feet.   5
The game before us was more than baseball.
It was a figure—Hector Moreno
Quick and hard with turned muscles,
His crouch the one I assumed before an altar
Of worn baseball cards, in my room.   10

I came here because I was Mexican, a stick
Of brown light in love with those
Who could do it—the triple and hard slide,
The gloves eating balls into double plays.
What could I do with 50 pounds, my shyness,   15
My black torch of hair, about to go out?
Father was dead, his face no longer
Hanging over the table or our sleep,
And mother was the terror of mouths
Twisting hurt by butter knives.   20

In the bleachers I was brilliant with my body,
Waving players in and stomping my feet,
Growing sweaty in the presence of white shirts.
I chewed sunflower seeds. I drank water
And bit my arm through the late innings.   25

Gary Soto 539

When Hector lined balls into deep
Center, in my mind I rounded the bases
With him, my face flared, my hair lifting
Beautifully, because we were coming home
to the arms of brown people.   30

Oranges

*Do you have distant memories that remain particularly
vivid in your mind, down to the smallest detail? In
"Oranges," the speaker re-creates an incident that happened when he was twelve—his first walk with a girl he
admired. Notice the detailed descriptions of setting and
the visual imagery he uses to set the mood of this poignant
scene.*

The first time I walked
With a girl, I was twelve,
Cold, and weighted down
With two oranges in my jacket.
December. Frost cracking   5
Beneath my steps, my breath
Before me, then gone,
As I walked toward
Her house, the one whose
Porch light burned yellow   10
Night and day, in any weather.
A dog barked at me, until
She came out pulling
At her gloves, face bright
With rouge. I smiled,   15
Touched her shoulder, and led
Her down the street, across
A used car lot and a line
Of newly planted trees,
Until we were breathing   20

Before a drugstore. We
Entered, the tiny bell
Bringing a saleslady
Down a narrow aisle of goods.
I turned to the candies   25
Tiered like bleachers,
And asked what she wanted—
Light in her eyes, a smile
Starting at the corners
Of her mouth. I fingered   30
A nickel in my pocket,
And when she lifted a chocolate
That cost a dime,
I didn't say anything.
I took the nickel from   35
My pocket, then an orange,
And set them quietly on
The counter. When I looked up,
The lady's eyes met mine,
And held them, knowing   40
Very well what it was all
About.

     Outside,
A few cars hissing past,
Fog hanging like old   45
Coats between the trees.
I took my girl's hand
In mine for two blocks,
Then released it to let
Her unwrap the chocolate.   50
I peeled my orange
That was so bright against
The gray of December
That, from some distance,
Someone might have thought   55
I was making a fire in my hands.

_____

For Study and Discussion

Black Hair

1. The speaker in the poem twice says, "I was brilliant with my body." **a.** What does he mean by this? **b.** To what degree is his sense of physical prowess *vicarious*—experienced secondhand through the baseball player he admires?

2. In the first stanza, the speaker says, "The game before us was more than baseball." **a.** In what way was it "more" than a mere baseball game? **b.** How does the speaker's worship of his hero relate to his Mexican American heritage?

3. In the second stanza, the speaker makes brief but significant mention of his mother and father. **a.** What imagery does he use to speak of his parents? **b.** What is the significance of this description in relation to the rest of the poem?

Oranges

4. The poet emphasizes the winter setting of the poem with images of "Frost cracking" and of frozen breath. This imagery contrasts with the warmth of the budding romance between the speaker and the girl. **a.** What **mood,** or prevailing feeling, does this contrast help to create? **b.** How would the mood be different if the poem were set in spring?

5. The brightness of the oranges contrasts sharply with "The gray of December." **a.** What other visual images contrast with the setting? **b.** How does this pattern of imagery, highlighted by the title "Oranges," contribute to the poem's mood?

Literary Elements

Imagery

Imagery consists of words and phrases that evoke the sensations of sight, hearing, touch, smell, or taste. By appealing to the senses in this way, writers can create vivid and lasting impressions in the reader's mind. Writers often use sensory images to describe abstract concepts and emotions—to make abstractions tangible to the reader. For example, in "Black Hair," Gary Soto describes the month of July as a "ring of heat." This image appeals to touch as well as sight and is more striking and memorable than any abstract description of heat could be. The poet also uses precise images and terms to describe the baseball game—"the triple and hard slide, / The gloves eating balls into double plays." This imagery expresses the action and feel of the baseball game and also reveals the speaker's fervent enthusiasm for every aspect of the game.

Discuss images in the poem that the speaker uses to describe himself. What does he reveal about himself through these images? What makes the imagery effective? To what senses do the images appeal?

Vocabulary

Using Verbals to Create Active Descriptions

In many of his poems, Gary Soto creates precise, dynamic images through the skillful use of verbs. For example, in the first "Wind" poem from *The Elements of San Joaquin,* the active verbs "Peeled," "strokes," "Covers," "picks up," "swirls," and "drops" characterize the wind as a powerful force that shapes and alters the environment.

In "Black Hair" and "Oranges," Soto uses **participles**—verb forms that can function as both adjectives and verbs—to lend action to his descriptions. For example, the images of "mouths / Twisting hurt by butter knives" in "Black Hair" and of "Frost cracking" in "Oranges" both contain participles—"Twisting" and "cracking"—that actively describe the nouns they modify.

Identify at least three other participles in "Black Hair" and three in "Oranges." Keep in mind that there are two kinds of

Sandra Cisneros

(1954–)

Writer and teacher Sandra Cisneros (sahn'drah sees-neh'rohs) believes that "art is in all of us"—that the rhythms of everyday speech are a natural source of poetry. She explains to her students that all writing is based on oral speech and that, consequently, anyone can write— even those intimidated by the prospect of putting words on paper.

Cisneros has a unique method for helping her students to discover their natural writing voice, a method she calls "speaking in doughnut language." "Doughnut language" is the everyday speech you would use if you were sitting in a doughnut shop with a group of friends. She encourages students to use their "doughnut language" as the basis for their writing style, "dressing it up or down" as the occasion demands.

Although Cisneros has faith in the natural talent that resides in everyone, she points out that talent alone does not make a writer. In addition to talent, young writers need to have the conviction that "good isn't good enough"—that no matter how well one writes, one can do better. She asks students who want to be writers, "How badly do you want to write? Can you *not* write?" Perhaps most important, she tells her students that one must have the courage and persistence to pursue a writing career in a culture that is not highly supportive of the arts.

Cisneros found her own writing voice when she began to write about her personal experiences and perspective as a Chicana. As discussed in the biographical note on page 355, she believes strongly that part of her "job" as a writer is to address the experiences of working-class minority people, particularly those of Mexican American women.

The poems on the following pages are taken from *My Wicked Wicked Ways,* Cisneros's most recent collection of poetry. Like many of her works, these poems describe childhood and family experiences that, in one form or another, "haunt" the poet's memory.

(For additional biographical information about Sandra Cisneros, see pages 320 and 355.)

Abuelito[1] Who

Simple in language yet rich in associations, this poem captures the everyday immediacy of a child's sadness and sense of loss in the face of her grandfather's declining health. As you read, consider what the voice, or language style, of the poem reveals about its speaker. Why do you think the poet chose to write in the voice of a child?

Abuelito who throws coins like rain
and asks who loves him
who is dough and feathers
who is a watch and glass of water
whose hair is made of fur   5
is too sad to come downstairs today
who tells me in Spanish you are my diamond
who tells me in English you are my sky
whose little eyes are string
can't come out to play   10
sleeps in his little room all night and day
who used to laugh like the letter k
is sick
is a doorknob tied to a sour stick
is tired shut the door   15
doesn't live here anymore
is hiding underneath the bed
who talks to me inside my head
is blankets and spoons and big brown shoes
who snores up and down up and down up and down again   20
is the rain on the roof that falls like coins
asking who loves him
who loves him who?

---

1. **Abuelito** (ah-bweh-lee'toh): a term of endearment meaning "dear grandfather."

Muddy Kid
Comes Home

*The speaker of this poem reacts indignantly to the adult
view that "mud is uncouth." Perhaps you, too, were once
a "muddy kid" coming home to an adult's outcry that
"mud must stay put." As you read, you will see what
argument the speaker gives in defense of mud. Why does
she feel that it should be respected rather than scorned?*

And mama complains
Mama whose motto
Is mud must remain
Mama who acts
So uppity up   5

Says mud can't come in
Says mud must stay put
Mama who thinks that
Mud is uncouth

Cannot remember   10
Can hardly recall
Mud's what I was
When I wasn't at all

But mud must remain
Or Mama complains   15
Mama who cannot
Remember her name

Six Brothers

As a child, poet Sandra Cisneros often cast herself as the heroine of the many fairy tales she read, imagining herself and her family to be the victims of an "evil curse." This poem harks back to one of those childhood tales. As you read, consider why the poet compares her six brothers to the brothers in the Grimm's story The Six Swans. *What does this comparison reveal about her relationship with her brothers?*

_____

> *In Grimm's tale* The Six Swans *a sister keeps a six-year silence and weaves six thistle shirts to break the spell that has changed her brothers into swans. She weaves all but the left sleeve of the final shirt, and when the brothers are changed back into men, the youngest lacks only his left arm and has in its place a swan's wing.*

In Spanish our name means swan.
A great past—castles maybe
or a Sahara city,
but more likely
a name that stuck   5
to a barefoot boy
herding the dusty flock
down the bright road.

We'll never know.
Great-grandparents might   10
but family likes to keep to silence—
perhaps with reason
though we don't need far back to go.
On our father's side we have a cousin,

second, but cousin nonetheless,   15
who shot someone, his wife I think.
And on the other hand, there's
mother's brother who shot himself.

Then there's us—
seven ways to make the name or break it.   20
Our father has it planned:
oldest, you're doctor,
second, administration,
me, he shrugs, you should've been reporting weather,
next, musician,   25
athlete,
genius,
and youngest—well,
you'll take the business over.

You six a team   30
keeping to the master plan,
the lovely motion of tradition.
Appearances are everything.
We live for each other's expectations.
Brothers, it is so hard to keep up with you.   35
I've got the bad blood in me I think,
the mad uncle, the bit of the bullet.

Ask me anything.
Six thistle shirts. Keep a vow of silence.
I'll do it. But I'm earthbound   40
always in my admiration.
My six brothers, graceful, strong.
Except for you, little one-winged,
finding it as difficult as me
to keep the good name clean.   45

Traficante[1]

Often, writers use startling figurative language in order to get at the heart of unpleasant realities. As you read this poem, notice the patterns of imagery that Cisneros develops through figurative comparisons. What is your reaction to these images, and how do they influence your response to the subject matter of the poem?

for Dennis

Pink like a starfish's belly
or a newborn rat,
she hid the infected hand
for some time
before they noticed.   5
First the skin had been smooth
as the left hand.
Then the fence
had poked through,
a tiny slit, the mouth of a small fish.   10
A crispy scab had stitched it to a pucker
but this was picked on until the wound
turned a purple-pink
and gradually became swollen
and hurt to the touch.   15
She liked to draw the fat hand
into her sleeve,
keep it hiding there,
a fish in its cave.
Sometimes it would come out   20
and she would talk to it.
At school the teacher
pulled the hand out suddenly

---

1. **Traficante** (trah-fee-kahn′teh): merchant, trader.

and the child yelped.
The mother took her   25
to Traficante's Drugs
where the doctor had an office
behind the case of eyeglasses
all colors and different styles.
He asked to see the hand.   30
The fish poked out
from the cuff of a nubby sleeve,
darted back in, then was out again
and placed upon the table
beneath the bright lamp.   35
One finger pressed its side
and she whimpered.
The doctor took down from the shelf
the medical encyclopedia, vol. 2,
and holding her by the wrist   40
said turn around.
Mrs. Ortiz was having a prescription filled
for Reynaldo's fever and was asking
how much when the book came down.

For Study and Discussion

Abuelito Who

1. The speaker uses several **metaphors**—figures of speech that compare two dissimilar things—to describe her grandfather. **a.** What objects does she identify her grandfather with? **b.** What impression of the grandfather do these metaphors create?

2. The language and syntax of this poem is simple and childlike. **a.** What does this use of language say about the speaker? **b.** How does it help to characterize the grandfather?

Muddy Kid Comes Home

3. The speaker protests the mother's insistence that "mud must remain." Why does the speaker think that the mother's "motto" is unjust?

4. The last two lines of this poem are *ambiguous*—that is, they have more than one possible meaning. **a.** What is their literal meaning? **b.** In light of the second stanza, what other meaning might they have? **c.** How does your reading of the lines affect your interpretation of the poem?

Six Brothers

5. In the second stanza, the speaker remarks that her family "likes to keep to silence— / perhaps with reason." About what is her family secretive, and why?

6. The speaker describes her six brothers as "a team / keeping to the master plan." **a.** What is the "master plan" that she is referring to? **b.** How is she different from her brothers, and how does she feel about her family's "expectations" for her?

Traficante

7. The poet uses vivid, startling imagery to describe the girl's infected hand. **a.** To what does she compare the hand? **b.** What pattern of imagery do these comparisons develop? **c.** What effect do these images have in the poem?

8. The last line reveals the surprising way that the doctor uses the medical encyclopedia to treat the infected hand. **a.** What is his method of treatment? **b.** Do you think that the doctor would have used this method on any patient? (Consider lines 42–43.) If not, what might his brutality reveal about his view of the girl's social or economic status?

Literary Elements

Repetition and Alliteration

Writers often use **repetition** of a word, phrase, or structure to create emphasis in a work. For example, in "Muddy Kid Comes Home," the repeated line "mud must remain" humorously emphasizes the mother's refusal to be swayed by the speaker's protests.

This line also contains a good example of **alliteration**—a particular kind of repetition in which the same sound is repeated within closely grouped words. The alliteration of *m* and *u* sounds that occur in this line and the other alliterated sounds throughout the poem lend a sing-song rhythm to the poem, helping to create its tone of childlike indignation.

Copy Sandra Cisneros's poem "Traficante" on a sheet of paper, and underline with colored pencils each example of alliteration in lines 1–13: for example, you might use a red pencil to underline the repetition of *s* sounds and a blue pencil to mark repeated long vowel sounds. (Keep in mind that alliteration consists of repeated sounds and not necessarily of the same letters repeated.)

What is the overall effect of alliteration in the poem? How do the repeated sounds you have underlined help to create the rhythm of the poem? What words, phrases, and images are emphasized by the poet's use of alliteration?

Writing About Literature

Analyzing an Extended Metaphor in a Poem

A **metaphor** is a figure of speech that draws a comparison between two essentially unlike things with the intent of giving meaning to one of them. For example, in Sandra Cisneros's poem "Traficante," the wound on the girl's hand is described as "the mouth of a small fish." The hand is not literally a fish, of course, but the metaphor describes the appearance of the wound and lends deeper meaning to the description by calling forth striking associations.

In "Six Brothers," Cisneros uses an **extended metaphor**—a metaphor that is developed, or extended, throughout the poem—to describe her relationship to her six brothers. In an essay of four or five paragraphs, analyze this extended metaphor and its function in the poem.

Prewriting. Cisneros's introductory note about the Grimm's fairy tale *The Six Swans* explains the basis for the metaphor. Trace the development of the metaphor throughout the poem, identifying specific details that will help to illustrate your discussion. Then, group these details according to four main points of comparison:

1. the things the speaker's family literally has in common with the family in the tale;
2. the figurative similarities between the speaker and the sister in *The Six Swans*;
3. the ways in which her brothers are like "the six swans";
4. the ways in which her relationship with her brothers mirrors the relationship between the sister and brothers in the tale.

Conclude your essay with a brief discussion of how the metaphor gives greater meaning to the speaker's descriptions of herself and her brothers within the poem.

Writing. As you write your essay, be sure to specify the points of comparison between the speaker's family and the family in *The Six Swans,* using adjectives and verbs that clearly indicate the similarities. For example, rather than state simply that the speaker "is like" the sister in the fairy tale, identify how they are alike, as in the following sentence:

Like the sister in *The Six Swans,* the speaker is "earthbound" while her brothers are, figuratively speaking, able to soar like birds—to achieve worldly success according to their father's "plan."

Lorna Dee Cervantes

(1954–)

In addition to devoting herself to her
work as an activist, editor, and educator,
Lorna Dee Cervantes (lohr'nah dee
sehr-bahn'tehs) has established herself as a talented poet who speaks
directly and passionately to her readers.

Cervantes was born in San Francisco, a descendant of *Californios*—
Spanish families who settled California in the seventeenth and
eighteenth centuries. Like many other Mexican American writers of her
generation, Cervantes grew up during a time of intense social upheaval
brought about by the merging currents of the Chicano movement, the
civil rights movement, and opposition to the United States' involvement
in Vietnam.

Cervantes experienced poverty firsthand from an early age. Her
parents separated when she was five years old, and she moved with her
mother, grandmother, and brother to San Jose, California, where she
and her family faced great hardship as they struggled to survive. Seeking refuge from the harsh realities that surrounded her, Cervantes began
to write at the age of eight, composing simple verses that formed the
basis of a collection of poetry she compiled several years later.

While still in high school, Cervantes became actively involved in the
Chicano movement as well as the anti-nuclear movement. She dedicated much of her time and energy to a fledgling theater group that
later toured California and participated in a theater festival in Mexico
City in 1974. After graduating from high school in 1972, Cervantes
began her college coursework and founded the Chicano literary
magazine *Mango.* From 1976 to 1982 she diligently kept the magazine
in circulation, printing it in her own kitchen. Cervantes left the

magazine in 1982 to attend college full time and received a degree in Creative Arts from San Jose State University in 1984.

Several of Cervantes's poems have received wide recognition, appearing in numerous anthologies and literary magazines. Her first published work, "Refugee Ship," was printed in a Mexico City newspaper in 1974. Her promise as a young poet was fulfilled in 1981 with the publication of her first book of poetry, *Emplumada,* as part of the University of Pittsburgh Press Poetry Series.

Cervantes writes with a clear and precise voice, presenting her readers with vivid, memorable images. Often addressing issues of self-esteem and personal freedom in her works, she also focuses on the difficulties of being caught between two cultures. The two poems that appear on the following pages reflect the central role that Cervantes's Mexican American heritage has played in her life and work. Alternating between Spanish and English in these poems, she both affirms her Hispanic roots and expresses the conflicts that arise from acculturation into Anglo society.

Cervantes currently lives in Boulder, Colorado, where she is working toward her doctorate and teaching poetry at the University of Colorado.

Freeway 280

*Although the small, well-tended neighborhood that the
speaker remembers has been torn down and replaced by a
freeway, the abandoned lots below the lanes still give
evidence of "old gardens" and human history. As you read,
consider what these overgrown gardens represent for the
speaker. Why does she return to the site of the old neighborhood? What does she hope to find there?*

Las casitas[1] near the gray cannery,
nestled amid wild abrazos[2] of climbing roses
and man-high red geraniums
are gone now. The freeway conceals it
all beneath a raised scar.   5

But under the fake windsounds of the open lanes,
in the abandoned lots below, new grasses sprout,
wild mustard remembers, old gardens
come back stronger than they were,
trees have been left standing in their yards.   10
Albaricoqueros, cerezos, nogales . . .[3]
Viejitas[4] come here with paper bags to gather greens.
Espinaca, verdolagas, yerbabuena . . .[5]

I scramble over the wire fence
that would have kept me out.   15
Once, I wanted out, wanted the rigid lanes
to take me to a place without sun,
without the smell of tomatoes burning
on swing shift in the greasy summer air.

1. **Las casitas** (lahs kah-see'tahs): the small houses.
2. **abrazos** (ah-brah'sohs): hugs, embraces.
3. **Albaricoqueros, cerezos, nogales** (ahl-bahr-ree-koh'keh'rohs,
   seh-reh'sohs, noh-gah'lehs): apricot trees, cherry trees, pecan trees.
4. **Viejitas** (byeh-hee'tahs): elderly ladies; dear old women.
5. **Espinaca, verdolagas, yerbabuena** (ehs-pee-nah'kah, behr-thoh-lah'gahs,
   yehr-bah-bweh'nah): spinach, purslane, peppermint.

Lorna Dee Cervantes 557

Maybe it's here   20
en los campos extraños de esta ciudad[6]
where I'll find it, that part of me
mown under
like a corpse
or a loose seed.   25

---

6. **en los campos extraños de esta ciudad** (ehn lohs kahm'pohs
ehx-trah'nyohs deh ehs'tah syoo-thahth'): in the strange fields of this
city.

Refugee Ship

*Perhaps you, like the speaker in this poem, have experienced
strong feelings of rootlessness. "Orphaned" from the
Hispanic heritage that is nevertheless her birthright, the
speaker feels as though she is trapped aboard a "refugee
ship / . . . that will never dock." The powerful impact of
this poem lies in the poet's deft use of figurative language
to describe her sense of being caught between two cultures.*

Like wet cornstarch, I slide
past my grandmother's eyes. Bible
at her side, she removes her glasses.
The pudding thickens.
Mama raised me without language,   5

I'm orphaned from my Spanish name.
The words are foreign, stumbling
on my tongue. I see in the mirror
my reflection: bronzed skin, black hair.

I feel I am a captive   10
aboard the refugee ship.
The ship that will never dock.
El barco que nunca atraca.[1]

---

1. *El barco que nunca atraca* (ehl bahr'koh keh noon'kah ah-trah'kah): The
ship that never docks.

558 Lorna Dee Cervantes

For Study and Discussion

Freeway 280

1. The speaker describes the freeway as a "raised scar." What does this image suggest about how the speaker views the freeway?

2. In the abandoned lots below the freeway, wild plants thrive and "old gardens / come back stronger than they were." What aspect of the speaker's life and cultural heritage might these gardens symbolically represent in the poem? In light of this symbolic meaning, what is significant about the gardens' resiliency?

3. The speaker says that she once "wanted out." **a.** What did she want to escape from, and where did she want to go? **b.** What does she hope to find or regain "en los campos extraños de esta ciudad" [in the strange fields of this city]?

Refugee Ship

4. In the first stanza, the speaker says: "Like wet cornstarch, I slide / past my grandmother's eyes." **a.** What is the significance of the grandmother's presence in the poem? **b.** What does the image of "wet cornstarch"—a pale, formless substance—suggest about the speaker's feelings?

5. The speaker clearly was not raised "without language" in a literal sense; rather, the statement in line 5 has a figurative meaning within the poem. **a.** What is this meaning? **b.** How does "without language" relate to "orphaned" in line 6?

6. The image of a refugee ship is a **metaphor,** or figurative comparison, that expresses the speaker's feelings about her cultural heritage. In what sense is she "captive" aboard a "ship that will never dock"?

7. In both "Freeway 280" and "Refugee Ship," the speaker describes feelings of being trapped or confined by her environment or her culture. Have you ever had such feelings? What did you do about them?

Lorna Dee Cervantes 559

Writing About Literature

Analyzing the Relationship Between Language and Theme in Two Poems

Many Mexican American writers, such as the poet Alurista, alternate between English and Spanish in their works—a practice called **code-switching**. The use of code-switching is a means of expressing the dual nature of the writers' cultural background and of affirming the importance of their Hispanic heritage. In an essay of two or three paragraphs, discuss how Lorna Dee Cervantes uses code-switching in "Refugee Ship" and "Freeway 280" to express aspects of her experience as a Mexican American.

Prewriting. Before you begin to examine Cervantes's use of Spanish words, it may be helpful to review the questions under **For Study and Discussion** that address themes and images in the two poems. Next, carefully examine Cervantes's use of code-switching in light of these thematic concerns. How often and in what context does she use Spanish words and phrases in the poems? How do these words and phrases help the poet to express particular features or elements of her Mexican American background? What kind of statement about her background might she be making through her use of language in each poem? You can organize your essay by devoting one paragraph to each poem or by developing each paragraph around a particular theme or a specific aspect of the poet's Mexican American background.

Writing and Revising. When quoting Spanish words and phrases from the poem, be particularly conscious of fitting the quotations smoothly into your sentences. For example, avoid grammatical inconsistencies such as the following:

> In "Freeway 280," "Las casitas" was demolished to make way for a freeway. (plural noun *casitas* [houses] as subject of singular verb *was*)

If you are uncertain of the grammatical form of a Spanish word or phrase, refer to the translation given in the footnote.

Creative Writing

Using Figurative Language in a Poem

Through the use of figurative language, writers can create power-ful images that help to express meanings in their works. For example, in Lorna Dee Cervantes's poem "Freeway 280," the freeway is a **symbol**—something that stands for itself and at the same stands for something larger than itself. The freeway is both an actual road that the speaker describes and also a symbol of the indifferent march of progress that has "mown under" an older, simpler way of life. In "Refugee Ship," Cervantes develops a **metaphor**—a kind of figurative language that draws a comparison between two basically dissimilar things—to express her feelings of being alienated from both her Hispanic roots and the Anglo culture in which she lives. The "refugee ship" is not a ship in the literal sense but rather a metaphor that the poet uses to describe her emotions. Her sense of being suspended between two cultures is comparable to the feelings of someone who is trapped aboard a refugee ship "that will never dock."

Write a poem in which you use a figure of speech such as a symbol or a metaphor to describe your feelings about a person, place, or thing that has played an important role in your life.

Prewriting. Choose a topic that you would enjoy writing about and that has strong associations for you. For example, do you, like the speaker in "Freeway 280," feel strongly about a place that has been greatly altered by time and progress? Or, like the speaker in "Refugee Ship," do you feel deeply influenced by some aspect of your cultural heritage? After you have decided on a topic, brainstorm a list of the feelings, thoughts, and images that you associate with that person, place, or thing. What object might stand as a symbol or a metaphor for how you view your subject? In what way does that object represent or suggest your thoughts and feelings?

Lorna Dee Cervantes 561

Writing and Revising. As you write and revise your poem, keep in mind that figurative language can suggest different things to different people. Choose your words and descriptive details carefully to make clear to your reader the meaning you intend. For example, in developing the metaphor of a refugee ship, Cervantes uses the word *orphaned* to indicate specifically how she is like someone stranded aboard a refugee ship: just as refugees are, in a sense, orphaned from the life and culture they leave behind, so the speaker is "orphaned" from her Hispanic heritage.

Alberto Ríos

(1952–)

Like many Mexican Americans, Alberto Ríos (ahl-behr'toh ree'ohs) has come to re-embrace the Hispanic heritage that he had learned as a child to reject. Although his first language was Spanish, Ríos was told by his teachers to speak only English in elementary school. Taught that Spanish was "bad," he consequently grew ashamed not only of his native language but also of his own Spanish-speaking relatives and the culture they represented. In high school and college, he had to "re-learn" the language that had once been so familiar—a process that has fostered a fresh sense of the worth and dignity of his cultural roots.

Much of Ríos's poetry reflects this rediscovery of his Hispanic heritage and of memories and emotions that stem from his childhood. A talented and versatile writer, Ríos uses simple yet resonant images that—as one critic has noted—are capable of transforming and illuminating even the most ordinary of objects and events. Although he writes in English, his poems often echo the rhythms and syntax of Spanish.

Ríos's first book of poems, *Whispering to Fool the Wind*, won the Academy of American Poets Walt Whitman Award in 1981. One of the poems on the following pages is taken from his first collection; the other two appear in *Five Indiscretions*, his most recent book of poetry.

(For additional biographical information about Alberto Ríos, see page 338.)

On January 5, 1984, El Santo[1] the Wrestler Died, Possibly

Many entertainers and other media figures gain a kind of immortality, remaining etched on the memory of their public even after their deaths. The legendary "el santo" was a familiar figure to almost anyone growing up in Mexico during the last forty years. The wrestler was known for the silver mask that he reportedly wore "even when he slept." As you read, consider why the speaker says that el santo only "possibly" died. What makes el santo a powerful, imposing figure even in death?

The thing was, he could never be trusted.
He wore the silver mask even when he slept.
At his funeral as reported by all the Mexican news services
The pall bearers also put on their faces
Sequined masks to honor him, or so it was said.   5
The men in truth wore masks as much to hide from him
That he would not see who was putting him into the ground
And so get angry, get up, and come back after them
That way for which he was famous.
His partner el atómico pretended to think   10
There was no funeral at all.
He would have had to help el santo be angry
Come like the Samson running against the pillars
These men were, holding up the box
In which el santo was trapped;   15
Would have had to angle his head down, come at them
Mount them three men to a shoulder
As he ran through the middle, ducking under the casket

---

1. **El Santo** (ehl sahn'toh): the saint.

Bowling them down like all the other times
Giving el santo just a moment to breathe, get strong.   20
He will be missed
But one must say this in a whisper, and quickly.
One knows of the dead, of their polite habit of listening
Too much, believing what they hear, and then of their caring.
One knows of the dead, how it all builds up   25
So that finally something must be said.
One knows of the year in which the town of Guaymas[2]
Had its first demonstration of a tape recorder.
It confirmed only what was already known:
That people speak. And that the voice of the wind   30
Captured finally, played back slowly
Given its moment to say something of lasting importance
Made only a complaint.
If el santo were to hear of his being missed
He might get hold of the wind, this voice of the dead,   35
And say too much, the way the best wrestlers do
With all the yelling.
So one will always be responsible enough only to whisper
The best things about el santo
Out of concern for the crops and the sapling trees.   40
This much was decided at the funeral.

The decision to whisper was not too much.
One had to be suspicious of this man with a mask
Even as he reached out to shake your hand,
That you might be flung and bent around   45
Knocked on the head and forced to say
How glad you are to meet him, and his uncle;
How suspicious that hand, which he always raised
More slowly than a weightlifter's last possible push
As if he too were suspicious of you   50
That you might at the last second
Be the Blue Demon after all—*el demonio azul:*[3] *¡ahá!*
    he recognizes you, *¡but too late!* that you might
In this last moment avoid his hand raised to shake
Hook the crook of your arm into his   55

---

2. **Guaymas** (gwai'mahs): town in northwestern Mexico.
3. *el demonio azul* (ehl deh-moh'nyoh ah-sool').

And flip him with a slam to a cement canvas.
No, he could not be trusted
And he could not trust you.
In his last years very far from 1942
The year he gave his first bruise to another man   60
One received as a greeting no hand from him any longer.
A raised eyebrow, perhaps, *good morning to you,*
Just visible through the mask on his morning walk.
This was his greeting, one man to another, now.
But even then he could not be trusted   65
Had not slipped with age even an inch:
As he moved the hairy arm of his brow up and down
Like a villain taking possession of the widow's house,
If one quickly did not get out of his way—
Well, then, he kept it moving up and down, had gotten   70
  you
Had made you imagine his eyebrow
Making the sound of a referee's hand
Slam beating the canvas ten times
Telling you that you have lost.

_____

Nani[1]

In this poem, the speaker's ties to a beloved figure from his childhood seem to run deeper than language or speech, revealing themselves in simple gestures of devotion. Perhaps you have had a person like Nani in your own life— someone you feel close to despite barriers of language, culture, and age. As you read, consider how Nani bridges the gap between the speaker and his Hispanic heritage. In what way does she remind him of what he "could have been, was"?

Sitting at her table, she serves
the sopa de arroz[2] to me
instinctively, and I watch her,
the absolute *mamá*, and eat words
I might have had to say more   5
out of embarrassment. To speak,
now-foreign words I used to speak,
too, dribble down her mouth as she serves
me albóndigas.[3] No more
than a third are easy to me.   10
By the stove she does something with words
and looks at me only with her
back. I am full. I tell her
I taste the mint, and watch her speak
smiles at the stove. All my words   15
make her smile. Nani never serves
herself, she only watches me
with her skin, her hair. I ask for more.

I watch the *mamá* warming more
tortillas[4] for me. I watch her   20
fingers in the flame for me.

---

1. Nani (nah'nee): term of endearment for a grandmotherly figure.
2. sopa de arroz (soh'pah deh ahr-rohs'): cooked rice that is later steamed.
3. albóndigas (ahl-bohn'dee-gahs): spicy meatballs.
4. tortillas (tohr-tee'yahs): flat, unleavened bread made of cornmeal.

Near her mouth, I see a wrinkle speak
of a man whose body serves
the ants like she serves me, then more words
about this and that, flowing more   25
easily from these other mouths. Each serves
as a tremendous string around her,
holding her together. They speak
Nani was this and that to me
and I wonder just how much of me   30
will die with her, what were the words
I could have been, was. Her insides speak
through a hundred wrinkles, now, more
than she can bear, steel around her,
shouting, then, What is this thing she serves?   35

She asks me if I want more.
I own no words to stop her.
Even before I speak, she serves.

The Lesson of Walls

*In this poem, a boy named Florencio builds an "invisible"
wall that shields him from the eyes of others, allowing him
to make "ugly faces" without being seen. As you read "The
Lesson of Walls," you may wonder if Florencio's wall—
which is "Too beautiful to be described"—is an actual wall
or an imaginary one. What do you think you would learn
from living behind an "invisible" wall like Florencio's?*

Florencio built a wall and told no one why.
He was stubborn this way about things.
Too beautiful to be described by the ill-educated
tax assessor in this small but honorable town,
it was entered in no book and so did not exist   5

in that way that other walls are known.
Florencio stood behind his invisible wall
and so quite reasonably was invisible himself
and could do for the first time whatever he chose.
People came from the big cities on Sunday noons   10
to see this thing that did not by its nature exist
and Florencio, Florencio as he had always wanted
since the early days of his troublesome schooling,
made his five ugly faces at the faces of the people,
inverting his eyelids and pushing to the side his nose   15
so as to look like the devil that children imagine,
and he made sounds with his mouth to his pleasure.
But through the years finally he grew
bored of his invisible fame, and his mouth, or entirely
his face, became tired, so that it rested,   20
let its weight fall, and it rolled over onto itself
in its leisure making Florencio wrinkled and heavy.
One morning he took a workman's hammer to his wall.
People saw him again, and he found himself
drawing up his face, as one might pull up   25
a stomach in front of a favorite aunt.
He was young again, and unhappy, and happy.
This business of the invisible,
of a thing too beautiful for the weak
recreations of words and of penmanship,   30
had taught Florencio who was a young fine horse of a boy
again, why a man builds a common wall
ugly, two bricks uneven, why he lets the paint chip.

For Study and Discussion

On January 5, 1984, El Santo the Wrestler Died, Possibly

1. The word "possibly" adds a tentative note to the poem's title.
a. What images in the poem reinforce this tentativeness about el santo's death? b. Why are people "suspicious" of el santo even

though he is "dead"? Cite specific details from the poem in giving your answers.

2. In the last stanza, el santo is compared to "a villain taking possession of the widow's house." **a.** What does this image suggest about el santo? **b.** In light of the meaning of el santo's name (see footnote, page 564), what is ironic about this description?

3. Do you have heroes from real life or fantasy who seem all-powerful to you—as if even death could not defeat them? In what way are such figures kept alive in the minds of their admirers?

Nani

4. The speaker says that Nani's wrinkles "speak" to him. What do her wrinkles say to him about her life?

5. To speak to Nani, the speaker must use "now-foreign" Spanish words that no longer come easily to him. In what sense does Nani seem to represent the speaker's Hispanic heritage?

6. Food and the serving of food are an important part of the speaker's relationship with Nani. In what way does food provide a common bond between them?

The Lesson of Walls

7. Two different walls are described and contrasted in this poem: Florencio's "beautiful," "invisible" wall and a "common," "ugly" wall. What might these two walls symbolically represent in the poem?

8. The speaker tells us that Florencio "built a wall" but that the wall "did not exist" in the way that ordinary walls exist. **a.** Do you think he "built" an actual wall or an imaginary one? Explain. **b.** Why do you think he built his wall?

9. Florencio eventually grows tired of his wall and tears it down. **a.** What is "the lesson of walls" that he has learned? **b.** When he demolishes his wall, why is he both "unhappy, and happy"?

Literary Elements

Characterization

Characterization is the means by which a writer creates and reveals a character's personality. Like prose writers, poets can develop a character in any of several ways: through the character's actions, speech, or thoughts; through a physical description or a direct statement about the character; and through other characters' thoughts, feelings, or statements about the character. For example, in the poem "Nani," Alberto Ríos characterizes Nani through action (her cooking and serving of food) and physical description (her wrinkles) as well as through the speaker's observations and reflections about Nani and her importance in his life.

In what ways does Ríos characterize el santo in "On January 5, 1984, El Santo the Wrestler Died, Possibly"? Cite details from the poem to support your answer.

Writing About Literature

Analyzing the Importance of Language in Alberto Ríos's Poetry

In each of the three poems by Alberto Ríos, language and speech are of central importance to the poet's development of theme. For example, in "The Lesson of Walls," Florencio's wall is said to have been "Too beautiful to be described" and that consequently it "did not exist." According to the speaker, Florencio's wall was "invisible" because it could not be defined in words—it could not be seen because it could not be spoken about. In this poem, then, language has the power to make things real or unreal in the eye of the beholder. In an essay of three or four paragraphs, discuss the importance of language and speech in another or in several other of Ríos's poems.

Prewriting. As you reread the poems, look for specific references to language and speech. What do the characters in the poems say to and about each other, and what importance is placed on their words? In what ways do the characters "speak"—that is, communicate—without using words? Does the poet place greater emphasis on the characters' words or on unspoken communication between them? How does Ríos use speech as a metaphor for other kinds of communication? You have several options in choosing the focus of your essay. You may want to

    1. give a detailed analysis of a single poem,

    2. compare two or all of the poems, or

    3. contrast two or all of the poems.

Be sure to focus clearly on your chosen topic, avoiding analysis of other elements in the poem(s) unless they relate directly to your discussion.

Writing and Revising. In drawing comparisons or contrasts between two poems or between elements within a single poem, be sure to use parallel structure in your sentences. For example, consider the following sentence and its rewording:

    Not Parallel: In "Nani," words are less important than to express feelings without words. (noun *words* paired with infinitive phrase *to express feelings without words*)

    Parallel: In "Nani," spoken words are less important than unspoken feelings. (adjective modifying a noun paired with adjective modifying a noun)

Creative Writing

Writing a Narrative

People can hide or conceal themselves from others in many different ways. For example, Florencio in "The Lesson of Walls" stands behind an invisible wall that shields him from the eyes of onlookers and allows him to make "ugly faces," and the legendary wrestler el santo wore a silver mask that hid his face. Perhaps you too sometimes dream of becoming "invisible." Write a short narrative describing how you would make yourself invisible and why you would wish to do so.

Prewriting. Keep in mind that means of concealment need not be as drastic or obvious as Florencio's wall or el santo's mask. Decide if you want your narrative to be as fantastical as "The Lesson of Walls"—describing, for instance, a magical potion that renders you invisible—or if you want to portray yourself as someone who, like a detective, can move about silently without being observed.

Consider the advantages and disadvantages of being "invisible." Would you be able to play practical jokes, solve crimes, or, like Florencio, make funny faces at people? Would you eventually grow bored with being unnoticed? How would you go about becoming visible again?

Writing and Revising. As you write your first draft, concentrate on getting your thoughts down on paper. Then, after you have a rough draft, reread and revise what you have written, paying careful attention to spelling and punctuation. Look up the spelling of any words that you are uncertain about, and, if necessary, review rules of punctuation to be sure you have used commas, semicolons, and other marks correctly.

Leonard Adame

(1949–)

The movingly tender poems of Leonard Adame (ah-thah-meh') stand among the best personal poetry of the Contemporary Period. While Adame has not produced a large number of works, those that he has published reflect the intensity of feeling that he brings to his craft.

Adame was born and raised in California's San Joaquin Valley, the center of César Chávez's union activities among farm workers in the late 1960s. Although he lived in the midst of heated labor protests against growers and the political activism of Luis Valdez's theater group El Teatro Campesino, Adame seemed to pass through his high-school years relatively untouched by the mounting fervor of the Chicano movement. His most vivid memories of those years are of the countless hours he spent amongst piles of dirty dishes in his father's restaurant and of the summers that he stayed on his uncle's farm.

Adame's poetry has been published in several anthologies and collections as well as in the *American Poetry Review,* a prestigious literary magazine. His 1979 chapbook, *Cantos pa' la memoria* [Songs for memory], contains his most memorable poems devoted to members of his family. They reflect a healthy view of himself in relationship to his family and friends, summarized in the poet's own words: "My brother and two uncles have muscular dystrophy and are in wheelchairs. When I feel pompous and depressed, I remember them and kick myself. . . ."

His poem "In December's Air," which appears on the following page, exhibits Adame's sensitivity at capturing the emotional complexity of a moving scene from everyday life.

In December's Air

Freezing in their thin, torn clothes, the children in this poem tug at the speaker's heart as he watches them huddle together on the doorstep of Beacon Gas and Grocery. As you read, you, like the speaker, will learn more about the children and about why they wait so patiently in the cold. When you finish the poem, see if you think that the children are as pitiable as they first appear.

---

eleven-thirty:
a boy, a little girl,
the dog quiet on their laps,
waiting for Nick the attendant
near the doorstep   5
of Beacon Gas and Grocery

gathered like kids
in old photographs,
her nostrils frost-cracked,
their breath like steam   10
in december's air

i look and want
to be sorry
for the holes
in their t-shirts and shoes—   15
kneeling, i ask
their names,
where they live,
why they sit here;
i say nothing   20
of the cold
soaking through
their clothes like water . . .

Trinidad, Guadalupe,
Charley their dog,   25
waiting

to buy candy
with the fifty cents from Grandma . . .
    they point
to their house   30
three vacant lots
away: the one
with the light,
they say,
can you see   35
it?

For Study and Discussion

1. The speaker says the children are "gathered like kids / in old photographs." Why do they remind him of an old photograph? What image of the children does this comparison create?

2a. When he sees the children, why does the speaker "want / to be sorry" for them? **b.** By the end of the poem, do you feel that the children are to be pitied? Why or why not?

3. Names of people, places, and things in literary works often have symbolic meanings that reinforce the theme of the work. **a.** What later image in the poem echoes the name "Beacon" in line 6? **b.** What might this name symbolically represent in the poem?

Literary Elements

Mood

The literary term **mood** has a meaning similar to the meaning of *mood* in everyday life. Just as a person's "mood" affects his or her thoughts, actions, and perceptions, the mood, or prevailing feeling, in a literary work helps to determine the reader's attitude and expectations. The writer's descriptions of setting often play an important part in establishing mood. For example, in Gary Soto's poem "Oranges," which appears on page 540, the figures of the speaker and his first love are etched against a gray winter setting that contrasts with the speaker's emotions and with the warmth of the candy store, creating a mood of poignancy and nostalgia.

What is the mood of Leonard Adame's poem "In December's Air"? How does the setting help to create this mood? In what way does the poem's mood help to determine your feelings toward the brother and sister?

Pat Mora
(1942–)

Pat Mora (moh'rah) has dedicated
much of her professional life to the
preservation of her culture. Believing
that people's sense of identity is firmly
rooted in their culture, she has worked
to raise awareness among Mexican Americans of the rich history and
traditions that make up their heritage. Her artistic goals are similar: to
write about the Mexican American experience not only as a contemporary phenomenon but also as the culmination of centuries-old values,
languages, and customs.

Born and raised in El Paso, Texas, Mora has had a unique opportunity to observe firsthand the changes that occur in Mexican culture as
a result of daily contact with Anglo society. She was educated in local
schools and later received her undergraduate and graduate degrees in
English and speech from the University of Texas at El Paso (UTEP).

Mora has been the recipient of several prestigious awards and grants,
including two Southwest Book Awards for collections of her poetry—
Chants (1984) and *Borders* (1986). In 1987, the Kellogg Foundation
chose her as a National Fellow to encourage her work in cultural
preservation. She has taken an active role within the El Paso and UTEP
communities, notably as Director of the University Museum and as
Assistant to the President at UTEP—two positions she still holds today.

Mora's poetry often springs from her geographical surroundings: the
high desert that extends from Mexico in the south to the Rocky Mountains in the north, creating a common bond between two countries and
two diverse cultures. In viewing Mexican and American experience,
she chooses to emphasize the harmony rather than the disharmony
between the two countries and between Hispanic and Anglo cultures
within the United States. While she does not avoid addressing negative

aspects of life along the border, she also affirms the creative and regenerative forces that the desert's natural grandeur brings to its inhabitants.

Mora currently lives in El Paso, Texas, where she is working on three new books: *Tomas and the Library Lady,* a children's book; *Angles,* a collection of personal essays; and *Journeys,* a volume of poetry.

Mi Madre[1]

*Do you, like the speaker of this poem, feel drawn to a
particular kind of terrain—a place that offers you comfort
and seems to reflect your inner thoughts? Consider why
the speaker characterizes the desert as a madre, or mother.*

I say feed me.
She serves red prickly pear on a spiked cactus.
I say tease me.
She sprinkles raindrops in my face on a sunny day.
I say frighten me.   5
She shouts thunder, flashes lightning.
I say comfort me.
She invites me to lay on her firm body.
I say heal me.
She gives me *manzanilla, orégano, dormilón*[2]   10
I say caress me.
She strokes my skin with her warm breath.
I say make me beautiful.
She offers turquoise for my fingers, a pink blossom for
   my hair.
I say sing to me.   15
She chants lonely women's songs of femaleness.
I say teach me.
She endures: glaring heat
              numbing cold
              frightening dryness.   20
She: the desert
She: strong mother.

---

1. **Mi Madre** (mee mah'threh): my mother.
2. *manzanilla, orégano, dormilón* (mahn-sah-nee'yah, oh-reh'gah-noh,
   dohr-mee-lohn'): three spices commonly used as herbal medicines.

580 *Pat Mora*

Bailando[1]

Waltzing gaily on her ninetieth birthday, the speaker's aunt seems to have lost little of the vitality and spirit of her youth. Perhaps you, too, have a beloved older relative who serves as an inspiration to you. Consider your feelings about that person as you read Mora's poem. How does the speaker express the love and admiration that she feels for her aunt?

I will remember you dancing,
spinning round and round
a young girl in Mexico,
your long, black hair free in the wind,
spinning round and round   5
a young woman at village dances
your long, blue dress swaying
to the beat of *La Varsoviana*,[2]
smiling into the eyes of your partners,
years later smiling into my eyes   10
when I'd reach up to dance with you,
my dear aunt, who years later
danced with my children,
you, white-haired but still young
waltzing on your ninetieth birthday,   15
more beautiful than the orchid
pinned on your shoulder,
tottering now when you walk
but saying to me, "Estoy [3]*bailando*,"
and laughing.   20

---

1. **Bailando** (bai-lahn'doh): dancing.
2. *La Varsoviana* (lah bahr-soh-byah'nah): a very popular adaptation of a Polish polka.
3. *Estoy* (ehs-toy'): I am.

Graduation Morning

During her many years as housekeeper to his family, the woman in this poem became like a mother to the boy whose graduation she now attends. Having cared for him throughout his childhood, she feels intense emotions witnessing the event that marks his becoming an adult. As you read, notice the images and details that express the strong mutual affection between the woman and the boy.

---

for Anthony

She called him *Lucero*,[1] morning star,
snared him with sweet coffee, pennies,
Mexican milk candy, brown bony hugs.

Through the years she'd cross the Rio
Grande to clean his mother's home. "*Lucero,*   5
mi[2] *lucero,*" she'd cry, when she'd see him
running toward her in the morning,
when she pulled stubborn cactus thorns
from his small hands, when she found him
hiding in the creosote.   10

Through she's small and thin,
black sweater, black scarf,
the boy in the white graduation robe
easily finds her at the back of the cathedral,
finds her amid the swirl of sparkling clothes,   15
finds her eyes.

Tears slide down her wrinkled cheeks.
Her eyes, *luceros,* stroke his face.

---

1. *Lucero* (loo-seh'roh).
2. *mi* (mee): my.

For Study and Discussion

Mi Madre

1. **Personification** is a figure of speech in which something non-human is given human qualities. What human qualities does Mora ascribe to the desert in this poem, and what does this personification indicate about the speaker's relationship to the desert?

2. **Imagery** consists of words or phrases that appeal to the senses to create pictures, or images, in the reader's mind. To what senses do the images in this poem appeal? Give examples.

Bailando

3. The speaker's aunt seems to have changed little over the years. **a.** How is she still like the "young girl" she once was? **b.** How does the speaker indicate the passing of time and the aunt's aging?

4. It may be hard for you to imagine what your parents or older relatives were like when they were your age. From a photograph or from descriptions, compose a character sketch of a parent or relative that focuses on a happy moment in his or her youth—perhaps a festive occasion like one of the village dances that the speaker's aunt attended. How is that time in his or her youth like or unlike an experience you have had?

Graduation Morning

5. Although the poet does not directly state the boy's affection for the housekeeper, she indicates their mutual bond in indirect ways. In stanza 3, how does the poet reveal the boy's feelings for the elderly woman?

6. In lines 5 and 6 the woman calls the boy *Lucero,* which means "morning star." **a.** To what does the word *luceros* refer in the last line? **b.** What is the effect of repeating this word at the end of the poem?

Pat Mora 583

7. As the woman watches the boy's graduation, "Tears slide down her wrinkled cheeks." Why is the woman crying? What mixed emotions might she be feeling?

Literary Elements

Stanza Form

A **stanza** is a group of related lines that forms a division of a poem or song. The length and number of lines within a stanza are often closely related to a poem's content, emphasizing thematic connections between images and indicating shifts in thought. For example, in Pat Mora's poem "Mi Madre," each of the first eight stanzas consists of two lines that state a request and then give a response to that request: "I say feed me. / She serves red prickly pear on a spiked cactus." This repeated pattern unifies the poem structurally and also indicates divisions between thoughts. How is the ninth stanza different from the first eight? What does it have in common with them? What reasons might the poet have had for breaking from the two-line pattern? How does the last stanza differ from the first eight, even though it also consists of two lines? How does the last stanza create closure in the poem?

Examine the stanza form in Mora's "Bailando." How does the stanza structure relate to the content and theme of the poem? What thought or images does this stanza form unify or separate?

Writing About Literature

Analyzing Thematic Similarities in Two Poems

Although a work of poetry or prose is separate and complete in itself, writers often explore different facets of a particular theme throughout several works. For example, the four poems by Sandra Cisneros that appear on pages 546–551 all draw on the poet's childhood memories, focusing on various aspects of childhood experience and the emotions that accompany them. In an essay of two or three paragraphs, discuss at least two common elements that thematically link Pat Mora's "Bailando" and "Graduation Morning."

Prewriting. As you reread the poems, consider the following questions. What or who is the subject of each poem? In what light does the poet seem to view her subject matter? What kind of imagery does she use to describe her characters? What feeling, or **mood,** do these images create in each poem? Write the answers to these questions on a sheet of paper, using a separate column for each poem. Then compare your lists, looking for similarities that connect the two works. In organizing your essay, you may choose either to give a point-by-point comparison of the two poems, devoting each paragraph of your essay to a discussion of a particular element that the poems have in common, or to discuss each poem separately before comparing them in a concluding paragraph.

Writing and Revising. As you cite specific details from the poems, give the line numbers in parentheses after each quotation, placing marks of punctuation outside the closing parentheses. When revising your essay, check to make sure that you have given the correct line number(s) for each quotation.

Creative Writing

Using Personification in a Poem

Personification is a kind of figurative language that attributes human qualities to something nonhuman, such as an animal, object, place, or idea. Like metaphors and similes—other forms of figurative comparison—personification can add vividness and depth of meaning to a writer's descriptions. For example, in the poem "Mi Madre," Pat Mora uses personification to describe the desert. In giving human qualities to the desert, she not only creates striking images but also conveys the speaker's feeling of kinship with the harsh yet nurturing landscape.

Write a poem of your own, at least eight lines long, in which you use personification to describe something.

Prewriting. In deciding on a subject for your poem, choose something with which you are familiar. Think about the environment around you—the places, objects, weather, and animals that you regularly encounter or the kinds of ideas and emotions that carry strong associations for you. After you have chosen a subject, list the qualities it seems to possess, allowing yourself to freely associate ideas and putting down on paper whatever comes to your mind about the topic. You can then read through your list and decide which elements you would like to incorporate into your poem. If you could characterize your subject in human terms, what kind of person would it be? What would it think and feel? How would it act?

Writing and Revising. Take care to choose words and phrases that precisely express the human characteristics you mean to represent. For example, if you were writing about a large, very old oak tree, you might use words such as *stately, solemn,* and *dignified* rather than more general descriptive terms such as *big* and *solid.*

Ray González
(1952–)

As a Mexican American growing up in
El Paso, Texas, Ray González (gohn-
sah'lehs) was greatly influenced by the
desert landscape and rich yet conflict-
ridden history of the southwestern
United States.The physical and cultural setting of his early years deeply
imprinted itself on his spirit and later formed the backdrop for many of
his poems.

González's interest in writing began when he was a teen-ager. He
worked on his high school's newspaper and, after graduating, entered
the University of Texas at El Paso, fully intending to pursue a career in
journalism. However, upon taking his first creative writing class in
1970, he found himself swept up in the beauty and possibilities of
poetry and soon committed himself wholeheartedly to becoming a poet.

After receiving a degree in creative writing in 1975, González struggled for several years to establish himself as a poet. During this time he
supported himself through various jobs, working as a substitute teacher,
as a counselor and instructor in a detention center, and as editor of a
small newspaper. When he moved to Denver, Colorado, in the late
1970s, opportunities began to open up for him. He was offered a
position with the *Bloomsbury Review,* a literary magazine published in
Denver, where he still serves as Poetry Editor. He is also the guiding
force at Mesilla Press—a small literary press that he himself founded to
publish poetry pamphlets and anthologies.

Beyond his professional influence as an editor, González dedicates
much time and energy to promoting poetry throughout the Southwest
and the rest of the country. He is particularly committed to helping and
encouraging minority and younger writers. With this goal in mind, he
has conducted numerous writing workshops in public schools and is

actively working to start a statewide poetry festival in Colorado. In addition to offering presentations on poetry, publishing, and works by minority writers, González gives readings of his own poetry to audiences across the country. In 1988, he received a Governor's Award for Excellence in the Arts in recognition of his artistic talent and his efforts to raise public awareness of poetry as an art form.

The poem that appears on the following page is taken from González's award-winning second book of poetry, *Twilights and Chants.*

Booming Ground

*The title of this poem, "Booming Ground," refers to a part
of the ocean where many ships have lost their anchors.
Such places are familiar to the poet's friend Paul Hunter,
an experienced sailor in the Pacific Northwest. Through
Hunter, Ray González learns valuable lessons that only
sailors and the sea can teach. Look for these lessons as you
read. What applications do you think they might have for
setting a course not only at sea but in life as well?*

---

for Paul Hunter

We sit in your boat and
you tell us how you lost your
anchor in the booming ground
when you sailed to Alaska,
how you found out the man who sails is   5
the man who stays ahead of the sea,
on top of the gale that blows him
into deep fathoms of darkness.

We sit on the pier and watch
the ducks dive for food,   10
disappear for minutes,
then suddenly pop up for air.
If there is this kind of
motion in the heart,
the boat rocks with   15
its exhausted rhythm.

Without time to take us sailing,
I wonder why you brought us here,
but sitting in your small boat,
I come closer to water without fear.   20
I picture you sailing, alone,
into the sound, absorbed in
grey mist that hides you from yourself

because, as the gulls interrupt and
larger boats leave the docks,   25
I know you are telling us
the sailor who knows where
he is bound expects
too much from the sea.

For Study and Discussion

1. In the first stanza, the speaker refers to a lesson that his friend
had learned while sailing: that "the man who sails is / the man
who stays ahead of the sea." **a.** How does someone in a sailboat
stay "ahead of the sea"? **b.** What larger meaning beyond sailing
could staying "ahead of the sea" have?

2. The poem closes with a lesson the speaker learns from his
friend: that "the sailor who knows where / he is bound expects /
too much from the sea." **a.** How does this lesson relate to the
lesson in lines 5 and 6? **b.** What broader implications does this
lesson have for life in general?

3. The speaker likens the rocking of the boat to a "kind of / motion
in the heart." How does this description compare with your own
experiences of being on a boat? Have you ever had a similar
experience in which natural surroundings suggested a "kind of /
motion in the heart"?

Creative Writing

Writing a Poem About an Insight
Gained Through Experience

Just as Ray González was introduced by his friend Paul Hunter
to the experience he describes in "Booming Ground," you have
probably had someone present you with an opportunity to gain

a valuable insight by sharing in that person's favorite pastime. Write a poem of not more than twenty lines in which you relate such an experience and reveal what you learned from it.

Prewriting. Begin by thinking back over experiences you have had in which a friend or acquaintance has introduced you to an activity that was new to you. As you recall your memories, two or three such experiences will likely stand out as particularly noteworthy. Identify what made these experiences significant. Did your friend point out something in particular? Was some feature of the environment especially striking? Did some action or event surprise you? Did you have any unique sensations? As you think about your experiences, jot down descriptive words and phrases that come to mind. Review your lists and determine which experience you think you can best develop into a poem.

Writing and Revising. As you write and revise your poem, pay close attention to the sounds as well as to the meanings of the words you use. Reading your poem aloud while you make revisions will help you achieve the rhythmic effect that you want. Keep in mind that you can use rhythm to help emphasize elements of the poem and to establish a particular tone and mood.

Bernice Zamora

(1938–)

Ever since she can remember, Bernice Zamora (sah-moh'rah) has felt
compelled to write. As an adolescent, she wrote letters and kept a
dream diary as well as a journal. In her freshman year in college, she
wrote humorous essays that one of her professors circulated around the
English department so that the other teachers could enjoy them. Several
years later while in graduate school, Zamora wrote her first short story
that, when submitted by a friend to a creative writing symposium, won
second prize and later was published. At the age of thirty, Zamora
found her niche when she began writing poetry.

Zamora was born in Aguilar, a small village in southern Colorado.
Her ancestors were among the first Spanish settlers who centuries ago
were granted land by the Spanish Crown. Unfortunately, their farmland
was rocky and poor, and the men in the family turned to working in the
coal mines.

While she was still young, Zamora's family moved north to Denver
and then back south to Pueblo, where they finally settled. Zamora was
educated in local parochial and public schools and received her
undergraduate and graduate degrees from universities in Colorado. She
later earned a doctorate in English from Stanford University. Currently,
she teaches English at Santa Clara University in California.

Zamora's poetry has appeared in a number of literary magazines and
anthologies, and a collection of her work, *Restless Serpents,* was
published in 1976. Critics have described her poems as being both very
contemporary and very medieval, indicating the wide range of her
subject matter and her style. The topics that she addresses in her works
vary from ancient religious practices to social and political causes such
as the Chicano movement and, particularly, feminism. While her
personal beliefs are strong, her poetic voice is never overbearing or
heavy-handed; instead, she prefers to couch her views within a broad
philosophical context.

The two poems on the following pages exhibit the precise language and vibrant images characteristic of Zamora's works. The first poem, " 'The Extraordinary Patience of Things,' " takes its title and general theme from a poem by the American writer Robinson Jeffers. Although Zamora shares Jeffers' appreciation for the beauty and value of nature, she expresses in the poem her unique personal view of human beings' relationship to their environment. Like " 'The Extraordinary Patience of Things,' " the second poem, "Pueblo Winter," also focuses on the natural world. In both poems, Zamora's keen attention to detail calls forth broader philosophical insights about universal human concerns.

"The Extraordinary Patience of Things"

from "Carmel Point"

At some time in your life, you have probably seen a place like the one Bernice Zamora describes—a natural, once-peaceful setting that has been "walled in" by suburban development. How did you feel to see the landscape altered by human progress? Did you, like the poet, feel that the human presence was in some way a "spoiler" of the natural world? As you read Zamora's poem, keep in mind that it is based on Robinson Jeffers' "Carmel Point," which is given on page 596. Consider how " 'The Extraordinary Patience of Things' " is a response to Jeffers' poem. What words and images from "Carmel Point" does Zamora echo? How does her concluding statement differ from Jeffers'?

Pasturing horses blink as the spoiler
steals in next to milch cows. Poppy
and lupine fields, walked in by the
intruder, stoop with the cliffs
crumbling beneath them.   5

How fortunate that in time all our works
will dissolve, like us, and return to dust
or less than that.

—As for us:
We center our minds on our minds: 10
We humanize the unhuman and become confident.
As the very grain of the granite housing fossils.

Pueblo¹ Winter

*Just as the robins in this poem "watch each other watch /
each other," the poet also "lays witness" to the quiet yet
visually intricate natural scene she describes. As you read,
try to visualize the poem's setting. What does the title
"Pueblo Winter" suggest about the landscape?*

Sparrows in Pueblo perch on empty
elm branches cocking their heads
at each other or at each shadow
under the warming winter sun.

They watch each other watch   5
each other and seem, at times,
more passive than their shadows
under the warming winter sun

until a robin flights by to break
their bobbing trance. Another robin   10
joins the first. Both alight
on a chokeberry bush

scattering the flapping
sparrows to the pole lines above.
From the lines they watch   15
the robins on the cherry bush.

One robin pecks at a drying cherry
while the silent other lays witness
to the act; so, too, the sparrows
under the warming sun.   20

---

1. **Pueblo** (pweh´bloh): a city in southern Colorado.

For Study and Discussion

"The Extraordinary Patience of Things"

1. Zamora's poem takes its title from the first line of Robinson Jeffers' "Carmel Point," which is given below. Identify four specific images that appear in both poems. In what other way or ways are the two poems alike?

Carmel Point

The extraordinary patience of things!
This beautiful place defaced with a crop
    of suburban houses—
How beautiful when we first beheld it,
Unbroken field of poppy and lupin walled with clean cliffs;
No intrusion but two or three horses pasturing,
Or a few milch cows rubbing their flanks on the outcrop
    rock-heads—
Now the spoiler has come: does it care?
Not faintly. It has all time. It knows the people are a tide
That swells and in time will ebb, and all
Their works dissolve. Meanwhile the image of
    the pristine beauty
Lives in the very grain of the granite,
Safe as the endless ocean that climbs our cliff.—As for us:
We must uncenter our minds from ourselves;
We must unhumanize our views a little, and become
    confident
As the rock and ocean that we were made from.

2. In stanza two, Zamora says, "How fortunate that in time all our works / will dissolve." What does she mean by this?

3. The last stanza of Zamora's poem is a response to lines 12–15 of "Carmel Point." What statement does Zamora make about human nature? How does it compare with Jeffers' conclusion?

Pueblo Winter

4. The sparrows seem as though in a "trance" until "a robin flights by" and causes them to scatter. How does their stillness seem to reflect the winter setting of the poem?

5. A **refrain** is a word, phrase, or line that is repeated at regular intervals in a poem, usually at the end of a stanza. What refrain does Zamora use in "Pueblo Winter"? What is the effect of this repetition?

6. Have you ever stopped to watch a scene in the natural world such as the one Zamora describes? What caught your attention about the scene? What thoughts did you have as you watched it? Did your observations spark any larger insights about the world around you?

Vocabulary

Analyzing the Use of Specific Descriptive Names in a Poem

Specific names and terms can lend vividness and clarity to a writer's descriptions. For example, in " 'The Extraordinary Patience of Things,' " Bernice Zamora names specific animals and plants: "pasturing horses," "milch cows," and "poppy and lupine fields." These names create clearer, more precise visual images than would general references to "animals" and "fields" in the poem.

Giving at least three examples, discuss Zamora's use of descriptive names in "Pueblo Winter." In your discussion, respond to the following questions:

1. What visual images do these names create?
2. How do they help to describe setting?
3. How would the poem be different if the poet used general rather than specific terms?

Bernice Zamora 597

Creative Writing

Writing a Poem About an Outdoor Scene

Many painters, writers, and other artists train themselves to pay keen attention to even the smallest details of their environment. This practice of careful observation helps them to gather and accurately render perceptions of the world around them. For example, in "Pueblo Winter," Bernice Zamora gives a description of birds in a winter landscape. She records details that suggest her attentiveness to her surroundings—details that, together, form an intricate picture of a natural scene.

Spend a few minutes watching an outdoor scene such as a tree in which birds have nested, a field alive with insects, or perhaps a busy city street. While you watch, write down your impressions in as much detail as possible; then use these notes to re-create the scene in a poem of fifteen or more lines.

Prewriting. As you observe a scene, write down not only your sensory impressions—what you see, feel, smell, or hear—but also any thoughts you have about the things you observe. For example, does the rustling of leaves in the wind or the facial expression of a person on the street spark an image from your memory? What other kinds of associations or comparisons come to your mind? After you have taken notes for several minutes, you can look over your list of impressions and decide which contain the most vivid and interesting images and which you would most enjoy writing about in a poem.

Writing and Revising. Always try to use specific names and sensory details to create precise images. For example, rather than referring to "a tree," specify the kind of tree you saw—such as an elm, an oak, or a willow—and use descriptive words that indicate what features of the tree captured your attention.

Leroy Quintana
(1944–)

Like many Mexican American writers, Leroy Quintana (keen-tah'nah) has been strongly influenced by the oral tradition of his culture. Born in Albuquerque, New Mexico, Quintana was raised by his grandparents, who told him many traditional stories that sparked his desire to become a storyteller himself. He grew up living part of the time in the barrio in Albuquerque and part of the time in the rural town of Ratón, three hundred miles away, gaining from this change in environment a broad perspective on Mexican American cultural values and lifestyles.

After attending public schools, he went on to the University of New Mexico. However, his schooling was interrupted when he entered the U.S. Army in 1967. He served in Vietnam from 1967 to 1968 as an infantryman, seeing combat as part of a reconnaissance team with the 101st Airborne Division. Following his discharge, he returned to the University of New Mexico and earned a bachelor's degree in English.

Quintana took a job as a social services caseworker when he finished his master's degree in English and then taught English at New Mexico State University and El Paso Community College. In 1980, he became a writer for the *Albuquerque Tribune,* covering special features and sports. Two years later, he decided to pursue his interest in social work and moved to Silver City, New Mexico, where he earned a master's degree in psychology from Western New Mexico University and became a counselor. His next move was to San Diego, California, and there he went into private practice as a marriage, family, and child counselor.

Although he found his work as a counselor rewarding, Quintana's early drive to become a storyteller never really left him; and after several years of keeping his pen silent, he again began writing. Currently, he is a professor of English at Mesa College in San Diego and has recently completed an anthology of new poems about his boyhood. Quintana has also begun to expand beyond poetry and is working on some short fiction, a novel, and a screenplay.

In the selection on the following page, Quintana deals with one of his memories of Vietnam, expressing a sense of the bitter irony and resentment that many veterans of the Vietnam War felt about the way that they were treated, even right up to their "last day in Vietnam."

Last Day in Viet Nam

A week or two before returning to the United States, most combat troops left their units in the field and returned to base camp to process out of Vietnam. During this time they often were assigned to work details such as cleaning barracks and picking up litter. Not surprisingly, many soldiers resented such menial chores after months of grueling, dangerous duty. Yet, they knew that they had little choice but to comply, because they faced one of the fundamental ironies of warfare: that they who wield the swords of battle are in the end always subject to those who wield the pens of bureaucracy.

It was either a sweep and mop-up operation
through the barracks of our last sleep in the Nam

or have our orders cancelled. One quick stroke of the pen
all that was necessary. Forget that freedom bird waiting.

For the pen, vowed the sergeant,
is mightier than the sword.

For Study and Discussion

1. The phrase "sweep and mop-up operation" is a term for a combat action in which troops move through an area where a battle has taken place and eliminate any remaining pockets of enemy resistance. **a.** How is this phrase used ironically in "Last Day in Viet Nam"? **b.** What word or phrase in the poem indicates that "sweep and mop-up operation" is not being used to refer to a military action?

Leroy Quintana 601

2. The last two lines of the poem contain a **paradox,** a statement that reveals a kind of truth although it seems at first to be self-contradictory and untrue. **a.** In what way is the pen "mightier than the sword" in "Last Day in Viet Nam"? **b.** Do you think it is just and proper that "the pen . . . / is mightier than the sword"? Explain.

Vocabulary

Analyzing the Use and Origins of Specialized Vocabulary

A **specialized vocabulary** is the vocabulary used by a particular group of people who share the same occupation or field of interest such as sports or a hobby. In many cases this vocabulary consists of common words that have acquired special meanings, such as *walk,* which commonly means "to move on foot" but in baseball has the special meaning "to advance to first base as a result of not swinging at four pitches out of the strike zone." In some cases a special word is coined, such as *shortstop,* which is a baseball term for the infield position between second base and third base.

In "Last Day in Viet Nam," Leroy Quintana uses words and phrases that belong to the specialized vocabulary of American soldiers, particularly those who served in Vietnam. For example, "sweep and mop-up operation" refers to a specific military tactic. Identify two other terms from this specialized vocabulary that appear in the poem, and give the meaning for each term. In what way(s) does the poet's use of these terms contribute to the poem?

From a book or a film or some other source—perhaps from a Vietnam veteran—find five other terms, along with their definitions, that belong to the specialized vocabulary of soldiers who served in Vietnam. Check in a dictionary to determine which of these terms also have common meanings and which of them were specially coined by those who used them.

Creative Writing

Conducting an Interview

Like the speaker in this poem, nearly every veteran who served in a war zone has a tale to tell about his or her last day or so there. Not all soldiers had such a disagreeable experience as the speaker; some stories are deeply moving, others quite humorous, still others highly exciting. Interview a veteran of the Vietnam War, the Korean War, or World War II about his or her experiences just prior to returning to the United States. Summarize your interview in a short narrative to share in class.

Prewriting. Your first task will be to locate a veteran to interview. If you or your parents do not know one, call a veterans group such as the American Legion or Veterans of Foreign Wars, and ask one of the organization's officers to suggest someone. You may choose to conduct the interview in person or by telephone. In either case, you will need to write to or telephone the person you wish to interview and make an appointment. Be prepared when you first contact the person to state why you wish to interview him or her. When you conduct the interview, be sensitive in your questioning: remember, many veterans had very upsetting experiences at war. Begin the interview with one or two general questions, such as "What do you remember most clearly about your last day or two before returning home?" Then, let your interviewee freely relate his or her experiences. Take notes, being particularly careful to accurately record what he or she says. Review your notes with your interviewee to make sure they are correct and complete.

Writing. As you summarize your notes, focus on what the interviewee told you, and keep your own personal statements to a minimum. Keep in mind that factual accuracy is important but also that humorous and unusual anecdotes will enliven the narrative and make it more interesting to your audience.

Leroy Quintana 603

Rolando
Hinojosa-Smith

(1929–)

In his writing as well as in person, Rolando Hinojosa-Smith (roh-lahn'doh ee-noh-hoh'sah) is eloquent yet plain-spoken, good-humored yet deeply serious. His poems and novels reflect both the breadth of his personal experience and the keen, hard-won insight he brings to his own life and to his observations of human nature.

Although his mother was Anglo, Hinojosa-Smith spoke primarily Spanish until he enlisted in the U.S. Army at the age of seventeen. His immersion in Hispanic culture while growing up (he says he did not speak to any Anglo children until he was eleven or twelve years old) had a profound influence on his sense of personal identity. Hinojosa-Smith still regards himself as a Mexican American with strong ties to his native culture, but like many Mexican American writers he is equally fluent in Spanish and English and feels at home writing in both.

Hinojosa-Smith believes that his role as a writer is to present the "eternal verities" of human nature and experience—to address the lives and concerns not only of Mexican Americans but also of his fellow human beings as a whole. This conviction is clearly evident in his works. For example, his collection of poems titled *Korean Love Songs* describes the horror and waste of war from both a deeply personal and a universal perspective. Although he writes from the point of view of a Mexican American soldier, his experiences speak to all people who have suffered the devastating effects of armed conflict.

The poems on the following pages are from *Korean Love Songs,* which forms part of a series of autobiographical works that includes several novels. As the poems will reveal, the title *Korean Love Songs* hints at the sharp irony that is characteristic of Hinojosa-Smith's writing.

(For additional biographical information about Rolando Hinojosa-Smith, see page 412.)

from
Korean Love Songs

In June 1950, the North Korean People's Army invaded the Republic of South Korea. The United States, along with other members of the United Nations, quickly came to the aid of South Korean forces defending their country. Korean Love Songs is an anthology of poems that focuses on four young Mexican Americans from Texas who served in an artillery battery in the U.S. Eighth Army. As a veteran of the Korean War, Hinojosa-Smith draws on his own experiences to give a realistic account of the brutality and hardships endured by these young soldiers.

The Eighth Army at the Chongchon[1]

In the fall of 1950, the U.S. Eighth Army suffered defeat in a battle near the Chongchon River in North Korea and was forced to retreat in blinding snowstorms and zero-degree weather. During one week of fighting, American casualties numbered eight thousand men dead, wounded, missing in action, or taken prisoner.

Creating history (their very words)
by protecting the world from Communism. I suppose
One needs a pep talk now and then, but what
Gen. Walton H. (Johnny) Walker said
Was something else.   5

Those were darker days, of course,
And the blinding march South
Cannot be believed
Unless you were there. But the point is

---

1. **Chongchon:** a major river in North Korea.

That the Chinese   10
Were stoppable, so Gen. Walker believed.

And he was right; later on he was killed
At one of the fronts, standing up
On a jeep. We understood.

This wasn't Ketch Ridge or Rumbough Hill   15
Or the Frisco-Rock Island RR Junction at Sill,[2]
But then, it wasn't the Alamo either.

And those who survived
Remember what he said:
      "We should not assume that (the)   20
      Chinese Communists are committed in force.
      After all, a lot of Mexicans live in Texas."

And that from Eighth Army Commanding
Himself. It was touching.
And yet, the 219th[3]   25
Creating history by protecting the world from Communism,
Brought up the rear, protected the guns, continued the mission,
And many of us there
Were again reminded who we were
Thousands of miles from home.   30

---

2. **Ketch Ridge . . . at Sill:** These are names of places in Fort Sill,
   Oklahoma, which serves as the headquarters and training base for U.S.
   Army artillery. The four artillerymen in *Korean Love Songs* trained there.
3. **219th:** the number of the artillery battery in which the speaker was
   serving.

Rear Guard Action I

Nov.–Dec. 1950

The military unit in this poem, the 219th Artillery Battery, served rear-guard duty in Korea during the retreat of American forces in the frigid winter of 1950–1951. As a rule, artillery units move forward in a retreat to save the guns. In this action, however, the rapid advance of the enemy troops made it imperative that the artillery remain behind to protect the main army and thus save as many men as possible. In addition to resisting the advancing Chinese, rear-guard units such as the 219th picked up American soldiers, like the clerk in this poem, who had fallen behind, become lost, or for some other reason had been separated from their units.

As you read "Rear Guard Action I," keep in mind that the soldiers were enduring freezing temperatures with little protection from the elements. In this poem, Hinojosa-Smith clearly shows that deprivation, suffering, and death threaten everyone, even clerks, in a war zone.

This much is definite: Crying won't help.
Praying doesn't seem to either; not here and not now
  at any rate.
The Chinese have been driving hard,
And once again we find ourselves in familiar grid
  coordinates.

It's crystal ball clear: 5
The Chinese want the boys to be home in time for
  Christmas.

Moving South, picking up stragglers and other lost souls.
Yesterday evening, while we were busy
Checking, polishing, and babying the guns over and over,
Hatalski brought in another straggler   10
With death written all over him.

  "Here's another mouth to feed," he says.

Rolando Hinojosa-Smith 607

A company clerk whose company
Abandoned *him;* he was left to guard
Cabinets crammed with shot, leave, and pay records along with 15
    the usual morning reports.
He carried an unloaded carbine, and there were no rounds
    on his person.

"Well, Merry Christmas to you, Mr. Company Clerk,"
    said Frazier.

And with this, he goes down to his knees.
To a man we turn away, and it's back to the guns.   20
After a minute or two, softly,
Frazier says, "When you're through, Chappie,
    Give us a hand with the elbow grease."
He keeps crying, but he's willing to work.

"How long had you been there when the Sergeant
    found you?"   25
"Since last night."
"And they just left you there?"
"They said they'd be back . . . Where we headed now?"
"We're going South . . . to Kunu-ri."¹
"But what artillery outfit is this?"   30
"The 219th . . ."
"The 219th . . . you're attached to the Second Division."
    Frazier laughs and says, "Assigned,
But not attached."

The clerk nods and reaching into his pocket,   35
He pulls out a Baby Ruth wrapper and takes a small bite
Off the frozen candy bar.
"We'll all eat soon," Frazier tells him.
He nods again:

"The Chinese saw me standing there   40
By the cabinets. They saw me,
And walked right by. They waved.
Some of them waved at me."

---

1. **South . . . to Kunu-ri:** the direction of the retreating army; Kunu-ri was
    an area where the army was to assemble and regroup in order to give
    the men a chance to rest before continuing the march.

"Yeah . . . they're just ahead . . ."
"Ahead?" 45
"Setting up roadblocks, most probably."
"Jesus . . ."
"We'll get out; we'll just burn the hills
And them too."
"Jesus . . ." 50

Above All, the Waste

*The speaker in this poem tells of the fate of his friend, a
lieutenant serving as a forward observer for an artillery
battery. Lying in a hole some two hundred to four hundred
yards in front of the guns, forward observers play a vital
role in spotting the enemy and directing fire. The stress
of constantly facing the enemy and death at close quarters
broke many men, further adding to the "waste" of war. In
movies, books, and television programs, warfare often
comes across as an exciting adventure—a dramatic, sometimes even humorous, theater for heroics and derring-do.
But, if you know any war veterans, they will likely tell
you that war is primarily a grim business dealing in death
and waste, killing at least in part the souls and hearts, if
not the bodies, of all who participate.*

Lt. Phil Brodkey up and shot himself two days ago;
We found his helmet, the binocs,
    The paper, the pencil,
Two packs of cigarettes and a Japanese lighter,
All in a row; We found him face down. 5
Half in half out of his forward ob. hole.[1]

---

1. **forward ob. hole:** the forward observer's hole.

He used to say he was a Philadelphia Jew
Doing time; for once he was wrong.
He was a friend; he was resourceful and kind, calm, precise,
And something that most of us here are not: 10
He was very good at his job.
And yet, he cracked,
As I imagine many of us will,
In time.

My God, but I'd hate to see   15
The letter Bracken will send off to his family.
Maybe, just once, Bracken'll do the right thing:
He'll personally recommend him for the Purple Heart[2]
    and the Bronze[3]
And then leave the writing to one of the other firing
    officers.[4]

---

2. **Purple Heart:** a medal awarded by the U.S. Army for wounds sustained in combat.
3. **Bronze:** the Bronze Star Medal, a medal awarded for bravery in action.
4. **firing officers:** the title of the junior officers (usually lieutenants) in charge of the battery's cannon and their firing orders.

For Study and Discussion

The Eighth Army at the Chongchon

1. Officers often address their troops prior to battle in order to build morale and to convince their men of the importance and seriousness of their mission. How effective do you think General Walker's words (lines 20–22) were in motivating the Mexican American soldiers serving under him? Explain.

2. A tone of irony, almost of cynicism, prevails throughout "The Eighth Army at the Chongchon." Identify specific words, phrases, and incidents in the poem that express this irony, and explain how they do so.

Rear Guard Action I

3. The company clerk who had been left behind by his unit says that enemy soldiers had seen him and yet had "walked right by" and even waved at him. In your opinion, why didn't the Chinese troops kill the clerk?

4. When the clerk comments that the 219th is "attached to the Second Division," Frazier answers with a laugh, "Assigned, / But not attached." What does this phrase suggest about the circumstances and attitudes of the men in the 219th?

Above All, the Waste

5. The title of a literary work often provides insights into the theme, characterization, imagery, or some other element of the work. **a.** What insights into the poem does the title "Above All, the Waste" provide? **b.** Beyond the poem itself, what insights does this title give into the nature of war?

6. Bracken is Brodkey's commanding officer, and one duty of a commanding officer is to write to the family of any soldier killed while serving under that officer's command. However, the speaker in the poem says that he would "hate to see / The letter Bracken will send." Why does the speaker make this comment? What is "the right thing" the speaker thinks Bracken should do?

Writing About Literature

Analyzing How the Same Theme Is Expressed in Different Poems

Although not opposed as strongly as the war in Vietnam, the Korean War was criticized by many Americans, including a large number of those who served there. Because the military objective in Korea was only to repel and guard against North Korean troops invading the South, American and other United Nations forces often felt frustrated when they had to cut short a successful attack once the enemy had been driven back into North Korea.

Prevented from fighting toward a decisive victory, many American soldiers became disillusioned, particularly with their leaders. This disillusionment is clearly expressed in all three of these poems by Rolando Hinojosa-Smith, who is himself a veteran of the Korean War.

Write a short essay in which you discuss how at least two of the three poems by Hinojosa-Smith deal with the theme of disillusionment.

Prewriting. Reread the poems carefully several times, looking for specific examples of how the speaker or a character expresses disillusionment. As you read, ask yourself questions such as the following. In what way or about what is the speaker or character disillusioned? What or who has caused the disillusionment? What does the speaker's or character's disillusionment suggest about his leaders? about the speaker or character? about American society? about the Korean War? about war in general?

Once you have analyzed each poem, you can organize your thoughts in one of several ways. For example, you can compare within each paragraph how two or three of the poems express a particular aspect of disillusionment, or you can discuss in each paragraph how one poem expresses several aspects of disillusionment. In your final paragraph, you can wrap up your discussion by drawing a general conclusion about the causes or the implications of the speaker's or the character's disillusionment.

Writing and Revising. As you write and revise your essay, be sure to integrate quotations from the poems in your discussion. If you are unfamiliar with how to use quotation marks with other marks of punctuation such as commas, semicolons, and periods, review the section on quotation marks in your English grammar textbook. Take care to make quotations flow smoothly into your own sentences. When you proofread your paper, always double-check each quotation to ensure that you have used the author's exact wording and punctuation.

Creative Writing

Writing a Letter from the Point of View of a Character in a Poem

In all three of Hinojosa-Smith's poems, characters relate their experiences in the Korean War. If these characters had been real people, they would likely have exchanged letters with friends and family back home. Assume the role of one of the characters in any of the three poems, and write a letter home to a person who is close to you—your mother or father, a cousin or grandparent, your best friend or an imaginary wife or child—and tell him or her of the experience that is described in the poem. In writing your letter, you may wish to add details, but be sure to focus primarily on the experience as it is related in the poem.

Prewriting. Begin by clearly defining the character you will become. How old is he? Where does he come from? How does he feel about the war? What kind of language does he use? Next, identify the person to whom he is writing. What sort of language would he use in a letter to this person? What kinds of details would he include? What feelings and thoughts would he reveal? Finally, jot down notes about the experience, beginning with details from the poem. Weave these details into a narrative, adding information to fill gaps, to reveal more about the character you are assuming, and to heighten interest.

Writing and Revising. As you write your letter, be sure to adopt the diction, sentence structure, grammar, and other language conventions that the character would likely use in a personal letter such as you are writing. Even though you are writing this letter as a school assignment, do your best to make it as much like a personal letter as you can.

Rolando Hinojosa-Smith 613

Rosemary Catacalos

(1944–)

Like many other authors, Rosemary
Catacalos (kah-tah'kah-lohs) began writing while quite young. Yet she kept her
creations hidden in a journal until—again, like many writers—she
received the help and encouragement of a mentor.

Catacalos was born in St. Petersburg, Florida, where her father was
stationed during World War II. After the war, she moved with her
parents to their hometown of San Antonio, Texas. Somewhat solitary as
a child, Catacalos loved to read and spent a great deal of time writing
in her journal. On the blank pages that beckoned to her, she would
compose poetry, try her hand at prose, and simply "talk to herself" by
writing down her feelings, thoughts, and impressions.

While attending a local junior college in 1962, Catacalos met John
Igo, a creative-writing professor who became her critic and her con-
fidant. She entrusted him with her works; in return, Igo, recognizing her
talent as a poet, offered her many helpful suggestions for improvement
and encouraged her to continue writing. Emboldened, she did persevere, publishing her first series of poems in 1970 in a journal at the
University of Houston.

Catacalos worked as a copywriter, an arts publicist, and a newspaper
reporter before devoting herself in 1974 to arts-in-education projects
sponsored by the National Endowment for the Arts. From 1974 to 1985,
she conducted poetry workshops in elementary and secondary schools
throughout Texas. Over the years, Catacalos has compiled and edited
more than thirty chapbooks, or pamphlets, of her students' work.

In 1984, Catacalos published two collections of her own poetry: *As
Long As It Takes,* a handcrafted, limited-edition chapbook; and *Again*

for the First Time, a full-length book that received the Texas Institute of Letters Poetry award in 1985. Also in 1985, in addition to writing and producing a series of cable-television segments about artists' work in schools, Catacalos designed mailers featuring her students' poetry and drawings, which were sent as gifts to the children of Mexico in the aftermath of that country's devastating earthquake. These student works later became the focus of an exhibit at the United Nations offices in Mexico City.

From 1986 to 1989, Catacalos lived in San Antonio, Texas, where she was the literature program director of the Guadalupe Cultural Arts Center, a multidisciplinary center for Hispanic arts. In addition to coordinating a citywide program of literature readings, classes, and workshops, she organized the San Antonio Inter-American Bookfair in 1987, which attracted national attention for its programming designed to promote cultural understanding through the exhibition of literature. Recently, Catacalos was awarded a fellowship to pursue her creative writing at Stanford University in California.

Katakalos

*Perhaps the greatest success that you can achieve is to
earn the love and respect of those who know you best. In
this poem, Rosemary Catacalos expresses the deep admiration that she and others in her family have for "The Old
Man," her grandfather. Although "Old Sam" never
achieved great wealth or fame, he appears to have been as
successful as anyone can ever hope to be. What clues does
the poet furnish for the secret of her grandfather's success?*

The Old Man, we always called him.
We said it with respect.
Even when he embarrassed us
by wearing his plaid flannel work shirt
to church under the fine blue suit   5
one of his up-and-coming sons,
the three prides of his life,
had bought him.
Even when he spent hours
straightening used nails when   10
we could afford to buy him new ones
so he could build the hundreds
of crooked little plant stands
that still wobble in the corners
of our houses.   15

He had come off a hard island birthplace,
a rock long ago deserted by the gods
but still sopping with the blood
of its passing from hand to hand,
Greek to Turk, Turk to Greek   20
and back again,
as if everything had not always
belonged to the sea, he said,
and to the relentless light
that hurt the eyes   25
of statues and children alike.

616   *Rosemary Catacalos*

He was brought up on routine whippings
every Sunday, before-the-fact punishment
to fit any crime. His father, the miller,
followed the wisdom that parents   30
can't be everywhere at once
and in seven days any boy is bound
to do something deserving a beating.
Besides, by his own admission
he was not such a good shepherd,   35
always getting sidetracked caring
for some sick bird or dog or donkey
that followed him everywhere ever after
and got mixed up with the goats and sheep.

A draft dodger from the Turkish Army,   40
he braved the maze of Ellis Island
alone at sixteen,
escaping with his last name intact
and his first name changed to Sam.
New York fed him dog food   45
those first few months
when he couldn't read the labels
and only knew from the pictures
that the cans were meat and cheap.
He used to laugh about that.   50
Said it was just as good as some of
that Spam and stuff they sell nowadays.
Anyway, Sam was
the darling of immigrant flophouses,
giving away counsel and sometimes money,   55
always finding someone who was
a little worse off than he was.

He hoboed all the way to Seattle
where he pretended to be a high-flying carpenter
and was saved by *Hagia Sophia*[1] from a fall that   60
would otherwise have meant certain death.
Then he came to where they were
burning Greeks out of Oklahoma
and anyone who could kept moving

---

1. *Hagia Sophia* (ah-yee'ah soh'fee-ah): Saint Sophia; Greek for "holy
wisdom."

and opened a hamburger stand   65
a little farther south.
In San Antonio he rigged up
a brightly painted horse-drawn
popcorn and ice cream wagon
and made the rounds on the West Side,   70
never quite making more than a living
since he always told poor kids
to pay him whenever they got the money.
The hamburger stands came next.
The cafe on Produce Row that some   75
old market hands still remember.
The Ideal Spot on South Presa,
where every hobo and derelict
from here to either coast
knew he could collect a free meal.   80
Good Old Sam.

But his wife was always angry.
She wanted a house of her own,
something more than glass beads.
She hated the way he was always   85
attracting winos and gypsies
and cousins from everywhere
who camped on her red velvet cushions
while he was out working hard
to give it all away.   90
She was from Lagos, Jalisco,[2]
and when they'd met
it hadn't been so much about love
as it had been simply time to get married.
That's what she always said.   95
Sam never said much about it
one way or the other,
except to smile and tell us
she'd had a hard life.

Still, they must have had a   100
little something special going.
Seeing how back then

---

2. **Lagos, Jalisco** (lah'gohs, hah-lees'koh): a town and a state in Mexico.

he spoke only Greek,
a little broken English,
and she spoke only Spanish.   105
They were married through an interpreter.
Sam wore an ill-fitting suit
and carried a brown paper bag
full of sandwiches he had made
so as not to let the few guests go hungry.   110

Years later when they were old
she had never learned English
and he had never bought her a house.
He'd spent years in his by-now-perfect
Spanish trying to get her to see   115
how there was always some poor devil
who needed just a little help.
When she complained the loudest
he just listened patiently
and went about setting out his   120
sugar water in bottle caps
to feed the ants.
A smiling survivor.
A fat soft heart.
The Old Man.   125
We still say it with respect.

La Casa[1]

The American novelist Thomas Wolfe once observed that "you can't go home again." In "La Casa," the speaker makes this same observation from the point of view of a young Mexican American. As you read, consider how the younger generation's perspective on the "old house" differs from that of "all the mothers" who still live there.

The house by the *acequia*,[2]
its front porch dark and
cool with begonias,
an old house, always there,
always of the same adobe,[3]   5
always full of the same lessons.
We would like to stop.
We know we belonged there once.
Our mothers are inside.
All the mothers are inside,   10
lighting candles, swaying
back and forth on their knees,
begging The Virgin's forgiveness
for having reeled us out
on such very weak string.   15
They are afraid for us.
They know we will not stop.
We will only wave as we pass by.
They will go on praying
that we might be simple again.   20

---

1. **La Casa** (lah kah′sah): The House.
2. *acequia* (ah-seh′kyah): an irrigation ditch or canal.
3. **adobe** (ah-thoh′beh): mud brick that has been baked in the sun.

For Study and Discussion

Katakalos

1. The speaker feels a deep respect for "The Old Man." What qualities did Sam have that made him worthy of respect? Cite details from the poem to support your answer.

2. Sam's wife is described as "always angry." **a.** Why was she angry at her husband? **b.** What do you think kept them together in spite of conflicts and barriers of language and culture?

3. People give many different meanings to the word *success.* Have you known anyone who, like Sam, seemed worthy of great respect and admiration even though he or she was not successful in a material sense? What is your own definition of *success,* and how does this definition affect how you view others?

La Casa

4. The speaker describes the house as "always of the same adobe, / always full of the same lessons." **a.** How does the speaker indicate that "the house" is not a particular house but rather an image that represents many houses? **b.** What does the house symbolize in the poem?

5. When the speaker says, "we belonged there once," to whom is she referring, and where or to what did they once belong?

6. "All the mothers are inside" the house, praying for "The Virgin's forgiveness." **a.** What do they ask forgiveness for? **b.** Why are they "afraid" for their children?

Literary Elements

Conflict

In literature, **conflict** refers to a struggle between two opposing characters or forces. A struggle that occurs between two people, between a person and society, or between a person and nature is called **external conflict. Internal conflict,** on the other hand, involves a struggle between different elements or forces within a person. For example, in Rosemary Catacalos's poem "La Casa," an external conflict occurs between the "we" of the poem and the older generation who feel that their children have strayed from their culture and their way of life. Yet the children also experience an internal conflict in that they feel torn between the life style they have chosen and the "simple" life to which they once "belonged."

What are the conflicts in "Katakalos"? Are they primarily external or internal? Refer to specific passages in the poem to support your answer.

Writing About Literature

Comparing and Contrasting Tone in Two Poems

In both "Katakalos" and "La Casa," the poet adopts a very definite **tone,** or attitude, toward the older generation she describes. In an essay of two or three paragraphs, compare and contrast the speaker's attitudes toward her elders in each poem. Also discuss how the speaker feels toward the way of life the older generation represents for her.

Prewriting. You may find it helpful to review the discussion of conflict under **Literary Elements.** In what way or ways is the speaker in each of these poems in harmony or in conflict with her elders and their way of life? As you reread the poems, notice how the poet's choice of words helps to express the speaker's attitude. For example, what is the significance of the word *respect* in "Katakalos," and how does this word help to express the speaker's feelings toward Sam? For each poem, write down a list of words and phrases that the poet uses to characterize the older generation and to reveal the speaker's feelings. You can then compare and contrast these examples and use them to develop your discussion.

Writing and Revising. As you write and revise your paper, check to make sure that each of your sentences relates directly to the main idea of the paragraph in which it appears. For example, if you were devoting a paragraph to the speaker's admiration for Sam in "Katakalos," you would not want to include an example of how Sam "embarrassed" his children. Although such an example may be important to your general discussion, it would belong in a paragraph that focused on conflict, on Sam's behavior, or on another more closely related topic rather than in a paragraph about the speaker's admiration.

Drama of the
Contemporary Period

Contemporary Chicano theater burst on the scene in 1965 when Luis Valdez, a young actor and playwright with a degree in drama, joined César Chávez and his farm workers union in central California. Prepared to throw his creative energy behind the social revolution that was brewing among Mexican, Mexican American, and Filipino workers who had organized under Chávez, Valdez formed El Teatro Campesino [The Farm Workers' Theater], which began performing *actos*—short, one-act plays—in community and church halls and even on the edges of fields throughout central California. Comprised mostly of migrant workers, the group carried a strong social message: "Join the strike against exploitation; don't let yourselves be used."

Some of the original farm workers/actors later joined Valdez in San Luis Obispo, California, to found a professional theater group named after the original Farm Workers' Theater. El Teatro Campesino has matured and gained momentum over the past twenty years and now receives national acclaim as an outstanding and versatile theater company. The group continues to hold workshops and travels throughout the United States, Latin America, and Europe. *Soldado razo* [The buck private], which appears on page 628, is one of Valdez's later *actos*, which was first performed by El Teatro Campesino in 1971.

Following the example of El Teatro Campesino, Chicano theater groups began to form on college campuses and in many communities across the southwestern United States and California. Many of these groups created their own *actos* to promote the social and political message of the Chicano movement. Although some groups disbanded for lack of interest and financial support in the early 1970s, others continue to prosper and evolve.

While Valdez and El Teatro Campesino are a major force in the development of contemporary theater, a number of other playwrights have written and produced a variety of dramatic works that explore personal and philosophical as well as social themes. Many of these works are more experimental in form and structure than the early *actos* of Valdez and other politically oriented groups, using poetic language and containing symbolic and mythological elements. Works by Denise Chávez, a talented fiction writer and playwright, feature some of the more lyrical and innovative aspects of contemporary Chicano theater. Chávez writes and enacts memorable dramatic character sketches, performing in one-woman shows across the Southwest for both young and adult audiences. One of her longer plays, *The Flying Tortilla Man*, blends realistic explorations of characters' lives with a touch of magical fantasy.

Contemporary Mexican American theater has developed more slowly than other genres of this period, most likely due to the relative difficulty and expense of publishing and producing dramatic works. Yet theater has emerged as a vital creative outlet for many Mexican American writers and performers as well as an effective vehicle for social and political commentary.

Luis Valdez
(1940–)

As a playwright, actor, and director, Luis Valdez (lwees' bahl-thehs') has earned a place of prominence in contemporary American theater. Throughout his career, he has used theater as a vehicle for political activism, attempting to effect change and to make pointed social statements through his art.

Like other Chicano writers such as Tomás Rivera and Tino Villanueva, Luis Valdez grew up in a family of migrant farm workers. Born in Delano, California, he began to work in the fields at the age of six. Although his schooling was constantly interrupted as his family followed the crops across the fertile San Joaquin Valley, he finished high school and received a scholarship to San Jose State University.

College provided Valdez with the opportunity to pursue his lifelong enthusiasm for the theater, which dates back to his youth when he put on puppet shows and simple plays for family and friends. During college, he wrote his first full-length play. After graduating with a B.A. in English in 1964, he joined the nationally known San Francisco Mime Troupe, receiving invaluable experience in improvisational theater that would influence his later work.

Valdez became increasingly involved in the Chicano movement as it gained strength throughout the Southwest and California. He particularly championed the cause of the underpaid, overworked migrant farm laborers. In 1965, he returned to Delano to join César Chávez, the noted labor organizer and leader who was in the process of forming a union of migrant farm workers. Over the next several years, Valdez organized and sustained El Teatro Campesino [The Farm Workers' Theater]. Initially a band of amateur actors and musicians, most of them migrant workers, the troupe would gather after a grueling day in the fields to write, stage, and rehearse *actos*—simple one-act plays. They would then perform these short plays throughout the San Joaquin Valley in open fields, community centers, church halls, and anywhere else an audience would gather to hear their satirical commentary on contemporary social issues.

During the years of the Vietnam War, Valdez also wrote and directed plays that dramatized the horror of war—particularly the tragedy of the many young Mexican Americans who were losing their lives in Vietnam.

From 1969 onward, El Teatro Campesino began to tour the United States and Europe, performing plays and songs. The staging of *Zoot Suit* in 1978 at the Mark Taper Forum in Los Angeles brought Valdez commercial success: the play sold out within days of the opening. More recently, the film *La Bamba* (1987), written and directed by Valdez, played to full theaters across the country, receiving popular and critical acclaim.

Soldado razo [The buck private] is one of Valdez's later *actos*. First performed in 1971, it focuses on a young Mexican American who learns too late the grim lesson of war and meets his fate in Vietnam. In this as in other plays, Valdez uses dark, ironical humor to deliver a strong social message.

The Buck Private

Sauntering onto the stage, Death claims that he is off to Vietnam to "join the ranks" as a private. Ironically, Death has been serving there for quite some time already. As you read, consider why Luis Valdez uses Death as the narrator in this play.

Characters

Johnny	The Mother
The Father	Cecilia
Death	The Brother

Death (*enters singing*). I'm taking off as a private, I'm going to join the ranks . . . along with the courageous young men who leave behind beloved mothers, who leave their girlfriends crying, crying, crying their farewell. Yeah! How lucky for me that there's a war. How goes it, bro? I am death. What else is new? Well, don't get paranoid because I didn't come to take anybody away. I came to tell you a story. Sure, the story of the Buck Private. Maybe you knew him, eh? He was killed not too long ago in Vietnam.

[Johnny *enters, adjusting his uniform.*]

Death. This is Johnny, The Buck Private. He's leaving for Vietnam in the morning, but tonight—well, tonight he's going to enjoy himself, right? Look at his face. Know what he's thinking? He's thinking (Johnny *moves his lips*) "Now, I'm a man!"

[The Mother *enters.*]

Death. This is his mother. Poor thing. She's worried about her son, like all mothers. "Blessed be God," she's thinking; (The Mother *moves her mouth*) "I hope nothing happens to my son." (The Mother *touches* Johnny *on the shoulder.*)
Johnny. Is dinner ready, mom?

Mother. Yes, son, almost. Why did you dress like that? You're not leaving until tomorrow.

Johnny. Well, you know. Cecilia's coming and everything.

Mother. Oh, my son. You're always bringing girlfriends to the house but you never think about settling down.

Johnny. One of these days I'll give you a surprise, ma. (*He kisses her forehead. Embraces her.*)

Death. Oh, my! What a picture of tenderness, no? But, watch the old lady. Listen to what she's thinking. "Now, my son is a man. He looks so handsome in that uniform."

Johnny. Well, mom, it's getting late. I'll be back shortly with Cecilia, okay?

Mother. Yes, son, hurry back. (*He leaves.*) May God take care of you, mom's pride and joy.

[Johnny *re-enters and begins to talk.*]

Death. Out in the street, Johnny begins to think about his family, his girl, his neighborhood, his life.

Johnny. Poor mom. Tomorrow it will be very difficult for her. For me as well. It was pretty hard when I went to boot camp, but now? Vietnam! It's a killer, man. The old man, too. I'm not going to be here to help him out. I wasn't getting rich doing fieldwork, but it was something. A little help, at least. My little brother can't work yet because he's still in school. I just hope he stays there. And finishes. I never liked that school stuff, but I know my little brother digs it. He's smart too—maybe he'll even go to college. One of us has got to make it in this life. Me—I guess I'll just get married to Cecilia and have a bunch of kids. I remember when I first saw her at the Rainbow Ballroom. I couldn't even dance with her because I had had a few beers. The next week was pretty good, though. Since then. How long ago was that? June . . . no, July. Four months. Now I want to get hitched. Her parents don't like me, I know. They think I'm a good for nothing. Maybe they'll feel different when I come back from Nam. Sure, the War Veteran! Maybe I'll get wounded and come back with tons of medals. I wonder how the dudes around here are going to think about that? Damn neighborhood—I've lived here all my life. Now I'm going to Vietnam. (*Taps and drum*) It's going to be a drag, man. I might even get killed. If I do, they'll bring me back here in a box, covered with a flag . . . military funeral like they gave Pete

Gomez . . . everybody crying . . . the old lady—(*Stops*) What the hell am I thinking, man? Damn fool! (*He freezes.*)

[Death *powders* Johnny's *face white during the next speech.*]

Death. Foolish, but not stupid, eh? He knew the kind of funeral he wanted and he got it. Military coffin, lots of flowers, American flag, women crying, and a trumpet playing taps with a rifle salute at the end. Or was it goodbye? It doesn't matter, you know what I mean. It was first class all the way. Oh, by the way, don't get upset about the makeup I'm putting on him, eh? I'm just getting him ready for what's coming. I don't always do things in a hurry, you know. Okay, then, next scene. (Johnny *exits.*)

[Johnny *goes on to* Cecilia's *and exits.*]

Death. Back at the house, his old man is just getting home.

[The Father *enters.*]

Father. Hey, old lady, I'm home. Is dinner ready?

[The Mother *enters.*]

Mother. Yes, dear. Just wait till Juan gets home. What did you buy?
Father. A sixpack of Coors.
Mother. Beer?
Father. Well, why not? Look—This is my son's last night.
Mother. What do you mean, his last night? Don't speak like that.
Father. I mean his last night at home, woman. You understand—hic.
Mother. You're drunk, aren't you?
Father. And if I am, what's it to you? I just had a few beers with my buddy and that's it. Well, what is this, anyway . . . ? It's all I need, man. My son's going to war and you don't want me to drink. I've got to celebrate, woman!
Mother. Celebrate what?
Father. That my son is now a man! And quite a man, the twerp. So don't pester me. Bring me some supper.
Mother. Wait for Juan to come home.
Father. Where is he? He's not here? Is that so-and-so loafing around again? Juan? Juan?

Mother. I'm telling you he went to get Cecilia, who's going to have dinner with us. And please don't use any foul language. What will the girl say if she hears you talking like that?

Father. To hell with it! Who owns this damn house, anyway? Aren't I the one who pays the rent? The one who buys the food? Don't make me get angry, huh? Or you'll get it. It doesn't matter if you already have a son who's a soldier.

Mother. Please. I ask you in your son's name, eh? Calm down. (*She exits.*)

Father. Calm down! Just like that she wants me to calm down. And who's going to shut my trap? My son the soldier? My son . . .

Death. The old man's thoughts are racing back a dozen years to a warm afternoon in July. Johnny, eight years old, is running toward him between the vines, shouting: "Paaa, I already picked 20 trays, paaapá!"

Father. Huh. Twenty trays. Little bugger.

[The Brother *enters.*]

Brother. Pa, is Johnny here?

Death. This is Johnny's little brother.

Father. And where are you coming from?

Brother. I was over at Polo's house. He has a new motor scooter.

Father. You just spend all your time playing, don't you?

Brother. I didn't do anything.

Father. Don't talk back to your father.

Brother (*shrugs*). Are we going to eat soon?

Father. I don't know. Go ask your mother.

[The Brother *exits.*]

Death. Looking at his younger son, the old man starts thinking about him. His thoughts spin around in the usual hopeless cycle of defeat, undercut by more defeat.

Father. That boy should be working. He's already fourteen years old. I don't know why the law forces them to go to school till they're sixteen. He won't amount to anything, anyway. It's better if he starts working with me so that he can help the family.

Death. Sure, he gets out of school and in three or four years, I take him the way I took Johnny. Crazy, huh?

[Johnny *returns with* Cecilia.]

Johnny. Good evening, pa.
Father. Son! Good evening. What's this? You're dressed as a soldier?
Johnny. I brought Cecilia over to have dinner with us.
Father. Well, have her come in, come in.
Cecilia. Thank you very much.
Father. My son looks good, doesn't he?
Cecilia. Yes, sir.
Father. Damn right. He's off to be a buck private. (*Pause*) Well, let's see . . . uh, son, would you like a beer?!
Johnny. Yes, sir, but couldn't we get a chair first? For Cecilia?
Father. But, of course. We have all the modern conveniences. Let me bring one. Sweetheart? The company's here! (*He exits.*)
Johnny. How you doing?
Cecilia. Okay. I love you.
Death. This, of course, is Johnny's girlfriend. Fine, ha? Too bad he'll never get to marry her. Oh, he proposed tonight and everything—and she accepted, but she doesn't know what's ahead. Listen to what she's thinking. (Cecilia *moves her mouth.*) "When we get married I hope Johnny still has his uniform. We'd look so good together. Me in a wedding gown and him like that. I wish we were getting married tomorrow!"
Johnny. What are you thinking?
Cecilia. Nothing.
Johnny. Come on.
Cecilia. Really.
Johnny. Come on, I saw your eyes. Now come on, tell me what you were thinking.
Cecilia. It was nothing.
Johnny. Are you scared?
Cecilia. About what?
Johnny. My going to Vietnam.
Cecilia. No! I mean . . . yes, in a way, but I wasn't thinking that.
Johnny. What was it?
Cecilia (*Pause*). I was thinking I wish the wedding was tomorrow.
Johnny. Really?
Cecilia. Yes.
Johnny. You know what? I wish it was too. (*He embraces her.*)

Death. And, of course, now he's thinking too. But it's not what she was thinking. What a world!

[The Father *and* The Brother *enter with four chairs.*]

Father. Here are the chairs. What did I tell you? (*To* The Brother) Hey, you, help me move the table, come on.

Johnny. Do you need help, pa?

Father. No, son, your brother and I'll move it. (*He and* The Brother *move imaginary table into place.*) There it is. And your mom says you should start sitting down because dinner's ready. She made tamales, can you believe that!

Johnny. Tamales?

Brother. They're Colonel Sanders, eeehh.

Father. You shut your trap! Look . . . don't pay attention to him, Cecilia; this little bugger, uh, this kid is always saying stupid things, uh, silly things. Sit down.

Mother (*entering with imaginary bowl*). Here come the tamales! Watch out because the pot's hot, okay? Oh, Cecilia, good evening.

Cecilia. Good evening, ma'am. Can I help you with anything?

Mother. No, no, everything's ready. Sit down, please.

Johnny. Ma, how come you made tamales? (Death *begins to put some more makeup on* Johnny's *face.*)

Mother. Well, because I know you like them so much, son.

Death. A thought flashes across Johnny's mind: "Too much, man. I should go to war every day." Over on this side of the table, the little brother is thinking: "What's so hot about going to war—tamales?"

Brother. I like tamales.

Father. Who told you to open your mouth? Would you like a beer, son?

Johnny (*nods*). Thanks, dad.

Father. And you, Cecilia?

Cecilia (*surprised*). No, sir, uh, thanks.

Mother. Juan, don't be so thoughtless. Cecilia's not old enough to drink. What are her parents going to say? I made some Kool-Aid, sweetheart; I'll bring the pitcher right out. (*She exits.*)

Death. You know what's going through the little brother's mind? He is thinking: "He offered her a beer! She was barely in the eighth grade three years ago. When I'm 17 I'm going to join the service and get really drunk."

Luis Valdez 633

Father. How old are you, Cecilia?

Cecilia. Eighteen.

Death. She lied, of course.

Father. Oh, well, what the heck, you're already a woman! Come on son, don't let her get away.

Johnny. I'm not.

Mother (*re-entering*). Here's the Kool-Aid and the beans.

Johnny. Ma, I got an announcement to make. Will you please sit down?

Mother. What is it?

Father (*to* The Brother). Give your chair to your mother.

Brother. What about my tamale?

Mother. Let him eat his dinner.

Father (*to* The Brother). Get up!

Johnny. Sit down, Mom.

Mother. What is it, son? (*She sits down.*)

Death. Funny little games people play, ha? The mother asks, but she already knows what her son is going to say. So does the father. And even little brother. They are all thinking: "He is going to say: Cecilia and I are getting married!"

Johnny. Cecilia and I are getting married!

Mother. Oh, son!

Father. You don't say!

Brother. Really?

Mother. When, son?

Johnny. When I get back from Vietnam.

Death. Suddenly a thought is crossing everybody's mind: "What if he doesn't come back?" But they shove it aside.

Mother. Oh, darling! (*She hugs* Cecilia.)

Father. Congratulations, son. (*He hugs* Johnny.)

Mother (*hugging* Johnny). My boy! (*She cries.*)

Johnny. Hey, mom, wait a minute. Save that for tomorrow. That's enough, ma.

Father. Daughter. (*He hugs* Cecilia *properly.*)

Brother. Heh, Johnny, why don't I go to Vietnam and you stay here for the wedding? I'm not afraid to die.

Mother. What makes you say that, child?

Brother. It just came out.

Father. You've let out too much already, don't you think?

Brother. I didn't mean it! (The Brother *exits.*)

Johnny. It was an accident, pa.

Mother. You're right; it was an accident. Please, sweetheart, let's eat in peace, ha? Juan leaves tomorrow.

Death. The rest of the meal goes by without any incidents. They discuss the wedding, the tamales, and the weather. Then it's time to go to the party.

Father. Is it true there's going to be a party?

Johnny. Just a small dance, over at Sapo's house.

Mother. Which Sapo, son?

Johnny. Sapo, my friend.

Father. Don't get drunk, okay?

Johnny. Oh, come on, dad, Cecilia will be with me.

Father. Did you ask her parents for permission?

Johnny. Yes, sir. She's got to be home by eleven.

Father. Okay. (Johnny *and* Cecilia *rise*.)

Cecilia. Thank you for the dinner, ma'am.

Mother. You're very welcome.

Cecilia. The tamales were really good.

Johnny. Yes, ma, they were terrific.

Mother. Is that right, son? You liked them?

Johnny. They were great. (*He hugs her.*) Thanks, eh?

Mother. What do you mean thanks? You're my son. Go then, it's getting late.

Father. Do you want to take the truck, son?

Johnny. No thanks, pa. I already have Cecilia's car.

Cecilia. Not mine. My parents' car. They loaned it to us for the dance.

Father. It seems like you made a good impression, eh?

Cecilia. He sure did. They say he's more responsible now that he's in the service.

Death (*to audience*). Did you hear that? Listen to her again.

Cecilia (*repeats sentence, exactly as before*). They say he's more responsible now that he's in the service.

Death. That's what I like to hear!

Father. That's good. Then all you have to do is go ask for Cecilia's hand, right, sweetheart?

Mother. God willing.

Johnny. We're going, then.

Cecilia. Good night.

Father. Good night.

Mother. Be careful on the road, children.

Johnny. Don't worry, mom. Be back later.

Cecilia. Bye!

[Johnny *and* Cecilia *exit. The Mother* stands at the door.]

Father (*sitting down again*). Well, old lady, little Johnny has become a man. The years fly by, don't they?
Death. The old man is thinking about the Korean War. Johnny was born about that time. He wishes he had some advice, some hints, to pass on to him about war. But he never went to Korea. The draft skipped him, and somehow, he never got around to enlisting. (The Mother *turns around.*)
Mother (*She sees Death*). Oh, my God! (*Exit*)
Death (*ducking down*). Damn, I think she saw me.
Father. What's wrong with you? (The Mother *is standing frozen, looking toward the spot where* Death *was standing.*) Answer me, what's up? (*Pause*) Speak to me! What am I, invisible?
Mother (*solemnly*). I just saw Death.
Father. Death? You're crazy.
Mother. It's true. As soon as Juan left, I turned around and there was Death, standing—smiling! (The Father *moves away from the spot inadvertently.*) Oh, Blessed Virgin Mary, what if something happens to Juan.
Father. Don't say that! Don't you know it's bad luck?

[*They exit.* Death *re-enters.*]

[*The Greyhound Bus Depot.*]

Death. The next day, Johnny goes to the Greyhound Bus Depot. His mother, his father, and his girlfriend go with him to say goodbye. The Bus Depot is full of soldiers and sailors and old men. Here and there, a drunkard is passed out on the benches. Then there's the announcements: THE LOS ANGELES BUS IS NOW RECEIVING PASSENGERS AT GATE TWO, FOR KINGSBURG, TULARE, DELANO, BAKERSFIELD AND LOS ANGELES, CONNECTIONS IN L.A. FOR POINTS EAST AND SOUTH.

[Johnny, Father, Mother, *and* Cecilia *enter.* Cecilia *clings to* Johnny.]

Father. It's been several years since I last set foot at the station.
Mother. Do you have your ticket, son?
Johnny. Oh, no, I have to buy it.
Cecilia. I'll go with you.

Father. Do you have money, son?
Johnny. Yes, pa, I have it.

[Johnny *and* Cecilia *walk over to* Death.]

Johnny. One ticket, please.
Death. Where to?
Johnny. Vietnam. I mean, Oakland.
Death. Round trip or one way?
Johnny. One way.
Death. Right. One way. (*Applies more makeup.*)

[Johnny *gets his ticket and he and* Cecilia *start back toward his parents.* Johnny *stops abruptly and glances back at* Death, *who has already shifted positions.*]

Cecilia. What's wrong?
Johnny. Nothing. (*They join the parents.*)
Death. For half an hour then, they exchange small talk and trivialities, repeating some of the things that have been said several times before. Cecilia promises Johnny she will be true to him and wait until he returns. Then it's time to go: THE OAKLAND-VIETNAM EXPRESS IS NOW RECEIVING PASSENGERS AT GATE NUMBER FOUR. ALL ABOARD PLEASE.
Johnny. That's my bus.
Mother. Oh, son.
Father. Take good care of yourself then, okay, son?
Cecilia. I love you, Johnny. (*She embraces him.*)
Death. THE OAKLAND-VIETNAM EXPRESS IS IN THE FINAL BOARDING STAGES. PASSENGERS WITH TICKETS ALL ABOARD PLEASE. AND THANKS FOR GOING GREYHOUND.
Johnny. I'm leaving, now.

[*Embraces all around, weeping, last goodbyes, etc.* Johnny *exits. Then parents exit. The* Mother *and* Cecilia *are crying.*]

Death (*sings*). *Goodbye, Goodbye*
               Star of my nights
               A soldier said in front of a window
               I'm leaving, I'm leaving
               But don't cry, my angel
               For tomorrow I'll be back . . .
So Johnny left for Vietnam, never to return. He didn't want to

go and yet he did. It never crossed his mind to refuse. How can he refuse the government of the United States? How could he refuse his family? Besides, who wants to go to prison? And there was the chance he'd come back alive . . . wounded maybe, but alive. So he took a chance—and lost. But before he died he saw many things in Vietnam; he had his eyes opened. He wrote his mother about them.

[Johnny *and* The Mother *enter at opposite sides of the stage.* Johnny *is in full battle gear. His face is now a skull.*]

Johnny. Dear mom.
Mother. Dear son.
Johnny. I am writing this letter.
Mother. I received your letter.
Johnny. To tell you I'm okay.
Mother. And I thank the heavens you're all right.
Johnny. How's everybody over there?
Mother. Here, we're all doing fine, thank God.
Johnny. Ma, there's a lot happening here that I didn't know about before. I don't know if I'm allowed to write about it, but I'm going to try. Yesterday we attacked a small village near some rice paddies. We had orders to kill everybody because they were supposed to be V-C's, communists. We entered the small village and my buddies started shooting. I saw one of them kill an old man and an old lady. My sergeant killed a small boy about seven years old, then he shot his mother or some woman that came running up crying. Blood was everywhere. I don't remember what happened after that but my sergeant ordered me to start shooting. I think I did. May God forgive me for what I did, but I never wanted to come over here. They say we have to do it to defend our country.
Mother. Son what you are writing to us makes me sad. I talked to your father and he also got very worried, but he says that's what war is like. He reminds you that you're fighting communists. I have a candle lit and everyday I ask God to take good care of you wherever you are and that he return you to our arms healthy and in one piece.
Johnny. Ma, I had a dream the other night. I dreamed I was breaking into one of the hooches, that's what we call the Vietnamese's houses. I went in firing my M-16 because I knew that the village was controlled by the gooks. I killed three of

them right away, but when I looked down it was my pa, my little brother and you, mother. I don't know how much more I can stand. Please tell Sapo and all the dudes how it's like over here. Don't let them . . .

[Death *fires a gun, shooting* Johnny *in the head. He falls.* The Mother *screams without looking at* Johnny.]

Death. Johnny was killed in action November 1965 at Chu Lai. His body lay in the field for two days and then it was taken to the beach and placed in a freezer, a converted portable food locker. Two weeks later he was shipped home for burial.

[Death *straightens out* Johnny's *body. Takes his helmet, rifle, etc.* The Father, The Mother, The Brother, *and* Cecilia *file past and gather around the body. Taps plays.*]

For Study and Discussion

1. As narrator, the figure of Death plays a central role in *The Buck Private.* **a.** Referring to specific passages in the play, discuss the manner in which Death is characterized. **b.** In what ways does Death serve as a **foil,** or contrast, to Johnny and the other characters?

2. Each of Johnny's loved ones, as well as Johnny himself, hopes and/or expects that his time in Vietnam will have a positive outcome. In light of his certain death, these expressions of hope take on tragic significance. **a.** Citing passages from the play, contrast each character's private expectations with what actually happens to Johnny. **b.** In your opinion, has Johnny truly matured, or gained knowledge, before his death?

3. This play is *didactic* in nature—that is, it attempts to teach something to its audience. What message does the play communicate about the nature of war? Do you think that this message is presented effectively? Explain your answer.

Literary Elements

Irony

Irony, in literature as well as in life, involves a discrepancy—an inconsistency—between appearance and reality. In *The Buck Private,* for example, Death's announcement that he is "going to join the ranks" as a private is an example of **verbal irony:** his tongue-in-cheek statement knowingly contrasts with the true nature of his "mission" and commanding role in Vietnam. Death's grim humor also helps to highlight examples of **dramatic irony** in the play. Dramatic irony involves a discrepancy between what a character says or thinks and what the audience knows to be true. For example, Johnny's brief daydream about his own funeral is of "a military funeral like they gave Pete Gomez," with "everybody crying." Johnny's romanticized version of his death contrasts ironically with the cold fact of its reality. Although, as Death points out, Johnny gets "the kind of funeral he wanted," the ceremony is meaningless because he is not there to appreciate it and because the pomp of his military funeral contrasts sharply with the ignoble treatment of his body in Vietnam.

Find one additional example each of verbal irony and dramatic irony in the play. In each case, explain what is ironic about the statement and why it functions as verbal rather than dramatic irony or vice versa.

Writing About Literature

Using Stage Directions

As a literary form, drama possesses unique resources and limitations. While reading a dramatic work, keep in mind that it is meant to be performed onstage—that its impact depends largely upon the effectiveness of its visual presentation. Stage directions given by the author guide the director and the performers in their production of a play. Some basic elements of staging include scenery, costume, gesture and movement, and lighting. Read through *The Buck Private,* noting all stage directions given by the author. How do these directions contribute to the effectiveness of the play? Pretending that you are the director, discuss how you would interpret the stage directions given by the author to render the first scene of the play, which ends with Johnny's first exit. For example, instances in which Johnny and his mother move their lips while Death speaks their thoughts could be quite striking onstage. How would you "play up" these instances?

Prewriting. Before you respond, consider the following questions. What kinds of lighting would be most effective throughout this scene? How would you position the characters in relation to one another? Should Death slink around the perimeter of the stage or stroll self-assuredly across its center? What kind of uniform would Johnny wear? What props, if any, would you add to the set? As you describe your direction of the first scene, be sure to explain the reasons for your choices. Any directing decision is valid as long as it can be justified in relation to the work—that is, as long as it does not contradict the tone, mood, and message of the written play.

Writing. Use precise wording to describe the relative positions of the characters onstage. Often, words and phrases that seem to mean the same thing suggest subtle differences that could be important in stage directions. For example, "next to" and "close to" suggest different degrees of nearness; "in back of" is a more specific direction than "behind." Also keep in mind that "stage left", and "stage right" refer to left and right from the actors' perspective and not the audience's.

Denise Chávez
(1948–)

I was born in Las Cruces, New Mexico, in a time of extreme heat, in August. Since then, I have carried that heat with me, wherever I have lived. A sensitivity to heat, a release in rain, these are my earliest memories. . . . The change of seasons, so subtle in the south . . . has found its expression in my writing.

In this passage, Denise Chávez reveals the powerful influence that the stark southwestern landscape has had on her life and art. Not only the physical but also the cultural setting of New Mexico is woven into the fabric of her works, reflecting her early experiences as a Mexican American growing up in Las Cruces, a small city where Anglo and Hispanic cultures have flourished side by side for over one hundred and fifty years.

A gifted writer and actress, Chávez has distinguished herself as a new and exciting voice in Mexican American literature and theater. She has enthralled audiences across the southwestern United States with her dramatic one-woman shows in which she portrays memorable characters of her own creation, among them a streetwise, tough-talking adolescent; a pious widow; and a wise *curandera,* or healer. She has written and produced more than twenty plays and has published a collection of bittersweet, semi-autobiographical short stories, *The Last of the Menu Girls.* Her play *The Flying Tortilla Man,* which appears on the following pages, illustrates the importance of landscape and Mexican American history and culture in her writing.

Chávez studied drama at New Mexico State University, receiving her undergraduate degree in 1971. She then went on to receive a master's degree in drama from Trinity University in 1974 and, ten years later, an additional graduate degree in creative writing from the University of

New Mexico in Albuquerque. Her years of experience gained through giving readings, conducting community workshops, and working with various theater groups throughout the Southwest have helped her to win numerous awards for her writing, acting, and community work.

Chávez now lives in Houston, Texas, where she teaches drama at the University of Houston. Her current writing projects include a novel as well as a handbook for teaching writing to elementary and high-school students.

The Flying
Tortilla Man

Set in New Mexico, The Flying Tortilla Man *interweaves
fantasy, realism, humor, and adventure in a narrative that
the author Denise Chávez has described as a tale for
"children of all ages." When Chávez directed a student
production of the play in 1975, she used movable flats, or
boards painted with scenery, to depict different settings.
As you read, try to imagine the set and characters of the
play as they might look in a production. If you were
directing the play, how would you interpret Chávez's stage
directions for scenery, lighting, and costume?*

---

*"Beautiful or not, it is my native land. A relative or not,
he is a fellow countryman."*

Chinese Proverb

Characters

Carlos *age twelve*	Neno *age twelve*
Bennie *age fourteen*	Hermano Gil *age forty-five*
Elias *age thirteen*	Bertina *early fifties*
Oscar *age eighteen*	Cotil *age fifteen*
Tudi *age twenty*	Fatty Campbell *age fifty-five*
Nora *early thirties*	The Birds / Old Women

The Tortilla Man ageless

Scene 1

*It is late evening on a hot summer night in Cuchillo, New Mexico.
The heat permeates the walls of an aluminum building that houses a
small but prosperous tortilla factory. The odor of cooked maize hangs
heavy in the air. The building seems collapsible, barely grounded to*

644 Denise Chávez

the earth. The factory is in full swing preparing for the day's orders. A screen door is held in place by two long wooden planks.

The radio jumps to a lively Mexican station, XELO, and casts a lyrical spell over the grinding, pulsating machines. Several teen-age boys are at their posts, silhouetted against machines in an eerie, yellow-maize darkness that creeps inside the factory and finds relief in the midst of activity.

Carlos *carries a pan of maize from a large metal trough to a machine that rinses the corn. He is a thin yet muscular boy of unspoiled character, gentle and filled with a natural goodness, a dreamer.* Carlos *stands not far from* Elias, *who supervises the maize in the grinding machine and changes the pans of crushed corn that go to the cutter as a finished masa.*[1] Elias *is a mischievous adolescent with thick burnt red hair and fair skin, appropriately named "El Güero."*[2] *Next to* Elias *stands* Neno, *guarding the cutting machines. He is about the same age as* Carlos, *somewhat tired and sickly-looking, with a dark chinless face. Not far from* Neno *stands* Bennie, *who pushes the dough through the cutting machine roller. He is silent and shy, lean and greyhoundlike. At the end of the cooking conveyor belt sit* Oscar *and* Nora, *taking turns counting out a dozen tortillas and spreading them, fanlike, on the metal shelf where they are packaged by the roving* Bennie. Oscar *is fat, jolly and toothy.* Nora *is a cheerful woman, who is somewhat simple-minded, yet she works with amazing speed and agility.*

At the far end of the factory stands the office, a tucked-away bastion of power amid the heat and sweat. Inside is a large metal desk covered with orders and business papers. Beside the desk stands a counter full of frozen products from the factory: flour and corn tortillas, taco shells, tamales. At the desk, behind the closed and forbidding door, sits Tudi, *who oversees the factory with a hard, anxious eye. He is a good-looking, somewhat morose young man. He is not the actual boss but simply manages the factory in the owner's stead. The radio plays . . . all are intense and involved in the swinging, swaying creation of the tortillas.*

Neno. It's hot!

Oscar. So, why don't you work in an ice plant?

Elias. Quiet, you guys, this is my favorite song!

---

1. *masa* (mah'sah): dough.
2. *"El Güero"* (ehl gweh'roh): masculine term used to refer to a person with a fair complexion and blond hair.

Denise Chávez 645

Oscar (*laughing to himself*). This one, ese[3], are you kidding me?

[*All are momentarily caught up in the dramatically sad tune coming from the radio: another song about lost love.*]

Neno. What am I doing here? I can't think . . . I can't breathe . . . it's so hot!

Oscar. You're not paid to think, man; you're paid to sweat!

Neno. I gotta get out of here . . . my head is on fire. Trade with me, Elias . . .

Elias. Heck no, Neno. I got my own work to do. You start doing it once, and you'll want to do it all the time.

Carlos. I'll trade, Neno.

Elias. They play this song to me this one night and you guys won't shut up.

Oscar. What's so special about tonight? It don't feel so special to me.

Elias. It's a special request from my girl!

Oscar. You have a girl, Güero? Who would want a pale worm like you?

Elias. None of your business, horsemouth!

Oscar. You called in the song yourself tonight, corn face, before you came in to work. Isn't that right, Nora? Doesn't have a girl at all, unless it's Nora here. Are you sweethearts with La Nica,[4] Elias? NicaNora, NicaNora, NicaNora, old metate[5] face. (*Oscar sings to* Nora, *who is first oblivious to him and then joins in, clapping her hands and humming, in a strange and haunting way.* Neno *is beginning to look progressively worse, and* Elias *makes ugly scowling faces at* Oscar, *who encourages* Bennie *to join him in his crazed chanting.*) NicaNora, NicaNora, NicaNora, old metate face! Laugh, Nica, laugh!

Elias. You're jealous!

Oscar. Of La Nica? Heck, man, I see her every day—that's enough for me.

Nora. Funny, Oscar, funny! (Nora *continues to clap her hands.*)

Oscar. Be quiet, Nora, and get back to work! The Boss gonna get on our case. We got lots of work to do . . .

[Nora *hums.*]

---

3. **ese** (eh'seh): a slang term meaning "hey, man" (masc., *ese*; fem., *esa*).
4. **La Nica** (lah nee'kah): nonsense name given to Nora by Oscar.
5. **metate** (meh-tah'teh): stone slab used to grind corn; Oscar refers cruelly to Nora's complexion.

Carlos. Nora hasn't done anything to you, Oscar; leave her alone!

Oscar. *You* leave *me* alone, Mr. Corn Lifter. I was only making fun.

Elias. You tell him, Carlos . . . trying to make believe that La Nica is my girlfriend. That old hag, I'd rather drown in the irrigation ditch!

Carlos. Leave her alone, Elias!

Oscar. But she's his ruca,[6] ese . . .

Elias. If you're such a good boy, Carlos, be quiet . . . shut your mouth, okay?

Carlos. Where's Tudi? He's been gone a long time. I'm worried about Neno.

Nora. Tudi? Tudi?

Oscar. Shut up and get to work!

Carlos. Don't talk to her that way, Oscar. Show some respect!

Oscar. To a crazy woman?

Elias. You think you're so good, Carlos . . . well, you're the one that's crazy! That's what happens when you don't have real parents. When you're an orphan! And when you live with people that ain't your kin, in a house full of strangers!

Carlos. I have parents!

Elias. You call those two—the stringbean and the squash—your parents? Heck, man, they have a houseful of kids, like rabbits, over there at that place.

Carlos. They're good to me.

Elias. It's because they feel sorry.

Nora. Carlitos, good boy!

Elias. See, even La Nica feels sorry.

Oscar. Go on Elias; you're finally showing a little nerve. Nica might fall in love with your strength!

Bennie. You guys better be still. Tudi might come back!

Oscar. Let him come back. I'll show him who OSCAR SALCEDO is!

Elias. Híjole,[7] Oscar, you couldn't whip a mouse!

Oscar. Be careful, you bleached earthworm!

Elias. You're going to get it one of these days, you fat hyena!

Bennie. Be quiet! Be quiet, or we'll get in trouble! Tudi's in his office!

---

6. **ruca** (roo'kah): slang for "girlfriend."
7. **Híjole** (ee'hoh-leh): exclamatory phrase meaning "wow" or "is that so."

Oscar. So El Tudi is in the office, huh? I don't trust that guy. He always looks like a dog who wants to bark. Too much power. Wooo! What do you say, Nica?

Nora. Where's Tudi? Tudi is a nice man.

Carlos. Her name is Nora.

Oscar (*referring to* Nora *as he counts tortillas*). So what does she know anyway? All she can do is count to twelve. Ay, this heat! It gets into your blood and drives you crazy. After so many years, you start counting all the time. Stupid things you start counting for nothing. All this heat . . . it affects your brain. It starts suddenly, like with Neno, until one day you're as dry in the head as Nica, right, Nenito? Where'd he go?

Carlos. He's at the washer.

Bennie. Don't let Tudi see you, Neno; it'll go rough for us!

Elias. So who cares! You've all got baked corn for brains, anyway!

Neno. I don't feel good. I'm going outside. (Neno *starts for the door and suddenly faints.* Carlos, Elias, *and* Bennie *run to him, followed by* Nora. Oscar *remains behind.*)

Oscar (*paying no attention to the others, he continues talking*). You just keep counting, that's all . . .

Carlos. What's wrong, Neno?

Bennie. He's sick!

Elias. You're really a smart one, Bennie. Is that why you work here?

Bennie. What about you, Güero? The light too bright for you out there in the world? You need to be in this cave, eh?

Oscar (*still oblivious to the others,* Oscar *continues to count tortillas*). Ten . . . eleven . . . twelve . . .

Carlos. Help me take him outside. He needs some fresh air.

Oscar. He's got the rot. It just happens.

Elias. You must be an advanced case.

Oscar. Sooner or later. . .

Elias. Would you shut up?

Oscar. It gets you.

Elias. Is that why you're still here after all these years?

[*The boys carry* Neno *outside and lean him up against the steps.* Nora *has gone to the water trough near the maize bags and dips her apron in and returns to the steps. She uses her apron as a towel on* Neno's *forehead.* Neno *is in a daze.*]

Carlos. Thank you, Nora.
Nora (*in a soothing voice*). Neno, Nenito. Good boy, Nenito.

[Neno *unsteadily gets to his feet with the help of* Nora *and* Carlos.]

Elias. Oh, he's okay.

[Bennie, Elias, Carlos, Nora *and* Neno *file back inside the building.*]

Bennie. We'd better get back to work!
Oscar. Since when have you worked around here, Bennie? And you, Nica. Where have you been, you lazy good-for-nothing? Who do you think you are, wiping people's foreheads? And who does Neno think he is? Hey, I already did more than my share of work, so where is everybody?

[Nora *runs back, confused. Her movements are pointed and jittery.*]

Nora. Sorry, Nora so sorry. Oscar not mad with Nora. She's sorry.
Oscar. Back to work, back to work! They can hear you in the other room, the bosses, the big shots. They can hear you out here like rats in the night. Isn't that right, Nica, like rats?
Nora (*making a ratlike face*). Like rats, like rats.
Carlos. Leave her alone, Oscar . . . she hasn't done anything to you. She was only trying to help Neno out.
Oscar. It'll go bad for us all, Carlos. You get back to work.
Carlos. He's sick!
Oscar. He's got the corn rot and the fever that comes nights working at a place like this. It starts flowing in your blood.
Elias (*sarcastically*). What are you anyway, a doctor?
Oscar. And you're the nurse!
Carlos. I can't leave him alone. He's sick!
Oscar. Oh, that's right . . . you're the one who doesn't have anyone to take care of you, so you take care of the world.
Tudi (*coming in and looking around suspiciously*). What's going on? Why aren't you working?
Neno. I'll be okay in a few minutes.
Bennie. Didn't I tell you guys?
Tudi. Get to work! All of you!
Carlos. Neno isn't feeling well, Tudi, I . . .
Tudi. Get to work, Carlos. We have orders to fill. It's late. The night's almost over and we're behind. Go on, all of you!

Carlos. Neno is sick. He needs to rest. Maybe he should go home.

Tudi. We can't have this, Carlos. We have orders to fill. This isn't the first time someone has played a trick, pretending to be sick . . .

Carlos. Feel his head . . .

Tudi. Huerfanito,[8] you, Carlos . . . help Neno get back to his job. He'll make it, all right. Now, boys, I've been in the office, thinking. (Oscar *snickers.*) And I've come up with a new set of rules.

Oscar. Not again!

Tudi. Quiet! Number one: one break every three hours, depending how far behind we are. Number two: no eating or drinking on the job. Number three: no visiting of an extended nature.

Oscar. Number four: No breathing! Visiting, man, are you joking me? Who's there to visit en esta maldita cueva?[9]

Tudi. Number four: more than one absence constitutes dismissal. Number five: we will all work together as a happy, united working force, producing as best as we can, without strife and dissension.

Bennie. Dissension, what's dissension?

Tudi. Quiet! Now then, I'll be available to talk to you guys any time. Remember that I'm the boss in place of our BOSS, who is gone. I am the absolute head in his place, and I demand respect and will treat you accordingly. Come on, boys, let's be friends!

Oscar. After all that . . . man, are you pulling my leg? It's a joke, Tudi.

Carlos. I'm taking Neno home, Tudi.

Elias. Let them go, let them go. . . they're nothing but trouble.

Oscar. Those two didn't do a thing all night.

Nora. Nice boys, Tudi, they're my friends.

Tudi. La Nica's very talkative tonight. She seems to be on your side, Carlos. Why are you helping Neno anyway? You know none of them would ever lift a finger for you. You could die right here on the job.

Oscar. Carlos was just standing around doing nothing, Tudi.

---

8. **Huerfanito** (wehr-fah-nee'toh): little orphan.
9. **en esta maldita cueva** (ehn ehs'tah mahl-thee'tah kweh'bah): in this accursed cave.

Carlos. I was helping my friend. I'm taking him home.

Tudi. If you do that, you might not have a job when you get back.

Carlos. You just can't *not* help someone. Especially a friend, someone you work with. Look at him, Tudi . . . he looks bad. Friendship is more than just standing by while someone is sick. Neno and I are friends.

Tudi. Go on, Carlos. Get outta here. Just try and come back. You're always getting in my way. Take your friend home. Just take him home. He's worthless!

Neno. I'm feeling better; really, I am. I can go to work, Carlos. I can go . . . (*He appears ready to faint and then recovers a bit.*) I can go home alone, Carlos; you stay here. Let me go alone.

Carlos. I'm taking you home! I care more about you than all the tortillas in the world!

Elias. Ah, they'll be back, begging for a job!

Tudi. Just you wait and see what happens, Carlos. Go on with you! Don't come back!

Nora. Goodbye. Goodbye, my friends. See you soon.

Oscar. You make me laugh, Nica. You really make me laugh! (*He starts laughing. They all join in.* Carlos *and* Neno *exit.*)

[*It is a rainy, windy night. The lightning crackles the breeze, and the boys look small and helpless against the sky. They don't have too far to go to* Neno's *but they make their way slowly and cautiously, pausing under the archways and porches, huddling together against the fury of the oncoming storm.* Carlos *knocks at* Neno's *door. A woman answers and takes* Neno *in, then closes the door.* Carlos *stands there long after they have gone in, unsure of what to do. He then dashes out of the doorway and runs madly to the next shelter. A delicate-looking man of above-average height with a fine, smooth face and warm, small eyes is standing there, also seeking shelter. They look at one another for a few seconds, the boy and the man, both dreamers.*]

Tortilla Man. Where are you, boy?

[Carlos *is not sure he heard the old gentleman correctly. He is taken aback by the seemingly strange question. Often* The Tortilla Man *will ask questions that seem to make no sense whatsoever, and yet they really do.*]

Carlos (*in an uncertain voice*). Where am I going, sir?

Tortilla Man. Where are you?

Carlos. I don't understand.

Tortilla Man. That's what's wrong with everyone. They're out of touch; they don't know where they are, especially in the middle of a storm. They're lost, going from one place to another, from one thing to another.

Carlos. WHO are you?

Tortilla Man. You don't know me?

Carlos (*suddenly wary*). What do you want?

Tortilla Man. What makes you think I want anything?

Carlos. If you'll excuse me, sir, I'll have to leave you and get back to work.

Tortilla Man. If I were you, I'd stay around and talk awhile. It's too early to be running off, and besides, your Boss hasn't decided to take you back yet. Wait up, boy; talk to an old man . . . tell him where you are.

Carlos. Who are you? You seem to know a lot. You're not from here, are you?

Tortilla Man. I remember Cuchillo when there was nothing out here but rocks and weeds and the bare sky to wear as a hat . . . when you blessed yourself for another day in this wilderness and prayed for rain . . .

Carlos. You don't look *that* old . . .

Tortilla Man. No impudence, boy, just listen to me. For he who teaches you for one day is your father for life. I read that in a book.

Carlos. I can barely read, and I don't have a father.

Tortilla Man. You do now, boy. We're in the same line of work.

Carlos. Tortillas?

Tortilla Man. Well, yes and no. Mostly yes.

Carlos. I don't have a job now. I've been fired. I don't know whether I should go back and beg—they said I would—or whether I should go home . . . I mean, where I live. My parents, Hermano Gil[10] and Bertina, they'll be mad at me. I finally got this job and now it's gone!

Tortilla Man. You'll go back to the factory, of course. No one should ever avoid what needs to be done.

Carlos. Yes, I thought so, too. How did you know?

---

10. **Hermano Gil** (ehr-mah'noh heel'): called Brother Gil by people who know him.

Tortilla Man. We do the same work.

Carlos. You make tortillas, too?

Tortilla Man. In a way, yes, but we'll come to that later. We both make things grow, come alive.

Carlos. We do?

Tortilla Man. We do, Carlos!

Carlos. You know my name!

Tortilla Man. Boy, you look like a Carlos—long, gangly, a real weed, a Carlos who is growing.

Carlos. You talk funny!

Tortilla Man. Boy, you look funny, all wet and long!

[*They both laugh.*]

Carlos. Who are you?

Tortilla Man. I'm The Flying Tortilla Man.

Carlos. The Tortilla Man? You run a factory, like our boss? He's never there, so Tudi takes his place. I never have seen the boss; I don't even know who he is . . .

Carlos (*realizing* The Tortilla Man *might be his boss*). You aren't . . .

Tortilla Man. I make things grow.

Carlos. But tortillas don't grow! They're a dead thing . . . they're just corn that becomes bread and that's eaten and is gone . . .

Tortilla Man. But, Carlos, tortillas are more than that . . . they're life to so many people. They're magic offerings; they're alive as the land, and as flat!

Carlos. They are, huh? What's your real name?

Tortilla Man. Juan.

Carlos. You're Mr. Juan, The Tortilla Man; pleased to meet you.

Tortilla Man. Enchanted. We are enchanted to meet you.

Carlos. Who's we?

Tortilla Man. Why, the Magic Tortilla, of course.

Carlos (*looking around*). Where is it?

Tortilla Man (*putting his arm around* Carlos's *shoulder and speaking confidentially*). I couldn't bring it out in this rain, could I?

Carlos (*disappointed*). I guess not.

Tortilla Man. Now . . . back to work . . . they're waiting for you.

Carlos. They are?

Tortilla Man. Don't be impudent, boy . . . don't you trust me?

Denise Chávez 653

Carlos. Yes . . . yes, I do! But I know I don't have a job anymore.
Tortilla Man. Who says? You just wait and see. Carlos, you just wait and see. You just can't stop something from growing.
Carlos. I'll try . . . I'll try . . .
Tortilla Man. Grow, boy. Let them see you grow, in front of their eyes! (*He laughs an infectious, clear laugh that is warm and comforting.*) You'll see. It's waiting there to grow . . . they can't stop you. They can't stop you . . . they'll try . . . Now, goodbye, think of me, and run, run . . .

[Carlos *runs into the darkness of a now-clear night. He is full of energy. He suddenly stops to say something to* The Tortilla Man, *who has vanished.*]

Carlos. THANK YOU! Sir . . . Mr. Juan . . . goodbye . . . he says he makes things grow, but how? Magic tortillas? And he says the sky is a hat . . .

[Carlos *runs back to the factory and walks in. Everyone is working noisily. The radio competes with the tortilla machine for dominance.*]

Tudi (*seeing* Carlos, *he signals for him to come closer*). It's about time . . . what took you so long?
Carlos. I was getting some fresh air; it's too hot in here . . .
Oscar. There, what'd I tell you . . . the rot . . . it starts nights . . .
Elias. Shut up!!
Tudi. Well, get back to work! We have orders to fill and the night is half over, and we've just begun!
Oscar. You're lucky, man . . . you're just lucky. Isn't that right, Nica?
Nora. Hello, Carlitos. Hello. How's your Mama?
Oscar. What a memory!
Nora. Lucky boy, lucky boy.
Carlos (*back at his post, he rinses out the maize*). I'm fine, Nora . . . I'm just fine! How are you?

[*Blackout. End of scene one.*]

Scene 2

The orphanage where Carlos *lives with his foster parents,* Hermano Gil *and* Bertina. *It is a large, rambling house with about twenty-five children and teen-agers and two frazzled adults. The orphans are not*

juvenile delinquents, merely displaced and disoriented people.
Carlos's room is set off from the main house. It is a small junk-filled
closet / shed that serves as a storage area and utility rooom, as well
as Carlos's *room. Spread about the room are boxes full of cloth*
remnants, paper, old toys, and empty luggage; up against the wall,
near Carlos's *bed, are some old picture frames, an old hoe, and some*
posters, as well as a beat-up, much-used vacuum cleaner. Nonetheless,
despite its disarray, the room has a certain personal coziness, as if
someone has tried his best to make a living space of his own and half
succeeded. There is a small night table next to the bed and a chest of
drawers nearby. On the table is an old decorated cigar box, with
CARLOS written on the outside. It is Carlos's *private property and*
personal joy. Inside the box are an old dried feather, a small fossil,
a large rubber band tied into a series of amazing knots, a soft red
handkerchief, two glass marbles, and a picture of a sickly old woman
in black. It is a picture of Isa, Carlos's *guardian after the death of*
his mother, whom he hardly knew. Carlos *is sleeping. It is about six*
a.m. He has not been in bed very long. A man is singing. It is
Hermano Gil. *He is a short, smallish man who works in the kitchen*
of a Mexican restaurant. He is energetic and sprightly despite the
hour and his obvious inebriation. He has a dark complexion that
seems even darker in the half-light.

The house is asleep for the most part, and the lights have a dim,
early-morning quality. Carlos *sleeps in a twisted position. Suddenly,*
the door opens to his room, and his foster father, Hermano Gil,
wanders in, looking for something in the dark room. He accidentally
falls against the sleeping Carlos. Hermano Gil *gets up and continues*
his search for a suitcase of his that is somewhere in the room.

Hermano Gil. This is the last time I'll bother you, any one of
you . . . this time I'm leaving for good! I'll take a job as a singer.
(*He sings a few bars from a Mexican love ballad in Spanish.*) I'll
come up in the world at last. Half my life spent in someone
else's kitchen, cleaning up. That's no kind of life. Then I have
to come home to a house full of strangers. I told Bertina, "Don't
do it, Bert." I said, "I can't take it." She didn't listen. "I can't
be a father to the entire world; we have a daughter of our own.
Isn't that enough, woman? I'm leaving . . . I'm leaving . . . "

Carlos (*he has awakened and is sitting up on the bed, listening*).
Papa, wait, don't leave!

Hermano Gil. I'm not your Papa . . . let me pack.

Carlos (*in a tired and sleepy voice*). We'll miss you, Papa!

Denise Chávez 655

Hermano Gil. I have to leave. I can't go on living in a hallway in a house full of lost children. What am I talking about? I just work in a kitchen. (*looking at Carlos*) You're nothing to me!

Carlos. Don't say that, Papa. We love you!

Hermano Gil. All my life in a kitchen . . . for what? To run a house for stray dogs and cats . . . all my money going to feed twenty-five hungry mouths . . . as if Bertina and Cotil and I didn't have our own problems.

[Hermano Gil *sits down on the edge of the bed. He puts his hand on the side of his head and sighs. He is holding a ragged suitcase. As* Hermano Gil *is bemoaning his fate, he accidentally knocks over* Carlos's *cigarbox, and the contents fall to the floor.* Carlos *scrambles to retrieve the objects, but* Hermano Gil *has swooped them up and holds them in his dark and unsteady hands.*]

Carlos. Papa!

Hermano Gil. So why do you keep this junk? Isn't there enough here already to crowd into your life?

Carlos. These are *my* things—they mean something to *me*! They remind me of people and places and times I've loved. They're alive to me.

Hermano Gil. This seashell is dead, son. There was a life here once, but where is it now? Show me, if you can. Can it talk to you? Can it tell you how it feels to be buried in the sand and come up to the sky as a rock, a hardened thing, an outline of something that was once alive? No, son, these are dead things— they have no use. You keep them because you are a silly dreamer like I used to be and because you make up stories to pass away your silly time. Like how you are going to be a singer and come up in the world . . . (*Referring to his own broken life,* Hermano Gil *breaks down and cries.* Carlos *comforts him.* Hermano Gil *wipes his eyes and looks at the knots in the rubber band.*) This game of knots, this game of glass. Of what use is it? (*He cries a bit more and then looks at the picture.*) Who is this old pan face? She has the skin of an old wrinkled prune . . . This is what I mean, Carlitos! Your name is Carlos; I forget with all the names. I forget, son, so many people pass through here and go away with not so much as a thank you for the food. They leave their mugres[11]—stuff, son, stuff—behind for us to collect and store

---

11. **mugres** (moo'grehs).

in this room. (*He looks at the feather and the rock.*) What is this? What does this mean? This dirty old bird feather and this rock?

Carlos. It's not a rock, Papa; it's a fossil.

Hermano Gil. It's a dirty old rock and this is a chicken feather! Like the ones whose necks I used to wring when I was a boy . . . (*He imitates the wringing of a chicken's neck.*) Squawk!

Carlos. It's a seashell.

Hermano Gil. So it is, Juanito.

Carlos. Carlos, Papa . . . Let me have my things, please, Papa . . . please.

Hermano Gil (*referring to the photograph*). This is the deadest thing of all, in black, like a spider.

Carlos. That's Isa, my mother's aunt. She took care of me when Mama died.

Hermano Gil (*touched*). Here, son . . . (*He puts the objects on the bed.*) Keep your treasures. You may be a fool, but you have a heart, and no man—not even the worst of us— can go against that. Keep your treasures. You'll need them out there in the world. Keep your feathers, your rocks, and your old lady's knotted life. (*He gets up.*) I don't want anything to do with strangers anymore. You've worn me out. I'm tired of trying to feed and clothe the world.

[Carlos *takes his things and puts them back in the box. Then he goes to the chest of drawers and puts the box on top of it, under some clothing, just as* Cotil *comes in.* Cotil *is a conniving young lady of fifteen, who besides being prone to fits of unthinking and unsolicited malice, is a chubby romantic.*]

Cotil. Hiding things again, lazy boy?

Carlos. Good morning, Cotil.

Cotil. Papa, Mama wants you to get ready for work.

Hermano Gil. I told you, I'm leaving. This is it, Cotil. You're the only flesh and blood of mine in this infernal household. Why should I remain the father of this faceless screaming brood? Tell me!

Cotil. Mama wants you to come and eat, or the atole[12] will get cold.

Hermano Gil. EAT? Child, how can I eat the fruit of my labor with a mouth full of sand? Let the maggots take it!

---

12. **atole** (ah-toh'leh): hot corn cereal.

Cotil. Papa, you better go before Mama comes to get you. And you, lazy boy, get up. You've already slept long enough.

Hermano Gil. Leave him alone.

Cotil. If I do, Papa, he'll sleep all day.

Hermano Gil. He's one of the few people that works around here. Let him rest! Go away!

Cotil. I'll tell Mama!

Hermano Gil. Tell her . . . tell her!

Cotil. You'd better get up, Carlos. I'll tell Mama you steal and hide things. I'll show her where you put them.

Hermano Gil. Out, out!

Cotil. He's got you believing him, Papa!

Hermano Gil. Flesh of my flesh, blood of my blood . . . (Cotil *exits with a wicked smile.* Hermano Gil *rises and gets ready to go to breakfast.*) Can you put away the suitcase, Carlitos? I am a bit hungry, now that I think about it. Carlos, you and me, we'll go away someday, just the two of us, just the two of us old fossils and we'll never come back . . .

Bertina (*yelling from the kitchen*). Gil, honey, come on. Come and have breakfast, or you'll be late for work.

Hermano Gil (*speaking to* Carlos). We'll have to make a few plans before we can leave . . . I'm coming . . . I'm coming, Bert!

Carlos. I'm sorry, Papa; I'll help you. I'll go away and become rich, and I'll send you lots of money. I'll make you happy.

Hermano Gil. Ha! Go back to bed and dream some more, son. Rub your magic things together and pray for someone to show you the way. Ask for money first, then loaves of bread and fish. Pray for rain, boy. This is New Mexico and our souls are dry! No, boy, go back to bed, but first put up the suitcase, so I'll know where to find it the next time . . . Thanks, son . . . (Hermano Gil *pauses in the doorway.*) It's so nice, so nice to believe in miracles . . . so keep your dried-out turkey feathers, who knows . . . who really knows . . .

[Bertina *is at the door, with* Cotil *beside her.* Bertina *is in her early fifties, a plump, kindly woman who is gracious and tactful.*]

Cotil. I told you, Mama. I told you they were talking and plotting, making all kinds of plans. Carlos is a troublemaker, Mama. I've always told you that.

Hermano Gil. Hello, Bert. Good morning to my dear and beloved wife and darling daughter.

Cotil. Carlos is a snake, Mama!

Hermano Gil. Shut up, my darling girl. Now go run and sharpen your tongue while your Mama and I eat breakfast.

Bertina. Go on, Cotil; your father is hungry.

Cotil. But MAMA!

Bertina. I only say things once. You know that. What would you like for breakfast, Gilito?

Hermano Gil. I thought you decided already. You take care of things like that, Bert. You always do.

Bertina. We'll start with a little atole . . . chile . . . (*They exit.*)

Cotil. What about Carlos? He's still in bed, Mama!

Hermano Gil. Let the world sleep! I'm going to have my atolito. You have all day to run your mother ragged, Cotil. I don't know how she does it. I don't know how you do it, Bert. A house full of children, both young and old.

Bertina. I love them as I love you, Gilito . . . that's all. We're all God's children . . .

Hermano Gil. But twenty-five!!

Cotil (*standing at the door to* Carlos's *room*). I saw you hide that box, Carlitos Warlitos. Such a good boy wouldn't have secrets.

Carlos. I don't!

Cotil. Then show me what's in the box!

Carlos. They're personal things.

Cotil. Nothing is personal in this house.

Carlos. Let me sleep!

Cotil. You're a lazy orphan, and my Mama and Papa don't really love you. They only put up with you because you don't have parents or a house.

Carlos. Leave me alone . . . please, Cotil.

Cotil. I'll never leave you alone—never!

Carlos. You hate me, don't you?

Cotil. Yes! You orphan!

Carlos (*sitting on the bed*). Why? Why? I haven't done anything to you!

Cotil. You think you're better than us.

Carlos. No, I don't!

Cotil. You have secrets!

Carlos. Why do you hate me so much, Cotil? (*It is a tense, electric moment.*)

Cotil. I don't know . . . but I do! (*She slams the door and leaves.*

Denise Chávez 659

She thinks twice about it and returns.) Get up, you lazy, yawning nobody, or I'll tell Mama about your secrets!

[Cotil *exits and leaves* Carlos *very hurt and stunned.*]

Carlos. What have I done that everyone hates me? I'm quiet and I work hard and all they do is yell at me. Get to work! Get to work! You better straighten up and show respect! I don't understand. Who can tell me what's going wrong? (Carlos *goes to the chest of drawers and removes the box from underneath the clothing. He looks at the photograph and then at the fossil.*) Hello, Isa. What can you tell me today? Gone to see some friends? And you, Carlos, do you have any friends? (*Thinking aloud,* Carlos *remembers* Mr. Juan.) Where are you now, Mr. Juan? (*remembering* The Tortilla Man's *words*) He said they'll try and stop you. They'll try but they can't . . . because for some reason, a person wants to keep growing . . . (Carlos *goes back to sleep.*)

Scene 3

Early the next evening, outside the factory. The workers have not yet arrived. We can hear whispers in the distance.

Elias. I'm here behind the building. To the right. Did you have any trouble?
Cotil. I had to sneak out of the house.
Elias. Will you get into trouble?
Cotil. Oh, no! I can do just about anything and my Mama won't care. She likes me. I'm the favorite.
Elias. What about your Papa?
Cotil. What about him? He does what my Mama says.
Elias (*coming closer to* Cotil, *he puts his arms around her*). Cotil, how are you?
Cotil (*moving away*). We don't have much time. Is everything ready?
Elias. Yes, Cotil. Oscar and I have gone over the plans many times. There's no doubt that we'll get Carlos—and good this time. Who does he think he is, walking all over Oscar and me like we were rocks under his feet?
Cotil. He's that way. He needs to be taught a lesson. He strolls through our house like he owns it, like he was my own true brother.

Elias. I'm glad I'm not your brother! Why don't you stay awhile?

Cotil. I have to go or Mama will get suspicious. You see, lucky for us, Carlos left the house to do an errand for Papa, and I snuck into his room and got this . . . (*She brings* Carlos's *cigar box from behind her back and shows it to* Elias.) See, it says CARLOS on it. That way, when the robbery is reported, everyone will figure he stole the stuff.

Elias. I'm glad you came, my dove, my little sunshine.

Cotil. Let's get on with it, okay?

Elias. Okay, okay. This is the plan: after work we stick around, Oscar and I. He opens the locks—he's real good at that—then we go into the office and fool around the safe. We mess up the room and leave. When Tudi comes in tomorrow morning, he sees Carlos's box and he figures out who broke in.

Cotil. Are you sure it'll work?

Elias. Aren't I Elias Macias? Hey, babe, by tomorrow Carlos will be fired. We'll have put him in his place. It's taken time to settle accounts with that goody-goody. Say, babe, can't you stay awhile?

Cotil. I have to get home. I just wanted to make sure everything is going okay.

Elias. Will you think of me?

Cotil. I do every night, Elias, just before I go to sleep.

Elias. Really?

Cotil. Yeah, now go on . . . listen to the radio . . . for a sign from me . . .

Elias. Cotil, the guys don't believe I have a girlfriend. How come you don't want to go out with me in public? (Cotil *looks away from him with an annoyed expression.*) Well, okay . . . until tomorrow. We'll celebrate the downfall of that plaster saint. There's no one worse than someone who smiles a lot with phony goodness . . . Goodnight, Cotil.

Cotil. Goodbye. Make sure that all goes well. (*She exits.*)

Elias. My Cotil . . . will you dedicate a song for me tonight? Ay! (*He sighs and exits with* Carlos's *box.*)

[*It is now about eight p.m. Everyone starts to arrive. By the side of the road stand four old women in black, who later become* The Birds, Tin, Tan, Ton, *and* Mabel.]

Woman One (*referring to the boys coming in for work at the tortilla factory*). Those boys, it's disgraceful . . .
Woman Two. Where is he?
Woman Three. Who?
Woman Four. The boy.
Woman Two. I don't see him.
Woman One. The rascally thin one, over there, over there.
Woman Four. His parents were killed when he was nothing . . .
Woman One. He was very small, wrinkled from his mother . . .
Woman Three. Full of his father's sweat . . .
Woman Two. They were killed?
Woman Four. He's always been alone, like the sore on the side of the mouth, turned inside with a life of its own . . .
Woman One. There he goes . . .
Woman Two. Who?
Woman Four. He's all alone . . .
Woman Three. The boy . . .

[*The boys come up.* Tudi *is the first to arrive. He opens up the tortilla factory, turns on the lights and the machines.* Bennie *and* Oscar *are behind him, followed by* Carlos *and* Elias. Nora *wanders in last.* Elias *is carrying a paper bag with the cigar box inside. He and* Oscar *wink to each other.*]

Tudi. Hello, boys!
All. Hello, Tudi!
Carlos. How are you, Tudi?
Tudi. I just said hello.
Nora. Hello, hello. I'm fine.
Tudi. I'm ready for work. How about everyone else?

[*Various grumbles, moans, sighs, and a belch can be heard.*]

Oscar. I'm ready to go out on the town, to do anything but slave in this furnace.
Elias (*looking at* Oscar). We'll have to set off some fireworks later on, eh, Oscar? Won't we?
Tudi. What's this? All of a sudden two fighting dogs become friends. It must be the end of the world.
Elias. We've come to an understanding.
Oscar. Some common ground.
Tudi. Probably some common hate. Don't forget about rule number three: socializing too much.

Oscar. Oh, yes, sir, Mr. Tudi.

Nora. Hello, hello, hello. I'm fine.

Tudi. Okay, okay, let's get to work. (*Talking to* Oscar) Are you setting up, Oscar?

Elias. Yes, we've got it all worked out . . . right, Oscar?

Tudi. Ready, Carlos . . . Nora?

Nora. Ready, Tudi, ready.

Carlos. I'm glad to see you and Oscar have become friends, Elias.

Tudi. Something must be wrong.

Elias. Finally something is right. We discovered a way to settle old debts.

Tudi. Get to work, you bums. We've been here ten minutes and you haven't done a bit of work. Hurry up there, Nora!

Nora. Okay, Tudi, I hurry.

Oscar. Here it comes, folks . . . THE TORTILLA EXPRESS!!

[*The action is speeded up. The machines roar, night goes by. Suddenly, it is early morning and the work is done.* Tudi *is beginning to turn off the lights and lock up.*]

Elias. Hey, Oscar, did you hear about Neno?

Oscar. What happened, man?

Elias. You were right.

Tudi. You guys must really be sick. Are you actually agreeing with him, Elias?

Elias. Neno's got the corn rot.

Oscar. He does?

Carlos. What's this, Elias? What's wrong?

Elias. Neno's got the rot. He's in bed. He's really sick. They don't know if he's going to make it.

Tudi. He was always sickly. The first time I saw him he looked like a stale sausage, very dark with bloody eyes. He was never healthy.

Oscar. I've said it again and again . . . it'll get you sooner or later. It gets into your blood after awhile and then there's no going back. You're lost.

Carlos. Neno is really sick? We should go see him.

Elias. Not me! I might get the rot from being near him.

Oscar. He was never a friend of mine. Too puny and dark.

Elias. I never knew him that well.

Nora. Nora all finished with work. She go home.

Denise Chávez 663

Carlos. I'll walk you, Nora.

Oscar. Uuucheee, it's too funny!

Elias. They're sweethearts, Oscar!

Tudi. Get out of here, you worms! I haven't got all day to put up with a bunch of lazy, rascally caterpillars. I have to lock up.

Carlos (*speaking gently to* Nora). Neno's sick.

Nora. Where's Nenito?

Oscar. Why do you bother with her? She can't understand you. One . . . two . . . three . . . four . . . five . . . six . . . seven . . . eight . . . nine . . . ten . . . eleven . . . twelve—that's all she understands. The two of you keep trying to make sense, and no one can understand.

Carlos. Let's go, Nora.

Nora. Goodbye, my friends.

Tudi. Go on, I have my work to do.

Carlos. Have a nice day, Tudi!

Tudi. Haven't you left yet?

Elias. I'm going.

Tudi. Well, hurry up!

Elias. Bye, you guys.

Carlos. Bye, Elias.

Elias (*to* Oscar). Hey, man, I'll walk with you.

Tudi. So goodbye already . . . this must be the end of the world.

Oscar. Let's go.

[*They exit and disappear around the building. They wait until* Tudi *has locked up and has gone.* Carlos *and* Nora *have left.* Oscar *and* Elias *emerge from the shadows and furtively slip into the doorway.* Oscar *begins fiddling with the door lock.*]

Elias. Where'd you learn that?

Oscar. You think I've been making tortillas all my life? I'm a T.V.I.[13] graduate.

Elias. I never knew you were so smart, Oscar.

Oscar. Haven't I told you all this time?

Elias. But who listens?

Oscar. Did Cotil come?

Elias. She gave me something that will put our Carlos in real trouble. See, it's a box with his name on it. When we get inside

---

13. **T.V.I.:** abbreviation of Technical and Vocational Institute.

the office, we'll drop it on the floor for Tudi to find. It's all settled. We'll get him yet!

[*They go inside quietly. Once they open the office door, they rummage around the room, dropping the box, and then leave as quietly and as quickly as possible. While they have been doing this,* Nora *has returned, looking for* Neno. *She sees what is going on but does not fully comprehend its significance. She slips away. Meanwhile,* Carlos *has returned to wait for* The Tortilla Man *under the same stoop. He is tired and sleepy. He sits back, leaning up against the door, and falls into a heavy sleep. He hears the sounds of voices, then a solitary voice—first far away, then near. It is a soothing, melodious voice, the type one hears in dreams. It has a sweet clarity and richness that comes from a height and flows past the dreamer until it is there beside him.* Carlos *feels a coolness and a movement but is unsure of where he is. Suddenly he feels a warm tingling sensation on his face.* Carlos *is startled and jumps up. This sudden movement jars him out of the dream. He is now awake.*]

Carlos. Where am I? (*Although he finds himself in mid-air, on a smooth disc, he is reassured to see* The Tortilla Man.)

Tortilla Man. Don't be impudent, boy. Where do you think you are?

Carlos. Where am I?

Tortilla Man. Why do you ask so many questions? Just look around. Open your eyes and really see. We're flying over the Rio Grande now.

Carlos. We are??? (*He jumps around and makes the Flying Tortilla take a nose dive*).

Tortilla Man. I wouldn't do that if I were you, Carlosssssss . . . (The Tortilla Man *looks nervous, but quickly regains control of the ship.* Carlos *holds on for dear life. He is glued to the firm spongy mass under him and stares, wide-eyed. The Flying Tortilla is a flat spongy disc about six feet across and four feet wide. It is a blue color, with multicolored spots. Tough and durable, it has been made by a Master Tortilla Maker,* Mr. Juan *himself. It has no seats to speak of, just two slightly raised air pockets that serve as seats.* The Tortilla Man *is wearing a historical costume of the fifteenth century, complete with armor. He looks proud and distinguished and a bit older than before. On the side of the Flying Tortilla is a flag of an unknown country with a feather on top. At the sides are rudders of dough. In the middle are several large sacks of baking powder, used to raise and* *lower the ship, much like the sand bags used in balloons. Once airborne, the Magic Blue Corn Tortilla floats on air currents and the occasional boost from various birds who happen to be flying by.)* You should never do that, Carlos!

Carlos. Are we on an airplane or a ship?

Tortilla Man. I must have asked questions, too, when I was a boy, so I'll have to be patient. Yes, we are on a ship. The Magic Flying Blue Corn Tortilla. There seems to be no satisfying you with answers . . . that's good. Yes, Carlos, right now we are . . . let me see . . . *(The Tortilla Man looks at a compass, checks the feather, and moistens his finger with saliva, then holds it up a foot or so from his face.)* We are about two miles due west of Cuchillo as the birds fly.

Carlos *(embracing The Tortilla Man with a mixture of fear and glee).* We are?

Tortilla Man. Boy, once you get over your wonder, you can start dealing with life. Sit up there . . . you're slouched over like you're afraid.

Carlos *(peering over the edge of the Flying Tortilla).* I am!

Tortilla Man. You, my young explorer, afraid of this . . . *(The Tortilla Man begins to jump up and down on the tortilla).*

Carlos *(begging The Tortilla Man to stop).* Oh please, Mr. Juan, won't you stop doing that? I think I'll just sit here, if you don't mind.

Tortilla Man. This isn't like you, Carlos. We're on an adventure. You just can't sit there and watch the birds fly by. You have to jump in or, in this case, fly on . . .

Carlos. How far up are we?

Tortilla Man. About three cloud lengths and a half . . . I can check . . . *(He makes a motion to go to the back of the ship.)*

Carlos. No, that isn't necessary. Is this . . . a . . . tortilla?

Tortilla Man. Nothing but the best for me . . . blue corn.

Carlos. How does it fly?

Tortilla Man. Up, Carlos, up! Now then, here we have the front and lateral rudders. I had a lot of trouble perfecting them. It seems the birds would fly by and nibble on them between meals. Lost a lot of rudders that way. I used to carry a parachute for safety. But since I've put those letters on the side, it's been better.

Carlos. M.F.T.V.F. What does it mean, Mr. Juan?

Tortilla Man. Glad to see you relaxing, Carlos. I hate to see tense young people. Why, those letters mean MAGIC FLYING TORTILLA VERY FATTENING. Birds are very conscious of their figures. To an extreme you might say. They never stop talking about it, but oh, how they love to eat! You don't do that, do you, Carlos?

Carlos. Do you really talk to the birds?

Tortilla Man. Yes, and usually in a loud voice. They're hard of hearing. I talk to them when I have time. We're always so busy. Now for the rest of the tour. How you do ask questions! The best thing is not to ask but to listen. You'll find out things much faster that way. Not enough listening these days. Here is my flag, Carlos. My compass and baking powder bags. (*He pauses and looks at* Carlos.) I'm waiting for questions.

Carlos. What flag is that?

Tortilla Man. Why it's my own, of course. It's the flag of growth. (*The flag is in burnt desert colors. It shows the mountains, the rivers, and the plants of the desert. In the forefront is a plant with its root system exposed.*) This is the land, dry and burnt. To someone who doesn't know its ways, it is like thirst—there is no in-between. Our land is a land of mountains and rivers, dry things and growing things. Our roots are in the earth and we feel the nourishment of the sky. This is *my* flag . . . what's yours?

Carlos. I don't have a flag of my own.

Tortilla Man. You don't? Well, then you shall have to make one.

Carlos (*discovering his box on the Flying Tortilla*). My cigar box! What is it doing here?

Tortilla Man. You were thinking about it, perhaps?

Carlos. Why, that's my feather up there with your flag!

Tortilla Man. I needed a compass. You see, birds tell the direction by the way their feathers blow, and besides, it's a nice feather.

Carlos. My father calls it an old ugly chicken feather.

Tortilla Man. Has he ever had his own feather? (Carlos *shakes his head no.*) Well, then, how would he know?

Carlos. It *is* an old feather!

Tortilla Man. Don't let the birds hear you say that. They may never forgive us! They don't exactly hold grudges, but it'll go better for us if we keep on their good side; the other side can be most uncomfortable. They give us a push now and then when the air current is low, so we can really use their help. You see, we fly by current. I ignite special minerals and then sprinkle that mixture over baking powder and whoosh! We are off! The staying up part is the only thing I've never really quite figured out yet.

Carlos. Ohhhh! (*He looks down fearfully.*) How do you land?

Tortilla Man. By dropping bags of powder much the way a balloon drops sand.

Carlos. But, Mr. Juan, that's not the way it works!

Tortilla Man. It isn't? Oh, what does it matter? Why must everything work the same way for everybody?

Carlos. All of this is hard to believe.

Tortilla Man. Just look down there . . . isn't it breathtaking? That's my trail down there. The Juan de Oñate Trail.[14] That's the way I came up through Mexico and all the way north to Santa Fe. When I came through here, there was nothing . . . Imagine that!

Carlos. Oñate, the explorer? We learned about him in school. He was from Spain, but he came up from Mexico to explore. He was a conquistador. I did a report on him.

Tortilla Man. Him? You mean me!

Carlos. You? But you're The Tortilla Man, Mr. Juan.

Tortilla Man. So I am.

Carlos. How can you be two people at once? Mexican and Spanish? Modern and old?

Tortilla Man. Carlos, my boy, when are you going to stop asking questions? Too many questions! (*He pushes out two bags of baking powder.*) We're going to land and walk around. (*He adjusts the compass.*) Now then, take a seat, Carlos. The landing may be a bit rough. I think a bird heard you earlier.

Carlos. You mean about the feather?

Tortilla Man. Ssshhh! Birds are terrible spellers, so kindly spell out that word henceforth. Very good diction but lousy spellers. (*The Magic Tortilla floats down and lands on a rocky hill.*) I thought you'd like this place. I understand you collect fossils.

Carlos. Yes, I do!

Tortilla Man. Well, look around you, Carlos. We have some good ones here. This used to be under water many, many years

---

14. **Juan de Oñate Trail** (hwahn deh oh-nyah'teh): route of the Spanish explorer Juan de Oñate.

ago. All of this was once part of a great vast ocean.

Carlos. Where are we now?

Tortilla Man. It's hard to believe, I know, but we are at the bottom of the sea! Find your fossil. We have all the time in the world. Find your fossil!

[*They stand together a moment.* Carlos *picks up a fossil and puts it in his cigar box. They wander about collecting fossils for a while and then reboard the ship and head due north to an area of white sand. The* Tortilla Man *has brought a lunch, and they take a break. They collect some sand, which* Carlos *puts in his box, then head back to Cuchillo.*]

Tortilla Man. It's getting late, Carlos. Are you tired? We must go on . . .

Carlos. I could never be tired with you, Mr. Juan. I'm too happy.

Tortilla Man. You're a good boy, Carlos.

Carlos. That's the problem! I don't want to be a good boy! I want to be a person. Nobody really likes good boys.

Tortilla Man. That *is* a problem. I see what you mean. It seems you can't be too good or too bad. It's hard. The solution is just to be yourself. Be truthful, and you won't have to worry about being at any far end. You'll be in the middle with yourself.

Carlos. But it's so hard!

Tortilla Man. When will you learn not to be impudent, boy! Trust me, and trust yourself above all. Here we are!

[*They drag the Flying Tortilla with a rope that is attached. They then sit by the side of the river, happy but exhausted.*]

Carlos. I want this time to last forever!

Tortilla Man. It will, my friend, but shhh! Let's listen to the birds. They're talking . . . see, there they are on the Magic Flying Tortilla . . .

[*The* Four Old Women, *now* Birds, *peck at the Flying Tortilla.*]

Ton. I'm hungry, Tin . . .

Tin. Me too, Ton.

Tan. I haven't eaten in days.

Mabel. Weeks . . .

Ton. Months . . .

Tin. Years . . .

Tan. When was it, anyway?

Mabel. When The Flying Tortilla Man was on his way South . . .

Ton. I don't know if I would have lasted if he hadn't come by . . .

Tin. I was dying for even a moldy, dried-out crust, a few crumbs . . . anything!

Tan. How about a nice big juicy earthworm?

Mabel. I'm a vegetarian.

Ton. Against your religion, eh?

Mabel. No, against my waistline.

Tin. Always prancing about with her airs she is!

Ton. Look who's talking!

Tin. What about you, Ton-Tona?

Ton. Don't call me that, please.

Tin. Against your religion?

Tan. Oh, yes, a nice big juicy baked earthworm would be nice, with lots of gravy and a bird's nest salad . . . (*She cries out.*) Bird does not live by bread alone!

Mabel. Stop it! I feel faint!

Tan. Can it be? Can it be? Oh, dear, The Tortilla Man is coming back this way. He's spotted us. See him, Mabel? Girls, take courage. Here he comes. (*They all bow.*) Oh, great Tortilla Man!

Ton. Image of hope, blessed Tortilla!

Tin. Blessed be the Holy Name of Tortilla.

Mabel. Thank you, Mr. Juan. (*She stuffs her face with some tortilla.*) Food!

Tin. Now who's watching her figure?

Tan. Not me, I don't have problems!

Ton. Nor me!

Mabel. You're all as crazy as magpies!

Tin. That's a terrible insult, Mabel!

Tan. Will you be quiet! They're just about ready to take off, and I'm still hungry! I'm still so hungry I can't think or move!

Ton (*speaking to the others*). She never could!

Mabel. Girls, please, we have to be off. Mr. Juan is nearly ready to leave. Settle down and get in formation. That's right!

[*They dress right and do a drill. Then, they fly off.*]

Birds. Thank you, Mr. Juan!

Tortilla Man (*as he inspects the ship*). Rudders don't look too damaged. Really, those birds are all right, Carlos. They do give me a push now and then. Now hop aboard . . . we have to go home.

Carlos. Do we have to, Mr. Juan?

Tortilla Man. We have things to do. We have our work, our families. And there's the fiesta coming up. I have to get ready for that.

Carlos. I don't have a real family, and I'm so tired of making tortillas!

Tortilla Man. There you go again. It's not what you do but how you do it. And as for having a family, you have people who love you . . . and you have yourself. So many people don't have themselves, Carlos. So what does it matter how many brothers and sisters you have? Why all of us are brothers and sisters!

Carlos. I've heard all those things before!

Tortilla Man. Yes, but did you listen to them? Or ask yourself *why* people were saying such things? Now be still with yourself and don't talk about you know what—because our friends might be listening. They might think we're saying one thing when we really mean another. Carlos, are you tired? Rest there on the Magic Tortilla. Before you know it, we'll be in Cuchillo. Close your eyes, sleep, sleep!

[Carlos *is getting sleepy, almost against his will.*]

Carlos. I'm not really sleepy. It's been the happiest day of my life!

Tortilla Man. Stretch out there and rest!

Carlos. Just for a moment, Mr. Juan. A little nap, that's all I need. You won't leave me, will you?

Tortilla Man. No, I won't leave you, ever . . . remember these things, Carlitos, and sleep, sleep . . .

Carlos (*in a far away voice*). Mr. Juan, where's my box? I had it right here . . .

Tortilla Man. Sleep . . . you need it, boy, to be strong . . .

Scene 4

Outside the factory the next morning. Carlos *wakes to find himself in the same position he was in on the Flying Tortilla. His body is*

Denise Chávez 671

cold and cramped. *He is surprised to find himself on the steps of the tortilla factory.* Tudi *shakes him as* Oscar *and* Elias *stand nearby.*

Tudi. Wake up! Wake up, you rascal!

Carlos. Mr. Juan, where is my box? I had it right here.

Elias. There you are, Tudi. He admits his guilt.

Oscar. It was Carlos who broke into your office, Tudi, and tried to get in the safe.

Elias. Oscar and I were walking by and noticed the lights were still on. Then we saw Carlos sleeping here. That's when we called you, Tudi.

Tudi. Thank you, boys! I'll make it up to you. Fortunately, the snake wasn't able to get into the safe, but he sure made a mess of things. How did you get in, Carlos? Oh, you're going to be sorry that you ever saw this place. You'll never forget this day!

Carlos. I don't understand. I was with Mr. Juan!

Elias. Don't lie to us, you thief!

Oscar. He's a sneaky one. Don't believe him, Tudi.

Elias. I'm very surprised, Tudi. He always seemed so good.

Carlos. I don't understand all this . . . what's happening?

Tudi. Don't lie to me, Carlos. And here I was thinking of promoting you. Vandal, you broke into my office and tried to rob my safe; and when you couldn't break in, you made a mess of things!

Elias. And you dropped this . . . (*He shows off* Carlos's *cigar box.*)

Carlos. My box, where did you find it?

Oscar. He admits it! Remember this, Elias. We're witnesses!

Elias. We'll sue! Won't we, Tudi?

Tudi. We'll sue! You'll be sorry you were ever born. They'll probably send you to the boys' home in Springer.

Oscar. Not that!

Elias. That's where all the hardened criminals go. A cousin of mine is there, so I know.

Carlos. You're all wrong! I wasn't here at all. I was flying with Mr. Juan.

Elias. Who is this Mr. Juan, anyway?

Carlos. He's a friend of mine.

Oscar. Listen to that story, would you, Tudi!

Tudi. Stop lying to us, Carlos. You're making up these crazy stories to lead us off the track.

Carlos. You've got it all wrong. I can show you. Give me the box, please.

Elias. Oh no, that's important evidence.

Oscar. If you were flying around, show us your wings. Show us your wings! That's a funny one!

Tudi. Let's go!

Carlos. Where? I'm not guilty. I tell you, I'm not guilty!

Tudi. This is a matter for the Sheriff's Office.

Oscar (*he turns to* Carlos, *almost impressed*). You little thief, you've hit the big time!

Elias. Is Fatty in today? I thought he went fishing on Wednesdays.

Tudi. The law is always at hand.

Oscar. What does that mean?

Tudi. Sounds good, doesn't it?

Carlos. But you have it all wrong!

Oscar. Man, if I were you, I'd start praying. No one can face Fatty Campbell and not feel helpless fear.

Tudi. Go on, march. March, there. Go on, march! Oscar, you run ahead and tell Bertina and Hermano Gil. They'll want to hear about this. Tell them to meet us at the Sheriff's Office. Forward now, to justice!

Scene 5

The Sheriff's Office. It is near the Plaza on Calle del Sol street. It consists of several rooms. The lobby has a desk and chairs and a long, orange plastic couch for visitors. A magazine rack is near the couch and has old copies of Ford Times, The Ranch News, *and last Thursday's paper. On the wall is a calendar from Corney Hawkins Olds. Next to that is a Navy picture of Company 1435, U.S. Naval Training Center, Great Lakes, Illinois, and beside that is a horseshoe and a picture of President John F. Kennedy.*

Fatty. Where were you the night of the 10th?

Carlos. With Mr. Juan.

Elias. There he goes again with that fabulous story.

Fatty (*He admonishes* Elias). Whoa there, boy. Order in the court. What do you mean speaking out of turn!

Elias. Tell us the truth now, Carlos!

Carlos. *I have* been telling the truth.

Bertina. No child of mine was ever a disgrace to our home, son.

Hermano Gil. Please, Carlos, tell Mr. Fatty the truth.

Fatty. Order, order in the court! (Elias, Bertina, Hermano Gil *and the others settle down and look at* Fatty.) Ahem. It's about time. (*To* Carlos) Were you not found near the scene of the crime by these two young fellows? (*He peers at* Elias *and* Oscar *very closely.*) I think I know you two from somewhere.

Carlos. Yes, I was, Mr. Fatty. I fell asleep with Mr. Juan, and he must have carried me back to the factory.

Fatty. *Who* is this mysterious Mr. Juan?

Hermano Gil. Pay no attention to him, Sheriff.

Elias. He keeps talking about a Mr. Juan who flies.

Tudi. He's unstable. That's all there is to it. He needs help.

Bertina. Oh, shut your mouth, Tudi.

Hermano Gil. Bertina, my love . . . Bert, settle down.

Carlos. Mr. Juan is a friend of mine.

Tudi. It's all your fault, Bertina! I shouldn't have listened to you and given the boy a chance at the factory. Now look what he's done! He's ruined my business.

Bertina. It's not *your* business, you little toad. Nothing was stolen, your honor.

Hermano Gil. My love, please.

Fatty. Settle down, folks. I know emotions run high, but this is a court of law . . . and I am the law. Settle down there, folks!

Hermano Gil. Can we settle this out of court, Mr. Fatty?

Cotil. Of course not, Papa! This is a matter of public concern.

Hermano Gil. Nothing was stolen except a bag of frozen tamales . . . that's all . . .

[Elias *looks at* Oscar, *who shrugs his shoulders as if to say, "I was hungry."*]

Tudi. That's all! I'll sue, Gil. My reputation is ruined. Have you seen that mess in the office? I'll sue! I'll sue!

Fatty. Whoa there. As judge and jury, I take the reins of the law in my hands. Having viewed the evidence and spoken to the accused and the witnesses, I now proclaim the verdict of this court, Filmore P. Campbell presiding, this eleventh day of June, in the year of, etcetera. Isn't it about time for lunch, Gil? What time do you have?

674 Denise Chávez

Bertina. He's just a boy! He never meant to hurt anyone. He's a good boy, your honor.

Elias. So what's the verdict?

Fatty. Don't I know you from somewhere, sonny?

Cotil. Mama, we have to abide by the verdict.

Hermano Gil. I can't believe a boy of mine could do this. How could you, son?

Carlos. Papa . . . you must believe me . . . I'm innocent!

Elias. As innocent as a snake!

Cotil. He's a liar, Papa. Don't you know that already?

Elias. Sentence him!

Oscar. Show no mercy!

Fatty. I hereby sentence you, Carlos Campo, to a week's labor on the Plaza, early curfew, and a fine of twenty dollars for court costs. Case closed. We have the fiesta coming up, and we'll need all the help we can get. Report at five a.m. to Fernando at the water tower. Court dismissed. (*He speaks to* Elias.) I know you from somewhere. Don't you have a cousin . . . ?

Elias. You must be thinking of someone else, Mr. Fatty.

Tudi. I demand a retrial! Who's going to clean up my office? What about the tamales? My mother made them for me, and I was taking them home. I demand a retrial!

Fatty. Go back and sell a few tortillas!

Tudi. I'll sue!

Bertina. He's just a child! Can't you understand that?

Fatty. Clear the court . . . clear the court. It's my lunchtime. Someone mention tamales?

Tudi. *This* is justice?

Fatty. Insulting the court—five dollars!

Tudi. I'll write my congressman.

Fatty. Threatening the law—ten dollars.

Tudi. Now wait a minute!

Fatty. Harassing the court—fifteen dollars.

Elias. Man, Tudi, you better leave while you can. It doesn't look good for you.

Hermano Gil. After all these years, son, how could you break your father's heart? You were my only hope, Carlos. I felt as if you were my true son, my flesh and blood. Now you're a stranger!

[*He walks away with* Bertina *and* Cotil, *who is gloating.*]

Denise Chávez 675

Cotil. Papa, I told you he was a sneak!

Carlos. Papa! I'm innocent!

Hermano Gil. Don't talk to me. Let's go, Bert.

Bertina. That's all right, son. Dinner's at six. We're having papitas con chorizo.[15]

Hermano Gil. How can anyone eat with a mouthful of sand?

Cotil. Hey, Carlos, bad luck!

Elias. Where are you going now, Cotil?

Cotil. I'm busy. I'm going home with Mama. So don't you bother me.

Elias. How can you say that to me after all I've done for you?

Cotil. You were always too young for me.

Oscar. Hey, Elias, I know something we can do.

Elias. Leave me alone, man.

Oscar. So what happened to our friendship?

Elias. I have better things to do. Out of my way.

[*They all exit.* Carlos *and* Fatty *are left in the courtroom.*]

Fatty. Come on, sonny, cheer up. It's not the end of the world. When I was a kid, I got into a few scrapes. What's it matter, huh? You want part of a tuna fish sandwich? Some chips? Now, cheer up. Here's the evidence. Don't tell anyone I gave it back to you. Run along now. I haven't got all day. I haven't eaten my lunch yet. Now, sonny, you watch those stories . . . they'll get you in a mess of trouble.

Carlos. They aren't stories . . . it's the truth! It's really the truth!

Scene 6

Carlos's *room late that night. He is sitting on the bed, when he decides to get up and get his box from the chest of drawers.*

Carlos (*looking up at the ceiling*). Where were you, Mr. Juan, when I needed you? Where are you now? Why do you always leave me? (*Dejectedly*) I am as lonely and sad as the day the men from the church carry the body of God around the Plaza in that wooden box on Good Friday. The people are all in black, singing with dried voices and moaning to themselves. They

---

15. **papitas con chorizo** (pah-pee'tahs kohn choh-ree'soh): potatoes with sausage.

stop in front of doors that are closed. He said many things but not where he was from or where he went. He comes and goes, and I want to be angry with him, but I can't. I can feel him close sometimes, when it matters. He knows, he really knows me . . . and he cares. Mr. Tortilla Man, come back. Stay awhile with your Carlos. He needs friends. Because people hate him when he is good and love him when he is bad. (*He looks down at the cigar box.*) Should I open it? What of our fossils and sand? Will they be there? (*He opens the box.*) Where are they? What's this? It's a little note. "Remember, Carlos. Your friend, Mr. Juan, The Flying Tortilla Man." That's all, just a note and this—a small hard edge of tortilla. Of what use is it? (*He throws the tortilla away and then retrieves it.*) Oh, well. It's something! He said many things, but not where he came from and where he went. He said many things . . . "Remember," he said, "remember." But what? What?

[Carlos *goes to sleep and has fitful dreams. The* Old Women / Birds *call out his name in a dream sequence. "There he is . . . who . . . ," and he sees all the people from the court scene. He wakes up in a sweat, clutching the cigar box; then he drifts off to sleep again.*]

Scene 7

The next morning in the Plaza. Carlos *is sweeping the bandstand. He looks forlorn and miserable.* Nora *comes up to him.*

Nora. What's wrong with boy?
Carlos. Hello, Nora.
Nora. What's wrong with Carlitos?
Carlos. I lost my job.
Nora. So sad. I miss Carlos at job. Oscar and Elias no like Nora—make fun all time. Neno? Neno?
Carlos. He's still very sick.
Nora. Neno! I look for him last night. Saw Oscar and Elias at the job.
Carlos. What was that, Nora?
Nora. Neno good boy—lose job? I look for him last night after Carlos walk Nora home. See Oscar and Elias make mess.
Carlos. They said I tried to break into Tudi's office last night.
Nora. Oh no, no. Oh no, that Elias and Oscar do.
Carlos. No, Nora. They said that about *me*.

Nora. Oscar and Elias go in and throw things around.

Carlos. What are you saying?

Nora. Nora see them.

Carlos. Have you told anyone?

Nora. I tell you. Nora see Elias and Oscar make mess.

Carlos (*grabbing her hand*). Let's go, Nora. Let's go see Fatty!

Nora. I don't know Fatty.

Scene 8

The Sheriff's Office.

Fatty. This is a highly unusual case. I've taken the liberty to call in two witnesses.

Carlos. Nora told us how she saw Elias and Oscar break into Tudi's office and throw things around.

Fatty. That's fine, son; but what proof do we have?

Carlos. Nora told us! She's a witness!

Fatty (*taking Carlos aside*). Son, she's not well. Loca en la cabeza.[16] You know what I mean? I think she made it up to help you. (*He speaks to Oscar and Elias.*) What do you boys say?

Elias. Carlos is trying to defend himself. It was a good try, but it won't work.

Nora. Oscar with Elias.

Oscar. Go away, Nora.

Nora. She see. She see. Elias call Oscar stupid fat boy behind his back.

Elias. Don't listen to her, Oscar. She's not all there.

Nora. Elias hate Oscar. He told me. (*She looks at Oscar.*) Say that night that you a stupid boy and he smart one.

Elias. Don't believe her, Oscar!

Oscar. Well, how do you like that! After all we've been through! You never did like me, man. He was there, Fatty. He made me do it!

Elias. You stupid fool! Why'd you take those tamales? I told you not to!

Oscar. I was hungry! Fatty, it was Elias's idea. He told me about it and asked me to help. We were trying to get back at Carlos for being such a baby. I thought Elias was my friend, but he's the type that talks about you behind your back. He's

---

16. **Loca en la cabeza** (loh'kah ehn lah kah-beh'sah): Crazy in the head.

just a lousy tortilla bum with the rot!

Elias. Will you shut up!! He's the sick one, Sheriff. He's got the rot. He's making things up!

Oscar. I'm smarter than you, Elias, you little punk. I can pick any lock I want to. What can you do besides give directions and tell people what to do? What do you know, anyway?

Nora. Carlos come back to work now?

Carlos. I was innocent all the time, Mr. Fatty.

Fatty. So it seems. The law is never tricked. Justice rules. Call Bertina, Gil, and Tudi. Court's in session. The retrial is about to begin.

Carlos. Why did you do this, Elias?

Elias. It was Cotil's idea. She made me do it. She wanted to get back at you for everything.

Oscar (*looking at* Carlos). You were always a better friend to me than Elias, Carlos.

Carlos. It's all right, Oscar. I forgive you.

Oscar. It was Elias's fault. He's full of poison blood.

Elias. It's the rot, man. I got the rot! It was Cotil made me do it . . .

Carlos. I forgive you too, Elias.

Elias. You always talked too much, Nora.

Nora. Thank you, all my friends! Go to work now?

Scene 9

The Fossil beds. Carlos *and* The Tortilla Man *are sitting on a rock shelf reviewing the past few days' events. It is a peaceful twilight in New Mexico.*

Carlos. And so, Mr. Juan, everything finally worked out. Where were you all that time? You could have told the Sheriff that I wasn't guilty.

Tortilla Man. When will you learn not to be impudent, boy? The truth of the matter is that I was getting ready for the fiesta, and anyway, you handled things pretty nicely.

Carlos. I don't know what I would have done without Nora.

Tortilla Man. I told her to take care of you.

Carlos. Do you know her?

Tortilla Man. Oh, blessed tortillas, yes! We're dear old friends. And besides, I was with you all the time. Remember that night you looked inside your cigar box? You were thinking of me, and I heard you. I said hello. I'm sorry I had to take the sand and the fossil. You see, I thought it was the best way. Things can't be too easy for us, or we don't appreciate them. We don't grow that way! Here's your fossil and the sand. (The Tortilla Man *hands them to* Carlos.) Remember me when you see them.

Carlos. Will you go away before the fiesta, Mr. Juan? Neno was to play the part of the Indian scout, Jusephe,[17] but he's still a little weak, so they asked me to take the role. This is my first time in the fiesta play. When I grow up, I want to play the part of Oñate. But how can anyone play that part, if you're the real Oñate? Why don't *you* play the part?

Tortilla Man. We'll have to work out something by that time, Carlos.

Carlos. Elias and Oscar have to work in the Plaza now, in my place, but the Sheriff is letting them take part in the parade. All of us have roles in the pageant play! Will you be in the parade? You said something about getting ready for the fiesta.

Tortilla Man. Oh, I have a very small part. Nothing that anyone couldn't play if they really wanted to.

Carlos. Will I see you?

Tortilla Man. If you don't, I shall be very sorry. Now, remember to see, not to look. I might seem a bit different from myself, but it's me. You can never really change a person inside, no matter what you do.

Carlos. Mama is making the costumes. Cotil is playing the part of a Señorita, but she still won't talk to me.

Tortilla Man. She'll get over it.

Carlos. Even if you're not good, some people still don't like you.

Tortilla Man. Remember what I said, we're all from the same country. We have the sky which covers our heads and the earth which warms our feet. We don't have time to be anywhere in between where we can't feel that power. Some people call it love. I call it I.W.A.

Carlos. I.W.A.? What does that mean?

Tortilla Man. Inside We're Alike. Now I must leave you.

Carlos. Can we go for a ride on the Flying Tortilla some time?

Tortilla Man. Anytime you like, Carlos.

---

17. **Jusephe** (hoo-seh'feh): an Indian scout who served as guide for one of Juan de Oñate's expeditions.

[*The Magic Tortilla takes off with a huge blast, and soon* Carlos *and* The Tortilla Man *are floating in space. Flash to the Plaza, the town fiesta, in honor of the founding of Cuchillo by Don Juan de Oñate. The Plaza is decorated with bright streamers and flowers, and booths completely circle it. There are food booths as well as game booths. The parade begins at North Cotton Street. First come the Spanish soldiers in costume, with* Tudi *leading.* Elias *and* Oscar *wear a cow costume and are led by a radiantly beautiful* Nora. Hermano Gil *plays the part of one of Oñate's generals, and* Bertina *is a noblewoman. She is followed by* Cotil, *and behind Cotil is* Fatty, *in a tight-fitting suit of armor and a helmet with the insignia of the Spanish army. He is the Master of Ceremonies. The parade marches forward. Jusephe, played by* Carlos, *leads the Royal Entourage. Carlos is followed by Don Juan de Oñate (The Flying Tortilla Man), a small old man with twinkling eyes.*]

Elias. Hey, Oscar, who's that old man next to Carlos?
Oscar. Let me see. (Oscar *sticks his head out of the cow's rear end.*) That's El Boss, Señor López—he owns the factory. He lives at one of those rest homes, but every year he comes out and plays Oñate. He's been doing it as long as I can remember.
Elias. So that's the original Tortilla Man, eh? He looks as old as the hills and as dusty.
Oscar. I can't go on much longer . . . it's hot!
Elias. So go work in an ice plant. Get it? Man, you have no sense of humor.
Oscar. You wouldn't have a sense of humor if you were back here!

[*They march forward, and when* Fatty *gets to the bandstand, he makes an announcement.* Carlos *sees* Neno *and yells to him.* Neno *is sitting on the side, resting in the sun, and looks much better.*]

Carlos. Hey, Neno! Neno, how are you?
Neno. I'm getting better, Carlos . . . I'm going to make it!
Elias. Move over, Oscar. There's Neno. I don't want germs to float over this way.
Nora. Come on, little cow; go see Neno.
Oscar. Can't you do anything, Elias? She's going near you-know-who-with-you-know-what. The Rot!
Nora. Neno, Neno!
Fatty. As Master of Ceremonies and Sheriff of the Cuchillo Municipality, I, Filmore P. Campbell, welcome you inhabitants

Denise Chávez 681

to our annual fiesta in honor of the founding of Cuchillo by Don Juan de Oñate.

[*The crowd cheers, and there is a great noise of firecrackers and shouts. The Birds are seen from a distance, viewing all the festivities.*]

Mabel. There he is . . .
Tin. Who?
Tan. The boy.
Ton. Are you going to start that again?
Mabel. I don't know what you're talking about.
Tan. What are they doing down there?
Tin. Who?
Mabel. The people in the Plaza.
Tan. They're laughing and having a good time.
Tin. You mean the ones out there? (*She peers into the audience.*)
Mabel (*looking out as well*). Oh, yes, they've been here awhile, haven't they?
Tan. I think they've had a good time, too. Don't you, Ton?
Ton. They look a little happier than when they came in.
Tin. Do you think so?
Tan. But what about the people in the Plaza? What's all that about down there? That parade and all the noise?
Mabel. Horses make me nervous.
Ton. Everything makes you nervous or unhappy or fat.
Mabel. I like a good story now and then, something to pass the time.
Ton. Oh, you and your time!
Tan. It's so nice to just sit here and smell the sky and the sunshine, and feel the sounds of life . . .
Mabel. How can you smell the sky, you crazy bird? You have it all mixed up!
Ton. Leave Tan alone, Mabel. She's all right. She's just being Tan.
Mabel. I guess you're right. She just can't help being Tan. Poor dear!
Tin. Are they getting nervous out there? (*Referring to the audience*)
Ton. No, but I think it's time to go home now.
Tin. Why? I was having so much fun!
Ton. It's just time.
Tan. Will we come back here again?

Tin. We'd better. I'm getting hungry just thinking about it.

Mabel. What are you silly birds talking about?

Tan. What's all the noise about anyway?

[*They fly off.*]

Ton. When will you listen, silly bird?

Tan. What was that? I couldn't hear you! "Listen." Did you say, "listen"? (*In a faraway voice*) Can't you just smell the sky?

For Study and Discussion

1. The setting of a work often helps to establish its **atmosphere**—its prevailing mood or feeling. At the beginning of Scene 1, what atmosphere is created by Chávez's description of the tortilla factory? Give specific details to support your answer.

2. Dramatists reveal character primarily through dialogue. What do you learn about Carlos through his conversations with the other workers in the tortilla factory throughout Scene 1?

3. Carlos's first meeting with The Tortilla Man **foreshadows**, or hints at, later plot developments in the play. What details of this meeting suggest that The Tortilla Man will become an important influence in Carlos's life?

4. Hermano Gil makes his first appearance in Scene 2. **a.** Based on his dialogue with Carlos, how would you characterize Hermano Gil? **b.** What does his reaction to Carlos's cigar box reveal about Hermano Gil's frustrated hopes and dreams?

5. A **foil** is a character who sets off another character by contrast. In what way is Cotil a foil to Carlos?

6. Carlos seemingly has done little to provoke Cotil, Oscar, and Elias. **a.** In your opinion, what is the cause of their antagonism

Denise Chávez 683

toward Carlos? **b.** Do you see anything ironic about their method of bringing about his "downfall"? Explain.

7. In Scene 3, when Carlos finds himself "in mid-air" aboard the Flying Tortilla, he feels "a mixture of fear and glee." Have you ever dreamed of having such an adventure? How would you react if you were in Carlos's place?

8. Juan de Oñate was a sixteenth-century Spanish explorer who played an important role in the colonization of New Mexico. In what way is The Flying Tortilla Man, who claims to be Juan de Oñate, a kind of modern-day explorer? What details in the play reveal his adventurous spirit?

9. The Magic Tortilla bears The Tortilla Man's own unique "flag." What does this flag look like, and what does it suggest about The Tortilla Man's view of life?

10. Perhaps it seems unfair to you that The Tortilla Man would leave Carlos asleep on the factory steps on the night of the break-in, contributing to Carlos's appearance of guilt. In light of his obvious concern for Carlos, what reasons might The Tortilla Man have had for doing this?

11. In Scene 6, Carlos finds a note in his cigar box from "Mr. Juan" that tells him to "remember." What do you think The Tortilla Man wants him to remember?

12. Cuchilla's annual fiesta celebrates the founding of the town by Juan de Oñate. **a.** How does The Tortilla Man's role in the parade point up his many different identities? **b.** Who do you think he "really" is?

13. In *The Flying Tortilla Man,* Chávez blends magical fantasy with realistic characters and details. Do you enjoy stories that have fantastical twists to them? If so, what do you like about them?

684   *Denise Chávez*

Literary Elements

Stagecraft

An audience's experience of a play depends partly upon the dramatist's use of **stagecraft**—visual devices such as scenery, costume, gesture and movement, and lighting. Often, dramatists give detailed stage directions to guide the director, performers, and other stage personnel in their production of a play; yet writers may also choose to de-emphasize stagecraft, providing very few directions. In the plays of Shakespeare, for example, one finds relatively few details of stagecraft.

In reading a play, it is important to pay attention to the writer's stage directions as well as to dialogue in order to better visualize the characters, settings, and events. For example, at the opening of Scene 1, Chávez gives stage directions to indicate scenery, lighting, and characterization.

What stage directions does Chávez give for the costumes in the play? As elements of stagecraft, what significance do these costumes have?

Vocabulary

Analyzing Words in Stage Directions

In stage directions such as those in *The Flying Tortilla Man,* the dramatist's word choice is particularly important for guiding the director and actors in their rendering of atmosphere, setting, and character interaction. Like most writers, Chávez chooses her words carefully to convey the exact meaning she intends. For example, in the stage directions at the opening of Scene 1, Chávez describes Tudi as a "morose young man." *Morose* means "gloomy, sullen, and ill-tempered." The description of Tudi as "morose" suggests something about his appearance as well as his behavior toward others, indicating the facial expression and manner that the actor playing Tudi should assume.

Denise Chávez 685

The following words appear in stage directions within the play. Define each word, and discuss how it helps to specify aspects of setting, atmosphere, or characterization.

permeates—Scene 1 (page 644)
bastion—Scene 1 (page 645)
admonishes—Scene 5 (page 673)
gloating—Scene 5 (page 675)

Writing About Literature

Stating the Theme of a Play

The **theme** of a work is its controlling idea—the general insight about life that the writer wishes to convey. Often, writers express theme through characters, events, and details rather than through direct statements. In *The Flying Tortilla Man,* what insight or insights does Denise Chávez offer into human nature? Try to state the theme of the play in a brief paragraph.

Prewriting. As you review the events and characters of the play, consider the following questions. What does Carlos learn from The Tortilla Man? What are The Tortilla Man's views on life and human nature? How do The Tortilla Man's lessons apply to the conflicts Carlos faces throughout the play? How do they apply to human experience in general? What do you learn from the play? As you think about these questions, write down whatever thoughts come to your mind about general ideas or insights that underlie the play. Then, carefully consider what you have written, and determine which of these thoughts most closely express the play's central theme.

Writing and Revising. As you write and revise your paragraph, avoid retelling the storyline of the play. For example, rather than recount the conflicts Carlos faces, state only the general message about life that the author conveys through these conflicts and their resolutions.

Creative Writing

Writing Dialogue

While Denise Chávez's stage directions in *The Flying Tortilla Man* help the reader to visualize its characters and settings, the story unfolds mainly through the dialogue of its characters. Write a dramatic scene similar to those in *The Flying Tortilla Man,* composed entirely of dialogue between two or more original characters of your own invention.

Prewriting. First, decide upon the type of scene you would like to create. What is the setting? Who are the characters, and what are their circumstances? What topic are they discussing, and why are they talking about that particular topic? Is their conversation comical or tragic or suspenseful? Write a rough outline of the scene, planning what your characters will say and how you will reveal details of setting and characterization through their dialogue.

Writing and Revising. Because dialogue will be your only means of characterization, you will want to choose words and phrases carefully to indicate your characters' personalities and their feelings toward one another. For example, if your characters were strangers meeting on the street, you would want to indicate their unfamiliarity with one another through formalized expressions that strangers would likely use to address one another.

Glossary

Many words in the English language have several meanings. In this glossary, the meanings given are the ones that apply to the words as they are used in the selections in the textbook. Words closely related in form and meaning are generally listed together in one entry (**trivial** and **trivialization**), and the definition is given for the first form. Related words that generally appear as separate entries in dictionaries are listed separately (**philanthropic** and **philanthropist**). Regular adverbs (ending in -*ly*) are defined in their adjective form, with the adverb form shown at the end of the definition.

The following abbreviations are used:

> *v.* verb   *n.* noun   *pl.* plural
> *adj.* adjective   *adv.* adverb   *prep.* preposition

A

aback (ə-bak′): *adv.* Backward; behind. —**taken aback** Surprised; suddenly confused; upset.

abalone (ab′ə-lō′nē): *n.* An edible shellfish having a flat shell lined with mother-of-pearl.

absolution (ab′sə-lōō′shən): *n.* A release from guilt or punishment for sin; forgiveness.

acclamation (ak′lə-mā′shən): *n.* A shout or some other indication of general approval or welcome.

acetylene (ə-set′ə-lən *or* ə-set′ə-lēn′): *n.* A colorless gas, burned in air to make light or with oxygen to produce heat for such processes as welding.

admonish (ad-mon′ish): *v.* To warn.

aesthetics (es-thet′iks): *n.* A branch of philosophy that attempts to explain the nature of beauty or of beautiful things.

affidavit (af′ə-dā′vit): *n.* A written statement sworn to be true.

albeit (ôl-bē′it): *conj.* Even though; although.

alkaline (al′kə-līn′ *or* al′kə-lin): *adj.* Of, like, or containing an alkali, such as potash, soda, or ammonia.

ambience *or* **ambiance** (am′bē-əns): *n.* A surrounding atmosphere; aura.

covenant (kuv'ə-nənt): *n*. An agreement entered into by two or more persons; pact.

cranny (kran'ē): *n*. A narrow opening, crack, or chink, as in a wall. —**crannied** *adj*.

craven (krā'vən): *adj*. Cowardly.

creosote (krē'ə-sōt'): *n*. An evergreen shrub that has a pungent odor.

cutaway (kut'ə-wā'): *n*. A man's formal coat for daytime wear, cut slopingly away from the waist in front down to the tails at the back.

D

decapitate (di-kap'ə-tāt'): *v*. **decapitation** To cut off the head of; behead.

decry (di-krī'): *v*. **decries** To speak critically of; condemn.

degradation (deg'rə-dā'shən): *n*. The act of being brought down from a higher to a lower condition; debasement.

delirious (di-lir'ē-əs): *adj*. Temporarily out of one's mind; wild and raving.

deportment (di-pôrt'mənt): *n*. The way a person acts or behaves; conduct.

dervish (dûr'vish): *n*. **1** A member of any of various Muslim religious orders. Some dervishes worship by whirling or howling. **2** Any person that whirls or dances without restraint.

desecrate (des'ə-krāt'): *v*. To show no reverence for something that is sacred, or to use it in an unworthy way. —**desecration** *n*.

devotions (di-vō'shəns): *n., pl*. Prayers; worship.

didactic (dī-dak'tik *or* di-dak'tik): *adj*. Suitable or intended for teaching or for guiding moral conduct.

diminutive (di-min'yə-tiv): *n*. A word, affix, or name that indicates something of small size or the state or quality of being lovable, familiar, or contemptible.

disarray (dis'ə-rā'): *n*. A very untidy state; confusion; disorder.

discriminate (dis-krim'ə-nāt'): *v*. To recognize a difference between; distinguish.

disorient (dis-ôr'ē-ent): *v*. To cause (a person) to lose his or her sense of time, location, or identity.

dissension (di-sen'shən): *n*. Quarrelsome disagreement, often within a group; conflict.

circlet (sûr′klit): *n.* A small circular object, as a ring.

coerce (kō-ûrs′): *v.* To force or compel to do something, as by threats or violence.

cognizance (kog′nə-zəns): *n.* The knowing or understanding of something; attention.

cohort (kō′hôrt): *n.* **1** A band or group, especially of warriors. **2** A companion or follower.

colloquium (kə-lō′kwē-əm): *n.,pl.* **colloquia** *or* **colloquiums** A conference on a particular subject, usually attended by experts or scholars.

columbine (kol′əm-bīn′): *n.* A plant with variously colored flowers of five petals.

concertina (kon′sər-tē′nə): *n.* A small musical instrument resembling an accordion.

conch (kongk *or* konch): *n., pl.* **conchs** (kongks) *or* **conches** (kon′chiz) A large spiral seashell.

conquistador (kon-k[w]is′tə-dôr′): *n.* Any of the Spanish conquerors of Mexico and Peru in the 16th century.

consensus (kən-sen′səs): *n.* Agreement of a majority or of everyone; general opinion.

consign (kən-sīn′): *v.* To give or hand over.

consolation (kon′sə-lā′shən): *n.* A person or thing that comforts in sorrow or disappointment; cheer.

consort (kon′sôrt): *n.* A husband or wife, especially of a ruler.

constitute (kon′stə-t[y] o̅o̅t′): *v.* To be the elements or parts of; make up.

contraband (kon′trə-band′): *n.* Goods that cannot legally be imported or exported; smuggled goods.

contrive (kən-trīv′) *v.* **contriving** To figure out; plan or plot.

corbel (kôr′bəl): *n.* A bracket used for support.

cornet (kôr-net′): *n.* A brass musical instrument resembling a trumpet.

coulee (ko̅o̅′lē): *n.* A ravine or gulch, often dry in summer.

courtesan (kôr′tə-zən *or* kōr′tə-zən): *n.* A prostitute, especially one with wealthy, socially prominent, or courtly clients.

---

a add / ā ace / â care / ä palm / e end / ē equal / i it / ī ice / o odd /
ō open / ô order / o̅o̅ took / o̅o̅ pool / u up / û burn / yo̅o̅ fuse / oi oil /
ou pout / ng ring / th thin / th this / zh vision

ə = a *in* above   e *in* sicken   i *in* possible   o *in* melon   u *in* circus

exude (ig-zo͞od' *or* ik-syo͞od'): *v.* **exuding** To discharge or cause to discharge in a small amount , as through pores.

exultant (ig-zul'tənt): *adj.* Full of great joy, as in triumph; jubilant.

F

ferment (fûr'ment): *n.* Agitation; excitement.

fervent (fûr'vənt): *adj.* Very eager and in earnest; ardent. — **fervently** *adv.*

fitful (fit'fəl): *adj.* Ceasing from time to time; not steady; irregular.

flaunt (flônt): *v.* To draw much attention to; to show off.

floozy (flo͞o'zē): *n., pl.* **floozies** A promiscuous woman or girl.

fortitude (fôr'tə-t[y]o͞od'): *n.* Courage to meet and endure pain, hardship, or danger.

foxtail (foks'tāl'): *n.* Any of several species of grass having brushlike flower heads suggestive of a fox's tail.

fraulein (froi'līn'): *n.* The German word used to refer to an unmarried woman.

functionary (fungk'shən-er'ē): *n., pl.* **functionaries** A public official.

furtive (fûr'tiv): *adj.* Done in secret; stealthy. —**furtively** *adv.*

G

gangly (gang'glē): *adj.* Awkward, tall, and lanky.

gazelle (gə-zel'): *n.* A small, graceful antelope of Africa and Arabia with curved horns and large eyes.

gentile (jen'tīl): *n.* A person who is not Jewish. Formerly used by Christians to refer to non-Christians. A pagan or heathen.

gloat (glōt): *v.* To think about with an intense, often malicious or evil delight.

grandee (gran-dē'): *n.* A man of elevated rank.

H

hallowed (hal'ōd): *adj.* Regarded as holy or sacred; revered.

heath (hēth): *n.* An open area overgrown with coarse plants.

hobble (hob'əl): *v.* To hinder or hamper.

dissipation (dis′ə-pā′shən): *n.* Overindulgence in harmful pleasures.

dominion (də-min′yən): *n.* Supreme power or authority; rule.

E

edifice (ed′ə-fis): *n.* A building, especially a large and impressive structure.

eke (ēk): *v.* To make with great difficulty and effort—usually used with *out.*

emic (ē′mik): *adj.* Concerning the analysis of the internal structure or functional elements of a linguistic or behavioral system.

emissary (em′ə-ser′ē): *n., pl.* **emissaries** A person sent as a special representative or to carry out special orders.

emphatic (em-fat′ik): *adj.* Striking; decisive.

emulate (em′yə-lāt′): *v.* To try to equal or surpass; imitate so as to excel.

emulsion (i-mul′shən): *n.* A mixture in which many small droplets of one liquid remain evenly distributed throughout another.

enmity (en′mə-tē): *n.* Deep hatred, mistrust, or dislike.

entourage (än′tŏŏ-räzh′): *n.* The group of aides and attendants accompanying a person of importance or high rank.

entreat (in-trēt′): *v.* To ask earnestly; implore; beg.

epistle (i-pis′əl): *n.* A long, formal letter.

eucalyptus (yŏŏ′kə-lip′təs): *n.* An evergreen tree that is valued for its oil and wood.

exhilarate (ig-zil′ə-rāt′): *v.* To fill with happiness or high spirits; stimulate.

existential (eg′zis-ten′shəl *or* ek′sis-ten′shəl): *adj.* Related to the philosophy of existentialism, which holds that humans are totally free to choose how they act and are responsible for their actions.

expedite (ek′spə-dīt′): *v.* To make go faster or more easily; speed up.

expound (ik-spound′): *v.* To interpret; set forth in detail.

---

a add / ā ace / â care / ä palm / e end / ē equal / i it / ī ice / o odd /
ō open / ô order / ŏŏ took / ōō pool / u up / û burn / yŏŏ fuse / oi oil /
ou pout / ng ring / th thin / th this / zh vision
ə = a *in* above   e *in* sicken   i *in* possible   o *in* melon   u *in* circus

I

idiosyncrasy (id'ē-ō-sing'krə-sē): *n., pl.* **idiosyncrasies** A way of thinking or behaving that is peculiar to an individual; quirk; mannerism.

implore (im-plôr'): *v.* **imploring** To beg for urgently.

impound (im-pound'): *v.* To seize or to shut up in an area.

improvident (im-prov'ə-dənt): *adj.* Not planning for the future; lacking foresight or thrift.

impudent (im'pyə-dənt): *adj.* Offensively bold; rude; insolent. — **impudence** *adj.*

in fine (ən fīn): In other words.

inadvertent (in'əd-vûr'tənt): *adj.* Unintentional. — **inadvertently** *adv.*

incarnate (in-kär'nāt'): *v.* To represent in some concrete form or shape.

incessant (in-ses'ənt): *adj.* Not ceasing; continuing without letup. — **incessantly** *adv.*

incisive (in-sī'siv): *adj.* Sharp; keen; penetrating.

inconsolable (in'kən-sō'lə-bəl): *adj.* Not to be comforted or cheered; brokenhearted.

indeterminate (in'di-tûr'mə-nit): *adj.* Not definite.

indomitable (in-dom'i-tə-bəl): *adj.* Not easily defeated or overcome; persevering.

indulgence (in-dul'jəns): *n.* The act of yielding to or giving free rein to.

inebriation (in-ē'brē-ā'shən): *n.* Drunkenness.

inexplicable (in-eks'pli-kə-bəl *or* in'iks-plik'-ə-bəl): *adj.* Impossible to explain.

instigate (in'stə-gāt'): *v.* To spur or urge to some action, esp. to some evil.

intersperse (in'tər-spûrs'): *v.* To change or vary by putting in things here and there.

invariable (in-vâr'ē-ə-bəl): *adj.* Not changing or able to change; constant. — **invariably** *adv.*

irrespective (ir'i-spek'tiv): *adj.* Regardless.

---

a add / ā ace / â care / ä palm / e end / ē equal / i it / ī ice / o odd / ō open / ô order / o͝o took / o͞o pool / u up / û burn / yo͞o fuse / oi oil / ou pout / ng ring / th thin / th this / zh vision

ə = a *in* above   e *in* sicken   i *in* possible   o *in* melon   u *in* circus

---

J

Janizary (jan′ə-zer′ē): *n.* Dedicated supporter or attendant.

jerked meat (jûrkt mēt): *n.* Strips of meat (usually beef) cured by drying.

jowly (jou′lē): *adj.* Having full or droopy flesh on or below the lower jaw.

juncture (jungk′chər): *n.* Joint or union.

juniper (jōō′nə-pər): *n.* an evergreen shrub or tree with dark blue berries.

L

lament (lə-ment′): *v.* To feel or express great sorrow over; to mourn or grieve for.

languor (lang′gər): *n.* Inactivity or stillness.

lateral (lat′ər-əl): *adj.* Of, situated at, coming from, or directed toward the side.

lath (lath): *n.* A thin strip of wood, often used as a base for plastering.

laurels (lôr′əlz): *n., pl.* Honor; fame.

lethargy (leth′ər-jē): *n.* The condition of feeling tired, dull, and listless.

licentiousness (lī-sen′shəs-nis): *n.* Indecency; immorality; lewdness.

lupin *or* **lupine** (lōō′pin): *n.* A plant related to the pea, having long spikes of flowers and bean-shaped seeds in flat pods.

M

maize (māz): *n.* Corn, the plant or its seeds; Indian corn.

malice (mal′is): *n.* An intention or desire to hurt or injure someone; ill will; spite.

mallow (mal′ō): *n.* A type of herb having rounded leaves and pale pink, purplish, or white flowers.

mandate (man′dāt′ *or* man′dit): *n.* A formal, usually written command from someone in authority.

manifold (man′ə-fōld′): *n.* A pipe having several openings, so as to connect it with other pipes.

manzanita (man′zə-nēt′ə): *n.* Any shrub or small tree of the heath family found in the western United States.

marimba (mə-rim'bə): *n.* A kind of xylophone that has resonating tubes beneath tuned wooden bars.

martinet (mär'tə-net'): *n.* A person who always enforces rules strictly and exactly.

melancholy (mel'ən-kol'ē): *adj.* Very gloomy; sad; dejected.

mellifluous (mə-lif'lōo-əs): *adj.* Having a sweet, smooth sound; honeyed.

metaphysical (met'ə-fiz'i-kəl): *adj.* Highly abstract and often difficult to understand.

milch (milch): *adj.* Giving milk, as a cow.

minister (min'is-tər): *v.* To give help or attention to a sick person.

morose (mə-rōs'): *adj.* Gloomy or sullen.

motley (mot'lē): *adj.* Containing very different and often clashing elements.

N

naive *or* **naïve** (nä-ēv'): *adj.* Foolish; inexperienced; childlike; unsophisticated.

necropolis (nə-kräp'ə-lis): *n.* A graveyard, particularly one of an ancient city.

non-fraternization (non-frat'ər-nə-zā'shən): *n.* Refrainment from associating in a friendly way.

nubby (nub'ē): *adj.* Having small, rounded projections or swellings; lumpy.

O

oblivious (ə-bliv'ē-əs): *adj.* Not conscious or aware; unmindful.

obsession (əb-sesh'ən): *n.* The condition of being overwhelmed by a thought or feeling.

obsidian (əb-sid'ē-ən): *n.* A hard, glassy rock, usually black, formed by the cooling of hot lava.

oppressive (ə-pres'iv): *adj.* Burdensome; harsh; cruel.

opulent (op'yə-lənt): *adj.* Wealthy; characterized by abundance.

---

a add / ā ace / â care / ä palm / e end / ē equal / i it / ī ice / o odd /
ō open / ô order / o͝o took / o͞o pool / u up / û burn / yo͞o fuse / oi oil /
ou pout / ng ring / th thin / th this / zh vision
ə = a *in* above e *in* sicken i *in* possible o *in* melon u *in* circus

oracle at Delphi (ôr′ə-kəl at del′fī): *n*. A priest through whom the gods were supposed to speak or phophesy to the ancient Greeks and Romans. The place where this occurred: The oracle of Apollo was at Delphi.

P

palatial (pə-lā′shəl): *adj*. Of, like, or befitting a palace; grand.

pall (pôl): *n*. Something that covers, especially something that is dark or gloomy.

pallid (pal′id): *adj*. Pale or wan; lacking in color or strength.

palpitate (pal′pə-tāt′): *v*. **palpitating** To beat irregularly or more rapidly than normal; flutter.

palsied (pôl′zēd): *adj*. Trembling.

pander (pan′dər): *v*. To exploit the base desires and weaknesses of others.

paradox (par′ə-doks′): *n*. A statement that seems contradictory but may in fact be true.

paranoid (par′ə-noid′): *adj*. Having or showing symptoms of paranoia, a mental disorder in which a person often imagines persecution by others or imagines being a more important person than he or she actually is.

parochial (pə-rō′kē-əl): *adj*. Limited in scope; narrow.

parochial school: *n*. A school that is run and maintained by a church or other religious organization.

paunch (pônch): *n*. A big belly that sticks out.

pell-mell (pel′mel′): *adv*. In a confused or disordered way.

penance (pen′əns): *n*. A punishment that a person accepts and endures or an action that a person performs to show regret for sins committed and desire to be forgiven.

peremptory (pə-remp′tər-ē): *adj*. Not open to argument or refusal.

perfunctory (pər-fungk′tər-ē): *adj*. Lacking in enthusiasm; routine.

permeate (pûr′mē-āt′): *v*. To spread or spread through.

perpetuate (pər-pech′o͞o-āt′): *v*. To cause to last or to be remembered for a very long time.

philanthropic (fil′ən-throp′ik): *adj*. Charitable; benevolent.

philanthropist (fi-lan′thrə-pist): *n*. A person who devotes time and money to helping others.

potentate (pōt′[ə]n-tāt′): *n*. A person who has great power or authority; ruler.

precocious (pri-kō′shəs): *adj*. Unusually mature or advanced for one's age.

precursor (pri-kûr'sər): *n.* A person or thing that comes before and indicates what is to follow; forerunner.

pretense (pri-tens' *or* prē'tens): *n.* Something pretended, as a false act, appearance, or excuse.

pretentious (pri-ten'shəs): *adj.* Making a flashy, outward show.

pretext (prē'tekst'): *n.* A false reason or motive given to conceal a real one.

prevail (pri-vāl'): *v.* **prevail upon** To urge or persuade successfully.

prevalent (prev'ə-lənt): *adj.* Of or having general acceptance or frequent occurrence; common.

privation (prī-vā'shən): *n.* The lack of the necessities or common comforts of life.

profound (prə-found'): *adj.* **1** Intensely felt. **2** Deep; complete.

propitious (prō-pish'əs): *adj.* Favorable; helpful.

proverbial (prə-vûr'bē-əl): *adj.* Often spoken of or about.

pulmotor (po͝ol'mōt'ər): *n.* A device used for pumping air into the lungs of someone having difficulty breathing.

pulsate (pul'sāt'): *v.* **pulsating** To throb or beat rhythmically, as the pulse or heart does.

Q

quail (kwāl): *v.* To shrink with fear; lose heart or courage.

R

redress (ri-dres'): *n.* Correction or satisfaction, as for wrongs and injuries done.

relentless (ri-lent'lis): *adj.* Persistent. —**relentlessly** *adv.*

rent (rent): *v.* Past tense and past participle of *rend*—To tear apart; split; break.

reproachful (ri-prōch'fəl): *adj.* Filled with or expressing reproach; filled with or expressing blame.

reredos (rir'däs): *n.* An ornamental screen behind a church altar.

retama (rā-tä'ma): *n.* A spiny, yellow-flowered shrub or tree.

---

a add / ā ace / â care / ä palm / e end / ē equal / i it / ī ice / o odd /
ō open / ô order / o͝o took / o͞o pool / u up / û burn / yo͞o fuse / oi oil /
ou pout / ng ring / th thin / th this / zh vision
ə = a *in* above e *in* sicken i *in* possible o *in* melon u *in* circus

---

retrospect (ret′rə-spekt′): *n.* A viewing or consideration of past times or events.

rigamarole (rig′ə-mə-rōl′) *or* **rigmarole** (rig′mə-rōl′): *n.* Confused or senseless talk or writing; nonsense; poppycock.

rivulet (riv′yə-lit): *n.* A brook.

rudimentary (rōō′də-men′tər-ē): *adj.* Imperfectly developed; basic.

S

sacral (sa′krəl): *adj.* The region at the lower end of the human spinal column where a triangular bone joins both hipbones to form the back part of the pelvis.

sagebrush (sāj′brush′): *n.* A small shrub with white or yellow flowers, found on the dry plains of the western United States.

sashay (sa-shā′): *v.* To walk in a swaggering or conspicuous way.

saunter (sôn′tər): *v.* To walk in a slow, casual way; stroll.

scallop (skol′əp *or* skal′əp): *n.* One of a series of semicircular curves along an edge, as for ornament.

scourge (skûrj): *n.* A cause of great suffering or trouble, as war.

seethe (sēth): *v.* **seething** To boil, or foam and bubble as if boiling.

sexton (seks′tən): *n.* A janitor of a church, whose duties may include ringing the bell and digging graves.

sleazy (slē′zē): *adj.* Cheap and disreputable.

solace (sol′is): *n.* Comfort in times of unhappiness or trouble.

solicit (sə-lis′it): *v.* To ask or ask for earnestly. —**solicitously** *adv.*

sorghum (sôr′gəm): *n.* A tall plant that looks rather like corn, is filled with a sweet juice, and is grown as food for livestock and to make syrup.

speculation (spek′yə-lā′shən): *n.* A theory; conjecture.

spume (spyōōm): *n.* Froth; foam; scum.

stature (stach′ər): *n.* Quality achieved through growth or development.

statute (stach′ōōt): *n.* A rule or law, especially a law passed by a legislature.

stipulate (stip′yə-lāt′): *v.* To specify as a condition on an agreement.

stodgy (stoj′ē): *adj.* Dull, stuffy, and commonplace.

stoic (stō′ik): *adj.* Unaffected by pleasure or pain.

strife (strīf): *n.* Any bitter or angry fight, quarrel, or conflict.

stupor (st[y]ōō′pər): *n.* A dazed state in which the power to feel, think, or act is lost or greatly lessened.

stygian (stij′ē-ən): *adj.* Very dark and gloomy.

sublime (sə-blīm′): *adj.* Inspiring awe or deep emotion; noble.

subsistence (səb-sis′təns): *n.* The minimum amount of food, clothing, and other essentials necessary to stay alive.

subvert (səb-vûrt′): *v.* To undermine the character or principles of.

sundries (sun′drēz): *n., pl.* Items or things too small or too numerous to be separately named.

superimpose (sōō′pər-im-pōz′): *v.* To place over, above, or on top of something else.

supple (sup′əl): *adj.* Bending easily; flexible or limber.

surname (sûr′nām′): *n.* An added name; nickname.

symposium (sim-pō′zē-əm): *n., pl.* **symposiums** or **symposia** A meeting for the discussion of a particular subject.

T

talisman (tal′is-mən): *n.* Any magic charm. —**talismanic** *adj.*

tank (tangk): *n.* A pool used to stop the flow of liquids.

tarry (tar′ē): *v.* **tarried** To stay for a while; linger.

temper (tem′pər): *v.* To make less harsh or strong, as by adding something; moderate.

thistle (this′əl): *n.* A plant with prickly leaves, having purple or white flowers.

tome (tōm): *n.* A large book; volume.

transcendent (tran-sen′dənt): *adj.* Going beyond what is usual; remarkable in every way; extraordinary.

transfiguration (trans′fig-yə-rā′shən): *n.* A change in appearance or form.

traumatic (trô-mat′ik *or* trou-mat′ik): *adj.* Of, constituting, or caused by a severe emotional shock that has long-lasting psychological effects.

trivial (triv′ē-əl): *adj.* Ordinary; commonplace. —**trivialization, trivialities** *n.*

trousseau (trōō′sō *or* trōō-sō′): *n.* A bride's wardrobe, including her clothing and household linens.

tule reed (tōō′lē rēd): *n.* A large plant found in marshes.

---

a add / ā ace / â care / ä palm / e end / ē equal / i it / ī ice / o odd /
ō open / ô order / ŏŏ took / ōō pool / u up / û burn / yōō fuse / oi oil /
ou pout / ng ring / th thin / <u>th</u> this / zh vision
ə = a *in* above   e *in* sicken   i *in* possible   o *in* melon   u *in* circus

U

unsized (un-sīzd'): *adj.* Not containing a thin, sticky glaze used for stiffening porous materials such as fabric or paper.

unsolicited (un-sə-lis'i-tid): *adj.* Not asked for.

urbanize (ûr'bə-nīz'): *n.* To give the characteristics of a city to.

V

varietal wine (və-rī'ət-əl wīn): *n.* A wine that is distinguished by the type of grape it was made from.

verdure (vûr'jər): *n.* The fresh greenness of growing plants, or the plants themselves.

verity (ver'ə-tē): *n.* A principle or belief considered to be true.

vesicula (və-sik'yə-lə): *n.* A small bladderlike sac or cavity in the body, containing liquid.

vespers (ves'pərz): *n., pl.* In certain churches, a service of worship held in the late afternoon or evening.

vibrant (vī'brənt): *adj.* Full of energy; vigorous.

vigilant (vij'ə-lənt): *adj.* Alert to possible danger; watchful.

virile (vir'əl *or* vir'īl): *adj.* Having vigor and strength; forceful.

vis-à-vis (vē'zə-vē'): *prep.* In comparison with or in relation to.

W

waif (wāf): *n.* A homeless, lost, or abandoned creature, especially a child or a pet.

wickerwork (wik'ər-wûrk'): *n.* Branches or twigs woven together to make baskets, light furniture, and other objects.

wizened (wiz'ənd): *adj.* Shrunken and dried up; withered.

Additional Contemporary Mexican American Authors

Aguilar, Ricardo. Currently a Professor of Spanish at the University of Texas at El Paso, he has published extensively in Mexico. Best known as a poet, he also writes and publishes narrative prose in Spanish.

Barrio, Raymond. His best-known novel, *The Plum Plum Pickers*, depicts the harsh life of migrant farm laborers and has recently been translated into German.

Bornstein-Somoza, Miriam. She now holds a position as Professor of Spanish at the University of Denver. In addition to writing literary criticism, she also writes bilingual poetry.

Burciaga, José Antonio. Exhibiting his skills as both a graphic artist and a poet, Burciaga's early work *Cultura* is a collection of silk-screened poetry broadsides. He is also one of the authors, along with Bernice Zamora, of a collection of poetry titled *Restless Serpents*.

Campbell, Trini. Her book-length poem *Canto indio mexicano* was published in 1977. Since then, she has published consistently, concentrating on her United States–Mexico experiences.

Cota-Cárdenas, Margarita. She earned her Ph.D. in Spanish at Arizona State University, where she is currently an Associate Professor. She is both a poet and a narrative prose writer. *Noches despertando en conciencias* (poetry) was her first long publication.

Elizondo, Sergio. He is currently Professor of Spanish at New Mexico State University. His early collections of poetry, *Perros y antiperros* and *Libro para batos y chavalas chicanas*, were followed by several narrative prose works.

García-Camarillo, Cecilio. He was founding editor of two literary magazines—*Caracol* and *Rayas*. His poetry displays both classical and experimental features.

Gaspar del Alba, Alice. Best known for her poem "Easter: The Lame Bull," she studied creative writing at the University of Texas at El Paso.

Hernández-Tovar, Inez. She has taught at the University of Texas at Austin and at D-Q University in California. Her poetry has been published in *Revista Chicano-Riqueña* and *Tejidos*.

Herrera, Juan Felipe. A widely published California poet, his work has appeared in *Floricanto en Aztlán, Citybender,* and *Inside the Belly of the Shark.*

Herrera-Sobek, María. Currently holding the position of Professor of Spanish at the University of California at Irvine, she is known primarily as a researcher. Her poetry has appeared in *Revista Chicano-Riqueña.*

Keller, Gary (El Huitlacoche). Not only a poet and a prose writer but a publisher as well, he is perhaps best known for his humorous pieces and satires.

López-Flores, Margarita. A young poet from Chicago, Illinois, her "Poem for My Mother" won the Gwendolyn Brooks Prize in 1980.

Morales, Alejandro. His first novel, *Caras viejas y vino nuevo,* was published in Mexico. His subsequent novels, *Reto en el Paraíso* (Spanish) and *The Brick People* (English), were published in the United States.

Morton, Carlos. Dramatist and author of *El jardín* (a dramatic allegory of the story of the Garden of Eden), he has had his best-known work, *Johnny Tenorio,* performed in Spain and Germany. He is currently the Director of Chicano Studies at the University of Texas at El Paso.

Rivera, Marina. An Arizona poet, she has had her work published in *Revista Chicano-Riqueña* and other literary journals. Her poems have been collected in three books: *Mestiza, Sobra,* and *The Celia Poems.*

Rodríguez, Alfonso. Born in Crystal City, Texas, he has published poems in *The Americas Review, Bilingual Review,* and numerous anthologies. At present he is a professor of Spanish at the University of Northern Colorado.

Rodriguez, Richard. This widely acclaimed and highly controversial writer is best known for his autobiography *Hunger of Memory.* He has also had numerous articles and essays published in popular magazines such as *Time* and *U.S. News and World Report.* His opposition to bilingual education and his outspoken adherence to other views that run counter to the thinking of many Hispanics have led to his being ostracized by a sizable bloc of the Mexican American community.

Salinas, Raúl. His best-known work, *Un Trip Through the Mind Jail y Otras Excursiones* (poetry), traces the fifteen-year journey of his realization of self. He has published extensively, and his work has appeared in journals such as *The Washington Review, New Era, Vórtice,* and *Tejidos.*

Torre, Alfredo de la. He succeeded Cecilio García-Camarillo as editor of the literary magazine *Caracol.* His novel *El León Salió de la Jaula* won the Pajarito Publications Prize.

Trambley, Estela Portillo. Born in El Paso, Texas, she has worked in radio and television. Her dramas and her narrative prose are highly realistic and forceful. Her best known works are *The Paris Gown* (short fiction) and *Trini* (novel).

Vásquez, Richard. His work *Chicano* was one of the earliest prose narratives of contemporary Mexican American literature.

Annotated Bibliography

Literary Works

Anthologies

Anaya, Rudolfo A., and **Antonio Márquez,** eds. *Cuentos Chicanos: A Short Story Anthology.* Revised edition. Albuquerque: New America, University of New Mexico, 1980.
This carefully balanced selection of short stories by prominent writers such as Rudolfo Anaya, Ron Arias, Denise Chávez, and Alberto Ríos provides a good cross section of contemporary Mexican American short fiction.

Campa, Arthur. *Treasure of the Sangre de Cristo: Tales and Traditions of the Spanish Southwest.* Norman: University of Oklahoma Press, 1963.
This is an excellent resource for early folk stories. Campa has collected many examples from northern New Mexico and southern Colorado by interviewing elderly Spanish-speaking people who have preserved the folk tradition that originated in the sixteenth century when the Spanish began to explore and settle this part of the Southwest.

Harth, Dorothy, and **Lewis M. Baldwin,** eds. *Voices of Aztlán: Chicano Literature of Today.* New York: New American Library, 1974.
This collection offers a large number of varied selections, including short stories, drama, poetry, and portions of novels.

Ortego, Philip D. *We Are Chicanos: An Anthology of Mexican-American Literature.* New York: Washington Square Press, 1973.
This anthology offers valuable help in gaining a historical perspective on Mexican American literature. The selections are accompanied by thoughtful and incisive comments.

Rebolledo, Diane, Erlinda Gonzales-Berry, and **Teresa Márquez.** *Las Mujeres Hablan: An Anthology of Nuevo Mexicana Writers.* Albuquerque: El Norte Publications, 1988.
Divided along broad topical categories, the selections in this volume give an excellent overview of some of the best writing by Mexican American woman authors.

Valdez, Luis, and Stan Steiner, eds. *Aztlán: An Anthology of Mexican-American Literature.* New York: Random House, 1972.

Including works from Mexican as well as from Mexican American literature, the editors of this anthology have arranged the selections along general topical lines that help to show the interrelationship of the two literatures and the cultural continuity from one to the other.

Drama

Trambley, Estela Portillo. *Sor Juana and Other Plays.* Ypsilanti: Bilingual Press, 1983.

As one of a very few Mexican American woman dramatists, Portillo Trambley offers an important alternative view of her culture. Her plays range from light comedy to serious drama dealing with moral and ethical issues.

Valdez, Luis, and El Teatro Campesino. *Actos.* San Juan Bautista: Cucaracha Publications, 1971.

Valdez and El Teatro Campesino have played a key role in the evolution of contemporary Chicano theater. This collection contains a number of works that express the Chicano perspective and reveal much about an important era of Mexican American history.

Novels

Anaya, Rudolfo A. *Bless Me, Ultima.* Berkeley: Quinto Sol Publications, 1972.

Sensitive and delicately written, this novel portrays a Mexican American male's transition from boyhood to adulthood under the tutelage of Ultima, a wise *curandera* [faith healer] who introduces him to a magical and mysterious world unlike his own. In the process of unfolding his tale, Anaya draws upon his personal experience to provide a view of rural life in northern New Mexico.

Arias, Ron. *The Road to Tamazunchale.* Tempe: Bilingual Press, 1987.

Much of the action in this novel takes place in the dreams and imagination of its central character, Fausto Tejada, a terminally ill retired book dealer and collector. Arias uses a deft interplay of fantasy and reality to present insights about life, death, and contemporary society.

Barrio, Raymond. *The Plum Plum Pickers.* Binghamton: Bilingual Press, 1985.

Barrio focuses on the members of a Mexican American family who are forced to live the unstable, nomadic life of migrant workers in the agricultural fields of California. The poignant presentation of the wife's inner torment is particularly moving.

Candelaria, Nash. *Memories of the Alhambra.* Palo Alto: Cibola Press, 1977.

In search of his cultural roots, José Rafa travels to Mexico and then to Spain in a futile attempt to locate his family's origins. This novel develops a theme that lies at the core of many Mexican American works of fiction—the search for personal identity.

Corpi, Lucha. *Delia's Song.* Houston: Arte Público Press, 1988.

An important new voice in Mexican American fiction, Lucha Corpi affords a glimpse of the Chicana perspective in her novels. Her protagonist, Delia, struggles to give meaning to her life first through familial loyalty, then through political militancy, and finally through a personal relationship.

Gonzales, Lawrence. *El Vago.* New York: Atheneum, 1983.

This fast-paced novel traces the adventures of two young men who become outlaws and then active participants in Mexico's 1910 revolution. As the story unfolds, one of the young men is revealed to be Pancho Villa, who later became a revolutionary general and a national hero.

González, Genaro. *Rainbow's End.* Houston: Arte Público Press, 1988.

Like Hinojosa-Smith's *Partners in Crime*, this novel deals with crime along the Texas–Mexico border. González traces the evolution of Mexican and Mexican American social, financial, and family relationships. Heraclio Cavazos, his protagonist, is a patriarch who sees his cultural values change and finally disintegrate as members of his family become involved in illegal activities.

Hinojosa-Smith, Rolando R. *Rites and Witnesses.* Houston: Arte Público Press, 1982.

Hinojosa-Smith blends reportage, dialogue, and vignettes in his first novel, which lays bare the decadence of the Anglo social elite in South Texas.

___ . *Partners in Crime*. Houston: Arte Público Press, 1986. Departing from his usual novelistic approach and from the forms commonly used in Mexican American novels, the author creates a fast-paced mystery complete with cops, murder, and high intrigue.

Méndez, Miguel. *The Dream of Santa María de las Piedras*. Tempe: Bilingual Press, forthcoming in 1989.

Méndez uses poetic language to create moving, memorable characters and scenes of life among the Yaqui Indians and Mexican population along the Sonora–Arizona border.

Morales, Alejandro. *The Brick People*. Houston: Arte Público Press, 1988.

This story revolves around a bitter conflict between a wealthy, influential Anglo family and a poor but tenacious Mexican family in California during the nineteenth and early twentieth centuries. The bricks of the title are a metaphor for the workers brought to California from Central Mexico to help build the state during a time of unprecedented growth.

Rivera, Tomás. *. . . y no se lo tragó la tierra* [. . . and the earth did not devour him]. Trans. Evangelina Vigil-Piñón. Houston: Arte Público Press, 1987.

Rivera's 1971 award-winning work focuses on a nameless central character, a young boy, as he grows more aware of himself in his relationship to his family. Through his eyes, we experience the abrupt and frequent changes that plague the lives of migrant agricultural workers.

Trambley, Estela Portillo. *Trini*. Binghamton: Bilingual Press, 1986.

The author tells an inspirational tale common to many Mexican immigrants who illegally cross the United States–Mexico border seeking a better life. Her protagonist, Trini, suffers indignity and hunger but in the end triumphs, reaffirming the resilience of the human spirit.

Villarreal, José Antonio. *Pocho*. Garden City: Doubleday and Company, 1959.

In this first novel of the Contemporary Period, the author traces the social and psychological changes a Mexican immigrant family undergoes while learning to survive in a foreign culture. Villarreal suggests that in surrendering their language and customs, the members of the family also lose the values inherent in their culture.

Short Fiction

Chávez, Denise. *The Last of the Menu Girls.* Houston: Arte Público Press, 1987.

In this semi-autobiographical collection of short stories, Chávez offers a glimpse of what it was like to grow up Hispanic and female in a small New Mexico city during the 1950s, capturing the pain and exhilaration of the young narrator's uncertain steps toward womanhood.

Cisneros, Sandra. *The House on Mango Street.* Houston: Arte Público Press, 1983.

Cisneros was born and raised in the Mexican American community of Chicago. In this collection of stories, she recounts life in the barrio from the perspective of a young girl who grows up in a family of males and in a culture dominated by men. She uses the metaphor of a house to symbolize a series of broken dreams her young narrator suffers during her pre-adolescent years. Her stories feature engaging vignettes about a not-so-typical Mexican American experience of growing up in the Midwest.

Méndez, Miguel. *Tata Casehua y otros cuentos* [Papa Casehua and other stories]. Trans. Eva Price, Leo Barrow, and Marco Portales. Berkeley: Editorial Justa Publications, 1979.

Méndez is a masterful artist with words. His short stories, most of them about the miserable conditions of Yaqui Indians and Mexicans along the United States–Mexico border, are carefully crafted works rich in subtle meaning.

Ríos, Alberto. *The Iguana Killer: Twelve Stories of the Heart.* A Blue Moon and Confluence Press Book, 1984. Distributed by Kampmann & Company of New York.

Although this collection consists of individual short stories about intimate feelings and very personal perceptions, together the stories form an overview of what many immigrants experience, such as border crossings, bewilderment in a new culture, and gradual adaptation.

Soto, Gary. *Living Up the Street.* San Francisco: Strawberry Hill Press, 1985.

Soto is recognized primarily as a fine, award-winning poet, but this book firmly establishes him as a promising writer of short fiction. His prose is as eloquent and evocative in its simplicity as his poetry. His narrator in these stories relates with tenderness a wide range of experiences common to males growing up in a Mexican American barrio. This book of recollections is aptly described on its back cover as containing "unpretentious language of the heart."

Ulibarrí, Sabine. *El Cóndor and Other Stories.* Houston: Arte Público Press, 1989.

Ulibarrí is a master storyteller of folkloric tales. This latest collection of his stories contains both Spanish and English versions of eleven widely varied stories that feature a cast of fascinating characters.

Viramontes, Mary Helen. *The Moths and Other Stories.* Houston: Arte Público Press, 1985.

Viramontes is a most promising writer who brings to her short stories a feminist perspective of women in Mexican American culture. The female protagonists of her stories are in various stages of breaking out of their traditional roles and challenging the cultural expectations of what they can and should become.

Poetry

Alurista. *Return: Poems Collected and New.* Ypsilanti: Bilingual Press, 1982.

Alurista is known for his bold linguistic experiments combining English, Spanish, and barrio slang. This superb collection contains some of this important poet's earlier work, including strong social protest pieces characteristic of Chicano poetry of the 1960s.

Baca, Jimmy Santiago. *Martín and Meditations on the South Valley.* New York: New Directions, 1986.

In this recent poetic work, Baca uses powerful imagery and demonstrates a keen understanding of change and unpredictability in the lives of rural Hispanics who live on the edge of urban expansion.

Catacalos, Rosemary. *Again for the First Time.* Santa Fe: Tooth of Time Books, 1984.

This book—the first collection of Rosemary Catacalos's poetry—established her as one of the brightest stars on the Mexican American literary horizon. Of special note is her use of imagery that is both striking and accessible. The themes of her poetry range from the most intimate reflections on self to social commentary that expresses surprising, somewhat provocative views of Mexican American culture.

Cervantes, Lorna Dee. *Emplumada.* Pittsburgh: Pittsburgh University Press, 1981.

Clear, direct, and highly accessible, Cervantes's poetry focuses on personal and community change in the barrio during the past twenty-five years. Giving an intimate view from a woman's perspective, she captures the anguish generated by the constant presence of drugs and violence as well as the comfort and support provided by family and friends.

Cisneros, Sandra. *My Wicked Wicked Ways.* Berkeley: Third Woman Press. Chicano Studies, University of California, 1988.

Unlike the narrative voice of the young girl in Cisneros's book of short fiction *The House on Mango Street,* the speaker in many of these poems is a grown woman whose travels throughout Europe and the southwestern United States have left her feeling unsettled. Yet, like the narrator of *The House on Mango Street,* she seeks to come to terms with the pain and confusion of her childhood.

Elizondo, Sergio. *Libro para vatos y chavalas Chicanas* [A book for Chicano guys and gals]. Trans. Edmundo García Girón. Berkeley: Editorial Justa Publications, 1977.

As the title indicates, Elizondo directs his poetry to young Mexican Americans as he sets out what he believes to be essential lessons of his people's relationship to the dominant Anglo society. His graphic imagery is often moderated by his sharp wit.

Gonzáles, Rodolfo "Corky". *I Am Joaquín / Yo Soy Joaquín: An Epic Poem.* New York: Bantam, 1972.

The overriding message throughout Gonzáles's long epic poem is that Mexican Americans have endured centuries of social injustice and should continue to resist oppression. Gonzáles wrote this poem as a kind of declaration or rallying cry of freedom for young Chicanos during the 1960s. *I am Joaquín* takes on significant historical importance as the first Chicano literary work to clearly set forth a social agenda.

Mora, Pat. *Chants.* Houston: Arte Público Press, 1984.

Growing up in El Paso, Mora has developed a keen sense and appreciation for the desert's beauty. In many of her poems dealing with loneliness and despair, the desert provides solace. Her narrator is a modern woman who must make her way in a conflict-ridden urban landscape, yet the desert is ever present to remind her that inner peace is always possible.

Ríos, Alberto. *Five Indiscretions.* New York: Sheep Meadow Press, 1985.

Ríos's poetry is rich in images and echoes of Mexican American life and culture close to the United States–Mexico border. He seems acutely aware that the path he has chosen as a poet must always lead back to his culture, which ultimately acts as the source of his poetic inspiration. His depiction of characters from both his past and his present is always gentle.

Salinas, Luis Omar. *The Sadness of Days: Selected and New Poems.* Houston: Arte Público Press, 1987.

This collection contains representative works from the various stages in Salinas's evolution as a poet. Present throughout his poetry is a personal search and longing for peace in a confused and compassionless world. His narrator is an outsider who is always looking in, trying to integrate himself into the human community.

Sánchez, Ricardo. *Selected Poems.* Houston: Arte Público Press, 1984.

An explicitly militant poet, Sánchez has lost little of his strident tone since his early 1960s poetry. Always on the attack, he decries and condemns social injustice and, like Alurista and Elizondo, produces poetry highly representative of Chicano movement literature.

Villanueva, Tino. *Shaking Off the Dark.* Houston: Arte Público Press, 1984.

Villanueva's multiple meanings and levels of imagery will delightfully challenge those interested in the writing and refining of poetry.

Literary Criticism

Bruce-Novoa, Juan. *Chicano Authors: Inquiry by Interview.* Austin: University of Texas Press, 1980.

In this collection of interviews, Bruce-Novoa poses the same series of questions to prominent Mexican American writers such as Alurista, Anaya, Arias, Méndez, and Zamora. In their answers they comment on their own lives and works as well as their perceived role in American society.

Huerta, Jorge. *Chicano Theater: Themes and Forms.* Ypsilanti: Bilingual Press, 1982.

In this comprehensive reference work, Huerta traces the development of Chicano theater, beginning with the founding of El Teatro Campesino in 1965. He devotes much attention to Luis Valdez, El Teatro Campesino, and some of the theater festivals and groups that they spawned.

Jiménez, Francisco. *The Identification and Analysis of Chicano Literature.* Ypsilanti: Bilingual Press, 1979.

Jiménez has collected in this volume some of the most important studies on specific authors and works in contemporary Mexican American literature through the late 1970s.

Sánchez, Marta. *Contemporary Chicana Poetry: A Critical Approach to an Emerging Literature.* Berkeley: University of California Press, 1985.

Sánchez devotes an entire chapter to each of the following female poets: Alma Villanueva, Lorna Dee Cervantes, Lucha Corpi, and Bernice Zamora. Her view of each is both interesting and highly informative.

Tatum, Charles M. *Chicano Literature.* Boston: G. K. Hall & Company, 1982.

In this general history of Mexican American literature, Tatum traces its development from the sixteenth century through 1980, devoting a chapter apiece to theater, the novel, the short story, and poetry.

Autobiographies

Baez, Joan. *Daybreak.* New York: Dial Press, 1968.

This famous folk singer of the 1960s and 1970s tells about growing up conscious of her Hispanic roots, taking trips to Mexico to visit relatives, and gradually moving away from her culture during a period of great success as a performer.

Galarza, Ernesto. *Barrio Boy.* Notre Dame: University of Notre Dame Press, 1971.

Galarza traces an immigrant family's voyage beginning with their life in a mountain village in the interior of Mexico to their eventual destination in a northern California city barrio. His account is rich in detail and impressions that give a firsthand view of one of many different experiences of Mexican immigrants who continue to make the trek northward to the United States.

García, Andrew. *Tough Trip Through Paradise, 1878–1879.* Ed. Bennett H. Stein. New York: Ballantine Books, 1967.

This unusual autobiographical account chronicles the exploits of a Mexican American who leaves his home in Texas in search of adventure. Written in the plain-spoken style of a cowpuncher, García's fascinating, rough-and-ready tales bring alive the Wild West.

Otero, Miguel A. *My Life on the Frontier 1865–1882.* 2 vols. Albuquerque: University of New Mexico Press, 1987.

Otero tells about growing up in the Wild West towns of Kansas and Colorado at a time when survival often depended on one's skill with a six-gun. He provides captivating descriptiions of legendary figures such as Calamity Jane and Wild Bill Hickok.

Quinn, Anthony. *The Original Sin: A Self-Portrait.* New York: Bantam, 1974.

Well-known Mexican American actor Anthony Quinn vividly describes the difficulties of growing up poor in the barrio and his triumph over adversity to start an acting career.

Background Works

Art, Film, and Music

Keller, Gary, ed. *Chicano Cinema: Research, Reviews, and Resources.* Binghamton: Bilingual Press, 1985.

Keller's collection of essays on the emerging Mexican American cinema as well as on Mexican Americans in Anglo cinema provides an overview of this important artistic medium as well as studies of currents and images within it.

Mandheim, Beverly A. *Ritchie Valens, The First Latin Rocker.* Tempe: Bilingual Press, 1988.

Valens died in the same plane crash as Buddy Holly, bringing to a tragic close his promising career as an early rock musician.

Mandheim focuses on the roots of Valens's music and his contributions to the development of rock.

Paredes, Américo. *With His Pistol in His Hand: A Border Ballad and Its Hero.* Austin: University of Texas Press, 1986.

Paredes traces the development of the *corrido* about Gregorio Cortez, a legendary hero of the early twentieth century who was much admired for resisting Anglo injustices against Mexican Americans. The author includes many variants of the *corrido* that he has collected and researched over a period of many years.

Petit, Arthur G. *Images of the Mexican American in Fiction and Film.* College Station: Texas A & M Press, 1980.

In this impressive array of examples from American film and literature, the author shows how predominantly negative stereotyping of Mexican Americans has been instrumental in shaping Anglo attitudes toward this minority group.

Quirarte, Jacinto. *Mexican-American Artists.* Austin: University of Texas Press, 1973.

In an engaging, readable style, the author discusses the work of individual Mexican American artists and surveys the history and development of this artistic field. Many color plates and black/white photos make Quirarte's beautifully illustrated book both attractive and quite useful.

___. *Chicano Art History: A Book of Selected Readings.* San Antonio: Research Center for the Arts and Humanities, University of Texas, 1984.

An excellent companion guide to Quirarte's *Mexican-American Artists,* this collection updates developments in the field of Mexican American art and provides in-depth discussions on artistic currents, art groups, and individual artists.

Robb, Stanley. *Hispanic Folksongs of New Mexico and the Southwest: A Self-Portrait of a People.* Norman: University of Oklahoma Press, 1980.

Robb has collected several hundred examples of Hispanic folk songs from throughout the Southwest. He covers their important forms—including the *romance, décima, canción,* and *corrido* —and the ways in which they reflect the Spanish-speaking population's history and culture.

History and Social Sciences

Acuña, Rodolfo. *Occupied America: A History of Chicanos.* 3rd ed. New York: Harper & Row, 1988.

Basing his book on extensive research, Acuña has significantly reinterpreted Mexican American history. He takes issue with Anglo historians, showing how their view of Mexican Americans is largely false and distorted.

Chávez, John R. *The Lost Land: The Chicano Image of the Southwest.* Albuquerque: University of New Mexico Press, 1984.

Chávez outlines the changing image of the Southwest as viewed by the Hispanic population that has lived there since the sixteenth century. He illustrates that Mexican Americans consider the Southwest their homeland or patrimony and that unlike most other ethnic groups they are indigenous to the region in which they live.

García, Eugene, Isidro Ortiz, Francisco Lomelí, and **Luis Leal,** eds. *Chicano Studies. A Multidisciplinary Approach.* New York: Columbia Teachers College Press, 1984.

This collection of essays provides an excellent overview of Mexican Americans from several perspectives: history, social structure and politics, literature and folklore, and education.

Mirandé, Alfred, and **Evangelina Enríquez.** *La Chicana: The Mexican American Woman.* Chicago: University of Chicago Press, 1979.

In reviewing the changing role of the Mexican American woman, the authors deal with the following broad topics: cultural heritage in Mexico and the United States; working women, education, and the family; images of women in literature; and Chicana feminism.

General Index

Titles of all selections are shown in italics. Names of authors and other references are shown in regular type.

A 9
B 0
C 1
D 2
E 3
F 4
G 5
H 6
I 7
J 8